# Folkbiology

# Folkbiology

edited by Douglas L. Medin and Scott Atran

A Bradford Book
The MIT Press
Cambridge, Massachusetts
London, England

©1999 Massachusetts Institute of Technology

All rights reserved. No part of this book may be reproduced in any form by any electronic or mechanical means (including photocopying, recording, or information storage and retrieval) without permission in writing from the publisher.

This book was set in Sabon by Asco Typesetters, Hong Kong.

Printed and bound in the United States of America.

Library of Congress Cataloging-in-Publication Data

Folkbiology / [edited by] Douglas L. Medin and Scott Atran.
    p.  cm.
"A Bradford book."
Includes bibliographical references and index.
ISBN 0-262-13349-0 (hc : alk. paper). — ISBN 0-262-63192-X
(pbk. : alk. paper)
1. Ethnobiology. 2. Folklore. 3. Cognition and culture.
I. Medin, Douglas L. II. Atran, Scott, 1952–   .
GN476.7.F65   1999
306.4′5—dc21                                                    98-50861
                                                                      CIP

# Contents

# Contributors

**Scott Atran**
Centre National de la Recherche
Scientifique
CREA-Polytechnique
Paris, France
Phone: 33-4-68980847
Fax: 33-4-68980847
and
Institute for Social Research
The University of Michigan
Ann Arbor, MI 48103

**Terry Kit-fong Au**
Department of Psychology
University of California, Los Angeles
1282 A Franz Hall
Box 951563
Los Angeles, CA. 90095-1563

**Brent Berlin**
Department of Anthropology
University of Georgia
Room G40, Baldwin Hall
Athens, GA. 30602-1619
Phone: (706) 542-9079
Fax: (706) 542-8432

**K. David Bishop**
Physiology Department
University of California Medical
School
Los Angeles, CA. 90095-1751
Phone: (310) 825-6177
Fax: (310) 206-5661

**John D. Coley**
Department of Psychology
Northwestern University
2029 Sheridan Road
102 Swift Hall
Evanston, IL. 60208
Phone: (847) 467-2421

**Jared Diamond**
Physiology Department
University of California Medical
School
Los Angeles, CA. 90095-1751
Phone: (310) 825-6177
Fax: (310) 206-5661

**John Dupre**
Department of Philosophy
Birkbeck College, University of
London
Malet Street
London, England
WC1E 7HX
Phone: +44 171 631 6549

**Roy Ellen**
Anthropology and Human Ecology
Eliot College
University of Kent at Canterbury
Canterbury, Kent CT2 7NS
United Kingdom

**Susan A. Gelman**
Department of Psychology
525 E. University Avenue
University of Michigan
Ann Arbor, MI. 48109-1109
Phone: (313) 764-0268

**Michael T. Ghiselin**
California Academy of Sciences
Golden Gate Park
San Francisco, CA. 94118-4599
Phone: (415) 221-5100

**Grant Gutheil**
Department of Psychology
Yale University
Box 208205
New Haven, CT 06520-8205

**Giyoo Hatano**
6-7-12 Honkomagome
Bunkyo-ku
Tokyo, JAPAN, 113

**Lawrence A. Hirschfeld**
Department of Psychology
525 E. University Avenue
University of Michigan
Ann Arbor, MI. 48109-1109
Phone: (313) 764-0268

**David L. Hull**
Department of Philosophy
Northwestern University
Evanston, IL. 60208
Phone: (847) 491-3656

**Eugene Hunn**
Department of Anthropology
Box 353100
University of Washington
Seattle, WA 98195
Phone: (206) 543-6825
Fax: (206) 543-3285

**Kayoko Inagaki**
6-7-12 Honkomagome
Bunkyo-ku
Tokyo, JAPAN, 113

**Frank C. Keil**
Department of Psychology
Yale University
Box 208205
New Haven, CT 06520-8205

**Daniel T. Levin**
Department of Psychology
Yale University
Box 208205
New Haven, CT 06520-8205

**Elizabeth Lynch**
Department of Psychology
Northwestern University
2029 Sheridan Road
102 Swift Hall
Evanston, IL. 60208
Phone: (847) 467-2421

**Douglas L. Medin**
Department of Psychology
Northwestern University
2029 Sheridan Road
102 Swift Hall
Evanston, IL. 60208
Phone: (847) 467-1660
Fax: (847) 491-7859

**Julia Beth Proffitt**
Department of Psychology
Northwestern University
2029 Sheridan Road
102 Swift Hall
Evanston, IL. 60208
Phone: (847) 467-2421

**Bethany A. Richman**
Department of Psychology
Yale University
Box 208205
New Haven, CT 06520-8205

**Laura F. Romo**
Department of Psychology
University of California, Los Angeles
1282 A Franz Hall
Box 951563
Los Angeles, CA. 90095-1563

**Sandra R. Waxman**
Department of Psychology
Northwestern University
102 Swift Hall
Evanston, IL. 60208
Phone: (847) 467-2293

# 1

# Introduction

Douglas L. Medin and Scott Atran

How do people ordinarily come to understand the natural world? Whether one is a scientist, an educator interested in the relation between formal and informal science education, or a policy maker concerned with the human dimensions of global change this is a fundamental question. The chapters in this volume represent an interdisciplinary perspective on people's everyday knowledge of the biological world—folkbiology if you will.

## 1.1   Importance of Folkbiology

Although we will develop this issue more fully later, it is worth taking a moment to underline the central importance of folkbiology to our understanding of thought and behavior. Much of human history has been spent (and is being spent) in intimate contact with plants and animals, and it is difficult to imagine that human cognition would not be molded by that fact. In subsistence cultures, survival depends on a detailed appreciation of the habits, affordances, and interactions linked to the biological world. In technologically advanced cultures, which are increasingly faced with environmental degradation and nonsustainable use of natural resources, no less may be at stake.

Claims about the nature of human nature, with their associated policy implications, require the very best analyses that an interdisciplinary cognitive science has to offer. People's actions on the natural world are surely conditioned in part by their ways of knowing and modeling it. What are these modes of knowledge and mental models? How are they affected by goals, theories, and intimacy of contact with the biological world? What is universal, what is not, and what are the implications of such observations for our understanding of the development of biological cognition? These questions shape the contributions to the present volume. Before turning from these general questions to more specific ones, we lay out the case for an interdisciplinary approach to research, taking as our focal points cognitive psychology and ethnobiology.

## 1.2   Case for Interdisciplinary Approaches

### Critique of Cognitive Psychology

In many respects anthropology and psychology are perfect foils for each other because of their complementary strengths (and weaknesses). In this section we focus on limitations of cognitive psychology in order to set up a contrast with anthropology.

**Universality**   One of our psychology colleagues is fond of saying that he is only interested in studying what is "universal." Universality of course seems transparently desirable; it represents the ideal on the dimension of "findings of broad applicability." For the moment let's not quibble but rather adopt the view that the quest for universality is good science. However, it must be said that if cognitive psychology thinks that universals are desirable, then it has a peculiar way of going about its quest for them. Research in cognitive psychology almost exclusively targets a single, highly selected subset of a single culture and population: college freshmen and sophomores, and not freshmen and sophomores, in general, but rather those at major research universities taking introductory psychology. Only with considerable effort could one come up with a more select, narrow population to study.

To be sure, there are exceptions to this narrowness. Some cognitive psychologists do research where they try to isolate distinct subsets of participants to explore possible (subgroup) differences. For example, one might study the performance of male versus female students on some task of interest. Selecting within a select population often does yield differences. To outsiders, however, this may seem like planning two vacations to be as different as possible subject only to the constraint that one travel no more than a kilometer from home. The other prominent exception is well represented in this volume: research on cognitive development. Even in this case, however, populations are sampled with convenience and little else in mind (witness the frequency with which the population studied is children attending a university grade school). In short, it would not be much of a caricature to suggest that cognitive psychology does not quest for university but rather assumes it. If cognitive psychology has laws or generalizations to offer about how the mind works, it has so far shown little interest in putting them to the test of whether they fit humanity at large.

**Sampling of Stimulus Materials**     One of the strengths of cognitive psychology is its focus on systematic controlled comparisons. Historically this concern was so strong that psychologists studying learning employed nonsense syllables to limit any influence of prior experience or knowledge. Although this particular habit has been discarded in favor of using meaningful materials, experimentalists have concentrated on finding materials with particular desirable properties (in terms of controlling for extraneous factors) with little concern for the relation between such materials and the range of stimuli over which one might wish to generalize. The idea of systematic sampling is somewhat alien, perhaps because it is not always clear how to answer the question, "systematic, with respect to what?" For example, if a psychologist wants to compare reasoning involving living kinds versus human artifacts as stimuli, he or she typically would generate examples subject only to the constraint that undergraduates be familiar with them. Rarely, if ever, would it occur to the psychologist to ask what kinds of artifacts or what kinds of living kinds there are and how might one go about selecting a representative sample.

**Reference**     A related limitation of research in cognitive psychology is that conceptual behavior is often studied with little concern about reference. For studies involving adults, the stimuli are often words and seldom does the researcher establish any relation between these words and what their referents are. For living kinds other than mammals, college students often have little idea about reference beyond a very general level (e.g., "such-and-such is a tree"; see Coley et al., chapter 7 in this volume). For developmental studies concerned with living kinds, the stimuli are typically toys, which are at best representations of living kinds. Again reference is rarely established. Although for some questions of interest reference may not matter, our impression is that, as in the case of populations and stimuli, convenience and control tend to dominate a systematic analysis of the domain of interest.

### Ethnobiology as a Contrast

The above limitations of research in cognitive psychology would strike many ethnobiologists as odd. Consider how an ethnobiologist would undertake the study of folkbiology in some new culture. The project could hardly get underway without asking what living kinds are found in that culture, what terms exist in the language referring to living kinds, and what the relation is between those terms, and what's there (the issue of reference). How does one describe what living kinds exist in some cultural context? A reasonable starting point is to use scientific taxonomy as a reference or standard. For example, one might ask whether every kind that science recognizes as a distinct species has a distinct name (Diamond and Bishop, chapter 2 in this volume; see also Gould 1979). Upon finding that many kinds do not have distinct names, it is natural to ask what principles determine whether or not a species has a distinct name (Berlin, chapter 4 in this volume). For example, naming could be driven by relevance to humans (utility), perceptual discontinuities, or even size (Hunn, chapter 3 in this volume).

Scientific taxonomy is, of course, a hierarchical taxonomy, and as such it provides both a standard and a heuristic for asking other questions about universal aspects of folktaxonomies. There are two important analytic points involved here. One is that although the particular kinds of plants and animals to be found may vary across cultures, the abstract structure in terms of species, genus, family, order, class, division, and kingdom will be represented. Consequently scientific taxonomy provides something of a conceptual grid for crosscultural comparisons (Atran, chapter 6 in this volume). The second, related point is that scientific taxonomy allows one to establish corresponding ranks such that that it becomes meaningful to state that oak is at the same level or rank as is trout. This does not mean that they are psychologically at the same rank, but it does provide a basis for asking questions such as whether some culture differentiates mammals more than fish (Coley et al., chapter 7 in this volume). As it turns out, ethnobiologists have found that folk ranks and folktaxonomies only loosely approximate scientific taxonomies, but formal taxonomy has served as an effective standard for cross-cultural comparisons (Hunn 1975).

Note that the practices that are most natural for an ethnobiologist address each of the limitations that we have attributed to cognitive psychology. Folktaxonomic analyses provide a framework in which one can propose and evaluate hypotheses about cognitive universals (Berlin, Breedlove, and Raven 1973). The main criticism we can offer for the issues in question is that ethnobiologists have tended to focus on (1) small-scale subsistence cultures to the neglect of larger, more industrialized cultures and (2) culturally competent adults rather than children (see Stross 1973 and Dougherty 1979 for two interesting exceptions).

**Critique of Anthropology**
We turn now to limitations of anthropological approaches to folkbiology as seen through psychologists' eyes.

**Where (and What) Are the Data?** Again at the risk of caricature one might argue that ethnobiological observations often fall short of the minimum needed for scientific progress. In many cases ethnobiological facts and observations are presented in summary form without any clear indication of their source. Are the informants a representative sample or a few local wise people or experts? In some instances no mention is made at all of the informants as if the "facts" were free-floating entities in the culture. Without some more precise identification of the data, one cannot begin to assess basic requirements for science such as replicability. Only in the last decade or so, have some ethnobiologists started to question the summary notion of an "omniscient informant" in favor of an analysis of variation within human populations (Boster 1986).

**Commensurable Units of Analysis in Data and Theory** Philosophical argument to the contrary, cognitive psychologists bask in the belief that mental representations (and meanings) reside in the heads of individuals. To be sure, they might be sensitive to a social contribution in the construction of meaning but they know where mental representations hang out. Not so in anthropology. Ethnobiologists seem as uncomfortable as behaviorists in talking about mental representations, whereas most psychologists do not know what to make of anthropology's talk of "cultural representations." Are cultural representations just the mental representations of some ideal informant, or are they differentially shared by the minds of several or all informants? If the latter, then there are psychologically intriguing issues concerning the causal structure of such distributed knowledge (Hutchins 1995) and whether such knowledge might have emergent properties that cannot be reduced to the mental life of any single individual (Sperber 1996). Different questions surely require different levels and units of analysis; however, there must be a measure of commensurability between psychological and anthropological analyses if there is to be cooperation and cumulative progress in understanding. To be blunt, ethnobiologists can't make claims about how individuals perceive, organize, and act on the natural world without worrying about what's in the heads of individuals and how such mental representations are causally linked to one another and to individual actions.

An analogy may serve to make the point. Economists study systems at different levels of analysis, and historically they have tended to assume that aggregate behavior derives from optimal behavior on the part of individuals. One important contribution of psychological studies of decision making and choice behavior has been to destroy the illusion of optimality and replace it with a systematic, theoretical, and empirical analysis of decision and choice (see Tversky and Kahneman, 1986; Busemeyer, Hastie, and Medin 1995; Fischhoff 1997). Just so, we think that ethnobiology needs to include individuals as units of analysis for claims about individuals. Anthropology cannot simply assume that culture (including language) is assimilated in something of the same way a body warms to the sun (see Strauss and Quinn 1992 for a critique of this view from within anthropology).

If anything we may be guilty of downplaying this issue. At times within anthropology, the methodological point that anthropological observations are socially constructed has been elevated to a form of self-immolation that threatens to destroy the science part of anthropology as a social science and move it squarely into literature. As one of our anthropological colleagues is fond of saying, fieldwork should focus on research that is liable to "awe" our own, often complacent culture with the diversity of collective human imagination and action. We readily grant the importance of demonstrating the rich variation in human thought and experience, but we think that science could better help to make the case.

**Role of Models and Theories**    The tricky thing about knowledge is that there are no free peeks at mental representations. This is true both for the scientist and the informant. At one point researchers interested in developing computers as expert systems hoped that knowledge could be transferred from human expert to machine simply by asking the expert to report what he or she knew. This effort was largely unsuccessful because experts can't, by an act of will, simply make their knowledge accessible. Artificial intelligence "knowledge engineers" and psychologists have learned to use indirect measures of knowledge and to draw inferences from patterns of behavior. This is an important operating procedure in cognitive science: that is, developing and testing methods and models that foster inferences about knowledge representation and use. Models and theories are not complete strangers to ethnobiology, but neither are they intimate friends.

## Cognitive Psychology as a Contrast

The stock and trade of cognitive psychology is theoretical models of human cognition and a well-honed set of methodological tools for drawing inferences from behavior to internal processes. And tons of data (often from narrow, overcontrolled, decontextualized settings but data nonetheless). If anything, cognitive psychology suffers from rigor mortis.

We are convinced that a cognitive science of folkbiology that combines and integrates the strengths of its constituent subfields holds great promise for progress in understanding how people cognize the natural world. The chapters in this volume are in this spirit of promoting this sort of integration. The challenge of understanding biological cognition is daunting. Consider the presumably simpler task of understanding temperature regulation, a problem that has its own evolutionary history. Here it has been found that temperature regulation in human beings involves the integration of multiple parallel systems (e.g., shivering, sweating, putting on clothes) that vary in their refinement and redundancy (e.g., see Satinoff 1983 for a review). We should not expect anything less for something as intricate as people's understanding of the natural world.

Fortunately, progress can come in smaller steps. Folkbiology is a field blessed with many intriguing and important issues that lend themselves to an analysis in terms of culture and cognition. Let us turn to a sample of three of them.

## 1.3    Theoretical Issues in the Cognitive Science of Folkbiology

### Are Folkbiological Categories Recognized or Constructed?

A basic issue within ethnobiology concerns whether categories are recognized versus constructed (see Malt 1995; Brown 1995). One view—known within ethnobiology as the "intellectualist view"—is that the structure of kinds in nature is comprised of "chunks" that more or less impose themselves on minds (at least minds with a perceptual system like ours). This position is reinforced by the finding that folk categories often correspond to scientific species or genera and by cross-cultural agreement in folktaxonomic systems (e.g., Atran 1990; Berlin 1992; Atran, however, interprets agreement in terms of universal properties of mind rather than the structure of nature alone). The alternative, or "utilitarian," view is that folktaxonomic systems are influenced by goals, theories, and belief systems and that they may be culture-dependent constructions (Hunn 1982; Ellen 1993). Other intermediate positions hold that the intellectualist and utilitarian views are not necessarily mutually exclusive. For example, their relative influence may depend on factors such as rank in the hierarchy (Bulmer 1970): Cultures may differ more in the structure and use of categories such as tree or bird (corresponding roughly to class in scientific taxonomy) than they do for oak or robin (corresponding roughly to the generic or species level).

The contributions to this volume suggest a further blurring of earlier distinctions through more refined analyses. Hunn (chapter 3) suggests that perceptual criteria, such as size, may have a universal role to play even with higher-level categories. Ellen (chapter 5) argues that although folkbiological knowledge appears to be constrained by the perceptual salience of the species involved, it varies significantly and reliably across cultures according to subsistence need (this is especially evident at lower levels of the taxonomic hierarchy). Coley et al. (chapter 7) and Atran (chapter 6) show that despite striking similarities in taxonomic organization and taxonomy-based reasoning in an industrialized society and a small-scale subsistence culture, there are important differences both within and across these cultures that are related to different needs and experiences.

### Is Reasoning from Folkbiological Categories Similarity-Based or Theory-Based?

Especially within cognitive psychology, folkbiology is an appealing domain from the contending standpoints of both similarity-based and theory-based views of categorization and category-based reasoning. On the one hand, our perceptual system is surely an adaptation to the natural world and if similarity-based models are going to succeed anywhere, it should be here. On the other hand, the biological world is apparently a world of fairly stable clusters of complex features whose remarkable endurance in the face of constant change presumably owes to naturally occurring causal patterns. Understanding causal patterns in the world is a primary goal of theory-driven knowledge in science, and the history of science is coterminous with trying to understand biological causality in particular. If theory-based knowledge were to develop anywhere outside of science—in other cultures or in everyday thinking—it should be here.

From the perspective of similarity, there are evident patterns of covariation for biologically-related attributes: toothless two-legged beings generally have wings, feathers, and fly; leaves, flowers, and fruits generally go together with stems and roots; and so on. Perhaps most people in the world are aware of these covariations without necessarily understanding their causal origins or interrelations, such as the role of feathers in flight or of leaves in stem development. In other words, there could be quite a bit of biologically relevant data that is stored but not theoretically assimilated.

Nevertheless, people in different cultures acknowledge, and often try to better understand, at least some of the causal interrelations among covariant biological attributes. These include irreversible patterns of biological growth (maturation); the apparent constancy of covariant morphological, anatomical, and behavioral patterns across generations (reproduction and inheritance); the success of mutually constraining actions of interrelated attributes in maintaining life (bodily functioning); and the breakdown of interrelated bodily functions (illness and death). Moreover these "naive" attempts at causal explanation are themselves interrelated, often with the sort of resultant explanatory bootstrapping and integration of the database that could help to kick off scientific growth.

Suppose, as ethnobiologists generally agree, that people everywhere witness certain covariant biological patterns (roughly corresponding to perceptually salient species or genera) but interpret the causal relationships underlying these patterns in different ways. This might suggest that similarity-based reasoning is prior to theoretically based reasoning, at least in the biological domain. This was a message of developmental studies in the 1980s (Carey 1985; Inagaki and Sugiyama 1988; Keil 1989). More recent studies have lowered the age at which children are thought to reason causally about biological kinds. But the origins of causal reasoning in folkbiology remain a matter of controversy.

In this volume several authors debate whether understanding of biological causality originates from within the specific domain of folkbiology, or whether such notions emerge from types of causal reasoning that may not be specific or original to the cognitive domain of folk biology. For Carey, folkbiological reasoning initially stems from folk psychology. For Au and Romo (chapter 11), the early principles of folkbiological causality are largely mechanical principles derived from naive mechanics. For Hirschfeld and Gelman a belief in the causal power of underlying essences, which comes to characterize folkbiology, does not emerge first or only in regard to animals and plants but also for people and perhaps substances. For Keil, Levin, Richman, and Gutheil (chapter 9) the causal principles of folkbiology originate early in development from within folkbiology, although this does not rule out that such causal principles, or "modes of construal," may have wider application in other domains. Hatano and Inagaki (chapter 10) argue that the causal principles underlying biological reasoning are both original and specific to the cognitive domain of "naive biology" in children.

A closely related question concerns which factors shape the acquisition of biological knowledge and the extent to which their influence extends to adult (more or less steady state) knowledge. Researchers in the area of cognitive development have been actively studying the role of language in conceptual development (see Waxman, chapter 8 in this volume) and are increasingly turning to an analysis of the role of input conditions (Hatano and Inagaki, chapter 10 in this volume; Gelman, Coley, Rosengren, Hartley, and Pappas, 1998), at least at intermediate stages of development. To our knowledge, there have been no studies of the role of input conditions on adult biological conceptions.

### Is Folkbiology a "Naive" Form of Scientific Biology?
To some extent the fact that most psychologists prefer the labels "naive biology" or "intuitive biology" over the ethnobiologist's "folkbiology" implies somewhat different understandings and uses of scientific biology as a standard of comparison. For those interested in the structure and development of biological causality in our own culture, folkbiological concepts often appear to contain "rudimentary" or "inchoate" elements and clusters of more sophisticated scientific concepts. Although there has been little systematic study of the input conditions and processes by which scientific concepts are assimilated into lay thinking, there is hardly any doubt that science is pervasively involved in how people in our culture come to think about the biological world. The influence of science may be especially pronounced among the university subpopulations psychologists prefer to study, but most of the general population is heavily exposed to scientific concepts in one form another through schooling, nature programs on television, popular books, the press and so forth. Even where scientific biology may have no direct or discernible impact on lay biology, well-studied aspects of scientific structure and development, such as the roles of theory and theory change, can serve as effective heuristics for the exploration of lay understandings of the biological world (in this volume see Keil et al., chapter 9; Hatano and Inagaki, chapter 10; Au and Romo, chapter 11; Carey 1985; see also Murphy and Medin 1985).

The elaborate folkbiological inventories that ethnobiologists have shown time and again for many small-scale subsistence societies often match and occasionally even surpass in intricacy and accuracy the knowledge of field biologists working in the same locales as those societies (in this volume see Diamond and Bishop chapter 2; Berlin et al., chapter 4; see also Bartlett 1936, Simpson 1961, Bulmer and Tyler 1968). Moreover few ethnobiologists would consider it enlightening—indeed rather misleading—to characterize the significant differences between folk knowledge in other cultures versus science in terms of relative degrees of intuition or naiveté (in this volume see Ellen, chapter 5, and Atran, chapter 6). Admittedly, ethnobiologists might well agree with psychologists about referring to lay biology in our culture as "naive" in comparison to the relative sophistication of science as well as folk-biological knowledge in other cultures.

In this volume philosophers of biology who are familiar with the role of science in extending the frontiers of human awareness examine the knowledge associated with popular or folk understanding from yet a different perspective. A key issue is whether basic folk concepts, such as folk species or generics, are different in kind from contemporary scientific concepts, such as the idea of a species as a logical individual rather than a logical class (Ghiselin, chapter 13 in this volume). If they are not really different in kind but only in degree of sophistication, then there may be no reason for holding onto the lay concept at all, except perhaps as an optional psychological convenience for navigating the everyday world (see also Kripke 1972; Putnam 1975). If, however, folk and scientific concepts are different in kind, then perhaps they have separate but equal—or at least different—roles to play in attainment of knowledge (Dupre, chapter 14 in this volume; see also Braisby et al. 1996; Atran, 1998): the one for accommodating to the everyday world and the other for exploring the cosmos at large (including extended thoughts about evolutionary dimensions of space and time that would be largely irrelevant to ordinary understanding and action).

Finally one might accept that folk and scientific concepts may be different in kind, or that folk concepts are in some sense psychologically more convenient in a given culture or at a given stage of history or development, but argue that folk concepts ought to be replaced by scientific concepts (Hull, chapter 15 in this volume). For example, if it is true that people ordinarily believe that living kinds (including humans) have underlying essences (see Gelman and Hirschfeld, chapter 12 in this volume), then it is also likely that people will treat natural variation as deviance. If so, then the essentialist folk concept should be discarded along with other outworn "commonsense" myths, such as belief in witches or in race as a biological category, no matter how hard it is to unlearn them. Even if this should be case, however, understanding how people do in fact think about biological kinds (and other biologically related phenomena discussed in this volume such as diseases) may help us all to better cope with them.

## 1.4   Conclusions

If it is not obvious from this introduction, the chapters in this volume make clear the promise and significance of interdisciplinary approaches to the study of folkbiology. In addition to revealing something of the state of the art, these contributions lay the foundation for addressing other urgent questions that are beyond the scope of the present volume. Can human beings make the transition from locally sustainable adaptions to (technologically driven) global economies without irreparably damaging our environment or destroying local cultures? To address such issues, researchers may need to integrate questions about the structure of biological cognition with systematic analyses of how knowledge is linked to action in diverse ecological and cultural contexts (Atran and Medin 1997). In short, the present volume marks progress with respect to the interdisciplinary study of people's understanding of the natural world. In providing new intellectual tools to understand how humans come to know nature, this progress reinforces, not complacency, but rather an appreciation of urgency.

## References

Atran, S. 1990. *Cognitive Foundations of Natural History*. Cambridge: Cambridge University Press.

Atran, S. 1998. Folk biology and the anthropology of science. *Behavioral and Brain Sciences*, forthcoming.

Atran, S., and D. Medin. 1997. Knowledge and action: Cultural models of nature and resource management in Mesoamerica. In M. Bazerman, D. Messick, A. Tinbrunsel, and K. Wayde-Benzoni, eds., *Environment, Ethics, and Behavior*. San Francisco: Jossey-Bass.

Bartlett, H. 1936. A method of procedure for field work in tropical American phytogeography based on a botanical reconnaissance in parts of British Honduras and the Peten forest of Guatemala. *Botany of the Maya Area, Miscellaneous Papers I*. Washington: Carnegie Institution of Washington Publication 461.

Berlin, B. 1992. *Ethnobiological Classification*. Princeton: Princeton University.

Berlin, E., and B. Berlin. 1996. *Medical Ethnobiology of the Highland Maya of Chiapas, Mexico*. Princeton: Princeton University Press.

Berlin, B., D. Breedlove, and P. Raven. 1973. General principles of classification and nomenclature in folk biology. *American Anthropologist* 74: 214–42.

Boster, J. 1986. Requiem for the omniscient informer. In J. Dougherty, ed., *Directions in Cognitive Anthropology*. Urbana: University of Illinois Press.

Braisby, N., B. Franks, and J. Hampton. 1996. Essentialism, word use, and concepts. *Cognition* 59: 247–74.

Brown, C. 1995. Lexical acculturation and ethnobiology: Utilitarianism versus intellectualism. *Journal of Linguistic Anthropology* 5: 51–64.

Bulmer, R. 1970. Which came first, the chicken or the egg-head? In J. Pouillon and P. Maranda, eds., *Echanges et communications: Mé langes offerts à Claude Lé vi-Strauss*. The Hague: Mouton.

Bulmer, R., and M. Tyler. 1968. Karam classification of frogs. *Journal of the Polynesian Society* 77: 333–85.

Busemeyer, J., R. Hastie, and D. Medin. 1995. Decision making from a cognitive perspective. In *The Psychology of Learning and Motivation*, vol. 32. San Diego: Academic Press.

Carey, S. 1985. *Conceptual Change in Childhood*. Cambridge: MIT Press.

Dougherty, J. 1979. Learning names for plants and plants for names. *Anthropological Linguistics* 21: 298–315.

Ellen, R. 1993. *The Cultural Relations of Classification*. Cambridge: Cambridge University Press.

Fischhoff, B. 1997. Ranking risks. In M. Bazerman, D. Messick, A. Tenbrunsel, and K. Wade-Benzoni, eds., *Environment, Ethics, and Behavior; the Psychology of Environmental Valuation and Degradation*. The New Lexington Press, San Francisco.

Gelman, S. A., J. D. Coley, K. S. Rosengren, E. Hartman, and A. Pappas. 1998. Beyond labeling: The role of parental input in the acquisition of richly-structured categories. *Monographs of the Society for Research in Child Development*, no. 253.

Gould, S. 1979. A quahog is a quahog. *Natural History* 88: 18–26.

Hunn, E. 1975. A measure of the degree of correspondence of folk to scientific biological classification. *American Ethnologist*. 2: 309–27.

Hunn, E. 1982. The utilitarian factor in folk biological classification. *American Anthropologist* 84: 830–47.

Hutchins, E. 1995. *Cognition in the Wild*. Cambridge: MIT Press.

Inagaki, K., and Sugiyama, K. (1988) Attributing human characteristics: Developmental changes in over- and underattribution. *Cognitive Development* 3: 55–70.

Keil, F. 1989. *Concepts, Kinds, and Cognitive Development*. Cambridge: MIT Press.

Kripke, S. 1972. Naming and necessity. In. D. Davidson and G. Harman, eds., *Semantics of Natural Language*. Dordrecht: Reidel.

Malt, B. 1995. Category coherence in cross-cultural perspective. *Cognitive Psychology* 29: 85–148.

Mayr, E. 1969. *Principles of Systematic Zoology*. New York: McGraw-Hill.

Murphy, G., and D. Medin. 1985. The role of theories in conceptual coherence. *Psychological Review* 92: 289–316.

Putnam, H. 1975. The meaning of "meaning." In K. Gunderson, ed., *Language, Mind, and Knowledge*. Minneapolis: University of Minnesota Press.

Satinoff, E. 1983. A re-evaluation of the concept of the homeostatic organization of temperature regulation. *Handbook of Behavioral Neurobiology*, vol. 6: Motivation, pp. 443–74.

Simpson, G. 1961. *Principles of Animal Taxonomy*. New York: Columbia University.

Sperber, D. 1996. *La Contagion des idées*. Paris: Editions Odile Jacob.

Strauss, C., and N. Quinn. 1992. Preliminaries to a theory of culture acquisition. In H. Pick, P. Van Den Broek, and D. Knill, eds., *Cognition: Conceptual and Methodological Issues*. APA, Washington D.C.

Stross, B. 1973. Acquisition of botanical terminology by Tzeltal children. In M. Edmonson, ed., *Meaning in Mayan Languages*. The Hague: Mouton.

Tversky, A., and D. Kahneman. 1986. Rational choice and framing decisions. *Journal of Business* 59: S251–78.

# 2

# Ethno-ornithology of the Ketengban People, Indonesian New Guinea

Jared Diamond and K. David Bishop

To biologists, the term "species names" refers to scientific nomenclature according to the principles formulated by Linnaeus in the eigtheenth century. However, as a matter of fact all recorded peoples have had vernacular names, in their local language, for plant and animal species familiar to them. Many of our English vernacular names are much older than Linnaean scientific names and were used by Shakespeare and Chaucer. But the number of traditional English vernacular names is small compared to those used by many existing foraging peoples still heavily dependent on wild plant and animal species.

Those traditional vernacular names are of scientific interest for at least three reasons (Berlin 1992; Brown 1985, 1986; Bulmer and Tyler 1968; Dwyer 1976, 1979; Hunn 1975; Majnep and Bulmer 1977; Pawley 1991). First, ethnobiologists and anthropologists seek to understand how different peoples perceive, classify, and mentally process the world. Vernacular names provide a good database because they reflect how different peoples react to partly shared sets of stimuli. Do any generalizations apply to vernacular naming of species? Are there any patterns to the differences among peoples?

Second, biologists continue to debate whether species are discrete entities reflecting an objective reality, or whether they are merely biologists' arbitrary delineation of a continuum of Nature. If peoples with very different upbringings and motivations for naming nevertheless tended to recognize the same units of Nature, that would lend support to the view that those units correspond to an objective reality that is not a mere invention of scientists.

Finally, knowledge of vernacular names allows biologists to plumb the detailed knowledge that traditional peoples possess about local species. Biologists can thus tap into the wisdom that our forebears accumulated over millions of years of hunting/gathering existence. It is urgent to record this traditional knowledge now because much of it is of economic and intellectual value and traditional knowledge systems are rapidly crumbling.

Many ethnobiological studies have been carried out in New Guinea where most peoples continue to practice traditional foraging techniques and are still walking encyclopedias of biological lore (Bulmer and Tyler 1968; Diamond 1966, 1972, 1989a, 1989b, 1994; Dumbacher et al. 1992; Dwyer 1976; Gilliard and LeCroy 1961; Glick 1964; Hays 1979; Majnep and Bulmer 1977; McElhanon 1977; Schmid 1993). All these studies have had to wrestle with difficult methodological problems in crossing a profound cultural gap and establishing the communication required to ascertain vernacular names in New Guinea languages correctly (Berlin et al. 1991; Diamond, 1989b). There is an obvious risk to posing a leading question or one with a yes/no answer because that method provides no internal check on the correctness of the answer. A deeper problem is that the most reliable method to ascertain vernacular names is to obtain them while New Guineans are encountering and naming species as they normally do, that is, as live plants and animals in the forest. But this method can hardly be practiced by scientists without sufficient knowledge of New Guinea plant and animal species to identify them in the field. Because New Guinea is biologically rich, even specialists require years to acquire that ability for the plant and animal group on which they work. Hence anthropologists who are not also trained as biologists, and biologists seeking to elicit vernacular names outside of their group of special interest, suffer from the crippling disadvantage that they know far less about their subject matter than do their informants.

Faced with this difficulty, ethnobiologists usually resort to either of two methods. One method is to ask informants to name dead specimens. Unfortunately, as we have found by tests, this method often results in names conflicting with those given for live animals, inconsistent names, or no names at all. These failures are not surprising. New Guineans identify most animal species by voice, behavior, posture, ecological context, and other criteria absent from dead specimens. The second method, which yields even more unsatisfactory results, is to ask informants to give names to pictures of birds or other animals in a field guide. This second method possesses all the disadvantages of the first method, of eliciting names from dead specimens. It possesses the further disadvantages that informants have no idea of the actual size of the bird in question and may be inexperienced at conjuring up three-dimensional images from a two-dimensional picture.

Still a further common methodological problem in the ethnobiological literature is that informants are likely to withhold information from scientists whom they perceive to be ignorant about the subject. For example, one of us (J.D.) spent three field seasons interviewing Foré informants (a New Guinea Highlands people) about names of birds, Diamond's subject of expertise. Diamond went on to ask informants about other taxa, including mushrooms, about which Diamond is ignorant. Foré informants denied to Diamond that they had different names for different species of mushrooms. During the third session, when Diamond and his informants were spending time at a New Guinea forest camp and running out of food, the Foré brought in two large bags full of mushrooms that they had gathered, and proposed to eat them. Diamond objected that some mushrooms are poisonous: How could the Foré be sure that those particular mushrooms were edible? The Foré then responded with an hour-long lecture on dozens of species of mushrooms that they distinguished and named, and on where each mushroom grew and whether it was edible. When Diamond asked why his friends had not told him those mushroom names previously when he had inquired about them, they answered that they had seen for themselves that Diamond knew a lot about birds but that he was ignorant about mushrooms, so they had considered it a waste of time to go to the effort of giving him information that he was incapable of understanding. Ethnobiologist Ralph Bulmer, an expert on birds, reached a similar dead end when he attempted to interview New Guineans about stones.

In the present study we circumvent these methodological problems in a study of vernacular bird names of the Ketengban people of New Guinea. Both of us have long experience of New Guinea birds (Diamond since 1964, Bishop since 1977). We were able to deal with the Ketengbans on a basis of equality, as far as knowledge of birds and ability to identify them in the field were concerned. Most of our eliciting of bird names occurred under the natural conditions in which the Ketengbans actually identify birds—namely while they were walking in the forest and encountering living birds in our company. The Ketengbans offer the additional advantage that they were contacted by the outside world for the first time recently, with the result that they still spend much of their time hunting and their traditional knowledge of birds is still relatively intact. As it turns out, their understanding of birds is outstanding even by the standards of traditional New Guinea peoples, virtually all of whom are highly knowledgeable about New Guinea birds.

## 2.1 Ketengban Language and People

The Ketengban language is spoken in a small area in the Jayawijaya Mountains (Star Mountains) of the Central Dividing Range of Indonesian New Guinea (Irian Jaya Province) near its border with Papua New Guinea. Ketengban is not written, and no vocabulary or grammar has been published for it. It is one of the approximately 1,000 native New Guinea languages, all of them confined to New Guinea. With 10,000 speakers, Ketengban nevertheless ranks as a moderately important language by New Guinea standards, since the median number of speakers for a New Guinea language is approximately 2,000 people.

Grimes (1996) and Wurm (1982) summarize some information about the Ketengban language and people. Briefly, Ketengban is the easternmost of half-a-dozen very closely related languages that Wurm (1982) classifies as comprising the Goliath or Mek subphylum-level language family. That family is clearly related to (Wurm 1982), and in Grimes's (1996) classification a member of, the Trans–New Guinea language phylum. (Interestingly, among the Ketengban bird names that we recorded, Harriet Whitehead [personal communication] has recognized 18 as being similar to the names of bird species in the Seltaman language, a member of the Trans–New Guinea phylum's Ok language family, which immediately abuts to the east the Goliath family). The Trans–New Guinea phylum is unique to New Guinea and possibly related to some of New Guinea's several dozen other so-called Papuan or non-Austronesian language families. None of those families has a proven relationship with any other language family elsewhere in the world. Wurm (1982) and Foley (1986) discuss possible groupings of New Guinea language families among themselves, while Ruhlen (1987) mentions possible wider relationships of New Guinea languages.

The Ketengban people live in settlements between elevations of 1,400 and 2,100 meters and forage between elevations of 1,000 and 3,700 meters. As is typical for the New Guinea mountains, the Ketengban terrain is extremely steep and contributes to the isolation that led to the evolution of such localized languages. The climax habitat of the area is montane rainforest, but much of the area has been cleared for gardens. Ketengbans live by growing crops (especially sweet potato and taro), maintaining some pigs, and spending much time hunting. They utilize birds for food, as ecological indicator of habitats and seasons, and to obtain plumes worn as decorations.

Formerly Ketengban villages were chronically at war with each other as well as with neighboring linguistic groups. Their technology was Neolithic (ground stone axes). Those features of Ketengban life began to change in 1972, when first contact with the outside world was made by western missionaries. Today the Ketengban area contains a small primary school, whose teacher is from another New Guinea tribe (the Dani), instructs in the Indonesian language, and is the sole non-Ketengban person in the Ketengban area. There is a small airstrip (Okbab) at Borbon village, visited a few times per month by single-engine mission aircraft. An American missionary lived for some time at the airstrip but is no longer resident.

Notable changes in Ketengban life since first contact have been the end of warfare and of cannibalism. Most but not all Ketengbans now wear manufactured clothes, and many middle-aged and younger people speak the Indonesian language as a second language. Among Western material goods adopted, the most important besides clothes are metal tools, matches, and some cooking utensils available from a small store at the airstrip.

However, the Ketengbans still depend heavily on traditional farming and hunting and live largely outside the cash economy. They continue to reside in their traditional small villages. Because of the rugged terrain and other peoples surrounding the Ketengbans, it is impossible to travel overland from the Ketengban area to New Guinea's north coast, a 180 kilometer distance; the only known people to have accomplished the trek were some members of a Dutch expedition in 1959 (Brongersma and Venema, 1963). Few Ketengbans can afford the expense of a chartered plane flight to the coast. Hence, as we will see, much of their traditional knowledge of birds appears to be intact.

## 2.2   Our Study

We spent the period from March 24 to April 16, 1993, in the Ketengban area. During that time we walked over virtually their entire altitudinal transect (1,190 to 3,660 meters above sea level), but we spent most of our time at elevations of 1,800 to 3,660 meters. We spent seven days based at Borbon village, four days walking between Borbon and a campsite that we made at 3,350 meters, and thirteen days at camps in forest between 2,040 and 3,350 meters.

Because bird diversity in New Guinea increases at lower elevations, our resulting information about Ketengban bird names was fairly complete at high altutides but incomplete at low elevations. Hence from September 14 to October 5, 1994, we took three Ketengban men from Borbon village to a forest camp at 800 meters in the Van Rees Mountains, lying 500 km from the Ketengban area and with an avifauna almost entirely shared with comparable elevations in the Ketengban area. Our field work between 500 and 1,200 meters in the Van Rees Mountains permitted us to elicit Ketengban names for additional low-elevation species.

On most days we spent between 8 and 11 hours a day walking (mainly in forest) and observing birds, always accompanied by Ketengban guides. Between 5 and 12 Ketengban men lived with us in our camps, and 30 men accompanied us as porters and guides on days when we were moving between camps or to and from Borbon village. These men were our main sources of information. All were between about 10 and 60 years old; most were between 16 and 30. They were from Borbon, Sibip, and Omwom villages, which are within 3 kilometer of each other. All spoke the Okbab dialect of Ketengban, one of the Ketengban language's nine recognized dialects (Wurm, 1982). We detected no systematic differences of Ketengban bird names among informants from these three villages, but that is hardly surprising given the villages' close proximity.

In our limited available time we did not learn the Ketengban language (except for names of birds, other animals, and plants), and no Ketengban spoke English. All our conversations with them were in the Indonesian language, in which we and our Ketengban companions were both reasonably fluent. We recorded 169 Ketengban bird names, identified most of them definitely, and identified most others tentatively. We also recorded 127 Ketengban names for trees, 51 names for mammals, 34 names for frogs, 16 names for lizards, 9 names for snakes, 6 names for spiders, 4 names for butterflies, and a few names for other inesects and fungi, but we will not discuss these other Ketengban names because we do not know the scientific identities of most of them.

## 2.3   Our Methods

Our principal method for eliciting bird names consisted in asking Ketengban guides for the name of a bird that we and they both saw, or else heard, while walking together. In order to distinguish which individual bird we meant if there were several in sight or calling, we either pointed to the bird or imitated the call that we were hearing. In order to check that the Ketengban name given in reply actually was meant to refer to the bird about which we were inquiring, we asked our Ketengban guides to describe the bird to us in detail—in particular, its bill, tail, size, color, diet, and forest stratum in which it normally foraged. In that way we could ascertain whether they and we were really talking about the same bird, and whether they were really familiar with the species. All vernacular names ascertained in this way are marked in our accompanying list (table 2.1) by an asterisk. Such names constitute the majority of our names identified to species, 126 out of 143.

In addition we and our Ketengban guides carried out running conversations about other birds while we were walking together. Initially those conversations were unstructured. We merely asked our guides to name and describe to us other bird species that they and we had not yet encountered together. We asked them to compare those not-yet-

**Table 2.1**
Ketengban bird names

| English vernacular name | Scientific name | Ketengban name |
| --- | --- | --- |
| | **Cassowaries** | |
| Dwarf Cassowary | *Casuarius bennetti* | kwetmá |
| | **Herons** | |
| Intermediate Egret/ Great Egret | *Ardea intermedia/A. alba* | mekokrí |
| | **Ducks** | |
| Salvadori's Teal | *Salvadorina waigiuensis* | ʔdawé |
| | **Hawks** | |
| *Brahminy Kite | *Haliastur indus* | ambún |
| *Meyer's Goshawk | *Accipiter meyerianus* | sengsengpéna |
| *New Guinea Harpy-Eagle | *Harpyopsis novaeguineae* | bukól |
| *Brown Falcon | *Falco berigora* | muldanyí |
| *Long-tailed Buzzard | *Henicopernis longicauda* | bep |
| (a large hawk) | | nyarará |
| (a long-clawed bird-eating hawk) | | mapón |
| (a hawk) | | silbít |
| | **Megapodes** | |
| *Common Scrubfowl or Wattled Brush-turkey | *Megapodius freycinet or Aepypodius arfakianus* | lyeyé |
| | **Quail** | |
| Snow Mountain Quail | *Anurophasis monorthonyx* | dapém |
| | **Rails** | |
| *Chestnut Forest-Rail | *Rallicula rubra* | kamél |
| | **Pigeons** | |
| *White-breasted Fruit dove | *Ptilinopus rivoli* | be |
| *Other fruit pigeons | *Ptilinopus* sp. | telél |
| *Imperial pigeons | *Ducula* sp. | ikin-pirirí |
| *Papuan Mountain Pigeon | *Gymnophaps albertisii* | pokpók |
| *White-throated Pigeon | *Columba vitiensis* | kiknyí, bilawík |
| *Brown Cuckoo-Dove | *Macropygia amboinensis* | kwon |
| *Black-billed Cuckoo-Dove | *Macropygia nigrirostris* | tukór |
| *Great Cuckoo-Dove | *Reinwardtoena reinwardtsi* | molé |
| *Bronze Ground-Dove | *Gallicolumba beccarii* | omkóng |
| Victoria Crowned Pigeon | *Goura victoria* | ʔwabupu-pirigní |

Table 2.1 (continued)

| English vernacular name | Scientific name | Ketengban name |
|---|---|---|
| **Parrots** | | |
| *Dusky Lory | *Pseudeos fuscata* | ʔbasér |
| *Rainbow Lorikeet | *Trichoglossus haematodus* | ʔkel |
| *Papuan Lorikeet | *Charmosyna papou* | wetén |
| *Plum-faced Lorikeet | *Oreopsittacus arfaki* | ʔbeteték |
| *Yellow-billed Lorikeet | *Neopsittacus musschenbroekii* | piteléng |
| *Orange-billed Lorikeet | *Neopsittacus pullicauda* | nyisbélek, alarí |
| Red-breasted Pygmy-Parrot | *Micropsitta bruijnii* | ʔbura-siriríya |
| *Sulphur-crested Cockatoo | *Cacatua galerita* | nyarí |
| *Vulturine Parrot | *Psittrichas fulgidas* | kaktá |
| *Palm Cockatoo | *Probosciger aterrimus* | yongóli |
| Eclectus Parrot | *Eclectus roratus* ♀ | kayór |
| *Brehm's Tiger-Parrot | *Psittacella brehmii* | geki |
| *Painted Tiger-Parrot | *Psittacella picta* | geki |
| (a large high-altitude parrot) | | youm |
| (a large high-altitude parrot) | | durú |
| (a large high-altitude parrot) | | maiyé |
| (a small high-altitude parrot) | | kiké |
| *Western Black-capped Lory or Red-cheeked Parrot | *Domicella lory* or *Geoffroyus* sp. | nyaléng |
| (a parrot larger than *Psittacella* sp. (= geki)) | | ʔgeki-kasmón |
| (a parrot) | | nyelbí |
| **Cuckoos** | | |
| *Brush Cuckoo | *Cacomantis variolosus* | belwól |
| *Fan-tailed Cuckoo | *Cacomantis pyrrhophanus* | nyororóng |
| *Chestnut-breasted Cuckoo | *Cacomantis castaneiventris* | amokbórorong |
| *Rufous-throated Bronze Cuckoo | *Chrysococcyx ruficollis* | dekibelbéla |
| *White-crowned Koel | *Caliechthrus leucolophus* | dadarbóng |
| *Greater Black Coucal | *Centropus menbeki* | kunkai |

**Table 2.1** (continued)

| English vernacular name | Scientific name | Ketengban name |
|---|---|---|
| **Night birds** (owls, frogmouths, nightjars, owlet-nightjars) | | |
| Sooty Owl | *Tyto tenebricosa* | daru |
| Papuan Boobook Owl | *Ninox theomacha* | ʔsulelína |
| Papuan or Marbled Frogmouth | *Podargus papuensis* or *P. ocellatus* | sumé |
| Large-tailed Nightjar | *Caprimulgus macrurus* | ʔkoité |
| (a large dark night bird) | | solelóng |
| (a night bird) | | boromnyá |
| | **Swifts** | |
| *Glossy Swiftlet | *Collocalia esculenta* | pupaléma |
| *Mountain Swiftlet | *Collocalia hirundinacea* | pupaléma |
| | **Tree-swifts** | |
| *Moustached Tree-swift | *Hemiprocne mystacea* | gadekdéka |
| | **Kingfishers** | |
| *Mountain Kingfisher | *Halcyon megarhyncha* | amkeri-tololóp |
| | **Bee-Eaters** | |
| *Rainbow Bee-Eater | *Merops ornatus* | boromboromá |
| | **Hornbills** | |
| *Blyth's Hornbill | *Rhyticeros plicatus* | kawér |
| | **Swallows** | |
| *Pacific Swallow | *Hirundo tahitica* | katwín |
| | **Cuckoo-Shrikes** | |
| *Black-bellied Cuckoo-Shrike | *Coracina montana* | kenáli |
| *Stout-billed Cuckoo-Shrike | *Coracina caeruleogrisea* | but-nyón |
| *Hooded Cuckoo-Shrike | *Coracina longicauda* | sekró-sekró |
| | **Wagtails** | |
| *Grey Wagtail | *Motacilla cinerea* | selapél |
| | **Pipits** | |
| *Alpine Pipit | *Anthus gutturalis* | mong-míng |
| | **Thrushes** | |
| *Pied Chat | *Saxicola caprata* | kurumsóng |
| *Island Thrush | *Turdus poliocephalus* | tet |
| | **Logrunners** | |
| *Lesser Melampitta | *Melampitta lugubris* | golík |
| *Spotted Jewel-Babbler | *Ptilorrhoa leucosticta* | sapkór |
| *Blue-capped Ifrita | *Ifrita kowaldi* | serepserep, burunyétu |

**Table 2.1** (continued)

| English vernacular name | Scientific name | Ketengban name |
|---|---|---|
| | **Warblers** | |
| *Rusty Mouse-Warbler | *Crateroscelis murina* | demán |
| *Mountain Mouse-Warbler | *Crateroscelis robusta* | toktokpáni |
| *White-shouldered Fairy-Wren | *Malurus alboscapulatus* | selelyáu |
| *Tawny Grassbird | *Megalurus timoriensis* | soleká |
| *Large Scrub-Wren | *Sericornis nouhuysi* | nyétu |
| *Papuan Scrub-Wren | *Sericornis papuensis* | dupseldupsel |
| *New Guinea Thornbill | *Acanthiza murina* | nyelék-nyelék |
| *Grey Gerygone | *Gerygone cinerea* | mepumínin |
| *Brown-breasted Gerygone | *Gerygone ruficollis* | kirinénen |
| *Island Leaf-Warbler | *Phylloscopus trivirgatus* | biduplesér |
| | **Flycatchers** | |
| *Mountain Peltops | *Peltops montanus* | sereréng |
| *Dimorphic Fantail | *Rhipidura brachyrhyncha* | oklinglíng-gor |
| *Black Fantail | *Rhipidura atra* | kengsóng tanah |
| *Friendly Fantail | *Rhipidura albolimbata* | kengsóng |
| *Northern Fantail | *Rhipidura rufiventris* | jerung-jerung |
| *Black Monarch | *Monarcha axillaris* | butorbaríya |
| *Black-breasted Boatbill | *Machaerirhynchus nigripectus* | dokwerwér |
| | **Robins** | |
| *Canary Flycatcher | *Microeca papuana* | burendáyap |
| *Torrent Flycatcher | *Monachella muelleriana* | senenenyí |
| Garnet Robin | *Eugerygone rubra* | poldemógnong |
| *Mountain Robin | *Petroica bivittata* | ʔikipá |
| *Black-throated Robin | *Poecilodryas albonotata* | ikdín |
| *Ashy Robin | *Poecilodryas albispecularis* | ʔalopdíndin |
| *White-winged Robin | *Peneothello sigillatus* | weribétbet |
| *Blue-grey Robin | *Peneothello cyanus* | tunglóp |
| *Lesser Ground-Robin | *Amalocichla incerta* | ʔalopdíndin |
| | **Whistlers** | |
| Mottled Whistler | *Pachycephala leucostigma* | ʔsikisók |
| *Sclater's Whistler | *Pachycephala soror* | mawe |
| *Regent Whistler | *Pachycephala schlegelii* | mawe |
| *Lorentz's Whistler | *Pachycephala lorentzi* | mawe |
| *Black-headed Whistler | *Pachycephala monacha* | kwalemtéte |
| *Rufous-naped Whistler | *Pachycephala rufinucha* | sunkór |

**Table 2.1** (continued)

| English vernacular name | Scientific name | Ketengban name |
|---|---|---|
| *Hooded Pitohui | *Pitohui dichrous* | popoyáu |
| *Black Pitohui | *Pitohui nigrescens* | insuán |
| *Crested Pitohui | *Pitohui cristatus* | bop |
| *Wattled Ploughbill | *Eulacestoma nigropectus* | ?kerí |
| | **Orioles** | |
| *Brown Oriole | *Oriolus szalayi* | sotokubólem |
| | **Magpie-Larks** | |
| *Torrent-Lark | *Grallina bruijnii* | men-nyí |
| | **Butcherbirds** | |
| *Hooded Butcherbird | *Cracticus cassicus* | moro-moro |
| | **Crows** | |
| *Grey Crow | *Corvus tristis* | taim |
| | **Birds of Paradise** | |
| *Macgregor's Bird of Paradise | *Macgregoria pulchra* | kwérma, nalmómi |
| *Short-tailed Paradigalla | *Paradigalla brevicauda* | mómi |
| *Black Sicklebill | *Epimachus fastuosus* | búla-búla ♂, nyung ♀ |
| *Brown Sicklebill | *Epimachus meyeri* | buk-buk-nyí |
| *Splendid Astrapia | *Astrapia splendissima* | dang-dang |
| *Carola's Parotia | *Parotia carolae* | benim |
| *Superb Bird of Paradise | *Lophorina superba* | karén |
| *King of Saxony Bird of Paradise | *Pteridophora alberti* | gekró |
| *Lesser Bird of Paradise | *Paradisaea minor* | kwalép |
| *Crested Bird of Paradise | *Cnemophilus macgregorii* | siwari |
| | **Bowerbirds** | |
| Macgregor's Bowerbird | *Amblyornis macgregoriae* | siwari-weté |
| | **Australian Nuthatches** | |
| *Black Sittella | *Daphoenositta miranda* | omsetók |
| | **Tree-creepers** | |
| *Papuan Tree-creeper | *Climacteris placens* | dondon |
| | **Honey-Eaters** | |
| *Olive Straightbill | *Timeliopsis fulvigula* | ?serep-serep |
| *Red-collared Myzomela | *Myzomela rosenbergii* | kau |
| *Slate-chinned Longbill | *Toxorhamphus poliopterus* | benselepná |
| *Long-billed Honey-Eater | *Melilestes megarhynchus* | buse |

**Table 2.1** (continued)

| English vernacular name | Scientific name | Ketengban name |
|---|---|---|
| *Common Smoky Honey-Eater | *Melipotes fumigatus* | kasóp |
| *Belford's Melidectes | *Melidectes belfordi* | ulámu |
| *Ornate Melidectes | *Melidectes torquatus* | alemkár |
| *Short-bearded Melidectes | *Melidectes nouhuysi* | umak |
| *Black-throated Honey-Eater | *Meliphaga subfrenata* | burusópsop, kurusóm |
| *Scrub White-eared or Mountain Meliphaga | *Meliphaga albonotata* or *M. orientalis* | dulém |
| Leaden Honey-Eater | *Ptiloprora plumbea* | dénsiki |
| *Grey-streaked Honey-Eater | *Ptiloprora perstriata* | sewi |
| *Marbled Honey-Eater | *Pycnopygius cinereus* | sorom |
| *New Guinea Friarbird | *Philemon novaeguineae* | nyoklép |
| Meyer's Friarbird | *Philemon meyeri* | ?tubán |
| | **Berry-Peckers** | |
| *Papuan Flower-Pecker | *Dicaeum pectorale* | bersék |
| *Fan-tailed Berry-Pecker | *Melanocharis versteri* | simbát |
| Spotted Berry-Picker | *Rhamphocharis crassirostris* | ?bontók |
| *Tit Berry-Pecker | *Oreocharis arfaki* | korité |
| *Crested Berry-Pecker | *Paramythia montium* | kisokwa |
| | **White-eyes** | |
| *Western Mountain White-eye | *Zosterops fuscicapillus* | amoli-kelúlup |
| | **Finches** | |
| *Blue-faced Parrot-Finch | *Erythrura trichroa* | sirilyá or siriríya |
| *Streak-headed Mannikin | *Lonchura tristissima* | teyongdulel-lepnyi |
| | **Unidentified Ketengban names** | |
| A small, low-altitude, warbler species | like *Gerygone palpebrosa* | ??simitnóng |
| A small warbler species | like *Gerygone cinerea* | ??sekelepná |
| A medium-sized brown bird | | ??kapitóto |
| A small, ground-dwelling, high-altitude species | like *Sericornis beccarii* | ??watkár |
| A dark, low-altitude, flycatcher species | like *Monarcha trivirgatus, M. julianae* | ??kweléng-kweléng |

**Table 2.1** (continued)

| English vernacular name | Scientific name | Ketengban name |
|---|---|---|
| A low-altitude flycatcher species | like ♀ *Myiagra alecto* | ??aling |
| A low-altitude species, possibly yellow | *Campochaera sloetii, Monarcha chrysomela*, or *Ptiloris magnificus* | ??pará |
| A ground bird like a rail or wader | | ??pelúl |
| A long-billed ground-dwelling species | | burr |
| A dull small bird | like *Sericornis nouhuysi* (=nyetu) | ??umum-itu-nyétu |
| A high-altitude bird | | ??inyu |
| A low-altitude black bird | | ??murip |
| A ground bird | | ??koripon |
| An unidentified bird | | ??keretnyóng |
| An unidentified bird | | ??nyadu |
| An unidentified bird | | ??siployeng |
| An unidentified bird | | ??waiyepenyá |
| An unidentified bird | | ??nawi |
| An unidentified bird | | ??amokborbor |

Note:  Species are grouped by families (boldface headings). Vernacular and scientific names are from Beehler et al. (1986), based on Beehler and Finch (1985). Ketengban names are spelled and accented so as to indicate pronunciation for Americans; in Indonesia, the sound that we transcribe as "ny" (as in "canyon") would instead be transcribed "ng." A single question mark indicates that the identity of the Ketengban name with the bird species denoted by its English vernacular and scientific name is tentative but not certain. Two question marks indicate that the identity of the Ketengban name is more uncertain. Asterisks indicate Ketengban names that we identified in the field when we and Ketengban informants observed the same bird together. Identifications without asterisks are based instead on cases where informants gave us a Ketengban name and described the bird to us but we and they did not observe the bird together.

encountered species to other species for which we had already ascertained names. Gradually, as we became familiar with many Ketengban names, we structured the questioning by asking our informants to name and describe to us all night birds, or all grassland birds, or all ground-dwelling birds, or all birds similar to some species (e.g., a parrot or pigeon species) whose vernacular name we had already identified.

In addition we gave our guides a brief verbal description (e.g., by imitating song or behavior) of some bird species that we expected in the Ketengban area but had not yet encountered. If our informants claimed to know that species and offered a name for it, we then asked them to describe it in detail, so that we could again be sure that we and they were referring to the same species. At all costs we avoided yes/no questions, leading questions, and discussions that led simply to an answer of the form "Yes, I know that bird, its name is X." Those questions or outcomes would have left us no way of knowing whether we and the Ketengbans were actually talking about the same species.

On our last days with the Ketengbans, we showed them the color plates in the Beehler et al. (1986) field guide to New Guinea birds and asked them to name and describe bird species that they recognized from the plates. This method yielded only a few additional names beyond those of species that we had already observed with Ketengbans or that they had already described to us. All such tentative identifications are among those marked with a single or double question mark in table 2.1. We used this method mainly to elicit further vernacular names and descriptions, to test in future field studies.

## 2.4   Results

Table 2.1 summarizes the 169 Ketengban vernacular bird names that we obtained. We were able to identify 143 bird species (as recognized by ornithologists) with Ketengban names, definitely or tentatively. Our tentative identifications mainly involved species that informants described to us but that they and we did not encounter together. We now discuss in turn Ketengban taxonomic categories; the fineness of distinctions that Ketengbans made among bird species; how they identified birds, and how they had learned about birds; whether there are any bird species that are resident in the Ketengban area but that the Ketengbans do not name; whether, conversely, there are species to which they give more than one name; limits to Ketengban knowledge of birds; and the vernacular names themselves.

### Ketengban Taxonomic Categories

Scientific nomenclature for a local biota is hierarchical, with four major levels below the class level (birds being the class Aves). Those four levels are the order, family, genus, and species. In contrast, Ketengban names belong to only two levels: a low-level terminal category corresponding closely to species, and a high-level collective category corresponding approximately to classes or orders. The six collective Ketengban names that we obtained correspond respectively to birds, bats, mammals other than bats, snakes, lizards, and frogs. We found no evidence that Ketengbans name any category intermediate between their low-level terminal category and their high-level collective category. Even though Ketengbans readily understood our questions about naming all species in distinctive bird families, such as naming all parrot species or all hawk species, they offered no name for those intermediate categories (which scientists recognize as families or orders), despite their ability to grasp the bounds of the intermediate category. Most Ketengban names referred to a single bird species. We will discuss the exceptions to this rule below.

### Fineness of Ketengban Ornithological Knowledge

Even by the standards of professional western ornithologists, the Ketengbans possess impressive knowledge of distinctions between very similar, related bird species. Three examples will serve as illustrations:

One of the common small bird species of the Ketengban area is the Gray-streaked Honey-Eater *Ptiloprora perstriata*, familiar to Ketengbans as "sewi." However, Ketengbans also described a very rare and similar-appearing sibling species, the Leaden Honey-Eater *Ptiloprora plumbea*, which the Ketengbans knew as "dénsiki." Informants were familiar with its altitudinal range, diet, and posture and correctly described it as being smaller than the "sewi" and rarer.

Two of the smallest bird species of the Ketengban area are two related warblers, the Brown-breasted Gerygone *Gerygone ruficollis* and the Gray Gerygone *Gerygone cinerea*. Of these two small and dull-colored birds, the Gray Gerygone is especially obscure, being not only tiny but mainly confined to the tops of high trees and silent. Nevertheless, Ketengbans distinguished these two species as "kirinénen" and "mépuminin" respectively.

Two small songbirds, the Regent Whistler *Pachycephala schelegelii* and Lorentz's Whistler *Pachycephala lorentzi*, overlap in altitudinal range and forage in essentially the same way. Male and female Lorentz's Whistler are identical in plumage and so similar to female Regent Whistlers that their distinctness as species was not recognized by scientists until 1940, over twenty-five years after specimens of Lorentz's Whistler first reached Dutch museums. Nevertheless, Ketengban informants pointed out to us not only the plumage distinctions of which western ornithologists eventually became aware (i.e., that Lorentz's Whistler is sexually monomorphic, while Regent Whistler is sexually dimorphic), but they also pointed out to us behavioral differences that we were then able to confirm but of which we and other Western ornithologists had been previously unaware: that the two species differ markedly in song, and that Lorentz's Whistler extends above, Regent Whistler below, the shared zone of altitudinal overlap.

Ketengban informants similarly named and distinguished sibling species of cuckoo-doves (genus *Macropygia*), lories (*Neopsittacus*), cuckoos (*Cacomantis*), cuckoo-shrikes (*Coracina*), scrub-wrens (*Sericornis*), and fantails (*Rhipidura*).

## Ketengban Field Identification of Birds

How do Ketengbans succeed in distinguishing such similar species at a glance? Recall that western ornithologists find some of these species pairs or trios difficult to distinguish as specimens held and measured in the hand, or as living birds observed through binoculars. Yet Ketengbans without binoculars distinguished these sibling pairs or trios of species in the forest at a distance, through dense foliage, and often in dim light, mist, or silhouette.

Ketengbans do not distinguish species as we do, by "field marks" or by the fine details of plumage to which Peterson field guides call attention by arrows on plates. Instead, Ketengbans identify by song, silhouette, posture, behavior, and general appearance, without being concerned about fine details of plumage that are normally invisible to forest observers without binoculars anyway. Ketengbans have the advantage that they know what birds to expect in their area, match bird individuals encountered against this expected set of possible identifications, and are not distracted by related species to which western observers are unnecessarily alert but which in fact do not occur in the Ketengban area. For example, when Ketengbans see a flock of very small, fast-moving, virtually tailless warblers gleaning silently in the canopy of tall forest at elevations of 2,000 to 2,800 meters, they know that the birds are probably "mépuminin" (= Gray Gerygone) even if no details of plumage can be seen—because other gerygone species in New Guinea occur at low elevation or below the forest canopy or are usually solitary or likely to be singing.

As another example, two very similar species of small brown scrubwrens, the Large Scrub-Wren *Sericornis nouhuysi* and Papuan Scrub-Wren *Sericornis papuensis*, which we often find difficult to distinguish in the hand as museum specimens, were distinguished by the Ketengbans as "nyétu" and "dupsel-dupsel" respectively, and identified at a distance in the forest by their differing songs and somewhat different foraging technique (*S. nouhuysi* being more of a bark-gleaner, *S. papuensis* more of a leaf-gleaner). Three species of *Cacomantis* cuckoos inhabit the Ketengban area, are very similar in appearance, and two of them are fairly similar in song, but the three species differ (albeit with some overlap) in habitat and altitudinal range. We never saw any of the three species during our twenty-five days in the Ketengban area but heard them daily. The Ketengbans identified these unseen cuckoos infallibly by song.

In most cases we were also able to distinguish by song, or else by sight with binoculars, the species that the Ketengbans distinguished without binoculars. However, the Ketengbans also distinguished male and female Tit Berry-Peckers (*Oreocharis arfaki*, "korité"), and adult and juvenile Black-throated Honey-Eaters (*Meliphaga subfrenata*, "burusópsop") by voice, although we could not detect the sound distinctions that the Ketengbans attempted to explain to us. (To our ears, all the calls were a short "ss"). However, we were able to confirm with our binoculars, by plumage characters invisible to the Ketengbans without binoculars, that they were correct in their field distinctions between males and females or between adults and juveniles of these species.

## How Do the Ketengbans Learn to Distinguish Bird Species

We were especially puzzled that the Ketengbans recognized and named tiny, dull, silent, economically seemingly unimportant species of the forest canopy, such as the Gray Gerygone = "mépuminin." It was obvious to us that Ketengban children as well as adults spend much time in the forest, but it was not clear to us how they could have familiarized themselves so closely with small canopy species. Our informants told us that they had acquired that knowledge in two ways. First, as children they spend much time in the forest canopy because their play includes climbing trees, constructing hunting blinds in the canopy, watching canopy species, and attempting to shoot them with a child's bow and arrow. Second, canopy species sometimes descend closer to the ground at the forest edge or in second-growth trees, where they can be observed by an observer on the ground.

## Are There Any Unnamed Bird Species?

Previous authors (e.g., Hunn 1991) have pointed out that hunting peoples may not apply individual names to every species in their environment, only to so-called salient species—that is, species that are distinctively different from other species. Undistinctive species may not be distinguished by separate names, especially in the case of groups of small and economically unimportant species. These perceptions by other observers correspond to our own experience in the New Guinea lowlands, where similar-appearing sets of small songbirds may be lumped under the same name.

In the Ketengban area, however, there was no bird species that we and they encountered together under adequate observing conditions and that they did not name. Thus it is not the case that the Ketengbans name only salient species and either ignore or broadly lump nonsalient species. Conversely, none of the bird species that the Ketengbans described to us appears to be mythical.

## One Name, One Species?

Most Ketengban vernacular bird names that we succeeded in identifying (about 115) appeared to refer to a single bird species recognized by scientists. The exceptions are few enough that it is worth listing all of them individually. *Two names, one species* Males and females of the bird of paradise species known as the Black Sicklebill (*Epimachus fastuosus*) are distinguished as "búla-búla" and "nyung" respectively. The sexes differ considerably in appearance, the male being larger, much darker, and with a much longer tail. The sexes are also economically different because only the male is prized by the Ketengbans for its plumes. The Eclectus Parrot *Eclectus roratus* is also strikingly sexually dimorphic, males being emerald green and females scarlet red. This species too may have different Ketengban names for the two sexes, though we are not certain, since we learned the name of the female ("kayór") but not of the male.

There are also some sexually monomorphic species to which the Ketengbans apply two alternative names. This is certain for the Macgregor's Bird of Paradise *Macgregoria pulchra*, which is known as the "kwérma" but also as the "nalmómi"; the former name is not related to any other Ketengban vernacular name, whereas "nalmómi" is related to the name "mómi" for another bird of paradise species, the Short-tailed Paradigalla *Paradigalla brevicauda*, which shares blackish plumage and a yellow facial wattle with Macgregor's Bird of Paradise. The Black-throated Honey-Eater *Meliphaga subfrenata* was consistently named "burusópsop" by one knowledgeable informant, "kurusóm" by another informant.

A puzzling case involved lorikeets of the genus *Neopsittacus*, of which ornithologists recognize two species, the Yellow-billed Lorikeet *N. musschenbroekii* and the Orange-billed Lorikeet *N. pullicauda*. Ketengban informants insisted that there were actually three species, and they identified the Yellow-billed Lorikeet in the field consistently as "piteléng" but variously identified the Orange-billed Lorikeet as either "nyisbélek" or "alarí." Cases are known in which New Guineans insisted that rats originally considered by mammalogists as a single species should actually be assigned to two vernacular names, and it turned out that the New Guineans were correct that two species actually were involved. We cannot exclude the possibility that what ornithologists consider to be *Neopsittacus pullicauda* actually consists of two very similar species that the Ketengbans have learned to distinguish by behavior. However, we consider it more likely that in this case the ornithologists are correct and the Ketengbans are in error.

Finally, three remaining species (the pigeon *Columba vitiensis*, the ifrita *Ifrita kowaldi*, and the honey-eater *Meliphaga subfrenata*) were also variously referred to by two alternative names. From the circumstances in each case, we suspect that the Ketengbans were uncertain to which of two similar species the bird individual observed belonged.

In four cases we believe that the Ketengbans do apply the same vernacular name to two or more related species. In at least two of these cases, however, the Ketengbans were aware of the differences between the two species bearing the same name.

The first case involves the Friendly Fantail *Rhipidura albolimbata* and the Black Fantail *Rhipidura atra*. We and our informants first encountered the Friendly Fantail, which our informants named "kengsóng." One informant then told us that there was still one other type of "kengsóng" that he and we had not encountered together, that was black, and that foraged mainly near the ground rather than in the trees. The informant referred to this-as-yet-not-encountered "kengsóng" as "kengsóng tanah," where "tanah" is the Indonesian word for "ground." When we later encountered the Black Fantail, which is indeed black and forages near the ground, we were told that there at last was the "kengsóng tanah" about which our informant had been talking before.

Similarly, after encountering the Regent Whistler (*Pachycephala schlegelii*) and obtaining the name "mawe," we encountered the very similar Lorentz's Whistler (*Pachycephala lorentzi*) and were told that it was also named "mawe." However, our informant proceeded to tell us that two different though similar-appearing birds went under the same name, and he accurately described the ecological, plumage, and song differences between the two species. A third related species, Sclater's Whistler *Pachycephala soror*, was also named "mawe"; in this case we were not able to ascertain whether our informants recognized its distinctness from the other two whistler species.

The third case involved two similar species of tiger-parrots, Brehm's Tiger-Parrot *Psittacella brehmii* and the Painted Tiger-Parrot *Psittacella picta*. Both were named "geki," and we are uncertain whether our informants recognized the difference.

Finally, two similar species of swiftlets, the Glossy Swiftlet *Collocalia esculenta* and the Mountain Swiftlet *Collocalia hirundinacea*, were both named "pupaléma." In this case we pointed out to Ketengbans that there was both a blue-backed slower-flying species and a brown-backed faster-flying species involved, but our informants said that they were not aware of the distinction. That failure is not surprising, since both species usually fly too fast to be observed closely without binoculars, and since we have yet to encounter any New Guinea or Solomon Island people that distinguishes the two species. This is the only case in which we are reasonably confident that the Ketengbans failed to distinguish two bird species resident in their area.

### Areas of Ornithological Confusion for the Ketengbans

Apart from these cases of sibling species of *Collocalia* swiftlets and possibly tiger-parrots and whistlers, we encountered two other pairs or groups of birds with which the Ketengbans had consistent problems of field identification.

One case involves two species of robins, the Ashy Robin *Poecilodryas albispecularis* and the Lesser Ground-Robin *Amalocichla incerta*. Both are fairly common species that hop on the ground and have beautiful, high-pitched, whistled songs, but both are extremely secretive; we never saw either during our twenty-four days in the Ketengban area, though we heard them sing many times daily. This secretiveness makes the differences between the two robins difficult to learn for field observers, and a further difficulty is that both species sing their high-pitched beautiful whistled songs in varied patterns. The Ketengbans referred to both singers as "alopdíndin," and we do not know whether they would have applied different names to the two species if we had seen them together.

The other area of confusion involved the many species of lories (nectar-feeding parrots) in the Ketengban area. The Ketengbans gave us thirteen names for lories: "alarí," "basér," "beteték," "durú," "kel," "kiké," "maiyé," "nyaléng," "nyelbí," "nyisbélek," "piteléng," "wetén," and "youm." Field identification of lories is difficult because they are mostly green and red birds with similar shrill short calls and are usually seen either flying rapidly overhead in silhouette or else perched concealed within the green canopy. We found them confusing, and so evidently did the Ketengbans. We are reasonably confident that the name "piteléng" refers to Yellow-billed Lorikeets, "wetén" to the Papuan Lorikeet. We would have needed more field time with Ketengban informants to determine whether Ketengbans named other lory species consistently under more favorable conditions of observation.

### Ketengban Bird Names Themselves

In several cases the Ketengbans applied similar but differing names to similar species. As mentioned above, two black birds of paradise with yellow face wattles, the Short-tailed Paradigalla *Paradigalla brevicauda* and Macgregor's Bird of Paradise *Macgregoria pulchra*, are named "mómi" and "nalmómi," respectively. The Crested Bird of Paradise *Cnemophilus macgregorii* and Macgregor's Bowerbird *Amblyornis macgregoriae*, both of which are of similar size and with orange and brown plumage, have the similar names "siwari" and "siwari-waté," respectively. The Large Scrub-Wren *Sericornis nouhuysi*, a brown warbler, is called "nyétu," while a name for the Blue-capped Ifrita *Ifrita kowaldi*, a brown log-runner with warblerlike behavior, is "buru-nyétu." A small green, red, and blue finch, the Blue-faced Parrot-Finch *Erythrura trichroa*, is named "siríriya," while a small green, red, and blue pygmy-parrot species (*Micropsitta bruijnii*) is "bura-siríriya."

At least one Ketengban name, "golík" for the Lesser Melampitta *Melampitta lugubris*, is an onomatopoeic description of the bird's call. Although we are familiar with the songs and calls of most bird species of the Ketengban area, we did not recognize any other obviously onomatopoeic name.

Eleven species have Ketengban names consisting of a double syllable or pair of syllables: "búla-búla," "dang-dang," "don-don," "dupsel-dupsel," "jerung-jerung," "kweleng-kweleng," "moro-moro," nyelek-nyelek," "pok-pók," "sekró-sekró," and "serep-serep." A dozen other names contain doubled syllables added to other syllables, such as "boromboromá," "buk-buk-nyí," "okling-líng-gor," "sengsengpéna," "tok-tok-páni," and "weri-bét-bet."

As we noted previously for other New Guinea languages (Diamond, 1989a), the length of the vernacular name tends to vary inversely with the size of the bird: big birds tend to have short names, while small birds tend to have long names. The longest identified names—the hexasyllables "teyongdulel-lepnyi," "bura-siríriya," and "amkeri-tololóp"—belong to the small finch *Lonchura tristissima*, the pygmy-parrot *Micropsitta bruijnii*, and the small kingfisher *Halcyon megarhyncha*, respectively. The tiniest warblers (New Guinea Thornbill, Gray Gerygone, Brown-breasted Gerygone, Island Leaf-Warbler) all have tetrasyllables as names: "nyelek-nyelek," "mepumínin," "kirinénen," and "biduplesér" respectively. Most monosyllabic names belong to jay-sized or crow-sized birds ("be," "bep," "bop," "kwon," "nyung," "taim"). The largest New Guinea birds are the ostrichlike cassowary and the New Guinea Harpy Eagle, both with disyllabic names ("kwetmá" and "bukól").

## 2.5   Ketengban and Linnaean Delineations of Species

Are local "species" real units of nature, or are they taxonomists' arbitrary splitting up of a continuum of nature? Darwin himself was uncertain of the answer to this question. In the 1930s most population biologists reached a consensus that species do constitute realities of nature. Species delineate themselves as groups of individuals that interbreed with each other and that do not interbreed with other such reproductively defined groups. Groups thus defined also prove to differ from each other in ecology and behavior. This definition is now commonly referred to as the biological species concept (Mayr 1963). The ambiguities in this definition that result from local hybridization generally affect such a small fraction of candidate species as not to interfere with the application of the definition as a test.

Practical problems in applying the definition do arise from so-called sibling species: that is, species that are reproductively isolated from each other and that differ in their behavior and their ecological niches just as do other species, and that are unusual only in that we humans find them very similar in appearance. The reproductive isolation of sibling species from each other means that they have no difficulty distinguishing each other (e.g., by song, smell, or behaviors not obvious to us); only we humans find it hard to distinguish them.

The other practical problem with the definition, a real problem, comes in assessing whether geographically separated populations, such as those on different islands, represent distinct species or merely subspecies of the same species. However, that problem does not invalidate the proposed definition of species as reproductively isolated groups. Since geographically separated populations are not in contact with each other and do not have the opportunity to interbreed, these groups have not yet been put to the natural test of reproductive isolation, and all that taxonomists can do is to attempt to predict how they would behave toward each other if they came into contact.

While this definition of species as real, reproductively isolated groups of individuals is now accepted by most scientists, it is still vigorously questioned by a significant minority of scientists. Hence it is of interest to compare the species recognized by western taxonomists with the "species" named by traditional hunting peoples. The Ketengbans differ from Western scientists greatly in many human attributes relevant to biological classification: in motivation for classifying (intellectual reasons, versus practical reasons and effects of being immersed in natural environments), in language, in schooling, in amount of time spent with wild animals, in the importance of wild animals for human life, and in adjuncts to observation of wild animals (our binoculars and tape recorders versus their treetop blinds). It is nevertheless striking that the units into which the Ketengbans and western scientists classify birds correspond for the most part on a one-to-one basis. This can only mean that their and our shared classification describes a mutually perceived reality in the biological world, as Mayr (1963) and others have already noted.

## 2.6   Disappearance of Ketengban Knowledge

People have occupied New Guinea, obtaining their living in part or in whole as hunters and gatherers, for at least 40,000 years. The Ketengbans and other modern New Guinea peoples are thus heirs to the knowledge accumulated by at least 1,600 generations of humans. Even for birds, the organisms most intensively studied by Western scientists, much of what the Ketengbans know represents new information for scientists. For species much less studied by scientists—such as mammals, insects, and plants—the Ketengbans have even more to teach us. They represent walking encyclopedias of biology, most of whose pages are as yet unread by scientists.

Much of this knowledge of Ketengbans and other New Guinea peoples is likely to be commercially valuable to the rest of the world. For example, Ketengbans described the bird known to them as "sumé" (one of two species of frogmouth) as attracting insects into its open mouth by a smelly, sticky substance secreted on the bird's palate. Other New Guineans have given similar accounts (Diamond 1972, 1994). A natural insect attractant that evolved for use in a natural fly-trap could prove valuable. Only within the last two years was it discovered that some New Guinea birds concentrate an intensely poisonous substance in their feathers and skin and give off a warning odor, probably as a snake repellent (Dumbacher et al. 1992). Still other New Guineans describe at least two groups of New Guinea birds whose bodies liquefy and decay immediately upon death (Diamond 1994). Such knowledge makes it understandable why chemical and pharmaceutical companies find it worthwhile to hire ethnobiologists to interview foraging peoples about useful local plants and animals and to collect specimens for testing. Ethnobiological discoveries have spawned billion-dollar industries.

Throughout the world, such traditional systems of biological knowledge and classification are shrinking as traditional peoples become drawn into the modern world, with its increasingly homogenized culture. We noticed that this shrinkage is beginning to affect the Ketengbans as well. Children formerly spent much of their time with adults in the forest, where they inevitably became instructed about wild plants and animals, the subject of much normal conversation in the forest. Play for children often meant climbing trees and building blinds to observe and hunt small forest animals, including birds. Now children in their formative years spend most of their time in school being instructed about matters of the outside world, and visit the forest only during school vacations. School education, and all dealings with the outside world, utilize the Indonesian language, not the Ketengban language. Even in campfire conversations that we overheard among the Ketengbans, when we were in the distance and not participating and no non-Ketengban speaker was present, we heard Indonesian numerals and other words infiltrating the Ketengban language itself. Like other New Guinea peoples, the Ketengbans are undergoing a shift in values. They are losing interest in their traditional culture and instead want cash with which to purchase clothes, medicines, axes, schoolbooks, food, blankets, and umbrellas.

Scientists and environmentally concerned lay people are now focusing much attention on the accelerating biodiversity crisis, in which most of the world's plant and animal species are likely to reach the brink of extinction within the next century. In that crisis, humans are the villains, Nature the victim. Much less attention has been given to the corresponding crisis in which humans are both victims and villains: the accelerating disappearance of most of the world's languages themselves, and of the tens of thousands of years of traditional knowledge that they carry (Diamond 1994). For the Ketengbans, as we have seen, much of this knowledge is not only interesting but unique and valuable as well. What is happening to the Ketengbans is happening at varying rates to the thousand other peoples of New Guinea. A prime goal of biologists working in New Guinea should be to record as much as possible of these traditional knowledge systems before they vanish.

## Note

We acknowledge with pleasure the help of our Ketengban field associates, whose knowledge provided the material for our study, and the research support provided by the National Geographic Society through its Committee for Research and Exploration.

## References

Beehler, B., and B. W. Finch. 1985. *Species-Checklist of the Birds of New Guinea*. Moonee Ponds: Royal Australasian Ornithological Union.

Beehler, B., T. Pratt, D. Zimmerman, et al. 1986. *Birds of New Guinea*. Princeton: Princeton University Press.

Berlin, P. 1992. *Ethnobiological Classification: Principles of Categorization of Plants and Animals in Traditional Societies*. Princeton: Princeton University Press.

Berlin, B., J. S. Boster, and J. P. O'Neill. 1981. The perceptual bases of ethnobiological classification: evidence from Aguarana Jívaro ornithology. *Journal of Ethnobiology* 1: 95–108.

Brongersma, L. D., and G. F. Venema. 1963. *To the Mountains of the Stars*. New York: Doubleday.

Brown, C. H. 1985. Mode of subsistence and folk biological taxonomy. *Current Anthropology* 26: 43–64.

Brown, C. H. 1986. The growth of ethnobiological nomenclature. *Current Anthropology* 27: 1–19.

Bulmer, R. H., and M. J. Tyler. 1968. Karam classification of frogs. *Journal of the Polynesian Society* 77: 333–85.

Diamond, J. M. 1966. Zoological classification system of a primitive people. *Science* 151: 1102–04.

Diamond, J. M. 1972. *Avifauna of the Eastern Highlands of New Guinea.* Cambridge, MA: Nuttall Ornithological Club.

Diamond, J. M. 1989a. This-fellow frog, name belong-him dakwo. *Natural History* 98(4): 16–23.

Diamond, J. M. 1989b. The ethnobiologist's dilemma. *Natural History* 98(6): 26–30.

Diamond, J. M. 1994. Stinking birds and burning books. *Natural History* 103: 4–12.

Dumbacher, J., B. M. Beehler, T. F. Spande, et al. 1992. Homobatrachotoxin in the genus *Pitohui*: Chemical defense in birds? *Science* 258: 799–801.

Dwyer, P. D. 1976. An analysis of Rofaifo mammal taxonomy. *American Ethnologist* 3: 424–45.

Dwyer, P. D. 1979. Animal metaphors: An evolutionary model. *Mankind* 12: 13–27.

Foley, W. A. 1986. *The Papuan Language of New Guinea.* Cambridge: Cambridge University Press.

Gilliard, E. T., and M. LeCroy. 1961. Birds of the Victor Emanuel and Hindenburg Mountains, New Guinea. *Bulletin of the American Museum of Natural History* 123: 1–86.

Glick, L. B. 1964. Categories and relations in Gimi natural science. *American Anthropologist* 66: 273–80.

Grimes, B. 1996. *Ethnologue: Languages of the World.* 13th ed. Dallas: International Linguistics Center.

Hays, T. E. 1979. Plant classification and nomenclature in Ndumba, Papua New Guinea Highlands. *Ethnology* 18: 253–70.

Hunn, E. 1975. A measure of the degree of correspondence of folk to scientific biological classification. *American Ethnologist* 2: 309–27.

Hunn, E. S. 1991. Sahaptin bird classification. In A. Pawley, ed., *Man and a Half.* Auckland: The Polynesian Society, pp. 137–47.

Majnep, I. S., and R. Bulmer. 1977. *Birds of My Kalem Country.* Auckland: Auckland University Press.

Mayr, E. 1963. *Animal Species and Evolution.* Cambridge: Harvard University Press.

McElhanon, K. A. 1977. Selepet avifauna. *Work Papers in Papua New Guinea Languages* 22: 71–85.

Pawley, A., ed. 1991. *Man and a Half.* Auckland: The Polynesian Society.

Ruhlen, M. 1987. *A Guide to the World's Languages.* Stanford: Stanford University Press.

Schmid, C. K. 1993. Birds of Nokopo. *Muruk* 6: 1–61.

Wurm, S. 1982. *Papuan Languages of Oceania.* Tübingen: Narr.

# 3

## Size as Limiting the Recognition of Biodiversity in Folkbiological Classifications: One of Four Factors Governing the Cultural Recognition of Biological Taxa

Eugene Hunn

A key issue for anthropology is to account for cultural variation. The study of ethnobiological classification is one arena in which this issue has been addressed. Furthermore, since the cultural content of ethnobiological classifications is amenable to systematic comparison, ethnobiologists have tended to emphasize rigorous and systematic data collection and analysis as the basis for a search for scientific explanations of culturally variable phenomena. As a result a substantial consensus among ethnobiologists has been achieved during the past twenty years (Hunn 1982; Berlin 1992). This progress has depended heavily on our ability to clearly define and accurately measure certain variables (e.g., Hunn 1975; Geoghegan 1976; Berlin, Boster, and O'Neill 1981; Turner 1988). I hope to further that effort here.

To date variation in the degree to which folkbiological classifications have approximated the Western scientific system has been attributed to either "perceptual" or to "cultural salience" (Berlin 1992: 3–13). Perceptual salience is understood to include those aspects of the available external stimuli that, in the context of universal aspects of human sensory information processing, determine the likelihood that a particular biotic category will be "seen" and thus culturally recognized. Biosystematists have analyzed this factor in terms of "decided gaps" in patterns of the distribution of phenotypic characters of species and other taxonomic groups (Mayr 1969: 37; Simpson 1961: 191; Hunn 1977: 45–53). "Perceptual salience" has been operationally defined with respect to the Linnean taxonomy by treating the Western scientific taxonomy as an "etic grid" (Hunn 1976; Boster, Berlin, and O'Neill 1986; Boster 1987). The underlying assumption is that points of agreement between a given folk system and the Western scientific system—treated as two historically independent cultural creations must be due to extra-cultural constraints within the perceptual process. The residual variation is then attributed to "cultural salience."

I propose here two refinements of this scheme. Two factors fit neither the biologists' notion of *phenotypic salience*, as sketched above, nor the normal understanding of cultural salience, that is, the particular impor-tance of a plant or animal that can be understood only in terms unique to that culture. These additional factors I choose to call *ecological salience* and the *size factor*. I believe that it is best to treat each as an aspect of perceptual salience, broadly conceived, leaving cultural salience as a residual influence.

## 3.1   Ecological Salience

Ecological salience is independent of both phenotypic salience and size. The ecological salience of a set of organisms reflects the biogeographic and phenological interactions of a population of organisms to be classi-fied and the human population classifying them.

For example, plants and animals vary in total abundance and also in terms of the degree to which they are confined to one or another habitat within the geographic range of a particular human society. More abun-dant and more widely distributed organisms are more likely to be noticed than those less abundant and less widely distributed, other things being equal. Furthermore nocturnal animals or animals that are secretive will be less ecologically salient than diurnal and confiding species of equal abundance for most human communities. Migratory animals and annual plants are temporally restricted and thus less likely to gain cultural recog-nition than permanent residents or perennial plants of otherwise equiva-lent phenotypic salience.

Note that ecological salience has a cultural component, since the dis-tribution of human observers within the range of a society is culturally conditioned. Thus nocturnal animals are of particularly low salience for people who fear to leave their homes at night, while the salience of aquatic animals is a function of the importance of aquatic resources in the subsistence system of the society in question. Nevertheless, ecological salience is logically distinct from cultural salience as cultural salience has been previously understood, that is, as a matter of the variable "interest in" or "attention to" a set of organisms that is the direct consequence of the role that set plays in local cultural plans, namely the taxon's "activity signature" (Hunn 1982; see also Turner 1988 for a detailed discussion of how to measure "cultural salience"). Ecological salience may be understood as an index of the likelihood of meaningful encounters between the people of a community and a set of organisms as a function of the spatiotemporal distribution of the organism's population. For the present we may assess this factor on a crude ordinal scale, from most to least ecologically salient.

Unlike phenotypic salience and the size factor, which we analyze in detail below, the ecological salience of a set of organisms may vary substantially within a community as, for example, between men and women (see Boster 1985), between occupational specialists, or between individuals resident in different segments of the community (if the community's land base is extensive and topographically variable). Thus ecological salience may prove an important factor governing intracultural variation (see Hays 1974; Gardner 1976).

## 3.2  Size Factor

The size of an organism obviously affects its "perceptual salience" for folkbiological classification but should have no effect on Western scientific judgments as to its phenotypic distinctiveness and thus its phylogenetic classification. This contrast is due in large measure to the tools Western scientists employ to enhance their perception, specifically microscopes and photography, which are tools not available to folk systematists. Under a microscope an ant may appear as large as an elephant to the naked eye, and microscopic morphological details such as the pattern of the insect's antenna segmentation may appear as striking as the shape of the elephant's trunk. Of course a multitude of organisms invisible to the unaided eye does not "exist" for the folk systematist. Biologists calculate that the diversity of living organisms is inversely related to the logarithm of their size and the readily visible organisms represent but the "tip of the biodiversity iceberg" (May 1988: 1442–44). A clear corollary of this fact of nature is that folkbiological classifications will "capture" but a sample of the high end of the size range of species. I propose methods to measure the selectivity of human perception of biodiversity with respect to this key dimension of size assuming naked-eye technology.

I will use a logarithmic scale to characterize the size of organisms. This allows us to graph the full range of sizes of living organisms from whales to viruses in a limited space. For simplicity's sake, I take one meter as the standard unit. By coincidence 1.5 or 1.7 meters is close to the height of the average human observer, and it thus symbolizes the anthropocentric perspective I am analyzing here. I use base 10 for the logarithmic scale, which allows direct conversion from the metric system. The longest linear dimension is used because it is the size datum most readily available for a wide range of organisms. For example, on this logarithmic scale an organism one meter in height or length scores 0 on the size dimension (i.e., $10^0 = 1$); a whale 10 meters long (about 33 feet) scores a 1 (i.e., $10^1 = 10$); a giant coast redwood 100 meters high ranks a 2 1 (i.e., $10^2 = 100$); a wren 10 centimeters long (about four finches) rates a $-1$ (i.e., $10^{-1} = 0.1$); a large ant might score a $-2$ (i.e., $10^{-2} = 0.01$, or one centimeter, 4/10 of an inch); and so on. The range of variation among living organisms is plotted against this scale in figure 3.1.

The adequacy of such a measure can be evaluated only by applying it to specific cases, as I attempt below. Specifically, I demonstrate a positive correlation between what I call the scientific species recognition ratio (SSRR) as an index of the total salience of a set of organisms and the average size of those organisms, scaled as described above.

## 3.3   Procedures

It is first necessary to have as data a comprehensive list of the species known to occur in the range of the culture in question, though the analysis might also be performed on a sample of the species known to occur. (For example, we might study mammals by examining ten representative orders or families.) This is no problem if comprehensive field guides or floras exist. However, key groups of plants and animals in many areas of the world remain poorly documented. Invertebrates pose special problems, since it is rarely possible to specify the total set of scientific species.

| $10^n$ m/ value of $n$ | Length | Type of organism | | | | |
|---|---|---|---|---|---|---|
| | | Plants | Mammals | Birds | Fish/ herps | Inverte- brates |
| +2.0 | 100 m | Redwood tree Ponderosa Pine | Blue whale | | | |
| +1.5 | 30 m | Hemlock tree  Oak tree | Whale shark | | | Giant squid |
| +1.0 | 10 m | Juniper tree Willow tree | Elephant | | | Crocodile |
| +0.5 | 3 m | Corn stalk | Horse Deer | | Sturgeon | |
| 0.0 | 1 m | Rose bush  Tulip | Pig  Cat | Swan Eagle Duck hawk | Salmon | Giant clam |
| −0.5 | 30 cm | Heather | Mouse | Dove  Thrush | Turtle  Lizard | Lobster |
| −1.0 | 10 cm | Strawberry Mushroom | Shrew | Sparrow Hummingbird | Frog  Minnow | Mussel |
| −1.5 | 3 cm | Cranberry | | | | Spider |
| −2.0 | 1 cm | | | | | Fly |
| −2.5 | 3 mm | | | | | Mosquito |
| −3.0 | 1 mm | | | | | Chigger |
| −3.5 | 0.3 mm | | | | | |
| −4.0 | 0.1 mm | | | | | Protozoa |
| −4.5 | 30 µ | | | | | |
| −5.0 | 10 µ | | | | | Viruses |

**Figure 3.1**
Sizes of plants and animals scaled logarithmically

In fact only a small fraction of invertebrate species have been scientifically described in many tropical forest areas (Wilson 1989). Plants pose similar problems. Comprehensive floras are not available for most of the world. The expedient of basing one's analysis on the culturally recognized subset of plants and animals—lists of which are more readily obtained—will clearly bias this type of analysis.

Next we need a list for a given cultural group of all basic level folk biological categories recognized nomenclaturally by that group. (If binomially named contrast sets are significant, these may be treated by a separate analysis of the folk system at the level of terminal taxa.)

We must now specify the size of each scientific species. Again, we must assume that information on the sizes of all local plants and animals is available. An ambiguity inheres on the notion of "size." I have chosen to use total body length for animals and height for plants. This is somewhat crude, but it is often necessary to use whatever systematic measurements are available. The use of such a size measure will result in some distortion for elongated plants, such as vines, and animals, such as those with long tails or snakes, but this is a minor weakness of the method. Most references cite a range of values for the size of a species, such as 12 to 27 centimeters; others distinguish males from females. In these cases I simply take the midpoint of the cited range for adults as the size of the species.

The next step is to match the size measures with some measure of the degree to which the organisms are recognized taxonomically in the folk classification. There are several ways this may be done. For example, we may calculate how many scientific species are included within each basic level folk taxon within the domain or subdomain to be analyzed.

I illustrate this in table 3.1 with data from Sahaptin mammal classification. It is easy to see that the larger the animal, the finer the degree of taxonomic differentiation. Mammals that are overdifferentiated ($< 1.0$ scientific species per basic folk taxon) average more than one meter long ($\log_{10}$ of length is $+0.14$). (A common English example might be that of "bull," "cow," and "calf." There is no named taxon inclusive of all individuals of the species *Bos taurus*.) Those scientific species that correspond 1:1 to basic Sahaptin folk taxa average slightly less than a meter in length ($\log_{10}$ of length $= -0.05$). Those that are underdifferentiated, that is, cases where two, three, or more scientific species are "lumped"

Table 3.1
Comparison of basic level Sahaptin mammal taxa by size category

| Number of scientific species included | Average size ($\log_{10} m$) of species included | Number of basic folk taxa |
| --- | --- | --- |
| <1.0 | +0.14 | 4 |
| 1.0 | −0.05 | 37 |
| 2.0 | −0.45 | 11 |
| 3.0 | −0.84 | 3 |
| >3.0 | −0.88 | 2 |

together in a single basic folk taxon, average progressively smaller (see table 3.1). Species distinctions among mice, bats, and shrews are of little more interest to Sahaptin-speaking Indians of the Columbia River Plateau than they are to the average U.S. citizen today.

This method is rather crude, however, and fails to reflect the fact that there may be many exceptions to the general rule. I next describe a somewhat refined method of analysis of the size factor.

I select a *data set* to be analyzed and then define a set of *sampling units* for that data set. A data set corresponds to a domain or subdomain such as "Sahaptin birds" or "Tzeltal plants." (The sampling units used in the present study are described in figures 3.2 to 3.9.) A sampling unit will typically be a set of 5 to 50 closely related species known to occur in the local area. It is important that the sampling units be relatively homogeneous both phylogenetically and with respect to size. However, the data set should encompass substantial variation in the average sizes of the component sampling units. The sampling units of each data set should represent scientific taxa of the same taxonomic rank and degree of internal diversity, and thus be equivalent with respect to phenotypic variation.

I first calculate the mean value of the sizes of the species of each sampling unit, such units as "salmon," "coniferous tree," or "waterfowl." I then calculate the scientific species recognition ratio (SSRR) of each sampling unit. This is simply the number of basic level folk taxa used to classify the species of the sampling unit divided by the number of scientific species in that sampling unit. For example, Sahaptin speakers of the Columbia Plateau recognize 13 basic categories of coniferous trees that

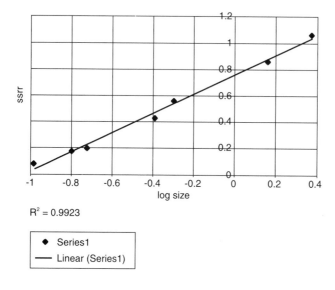

R² = 0.9923

| log size | ssrr | id | sampling unit | n | | |
|---|---|---|---|---|---|---|
| -0.99 | 0.08 | 1 | Chiroptera | 13 | multiple R | 0.996 |
| -0.8 | 0.18 | 2 | Insectivora | 11 | R square | 0.992 |
| -0.73 | 0.2 | 3 | Cricetidae | 15 | adjusted R square | 0.991 |
| -0.39 | 0.43 | 4 | Lagomorpha | 7 | standard error | 0.036 |
| -0.3 | 0.56 | 5 | Sciuridae | 17 | F = | 643.18 |
| -0.16 | 0.87 | 6 | Carnivora | 22 | signif F = | 0 |
| -0.37 | 1.07 | 7 | PerissArtio | 15 | | |

**Figure 3.2**
Plot of Sahaptin mammals, SSRR by size, by sampling unit

correspond to the 21 species of Coniferophyta known to occur in their traditional range. Thus the SSRR for the Coniferophyta = 13/21 = 0.62 for Sahaptin. The SSRR of a sampling unit may range from zero (when the species of the sampling unit are not recognized at the basic level of the folk taxonomy) to values greater than one in the case of over-differentiation in the folk system. Once average sizes and SSRRs have been calculated for each sampling unit of the data set, we may plot each sampling unit as a point on a graph. The logarithm of the average size (our independent variable) is scaled on the horizontal axis and the SSRR (our dependent variable) is scaled on the vertical. We may then calculate the correlation coefficient (Pearson's *r*) of these two variables for the data

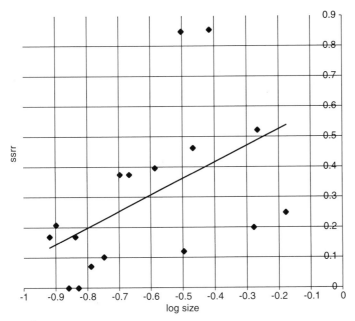

$R^2 = 0.2527$

| | |
|---|---|
| ◆ | Series1 |
| — | Linear (Series1) |

| log size | ssrr | id | sampling unit | n | | |
|---|---|---|---|---|---|---|
| -0.92 | 0.17 | 1 | Apodiformes | 6 | multiple R | 0.503 |
| -0.9 | 0.21 | 2 | tit+wren | 14 | R square | 0.253 |
| -0.86 | 0 | 3 | VireoParul | 13 | adjusted R square | 0.203 |
| -0.84 | 0.17 | 4 | Hirundinidae | 6 | standard error | 0.233 |
| -0.83 | 0 | 5 | misc dickeybird | 11 | F = | 5.07 |
| -0.79 | 0.07 | 6 | Ember+Cardue | 29 | signif F = | 0.04 |
| -0.75 | 0.1 | 7 | Tyrannidae | 10 | | |
| -0.7 | 0.38 | 8 | Turdinae | 8 | | |
| -0.67 | 0.38 | 9 | Icterinae | 8 | | |
| -0.59 | 0.4 | 10 | Picidae | 10 | | |
| -0.5 | 0.86 | 11 | Galliformes | 7 | | |
| -0.5 | 0.12 | 12 | Charadriiformes | 33 | | |
| -0.47 | 0.47 | 13 | Strigiformes+ | 15 | | |
| -0.41 | 0.86 | 14 | Corvidae | 7 | | |
| -0.28 | 0.2 | 15 | Anatidae | 25 | | |
| -0.27 | 0.53 | 16 | Falconiformes | 15 | | |
| -0.18 | 0.25 | 17 | misc waterbird | 16 | | |

**Figure 3.3**
Plot of Sahaptin birds, SSRR by size, by sampling unit

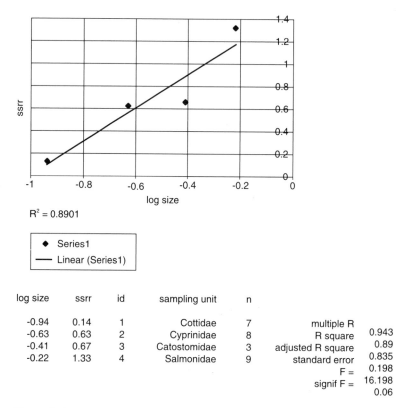

$R^2 = 0.8901$

| log size | ssrr | id | sampling unit | n | | |
|----------|------|-----|--------------|-----|----------------|-------|
| -0.94 | 0.14 | 1 | Cottidae | 7 | multiple R | |
| -0.63 | 0.63 | 2 | Cyprinidae | 8 | R square | 0.943 |
| -0.41 | 0.67 | 3 | Catostomidae | 3 | adjusted R square | 0.89 |
| -0.22 | 1.33 | 4 | Salmonidae | 9 | standard error | 0.835 |
| | | | | | F = | 0.198 |
| | | | | | signif F = | 16.198 |
| | | | | | | 0.06 |

**Figure 3.4**
Plot of Sahaptin fishes, SSRR by size, by sampling unit

set and compare the distribution of individual sampling unit values with respect to the best-fitting straight line (see figures 3.2–3.9).

A further methodological refinement involves treating each scientific species as a "sampling unit" (the single species point method) calculating an average size for each species, then calculating the SSRRs of each species according to a slightly variant procedure. The SSRR of a species in this procedure is 1 if it corresponds 1:1 to a basic folk taxon, it is 0.5 if it is one of two species included within a single basic folk taxon; it is 0.33 if it is one of three such species; and it may be 2.0 if it is "split" between two basic folk taxa; and so on. This methodological refinement eliminates the loss of detail that results from size averaging which characterizes the sampling unit method, but it has the disadvantage that the results

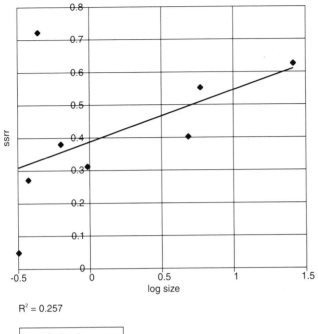

$R^2 = 0.257$

◆  Series 1
—  Linear (Series 1)

| log size | ssrr | id | sampling unit | n | | |
|---|---|---|---|---|---|---|
| -0.5 | 0.05 | 1 | Ranunculaceae | 38 | multiple R | 0.507 |
| -0.43 | 0.27 | 2 | Ericaceae | 27 | R square | 0.257 |
| -0.36 | 0.72 | 3 | Lomatium | 22 | adjusted R square | 0.133 |
| -0.2 | 0.38 | 4 | Apiaceae- | 21 | standard error | 0.199 |
| -0.02 | 0.31 | 5 | Rosaceae | 52 | F = | 2.075 |
| 0.68 | 0.4 | 6 | Salicaceae | 10 | signif F = | 0.2 |
| 0.77 | 0.55 | 7 | Urticales | 9 | | |
| 1.41 | 0.62 | 8 | Coniferophyta | 21 | | |

**Figure 3.5**
Plot of Sahaptin plants, SSRR by size, by sampling unit

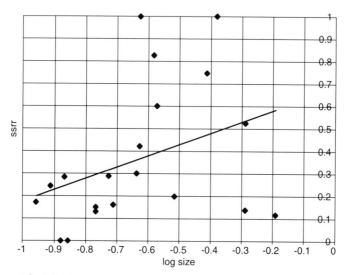

$R^2 = 0.1326$

| log size | ssrr | id | sampling unit | n | | | |
|----------|------|-----|----------------|-----|---|---|---|
| -0.96 | 0.17 | 1 | Apodiformes | 6 | multiple R | 0.364 | |
| -0.91 | 0.25 | 2 | "tits" | 4 | R square | 0.133 | |
| -0.87 | 0 | 3 | Parulinae | 13 | adjusted R square | 0.084 | |
| -0.86 | 0.29 | 4 | Troglodytidae | 7 | standard error | 0.3 | |
| -0.85 | 0 | 5 | Carduelinae | 7 | F = | 2.75 | |
| -0.76 | 0.14 | 6 | Tyrannidae | 14 | signif F = | 0.11 | |
| -0.76 | 0.16 | 7 | Emberizidae (R) | 25 | | | |
| -0.72 | 0.29 | 8 | Hirundinidae | 7 | | | |
| -0.71 | 0.17 | 9 | Turdinae | 6 | | | |
| -0.63 | 1 | 10 | Columbidae | 4 | | | |
| -0.63 | 0.3 | 11 | Icterinae | 10 | | | |
| -0.62 | 0.43 | 12 | Picidae | 7 | | | |
| -0.58 | 0.83 | 13 | Mimidae | 6 | | | |
| -0.57 | 0.6 | 14 | Strigiformes+ | 10 | | | |
| -0.51 | 0.2 | 15 | Charadriiformes | 15 | | | |
| -0.41 | 0.75 | 16 | Corvidae | 4 | | | |
| -0.38 | 1 | 17 | Cuculidae | 2 | | | |
| -0.29 | 0.53 | 18 | Falconiformes | 15 | | | |
| -0.28 | 0.14 | 19 | Anatidae | 14 | | | |
| -0.19 | 0.11 | 20 | Ardeiformes | 9 | | | |

**Figure 3.6**
Plot of Piman birds, SSRR by size, by sampling unit

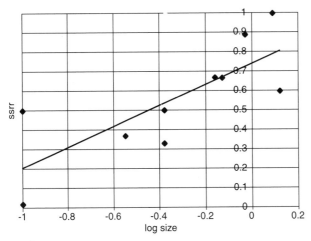

$R^2 = 0.6013$

| log size | ssrr | id | sampling unit | n | | |
|---|---|---|---|---|---|---|
| -1 | 0.5 | 1 | Insectivora | 2 | multiple R | 0.775 |
| -1 | 0.02 | 2 | Chiroptera | 60 | R square | 0.601 |
| -0.55 | 0.37 | 3 | Rodentia | 27 | adjusted R square | 0.551 |
| -0.38 | 0.5 | 4 | Lagomorpha | 2 | standard error | 0.189 |
| -0.38 | 0.33 | 5 | Sciuridae | 3 | F = | 12.066 |
| -0.16 | 0.67 | 6 | Edentata | 3 | signif F = | 0.008 |
| -0.13 | 0.67 | 7 | Marsupialia | 3 | | |
| -0.03 | 0.89 | 8 | Carnivora | 18 | | |
| -0.09 | 1 | 9 | Primates | 2 | | |
| 0.12 | 0.6 | 10 | PerissArtio | 5 | | |

**Figure 3.7**
Plot of Tzeltal mammals, SSRR by size, by sampling unit

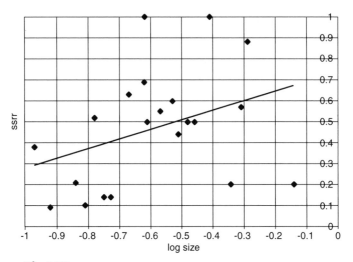

$R^2 = 0.124$

◆  Series1

—  Linear (Series1)

| log size | ssrr | id | sampling unit | n |
|---|---|---|---|---|
| -0.97 | 0.38 | 1 | Troglodytidae | 8 |
| -0.92 | 0.09 | 2 | Apodiformes | 23 |
| -0.84 | 0.21 | 3 | Parulinae+ | 43 |
| -0.81 | 0.1 | 4 | Hirundinidae | 10 |
| -0.78 | 0.52 | 5 | Fringillidae+ | 25 |
| -0.75 | 0.14 | 6 | Tyrannidae | 21 |
| -0.73 | 0.14 | 7 | Charadriiformes | 7 |
| -0.67 | 0.63 | 8 | Picidae | 8 |
| -0.62 | 1 | 9 | Mimidae | 3 |
| -0.62 | 0.69 | 10 | Icterinae | 13 |
| -0.61 | 0.5 | 11 | Columbidae | 10 |
| -0.57 | 0.55 | 12 | Turdinae | 9 |
| -0.53 | 0.6 | 13 | night birds | 15 |
| -.051 | 0.44 | 14 | Psittaciformes | 9 |
| -0.48 | 0.5 | 15 | toucan+ | 8 |
| -0.46 | 0.5 | 16 | Corvidae | 8 |
| -0.41 | 1 | 17 | Cuculidae | 4 |
| -0.34 | 0.2 | 18 | Anatidae | 10 |
| -0.31 | 0.57 | 19 | Falconiformes | 14 |
| -0.29 | 0.88 | 20 | Galliformes | 9 |
| -0.14 | 0.2 | 21 | Ardeidae | 5 |

| | |
|---|---|
| multiple R | 0.352 |
| R square | 0.124 |
| adjusted R square | 0.078 |
| standard error | 0.269 |
| F = | 2.689 |
| signif F = | 0.12 |

**Figure 3.8**
Plot of Tzeltal birds, SSRR by size, by sampling unit

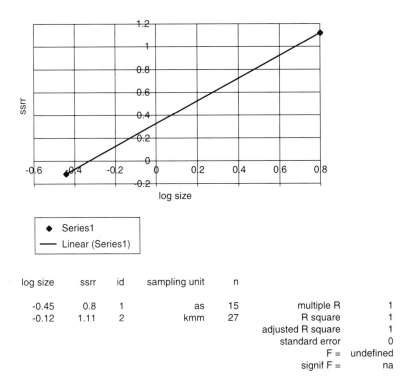

**Figure 3.9**
Plot of Kalam mammals, SSRR by size, by sampling unit

are harder to visualize and represent graphically. I have employed this technique as a check on the results of the less refined analysis.

## 3.4   Results

I have so far analyzed nine data sets, eight by the sampling unit method: Sahaptin mammals (figure 3.2), birds (figure 3.3), fish (figure 3.4), and plants (figure 3.5; Hunn 1989); Piman birds (figure 3.6; Rea 1983); Tzeltal mammals (figure 3.7) and birds (figure 3.8) (Hunn 1977); and Kalam mammals (figure 3.9; Bulmer and Menzies 1972–73). I have reanalyzed five of these (Tzeltal mammals and birds and Sahaptin mammals, birds, and fish) using the single species point method and added a sixth, Anindilyakwa Aborigine birds (Waddy 1988). The results are

**Table 3.2**
Correlation coefficients, slopes, and intercepts of size and SSRR for eight folk biological data sets

| Data set | Sampling units/ N of species | Pearson's $r/r^2$ | Pearson's $r$[a] | Slope | Y-inter-cept | $F$ |
|---|---|---|---|---|---|---|
| Sahaptin mammals | 7/121 | 0.99/0.99 | 0.81 | 0.73 | 0.76 | 643.0[b] |
| Sahaptin birds | 17/241 | 0.50/0.25 | 0.37 | 0.55 | 0.64 | 5.1[b] |
| Sahaptin fish | 4/34 | 0.94/0.89 | 0.69 | 1.49 | 1.51 | 16.0[b] |
| Sahaptin plants | 8/— | 0.51/0.26 | | 0.16 | 0.39 | 2.1 |
| Piman birds | 20/— | 0.36/0.13 | | 0.51 | 0.69 | 2.8 |
| Tzeltal mammals | 10/139 | 0.78/0.60 | 0.89 | 0.54 | 0.74 | 12.0[b] |
| Tzeltal birds | 21/270 | 0.35/0.12 | 0.36 | 0.45 | 0.73 | 2.7 |
| Kalam mammals | 2 | — | | 0.94 | 1.22 | — |
| Anindilyakwa birds | —/210 | — | 0.48 | — | — | |

a. The second set of correlation coefficients were calculated using the single species point method. The $N$ for those calculations is the $N$ of species, not of sampling units.
b. Significant at $p < 0.05$.

tabulated in table 3.2, and the full data set is shown for Sahaptin fish in table 3.3.

The Kalam data (figure 3.9) fall into only two sampling units that vary in size, too few data points for a meaningful statistical analysis. Nevertheless, the Kalam data fit the general pattern. The other seven data sets analyzed by the sampling unit method exhibit moderate to very strong positive linear associations between the logarithm of size and the SSRR. Sahaptin and Tzeltal mammals and Sahaptin fish exhibit high correlations, with $r$ varying from 0.78 for Tzeltal mammals to 0.99+ for Sahaptin mammals. The single species point method yielded correlations on the whole somewhat lower, suggesting that the grouping of species into sampling units may exaggerate the strength of association between size and folk taxonomic recognition. The difference between the results by the two methods is substantial in all three cases: for Sahaptin fish (0.94

vs. 0.69) and Sahaptin mammals (0.99 vs. 0.81), the single-species point method yields the lower value. This is reversed, however, for Tzeltal mammals (0.78 vs. 0.89). The results of both methods indicate that size is the predominant factor determining the level of classificatory detail in these folk domains.

For Sahaptin plants and the four bird sets Pearson's $r$ is at a moderate level of 0.35 to 0.50. The two methods yield comparable results for Sahaptin (0.50 vs. 0.37) and Tzeltal birds (0.35 vs. 0.36), while the figure calculated by the single species point method for the Anindilyakwa bird data at 0.48 is right in the ball park. Size remains significant, accounting for 12 to 25 percent of the variance, but clearly factors other than size are significant here. We may gain some appreciation of what those other factors might be by inspecting more closely the sampling unit data in graphic form (see figures 3.2–3.9). The graphs of several data sets (figures 3.3, 3.5, 3.6, and 3.8) show sampling units falling well above or below the regression line. For example, the genus *Lomatium* in the Sahaptin plant domain shown in the upper left corner of the graph in figure 3.5 falls far above the line; that is, it is more highly differentiated than we would expect given the average size of plants of this genus. Why? In this case it is obvious, since the genus *Lomatium* includes a large number of important food and medicinal plants (Hunn and French 1981). Their extraordinary cultural salience has overcome the expected effect of their small stature. It is curious that among birds three small families stand out for Pima and Tzeltal alike as exhibiting "enhanced salience": doves, cuckoos, and mimic thrushes. All are notably vocal, while most of the included species are also conspicuous and abundant in their respective ranges. These are elements of ecological salience. For Sahaptins, grouse and corvids exhibit enhanced salience: both groups are common permanent residents that are vocally conspicuous, while grouse are hunted for food.

How are we to interpret the opposite case, when a sampling unit falls well below the regression line? It could of course simply represent chance variation. This may account for the two most deviant cases among Tzeltal mammals (figure 3.7), the insectivores falling above the line and the ungulates falling below. In neither case is it obvious why the first should be of unusually high salience, the other of low salience. In

**Table 3.3**
Analysis of data set of Sahaptin fish

| Common name | Latin name | Sahaptin name | SSRR | Size/m | Log size |
|---|---|---|---|---|---|
| Lamprey | *Entosphenus tridentata* | **k'suyas/asum** | 1.00[a] | 0.77 | -0.11 |
| Lamprey | *Lampetra ayresi* | **k'suyas/asum** | 0.33 | 0.3 | -0.52 |
| Lamprey | *Lampetra richardsoni* | **k'suyas/asum** | 0.33 | 0.18 | -0.74 |
| White sturgeon | *Acipenser transmontanus* | *wilaps* | 1.00 | 3 | 0.48 |
| Mountain whitefish | *Prosopium williamsoni* | *simay* | 1.00 | 0.3 | -0.52 |
| Cutthroat trout | *Oncorhynchus clarki* | *ayay/aytmin* | 0.50 | 1 | 0.00 |
| Rainbow trout | *Oncorhynchus mykiss* | *ayay/aytmin* | 0.50 | 0.6 | -0.22 |
| Steelhead trout | *Oncorhynchus mykiss* | *shushaynsh* | 2.00 | 0.77 | -0.11 |
| Dolly Varden | *Salvelinus malma* | *ashchinsh* | 1.00 | 0.64 | -0.19 |
| Pink salmon | *Oncorhynchus gorbuscha* | *wats'ya* | 1.00 | 0.76 | -0.12 |
| Dog salmon | *Oncorhynchus keta* | *mit'ula* | 1.00 | 1.02 | 0.01 |
| Blueback | *Oncorhynchus nerka* | **kalux** | 1.00 | 0.84 | -0.08 |
| Silver salmon | *Oncorhynchus kisutch* | *sinux* | 1.00 | 0.98 | -0.01 |
| Chinook salmon | *Oncorhynchus tschawytscha* | *tkwinat* | 1.00 | 1.47 | 0.17 |
| Jack chinook salmon | *Oncorhynchus tschawytscha* | *tkwilat-tkwilat* | 2.00 | 1.00 | 0 |
| Eulachon | *Thaleichthys pacificus* | *wilxina* | 1.00 | 0.25 | -0.60 |
| Carp | *Cyprinus carpio* | *nch'i-psani* | 1.00 | 0.64 | -0.19 |
| Goldfish | *Carassius aruatus* | *luts'anmi xulxul* | 1.00 | 0.26 | -0.59 |

| Chiselmouth | *Acrocheilus alutaceus* | *lalapti* | 1.00 | 0.30 | −0.52 |
| Red-sided shiner | *Richardsonius balteatus* | *palali* | 1.00 | 0.13 | −0.89 |
| Dace | *Rhinichthys osculus* | *mukw'iya* | 0.33 | 0.10 | −1.00 |
| Dace | *Rhinichthys cataractae* | *mukw'iya* | 0.33 | 0.10 | −1.00 |
| Dace | *Rhinichthys falcatus* | *mukw'iya* | 0.33 | 0.10 | −1.00 |
| Northern squawfish | *Ptychocheilus oregonensis* | *lukw'aa* | 1.00 | 0.64 | −0.19 |
| Peamouth | *Mylocheilus caurinus* | *chuksh* | 1.00 | 0.36 | −0.44 |
| Large-scale sucker | *Catostomus macrocheilus* | *xuun* | 1.00 | 0.60 | −0.22 |
| Bridge-lip sucker | *Catostomus columbianus* | *yayk* | 1.00 | 0.44 | −0.36 |
| Sculpin | *Cottus confusus* | *kw'asla* | 0.14 | 0.10 | −1.00 |
| Sculpin | *Cottus beldingi* | *kw'asla* | 0.14 | 0.13 | −0.89 |
| Sculpin | *Cottus rhotheus* | *kw'asla* | 0.14 | 0.15 | −0.82 |
| Sculpin | *Cottus cognatus* | *kw'asla* | 0.14 | 0.08 | −1.10 |
| Sculpin | *Cottus asper* | *kw'asla* | 0.14 | 0.15 | −0.82 |
| Sculpin | *Cottus marginatus* | *kw'asla* | 0.14 | 0.08 | −1.10 |
| Sculpin | *Cottus bairdi* | *kw'asla* | 0.14 | 0.14 | −0.85 |

a. The differing values for the SSRR of the three sturgeon species reflect the recognition of a covert prototype within the category labeled **k'suyas/asum** (the two nomenclatural variants are dialectal synonyms). That is, the prototypical species *Entosphenus tridentata* is evaluated as in 1:1 correspondence with the prototype of the category, while the two less typical (and rarer) species are analyzed as corresponding 3:1 to the more inclusive Sahaptin category. Pearson's *r* for the correlation of SSRR and the log of size is 0.69.

both cases the number of species in the sampling units is small ($n = 2$ for the insectivores, $n = 5$ for the . ungulates). However, for more representative sampling units, the farther the point is out of line, the less likely its position is due to chance. The three bird sets provide cases in point. The three most deviant cases among Sahaptin birds (figure 3.3) all fall well below the regression line; all are groups of aquatic birds (miscellaneous waterbirds, waterfowl, and shorebirds). Among Piman birds (figure 3.6), likewise waders (Ardeiformes) and waterfowl (Anatidae) are far out of line with statistical expectations based on the size factor. The most deviant Tzeltal birds (figure 3.8) are also the waterfowl and waders. I believe in these cases it is a matter of the relatively low ecological salience of groups of birds that include mostly migratory, aquatic species in environments with limited aquatic habitat. We may also ask what is the significance of variation between domains in the slope of the regression line (see table 3.2)? Some rise steeply, others more gradually. I believe that the slope may be simply an artifact of the range of variation available to be measured within a given group. Certainly Sahaptin plants—which in this case exhibit a gradual slope (0.16)—range over a wider size range, and at the same time exhibit a narrower range of SSRR variation, than do fish, which exhibit a very steep slope (1.49). Most of the remaining data sets range within the narrower limits of $0.60 \pm 0.10$.

The majority of the data sets so far analyzed also exhibit a convergence on a value of 0.70 for the $y$-intercept (i.e., the point on the SSRR dimension to be expected when size is one meter). Sahaptin plants exhibit a rather low value of 0.39, while Sahaptin fish and Kalam mammals exhibit very high values, $> 1.2$ for the $y$-intercept. In the Kalam case the regression line roughly parallels that of Sahaptin and Tzeltal mammals (see figures 3.2 and 3.7) but is elevated. This may indicate a pervasive influence of cultural salience, since Tzeltal are mostly subsistence farmers. Traditional Sahaptin subsistence emphasizes fishing and gathering (Hunn and Selam 1990), while the Kalam are avid hunters (Majnep and Bulmer 1977). There also appears to be a convergence at a value of $-1.00$ for the $x$-intercept, which suggests a lower size limit for the "unmotivated" recognition of species in folk taxonomies. The three bird domains exhibit striking similarity in both slopes and $y$-intercepts. Here the relationship of size to total salience seems to transcend cultural and regional differences.

## 3.5   Conclusions

The analysis sketched here illustrates the value of defining parameters of cultural variation in explicit, quantifiable terms whenever possible. We now have a manageable method that allows us to abstract the effect of size on the precision with which living organisms are classified in folk systems. By carefully controlling for the effect of size, we may more clearly recognize and define the role of phenotypic, ecological, and cultural salience in determining the level of classificatory detail accorded a given taxonomic group in a particular culture. This informs us not only about the universal constraining power of this one aspect of biological reality on cultural practice but serves also to highlight the play upon the surface of objective constraint of culturally specific perspectives and motives.

The two methods applied here should be used together. The rather ad hoc sampling units employed for data points in the sampling unit method makes it difficult to evaluate the statistical significance of the results. This limitation is avoided in the single species point method. However, the sampling unit method more clearly highlights variation in the level of classificatory detail between groups of organisms.

An additional refinement that should be pursued in the future is the calculation of multiple and partial regression statistics incorporating values for the phenotypic, ecological, and cultural salience of each species or sampling unit. This would allow the determination of the degree to which each of the four factors—phenotypic salience, ecological salience, the size factor, and cultural salience—acts independently or interactively to motivate the cultural recognition of natural discontinuities.

Finally the fact that size strongly constrains the recognition of biodiversity in traditional ecological knowledge systems suggests caution. Folkbiologists are highly knowledgeable about the biotic resources of their immediate environment and in many cases clearly cherish and husband those resources. However, a very large portion of the total biodiversity of their traditional lands is culturally unrecognized for the simple reason that it is invisible.

## References

Berlin, B. 1973. The relation of folk systematics to biological classification and nomenclature. *Annual Review of Ecology and Systematics* 4: 259–71.

Berlin, B. 1976. The concept of rank in Ethnobiological classification: Some evidence from Aguaruna folk botany. *American Ethnologist* 3: 381–99.

Berlin, B. 1992. *Ethnobiological Classification: Principles of Categorization of Plants and Animals in Traditional Societies*. Princeton: Princeton University Press.

Berlin, B., J. Boster, and J. P. O'Neill. 1981. The perceptual bases of ethnobiological classification: Evidence from Aguaruna Jivaro Ornithology. *Journal of Ethnobiology* 1: 95–108.

Berlin, B., D. E. Breedlove, and P. H. Raven. 1974. *Principles of Tzeltal Plant Classification: An Introduction to the Botanical Ethnography of a Mayan Speaking People of Highland Chiapas*. New York: Academic Press.

Boster, J. 1987. Agreement between biological classification systems is not dependent on cultural transmission. *American Anthropologist* 89: 914–20.

Boster, J. S. 1985. "Requiem for the Omniscient Informant": There's life in the old girl yet. In J. W. D. Dougherty, ed., *Directions in Cognitive Anthropology*. pp. 177–97.

Boster, J., B. Berlin, and J. P. O'Neill. 1986. The correspondence of Jivaroan to scientific ornithology. *American Anthropologist* 88: 569–83.

Bulmer, R. N. H., and J. I. Menzies. 1972, 1973. Karam classification of marsupials and rodents. *Journal of the Polynesian Society* 81: 472–99, 82: 86–107.

Gardner, P. M. 1976. Birds, words, and a requiem for the omniscient informant. *American Ethnologist* 3: 469–80.

Geoghegan, W. H. 1976. Polytypy in folk biological taxonomies. *American Ethnologist* 3: 469–80.

Hays, T. E. 1974. *Mauna: Explorations in Ndumba Ethnobotany*. PhD dissertation. University of Washington, Seattle.

Hunn, E. S. 1975. A measure of the degree of correspondence of folk to scientific biological classification. *American Ethnologist* 2: 309–27.

Hunn, E. S. 1976. Toward a perceptual model of folk biological classification. *American Ethnologist* 3: 508–24.

Hunn, E. S. 1977. *Tzeltal Folk Zoology: The Classification of Discontinuities in Nature*. New York: Academic Press.

Hunn, E. S. 1980. Sahaptin fish classification. *Northwest Anthropological Research Notes* 14: 1–19.

Hunn, E. S. 1982. The utilitarian factor in folk biological classification. *American Anthropologist* 84: 830–47.

Hunn, E. S., and J. Selam. 1990. *Nch'i-Wana (The Big River): Mid-Columbia Indians and Their Land.* Seattle: University of Washington Press.

Hunn, E. S., and D. H. French. 1981. Lomatium: A key resource for Columbia Plateau native subsistence. *Northwest Science* 55: 87–94.

May, R. M. 1988. How many species are there on earth? *Science* 241: 1441–49.

Rea, A. M. 1983. *Once a River: Bird Life and Habitat Changes on the Middle Gila.* Tucson: University of Arizona Press.

Rosch, E. H. 1978. Principles of categorization. In E. H. Rosch and B. Lloyd, eds., *Cognition and Categorization.* Hillsdale, NJ: Lawrence Erlbaum, pp. 27–48.

Turner, N. J. 1988. "The importance of a Rose": Evaluating the cultural significance of plants in Thompson and Lillooet Interior Salish. *American Anthropologist* 90: 272–90.

Waddy, J. A. 1988. *Classification of Plants and Animals from a Groote Eylandt Aboriginal Point of View,* 2 vols. Darwin: Australian National University.

Wilson, E. O. 1989. Threats to biodiversity. *Scientific American,* September 1989, pp. 108–16.

# 4

## How a Folkbotanical System Can Be Both Natural and Comprehensive: One Maya Indian's View of the Plant World

Brent Berlin

One of the first universal principles of ethnobiological classification states that no folk system is comprehensive in that taxa at its lower ranks, say folk genera and folk species, partition the full range of plant diversity for a local habitat. After the most prominent botanical species[1] are named in some particular system, there will always remain hundreds of others that are not given linguistic recognition. A second general principle claims that the conceptual ordering of those taxa that *are* recognized will be based on the affinities that humans observe among the species themselves, independently of these species' cultural importance (see Berlin 1992). The application of this principle implies that when the outlines of an ethnobiological system of classification are known, they will reflect in great part the order inherent *in nature*, not an order arbitrarily laid *on nature* by humans' economic or symbolic concerns.

In this chapter, I present data on the folk botanical system of classification of Alonso Méndez Ton, a Tzeltal Maya Indian from the Highlands of Chiapas, Mexico. Analysis of the data supports the second principle, naturalness, but requires qualification of the strict application of the first principle, comprehensiveness. The data show that *comprehensiveness* is achieved when species not afforded standard linguistic recognition are nonetheless stated to be *similar to* (or *related to*) some set of folk taxa in the system that are themselves named. The data show that naturalness is achieved when it is observed that those plant species said to be "similar to" named species are also found to share readily observable morphological characteristics with those species to which they are said to be close. Often this morphological similarity reflects taxonomic affinity as well (i.e., perceptually related species are often members of the same genus or same family as the target species). Both findings are supported by data drawn from Alonso's classification of more than 5,000 botanical collections representing some 3,000 species carried out as part of a general botanical collecting program over a period of several years. It is proposed that Alonso's folk system of classification is based on psychological principles that underlie what we know today as scientific systematic botany.

## 4.1   Comprehensiveness

If it is generally true that only a subset of the organisms in any given region are usually extended conceptual recognition in folk systems of biological classification, one is led to ask, 'Just how are species that are *not* recognized linguistically actually treated conceptually?' Most Americans, when asked for the name of an unfamiliar plant, might simply respond with causal remarks such as "I don't know, it's just a bush" or "it's some kind of tree, I don't have a name for it". But thirty years ago, when Dennis Breedlove and I began our general ethnobotanical work among the Tzeltal Maya, we soon noted that these types of "I don't know" or "it's just a (tree), (grass) ..." responses were extremely rare among our Tzeltal collaborators. In *Principles of Tzeltal Plant Classification*, we wrote:

General botanical collecting quickly revealed that the Tzeltal lacked true plant names for much of the local flora. On the other hand, when presented with a particular plant [species that was unfamiliar to them] informants would rarely respond that the species had no name. Instead, they would systematically attempt to relate it to one of the categories in their named taxonomy. For example, an informant might state that such and such a plant was *kol pahaluk sok X* "it's similar to X," where X represents the Maya name of a known, lower-level category.... These classificatory responses allowed us to determine [what we called] the *basic ranges* of each recognized category (i.e., all "genuine exemplars") and the *extended ranges* of these genuine categories (i.e., all the "it's similar to X" exemplars). (Berlin, Breedlove, and Raven 1974: 53)[2]

When our Maya collaborators made a statement such as "it's like an X," or "it's similar to X," they were engaging in what might be called first-approximation botanical classification. The process is something like the following: First, a specimen of some unfamiliar species is examined and its perceptual characteristics are evaluated, a process that we can call *identification.* Once identified, the species is conceptually assigned to a place "near to" a known species to which it is seen to be most similar, one already given linguistic recognition in the folk system, a process that we can call *classification*.[3] This kind of basic, first-order classificatory behavior, of course, is no different than that of the field botanist who makes a preliminary determination of a particular species as "near to X," as in *Smilax* aff. *bona-nox*, a designation that the species will bear until a more definitive determination can be made at leisure, normally on the basis of comparison with herbarium material. If applied in a general, encompassing fashion, classifying plants in this manner allows for a folk botanical system of classification to be nearly comprehensive in that most plant species of a local habitat can either be assigned to one of the recognized lower-level folk categories of the folk system or to one of the named lower-level folk taxa if not recognized as a legitimate member of a named category but seen as "conceptually related to" it.

Knowledge of the extent to which such a system of classification actually works depends ideally on data comprised of large numbers of general botanical collections that have been comprehensively classified by numerous native collaborators. Barring large numbers of collaborators, an initial glimpse into the nature of such a system can be gained by the classification system that emerges from the remarkable botanical collections of Alonso Méndez Ton (hereafter, AMT), a Tzeltal Maya botanical collaborator who worked continually with Breedlove and me in our already mentioned ethnobotanical research in the 1960s and 1970s (see Berlin 1984 for a brief description of AMT's botanical contributions). Shortly after beginning our ethnobotanical work among the Tzeltal, Breedlove and I quickly recognized AMT's talents as a botanical collector, and in a few short months he was in the field working alone, making his own fine botanical collections (figure 4.1). At the completion of our project, AMT continued collecting, both as an assistant in Breedlove's *Flora of Chiapas* project and later as a brigade leader for one of the National Autonomous University of Mexico's *Flora of Mexico* collecting teams. Over a period of about five or six years, AMT had more than 5,000 botanical collection numbers to his credit (most in sheets of five) taken from numerous, widely separated localities throughout the state of Chiapas (figure 4.2).[4]

**Figure 4.1**
Alonso Méndez Ton, circa 1961, Chiapas, Mexico

The large majority of AMT's botanical collections were made in areas far removed from *kulak'tik*, a small hamlet of the municipality of Tenejapa where AMT grew up. Many of the species he collected, pressed, and dried were only slightly familiar to him, and it is certain that he had never seen a major portion of them. Nonetheless, only 44 of the full 5,552 set of numbers are given the entry "no name"in AMT's collection books, less than one percent of the total inventory.

Linguistically AMT's Maya plant names (*sensu laxu*) can be analyzed as one of two types: The first set is indicated by a noun accompanied by the qualifier *batz'il* (abbreviated as "*b.*") meaning 'true' or 'genuine', such as *batz'il atz'am te'* meaning 'genuine *atz'am te'* (*Rapanea myricoides*). Another set is comprised of nouns modified by the expression *kol pahaluk sok* (abbreviated as "kps"), literally glossed as 'it is somewhat the same as' < *pahal* 'same', -uk subjunctivizing suffix 'as it were', thus pahaluk X 'likened to X'. One can freely gloss the descriptive phrase *kps atz'am te'* as meaning 'similar to *atz'am te''* (*Rapanea juergensenii*).

Both of these types of expressions can be seen on any a page of AMT's collection notebooks. Figure 4.3 shows collections made by AMT on the

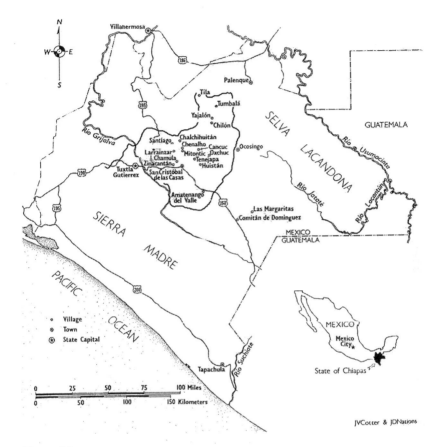

**Figure 4.2**
Chiapas, Mexico. Areas where AMT has collected are the Maya municipalities in
the central part of the state are enclosed by a solid black line.

first day of October 1968 at a small "rancho" called *mumuntik* in the
municipality of Ocosingo in the northeastern part of Chiapas. For ease of
reading, I have underlined the Maya names in each collection.

The short Maya text following each name is a brief botanical description of the specimen. For example, collection number 3429 reads "*b.
ichil ak'* (genuine *ichil ak'* [later determined as *Clematis grossa*, a clam-
bering vine in the Ranunculaceae]) and is described as *lom nahtik yak'ul
ya xmo ta te', sakik xnich* '([a] very long vine climbing in trees, with
white flowers'). The entry for the immediately following collection, 3430,
is *kps ichil ak'* (similar to *ichil ak'*). AMT describes this specimen as *lom

Figure 4.3
Scanned image of a page from AMT's collection notebook, 10 January 1968

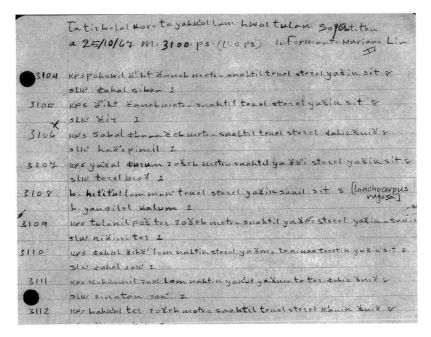

**Figure 4.4**
Scanned image of a page from AMT's collection notebook, 25 October 1967

*nahtik yak'ul ya xmo ta te'*, *tzajik sit* ([a] very long vine climbing in trees, with red fruits). This collection was ultimately determined as *Serjania hispida*, a sprawling vine in the Sapindaceae. While in different botanical families, *Clematis* and *Serjania* share many common characters of gross morphology and overall aspect. Furthermore, although there are a number of species of *Serjania*, none of them receives a single, stable, distinctive "genuine name". This genus is always incorporated into AMT's classification system as "a vine similar to *ichil ak'*, *Clematis grossa*." Another set of entries from AMT's collection notebook can be seen in figure 4.4. These collections were made in the company of another Tzeltal Indian from the municipality of Soyatitán, in northern Chiapas, on October 25, 1967. This far northern municipality is considerably lower in elevation than AMT's native municipality of Tenejapa (these collections were made at about 1,000 meters). All of the collections indicated on this page of his notebook are given kps entries save 3108 *b*. *hit'it'ul* 'genuine *hit'it'ul*', *Lonchocarpus rugosa*, a species familiar to him in that it is found along the lowland water courses of his native municipality.[5]

As a result of AMT's long-term collecting efforts in Chiapas, it is possible to state with some confidence the actual number of basic folk generic taxa that comprise his system of ethnobotanical classification. As we have come to expect from the ethnobotanical systems of traditional horticulturalists, AMT shows an inventory of approximately 500 folk genera (485 to be exact). He employs several hundred names and only these names—either in the form "genuine X" or "related to X"—to classify all of the botanical diversity with which he has come in contact during his collecting efforts in Chiapas, a diversity representing some 900 scientific genera and nearly 3,000 valid botanical species (this number comes close to representing the full set of species for the Chiapas central plateau). Conceptually AMT's ethnobotanical system is comprehensive of the region's botanical diversity.[6]

## 4.2   Naturalness

If AMT's ethnobotanical system is close to comprehensive, is it natural? What are the patterns revealed in his conceptual organization of the considerable botanical diversity with which he is confronted? How consistent is his system of classification? Are the patterns revealed understandable in terms of a perceptually based theory of botanical classification based on overall morphological similarity which, in the main, also reflects the natural affinities of botanical species?

To fully answer these questions would require a long monograph, currently in preparation. In brief, the general outlines of the structure and content of AMT's view of the plant world can be seen by examining in some detail a number of typical examples from the massive ethnobotanical database created as a result of his efforts.

One of the most straightforward examples can be seen in AMT's conceptual treatment of the several species of *Lantana* in his collections (see table 4.1). Table 4.1 indicates that AMT employs the Maya term *ch'ilwet* to refer to 31 botanical collections. The term ranges over a number of species of *Lantana*, as well as *Phyla stoechadifolia* and *Lippia graveolens*. AMT provided the name *batz'il ch'ilwet* to 9 of the 10 collections

Table 4.1
Tabular representation of AMT's concept of *ch'ilwet*

| Botanical species | AMT's names | | Total collections |
| | batz'il ch'ilwet | kps ch'ilwet | |
|---|---|---|---|
| *Lantana camara* | 9 | 1 | 10 |
| *Lantana hispida* | 5 | 1 | 6 |
| *Lantana hirta* | 2 | 2 | 4 |
| *Lantana velutina* | | 3 | 3 |
| *Lantana scorta* | | 2 | 2 |
| *Lantana costaricensis* | | 1 | 1 |
| *Lantana frutilla* | | 1 | 1 |
| *Lantana trifolia* | | 1 | 1 |
| *Phyla stoechadifolia* | | 2 | 2 |
| *Lippia graveolens* | | 1 | 1 |
| Total | 16 | 15 | 31 |

of *L. camara*, 5 of the 6 collections of *L. hispida*, and 2 of the 4 collections of *L. hirta*. The remaining species in the set receive "*kol pahaluk sok ch'ilwet*" designations.

The distribution of AMT's responses allow one to make fairly clear inferences about his concept of *ch'ilwet*. First, it will be noted that all of the plants in the set are closely related species of the same family, the Verbenaceae. *L. camara* and *L. hispida* are seen as the best exemplars or prototype of the category, most likely due to their relative frequency of occurrence in the area vis à vis other species of the genus. They are highly common, quite similar species with brightly-colored orange and white flowers found on exposed rocky slopes throughout much of Highland Chiapas. (Sometimes the genus is subdivided into folk species where flower color is marked by the specific epithet, e.g., tzajal *ch'ilwet* '[red ch'ilwet'] and *sakil ch'ilwet*' [white ch'ilwet']).

Several other species of the genus (*L. hirta*, *L. velutina*, *L. scorta*, *L. costaricensis*, *L. frutilla*, and *L. trifolia*) are considered to be conceptually related to the prototype. These species are less common and show fewer characters in common with the two major species. *Phyla stoechadifolia*

**Table 4.2**
Tabular representation of AMT's concept of *ajoj*

| | AMT's names | | |
| --- | --- | --- | --- |
| Botanical species | batz'il ajoj | kps ajoj | Total collections |
| *Saurauia scabrida* | 11 | | 11 |
| *Saurauia comitis-rossei* | 3 | 1 | 4 |
| *Saurauia oreophila* | 2 | 5 | 7 |
| *Saurauia angustifolia* | 1 | | 1 |
| *Saurauia conzattii* | | 1 | 1 |
| *Saurauia hegeliana* | | 2 | 1 |
| *Saurauia villosa* | | 1 | 1 |
| *Kohleria elegans* | | 3 | 3 |
| *Kohleria deppeana* | | 1 | 1 |
| *Palicourea* sp. | | 1 | 1 |
| *Palicourea tridiocarpa* | | 1 | 1 |
| *Achimenes grandiflora* | | 1 | 1 |
| *Comocladia guatemalensis* | | 1 | 1 |
| *Sommera grandis* | | 1 | 1 |
| Total | 17 | 19 | 36 |

and *Lippea graveolens* are related genera in the same family. *Lippia graveolens* is represented by but a single collection in the dataset. In addition to its designation as "*kps ch'ilwet*," the only other collection of *Phyla stoechadifolia* was said to be "related to" *yakan k'ulub wamal* a folk genus with a botanical range of *Verbena litoralis*, also perceptually similar to *ch'ilwet* and in the same family. The single collections of *L. camara* and *L. hirta* identified by AMT as "like ch'ilwet," as well as the two collections of *L. hirta* identified as "genuine ch'ilwet" are likely errors. Such misidentifications on AMT's part are rare and clearly explainable as part of dealing with normal species variation associated with botanical identifications in the field context, as any field botanist will readily admit.

A slightly more complex example can be seen in AMT's concept of the folk genus *ajoj*. *Ajoj* is the folk generic name afforded several species of the genus *Saurauia* (Actinidiaceae; see table 4.2). These plants are soft-wooded, low-branched trees and shrubs with rather large (20–30 cm) leaves covered with dense rusty pubescent intricately branched hairs. It is one of the most common trees in the pine-oak-liquidambar forests of Chiapas.

Table 4.2 shows that the prototypical species in this set is *S. scabrida*, represented by eleven of AMT's collections. In addition three of the four collections of *S. comitis-rossei* are considered to be "genuine members" of this category, as is a single collection of *S. angustifolia*.

Five other species of *Saurauia* are included in the extended range of the concept and treated as "similar to genuine *ajoj*". The most prominent of these is *S. orephila* (with five collections). In addition two species of *Kohleria* and two species of *Palicourea* are also recognized as perceptually similar to *ajoj*, as are single collections of *Achimenes grandiflora*, *Comocladia guatemalensis*, and *Sommera grandis*. While these genera represent different families (Gesneriaceae, Anacardiaceae, and Rubiaceae), they are all generally similar to *Saurauia* in their overall aspect.

A final example from AMT's folk system can be seen in his classification of the two conceptually related folk genera, *atz'am te'* and *tilil ja'*, two prominent small trees with a primary botanical range of *Rapanea myricoides* and *Parathesis chiapensis*, both members of the Myrsinaceae. *R. myricoides* is a delicately branched shrub with narrowly elliptic leaves, 5 to 9 cm long. Fruit appears in small clusters along the stems and often like glistening beads of salt (hence the name *atz'am te'* ['salt tree']. *P. chiapensis* is also a small tree with somewhat broadly elliptic leaves. Both species are common and conspicuous understory shrubs throughout the region.

Table 4.3 shows that genuine *atz'am te'* finds a clear focus on *Rapanea myricoides* (13 collections). Species that are considered conceptually close to *atz'am te'* include *R. juergensenii* (7 collections), *Ardisia escallonioides* (3 collections), and a single collection of *Wimmeria acuminata*.

The folk taxon *tilil ja'* is centered on the closely related tree *Parathesis chiapensis* (11 collections). This taxon's conceptual relatives include other species of *Parathesis* (i.e., *P. donnell-smithii*, *P. melanostica*, *Parathesis microcalyx*, and *P. leptopa*), as well as *Gentlea micrantha* and several species of *Ardisia* (*A. compressa*, *A. liebmannii*, *A. alba*, *A. karwinskyana*, and a single collection of *Dendropanax*). Both *atz'am te'* and

**Table 4.3**
Tabular representation of AMT's concepts of *atz'am te'* and *tilil ja'*

| Botanical species | AMT's names | | | | |
| | batz'il atz'am te' | kps atz'am te' | batz'il tilil ja' | kps tilil ja' | Total collections |
|---|---|---|---|---|---|
| *Rapanea myricoides* | 13 | | 1 | | 14 |
| *Rapanea juergensenii* | | 7 | | | 7 |
| *Ardisia escallonioides* | | 3 | | 3 | 6 |
| *Wimmeria acuminata* | | 1 | | | 1 |
| *Parathesis chiapensis* | | | 11 | 3 | 14 |
| *Parathesis donnell-smithii* | | | 3 | 5 | 8 |
| *Parathesis melanosticta* | | | | 3 | 3 |
| *Parathesis microcalyx* | | | | 2 | 2 |
| *Parathesis leptopa* | | | | 1 | 1 |
| *Gentlea micrantha* | | | | 8 | 8 |
| *Ardisia compressa* | | | | 7 | 7 |
| *Ardisia liebmannii* | | | | 2 | 2 |
| *Ardisia alba* | | | | 1 | 1 |
| *Ardisia karwinskyana* | | | | 1 | 1 |
| *Dendropanax arboreus* | | | | 1 | 1 |
| *Synardisia venosa* | | | | 1 | 1 |
| Total | 13 | 11 | 15 | 38 | 77 |

*tilil ja'* are linked perceptually *via Ardisia escallonioides*, a species similar in overall aspect to both *Rapanea* and *Parathesis*. The basic and extended ranges of these two folk genera nearly cover the full set of all species in the Myrsinaceae as attested in AMT's collections, and only *Wimmeria* (Celastraceae) and *Dendropanax* (Araliaceae), both assigned "similar to X" designations, are in distinct botanical families.

## 4.3    Discussion

Each of the examples representing species from families as diverse as the Verbenaceae, Actinidiaceae, and Myrsinaceae are multiplied many times in AMT's collections, ultimately exhausting the several thousand species found in some of Chiapas' most varied ecological zones. In almost all of his classificatory decisions dealing with the placement of each of his 5,000 collections, this Maya Indian's view of the plant world proves to be perceptually based, remarkably consistent, and, for the most part, botanically informed as to the natural affinities of the species involved.

When his classification of the flora does not conform with currently recognized phylogenetic boundaries of Western botany, it is generally the case that the organisms in question nonetheless share many perceptual features in common which justify his grouping them as members of the same conceptual category. AMT is not a trained botanist, guided by the conceptual framework found in evolutionary theory, full of notions concerning the likely phylogeny of the Chiapas flora. He lacks any basic formal education, having completed only the second grade in Mexico's notoriously bad rural schools. Breedlove's and my influence on him could hardly account for his performance, our contributions to his training being nothing more than preparing him in standard botanical collecting methods and instruction in the techniques of modern linguistic transcription.

What we see here is the systematic application of an ethnobotanical system of classification comprised of no more than 500 folk genera which conceptually organize the biodiversity of one of the most botanically complex regions of Mexico. AMT's recognition of genuine exemplars of basic, folk generic botanical categories, as well as the perceptually closely related species seen to be conceptual affiliates of these basic categories, allows him organize his regional botanical reality in a highly comprehensive manner. Few professional botanists could excel the accuracy of his field determinations, all made on the spot without benefit of comparative herbarium materials (Breedlove has marveled at this on countless occasions). Thus, as the ethnobiological principle of naturalness is confirmed by AMT's system of ethnobotancial classification, our general principle on comprehensiveness must be modified, or at least clarified, so as to recognize the all-encompassing properties that AMT's view of the plant world so clearly reflects.

One might speculate that the folk system demonstrated by Alonso Méndez Ton is an early, though uncodified, formulation of the cognitive-linguistic ordering of nature that we know today as Western systematic biology. Perceptually distinctive species are first given linguistic recognition, the remaining plant world being largely ignored ("it's just a tree," "it's some kind of vine"). With enlarging experience, additional species are next incorporated into the older system by being recognized as similar to those with already codified names ("it's similar to X," "it's Y's companion," "it's a relative of Z"). Finally with the development of classical botany, and especially with Linnaeus's nomenclatural standarizations, species said to be "similar to X" are recognized, if slightly different, as new species of established genera, or, if they are distinctive enough, become established as new genera and are given their own distinctive generic names.[7] In AMT's natural and comprehensive system of classification, we see the unfolding of the first stages of this universal conceptual process.

## Postscript

The data described in the foregoing pages are suggestive of *how* AMT's system of ethnobotanical classification works. None shed any light on *why* it works. The following speculations are presented as a plausible hypothesis requiring much further testing.

The basic intuition is this: AMT (and, by implication, people in general) learn their natural kinds in the localized ecosystems where they become socialized and enculturated. With specific reference to ethnobotany, this means those plant species that one first comes in contact with during early socialization. These are the plants that one first learns as a child. I propose that these species become the prototypes of the common categories of natural kinds that a person uses throughout their adult lives.

When one travels of moves away from one's childhood habitat and is confronted with a set of totally new species (new natural kinds), one has at least three classificatory choices in dealing with these unfamiliar organisms. The first, that chosen by many urban dwellers today, is to claim total ignorance ("Hmmm ... I've never seen that before, I don't know what it's name is" or "I guess it's just a tree of some kind").

A second strategy is to learn the names that the locals use for these new species. It is usually easy enough to acquire the local names of species by asking local guides or experts. This is the strategy that tourists use when they take trips to foreign lands and children use when they go to zoos. Children are quite willing to accept the names for the new creatures they see when these new names are provided by their parents (the "experts" who don't know the animals but who can read the labels on the cages).

The third strategy, and the strategy exhibited in AMT's naming behavior, is to conceptually relate any new natural kinds he may come in contact with to the prototypes he learned as a child, a process that I believe Medin refers to as "exemplar comparison" (Medin 1989). The careful observer employing this strategy will notice that X is "similar to" its prototype, Y, on the basis of the perceptual affinities of the newly encountered target species to the original prototype. This is why AMT's "similar to x" responses are natural and make good botanical sense.

Furthermore I believer that good distributional evidence can be brought to bear that will show that AMT gives "like X" responses are given to species that do *not typically occur in the region where he formed his prototypical images.* Thus *Rapanea juergensenii* is a higher elevation species that is similar to the members of *R. myricoides* that AMT learned as his prototypical, lower-to-mid elevation *atz'am te'*, but clearly distinctive enough not to be seen as a *good* exemplar of that prototype (figure 4.5).

It also appears that a number of polytypic species (e.g., *Rapanea*) that occur naturally in the same habitat are often given distinctive folk generic names by those individuals who have grown up in those habitats. Thus, while *R. myricoides* is known as *atz'am te'*, by Tenejapans who reside in the upper elevations of the municipality, *R. juergensenii* is known by its own distinct name, *k'olol te'*, since they see it habitually and can easily distinguish it from it's similar (but not *so* similar) sympatric conspecific, *R. myricoides*. In this they contrast with AMT's more generalized view of the species.

A full test of these intuitions requires returning to the original data and determining just where AMT's collections were made, a task which I tackle in a monographic work currently in preparation (Berlin n.d.). My guess is that species commonly collected in areas near AMT's natal hamlet will all be given *"batz'il"* or genuine names, while those collected

*batz'il atz'am te'*

Rapanea myricoides

kps *atz'am te'*

R. juergensenii

**Figure 4.5**

in regions of lower or higher elevations *or* in regions removed by geographic distance at the same elevation will have "kol pahaluk sok" or "similar to X" names.

Furthermore plants collected early on in AMT's days as a collector are more likley to be *near his native home site*, (and more likley to receive *batz'il* names), while those collected later in his career are more likely to be found in unfamiliar habitats (and more likely to receive *kps* names). While I do not yet have all of the locality data to back up this claim, the distribution of his naming responses over some 4,000 collections is fairly suggestive (see figure 4.6).

These data may provide ecological support for the notion of prototype that has been lacking in much of the discussion on the subject, at least in my own thinking about it. Of course, the question remains as to why people should choose to notice only 500 or so natural prototypes in the area where they first learn natural kinds in the first place.

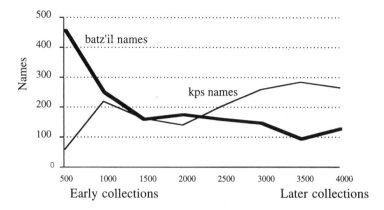

**Figure 4.6**
Number of AMT's 'genuine' and 'similar to' naming responses, collections 1–4,000

## Notes

1. E. Hunn proposes several factors that relate to what counts in assessing prominence, size of organism being one of the most important (see Hunn n.d.).

2. An identical process has been noted by Breedlove and Laughlin in their description of Tzotzil ethnobotany. "When evoking botanical names, two descriptive terms dominated our conversations—*batz'i*, "genuine" or "true" and *yit'ix*, "bastard" or "false." With such a handy term [as *yit'ix*] any unknown plant can be easily [classified] (1993: 110).

3. Several competing psychological models have been proposed for this cognitive process. Medin (1989) discusses the most prominent: overall similarity, exemplar-based, or some combination of the two. An exemplar-based strategy seems most likely to account for the behavior described here.

4. AMT efforts during this period were devoted to making general botanical collections, that is, collections of "anything and everything in flower or fruit." This included, of course, many hundreds of species for which he lacked Maya names. His collections represent a significant contribution to our knowledge of the flora of Chiapas, and in partial recognition for his efforts, some 20 new species have been named in his honor (e.g., *Ilex tonii* Lundell, *Calypthrantes tonii* Lundell). His collections are currently housed at the California Academy of Sciences, San Francisco, and at the Herbarium of the National Autonomous University of Mexico in Mexico City.

5. Note that most of the names that AMT transcribes for his Maya companion are entirely different from his own, indicative of the widespread regional linguistic variation in the area. The abbreviation *slk'* is the equivalent of "kol pahaluk sok" in the Soyatitán dialect of Tzeltal.

6. My intuitive impressions concerning AMT's remarkable performance suggests something about what Medin calls "nontrivial exposure to the natural world" (personal communication), coupled with the thoughtful observation of an expert. The latter, I think, plays a minor role if my personal interaction with indigenous ethnobiologists over the last thirty years is any indication. Of course nontrivial exposure to the natural world could make one an expert by definition, but as with everything else, sheer native intelligence is surely a major unquantifiable factor in this whole story.

7. AMT was in his early twenties when he began working with the Stanford University project in 1960. Shortly afterward, he became a collaborator in the University of Chicago's Man and Nature Project, headed by Norman A. McQuown. He later worked as my primary informant on a project dealing with an interesting class of bound morphemes called numeral classifiers, a project that ultimately led to Berlin (1968). At that time he barely knew how to write but quickly learned technical linguistic transcription and immediately grasped the nature of systematic linguistic elicitation. Finally he joined Breedlove and me as an ethnobotanical collaborator and worked with us for the next several years. So far as we know now, he had not been previously employed but worked as a traditional Tzeltal farmer in the municipality of Tenejapa where he was born. Toward the end of the decade, he married an American ex-patriot with whom he lived for several tumultuous years before an acrimonious divorce. Today Alonso Méndez Ton works as a well-paid gardener for a wealthy landowner in Bolinas, California. He seldom returns to Chiapas.

8. For a discussion of the issues involved in the linguistic processes involved in this nomeclatural elaboration, see Atran (1990), Bartlett (1940), Berlin (1972, 1986), Brown (1986), Cain (1956, 1958, 1959a, 1959b), Greene (1983 [1909]), Hunn and French (1984), and Walters (1986).

## References

Atran, S. 1990. *Cognitive Foundations of Natural History*. Cambridge: Cambridge University Press.

Bartlett, H. H. 1940. The concept of the genus. I. History of the generic concept in botany. *Bulletion of Torrey Botanical Club* 67: 349–62.

Berlin, B. 1968b. *Tzeltal Numeral Classifiers: A Study in Ethnographic Semantics*. The Hague: Mouton.

Berlin, B. 1972. Speculations on the growth of ethnobotanical nomenclature. *Language and Society* 1: 51–86.

Berlin, B. 1984. The Contributions of Native American Collectors in the Ethnobotany of the Neotropics. In Ghillean Prance and Nancy Kulunki, eds., *Ethnobotany of the Neotropics*. New York Botanical Garden, Institute of Economic Botany, pp. 24–33.

Berlin, B. 1986. Comment on "The growth of ethnobiological nomenclature by C. H. Brown." *Current Anthropology* 27: 12–13.

Berlin, B. 1992. *Ethnobiological Classification: Principles of Categorization of Plants and Animals in Traditional Societies.* Princeton: Princeton University Press.

Berlin, B. n.d. *One Maya Indian's View of the Plant World: Psychological and Ecological Factors of an Ethnobotanical System of Classification.* Laboratories of Ethnobiology, University of Georgia.

Berlin, B., D. E. Breedlove, and P. H. Raven. 1974. *Principles of Tzeltal Plant Classification.* New York: Academic Press.

Brown, C. H. 1986. The growth of ethnobiological nomenclature. *Current Anthropology.* 27: 1–18.

Breedlove, D. E., and R. M. Laughlin. 1993. *The Flowering of Man: A Tzotzil Botany of Zinacantán.* Washington: Smithsonian Institution Press.

Cain, A. J. 1956. The genus in evolutionary history. *Systematic Zoology.* 5: 97–109.

Cain, A. J. 1958. Logic and memory in Linnaeus's system of taxonomy. *Proceedings of the Linnaen Society of London,* Session 169: 144–63.

Cain, A. J. 1959a. Taxonomic concepts. *Ibis* 101: 302–18.

Cain, A. J. 1959b. The post-Linnaean development of taxonomy. *Proceedings of the Linnaen Society of London,* Session 170: 234–44.

Greene, E. L. 1983 [1909]. *Landmarks of Botanical History,* 2 vols. F. N. Egerton, ed., Stanford: Stanford University Press.

Hunn, E. n.d. For factors governing the cultural recognition of biological taxa. Unpublished ms, University of Washington, Seattle.

Hunn, E., and D. French. 1984. Alternatives to taxonomic hierarchy: The Sahaptin case. *Journal of Ethnobiology* 3: 73–92.

Medin, D. 1989. Concepts and conceptual structure. *American Psychologist.* 12: 1469–81.

Walters, S. M. 1986. The name of the rose: A review of the ideas on the European bias in angiosperm classification. Tansley Review Paper 6, *New Phytologist* 104: 527–46.

# 5

## Modes of Subsistence and Ethnobiological Knowledge: Between Extraction and Cultivation in Southeast Asia

Roy Ellen

The successful adaptation of humans to rain forest environments depends on their ability to maintain population-land ratios at a level that permits sustainable extraction, which in turn depends on their capacity to organize and apply knowledge of rain forest structure and composition. This chapter examines our current understanding of this knowledge in a Southeast Asian context and considers how it relates to reliance on varying modes of subsistence. Emphasis will be placed on the differences among populations that focus predominantly on direct extraction, populations that focus on plant cultivation, and populations that seem to be in various respects transitional.

In seeking to explore these relationships, I argue that it is necessary to reflect more carefully on what is meant by "indigenous ethnobiological knowledge" and to distinguish between knowledge encoded in language and knowledge not so encoded, between—if you will—formal knowledge (as registered in the words which people use to label types of plants and animals) and the substantive knowledge which people actually apply when engaged in the regulation and extraction of resources, activities that ultimately enhance their adaptiveness. I conclude by observing that such comparative data on size of formal ethnobiological inventories suggest (following Berlin) that they are strongly constrained by biodiversity but that they especially at the margins reflect a history of contact between, and therefore the sharing of knowledge among, peoples with different subsistence specializations living in areas dominated by a general equatorial rain forest ecology. It would appear that while the knowledge of agricultural peoples in these areas is more likely to be lexically encoded than that of nonagricultural peoples, that of nonagricultural peoples is less likely to be encoded, though arguably not measurably less in substantive terms. I conclude that differences between populations relying to varying degrees on agricultural production may be linked to group size and social organization, through the necessity and opportunities to share, organize, and label collective knowledge to which these variables are connected. However, in order to reach this point in the argument, we need first to look at rain forest as an ecological system with a complex cultural history that is able to support various combinations of human subsistence strategies.

## 5.1  Cultural History of the Southeast Asian Rain Forest

We are sometimes persuaded to imagine that the Southeast Asian rain forest is a fragment of some vast unchanging past that has intruded into the present. Although the rain forest does have a long ecological history and was at its geographical zenith about 10,000 years bp (= before present), it is far from stable and unchanging (Flenley 1979: 1, 77–100; Maloney 1998; Whitmore 1990: 94). Indeed its areal distribution today probably exceeds that of 20,000 bp when most of the land mass was covered in monsoon forest and savanna (Glover 1977: 160). Moreover its history, at least for the last 10,000 years, has also been a cultural history: not only the context in which human social and ecological change has taken place but an environment in which humans have been instrumental, by turns, maintaining and altering. Human beings have been in Southeast Asia for perhaps nearly 50,000 years (Bellwood 1985: 93), and they have been cultivating grains, root tubers, and tree crops in one form or another for something in excess of 7,000 years (Glover 1977: 162; Gorman 1971). Whether through simple extraction or low-intensity farming, the cumulative long-term effects of these disturbances on forest composition and structure, compared with those of other large mammals living at similar densities, must have been considerable, at least in some areas (Dunn 1975; Flenley 1979: 122; Hutterer 1983: 196; Medway, Lord 1977). This has both improved the rain forest as a human resource base and contributed to its structural patchiness and biodiversity.

Moreover persistent interventions over many hundreds of years have had important coevolutionary consequences. Rapid expansion of agriculture, and its intensification to the point where humans had to constantly intervene to prevent reestablishment of forest and to artificially ensure nutritional and water sufficiency, has probably been a recent development, perhaps no more than 2,000 years in the areas where it was practiced earliest (Bellwood 1985; Higham 1989). Until that time human agriculture would have been just one element contributing to the complex and diverse phenomenon that we now call equatorial rain forest.

Long-term human impact has taken various forms, and we can obtain some measure of it by examining ethnographic evidence drawn from what we know about contemporary and historically recent food collectors and small-scale agriculturalists in the region. Following Rambo (1979: 61), it is helpful to organize this under the headings: habitat modification, direct selection, dispersal, and domestication.

Even groups subsisting at low population densities modify their habitats such as by increasing river sediment loads as a result of agricultural soil disturbance and erosion; by introduction of humanly transmitted pathogens and other toxins (including fish poisons such as the root of *Garcinia dulcis*; Rambo 1985: 58); and by changing soil nutrient levels, disturbing the structure and causing surface erosion (ibid., p. 63). Clearance for swiddens not only transforms forest structure through temporary cultivation and regrowth but also through the selective removal of trees. Large trees with hard woods have a selective advantage in being more difficult to remove using restricted technology. Rambo (1985: 68) has reported this for *Koompassia exselsa* among the Semang of the Malaysian peninsula. On Seram, in the east of the archipelago, the presence of particular trees, such as *Canarium vulgare, Sterculia* sp. and *Diospyros ebenaster*, pose similar formidable difficulties for Nuaulu swiddeners (Ellen 1985b: 568). But plants may be preserved deliberately as well as by default, and many techniques are reported in the literature that involve degrees of protection of otherwise wild species (Rambo 1985: 71). Collection of forest products specifically for trade (e.g., resins, rattans, and seeds) has probably had a major selection pressure (Dunn 1975; Ellen 1985b: 577; Rambo 1979: 60) in the Malaysian peninsula especially on rattans. Humans alter the forest inadvertently by helping disseminate certain seeds of wild plants (abandoned camps, gardens, and villages providing particularly good examples of this; Fox 1953; Rambo 1985: 70), while anthropogenic secondary growth may constitute habitats for new kinds of plants and grazing animals. Human settlement has led to the deliberate introduction of many varieties of cultivated trees: *Tectona grandis* and *Toona sureni* are now well-established in the lowland forest of Seram, though were probably introduced during the seventeenth century, while the ornamental *Delonix regia* cannot have been planted before the nineteenth (Ellen 1985b: 563). In some places quick-growing species are planted in swiddens to ensure rapid and appropriate regrowth and to supply fuel (Whitmore 1990: 135). Also the selective extraction of wild species, strategic burning, and swiddening at optimal conditions may combine to give rise to distinctive patches and new opportunities for colonization.

## 5.2   Modes of Rain Forest Subsistence

From what I have said above in their impact on rain forest ecology, it is sometimes rather difficult to distinguish between the effects of those nonagricultural forms of human extraction we call hunter-gathering and low-intensity agriculture. Let us take this idea a little further. We impose concepts such as *subsistence technique* and *mode of subsistence* on what is ecologically and technologically continuous. While we cannot do without such typologies (Ellen 1988), they are fraught with difficulties in their application. When, for example, does hunting become husbandry or vegetable gathering become farming? Consider also the distinction between fishing and hunting. The only differences between a Nuaulu archer using a forked arrow to catch a bird rather than a fish are the animals predated upon, their behavior, and the fact that water is a denser medium than air, with different physical (including refractive) properties that affect the specific motor and sensory organization of aiming and firing. There are similar problems with other key distinctions in the analysis of subsistence: *extraction, modification, cultivation,* and *domestication,* and more generally *food collecting* versus *food production.* There is now plenty of evidence for the manipulation and regulation of plant resources in otherwise food-collecting populations of the Southeast Asian rain forests in ways that maintain or increase yield (Hutterer 1983:

173): for example, replanting the heads of wild tubers, protection of valuable fruit-bearing trees, and deliberate burning of bamboo clumps in order to facilitate the extraction of desirable haulms and to promote the growth of green shoots (Rambo 1985: 70). Those peoples engaged in "wild" palm sago extraction, extract selectively, detach, and protect suckers thrown out by mature palms and exercise certain forms of ownership (Ellen 1988). Often such activity is sufficiently organized, purposeful, and significant to warrant the description "rain forest management," which from the genetic evidence is the outcome of what is now recognized as a significant historic pathway to domestication and cultivation in the region (Harris 1973: 397–98, 1977; Hutterer 1983: 183).

Any one rain forest population, however, will always be dependent on a range of different techniques, a technological breadth empirically evident even if we acknowledge the conceptual difficulties mentioned above. Moreover individuals may specialize in different techniques and divide their utilization of different techniques on a time basis, one day hunting, another gardening, and so on. A mode of subsistence is therefore always an *aggregate* of extractive processes. Most variation in modes of subsistence lies in the combination and relative significance of different techniques rather than in differences between the techniques themselves (Ellen 1982: 128), while the comparative ecological effects of the same technique practiced in different ways may be more significant than the effects of using different techniques. Thus, if it is difficult to agree on definitions of techniques, it becomes much more difficult to define assemblages of strategies used by particular populations, to establish what criteria we should recognize, and to distinguish them.

Those people we conventionally label food-collectors (or hunters and gatherers), and even those who so perceive themselves, often do things other than hunting and collecting. Indeed practices that may assume a critical position in terms of identity and ideology may be rather unimportant in terms of objective ecological measurements (e.g., Barnard 1983; Bird-David 1988). In Southeast Asia some groups extract from species that are recognizably domesticates (e.g., certain kinds of fruit tree; Hutterer 1983: 176), plant tubers or sow seeds in encampments, and clear swiddens with varying degrees of regularity and permanence (e.g.,

Rambo 1985: 43). There is no hard evidence to suggest, as was once claimed (e.g., Schebasta 1973), that this is a particularly recent development. Rather, the evidence indicates remarkable subsistence variability among contemporary and historically recent Southeast Asian collectors, both between and within groups from different areas (Griffin 1985: 349–50, 352). It is more plausible to assume that southeast Asian food collectors have intermittently practiced agriculture for a long time, a conclusion borne out not only because many contemporary and historical hunting and collecting groups live in areas that would support agriculture but because they also clearly have a longstanding knowledge of agricultural practices (Hutterer 1983: 173).

Similarly many peoples regarded overall as cultivators may actually extract little food from farming practices and rely mainly on sago collecting and hunting, or may cultivate nondomesticates as well as domesticates (Hutterer 1983: 176). If suitable food sources are available, then a remarkable degree of sedentism is possible without cultivation in the usual sense, and with it the mobilization of large amounts of food for social purposes. In parts of Southeast Asia and Melanesia extensive reserves of palm sago make this possible. For example, the Penan of Sarawak make considerable use of *Eugeissona utilis* (Brosius 1995), while for the Nuaulu, *Metroxylon sagu* is the mainstay of clan-based social organization in permanent locations, although the degree of dependence is often obscured by simultaneous involvement in swidden cultivation (e.g., Ellen 1988). Indeed the humid tropics alone exhibit every degree of agricultural permanence, from fixed fields to patches utilized for less than one calendar year and then abandoned, and swiddening is certainly not the uniform system implied three decades ago by Clifford Geertz (Ellen 1986: 192).

Since the mid-1970s there has been both a growing appreciation that differences between those labeled "hunter-gatherers" and agriculturalists are often exaggerated (Harris 1989: 14; Hutterer 1983: 172), and a recognition that many food-collecting groups have become "encapsulated" (Woodburn 1988) in wider social formations of which they are in some cases no more than specialized components. The extent to which forest food collectors can sustain themselves on the basis of direct extraction alone has recently been questioned (Headland 1987; Headland and

Bailey 1991), with the implication that they must always have had access to other starch staples, perhaps through trade, or have depended on combinations of techniques in the way suggested here. One of the few exceptions may have been where such peoples could rely on starch palms.

According to this view a key adaptive role must have been played by energy subsidies obtained through exchange. Indeed trade and exchange has existed for centuries between interior or upriver peoples, including remote foraging populations, linking them to peoples of the forest fringes, the estuaries or coasts, and ultimately the global economy. Such populations are involved in collecting forest products that enter the world system (Dunn 1975; Hoffman 1984; Brosius 1995) and are often dependent on inputs from non-food-collecting groups for their biological and social reproduction (Morris 1982; Peterson 1978). In some cases there is historical, ethnographic, and linguistic (though not specifically ethnobotanical) evidence to indicate that food-collecting groups may well have evolved as specialist foragers in regional systems where their ancestors once practiced agriculture (Hutterer and Mcdonald 1982: 7). But rarely, if at all, have such people become completely economically isolated and reproductively autonomous. Thus we have here an argument that parallels the recent findings of historical ecology in the Amazon basin (Balée 1992).

It is advisable therefore to begin with the assumption that most human subsistence systems are to a degree connected and that few have ever been isolated for more than a few generations at a time (Ellen 1994a). One implication of this view for our understanding of subsistence is that it subverts simple models of homeostatic adaptation. Rather, such systems are more likely to expand until checked by other endogenous stresses and external barriers, both social and ecological. It is thus far more realistic to treat much adaptation as occurring through links with other populations (see Ellen 1990) and social evolution as the coevolution of systems of various degrees of connectedness.

## 5.3  Subsistence and Knowledge

The question now arises as to what all this has to do with ethnobiological knowledge. We recognize, of course, that individual subsistence techniques, and therefore different overall combinations of strategies employed by particular populations, have different ecological profiles: in terms of energy transfer, limiting factors and carrying capacity, the degree of human effort required, their effects on the landscape, and the cultural regulation of environmental relations. But, by the same token—and much less attention has been paid to this—they must presumably also have different knowledge profiles. Older theories of human subsistence adaptation privilege tools (i.e., physical artifacts) rather than know-how. This, of course, betrays a particular kind of materialist bias, and we now realize that much cultural activity directed at subsistence does not involve tools as we conventionally understand them, that technology is more than equipment, and that "primitive technologies" (meaning restricted equipment) in no sense should imply restricted knowledge. Thus ecological history is not simply the history of material techniques but the history of knowledge, much of which will necessarily be ethnobiological.

But what do we mean by an "ethnobiological knowledge profile," and how might we begin to measure it? One way might be to use the names applied to plants and animals as some proxy of overall knowledge. Brown (1985), for example, has argued that plant cultivation leads to an expanded inventory of biological terms and has produced evidence in support of this which shows that the inventories for food-collectors and hunters are shorter than those for farmers. And this applies as much to animals (table 5.2) as it does to plants (table 5.1). More recently, Berlin (1992) has produced similar but revised comparative data using indigenous "generic" terms. For convenience, I have summarized some of the key statistical data in table 5.3. If we inspect Brown's figures, what is immediately apparent is that most of his nonagricultural peoples are from temperate and subarctic latitudes, where biodiversity is less than in the tropics. Tropical food-collectors are only represented by the Casigurun Dumagat (Agta) and the Tasaday, both of which provide inventories higher than those given for other nonagriculturalists. Indeed (though we may wish to exclude the Tasaday on the basis that the data are controversial) there is evidence to suggest that tropical food-collectors probably have more names for both plants and animals than Brown's evidence suggests. Headland, the ethnographic source for the Agta data, has subsequently favored (Headland 1985) a figure of 603+

**Table 5.1**
Data on ethnobotanical inventories for Southeast Asia

| Language | Total plant terms[a] | Percentage plant binomials[a] | Total plant generics[b] | Source |
|---|---|---|---|---|
| 1. Ifugao | 2,131 | — | — | Conklin (1980) |
| 2. Hanunóo | 1,879 | 51.1 | 956 | Conklin (1954) |
| 3. Eastern Subanun | 1,400+ | — | — | Frake (1969) |
| 4. Jörai | 1,182 | 64.7 | | Dournes (1968) |
| 5. Tobelorese | 1,162 | 27.3 | 689 | Taylor (1980) |
| 6. Nuaulu | 1,000 | 60.1 | | Ellen (1996) |
| 7. Bunaq | 935 | | | Friedberg (1990) |
| 8. Sri Aman Iban | 800 | | | Christensen (n.d.) |
| 9. Palawan | 776 | | | Revel (1990) |
| 10. Taubuid | | | 598 | Pennoyer (1975) |
| 11. Ndumba | 766 | 44.8 | 385 | Hays (1974, 1979, 1983) |
| 12. Merimbun Dusun | 612+ | | | Ellen (1994[b]: 8–9) |
| 13. Bontoc | 354 | 9.0 | | Reid and Madulid (1972) |
| 14. Semelai | 260+ | | | Gianno (1990) |
| 15. Tasaday | 215 | 11.6 | | Yen (1976) |
| 16. Gasigurun Dumagat (Agta) | 208 | 2.4 | | Brown (1985) |
| 17. Revised Agta figures | 603 | | 400 | Headland (1985) |
| 18. Pinatubo | 600 | | | Fox (1953) |

Note: Data below the broken line are for nonagricultural peoples.
a. Data in these columns from Brown (1985), except 6, 7, 8, 11, 12, 14, 17, 18, and 19, which are taken direct from the sources given in the final column.
b. Data from Berlin (1992: 98).

Table 5.2
Data on ethnozoological inventories for Southeast Asia and Melanesia

| Language | Total animal terms[a] | Percentage animal binomials[a] | Total animal generics[b] | Source |
|---|---|---|---|---|
| 1. Ifugao | 597 | — | | Conklin (1980) |
| 2. Palawan | 469 | | | Revel (1990) |
| 3. Kyaka Enga | 466 | — | | Bulmer (1985) |
| 4. Nuaulu | 462 | 59.1 | | Ellen (1993) |
| 5. Hanunóo | 461 | — | 461 | Conklin (1954) |
| 6. Tobelorese | 443[c] | | 420 | Taylor (1990) |
| 7. Ndumba | 323 | 5.3 | 186 | Hays (1974) |
| 8. Kalam | | | 345 | Majnep and Bulmer (1977) |

a. Data from Brown (1985), except 2 and 4, which are taken direct from the sources given in the final column.
b. Data from Berlin (1992: 100).
c. Terminal categories only.

plant terms, which Berlin (1992: 285) plausibly converts into approximately 400 plant generic terms. Data collected by Fox (1953) suggest 600+ for the Pinatubo Negrito, a figure that Berlin points out corresponds closely to that for neighboring Taubuid cultivators (see Pennoyer III 1975). On the other hand, tropical forest cultivators are much better represented, and these are among groups that yield the largest inventories, between 800 and 2,000 plant categories (Brown 1985: 44). The main problem then is the quality of the data of tropical forest food-collectors (for which we have no complete ethnobotanical descriptions; Berlin 1992: 99) compared with those for cultivators in the same environment.

If we look at Berlin's revised data (table 5.1), we find a much more reduced range for the numbers of generic terms reported for agriculturalists and nonagriculturalists generally, and particularly between those living in rain forest environments. What this suggests is that the objective diversity (the biological richness) of rain forests is linked to an increase in the number of terms for both cultivators *and* food-collectors (Berlin 1992: 99) and that further research on nonagricultural peoples is likely

**Table 5.3**
Summary of aggregate data on ethnobiological inventories

| | | Mean | Number of cases | Source |
|---|---|---|---|---|
| 1. | Total plant terms (worldwide) | 510 | 39 | Brown (1985: 44) |
| 2. | Total plant terms (cultivators, worldwide) | 858 | 19 | Brown (1985: 44) |
| 3. | Total plant terms (noncultivators, worldwide) | 179 | 20 | Brown (1985: 44) |
| 4. | Total plants terms (Southeast Asia) | 851 | 16 | Brown (1985: 44)[a] |
| 5. | Total plants terms (Southeast Asian cultivators) | 1058 | 12 | Brown (1985: 44)[a] |
| 6. | Plant generics | 358 | 17 | Berlin (1992: 98) |
| 7. | Plant generics (noncultivators, worldwide) | 197 | 7 | Berlin (1992: 98) |
| 8. | Plant generics (cultivators, worldwide) | 520 | 10 | Berlin (1992: 98) |
| 9. | Total animal terms | 443 | 17 | Brown (1985: 44) |
| 10. | Total animal terms (cultivators, worldwide) | 544 | 10 | Brown (1985: 44) |
| 11. | Total animal terms (noncultivators, worldwide) | 299 | 7 | Brown (1985: 44) |
| 12. | Total animal terms (Southeast Asian cultivators) | 460 | 7 | Brown (1985: 44), Revel (1990), Ellen (1993) |
| 13. | Animal generic | 390 | 10 | Berlin (1992: 100) |

a. Plus revisions indicated in table 5.1, note a.

to increase the number of terms so far available for such groups. Despite all this there is *still* some evidence to suggest that equatorial food-collectors have fewer names than cultivators living in the same environment.[1] If we assume for the sake of argument that the inventories for rain forest cultivators *are* longer, why should this be so?

One possible explanation is that it is linked to greater functional diversity in domesticated or cultivated stock, an explanation favored by both Brown and Berlin. According to this view, single plant species that have been much modified through domestication are more likely to be subdivided terminologically. Those that are "cultivated" (i.e., to use Berlin's definition, "deliberately planted and managed by constant and direct intervention"; 1992, p. 120 are likely to be more finely subdivided than those that are just "protected" (i.e., "not consciously destroyed in normal horticultural activities"). In other words, there is a greater degree of polytypy, and in addition polytypy is dramatically greater for both cultivated and protected plants than for wild species, both "significant" and "useless." Berlin also suggests (p. 274) that agricultural peoples are more likely to recognize subgeneric categories and name more generics. Both Brown and Berlin deduce from their data that the languages of agricultural populations are more likely to have binomials than those traditional nonagricultural peoples living in the same habitat. Binomialization is therefore a response to the need for an expanded ethnobiological repertoire (Brown 1985: 49; Hunn and French 1984: 89). Brown, and Hunn and French, independently, have speculated that high inventories reflect the risks of crop failure faced by farmers compared with food collectors who, at a lower population density, can afford to be more selective, and I have suggested that this might also reflect the importance among cultivators of distinguishing weeds (Ellen 1985a: 56; Ellen 1991: 98–99). Brown also argues that plant cultivation leads to expansion of inventories of animals as well as plants, which has again been suggested reflects the need for a subsistence buffer against the risk of crop failure, and perhaps the increased significance of insects and birds as predators (Ellen 1985a).

To this we can also add the observation (Voekes, pers comm.) that the mobile lifestyle of nonagriculturalists is linked to the absence of any incentive to construct any dwelling more substantial than a temporary shelter, and therefore to the utilitarian argument that such groups are unlikely to require detailed knowledge of the constructional properties of different types of timber and the terminological distinctions between species of forest tree which we might expect to accompany such knowledge.

There is, however, one important caveat to enter at this stage in regard to explanations of this type. The Brown-Berlin hypothesis employs a disaggregated category of "agriculture." This is partly, I suspect, in order to ensure a respectable number of case studies from which data can be drawn. But there is good reason to believe that the consequences of low-intensity swidden cultivation for ethnobiological knowledge are different from those found in intensive permanent field agriculture, and that low-intensity agriculture is itself highly variable in terms of certain key particulars (Hames 1983). This is because, for one thing, there is greater biological variety in most Southeast Asian swiddening environments at other than possibly the varietal level (e.g., Conklin 1957). Crop diversity follows from a greater likelihood of serial and simultaneous polycropping in the same plot, different planting arrangements for different stages in the swidden cycle, an increased tendency to establish plots in different kinds of forest, and varying possibilities for regrowth. We have as yet insufficient terminological data for intensive agriculturalists in the humid tropics. However, on the basis of the data provided in table 5.1, it would seem that among low-intensity swiddeners (cases 2 to 12, possibly excluding 6) there is no easy correlation between objective biological diversity and extent of lexical expression.

## 5.4   Situational Basis of Ethnobiological Knowledge: Depth rather than Lexical Breadth

There is another way of looking at the problem of why it is that cultivators should have more extensive ethnobiological terminologies than noncultivators, and this emphasizes less why there are more terms among cultivators (or particular kinds of cultivators), than why there are fewer among noncultivators. In order to pursue this, we have first to question the extent to which terminologies really do reflect knowledge and examine how demographic and social factors affect the presentation of that knowledge.

In one sense terminologies must reflect knowledge of a kind—knowledge of *names* at the very least, with a high probability that these names will correspond to categories that map some part of the objective biological world. It is also probable that the existence of names indicates knowledge beyond this: knowledge of organism morphology, behavior, and use. However, I would like to argue that this latter *substantive* knowledge is more likely to vary than *formal* lexical knowledge, both within populations and between them. If we accept, as I do, Berlin's (and Lévi-Strauss's) contention that the number and kinds of folk terms for biota broadly reflect objective diversity and discontinuities, and with this the shared properties of human sensory perception, then there will be occasions when this diverges from detailed in-depth knowledge of particular parts of the biological world. Even though such knowledge may be constrained by the perceptual salience of the species involved, it is also much more likely to vary according to subsistence need. Thus the unimportance of frogs as food for Nuaulu inhabiting the coastal lowland forests of Seram, in relation to their relatively high lexical differentiation, is plausibly responsible for some of the uncertainty and variability with which respondents supply names (figure 5.1) (Ellen, Stimson, and Menzies 1976). It is the outcome, if you like, of interaction between shallow knowledge *for* and extended knowledge *of*. We can perhaps see something similar at work in all those terms for sweet potatoes in the New Guinea highlands (Heider 1969).

The assertion that bare lists of terms are of limited application (see Alcorn 1981: 228), and are to be treated warily as a proxy for functional knowledge, is wholly consistent with those many observations to the effect that food-collectors (and many intermediate groups) are particularly well adapted to the rain forest (Rambo 1980), and even that lack of this knowledge effectively locks many farming peoples out of the rain forest (Hutterer 1977: 793), who can therefore only obtain its products as dependents of forest people. But this is a vague assertion, and we need to know what parameters characterize such substantive applied knowledge.

To begin with, there is *knowledge of individual organisms* (behavior, feeding habits, connections with other species, overall folk autoecology, their usefulness and potential). This knowledge is highly variable from one organism to the next. Nuaulu (Ellen 1993b), for example, have a

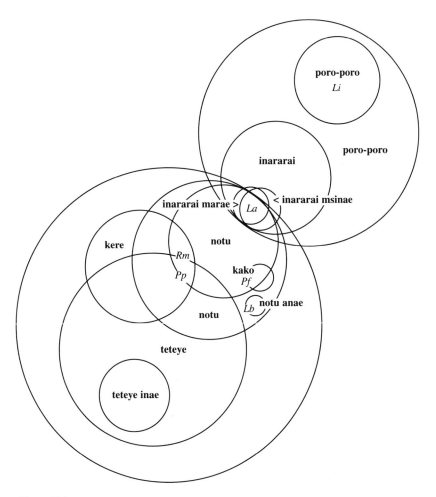

**Figure 5.1**
Nuaulu frog classification arranged as a Venn diagram, and indicating extensive
overlap between terms provided by informants for specimens (bold) and their
phylogenetic content (italic abbreviations). *La = Litoria amboinensis*, *Lb =
Litoria sp. (bicolor* group), *Li = Litoria infrafrenata*, *Pf = Phyrnomantis fusca*,
*Pp = Platymantis papuensis*, *Rm = Rana modesta*, *R? = Rana sp.* Reproduced
from Ellen (1993b).

wide-ranging knowledge of wild pig (**hahu**: *Sus scrofa*), enough to fill a short ethnoecological monograph, whereas few persons have anything but a passing acquaintance with worm snakes (**teke tuamana**: Typhlopidae), which they rarely see and have little interest in. Those who have attempted to measure degree of utility, have conclusively shown it to be asymmetrically distributed with respect to named species, and that it is only when we examine our data in this way that we can see that what constitutes a "use" is highly problematic, and that one use is by no means commensurate with another (Hays 1974, 1982, 1991).

Second, there is *knowledge conferring fitness in marginal situations* (i.e., where selective pressure is at its maximum). This is less likely to be formal lexical knowledge, though I accept Berlin and Boster's proposition that the propensity to categorize and name in a particular way (Boster 1996) is adaptive. It is more likely to be knowledge of reproductive biology (e.g., mast-finiting of dipterocarps; see Dove and Kammen 1997); knowledge of what parts are useful and how to process them, knowledge of the damage they can do to humans and other organisms on which humans are dependent (toxic yams, insect pests, dangerous snakes, etc.), the role of other organisms in the dispersal of seeds, and the use made of the plant by other nonhuman organisms as food. In other words, plants and animals have to be understood as part of the web of forest life, not simply in isolation. Thus it is adaptively more important to distinguish varieties of yam from one another because one contains toxic levels of dioscorine and the other is edible, than to distinguish them on the basis of perceptual criteria alone (e.g., size of leaf), though such features may indeed flag crucial functional distinctions. This kind of knowledge is the result of generations of accumulated experience, experimentation and information exchange.

Third, what may be more important in the long run than either breadth of formal knowledge or depth of substantive knowledge of individual organisms is *knowledge of general principles* based on the observation of many different species. It is quite clear that general ethnobiological lessons are learned from observing particular instances, and that in the transmission of knowledge overarching deductive models of how the natural world works are privileged over accumulated inductive knowledge. Thus both preemptive and retrospective control of resources (Ellen

1994a) are well-understood by food-collectors as well as cultivators. The evidence of regulation of rainforest resources by food collectors suggests, along with the preadaptation of knowledge and equipment (e.g., grinding stones; Kraybill 1977), that the cultural preconditions for the emergence of agriculture existed long before its emergence as a major mode of subsistence, partly in the form of depth knowledge of the kind to which I have been just referring and partly the breadth associated with broad spectrum collecting practices (Gorman 1971: 316). The main elements of agriculture, individually or combined (tilling, artificial selection by weeding, etc.), coordinated seasonal harvesting, storage, planting (usually of cuttings, vegetation clearance) are all known for so-called preagricultural systems, with the possible exception of seed selection and artificial dispersal (Yen 1989: 57). Moreover agricultural systems have simplified ecologies compared with rain forests, and what separates much agriculture from food collecting, at least of the broad spectrum variety, is the little equipment actually used. In many vegecultural systems the digging stick and bush knife are the only permanent tools employed, while different kinds of hunting and collection may involve a complex array of possible physical devices. Thus the knowledge base required for effective agriculture is actually smaller (though more focused) than that required for hunting and gathering.

Fourth, it has become clear that systematic encyclopedic knowledge is situated within folk-models, which reflect an ability to connect observations at the species level with informed perceptions about forest structure and dynamics (*folk-synecology*). Thus Posey (1988) has shown how Amazonian Kayapó maintain buffer zones between gardens and forest that contain plants with nectar-producing glands on their foliage which have the effect of drawing away aggressive ants and parasitic wasps from crops. Of course, what constitutes "forest" is something we might expect to vary cross-culturally. However, even if we restrict ourselves to focal shared meanings, it is clearly a complex categorical construction (e.g., Ellen 1993c) much like the modern scientific model of rain forest as a continuous aggregation of different biotopes and patches, varying according to stages in growth cycles, degree of regeneration, underlying geology, altitude, geography and natural contingency, or in emic terms a mosaic of resources and a dense network of particular places and paths (see Dwyer 1996). For forest-fallow swidden, cultivators' synecological knowledge may include understanding the relationship between vegetative growth and soil type, the consequences of cutting and burning, of the regrowth stages following abandonment, and the deliberate application of all this in a way that assists the recovery of degraded areas (Conklin 1957; Sillitoe 1993). Moreover such empirical knowledge of plants as I have referred to so far does not exist apart from a broader socially informed understanding of the world, in some kind of hermetically sealed vacuum from which other aspects of culture are excluded. Detailed knowledge of plant reproduction or symbiosis may, for example, comfortably coexist with beliefs about the world that have not been empirically tested in a conventional scientific sense. Everything is seen as connected through chains of mutual causation to give rise to a complex notion of nature, and if not "nature" in the narrow sense, then of the world.

Although much of this knowledge will often find specialized lexical expression, it is not an absolute requirement for memory storage, intergenerational transmission, or practical application. We have long known —partly through the innovative work of Berlin himself—that many people can manage without extensive color terminologies, since the close "semantic contact" between forest peoples and their environment provides alternative—often more specific and revealing—ways of linguistically encoding difference without resort to the abstract categories provided in the domain of color (Bousfield 1979). It has now also be acknowledged that the privileged level in encoding the biological world—the level at which names readily come to mind—also varies: populations with less direct subsistence contact with the variety of forms tend to encode at more abstract levels, using more inclusive categories (Atran 1987; Ellen 1993a: 87–92; Coley et al. 1997). Conversely, as cultural importance and relevant experience declines, so folkbiological classifications "decay from the bottom up" (Dougherty 1978). Yet this hypothesis is problematic insofar as the prediction is not always met that the more contact a people have with the detailed contents of a domain, the more "expert" they become. It is probably not met with regard to color, and I believe the paucity of names at lower levels in the organization of biological knowledge among tropical nonagricultural peoples also suggests that the correlation just cannot be that simple. As the work of Berlin and Brown demonstrates, the ranks of folk specific and varietal are rare among nonagricultural peoples, though it is demonstrably not the case that the knowledge—breadth or depth—of nonagricultural peoples is in any sense inferior or less. If this is so, then the most probable explanation for the particular disjunction, among nonagricultural peoples, between formal lexical knowledge and the substantive knowledge of the kind just attested to, is that substantive knowledge is no less but that shared knowledge (and therefore lexically encoded knowledge) is reduced. Such a reduction would appear to be related to the social, demographic, and mobility circumstances of nonagricultural peoples where knowledge is gained essentially through personal experience not reflected in shared lexica. This is basically the argument first mooted by Morris (1976: 544), and rejected by Berlin, but it seems to me that it is well worth further attention. And, by extension, the same argument may apply—to a lesser degree—among low-intensity cultivators.

## 5.5   Retrospect and Prospect

This chapter has attempted to ask what precisely we mean by indigenous ethnobiological knowledge. By examining data for peoples of the Southeast Asian rain forests, it develops the distinction between formal linguistically encoded knowledge (which passively recognizes diversity and functionality) and substantive knowledge (which is dynamically adaptive). It has suggested how the two might be connected and—more important —disconnected. In particular, it permits a number of specific conclusions:

1. As Berlin (1992: 280) has pointed out, we do not have adequate ethnobiological descriptions of people moving from collecting to incipient agriculture, but we do have a lot of general ethnographic data on collectors who are also incipient agriculturalists, and vice versa, for the Southeast Asian rain forest. Indeed Berlin's dataset is essentially of farming populations who also extract wild resources, rather than one that is sufficiently balanced and distributed to permit the confident comparison of agricultural and nonagricultural populations. It may be that such a balanced comparison is not really possible. The reason may be simply not that there are no longer sufficient quality data for nonagricultural populations but that what might be seen as discrete bodies of

knowledge tied to particular social and ethnic groups are more realistically conceptualized as a division of ethnobiological knowledge reflecting the subsistence specialisms of people who have long been in contact and who in some cases share a common origin.

2. Ethnobiological inventories are strongly constrained by objective biological diversity. We would therefore expect the inventories of tropical rain forest agricultural and nonagricultural peoples to be be more similar than cultivators and collectors considered globally.

3. Given the subsistence overlap in terms of available strategies between those generally described as cultivators and collectors, and the varied combinations possible, ethnobiological inventories are likely to have a clinal distribution between the two hypothetical extremes.

4. Populations less dependent on regular agriculture will have a greater substantive knowledge of noncultivated resources, even if this is not encoded lexically. Contrariwise, populations more dependent on regular agriculture are more likely to have less substantive knowledge of non-cultivated resources, even if terms are lexically encoded.

5. Groups living at low population densities and in small settlements with relatively high turnover in composition will be less likely to have maximal degrees of shared knowledge and will be characterized by shorter terminological inventories. This might be expected to apply to both nonagricultural modes of subsistence and to low-intensity farming.

6. Given the similarity between rain forest populations engaged in varying degrees of extraction and cultivation, the main discontinuity in patterns of knowledge may not come with cultivation itself but with agricultural intensification and the marginalization of rainforest resources. Intensification involves increasing knowledge specialization and higher labor inputs. The higher population growth which generally accompanies the process also places additional pressure on rain forest extraction, especially timber, decreasing biological richness and making forest less accessible. Under these conditions it is most unlikely that knowledge of many species can be effectively reproduced. I would expect that what is true for Southeast Asia will also be the case for other parts of the humid tropics.

## Acknowledgments

An earlier version of this chapter was presented at session C of the Pithecanthropus Centennial Conference held in Leiden in July 1993. I am grateful to the University of Kent at Canterbury for making attendance at that conference possible, and to Alan Barnard for inviting me. The research involved in writing the original version, and in its subsequent revision, was partly supported through two British Economic and Social Research Council awards to the author, one (R000 23 3088) for a project entitled "The ecology and ethnobiology of human-rainforest interaction in Brunei," the other on "Deforestation and forest knowledge in south central Seram" (R000 23 6082); in association with the EC-funded programme, *Avenir des peuples des forêts tropicales* (APFT). I am grateful to Laura Rival, Jay Bernstein, and to the participants of a seminar at the Oxford Centre for Environment, Ethics and Society for their comments. The usual disclaimers apply.

## Note

1. Within particular groups of plants, some are more likely to be labeled than others. We might expect these to be more salient for reason of being, say, the largest, with the most unusual habit, the most striking flower, the most useful property, or the most commonly occurring. However, neither high levels of occurrence nor apparently striking flowers are sufficient to generate names where plants are of otherwise little use, as for example with many pan-tropical weeds included within the Nuaulu category *monote* (Ellen 1991).

## References

Alcorn, J. B. 1981. Factors influencing botanical resource perception among the Huastec: Suggestions for future ethnobotanical enquiry. *Journal of Ethnobiology* 1: 221–30.

Atran, S. 1987. Origins of the species and genus concept. *Journal of the History of Biology* 20: 195–279.

Balée, W. 1992. People of the fallow: A historical ecology of foraging in lowland South America. In K. Redford and C. Padoch, eds., *Conservation of Neotropical forests: Working from Traditional Resource Use*. New York: Columbia University Press, pp. 35–57.

Barnard, A. 1983. Contemporary hunter-gatherers: Current theoretical issues in ecology and social organisation. *Annual Review of Anthropology* 12: 193–214.

Bellwood, P. 1985. *Prehistory of the Indo-Malaysian Archipelago*. New York: Academic Press.

Berlin, B. 1992. *Ethnobiological Classification: Principles of Categorization of Plants and Animals in Traditional Societies*. Princeton: Princeton University Press.

Bird-David, N. H. 1988. Hunters and gatherers and other people—A reexamination. In T. Ingold, D. Riches, and J. Woodburn, eds., *Hunters and Gatherers: History, Evolution and Social Change*, vol. 1. London: Berg.

Boster, J. 1996. Human cognition as a product and agent of evolution. In R. F. Ellen and K. Fukui, eds., *Redefining Nature: Ecology, Culture and Domestication*. London: Berg.

Bousfield, J. 1979. The world seen as a colour chart. In R. F. Ellen and D. Reason, eds., *Classifications in Their Social Context*. London: Academic Press, pp. 195–220.

Brosius, J. P. 1995. Bornean forest trade in historical and regional perspective: The case of Penan hunter-gatherers of Sarawak. In J. Fox, ed., *Society and Non-timber Forest Products in Tropical Asia*. East-West Center Occasional Papers (Environment Series) 19, Honolulu: East-West Center, pp. 13–26.

Brown, C. H. 1985. Mode of subsistence and folk biological taxonomy. *Current Anthropology* 26: 43–53.

Bulmer, R. 1985. Trees, grerbs, wugs, shwms and quammals: The new universal natural history of Cecil H. Brown. *Journal of the Polynesian Society* 94: 431–37.

Christensen, H. 1996. Plant names and plant classification in an Iban community in Sarawak, Malaysia. Unpublished manuscript.

Coley, J. D., D. L. Medin, S. Atran, and E. Lynch. 1997. Does privilege have its rank? Folkbiological taxonomy and induction in two cultures. *Cognition* 64: 73–112.

Conklin, H. C. 1954. *The Relation of Hanunóo Culture to the Plant World*. PhD dissertation. Yale University, New Haven.

Conklin, H. C. 1957. *Hanunóo Agriculture, A Report on an Integral System of Shifting Cultivation in the Philippines*. Rome: Food and Agricultural Organization of the United Nations.

Conklin, H. C. 1980. *Ethnographic Atlas of Ifugao: A Study of Environment Culture and Society in Northern Luzon*. New Haven: Yale University Press.

Dougherty, J. W. 1978. Salience and relativity in classification. *American Ethnologist* 5: 66–80.

Dournes, J. 1968. *Bois-bambou. Journal d' Agriculture Tropicale et de Botanique Appliquée* 15 (4–6).

Dunn, F. L. 1975. *Rainforest Collectors and Traders: A Study of Resource Utilization in Modern and Ancient Malaya*. Monograph 5. Petaling Jaya: Malaysian Branch of the Royal Asiatic Society.

Dwyer, P. D. 1996. The invention of nature. In R. F. Ellen and K. Fukui, eds., *Redefining Nature: Ecology, Culture and Domestication*. London: Berg.

Ellen, R. F. 1982. *Environment, Subsistence and System. The Ecology of Small-Scale Social Formations*. Cambridge: Cambridge University Press.

Ellen, R. F. 1985a. Comment on "Mode of subsistence and folk biological taxonomy" by Cecil H. Brown. *Current Anthropology* 26: 55–56.

Ellen, R. F. 1985b. Patterns of indigenous timber extraction from Moluccan rain forest fringes. *Journal of Biogeography* 12: 559–87.

Ellen, R. F. 1986. Review of *Swidden Agriculture in Indonesia*, by M. R. Dove. *Journal of Tropical Ecology* 2: 191–92.

Ellen, R. F. 1988. Foraging, starch extraction and the sedentary lifestyle in the lowland rainforest of central Seram. In T. Ingold, D. Riches, and J. Woodburn, eds., *Hunters and Gatherers 1: History, Evolution and Social Change*. London: Berg.

Ellen, R. F. 1990. Trade, environment and the reproduction of local systems in the Moluccas. In E. F. Moran, ed., *The Ecosystem Approach in Anthropology: From Concept to Practice*. Ann Arbor: University of Michigan Press.

Ellen, R. F. 1991. Grass, grerb or weed? A Bulmerian meditation on the category "monote" in Nuaulu plant classification. In A. Pawley, ed., *Man and a Half: Essays in Honour of Ralph Bulmer*. Auckland: Uniprint.

Ellen, R. F. 1993a. *The Cultural Relations of Classification: An Analysis of Nuaulu Animal Categories from Central Seram*. Cambridge Studies in Social and Cultural Anthropology 91. Cambridge: Cambridge University Press.

Ellen, R. F. 1993b. *Nuaulu Ethnozoology: A Systematic Inventory*. Monograph 6. Canterbury: University of Kent Centre for Social Anthropology and Computing in cooperation with the Centre for South-East Asian Studies.

Ellen, R. F. 1993c. Rhetoric, practice and incentive in the face of the changing times: a case study of Nuaulu attitudes to conservation and deforestation. In K. Milton, ed., *Environmentalism: The View from Anthropology*. London: Routledge.

Ellen, R. F. 1994a. Modes of subsistence: hunting and gathering to agriculture and pastoralism. In T. Ingold, ed., *Companion Encyclopaedia of Anthropology: Humanity, Culture and Social Life*. London: Routledge.

Ellen, R. F. 1994b. The ecology and ethnobiology of human-rainforest interaction in Brunei (a Dusun case study). End of project report submitted to the Economic and Social Research Council (R00 23 3088), pp. 1–17.

Ellen, R. F. 1996. Nuaulu plant names and categories: A systematic ethnobotanical inventory. Unpublished computer database.

Ellen, R. F., A. F. Stimson, and J. Menzies. 1976. Structure and inconsistency in Nuaulu categories for amphibians. *Journal d'Agriculture Tropicale et de Botanique Appliquée* 23: 125–38.

Flenley, J. R. 1979. *The Equatorial Rain Forest: A Geological History*. London: Butterworths.

Flenley, J. R. 1985. Man's impact on the vegetation of Southeast Asia: The pollen evidence. In V. N. Misra and P. Bellwood, eds., *Recent Advances in*

Indo-Pacific Prehistory: Proceedings of the International Symposium Held at Poona, December 19–21 1978. Leiden: Brill, pp. 297–305.

Fox, R. B. 1953. The Pinatubo Negritos: Their plants and material culture. *Philippine Journal of Science* 81: 173–414.

Frake, C. O. 1969. The ethnographic study of cognitive systems. In S. A. Tyler, ed., *Cognitive anthropology*. New York: Holt, Rinehart and Winston.

Friedberg, C. 1990. *Le Savoir botanique des Bunaq: Percevoir et classer dans le Haut Lamaknen (Timor, Indonésie)*. Mémoires du Muséum National d'Histoire Naturelle, Botanique 32. Paris: Muséum National d'Histoire Naturelle.

Gianno, R. 1990. *Semelai Culture and Resin Technology*. Memoirs of the Connecticut Academy of Arts and Sciences 22. New Haven: Connecticut Academy of Arts and Sciences.

Glover, I. C. 1977. The Hoabinhian: Hunter-gatherers or early agriculturalists in South-East Asia? In J. V. S. Megaw, ed., *Hunters, Gatherers and First Farmers beyond Europe*. Leicester: Leicester University Press.

Golson, J. 1985. Agricultural origins in southeast Asia: A view from the east. In V. N. Misra and P. Bellwood, eds., *Recent Advances in Indo-Pacific Prehistory: Proceedings of the International Symposium Held at Poona, December 19–21 1978* Leiden: Brill, pp. 307–14.

Gorman, C. F. 1971. The Hoabinhian and after: Subsistence patterns in Southeast Asia during the last pleistocene and early recent periods. *World Archaeology* 2: 300–20.

Griffin, O. Bion. 1985. A contemporary view of the shift from hunting to horticulture: The Agta case. In V. N. Misra and P. Bellwood, eds., *Recent Advances in Indo-Pacific Prehistory: Proceedings of the International Symposium Held at Poona, December 19–21 1978*. Leiden: Brill, pp. 349–52.

Hames, R. 1983. Monoculture, polyculture, and polyvariety in tropical forest swidden cultivation. *Human Ecology* 11: 13–34.

Harris, D. R. 1973. The prehistory of tropical agriculture: an ethnoecological model. In C. Renfrew, ed., *The Explanation of Culture*. London: Duckworth.

Harris, D. R. 1977. Alternative pathways toward agriculture. In C. A. Reed, ed., *Origins of Agriculture*. The Hage: Mouton.

Harris, D. R. 1989. An evolutionary continuum of people-plant interaction. In D. R. Harris, ed., *Foraging and Farming: The Evolution of Plant Exploitation*. London: Unwin Hyman.

Hays, T. E. 1974. *Mauna: Explorations in Ndumba Ethnobotany*. PhD dissertation. University of Washington, Seattle.

Hays, T. E. 1979. Plant classification and nomenclature in Ndumba, Papua New Guinea Highlands. *Ethnology* 18: 253–70.

Hayes, T. E. 1982. Utilitarian/adaptationist explanations of folk biological classification: Some cautionary notes. *Journal of Ethnobiology* 2: 89–94.

Hays, T. E. 1983. Ndumba folk biology and general principles of ethnobiological classification and nomenclature. *American Anthropologist* 85: 592–611.

Hays, T. E. 1991. Interest, use, and interest in uses in folk biology. In A. Pawley, ed., *Man and a Half: Essays in Pacific Anthropology and Ethnobiology in Honour of Ralph Bulmer*. Auckland: The Polynesian Society, pp. 109–14.

Headland, T. N. 1985. Comment on "Mode of subsistence and folk biological taxonomy" by Cecil H. Brown. *Current Anthropology* 26: 57–58.

Headland, T. N. 1987. The wild yam question: How well could independent hunter-gatherers live in a tropical rainforest ecosystem. *Human Ecology* 15: 463–92.

Headland, T. N., and R. C. Bailey 1991. Introduction: Have hunters and gatherers ever lived in tropical rainforest independently of agriculture? *Human Ecology* 19: 115–22.

Heider, K. G. 1969. Sweet potato notes and queries, or, the problem of all those names for sweet potatoes in the New Guinea highlands. *Kroeber Anthropological Society Papers* 4: 78–86.

Higham, C. 1989. *The Archaeology of Mainland Southeast Asia: From 10,000 BC to the Fall of Angkor*. Cambridge: Cambridge University Press.

Hoffman, C. 1984. Punan foragers in the trading networks of Southeast Asia. In C. Schrire, ed., *Past and present in hunter-gatherer studies*. London; Academic.

Hunn, E. S., and D. H. French. 1984. Alternatives to taxonomic hierarchy: The Sahaptin case. *Journal of Ethnobiology* 3: 73–92.

Hutterer, K. L. 1977. Review of *Rain Forest Collectors and Traders* by F. L. Dunn. *Journal of Asian Studies* 36: 792–93.

Hutterer, K. L., and W. K. Mcdonald, eds. 1982. *Houses Built on Scattered Poles*. Cebu City: University of San Carlos.

Hutterer, K. L. 1983. The natural and cultural history of Southeast Asian agriculture: Ecological and evolutionary considerations. *Anthropos* 78: 169–212.

Kraybill, N. 1977. Pre-agricultural tools for the preparation of foods in the old world. In C. A. Reed, ed., *Origins of Agriculture*. The Hague: Mouton.

Majnep, I. S., and R. Bulmer. 1977. *Birds of My Kalam Country*. Auckland: Auckland University Press.

Maloney, B. K. 1998. The long-term history of human activity and rainforest development. In B. K. Maloney ed., *Human Activities and the Tropical Rainforest: Past, Present, and Possible Future*. Dordrecht: Kluwer, pp. 65–85.

Medway (Lord). 1977. The Niah excavations and an assessment of the impact of early man on mammals in Borneo. *Asian Perspectives* 20: 51–69.

Morris, B. 1976. Whither the savage mind? Notes on the natural taxonomies of a hunting and gathering people. *Man* 11: 542–57.

Morris, B. 1982. *Forest Traders: A Socioeconomic Study of the Hill Pandaram*. London School of Economics Monographs on Social Anthropology, 55. London:

Athlone. Pennoyer, F. D., III. 1975. *Taubuid Plants and Ritual Complexes*. PhD dissertation. Washington State University, Pullman.

Peterson, J. T. 1978. *The Ecology of Social Boundaries: Agta Foragers of the Philippines* Illinois Studies in Anthropology 11. Urbana: University of Illinois Press.

Posey, D. 1988. Kayapó Indian natural-resource management. In J. S. Denslow and C. Padoch, eds., *People of the Tropical Rainforest*. Berkeley: University of California Press.

Rambo, A. T. 1979. Primitive man's impact on genetic resources of the Malaysian tropical rain forest. *Malaysian Applied Biology* 8: 59–65.

Rambo, A. T. 1980. Of stones and stars: Malaysian Orang Asli environmental knowledge in relation to their adaptation to the tropical rainforest ecosystem. *Federation Museums Journal* 25: 77–88.

Rambo, A. T. 1985. *Primitive Polluters: Semang Impact on the Malaysian Tropical Rain Forest Ecosystem*. Anthropological papers, Museum of Anthropology 76. Ann Arbor: University of Michigan.

Reid, L. A., and D. Madulid 1972. Some comments on Bontoc ethnobotany. *Philippine Journal of Linguistics* 3: 1–24.

Revel, N. 1990. *Fleurs de Paroles: Histoire Naturelle Palawan*, vols. 1 and 2. Paris: Peeters/SELAF.

Schebasta, P. 1973. *Among the Forest Dwarfs of Malaya*. Kuala Lumpur: Oxford University Press.

Sillitoe, P. 1993. Local awareness of the soil environment in the Papua New Guinea Highlands. In K. Milton, ed., *Environmentalism: The View from Anthropology*. London: Routledge.

Taylor, P. M. 1990. *The Folk Biology of the Tobelo People: A Study in Folk Classification*. Smithsonian Contributions to Anthropology 34. Washington: Smithsonian Institution Press.

Voekes, R. A. 1994. Useful plants of the Penan: A quantitative comparison of hunter-gatherer and swidden cultivator ethnobotanical knowledge. Paper presented at the Third International Conference on Geography of the ASEAN Region, October 25–26, University of Malaya, Kuala Lumpur.

Whitmore, T. C. 1990. *An Introduction to Tropical Rain Forests*. Oxford: Clarendon Press.

Woodburn, J. 1988. African hunter-gatherer social organization: Is it best understood as a product of encapsulation? In T. Ingold, D. Riches, and J. Woodburn, eds., *Hunters and Gatherers 1: History, Evolution and Social Change*. London: Berg.

Yen, D. E. 1976. The ethnobotany of the Tasaday: III. Notes on the subsistence system. In D. E. Yen, and J. Nance, eds., *Further Studies on the Tasaday*.

Panamin Foundation Research Series 2. Makati, Rizal, Philippines: Panamin Foundation.

Yen, D. 1985. Wild plants and domestication in the Pacific islands. In *Recent Advances in Indo-Pacific Prehistory: Proceedings of the International Symposium Held at Poona, December 19–21 1978*. Leiden: Brill, pp. 315–26.

Yen, D. 1989. The domestication of environment. In D. Harris and G. C. Hillman, eds., *Foraging and Farming: The Evolution of Plant Exploitation*. London: Unwin Hyman.

# 6

# Itzaj Maya Folkbiological Taxonomy: Cognitive Universals and Cultural Particulars

Scott Atran

"One of the most difficult matters in all of controversy," lamented Bertrand Russell, "is to distinguish disputes about words from disputes about facts" (Russell 1958: 114). This is so particularly in the early stages of an interdisciplinary field such as folkbiology. In other chapters we see psychologists split between those who believe that so-called domain-specific theories drive folkbiology from early childhood on (chapters 9 and 10, this volume) and those who believe that children initially have no so-called biological theories to speak of, and therefore no folkbiology (chapter 11, this volume; Carey 1996). Within this debate the existence of folkbiology depends on the existence of "intuitive" or "folk" theories, since everyone seems to agree that whatever such theories may be, they are neither explicit nor scientific. My take is that folkbiological knowledge, even among educated lay Americans (or Japanese), need never become theoretical in any meaningful sense (Atran 1998).

In what follows I outline a small but crucial part of the folkbiological system of a people unschooled in Western notions of theories: the folkbiological taxonomy of the Itzaj Maya. Such taxonomies are crucial to understanding folkbiology for two reasons: biological taxonomies seem to be culturally universal, and they are well structured enough to impose constraints on any and all possible theories, thereby rendering biological theories possible as well as evolutionary theory (at least historically). Western biological theories emerged by decontextualizing nature, by curiously tearing out water lilies from water so that they could be dried, measured, printed, and compared with other living forms detached from local ecology and most of the senses. For Itzaj, folkbiological taxonomy appears to hearken to a somewhat different calling in human life and cognition. However one chooses to characterize this system in terms of theory, there seems no denying the fact that if this is not evidence of folkbiology, nothing else is sure to be.

Humans everywhere classify animals and plants into specieslike groupings that are as obvious to a modern scientist as to a Maya Indian (Simpson 1961; chapter 2, this volume). Such groupings are primary loci for thinking about biological causes and relations (Mayr 1969). Historically they tended to provide a transtheoretical basis for scientific biology in that different theories—including evolutionary theory—have sought to account for the apparent constancy of common species and the organic processes centering on them (Wallace 1889: 1). In addition these privileged groupings have "from the most remote period ... been classed in groups under groups" (Darwin 1859: 431). This taxonomic array provides a natural framework for inference, and an inductive compendium of information, about organic categories and properties (Atran 1990). It is not as conventional or arbitrary in structure and content, nor as variable across cultures, as the assembly of entities into cosmologies, materials, or social groups (Berlin 1992).

The universal character of folkbiological taxonomy does not mean that folkbiological categories are culturally irrelevant. On the contrary, insofar as they reflect a cognitively biased, phenomenal appreciation of the surrounding environment, they help to set the constraints on life that make a culture possible. It is little wonder then that folkbiological taxonomies tend to be among the most stable, widely distributed, and conservative cognitive structures in any culture. Once set into place, such a structure would likely survive even catastrophic historical upheaval to a clearly recognizable degree. Ancient and contemporary Maya societies would be no exception. Even with the social order and cosmological system sundered, the folkbiological structure would persist as a cognitive basis for cultural survival under two conditions: first, there must be significant biological continuity in the ecological distribution of species; second, their must be significant linguistic continuity with the dialect that first encoded the knowledge.

Itzaj Maya folkbiology provides evidence for generalizations about the specific taxonomic structure that delimits the universal domain of folkbiology, but also evidence for the influence of local ecology and culture. The Itzaj are the last Maya Indians native to the Peten tropical forest of northern Guatemala, once an epicenter of classic Maya civilization. The Spanish conquest of the Itzaj in 1697 put a brutal end to the last independent Maya confederacy. Although the Itzaj cosmological system was destroyed, Itzaj folkbiological knowledge—including taxonomic competence and practical application—remains strikingly robust (Atran 1993; Atran and Medin 1997; Atran and Ucan Ek' 1999). Presently, however, Itzaj forest culture verges on extinction: the language, banned for decades by government authorities with threats of fine and punishment, is dying among the young, and the forest is being razed at an awesome rate by loggers, immigrant slash-and-burn farmers, and cattle ranchers. We are working with Itzaj to establish a bioreserve.

## 6.1 Principles of Folkbiological Taxonomy

Over a century of ethnobiological research has shown that even within a single culture there may be several different sorts of special-purpose folkbiological classifications, which are organized by particular interests for particular uses (beneficial/noxious, domestic/wild, edible/inedible, etc.). Only in the last decades has intensive empirical and theoretical work revealed a cross-culturally universal general-purpose taxonomy (Berlin, Breedlove, and Raven 1973) that supports the widest possible range of inductions about living kinds that are relevant to everyday life (Atran 1990). This includes indefinitely many inductions about the plausible distributions of initially unfamiliar biologically related traits over organisms given the discovery of such traits in some organism(s), or the likely correlation of known traits among unfamiliar organisms given the discovery of only some of those traits among the organisms. For example, learning that one cow is susceptible to mad cow disease, one might reasonably infer that all cows may be susceptible to the disease but not that all mammals or animals are.

This default folkbiological taxonomy, which serves as an inductive compendium of biological information, is composed of a stable hierarchy of inclusive groups of organisms, or taxa. At each level the taxa, which are mutually exclusive, partition the locally perceived biota in a virtually exhaustive manner. Lay taxonomy is composed of a small number of absolutely distinct hierarchical levels, or *ranks* (Berlin 1992): the levels of *folk kingdom* (e.g., animal, plant), *life form* (e.g., bug, fish, bird, mammal, tree, herb/grass, bush), *generic species* (e.g., gnat, shark, robin, dog, oak, clover, holly) *folk specific* (poodle, white oak), and *folk varietal* (toy poodle; spotted white oak). Ranking is a cognitive mapping that projects living kind categories onto a structure of *absolute levels*, that is, fundamentally *different levels of reality*. Taxa of the same rank tend to display similar linguistic, biological, and psychological characteristics. Ranks, not taxa, are apparently universal.[1]

### Kingdoms and Life Forms

The most general rank in any folkbiological taxonomy is the folk kingdom,[2] that is, plant or animal. Such taxa are not always explicitly named, since they represent the most fundamental divisions of the (non-human) biological world. These divisions correspond to the notion of ontological category in philosophy (Donnellan 1971) and psychology (Keil 1979). From an early age, it appears, humans cannot help but conceive of any object they see in the world as either being or not being an animal, and there is evidence for an early distinction between plants and nonliving things (Gelman and Wellman 1991; Keil 1994; Hickling and Gelman 1995; Hatano and Inagaki 1996). Conceiving of an object as a plant or animal seems to carry with it certain presumptions that are not applied to objects thought of as belonging to other ontological categories, like the categories of person, substance, or artifact.[3]

The next rank down is that of life form.[4] The majority of taxa of lesser rank fall under one or another life form. Most life-form taxa are named by lexically unanalyzable names (primary lexemes), and they have further named subdivisions, such as tree or bird. Biologically, members of a single life form are diverse. Psychologically, members of a life form share a small number of perceptual diagnostics, such as stem habit or skin covering (Brown 1984). Life-form taxa may represent general adaptations to broad sets of ecological conditions, such as the competition of single-stem plants for sunlight and tetrapod adaptation to life in the air (Hunn 1982; Atran 1990). Classification by life form may occur relatively early in childhood. For example, familiar kinds of quadrupeds (e.g., dog and horse) are classed apart from sea versus air animals (Mandler, Bauer, and McDonough 1991; Dougherty 1979 for American plants).

Itzaj kingdoms and life forms provide evidence for this universal cognitive structure in a Maya idiom. There is no common lexical entry for the plant kingdom; however, the numeral classifier *-teek* is used with all and only plants. Plants generally fall under one of four mutually exclusive life forms: *che'* (trees), *pok∼che'* (herbs, shrubs = undergrowth), *ak'* (vines), and *su'uk* (grasses). Each life form conforms to a distinct stem habit. Some introduced and cultivated plants are unaffiliated with any of these life forms and are simply denoted *jun∼teek* (lit. "one plant," e.g., *jun∼teek ixi'im* = a maize plant). This is also true of many of the phylogenetically isolated plants such as the cacti. All informants agree that mushrooms (*xikin∼che'*, lit. "tree-ear") have no "heart," or *pusik'al* and are not plants but take life away from the trees that host them. Lichens and bryophytes (mosses and liverworts) are not considered to be plants, to have an essence or to live.

In Itzaj, the term for animals (*b'a'al∼che'* = "forest-thing") polysemously refers to (1) the whole animal kingdom (including invertebrates, birds, and fish), (2) a more restrictive grouping of quadrupeds (i.e., *b'a'al∼che'+k-u-siit'* = "jumping animals" or amphibians, *b'a'al∼che'+k-u-jil-t-ik u-b'aj* = "slithering animals" or reptiles, *b'a'al∼che'+k-u-xi'-mal* = "walking animals" or mammals), and (3) typically the mammals alone. Birds (*ch'iich'* including *sotz'* = bats) and fish (*käy*) exhibit patterns of internal structure that parallel those of the "unnamed" mammal and herpetofauna life forms.[5] Like the named life form, *ch'iich'*, the mammal group forms an inferentially self-contained category over which inductive generalizations can be made about biologically related properties. To a significant extent, patterns of induction are the same for the Itzaj life forms, *b'a'al∼che'* (sense 3) and *ch'iich'*, as they are for the American folk categories mammal and bird (Atran, et al. 1997). Snakes (*kan*) also form an inferentially self-contained group (Atran 1994); however, snakes are consistently and exclusively sorted with the lizards at one (intermediate) level and with the rest of the herpetofauna at the next (life-form) level.[6]

Like the life form of invertebrates (*mejen+b'a'al~che'* = "small animal"), herpetofauna seem to form a "residual" life-form category that does not have a conceptually distinctive role in "the economy of nature." This contrasts with the other plant and life-form categories, which seem to have mutually defined ecological roles (see Atran 1990; Berlin 1992): birds and trees in the air (*ik'*) and upper forest tier, mammals and herbs on the ground (*lu'um*) in the forest understory, vines in the connecting "middle" (*tan~chumuk*) tiers, grasses in the open lands (*chäk'an*), and fish in the water (*ja'*). To be sure, the boundaries between these adaptive zones are permeable by members of each life form; however, each of these life forms has its respective habitat, or "home" (*otoch*). Accordingly, because the chicken (*aj-kax*) has its home exclusively on the ground and cannot live in the air like other birds, it is not a bird, nor is it included under any of the other life forms (although for Tzeltal Maya the chicken is the prototypical bird; Hunn 1977).

For the *mejen+b'a'al~che'*, whose morphologies and ecological proclivities are very distant from humans and other vertebrates, correspondence of folk to modern systematics blurs as one descends the ranks of the scientific ladder, and violations of scientific taxonomy tend to be more pronounced. Still, in this respect as in others, Itzaj taxonomy differs little from that of any other folkbiological system, such as that which initially gave rise to systematics, including evolutionary systematics. For Linnaeus, a natural system is rooted in "a natural instinct [that] teaches us to know first objects closest to us, and at length the smallest ones: for example, Man, Quadrupeds, Birds, Fish, Insects, Mites, or first the large Plants, last the smallest mosses" (1751: sec. 153).

## Generic Species

The core of any folk taxonomy is rank of generic species, which contains by far the most numerous taxa in any folkbiological system. Most cultures have a set of life forms, but all cultures have a set of generic species. People in all cultures spontaneously partition the ontological categories animal and plant into generic species in a virtually exhaustive manner. "Virtually exhaustive" means that when an organism is encountered that is not readily identifiable as belonging to a named generic species, it is still *expected* to belong to one. The organism is assimilated to one of the named taxa that it resembles (see chapter 4, this volume). This partitioning of ontological categories seems to be part and parcel of the categories themselves: no plant or animal can fail to uniquely belong to a generic species.

Taxa of the generic-species rank generally fall under some life form, but there may be outliers that are unaffiliated with any major life form taxon.[7] This is often so for plants and animals of particular cultural interest, such as cassowaries for the Kalam of New Guinea (Bulmer 1970) and maize (*ixi'im*) for Itzaj and other Maya (see Berlin, Breedlove and Raven 1974; Barrera Marín, Barrera Vásquez, and López Franco 1976). Like life-form taxa, generic-species taxa are usually named by primary lexemes. Examples are oak and robin in English, or *'oop* (custard-apple tree) and *pek'* (dog) in Itzaj. Sometimes generic species are labeled as binomial compounds, such as hummingbird or *k'u~che'* ("god's tree" = tropical cedar). On other occasions they may be optionally labeled as binomial composites, such as oak tree (as opposed to poison oak) or *ix-k'o'och( +che')* = "the *k'o'och* tree" (*Cecropia*), as opposed to the *k'o'och* herb = *Ricinus communis*). In both cases the binomial makes the hierarchical relation apparent between the generic species and the life form.

Generic species often correspond to scientific genera or species, at least for those organisms that humans mostly readily perceive, such as large vertebrates and flowering plants. On occasion, generic species correspond to local fragments of biological families (e.g., vulture), orders (e.g., bat), and especially with invertebrates, higher-order taxa. Generic species also tend to be the categories most easily recognized, most commonly named, and most readily learned in small-scale societies (Stross 1973).

The term "generic species" is used here, rather than "folk genera/folk generic" (Berlin 1972) or "folk species/folk specieme" (Bulmer 1970), for three reasons.[8] First, a principled distinction between biological genus and species is not pertinent to local folk around the world. The most phenomenally salient species for humans, including most species of large vertebrates, trees, and phylogenetically isolated groups such as palms and cacti belong to monospecific genera in any given locale. Closely related species of a polytypic genus are often hard to distinguish locally, and no readily perceptible morphological or ecological "gap" can be discerned between them (Diver 1940). Second, "generic species" reflects a more accurate sense of the correspondence between psychologically privileged folkbiological groups and historically privileged scientific groups (Stevens 1994). A distinction between genus and species did not appear until the influx of newly discovered species from the world over compelled European naturalists to mnemonically manage them within a worldwide system of genera built around (mainly European) species types (Atran 1987). Third, "generic species" reflects their dual character. As privileged mnemonic groups, they are akin to genera in being those groups most readily apparent to the naked eye (Cain 1956). As privileged causal groups, they are akin to species in being the principal loci of evolutionary processes responsible for the appearance of biological diversity (Mayr 1969).

The correspondence of the generic species to scientific species or genera is not isomorphic; it varies according to patterns of species distribution within biological families and other factors. Nevertheless, generic species usually encompass single biological species and usually do not extend beyond biological genera for the larger vertebrates and flowering plants. For example, in a comparative study we found that two-thirds of tree genera in both the Chicago area—40 of 48—and a sample portion of the Itzaj area of Peten—158 of 229—are monospecific (AHG/APESA 1992; Medin et al. 1997). Moreover 365 generic species of Peten trees and other plants, which Itzaj have thus far identified to us as useful to them, correspond to 437 biological species distributed over 100 biological families (Atran and Ucan Ek', 1999). A comparative study of mammal classification among Itzaj and undergraduates from rural Michigan reveals a similar pattern. The great majority of mammal taxa in both cultures correspond to scientific species, and most also correspond to monospecific genera: 30 of 40 (75 percent) basic Michigan mammal terms denote biological species, of which 21 (70 or 53 percent of the total) are monospecific genera; 36 of 42 (86 percent) basic Itzaj mammal terms denote biological species, of which 25 (69 or 60 percent of the total) are monospecific genera (López et al. 1997).

The rank of generic species is the level at which morphological, behavioral, and ecological relationships between organisms maximally covary. The majority of Itzaj folkbiological taxa belong to this level. It is this level that Itzaj privilege when they see and talk about biological discontinuities. Generic species represent cuts in nature that Itzaj children first name and form an image of (for Highland Maya, see Stross 1973) and that Itzaj adults most frequently use in speech, most easily recall in memory, and most readily communicate to others (for Highland Maya, see Berlin et al. 1974; Hunn 1977). It is the rank at which Itzaj, like other folk around the world, are most likely to attribute biological properties, including characteristic patterns of inheritance, growth, physiological function, as well as more "hidden" properties such as hitherto unknown organic processes, organs, and diseases (Atran et al. 1997).

## Folkspecifics and Varietals

Generic species may be further divided into folkspecifics. In general, whether or not a generic species is further differentiated depends on cultural importance. Itzaj subdivide 365 useful plant generic species into 341 subordinate taxa. But even useful generic species are more likely to be monotypic than polytypic: Itzaj have no subdivisions for three-fourths of useful trees (146 of 200) and other useful plants (119 of 165), and they subdivide the remaining one-fourth into 263 specifics, 72 varietals, and 6 subvarietals (Atran and Ucan Ek' 1999).

Folkspecific taxa are usually labeled binomially, with secondary lexemes. Such compound names make transparent the hierarchical relation between generic species and subordinate folkspecifics, like white oak and mountain robin. However, folkspecifics that belong to generic species with a long tradition of high cultural salience may be labeled with primary lexemes, like winesap (a kind of apple tree) and tabby (a kind of cat). Foreign organisms suddenly introduced into a local environment are often initially assimilated to generic species as folkspecifics. For example, the Lowland Maya originally labeled the Spanish pig "village peccary," just as they termed wheat "Castillian maize." Similarly the Spanish referred to the indigenous pacas and agoutis as "bastard hares," just as they denoted the Maya breadnut tree "Indian fig" (Beltrán 1742). Over time, as introduced species acquire their own distinctive role in the local environment, they tend to assume generic-species status and, as with most other generic species, are labeled by a single lexeme (e.g., "corn" in American English now refers exclusively to maize). Thus the original

Lowland Maya word for the peccary, *k'ek'en*, now refers exclusively to the introduced pig, whereas the native peccary is obligatorily marked in the composite expression *k'ek'en(+)che'* = "forest *k'ek'en*."

The subordinate ranks of folkspecific and varietal corresponds to ranges of perceptible natural variation that humans are most apt to appropriate and manipulate as a function of their cultural interests. Partitioning into subordinate taxa usually occurs as a set of two or more taxa that lexically contrast along some readily perceptible dimension (color, habitat, size, etc.). For Itzaj, 59 percent of the subordinate taxa are distinguished by color contrasts. But such contrast sets often involve cultural distinctions that language and perception alone do not suffice to explain (Hunn 1982). An example is the Itzaj Maya contrast between red mahogany (*chäk[+]chäk-äl~te'*) and white mahogany (*säk[+]chäk-äl~te'*). Red mahogany actually appears to be no redder than white mahogany. Rather, red mahogany is preferred for its beauty because it has a deeper, darker wood grain than white mahogany. But why "red" as opposed to "white," rather than simply "dark" as opposed to "light"?

A majority of Itzaj folkspecifics reflect color contrasts, and the most habitual contrast is between *chäk* and *säk*, which represents 38 percent of all color contrasts (Atran and Ucan Ek', 1999)—this, despite the fact that distinctions involving "green," "yellow," or "black" may be no less obvious to the naked eye. One interpretation is that use of contrasting color specifics, which almost invariably involve just the five primary colors, is related to the overriding importance of these colors in Maya cosmology (see Bruce 1968 for Lakantun; Barrera Marín et al. 1976 for Yukatek). This cosmology traditionally associates red with the true wind of the East, which brings steady rain and bounty, and white with the false wind of the North, which brings drizzle and deception. This is not to deny that color contrasts generally signal perceptible distinctions among folkspecifics. It merely suggests that color perception alone may underdetermine whether, say, "red" versus "white" is really more apparent for a given case than "black" versus "yellow."

Occasionally an important folkspecific will be further subdivided into contrasting varietal taxa, such as short-haired tabby (cat) versus long-haired tabby (cat), or *ix-chäk[[+]]tzäma'[+](b'u'ul)* = "the red *tzäma'* (bean)" versus *ix-säk[[+]]tzäma'[+](b'u'ul)* = "the white *tzäma'* (bean)."

Varietals are usually labeled trinomially, with tertiary lexemes that make transparent their taxonomic relationship with superordinate folkspecifics and generic species. An example is spotted white oak versus swamp white oak, or *ix-k'än*[[+]]*put-il*[+]*kaj* = "the yellow village papaya" versus *ix-säk*[[+]]*put-il*[+]*kaj* = "the white village papaya."

## Intermediate Taxa

Intermediate levels also exist between the generic-species and life-form levels. Taxa at these levels usually have no explicit name (e.g., rats + mice but no other rodents), although they sometimes do (e.g., felines, palms). Such taxa—especially unnamed, "covert" ones—tend not to be as well delimited as generic species or life forms, nor does any one intermediate level always constitute a fixed taxonomic rank that partitions the local fauna and flora into a mutually exclusive and virtually exhaustive set of broadly equivalent taxa. Still there is an evident preference for forming intermediate taxa at a level roughly between the scientific family (e.g., canine, weaver bird) and order (e.g., carnivore, passerine) (Atran 1983; Berlin 1992).

Like folk around the world, Itzaj also have a number of relatively stable intermediate categories, both named and unnamed. Such categories may be nested one within the other. For example, the named category of snakes is embedded in the larger unnamed category of squamates (snakes and lizards).. In turn the squamates are embedded in the (unnamed) life form that includes all herpetofauna. Other examples of named intermediate categories are *aj-ch'uuy* (diurnal raptors), *'aak* (turtles), *kab'* (bees), and *sinik* (ants). A number of intermediates are also polysemously named after prototypical species: *b'alum* (jaguars in particular, and large felines in general), *juj* (iguanas in particular, and lizards in general), *ya'* (chicle tree in particular, and resinous Sapotaceae trees in general), and *xa'an* (guano palm and palms in general). In such cases the intermediate can generally be disambiguated from its prototypical generic species as *uy-et'~ok* X ("companions of X") or *u-ch'ib'-al* X ("lineage of X"), where X is the name of the generic species. Like the named intermediates, unnamed intermediates are usually restricted to locally occurring fragments of biological orders, families, or genera. Examples include *Araneida* (tarantulas and other spiders), *Anura* (frogs and toads),

*Psittacidae* (parrots and macaws), *Dasypractidae* (agoutis and pacas), *Meliaceae* (mahogany and tropical cedars), and *Annona* (custard apples).

## 6.2  Lowland Maya Nomenclature and Notation

The systematic qualification of folkbiological categories by attributives often indicates binomial folkspecific taxa of cultural importance. Yet reliance on nomenclature alone can be misleading. To highlight cognitive distinctions between superficially similar expressions, a set of nomenclatural marks are introduced. These notations represent "hidden" cognitive features of folkbiological categorization that are not apparent from spoken linguistic forms. In what follows, all terms that express taxonomic ranking are composite expressions rather than compounds or descriptive phrases (see Conklin 1962). Morpheme breaks are indicated by a hyphen.

Composite expressions consist of a qualifier plus a stem. The stem designates a category immediately superordinate to the category in question. For example, the composite *mejen+b'a'al∼che'*, which designates the Itzaj life form "invertebrate," consists of the stem for the superordinate kingdom (*b'a'al∼che'* = animal) plus a qualifier (*mejen* = small). For the few life forms that are composite expressions, the relationship between stem and qualifier is indicated by a plus sign. By contrast, the expression *nojoch b'a'al∼che'* ("big animal") is a descriptive phrase rather than a composite. Although *nojoch b'a'al∼che'* could refer to all animals that are not *mejen+b'a'al∼che'*—birds, mammals, fish, and reptiles—this reference is not systematic, and the distinction between "big animal" and "small animal" does not represent a taxonomic partition of animal. This is not to deny that *mejen b'a'al∼che'* can also be used descriptively: to denote any "small animal," which may or may not be an invertebrate depending on the context in which the descriptive phrase is used. The relationship between terms in a descriptive phrase is indicated by a blank space between the terms.

Notice in these examples that the animal kingdom is denoted by a compounding of two terms: *b'a'al* = "thing," together with *che'* = "tree/forest." A compound is formed by uniting two terms, whose different meanings may or may not be related, in order to form a single new meaning. The relationship between compounded terms is indicated by a tilde ( ~ ). The expression *b'a'al~che'* is not a composite because *b'a'al* is not a kind of *che'* (i.e., "thing" is not a kind of "tree"). Neither is the expression a descriptive phrase because *b'a'al* does not qualify *che'* (i.e., "thing" does not modify "tree"). Another example is *k'u~che'* ("god tree"). This compound expression refers exclusively to the generic species, tropical cedar (*Cedrela mexicana*). For the Maya, tropical cedar was traditionally a sacred tree, and the etymological significance of the compound name is thus apparent on inspection. But few present-day Itzaj are spontaneously aware of the constituent meanings; no more, say, than most Americans automatically think of the compound term "eggplant" as, first of all, describing an eggy plant.

Composite expressions also occur for a few generic species when their names indicate an intermediate category. For example, the tapir, *tzimin*(+)*che'* ("forest beast"), forms an intermediate category together with horse, *tzimin*, which is optionally marked by the composite expression *tzimin*( + *kaj*) ("village beast") or *tzimin*(+*kastil*) ("Spanish beast").[9] Terms that are intermediate composite expressions are indicated by a plus sign in parantheses. Optional composite expressions are indicated by enclosing a plus sign within parentheses together with the stem or qualifier. For example, *tzimin*(+*kaj*) has the form STEM(+QUALIFIER), whereas *aj-tzaab'*(+*kan*) ("rattle snake") has the form QUALIFIER (+STEM).

Most folkspecifics are composite expressions consisting of a generic-species stem plus a qualifier. This relationship is indicated by a plus sign in brackets, for example, *ix-ch'uuk*[+]*'ik* ("sweet chile"). Varietals are nearly always composites whose superordinate specific is itself a composite. This embedded composite relationship is indicated by a plus sign in double brackets, for example, *ix-noj*[[+]]*ch'uuk*[+]*'ik* ("big sweet chile"). The female gender marker, *ix*, and the male gender marker, *aj*, are usually obligatory for folkspecifics and varietals in that they designate an item in a contrast set. They are also occasionally attached to certain generic species, with *ix* habitually attached to plants (e.g., *ix-yaat*, a small herbaceous palm) and smaller animals (*ix-litz'*, a small lizard), and *aj* to larger vertebrates (*aj-koj*, mountain lion) and some trees (*aj-k'uxu'*, annota). The prototypical generic species of an intermediate taxon is generally not marked by gender (e.g., *b'alum, juj, ya', xa'an*) (for details, see Lois 1998).

To see how the notation helps clarify cognitive status, consider some representative folkbiological expressions from table 6.1, which represents the intermediate taxon *uy-et'~ok xa'an*.

1. *jach xa'an* = "true guano." This descriptive phrase is usually employed to indicate the protypical status of *Sabal mauriitiformis* among the intermediate category of (usually) taller palms, *xa'an*. On occasion, however, it can be descriptively used to indicate a specific kind of *S. mauriitiformis* as the prototypical folkspecific, namely *aj-b'äyäl*[+]*xa'an* (see example 4 below).

2. *b'otan*(+*xa'an*) = "botan guano." This composite expression refers exclusively to the generic species, *S. mauriitiformis*. Usually the generic species is simply denoted *xa'an*; however, use of the composite *b'otan*(+*xa'an*) allows the generic species, *xa'an*, to be disambiguated from the intermediate palm category, *xa'an*. Most often *b'otan* is used without the composite stem, to refer either to the generic species *S. mauriitiformis* or to its mature form alone.

3. *aj-b'on*(+)*xa'an* = "cabbage-palm guano." This refers exclusively to the generic species *Sabal mexicana*, the closest taxonomic ally of *S. mauriitiformis*. A minority of informants consider the composite stem optional and simply refer to *aj-b'on* or *b'on*. But for all other generic species of the intermediate palm category, *xa'an*, inclusion of the composite stem is always optional: for example, *aj-kuum*(+*xa'an*) = *Crysophilia staurocauta*), *tuk'*(+*xa'an*) = *Acrocomia mexicana*, and so on.

4a. *aj-b'äyäl*[+]*xa'an* = "basket whist guano." This is the prototypical folkspecific of *Sabal mauriitiformis* (see also example 5 below).

4b. *b'äyäl*(+*xa'an*) = "basket whist guano." Only a few informants extend the limits of the intermediate palm category, *xa'an*, to palms of the genus *Desmoncus*. In general, this generic species of climbing palms is simply denoted *b'äyäl*.

5. *b'äyäl*(+*ak'*) = "basket whist vine." Most informants consider *Desmoncus* palms to belong to the life-form category, *ak'* "vine", and will optionally include the life-form stem when referring to the generic species. In some contexts (e.g., our experiments with palms), Itzaj use this composite to distinguish basket whist from the protoypical guano folkspecific, *aj-b'äyäl*[+]*xa'an*. (Generic species that include the life-form stem may be considered composites, rather than compounds if the stem is strictly optional.)

Table 6.1
Petén Maya Palms (ARECACEAE) and their close folkbotanical allies

| English name  Source: mainly Standley & Steyermark (1946–1977) for British Honduras (local Spanish name) | 16th–17th century Cholti-Lakantun name  Sources: Villagutierre (1701/1985) Hellmuth (1977)  (Present Lakantun)  Sources: Nations & Chan K'in José Valenzuela (n.d.)  {Present Mopán}  Sources: Interviews with Mopán speakers from San Luis, Petén | 16th–17th century Yukatek name  Sources: Landa (1566/1975), Roys (1931)  (Present Yukatek)  Sources: Barrera Marín et al. (1976), interviews with Yukatek speakers | Itzaj generic species | Scientific name (Itzaj life-form affiliation) |
|---|---|---|---|---|
| | | | Morphological dimensions:  u-che'-il = tree trunk  u-pok~che'-il = herb stem  u-le' = leaf  k'i'ix = spines  Location:  noj k'aax = upland high forest  kab'al k'aax = transitional forest  u-k'aax-il kab'al lu'um = 'ak'al~che' = low "Bajo" forest or wetland  u-k'aax-il b'otan = botanal  u-k'aax-il kuum = escobal  u-k'aax-il tutz = corozal  chäk'an = savanna/grassland  ju'~che' = secondary vegetation (overgrown or "fallowed" land)  kol = milpa (agricultural field)  päk'aal = "plantation" (tree orchard or kitchen garden)  "Gender" prefix marking noun class for generic species & contrast set for specifics/varietals  aj- = masculine marker  ix- = feminine marker | Itzaj plant life forms:  che' = tree  (che'-im-b'il = treelike)  pok~che' = bush/herb  (pok~che'-im-b'il = herb-like)  ak' = vine  (ak'-im-b'il = vinelike)  Main plant parts:  ich = fruit  k'o' = palm heart  le' = leaf  motz = root  nek' = seed  noy = fleshy part of fruit  top' = flower  tz'ak = medicine |

**Table 6.1** (continued)

| Sabal palm (palma de guano) | xa'an (xa'an) {xa'an} | xan (b'otan xa'an) | | |
|---|---|---|---|---|
| | | (b'ayaal (xa'an)) | | |

Itzaj *specifics/varietals*
Folk specific attributives [+]
Varietal attributives [[+]]
Subvarietals [[[+]]]

Primary colors
**säk** = white/gray
**k'än** = yellow
**ya'ax** = green/blue
**chäk** = red/brown
**b'ox** = black

Possessive markers
**u-** = possessive prefix
**-il** = possessive suffix

**jach** = "true"

[+]*nojoch~u-chun = aj-noj ~ chun*[+] ("large trunk") = *aj-ton*[+]=*u-xib'-al*[+] ("male")
–coarser leaf

*aj-b'äyäl*[+] {**b'ab'** = wing & **y** = possessive pronoun & **al** = child}
–finer leaf (**u-le' b'ek'ech**) = **jach xa'an**

*xa'an = b'otan* {**b'o'** = shade & **tan** = presence} = guano palm, Sp. "guano" **u-che'-il:** 20–27 m × 20–35 cm **u-le':** 1.5–2.5 m **noj k'aax, u-k'aax-il b'otan**—specific types

*Sabal mauritiiformis* (unaffiliated except **b'otan** = **che'**) **noj k'aax:** when young **k'o'~xa'an** is edible and **le'** when young is preferred thatch for roofing houses; **b'otan** wood is used for fencing (**kot**) and preparation of lime (**ta'an**)

| | | | | | |
|---|---|---|---|---|---|
| | | (b'on xá'an) | *aj-b'on* (+*xa'an*) {**bo'** = shade & **-om** = agentive suffix} = cabbage palm, Sp. "palma castilla"<br>**u-che'-il**: 10–12 m × 30–40 cm<br>**u-le'**: 1–2 m<br>kab'al k'aax, kaj, päk'aal, kol, ju'~che' | | *Sabal mexicana* (**che'-im-b'il** or unaffiliated) edible **ich**; leaf fibers (**u-k'o' u-le'**) for making hats (**p'ook**) & baskets (**xak**); salt (**taab'**) made from burning **le'** and **k'o'** |
| (tasiste) | {tasiste} | (tasiste) | *tasiistej*<br>**u-che'-il**: 2–5 m × 5–10 cm<br>**u-le'**: 1–2 m, k'i-k'i'ix u-chun u-le' (spiny petiole)<br>chäk'an, kab'al lu'um | | *Acoelorrhaphe wrightii* (**che'-im-b'il** or unaffiliated) **le'** for making hats & baskets |
| coconut (coco) | {chäk kooko} | (kastelan tuk' = "Spanish cocoyol, "tuk'-il pol) | *kookoj*<br>**u-che'-il**: 3–20 m × 20–30 cm<br>**u-le'**: 3–5 m<br>kaj; päk'aal—specific types by color size and shape of fruit casings (**u-pach uy-ich**) & stem size | aj/ix-k'än[+] | *Cocos nucifera* (**che'-im-b'il** or unaffiliated) edible **k'o'** and **ich**, also for beverage (**u-ja'-il uy-ich**); **le'** for adornment (**uy-utzil-il**) & thatch; soft stem (**mum u-tz'u'**) for low-quality fencing |
| | {säk kooko} | | | aj/ix-ya'ax[+] | |
| | | | | [[+]]'uch-b'en | |
| | | | | [[+]]tu'um-b'en | |
| | {kab'al kooko} | | | aj/ix-kab'al<br>[+] = [+]<br>'enaanoj<br>(dwarf) | |
| | | | | [[+]]ya'ax | |
| | | | | k'än[[+]] | |
| | | | | [[+]]'uub'aj =<br>"grape" | |
| | | | | [[+]]naraanjaj<br>= "orange" | |

**Table 6.1** (continued)

| (cambo) | {k'ämb'o} | kamb'o' | *aj-k'än~b'oo'* {**k'än** = yellow & **b'oo'** = shade/palm spathe, because of yellowish inflorescence} **u-che'-il:** 10–20 m × 10–15 cm, **u-le':** 2–3 m **noj k'aax, kab'al k'aax** | *Gaussia maya* (**che'-im-b'il** or unaffiliated) edible **k'o'** of inferior quality; **le'** as thatch |
|---|---|---|---|---|
| royal palm (palma real) | | palmareaal | *aj-ya'ax~pach* (**ya'ax** = green & **pach** = bark, because of green trunk); more common name today is *palmareyaal* **u-che'-il:** 15–25 m × 30–40 cm, **u-le':** 2 m | *Roystonea dunlapiana* (**che'-im-b'il** or unaffiliated) sweet (**ch'uuk**) edible **k'o'**; **le'** for thatch and adornment |
| broom palm, give & take palm (escoba) | (kun) {miis} | (kuum, miis) | *aj-kuum = aj-miis* = "broom" panids of 200–300 fruits **u-che'-il:** 8–10 m × 8–10 cm, **k'i'ix** **u-le':** 1–2 m **noj k'aax, kab'al k'aax, u-k'aax-il kuum** | *Crysophilia staurocata* (**che'-im-b'il** or unaffiliated) dried **le'** for brooms (**miis**), thatch, hats & baskets; edible **k'o'; tz'ak u-ta'an-il u-k'o'** ash gratings for compress against bleeding & thrown into water as fish poison because astringent (**suutz'**); roasted bitter (**k'aj**) **k'o'** eaten for malaria; burned **k'o'** for salt & sap lick; **u-che'-il** for marl wall supports (**koloj~che'**) & maize storage bin (**ma-kan~che'**) |

| Common name | Folk category | | Description | Variety | Sub-variety | Scientific name & uses |
|---|---|---|---|---|---|---|
| corozo palm (corozo, manaca) | (tuch, *Scheelea Preussi*) {säk tutz} | (mop, tutz') | *tutz* {"oval," because of fruit shape} panids of 600–1,000 fruits **u-che'-il**: 10–20 m × 40–50 cm **u-le'**: 8–10 m **kab'al k'aax, u-k'aax-il tutz**—specific types by color of fruit flesh (**u-noy uy-ich**) and size | *aj/ix-säk*[+] = *jach tutz* | | *Orbignya cohune* (**che'-im-b'il** or unaffiliated) **le'** for thatch; edible upper third of **k'o'** (**aj-kuul**); **k'o'** yields sweet liquid extract for beverage (also for fermenting); **ich** kernels (**ja-b'-en~tun**) used to scrub pots, boiled for cooking oil, hair and body oil, and to fuel prayer lamps; edible **noy** is a famine food which, with **'oox** (*Brosimum alicastrum*), has saved Itzaj time and again (e.g., 1930s) |
| | {k'äntutz} | | | *aj/ix-k'än*[+] | | *Scheelea lundelli* idem. |
| cocoyol palm (cocoyol) | yu (tuk) {ya'ax mäp} | tuk (tuk') | *tuk'* {"hard," after hard kernel} **u-che'-il**: 12–15 m × 30–40 cm, **k'i'ix u-le'**: 3–4 m **ju'~che', päk'-aal, chäk'an**—types by fruit color, size and ease of peeling | *aj/ix-ya'ax*[+] | | *Acrocomia mexicana* (**che'-im-b'il** or unaffiliated) edible **k'o'**; **ich** boiled & skin removed, then finish cooking in sugar or honey to make jam (**ch'uuk-b'il**) from **noy** and candies from **nek'** |
| | {k'än mäp} | | | *aj/ix-k'än*[+] | | |
| | | | | *aj/ix-sus*[+] {**suus** = scrape}—easier to peel off **noy** | *mejen*[[+]] | |
| | | | | | *nukuch* [[+]] | |

Table 6.1 (continued)

| | | | |
|---|---|---|---|
| Warree cohune (chapay) | (akte) {chapay} | *chapay*<br>u-che'-il: 3–6 m × 3–6 cm, k'i'ix<br>u-le': 1–1.5 m<br>kab'al k'aax, chäk'an | *Astrocaryum mexicanum* (**che'-im-b'il** or unaffiliated) edible **k'o'** & cooked **top'**, especially for Easter when meat eating is forbidden |
| poknoboy (huis-coyo-l, jahuacté) | {jalak-te'} | (jawakte') | *mach'* (Sp. *jahuacté macho*)<br>u-che'-il: 3–8 m × 3–8 cm, k'i'ix<br>u-le': 1–2 m<br>kab'al k'aax | *Bactris mexicana* (**che'-im-b'il**, or unaffiliated) stem fiber (**u-k'o' u-che'-il**) for fishtraps (**ix-pat**) |
| | | | *jawaaktej*<br>u-che'-il: 4–5 m × 2.5–5 cm, k'i'ix<br>u-le': 1–1.5 m<br>kab'al lu'um, chäk'an | *Bactris balanoidea* (**che'-im-b'il**, or unaffiliated) edible **ich** |
| basket whist | {b'äyäl} | bayal (b'ayaal) | *b'äyäl* (+*ak'*)<br>u-che'-il: climber to 20 m × 4 cm, k'i'ix<br>u-le': 1–2 m<br>noj k'aax, kab'al k'aax, ju'~che' | *Desmoncus ferox, D. quasilarius, D. uaxactunensis* (**ak'-im-b'il** or unaffiliated) edible **k'o'**; vine-stem fibers (**u-k'o' u-'ak'-il**) as for furniture, hats, baskets, & fishtraps |

| | | | | | |
|---|---|---|---|---|---|
| (pacaya) | (ch'ip) {säk ch'ib'} | (ch'ib) | *ch'ib'* **u-che'-il:** 4–7 m × 1–3 cm **u-le':** 0.5–1.5 m **u-k'aax-il b'otan, kab'al lu'um** | | *Chamaedorea tepejilote* (**che'-im-b'il, pok~che'-im-b'il** or unaffiliated) edible cooked **top'**; stems for poor quality fishtraps of limited duration; **le'** for Palm Sunday branches as church adornment (**uy-utzi-l-il k'u~naj**) |
| (pata de vaca) | {yok vakax} | (jade) | *ix-'ok~wakax* {**ok** = foot & **wakax** = cattle: from Sp. "vacas"} **u-che'-il:** 3–4 m × 1.5–2.5 cm **u-le':** 20–40 cm **noj k'aax** | | *Geonoma decurrens* (**pok~che'-im-b'il** or unaffiliated) **le'** for ornamentation and commerce (see *ix-xyaat*) |
| (xate) | (boi) {mejen xiaat} | (xyaat) | *ix-yaat* **u-che'-il:** 1–5 m × 0.5–2 cm **u-le':** 15–50 cm **noj k'aax**— specific types by stem and leaf size | *u-ch'up-al*[+] = "female," Sp. "hembra," "chico" -smaller, finer leaf | *Chamaedorea elegans* (**pok~che'**) **le'** as ornamentation at local festivities; also collected & sold as export item for adorning flower arrangements [note: falsely rumored to be used by "foreigners" (**tz'ul**) as ingredient in medicines, aphrodisiacs and contraceptives] |

Table 6.1 (continued)

| | | | Variety | Scientific name / uses |
|---|---|---|---|---|
| {macho xiaat} | | u-xib'-al[+] aj-ton[+] = "male," Sp. "jade"—wider, longer leaf and stem | | *Chamaedorea oblongata* idem., (pok~che'-im-b'il or unaffiliated) |
| | | kamb'ray—largest leaf and stem | | *Chamaedorea seifrizii* idem., also used locally as church adornment |
| **ZINGIBERALES** | | | | |
| (caña cristo) | (nunkach pasa') | (paj tzab') | chuuj~le' {chuuj = handful & le' = leaf} = kanya~ch'o' ("rat cane") u-pok~che'-il: 1–1.5 m u-le': 10–20 cm × 5–8 cm—specific types by scale & flower color kab'al lu'um | ix-chäk[+] = jach chuuj~le' ix-säk[+] | Costaceae: *Costus pictus* (pok~che') k'aax: moist and acidic peeled stem for alleviating thirst in emergencies, also used to flavor soups (only before flowering); tz'ak u-le' combined with ix-'ob'eel (*Piper auritum*) to bathe child 9 times for ix-pak'-il ("child fright," Sp. *susto*) & tukul ("child pensiveness," Sp. *pesar*) |
| (platanillo) | {chiki-lab'} | | ix-chikila' u-pok-che'-il: 1–3 m u'-le': 35–45 cm × 15–25 cm kab'al lu'um, u-k'aax-il kuum | | Cannaceae: *Canna lutea* (pok~che') k'aax: household adornment (uy-utzil-il jol~naj) |

| | | | | | |
|---|---|---|---|---|---|
| (kut) | | *kut'*<br>**u-pok-che'-il:** 1–3 m<br>**u-le':** 60–70 cm × 20–25 cm<br>**kab'al k'aax, u-k'aax-il tutz** | | | Marantaceae: *Calathea Allouia* (**pok~che'**) **k'aax**: edible young spikes (**top'**) |
| (maxan) | {le'che'} | *muxan*<br>**u-pok~che'-il:** 1–3 m<br>**u-le':** 40–80 cm × 25–50 cm<br>**kab'al k'aax**<br>—specific types by leaf color | *ix-säk*[+] = *jacb muxan*<br>*ix-ya'ax*[+] | | *Calathea lutea* (**pok~che'**) **le'** used for preparing tamales & tortillas and as emergency thatch; **tz'ak** pruinose underside (**tzakam** = powder) of **le'** mixed with **u-noy k'uxu'** (*Bixa orellana*) & water and ingested to relieve sore throat (**ix-yaj~kal-il**) associated with certain skin allergies producing welts "your body swells" = (**k-u-sip'-tal a'-b'äk'-el**) & chicken pox (**tämäkäs**) |
| banana/ plantain (guineo, plátano) | (patan) {ja'as} | *ja'as*<br>**u-pok~che'-il:** 2–4 m × 50–80 cm<br>**u-le':** 1–2 m × 30–80 cm<br>**päk'-aal, kol** | *ix-gineeyoj* (banano) —types by fruit color, size, shape, & texture | *ix-kab·al*[[+]] = *aj-'enaanoj*[[+]] = dwarf-small stem<br>[[+]]*mansaanaj* = apple<br>*ix-b'amaanoj*[+] = sweet banana | Musaceae: *Musa acuminata* × *M. balbisiana* (**pok~che'-im-b'il** or unaffiliated) edible **ich**; **le'** used for preparing tamales & tortillas |
| | | | | *ya'ax* [[[+]]]<br>*k'än* [[[+]]] | |

**Table 6.1** (continued)

| ja'as (plátano) —types by fruit color, size, shape, & texture | *ix-majuunchej = ix-morookaj = ix*-[[+]]-*k'ek'en*—large fruits | | |
|---|---|---|---|
| | *aj-b'ox~ja'as* [[+]] (Sp. *guineo morado*) | *k'än* [[[+]]] | **le'** for tamal; edible **ich**; edible inner peel of **motz**; **b'ox~ja'as** scraped & fermented to make vinegar for flavoring meat; crushed & rubbed on for back ache; **tz'ak uy-itz u-le'** as ointment ("tinctures where it burns" **k-u-b'on-b'-ol tu'ux 'el-el**) |
| | | *chäk* [[[+]]] | |
| | *aj/ix-ixik*[[+]] Sp. plátano macho | | **le'** for tamal; edible **ich**; **tz'ak u-k'o'** boiled as tea with **su'sk~limoon** (*Cymbogon citratis*), **u'k'o' jab'in** (*Piscidia piscipula*) and **uy-ok~wakax** (*Bauhinia divaricata*) for "evil wind" (**k'a~k'as~'ik**) and colds (**se'en**); **tz'ak uy-ich** just before ripening peel, toast, grind, mix in water & sugar and ingest to control menstrual bleeding & for fever |
| | *ix-jäl*[[+]] Sp. plátano hembra | | |
| | *aj-chäk*[[+]] | | |

6. *k'i'ix xa'an* = "spiny guano." This descriptive phrase can be used to denote some or all of the armed palms. Although for some informants it can describe a stable intermediate grouping of armed palms, there is no cultural consensus in the use of the phrase. For example, although most informants will agree that it describes the armed "treelike" palms *aj-kuum* and *tuk'* (see example 3 above), few allow that it describes the armed "vine," *b'äyäl* (see example 4b above).

7a. *k'än xa'an* = "yellow guano." This can be understood as describing any guano that is withering, guano that appears to shimmer yellow in the sun, and the like.

7b. *k'än∼xa'an* = "yellow guano." This compound refers exclusively to nargusta trees (*Terminalia amazonia*, Combretaceae), whose leaves branch out in a pattern similar to *Sabal mauritiiformis* though they are not folktaxonomically related to *xa'an.*

7c. *k'än∼xa'an∼che'* = "yellow guano tree." This tree (*Calypranthes magistrophylla*) resembles *Terminalia amazonia* in its overall size and yellow sapwood; however, it is considered neither a companion of *k'än∼xa'an* nor of *xa'an.*

8. *ix-jäl[+]ja'as = u-ch'up-al[+]ja'as* = "female plantain." This composite refers to a specific kind of plantain that taxonomically contrasts with the "male plantain," *ix-ixik[+]ja'as = u-xib'-al[+]ja'as.* Itzaj are well aware that plantains and bananas are propagated without regard to sex from underground buds on the rhizome. Itzaj thus use the sexual analogy to highlight a morphological contrast rather than to describe or type a truly sexual distinction. It is unclear, however, whether stable kinds of plantains should be considered folkspecifics of the generic species, plantain, or folkvarietals of a generic species that includes both plantains (*ja'as*) and bananas (*ix-gineeyoj*). In the latter event, *ja'as* would refer polysemously to both the intermediate category of plantains and bananas, and to the generic species of plantains alone. In that case the composite expression for "female plantain" would be *ix-jäl[[+]]j'a'as.*

9. *b'ox∼ja'as* = "black plantain." This compound expression actually refers to a specific kind of banana (*xi-gineeyoj*) rather than plantain (*ja'as*). The terms of the compound expression loosely describe taxonomically relevant properties of the fruit, whose peel and pulp are dark reddish and whose length resembles plantains. Depending on whether the kind is considered a specific or a varietal (see example 8 above), its composite expression would be *aj-b'ox∼ja'as[+]gineeyoj* or *aj-b'ox∼ja'as[[+]]gineeyoj[+]ja'as.*

10a. *chäk ja'as* = "red plantain." This could describe any plantain or banana whose peel or fruit took on a reddish cast. It can also elliptically refer to the redder (as opposed to yellower) variety of *b'ox~ja'as*. In the latter case the full composite form would be *ix-chäk*[[+]]*b'ox~ja'as* if considered a varietal, or *ix-chäk*[[[+]]]*b'ox~ja'as* if considered a subvarietal (see example 9 above).

10b. *ix-chäk-äl~ja'as* = "reddish plantain." This refers exclusively to the red mamey tree (*Pouteria mammosa*), which has no taxonomic relationship nowadays with plantains and bananas. Historically, however, the native mamey was originally labeled *ja'as*. It was initially perceived as related to the introduced plantains and bananas in much the way that the tapir and horse were perceived to be related. When the Spanish introduced the horse, a perissodactyl, the Maya classified it as a specific kind tapir, the only native perissodactyl. Over time the importance of the horse in the Maya vision of "the economy of nature" came to outweigh the tapir's. The original unmarked term for tapir, *tzimin*, was passed on to the horse, and the tapir acquired the obligatory marking *tzimin*(+)*che'* ("forest *tzimin*"). But an intermediate-level taxonomic link persists for Yukatekan Maya (Itzaj, Lakantun, Mopán, Yukatek), indicating awareness of a significant biological relationship between the tapir and horse. By contrast, these Lowland Maya ultimately recognized the initial morphological analogy between the native mamey fruit and the introduced plantains and bananas to be biologically superficial and taxonomically insignificant.

In sum, surface expressions of folkbiological nomenclature, while valuable as a starting points in ethnotaxonomic inquiry, can only be indirect guides to the current status of cognitive categories. For further clarity, cultural context may be crucial and historical analysis enlightening. Controlled psychological testing, however, can sometimes be decisive on these and other issues concerning the cognitive nature of folkbiological taxonomy and taxonomy-based reasoning.

## 6.3    Taxonomic Categories and Category-Based Inference

To illustrate the character of Itzaj folkbiological taxonomy, I will summarize some recent experimental findings gathered with colleagues. The experimental strategy was as follows: First, we asked individual informants to perform successive sorting tasks of name cards or colored picture cards (or specimens in Itzaj pilot studies) in order to elicit individual taxonomies. Then we used statistical measures to see whether or not the data justified aggregating the individual taxonomies for each informant group into a single "cultural model" that could confidently retrodict most (of the variance in) informant responses. Finally, we used the aggregated cultural taxonomies to perform various category-based inference tasks with the same or different informants. Our intention was to see whether and how how people reason from their cultural taxonomies to determine the likely distribution of unfamiliar biologically related properties. At each stage of the sorting and inference tasks, we asked informants to justify their responses. Task preparation and interpretation involved researchers from several countries and disciplines.

By and large, the Itzaj males in our studies were traditional farmers and woodsmen, while females tended household. In nearly all studies equal numbers of men and women were represented. There is some evidence of differences in knowledge (e.g., men often know more about forest trees and animal habits, women often know more about medicinal herbs that grow around the village); however, with the exception of one inference task concerning bird typicality (discussed below), there were no statistically significant differences between men and women in tasks concerning the structuring of taxonomic categories or category-based inference. The folktaxonomic data presented below are intended to be illustrative rather than exhaustive.

### Ranking and Inductive Privilege
The study summarized here uses a standard tool of cognitive psychology —inductive inference—to explore the cognitive validity of folkbiological ranks in general. In particular, the study tests whether or not there is a psychologically privileged rank that maximizes the strength of any potential inference about biologically relevant information. The crucial question is whether and where in the taxonomic hierarchy a breakpoint or sharp change in inductive strength occurs. Similar studies were performed with Lowland Maya and midwestern Americans (for comparative results, see chapter 7, this volume).

Based on extensive fieldwork and preliminary sortings, we chose Itzaj folkbiological categories of the kingdom (K), life form (L), generic species (G), folkspecific (S), and varietal (V) ranks. We selected three plant life forms: *che'* = tree, *ak'* = vine, *pok~che'* = herb/bush. We also selected three animal life forms: *b'a'al~che'+kuxi'mal* = "walking animal," namely, mammal, *ch'iich'* = birds including bats, and *käy* = fish. Three generic-species taxa were chosen from each life form such that each generic species had a subordinate folkspecific and each specific had a salient varietal.

Pretesting showed participants willing to make inferences about hypothetical diseases. The properties chosen for animals were diseases related to the "heart" (*pusik'al*), "blood" (*k'ik'el*), and "liver" (*tamen*). For plants, diseases related to the "roots" (*motz*), "sap" (*itz*), and "leaf" (*le'*). These properties were chosen according to Itzaj beliefs about the essential underlying aspects of life's functioning. Thus the Itzaj word *pusik'al*, in addition to identifying the biological organ "heart" in animals, also denotes "essence" or "heart" in both animals and plants. The term *motz* denotes "roots," which is considered the initial locus of the plant *pusik'al*. The term *k'ik'el* denotes "blood," conceived as the principal vehicle for conveying life from the *pusik'al* throughout the body. The term *itz* denotes "sap," which functions as the plant's *k'ik'el*. The *tamen*, or "liver," helps to "center" and regulate the animal's *pusik'al*. The *le'*, or "leaf," is the final locus of the plant *pusik'al*. For inferences, properties had the form, "is susceptible to a disease of the ⟨root⟩ called ⟨X⟩." For each question, X was replaced with a phonologically appropriate nonsense name (e.g., "eta") in order to minimize the task's repetitiveness.

Each participant responded to a list of over fifty questions in which he/she was told that all members of a category had a property (the premise), and asked whether "all," "few," or "no" members of a higher-level category (the conclusion category) also possessed that property. The premise category was at one of four levels: life form (e.g., L = bird), generic species (e.g., G = vulture), folkspecific (e.g., S = black vulture), or varietal (e.g., V = red-headed black vulture). The conclusion category was drawn from a higher-level category: kingdom (e.g., K = animal), life form (L), generic species (G), or folkspecific (S). Thus there were ten possible combinations of premise and conclusion category levels: L → K, G → K, G → L, S → K, S → L, S → G, V → K, V → L, V → G, and V → S. For example, a folkspecific to life-form (S → L) question might be, "If all black vultures are susceptible to the blood disease called eta, are all other birds susceptible?" If a participant answers "no," then the follow-up question would be, "Are some or a few other birds susceptible to disease eta, or no other birds at all?"

Representative findings are given in Figure 6.1. Responses were scored in two ways. First, we totaled the proportion of "all or virtually all" responses for each kind of question (e.g., the proportion of times respondents agreed that if red oaks had a property, all or virtually all oaks would have the same property). Second, we calculated "response scores" for each item, counting a response of "all or virtually all" as 3, "some or few" as 2, and "none or virtually none" as 1. A higher response score reflected more confidence in the strength of an inference. These scores were analyzed using *t*-tests with significance levels adjusted to account for multiple comparisons. All results reported are significant beyond chance.

Figure 6.1a summarizes the results from all Itzaj informants for all life forms and it diseases, and it shows the proportion of "all" responses (black), "few" responses (checkered), and "none" responses (white). For example, given a premise of folkspecific (S) rank (e.g., red squirrel) and a conclusion category of generic-species (G) rank (e.g., squirrel), 49 percent of responses indicated that "all" squirrels, and not just "some" or "none," would possess a property that red squirrels have. These results were obtained by totaling the proportion of "all or virtually all" responses for each kind of question (e.g., the proportion of times respondents agreed that if red oaks had a property, all or virtually all oaks would have the same property). Thus a higher-response score represented more confidence in the strength of the inductive inference.

Following the main diagonal of figure 6.1a refers to changing the levels of both the premise and conclusion categories while keeping their relative level the same (with the conclusion one level higher than the premise). Induction patterns along the main diagonal indicate a single inductively privileged level. Examining inferences from a given rank to the adjacent higher-order rank (V → S, S → G, G → L, L → K), we find a sharp decline in strength of inferences to taxa ranked higher than generic species, whereas V → S and S → G inferences are nearly equal and similarly strong.[10] Moving horizontally within each graph in figure 6.1a corresponds to holding the premise category constant and varying the level of the conclusion.[11] Itzaj show the largest break between inferences

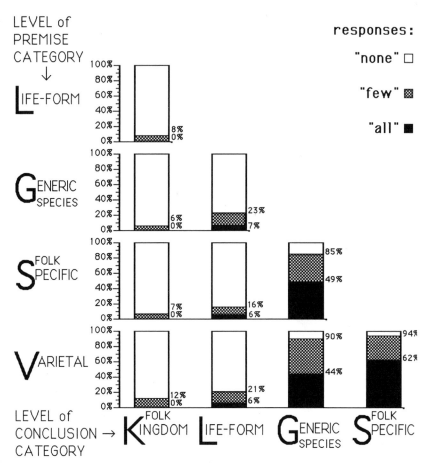

**Figure 6.1a**
Itzaj results: All lifeforms, all diseases, both sexes

to generic species versus life forms. The same pattern for "all" responses is evident for Americans along the main diagonal of Figure 6.1b, while in the combined response scores ("all" + "few") there is evidence of increased inductive strength for higher-order taxa among Americans versus Itzaj. Americans also show a consistent pattern of rating inferences to life-form taxa higher than to folk-kingdom taxa: $G \rightarrow K$ or $G \rightarrow L$, $S \rightarrow K$ or $S \rightarrow L$, and $V \rightarrow K$ or $V \rightarrow L$. This indicates a secondary privileging of life-form taxa for Americans, which arguably owes to attrition of experience at the generic-species level (vs. enhancement of experience for Itzaj).[12]

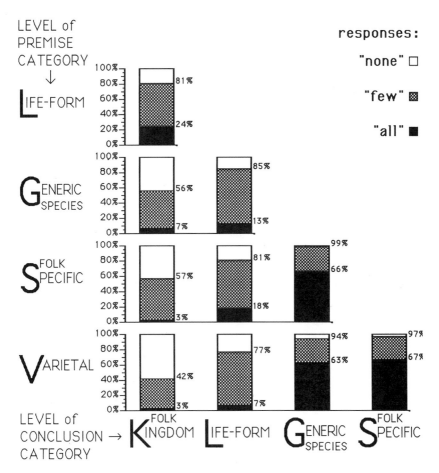

**Figure 6.1b**
Michigan results: All lifeforms, all diseases, both sexes

Moving both horizontally and along the diagonal of figure 6.1a, there is a modest but significant difference between inductions using conclusions at the generic-species versus folkspecific levels: V → G and S → G are modestly weaker than V → S. Most of the difference owes to induction patterns for the Itzaj tree life form. There is evidence that Itzaj confer special privileged status on trees at the folkspecific level (e.g., savanna nance tree): figure 6.2 shows inductive privilege at the folkspecific level for the life form *che'* (tree). A strong ethic of reciprocity in silviculture still pervades the Itzaj, which involves Maya tending trees in

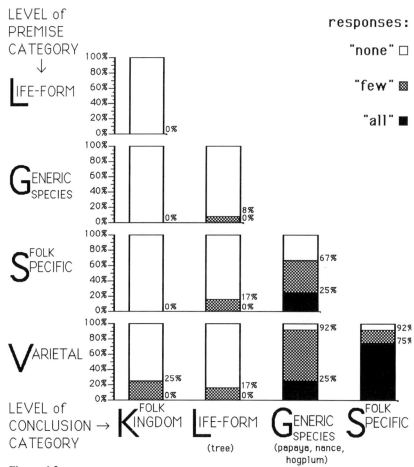

**Figure 6.2**
Itzaj tree lifeform

order that the forest tend to the Maya (Atran and Medin 1997). Knowledge and expertise concerning trees thus seem to translate into an upgrading of biological interest in tree folk specifics. In sum, Itzaj patterns of induction across folkbiological ranks reflects the overall privilege of the generic-species as well as the secondary importance of lower-level distinctions, at least for kinds of trees (see chapter 5, this volume). Argurbly, preference for the generic species represents an evolutionary adaptation to relevant and recurrent features of ancestral hominid environments (Atran 1998).

## Itzaj Mammal Taxonomy

What follows is a brief account of findings in regard to all mammals represented in the local environment of the Itzaj. We included bats, although Itzaj do not consider them mammals (because we wanted to compare how Americans and Maya treat bats; see López et al. 1997). We asked informants to sort name cards of all local mammal generic species into succesive piles. Pretesting name cards were Mayan words in Latin letters, and informants were asked to succesively sort cards according to the degree to which they "go together as companions" (*uy-et'~ok*) of the same "natural lineage" (*u-ch'ib'-al*). When an informant indicated no further desire to successively groups cards, the first piles were restored, and the informant was asked to subdivide the piles until he or she no longer wished to do so.

The "taxonomic distance" between any two taxa (cards) was calculated according to where in the sorting sequence they were first grouped together. While a majority of Itzaj informants were functionally illiterate, they had no trouble in manipulating the name cards as mnemonic icons. There were no observed differences in handling of cards between literate and illiterate Itzaj, and no statistically significant differences in results. We chose names cards over pictures or drawings to minimize stimulus effects and to maximize the role of categorical knowledge.

Results indicate that individual Itzaj mammal taxonomies are all more or less competent expressions of a consensual cultural model of the mammal world.[13] To compare the structure and content of the cultural model with a scientific model, we mathematically correlated each group's aggregate taxonomy with a classical evolutionary taxonomy, that is, one based on a combination of morphological and phylogenetic criteria (Atran 1994; López et al. 1997). The overall correlation between evolutionary and Itzaj taxonomies was strong ($r = 0.81$). A comparison of higher-order taxa only (i.e., excluding generic species) still shows a robust correlation ($r = 0.51$).[14]

Agreement between higher-order groups and science is maximized at the level of the scientific suborder (i.e., the level between family and order), both for Itzaj and Michigan subjects, indicating an intermediate-level focus in the folk taxonomies of both cultures. On the whole, taxa formed at this level are still imageable. Consider the mammal sorting of one Itzaj woman in figure 6.3, which is fairly representative of the aggregate taxonomy (i.e., her first-factor, or competence, score in a principal components factor analysis was >0.9). For example, taxa formed at level 3 in figure 6.3 (the Itzaj counterpart of scientific rankings at the level of the suborder or below) are not only representable by an abstract image but are sometimes named as well. At level 3, for example, *b'alum* includes the large felines (margay, ocelot, jaguar, and mountain lion). At level 2, *'och* includes the skunk, oppossum, porcupine, and weasel, which are morphologically and behaviorally close (in figure 6.3) but scientifically distant (in figure 6.4).

Closer comparison suggests cognitive factors at work in folkbiological classification that are mitigated or ignored by science. For example, certain groupings, such as felines + canines, are common to both Itzaj and Michigan students (see López et al. 1997), although felines and canines are phylogenetically further from one another than either family is to other carnivore families (mustelids, procyonids, etc.). These groupings of large predators indicate that size and ferocity or remoteness from humans is a salient dimension (see Rips et al. 1973). This is a dimension that a corresponding evolutionary classification of the local fauna does not highlight.[15]

**Figure 6.3**
Superordinate levels in mammal taxonomy (b'a'al~che'+k-u-xi'-mal) of an Itzaj woman. As exhibited by average link cluster analysis (the preferred clustering technique in systematics), this tree shows that the folkbiological taxonomy of mammals for the subject has a total of six levels, with only three groups of mammals at level 1: FOX and JAGUARUNDI, JAQUAR and OCELOT, and POCKET MOUSE, RAT, and SHREW. It also shows that MOUNTAIN LION goes together with JAGUAR and OCELOT at level 2, with MARGAY at level 3, with CAT, FOX, and JAGUARUNDI at level 4, with COYOTE and DOG at level 5, and with the rest of the mammals at level 6 (e.g., OTTER). The lowest level at which two given mammals go together in the taxonomy represents the taxonomic distance between them. Thus low taxonomic distance corresponds to high folkbiological relatedness. In the example, MOUNTAINLION is closely related to JAGUAR (2), fairly related to CAT (4), and not very related to OTTER (6). Note that the topological structure of corresponding scientific trees for Itza mammals in figure 6.4 resembles this individual's tree and that the correlation of "topological distance" between these trees is 0.5. Note also that Itzaj consider BAT (aj-sotz') to belong to BIRD (ch'iich), not MAMMAL. Itzaj cross-classify OTTER (u-pek'-il~ja') with acquatic herpetofauna.

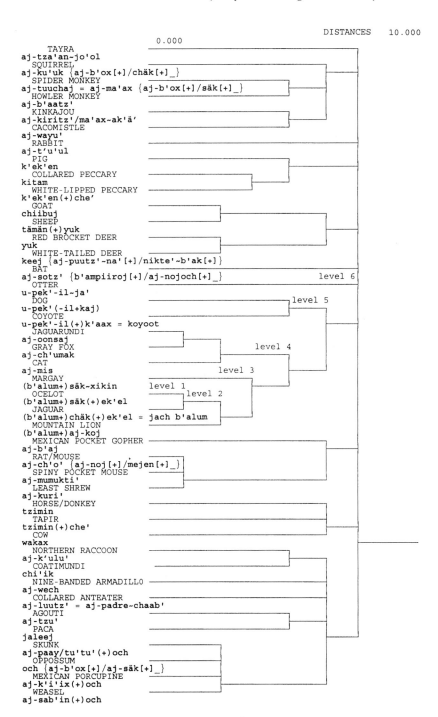

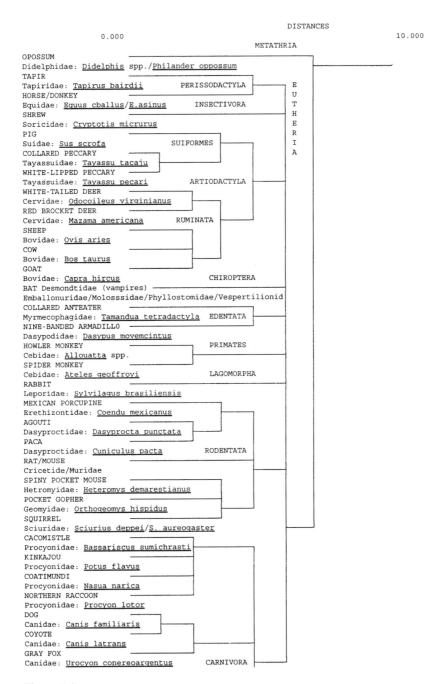

**Figure 6.4**
Scientific tree for Itzaj mammals. The six levels represented in the tree, from left to right, are genus, family, suborder, order, subclass, and class.

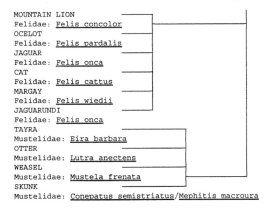

```
MOUNTAIN LION
Felidae: Felis concolor
OCELOT
Felidae: Felis pardalis
JAGUAR
Felidae: Felis onca
CAT
Felidae: Felis cattus
MARGAY
Felidae: Felis wiedii
JAGUARUNDI
Felidae: Felis onca
TAYRA
Mustelidae: Eira barbara
OTTER
Mustelidae: Lutra anectens
WEASEL
Mustelidae: Mustela frenata
SKUNK
Mustelidae: Conepatus semistriatus/Mephitis macroura
```

**Figure 6.4** (continued)

An additional nonscientific dimension in Itzaj classification, not present in American folk classification, relates to ecology. For example, Itzaj form a group of arboreal animals, including monkeys as well as tree-dwelling procyonids (kinkajou, cacomistle) and squirrels (a rodent). The ecological nature of this group was independently confirmed. We asked informants to tell us which plants are most important for the forest to live. Then we aggregated the answers into a cultural model, and for each plant in the aggregate list we asked which animals most interacted with it (without asking directly which animals interact with one another). The same group of arboreal animals emerged as a stable cluster in interactions with plants (Atran and Medin 1997).

### Itzaj Palm Taxonomy

The biasing roles of size and habit are also apparent in the comparison of Itzaj palm classification with a scientific classification of local palms and their folkbotanical allies, the zingiberales (e.g., bananas and plantains). Sorting results show that Itzaj taxonomy correlates positively and significantly with the scientific taxonomy when the generic-species level is included ($r = 0.71$) accounting for half the variance ($r^2$). Furthermore there is a more modest but significant correlation when the folk generic-species level is excluded ($r = 0.44$). These results indicate that Itzaj roughly tend to agree with science in their classification of palms and folkbotanical allies: scientifically distant or close plants tend to be seen on the whole as distant or close on scientific grounds as well. The correlation with science in the case of palms closely parallels the mammal case.

The overall correlation between Itzaj and scientists (which accounts for slightly over half of the variance) reflects the fact that when scientists and folk carve up the biological world, they tend to make the same basic cuts. The lower correlation involving only superordinate palm groupings suggests that folk discriminate these groupings on the basis of somewhat different criteria than does scientific systematics (see figures 6.5 and 6.6). As with the case of mammals (for both Itzaj and American folk), the chief difference appears to be folk reliance on the dimension of size (see chapter 3 by Hunn, this volume). For example, Itzaj readily acknowledge a similarlity in leaf and overall morphological aspect between all of the *Chamaedorea*; however, because *ch'ib'* tends to be markedly taller than the other *Chamaedorea*, it is classed with other treelets (in figure 6.5) rather than with the other *Chamaedorea* "herbs" (*pok~che'*). Similarly, although there is some local acknowledgment of an affinity between all of the Hyophorbeae (in figure 6.6), the treelike character of *aj-k'än~b'oo'* places it with coconut trees and royal palms rather than with the herblike *Chamaedorea*.

In sum, the evidence points to both marked convergence and divergence between folk and science. But the lack of a perfect correlation does not necessarily mean that where they diverge, folk present a "wrong" image of biological reality and science a "right" one. Thus in the folk case stem and leaf size (and habit) is intimately bound up with an appreciation of the ecological role that the taxa play in the local setting. At best, such an appreciation is only of secondary concern to systematics (as a source of information about the genealogical relationships among organisms). Nevertheless, folk appreciation is equally factual. Indeed the very notion of tree, although banned from systematics since at least Linneaus (1751, sec. 209), can hardly be thought to represent a "false" picture of the world. Linnaeus—no less than any contemporary field botanist—would invariably rely on everyday concepts like tree, vine, or herb to understand the composition of any local flora. In the local context of Peten, knowing that *ch'ib'* and *aj-k'än~b'oo'* are not part of the lower undergrowth to which the rest of the hyophorbaceous *Chamae-*

*dorea* belong is not only Maya common sense, it also reflects what is truly perceived.

## Itzaj Snake Taxonomy

There are also evident folk biases in Itzaj classification of snakes = *kan*. Itzaj group snakes into basically three clusters (figures 6.7 and 6.8): (1) long and thin "vine snakes" = *u-kan-il*(+)*ak'* and "fasting snakes" = *aj/ix-suk'in*(+)*kan*, which are thin, mostly inactive snakes that are either nocturnal and arboreal or burrowing, (2) snakes that eat other snakes (e.g., the large boa constrictor, or "oppossum snake" = *aj-'och*(+)*kan*, and the large "rat snake" = *aj-kan*(+)*ch'o'*), and (3) the supposedly lethal snakes, including the fer-de-lance = *k'ok'o'*, the tropical rattlesnake = *aj-tzaab'*(+*kan*), and the coral snakes. But the primary cognitive dimension in the snake classification is venomous versus non-venomous. Questioning shows that people fear certain snakes. Only some of these are actually poisonous, but all those feared are nevertheless thought to sprout wings and extra heads, and to fly off to the sea with their last victims—a likely cultural survival of the Precolumbian cult of *kukul*~*kan* ("feathered serpent"). Interviews suggest that supposed danger is a very strong factor in snake sortings, and supports one interpretation of a multidimensional scaling of these sortings (figure 6.8).[16]

A first interpretation might be that in some cases the biological target is more determined by culturally specific interests than by readily perceptible phenotypic gaps in the distribution of local biota. Evidence from biology and social history, however, indicates a more complex story. Humans everywhere, it seems, are emotionally disposed to fear snakes (Seligman 1971) and to socially ritualize this phobia (Marks 1987) in recurrent cross-cultural themes, such as "the cult of the serpent." The fact that people are spontaneously more inclined to exhibit and express fear of snakes than fear of much more lethal cultural artifacts—like swords, guns, and atom bombs—intimates an evolutionary explanation: naturally selected phobias to resurgent perils in ancestral environments may have provided an extra margin for survival, whereas there would be no direct natural selection of cognitive responses to the more recent dangers of particular cultural environments. To an extent, then, Itza snake classification seems an exception that proves the rule: folk-

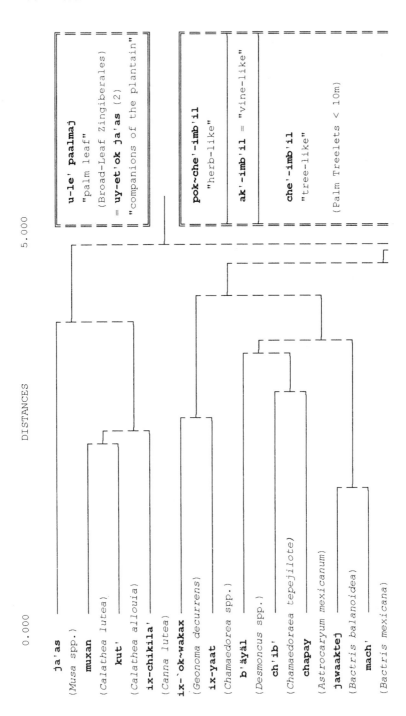

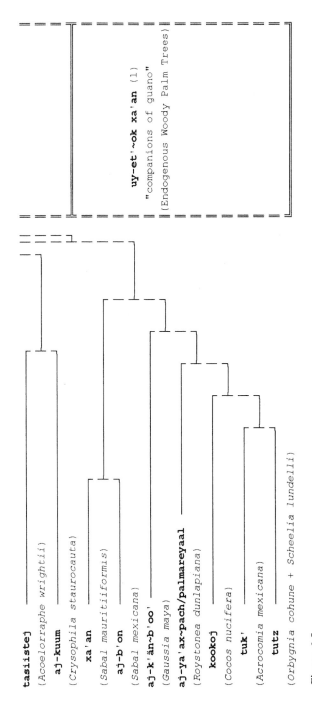

**Figure 6.5**
Itzaj Maya palm taxonomy (uy-et'~ok xa'an): Average link cluster analysis. Note that (1) **uy-et'~ok xa'an** typically refers to "close relatives" (**u-ch'ib'-al**) of *Sabal mauritiiformis* but is occasionally extended to the usually covert intermediate of all local palms and their zingiberale allies, and (2) **chuuj~le'** (*Costus pictus*), a "companion" (**et'~ok**) of **muxan, ix-chikila'**, and **kut'**, was initially unidentifed and excluded from taxomonic sorting experiments.

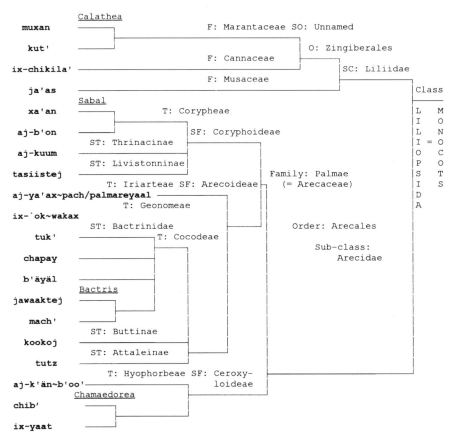

**Figure 6.6**
Scientific taxonomy for Itzaj palms and folkbotanical allies. Taxonomic levels in ascending order, left to right, are (1) genus, (2) *ST* = subtribe, (3) *T* = tribe, (4) *SF* = subfamily, (5) *F* = family, (6) *SO* = suborder, (7) *O* = order, (8) *SC* = subclass, and (9) class.

taxonomies are more or less naturally selected conceptual structures—habits of mind—that are biologically pretuned to capture relevant and recurrent contents of those natural environments—habits of the world—in which hominid evolution occurred.

For snakes, the correlation between Itzaj classification and evolutionary classification is not highly significant, although the correlation between science and the Itzaj herpetofauna as a whole is comparable to the mammal case. Nevertheless, there is a clear morphobehavioral basis for Itzaj snake classification, which is phenomenally salient in the context of forest life and survival. Thus Itzaj classification of snakes into deadly versus nondeadly violates evolutionary classification because nonlethal colubrids are often classed with the lethal pitvipers and corals. A closer look at the violations reveals that ostensibly poisonous colubrids are often biological mimics of the venomous snakes. Mimics are species (1) whose ecological range overlaps with a venomous species or group of species, (2) whose mimetic features are restricted to external characteristics, and (3) which are less able to defend themselves than are their models.

For example, Itzaj classify the following colubrid species with the true corals (*Micrurus* spp.): *Lampropeltis triangulum, Oxyrhopus petola, Pliocercus elapoides, Rhinobothryum bovalli, Scaphiodontophis annulatus, Sibon sartori, Tintilla moesta,* and *Stenorrhina freminvillei* (only red specimens of this species, which is highly variable in color). Even expert herpetologists often have trouble distinguishing some of these species from true corals at a glance. Moreover: "It seems clear that potential predators, for whatever reason, may be discouraged by the bright colors displayed by *Micrurus* ... and that other broadly sympatric ... harmless snake species derive benefit from being colored similarly" (Campbell and Lamar 1989: 379). In this case then human cognition of nature's mimics resembles the instincts of other species. Similar considerations apply to mimics of the pitvipers, such as *Xenodon rabdocephalus.* It resembles the fer-de-lance in size and skin patterning, and it can it change its shape to look venomous. Juvenile specimens of *Senticollis triaspis* also resemble the fer-de-lance, although adult specimens generally do not. Here awareness of morphological similarities has obvious precautionary survival value.

DISTANCES

10.000

0.000

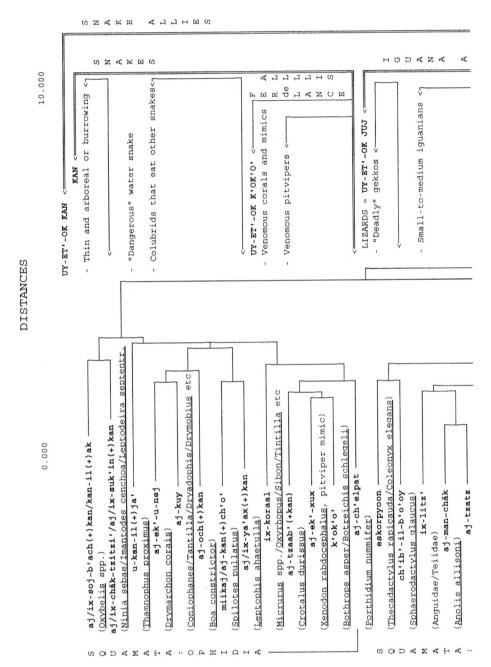

UY-ET'.-OK KAN

KAN
- Thin and arboreal or burrowing

- "Dangerous" water snake
- Colubrids that eat other snakes

UY-ET'.-OK K'OK'O'
- Venomous corals and mimics
- Venomous pitvipers

LIZARDS = UY-ET'.-OK JUJ
- "Deadly" gekkos
- Small-to-medium iguanians

aj/ix-soj-b'ach(+)kan/kan-il(+)ak
(Oxybelis spp.)
aj/ix-chäk-tzitzi'/aj/ix-suk'in(+)kan
(Ninia sebae/Imantodes cenchoa/Leptodeira septentr.
u-kan-il(+)ja'
(Thamnophus proximus)
aj-ek'-u-nej
(Drymarchon corais)
aj-kuy
(Coniophanes/Tantilla/Dryadophis/Drymobius etc
aj-och(+)kan
(Boa constrictor)
mikaj/aj-kan(+)ch'o'
(Spilotes pullatus)
aj/ix-ya'ax(+)kan
(Leptophis ahaetulla)
ix-koraal
(Micrurus spp./Oxyrhopus/Sibon/Tintilla etc
aj-tzaab'(+kan)
(Crotalus durissus)
aj-ek'-xux
(Xenodon rabdocephalus, pitviper mimic)
k'ok'o'
(Bothrops asper/Botreichis schlegeli)
aj-ch'elpat
(Porthidium nummifer)
eskorpyoon
(Thecadactylus rapicauda/Coleonyx elegans)
ch'ib'-il-b'o'oy
(Sphaerodactylus glaucus)
ix-litz'
(Anguidae/Teiidae)
aj-man-chäk
(Anolis allisoni)
aj-tzatz

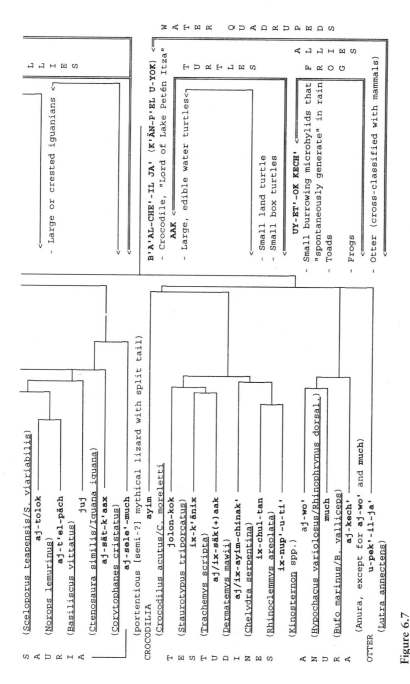

**Figure 6.7**

Aggregate Itzaj taxonomy of Herpetofuana (ba'a'l~che'+k-u-jil-t-ik-ub'aj): Average link cluster analysis

| variable | plot | dimension 1 | 2 | species |
|---|---|---|---|---|
| aj-chäk-tzitzi' = aj-suk'in(+)kan ("fasting snake") | A | 1.16 | 1.04 | Ninia sebae (red coffee snake) / Imantodes cenchoa/Leptodeira septentrionalis |
| ch'elpat | B | -.78 | .09 | Porthidium nummifer (jumping tommy pitviper) |
| aj-ek'-u-nej | C | .21 | -.74 | Drymarchon corais ("black-tail") |
| aj-ek'-xux | D | -.62 | .45 | Xenodon rabdocephalus (false fer-de-lance) / Senticollis triaspis (juveniles only) |
| u-kan-il(+)ja' | E | -.69 | -1.03 | Thamnophus proximus ("water snake") |
| ix-koraal including "false corals," e.g., | F | -.77 | .36 | Micrurus diastema/M. nigrocintus (coral) / Oxyrhopus petola/Sibon sartori/Tintilla moesta |
| aj-kuy zumbadora including species variable in color and cross-classified | G | .53 | -.56 | Coniophanes schmidti/Tantilla canula / Dryadophis melanalomas/Drymobius margeriitif./ Stenorrhina freminvillei, etc. |
| aj-k'än[+]k'ok'o' | H | -.94 | .35 | Bothrops asper ("yellow fer-de-lance") |
| aj-ya'ax[+]k'ok'o' | | | | Botreichis schlegeli ("green fer-de-lance") |
| miikaj | I | .38 | .21 | Spilotes pullatus ("rat snake"=aj-kan(+)ch'o') |
| aj-och(+)kan | J | .58 | -.84 | Boa constrictor ("oppossum snake") |
| ix-soj-b'ach(+)kan = kan-il(+)ak' "vine snake," e.g., | K | 1.60 | .02 | Oxybelis aeneus ("dry-bone snake") / Oxybelis fulgidus ("green vine snake") |
| aj-tz'aab'(+kan) | L | -.92 | .26 | Crotalus durissus ("rattle snake") |
| ix-ya'ax(+)kan | M | .25 | .40 | Leptophis ahaetulla ("green snake") |

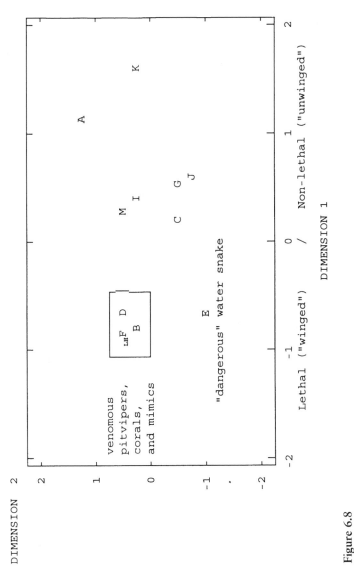

**Figure 6.8**
Multidimensional scaling of Itzaj snake (kan) classification. In the upper panel, the coordinates are in two dimensions. The stress of the final configuration is 0.10861; the proportion of variance (rsq) is 0.93985. In the lower panel, *H, L* are the prototypical snakes, **jach kan** = "true snake."

The fact that Itzaj classify specimens of mimics with lethal snakes does not always mean that Itzaj think of the mimics as essentially venomous. For example, Itzaj sometimes label specimens of green-colored arboreal colubrids as *aj-ya'ax*[+]*k'ok'o'*, whose prototype is the relatively rare palm pitviper, *Botreichis schlegeli*. But Itzaj say it is hard to tell in glancing up a tree if a given specimen is "really" an exemplar of *aj-ya'ax*[+]*k'ok'o*, or an exemplar of some other green snake taxon, such as a juvenile *aj/ix-ya'ax*[+]*soj~bach* ("green dry-bone," a vine snake whose protoytpe is *Oxybelis fulgidus*) or *aj/ix-ya'ax*(+)*kan* ("green snake," a semivenomous nonlethal colubrid whose prototype is *Leptophis ahaetulla*). The "true" test of which taxa a given specimen belongs to depends on its "heart" or "essence" (*pusik'al*); for example, an essential character of *aj-ya'ax*[+]*k'ok'o'*, as opposed to other green snake species, is that it kills its victim: "If you feel the gas spread within you, and the blood flows from your pores, and you die within the day, then it's *aj-ya'ax*[+]*k'ok'o'*." Unfortunately, only the dead may be sure to know to which taxon a given specimen belongs. Of course, there are also "mistaken" cross-classifications, such as identification of the green-speckled specimens of *Drymobius margeriitiferus* with any of the three green snake taxa. Here as well initial *classificatory identification* seems motivated by the survival strategy, "better safe than dead." Still the *principled classification* of taxa by essences potentially distinguishes morphologically similar species. This principled classification involves cognitive strategies that go far beyond the evidence at hand and the recognitory instincts of other species.

### Itzaj Bird Taxonomy

In an experiment with color drawings of 104 local bird species (plus 2 bat species), we asked Itzaj to pilesort as in name card experiments with mammals, palms, and herpetofauna. We used drawings instead of name cards to directly compare how Itzaj classify their birds with how folk in other cultures classify these same birds. As with mammals, palms, and herpetofauna (including snakes), aggregated individual sortings yield a highly consensual taxonomy; that is, a single factor accounted for most of the variance in a principal components analysis, and all individual first-factor scores were positive. Itzaj bird classification is well-correlated with evolutionary taxonomy ($r = 0.75$), with over half the variance accounted for.[17]

To make sense of remaining variance, consider higher-order sortings in figure 6.9 representing the consensual bird taxonomy. Itzaj, local Spanish, and common English names of folktaxa are given in listing 1, along with scientific orders, families, and species to which the taxa belong (figure 6.10). Stimuli broadly represent local distributions of higher- and lower-order scientific taxa, but there are notable absences. Individual variation in naming mostly revolves around closely related taxa (e.g., names for exemplars of the intermediate parrot taxon, *ix-t'ut'*).

Stimulus effects sometimes lead to misidentification because morphological attributes on picture cards give no evidence of the distinctive calls and behaviors often used to identify birds in nature and locate them in culture. Many Itzaj bird names are onomatopoeic, with constituent sounds also often accorded meaning. For example, Itzaj women tend to consider mournful cooing of the short-billed pigeon (*ix-ku'uk~tzu'uy-een* = "squirrel tricked me") as the lament of the bird mother who confided her child to the squirrel trickster. With jaguar approaching, squirrel offered to hide the mother's child as she escaped, then ate the child. Itzaj men, who venture deeper into the forest, say the bird can also be called *ix-k'uk'~suku'un* ("budding brother"). Itzaj confound it with other birds of the intermediate pigeon taxon (*ix-tuut/ix-paloomaj*) only when it is not heard.

Correspondence of distinctive perceptual and behavioral markers with cultural meanings occurs at the life-form, intermediate, generic-species, folkspecific, and varietal levels. For example, although bats (*sotz'*) are classed with birds, their "dualizing" behavior with mammals emerges in folktales: they are deceitful creatures who, in legendary battles between life forms for forest supremacy, betray their (bird) kind for their own advantage. The deluder pretends to suckle its young in the company of mammals and desire only fruit, then sneaks at night to suck out the lifeblood of both mammals and birds. Itzaj believe that while some bats eat fruit, all suck blood. The especially furtive and small vampire bat (*aj-tz'utz'~k'ik'*[+]*sotz'* = "blood sucker" = *Desmodus rotundus*) is the deadliest offender, but larger frugivorous bats (*aj-nojoch*[+]*sotz'*) also dine on friend and foe.

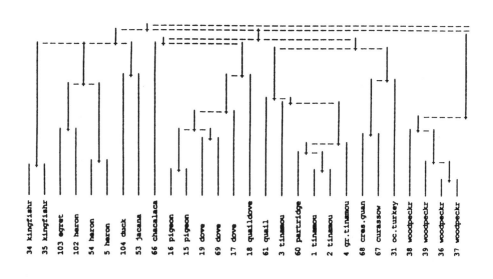

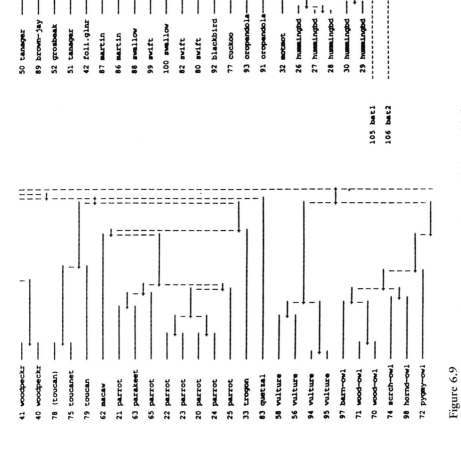

Figure 6.9
Itzaj bird taxonomy (for aggregate sortings, with bats added)

"scientific" cluster
AVERAGE LINKAGE METHOD

Psittaciformes
62 macaw
25 parrot
20 parrot
24 parrot
65 parrot

Columbiformes
19 dove
17 dove
15 pigeon
16 pigeon
18 quaildove
69 dove

Piciformes
41 woodpeckr
39 woodpeckr
38 woodpeckr
36 woodpeckr
37 woodpeckr
40 woodpeckr
78 (toucan)
75 toucanet
79 toucan

Trogoniformes
33 trogon
83 quetzal

Strigiformes
97 barn-owl
74 scrch-owl
71 wood-owl
70 wood-owl
72 pygmy-owl
98 hornd-owl

Ardeiformes
103 egret
54 heron
5 heron
102 heron

Apodiformes
99 swift
80 swift
82 swift

Falconiformes
96 kestrel
14 falcon
13 for.falcon
12 for.falcon
57 falcon
59 hawkeagle
11 hawkeagle
10 hawk
7 kite
6 kite
8 hawk
9 hawk
55 kite
94 vulture
56 vulture
58 vulture
95 vulture

Caprimulgiformes
81 poorwill
73 potoo

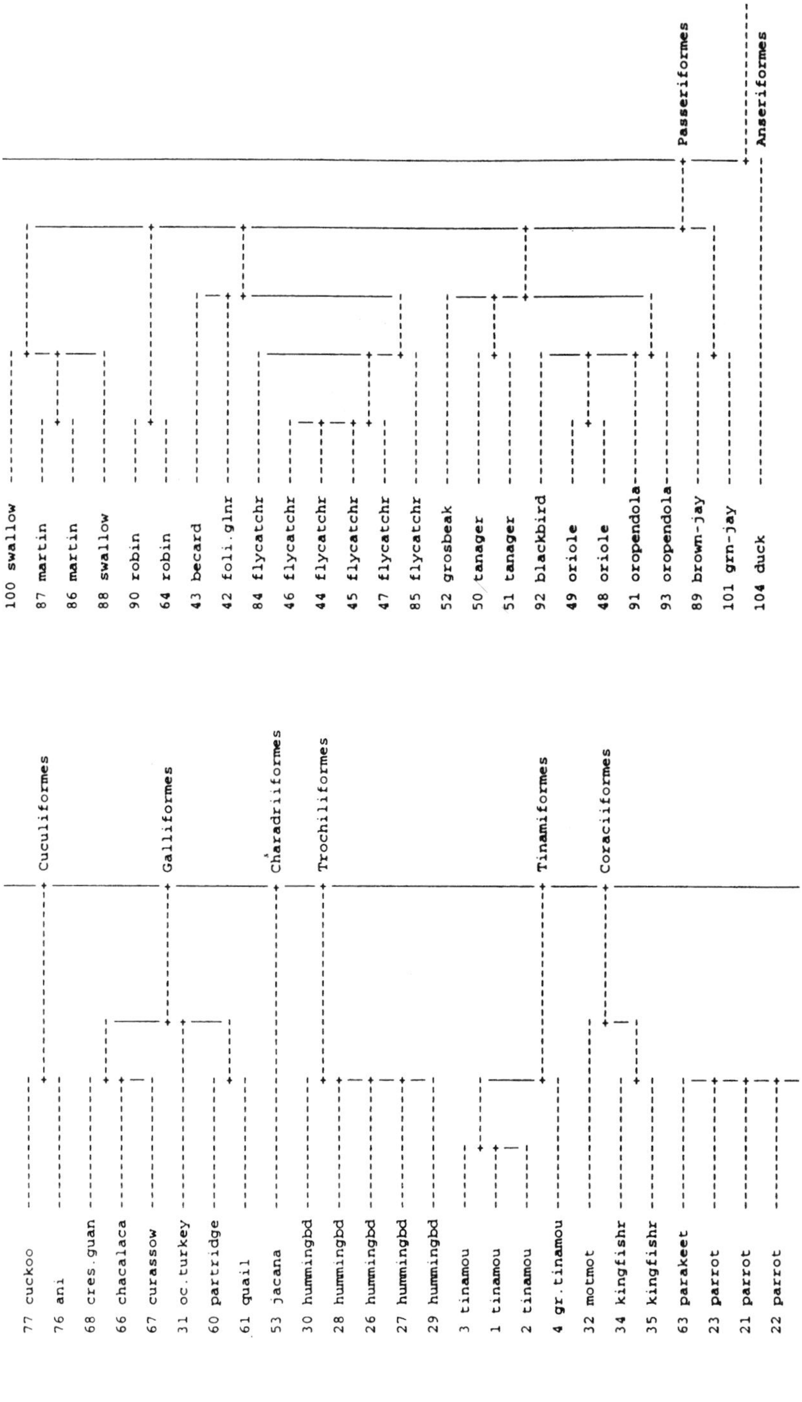


Figure 6.10
Scientific tree of Itzaj birds

The intermediate owl group (*aj-b'uj*) augurs death. Owl generic species distinguish kinds of death augured: the dirge of the barn owl (*aj-xooch'* = *Tyto alba*) foretells a foreigner's (*tz'ul*) demise, the dimunitive appearance of the pygmy owl (*ix-nuk* = *Glaucidium brasilianum*) portends widowhood, the horned screech owl (*aj-b'uj*[+]*kaachoj*/*aj-kukus*[+]*b'uj* = *Otus guatemalae*) is an omen of a violent end. Still the true overlord of life and death in the forest (*jach u-yum-il k'aax*) remains the jaguar, or "red black *b'alum* " = (*b'alum*+)*chäk*(+)*'ek'el*, although mountain lions (*aj-koj*) may be more ferocious. In short, cultural meanings reflect upon taxonomy.

The broadest bird division that some informants explicitly provide in justifying higher-order sortings is (I) edible = *k-u-jan-b'-äl* versus (II) inedible = *ma' tan-u-jan-b'-äl*. But a more consensual, if covert, division, involves a nuanced mix of habit and habitat:

(IA) "Fish-eating water birds" = *u-ch'iich'-il ja' k-u-jan-t-ik käy*: (IA1) Coraciiformes in part (kingfishers = *aj-ch'el*), (IA2) Ciconiiformes (egrets = *aj*/*ix-säk*~*b'ok* and herons = *aj*/*ix-t'on*~*k'uum*), (IA3) Anseriformes (ducks = *u-kutz-il*~*ja'*), and Charadriiformes (jacanas = *ix-ch'iich'-il*~*naab'*). Other swimming birds called *u-kutz-il*~*ja'* but not represented in the sample include Gruiformes (coots, grebes, scamps, teals, etc.). The sandpiper, *ix-tu'wi'is* (Scolopacidae: *Actitis macularia*), is a Charadriiforme that visits wetlands but is not represented. Also not represented in (IA)'s sample are the Pelecaniformes, including the cormorant, *ix-mulach* (Phalacrocoracidae, *Phalacrocorax brasilianus*), and the brown pelican, *aj-je'me'* (Pelecanidae: *Pelecanus occidentalis*).

(IB) "Edible fruit-eating ground birds" = *u-ch'iich'-il lu'um k-u-jan-b'-äl k-u-jan-t-ik ich*: (IB1) Columbiformes (pigeons, doves = *ix-tuut*) and (1B2) Galliformes (tinamous, quails, turkeys). One Galliforme, the raucous and gregarious chachalaca = *ix-b'ach*, is closer folktaxonomically to (1B1) than (1B2). Remaining Galliformes divide as (1B2a) *uy-et'*~*ok ix-män*~*kolol* = "companion of the great tinamou" (small Cracidae and Phasiandae) and (1B2b) "companion of the wild turkey" = *uy-et'*~*ok u-kutz-il*(+)*k'aax*, or "true birds" = *jach ch'iich'* (large Phasiandae and Cracidae).

(IC) "Edible fruit-eating tree birds" = *u-ch'iich'-il che' k-u-jan-b'-äl k-u-jan-t-ik ich*. These subdivide into those that (IC1) "eat worms" =

*k-u-jan-t-ik nok'ol*, Piciformes in part (woodpeckers = *aj-ch'eje'/aj-kolon~te'*), versus (IC2) "are beautiful" = *yutzil*, or brightly colored, including Piciformes in part (toucans = *aj-pichik', aj-piitoj*), Psittaciformes (macaws = *aj-mo'* and parrots = *ix-t'ut'*), and Trogoniformes (trogons = *ix-kokochan*). The quetzal (*ketzal*), Guatemala's rare national bird, is a spectacular trogon of the distant cloud forest that stands alone.

(IIA) "Inedible flesh-eating birds" = *ch'iich' ma' tan-u-jan-b-äl k-u-jan-t-ik b'äk'*. These subdivide into those that eat flesh, which is (IIA1) "rotten" = *tu'*, Falconiformes in part (Cathartidae: vultures = *aj-ch'om*), versus (IIA2) obtained "by killing" = *k-u-kin-s-ik*. The latter further subdivides into those that feed: (IIA2a) "by night" = *ti ak'ä'*, Strigiformes (owls = *aj-b'uj*), versus (IIA2b) "by day" = *ti k'in*, Falconiformes in part (Accipitridae, Falconidae: hawks, kites, falcons = *aj-ch'uuy/aj-mujan*). The jet-black ani (Cuculiformes in part = *aj-ch'ik~b'ul*), with its grooved-bill and fondness for hunting small reptiles and mammals at the forest edge, is marginally attached to (IIA2b), although some informants place it with the blackbird (*aj-pich'*) in (IIB).

(IIB) "Inedible fruit-eating birds" = *u-ch'iich' ma' tan-u-jan-b'-äl k-u-jan-t-ik ich*: Cuculiformes in part (cuckoos), Apodiformes (swifts, hummingbirds), Caprimulgiformes (poorwills, potoos), Coraciformes in part (momots), and Passeriformes (becards, flycatchers, orioles, robins, tanagers, jays, foliage gleaners, grosbeaks, martins, swallows, blackbirds, oropendolas). Subdivisions are (IIB1) becards (*ix-ma'~tuch*) and Caprimugliformes (*aj-pujuy*); (IIB2) *ix-wirisu'*, including most Passeriformes; (IIB3) *ix-kusam*, including martins, swifts, and swallows; (IIB4) cuckoos (*aj-käpäk~cho'/aj-chäk~cho'*), oropendolas (*aj-k'ub'ul*), and motmots (*aj-b'uk~pik*); (IIB5) *tz'unu'un*, hummingbirds. Also known as "birds that eat flower honey" (*ch'iich' k-u-jan-t-ik u-kab'-il top'*), hummingbirds are harbingers of promiscuity.

Some informants link Caprimugliformes to owls (IIA2b) because both groups are nocturnal hunters, but occasional sortings (and misidentifications) of potoos with antshrikes (not included in sample) and becards "pulls" the group into (IIB). The prototypes of (IIB2) are the "queens" (*ix-reeynaj*[+]*wirisu'*), which are flycatchers notable for their white head stripe. The category includes otherwise unremarkable passerines, although orioles (*ix-tzi'il*), robins (*ix-k'ok'*), and tanagers sometimes stand apart (including *Tanagra* = *chichin~b'äkäl*, not represented). Other somewhat distinctive passerines not represented in our sample include warblers (*ix-pitz'-i'~'oox*, Parulidae) and the black-headed *Saltator atriceps* (*ix-tz'apin*, Emberezidae). Swifts are confounded with martins and swallows in (IIB3) because of morphobehavioral similarities, especially tail-feathers and flight. Although Cuculiformes have aspects of both (IIA) and (IIB) because they eat both fruit and small vertebrates, cuckoos (*aj-käpäk~cho'*) are attached to (IIB) along with the blue-crowned momot (*aj-b'uk~pik'*). Momots, unlike some other Coraciformes such as kingfishers (see IA), are akin to squirrel cuckoos in size, eating habit, habitat, and elegant tail-feathers (also a feature of oropendolas). The Itzaj name, *aj-b'uk~pik'*, imitates the motmot's call in the forest understory, whereas the Yukatek name, *toj-toj*, imitates its call from scattered tree tops (there is less understory left in Yucatan). Itzaj variation in naming and misidentification is far greatest for Passeriformes, with some families split among local taxa (Corvidae, Thraupidae, Icteridae). Scientists too have difficulty distinguishing passerine families, which have come to occupy such a wide variety of ecological niches with little concomitant change in structure.

(IIC) "Inedible blood-sucking birds" = *u-ch'iich' ma' tan k-u-jan-b'-äl k-uy-uy-ik k'ik'*, Chiroptera (bats). The bat = *sotz'* was initially excluded from bird sortings (for reasons of cross-cultural comparison), but subsequent sorting trials revealed this folktaxonomic position.

In sum, Itzaj bird taxa largely preserve scientific species, genera, families, and orders. But ecology on a human scale takes on increasing significance as one ascends the life-form taxonomy. Knowledge of which birds can be hunted, and where, is inseparable from knowledge of where and how birds themselves obtain food. Such knowledge, in turn, is intimately linked to awareness of relationships between birds and the forest fauna and flora that birds depend on. This awareness includes patterns of predation and seed dispersal that keep the forest alive. For Itzaj, to infer how the forest can stay alive is to imagine how they can survive (Atran and Medin 1997).

### Itzaj Typicality Judgments and Typicality-Based Inference

Itzaj Maya and students from rural Michigan both project biological properties from typical taxa to an inclusive taxonomic group better than from less typical taxa: $p < 0.05$ on all two-tailed $t$-tests, $n = 12$–$24$ Americans (6–12 men + 6–12 women) and 12–16 Itzaj (6–8 men + 6–8 women). The metric for typicality is given by the taxonomy itself as the lowest average taxonomic distance. In other words, the typicality of an item (e.g., a generic species) is the average taxonomic distance of that item to all other items in the inclusive category (e.g., life form). Items that are more typical provide greater coverage of the category than less typical items. Thus Itzaj choose jaguar/mammal or mountain lion/mammal over squirrel/mammal or raccoon/mammal, judging that all mammals are more likely to be susceptible to a disease that jaguars or mountain lions have than to a disease that squirrels or raccoons have. This is because Maya consider jaguars and mountain lions more typical of mammals than are squirrels and raccoons. In fact jaguars and mountain lions are not typical for Itzaj just because they are more directly related to other mammals than are squirrels and raccoons; they also more closely represent an ideal standard of the "true animal/mammal" (*jach b'a'al∼ che'*) against which the appearance and behavior of all other animals may be judged (see Barsalou 1985). This is evident from Itzaj justifications as well as from direct ratings of which mammals Itzaj consider to be the "truest."

By contrast, American informants choose the items squirrel/mammal or raccoon/mammal over bobcat/mammal or lynx/mammal, presumably because they consider that squirrels and raccoons are more typical of mammals for Americans than are bobcats and lynxes. Note that typicality in these cases cannot be attributed to frequency of occurrence or encounter. Our American subjects were all raised in rural Michigan where the frequency of encounter with squirrels, raccoons, bobcats, and lynxes is nowadays about as likely as the corresponding Itzaj encounter with squirrels, raccoons, jaguars, and mountain lions. Both the Americans and Maya were also more or less familiar with all animals in their respective tasks.

Similarly birds at the top of Rosch's (1975b) American typicality list (e.g., plain-colored passerines like sparrows) are never considered "true representatives" (*jach*) of bird (*ch'iich'*) for Itzaj, whereas birds at the bottom of Rosch's typicality list are (e.g., galliformes such as turkeys). This is the case despite the fact the frequency of occurrence and encounter with plain-colored passerines is about the same in rural Michigan and central Peten, and always greater than frequency of occurrence and encounter with galliformes. In one study we asked midwestern Americans and Itzaj to indicate the "truest" birds among a series of 104 scaled color drawings of the birds of Peten. The Americans invariably placed passeriformes, such as flycatchers and orioles, at the top of their list and galliformes, such as the ocellated turkey, crested guan, and great curassow, at the bottom. Itzaj did just the reverse. When asked which birds were more likely to share a disease with other birds, Americans and Itzaj both strongly preferred their respective "truest" birds. We used "true" rather than "typical" because "typical" correlates closely with "true" for the Americans and because the Itzaj have no term that directly glosses "typical."

In justifying choices, Americans argued that the less remarkable and more frequently encountered passeriformes were more like most other birds than the remarkable galliformes were more like most other birds. By contrast, Itzaj tended to argue that diseases of the galliformes would have greater impact on other living things in the forest, including other birds. This is because of their remarkable size, behavior, and value (in the food chain) to other salient birds (predators), mammals (large carnivores), trees (large nut and fruit trees), and humans.

Comparing direct ratings of "true" with "taxonomic typicality," we found that passeriformes actually had a higher taxonomic-typicality rating (i.e., lower average taxonomic distance) than galliformes for both Itzaj and Americans. This suggests that the concept of typicality inherent in the taxonomy is not the only determinant of typicality-based biological reasoning for Itzaj. Among Itzaj, both "true" and "taxonomically typical" have roles to play where these two notions diverge, as with birds ("true" and taxonomically typical" more closely coincide for mammals and palms). For example, we pitted passeriformes against diurnal raptors (Accipitridae + Falconidae). For Itzaj, passeriformes have medium to high taxonomic typicality, whereas the diurnal raptors have the highest taxonomic-typicality ratings. Itzaj considered the diurnal raptors much stronger candidates than passeriformes for biological inference to all birds. But when dirunal raptors are contrasted with galliformes, overall Itzaj choose galliformes as often as diurnal raptors, although galliformes have the lowest taxonomic-typicality ratings.

Surprisingly 75 percent of men chose the raptors, whereas 75 percent of the women chose the galliformes, with the sex difference being significant ($p = <0.05$ on a two-tailed $t$-test, $n = 8$ women + 8 men). In their justifications men tended to claim that because raptors fly over the entire forest and eat other birds (including other raptors), they can better acquire and spread the biologically related properties (e.g., diseases) of other birds. By contrast, the women inclined to argue that because the galliformes roam over the forest floor and eat all manner of seeds, fruits, and insects they can better acquire and spread their properties throughout the forest (including through their excrement) to other birds that either feed on the galliformes themselves or feed on the myriad other things on the forest floor that galliformes are in contact with.

In each case for which we have Itzaj typicality ratings, the "truest" (and often most taxonomically typical taxa) are large, perceptually striking, culturally important and ecologically prominent: the jaguar and its allies or the tapir for the mammal life form, the ocellated turkey and its allies or the laughing and collared falcons for the bird life form, the fer-de-lance and its allies for the named intermediate category of snakes, the guano palm and its allies for the unnamed intermediate palm category. The dimensions of perceptual, cultural, and ecological salience are all seemingly necessary to a determination of typicality, but none alone appears to be sufficient.

Thus each typical representative can grow large but is not the necessarily largest of its group (cows are bigger than jaguars and tapirs, certain herons and vultures are taller or more massive than ocellated turkeys or falcons, boa constrictors are longer and more massive than fer-de-lance, corozo palms are more massive than guano palms). Each is otherwise physically striking, but in a different way (the jaguar's luxuriant coat and the tapir's elephantlike snout, the ocellated turkeys iridescent feathering and the falcon's loud call, the fer-de-lance's yellow throat, the young guano's palm-leaf cover of the forest floor and the mature guano's strikingly tall and leafless trunk). Each is culturally important but in a different way (jaguars and the falcons are predatory lords of the forest, tapirs and ocellated turkeys define the country's bounty, fer-de-lance is the most feared creature of all, guano palms provide materials for all types of shelter).

Each is salient to to the forest's ecological composition and to people's place in it but in a different way (the jaguar's and tapir's habitats—some 50 km²—determines the extent of a forest section, the presence of the ocellated turkey and black hawk-eagle indicate where game is abundant, where the fer-de-lance strikes determines where people should fear to tread, where there are guano palms human settlement is possible). Indeed the three dimensions seem to be so bound up with one another that it is difficult, if not impossible, to completely distinguish them for any particular case. In other words, typicality for the Itzaj appears to be an integral part of the human (culturaly relevant) ecology. Thus the Itzaj say that wherever the sound of the jaguar is not heard, there is no longer any "true" forest nor any "true" Maya. Nothing of this sort arises for American judgments of biological typicality and typicality-based biological inference. For example, the wolverine is emblematic in Michigan but carries no privileged inductive load.

### Ecological Context and Causal Reasoning versus Diversity-Based Categorical Inference

Concern with ecology is also likely one reason for Itzaj "failure" to apply the so-called diversity principle to biological reasoning with animal (e.g., mammal) and plant (e.g., palm) taxa (Osherson et al. 1990). On this principle, when things are equal (e.g., when taxa are equally typical), a biological property shared by two taxonomically close taxa (e.g., a wolf and a coyote) is less likely to be shared by a superordinate group of taxa (e.g., mammals) than a property shared by two taxonomically distant taxa (e.g., a wolf and a gopher). The diversity principle roughly corresponds to the fundamental principle of induction in scientific systematics: a property shared by two organisms (or taxa) is likely shared by all organisms falling under the smallest (or lowest ranked) taxon containing the two (Warburton 1967).

Thus American folk seem to use their biological taxonomies much as scientists do when given unfamiliar information in order to infer what is likely in the face of uncertainty: informed that goats and mice share a hitherto unknown property, they are more likely to project that property to mammals than if informed that goats and sheep do. By contrast, Itzaj tend to use similarly structured taxonomies to search for causal ecological explanations of why unlikely events should occur. In many cases ecological considerations lead Itzaj informants to conclude that the arguments with the more diverse premises are actually the weaker. For example, Itzaj generally favored argument (i) over argument (ii), where $X$ and $Y$ are unfamiliar biologically related properties, such as unknown diseases.

(i)    Tinamou (*ix-noom*) and quail (*ix-kob'an*) have $X$; therefore any bird (*ch'iich'*) has $X$.

(ii)    Toucan (*aj-pittoj*), chachalaca (*ix-b'ach*), have $Y$; therefore any bird has $Y$.

One Itzaj man argued that the taxonomic allies, rufescent tinamou and spotted wood quail, eat many of the same things off the same ground, including disease-bearing insects and worms. They also leave many half-eaten and disease-ridden things behind for other birds to eat. Raptors eating any of the birds that eat what tinamous and quails eat will, in turn, also be susceptible to the disease. Taxonomically more distant toucans and chachalacas eat fresh fruits apart in trees; hence they are less likely to get and spread a disease. In other words, more (kinds of) birds are apt to have $X$ than $Y$. In this, as in many other cases, taxonomic distance is inversely related to the likelihood that ecological (causal) chains linking habit (especially eating habit) and habitat can be maintained to spread the property to other members of the life form.

Consider, for example, why one Itzaj woman preferred (iii) to (iv):

(iii)    Brown jay (*aj-pa'ap*) and robin (*ix-k'ok'*) have $Y$, therefore any bird has $Y$.

(iv)    Hummingbird (*tz'unu'un*) and kingfisher (*ch'el*) have $X$, therefore any bird has $X$.

She argued that jay and robins both eat fresh as well as rotting things in trees, which can fall to the ground for many other birds to eat. By contrast, kingfishers eat only fish that may fall into water where few other birds venture, and hummingbirds eat only the nectar of flowers that rarely convey disease. As a result more birds are apt to have $Y$ than $X$. For birds (figure 6.9) and mammals (figure 6.3), when typicality is held constant across premises, Itzaj consider arguments with more similar premises to be stronger than arguments with more diverse premises ($p < 0.05$).

Notice that from an epidemiological perspective, Itzaj use of related taxa to generate plausible ecological chains for the spread of a disease across other taxa can be as valid a reasoning strategy as the use of distant taxa to judge widespread intrinsic susceptibility to the disease. A priori, a biologically intrinsic or an ecologically extrinsic stance might be correct. Thus diseases are clearly biologically related, but distribution of a hitherto unknown disease among a given animal population could involve epidemiological factors that depend on both inherent biological susceptibility and ecological agency.

For palms (figure 6.5), although similar premises are chosen more frequently than diverse premises, the difference fails to reach significance. Nevertheless, Itzaj preference for causally based ecological reasoning is evident here as well. For example, one person favored argument (v) over argument (vi), arguing that because the coconut and the royal palm are tall and treelike, their disease is more able to spread to other palms:

(v)    Coconut (*kookoj*) and royal palm (*palmareyaal*)/all palms (*tulakal uy-et'ok xa'an*).

(vi)    Coconut (*kookoj*) and basket whist (*b'äyäl*)/all palms.

In this case, as in many others, size is indicative of the broader ecological coverage of the forest's canopy. In other cases ecological considerations again led diversity-based inductions. For example, one informant accepted (vi) as being stronger than (v) by saying: "Don't you see that the coconut is a big tree and the basket whist clings to it worse than a vine, isn't that so? It can encounter the coconut, climb it, and catch the same disease the other has [and give it to the other palms]." In other words, vinelike basket whists can help spread the disease of treelike coconuts to all other palms, whereas the treelike royal palm would presumably contribute little more to the spread of the disease than would the coconut alone. In this case, as in others, the focus seems to be on broader ecological coverage in terms of the vertical, or storied, relationships between forest species rather than in terms of horizontal relationships of broad spatial coverage.

In the absence of a theory—or at least presumption of a theory—of causal unity underlying disparate species, there is no compelling reason to consider a property discovered in two distant species as biologically intrinsic or essential to both. It may make as much or more sense to consider the counterintuitive presence of a property in dissimilar species as the likely result of an extrinsic or ecologically "accidental" cause. For Itzaj, taxonomic distance can provide one indication of the extent to which ecological agents are likely to be involved in predicting biological properties that do not conform to surface relationships. This may account for negative diversity on some tasks (López et al. 1997). This does not mean that Itzaj fail to grasp or use a diversity principle. In justifications, Itzaj clearly reject a context-free use of the diversity principle in favor of context-sensitive reasoning about likely causal connections. In tasks designed to assess risk-diversification strategies (e.g., sampling productivity from one forest plot or several), Itzaj consistently showed an appreciation of the diversity principle in these other settings (Atran 1995; López et al. 1997).

More generally, what "counts" as a biological cause or property may be somewhat different for folk, like the Itzaj, who necessarily live in intimate awareness of their surroundings, and those, like American folk, whose awareness is less intimate and necessary. For Itzaj, awareness of biological causes and properties may directly relate to ecology, whereas for most American folk the ecological ramifications of biological causes and properties may remain obscure. Historically the West's development of a worldwide scientific systematics explicitly involved disregard of ecological relationships and of the colors, smells, sounds, tastes, and textures that constitute the most intimate channels of Maya recognition and access to the surrounding living world. For example, the smell of animal excrement so crucial to Maya hunters, or the texture of bark so important to their recognition of trees in the dark forest understory, simply have no place in a generalized and decontextualized scientific classification (Atran 1990).

### Relevance of Taxonomy-Based Inference
The idea that folkbiological taxonomies provide a universal framework for general-purpose inductions, while also supporting context-sensitive

causal inferences, leads to speculation about whether or not a single model of taxonomy-based inference can account for all of these phenomena. Our experimental studies suggest that similarity-based models of taxonomic categorization and category-based induction cannot explain our results. The first study on the relationship between rank and inductive privilege suggests that similarity-based models of taxonomic categorization (e.g., Rosch et al. 1976; Hunn 1976) cannot account for the generic species level being the privileged rank for both Itzaj and Americans. This is because American perceptions and experiences tend to privilege life forms for recognition, recall, and communication, whereas Itzaj perceptions and experiences tend to privilege generic species or folk specifics (in the case of trees) for daily use. Yet Americans privilege generic species just as Itzaj do for inductions regarding biologically relevant properties (chapter 7, this volume). For the most part, this is true regardless of familiarity or experience with species.

The bird-inference studies show that even taxonomically defined criteria of typicality do not suffice to uniformly explain patterns of projection among different categories of the same rank (e.g., mammals versus birds) or among different subpopulations of the same culture (e.g., men versus women). Where taxonomically defined typicality tends also to coincide with causal ideals, as in the case of Itzaj mammals or palms, then patterns of property projection tend to parallel American patterns. But where ratings of taxonomic typicality and idealness diverge, as in the case of birds, neither may have a clear advantage in determining inference.

The diversity studies show that similarity-based models of taxonomic induction (e.g., Osherson et al. 1990; Sloman 1993) cannot account for observed asymmetries in patterns of category-based induction. Thus, whereas both Americans and Itzaj use their respective taxonomies to project biologically related properties (e.g., disease) in accordance with taxonomically defined patterns of similarity and typicality, Itzaj do not also project properties in accordance with diversity, although Itzaj clearly apply diversity-based reasoning to other tasks. Yet typicality and diversity presumably reflect the same similarity-based notion of coverage. The fact that certain American groups, such as ecologically knowledgeable parks maintenance workers, also do not reason in accordance with diversity demonstrates that this phenomenon is not restricted to a single culture or type of culture (e.g., small-scale or "traditional" versus industrialized or urban) (chapter 7, this volume).

As an alternative to similarity-based models of taxonomic categorization and category-based inference, which fail to account for our results, we are exploring a relevance-based model of inference. The central idea in a relevance-based model involves an optimizing function between the cognitive costs in mobilizing and making sense of information, and the cognitive benefits in utilizing that information (Sperber and Wilson 1986). On the one hand, certain cognitive benefits, such as correctly anticipating where maximum biological information is to be found in the world, may outweigh the costs of mobilizing information that is somewhat detached from what is most readily perceived or familiar in a local context. This would favor the universal privilege of the generic-species rank in folktaxonomy. On the other hand, certain cognitive benefits, such as understanding the causal connections between biological items that make up the local ecology, and the cognitive costs associated with this understanding, may depend on cultural experience or expertise. This could help to explain how different cultural contexts lead to different predictions of inductive power or argument strength in cases involving typicality and diversity.

To illustrate, consider the diversity task in terms of its relevance. Suppose that the more taxonomically related two items are, the more people expect them to share biologically related properties. This entails that the more taxonomically distant two items are, the more people do not expect them to share properties. This principle corresponds to the similarity phenomenon in Osherson et al. (1990). Suppose also that people are given a situation where taxonomically distant items share a property, just as taxonomically close items share a property. This corresponds to the experimental setup in the diversity task. On the previous principle, an unexpected relationship is being presented as just as true (or likely, plausible, etc.) as the expected relationship. The problem then is to activate background assumptions and knowledge that could in fact make the unexpected relationship true, and do so with the least cognitive effort.

The presence of a superordinate category mobilizes this search for the relevant background information. Take, for example, the case of rat, pocket mouse/mammal versus tapir, squirrel/mammal (in López et al.

1977). The category mammal frames the problem as: "What is it about mammals in general that makes the (taxonomically more distant, hence relatively) unexpected relationship between tapir and squirrel true?" Itzaj seem to mobilize the following background assumptions: "Mammals in general have varied and particular ecologically based causal relationships that govern their interactions, in addition to the host of shared properties and relationships one would expect of closely related taxa; however, the more unlikely the relationship in terms of (taxonomically) shared expectations, the more likely the relationship can be accounted for only in terms of particular causal relationships."

The most relevant causal relationships—that is, those most easily generated or activated from background knowledge and experience—are then mobilized to render the taxonomically unexpected relationship true, or at least understandable, in the context of these background assumptions and knowledge. In other words, conditions of relevance compel Itzaj to search for information that most readily renders understandable the proposition: "If $X$ were the case, then tapir, squirrel/mammal would be true." According to one woman, if bats were to bite and infect tapirs and squirrels, bats could also bite and infect other mammals. Invocation of causal properties to "fill in" $X$ plausibly stems from Itzaj being primed by their life circumstances to consider such causal relationships crucial to daily subsistence and long-term survival.

Once mobilized to explain these taxonomically unexpected relationships, causal interpretations would also be mobilized to account for the (taxonomically) expected relationship. This is necessary if the induction problem is to be equally relevant for both arguments: the one involving taxonomically distant premise categories, and the one involving taxonomically close premise categories. The induction problem becomes: "Which causal relationship is more easily generalized from any of the original items (premise categories) to all other items that fall within the superordinate's range (conclusion category)?" Because rats and pocket mice forgo an external agent, such as a bat, to share and spread their disease, other mammals will more likely get it.

On the average, we should find that the more taxonomically distant and unexpected the relationship, the more particular and idiosyncratic the causal connection, and the less generalizable that causal relationship is to other items. But this need not always be the case. This is because the causal relationships mobilized from background knowledge, although they will tend to be particular to the specific items in question, may create causal contexts with a wider scope than the causal contexts evoked to connect taxonomically closer items. Thus we have seen Itzaj invoke causal scenarios of differing scope for the same arguments, which sometimes leads to contrasting judgments about argument strength. For midwesterners, taxonomically distant items do not engender a causal account. The students may not readily think about causal relationships among living kinds because they do not depend on such knowledge for their everyday lives. Little background knowledge of the living world is directly available to them, or in need of ready access.

Like Itzaj, the Americans students assume that taxonomically close items share more properties more strongly than do taxonomically distant items. Like Itzaj, they therefore face the problem: "What is it about horses and squirrels in particular, or mammals in general, that would make the unexpected relationship between horses and squirrels as true as the expected relationship between rats and mice?" As for the Itzaj, conditions of relevance compel the students to search for information that most readily renders understandable the proposition: "If $X$ were the case, then horse, squirrel/mammal would be true." Because the students know next to nothing about the ecological, or causal, connections between horses and squirrels in particular—and usually need to care about such connections even less—the students "fall back" on the relevant area of taxonomy alone (i.e., the area delimited by the superordinate category highlighted by the task). Their answer to the problem is: "Horses and squirrels share properties because they are mammals." Unlike the case for Itzaj, where $X$ is replaced by a variety of causal scenarios, for most of the students $X$ is simply replaced by the (empty) knowledge that the items are mammals, or that they belong to some relatively large subset of mammals.

Once mobilized to explain taxonomically unexpected relationships, a category-based (rather than causally based) interpretation will also be acitvated to account for (taxonomically) expected relationships. This is necessary if the induction problem is to be equally relevant for both arguments: one involving taxonomically distant premise categories (horse, squirrel), and the one involving taxonomically close premise categories (rat, mouse). The induction problem then becomes: "Which taxonomic relationship is more easily generalized from any of the original items (premise categories) to all other items that fall within the superordinate's range (conclusion category)?" On the average, we should find that the more taxonomically distant and unexpected the relationship, the more generalizable that causally empty relationship is to other items. This is not the case for all Americans. For example, midwestern parks maintenance workers, who are ecologically knowledgeable and depend for their livelihood on that knowledge, reason on diversity tasks in patterned ways that closely parallel those of the Itzaj.

## 6.4   Conclusion

Itzaj folkbiological taxonomy manifests the culturally universal feature of uniquely assigning readily perceptible (nonhuman) organism to specieslike groups and further ranking these mutually exclusive generic species into higher- and lower-order groups. Like folkbiological taxonomies everywhere, it also provides a general inferential framework for category-based inductions. This allows people to readily predict and project the likely distribution of familiar or unfamiliar biologically related properties across living kinds and thus to extend knowledge in the face of uncertainty. The generic species is the privileged locus for isolating such properties and making predictions.

Itzaj folkbiological taxonomy also exhibits features that are culturally particular, or at least constrained by the requirements of life in a small-scale society. For Itzaj, ecology matters significantly for categorization and category-based inference. These findings, however, do not uphold the customary distinction in anthropology, and in history and philosophy of biology, between general-purpose scientific classifications that are designed to maximize inductive potential and special-purpose folk-biological classifications (Gilmour and Walters 1964; Bulmer 1970), which are driven chiefly by functional (Dupré 1981), utilitarian (Hunn 1982), or social (Ellen 1993) concerns. On the contrary, like scientific classifications Itzaj folkbiological taxonomies appear to be general-purpose systems that maximize inductive potential for indefinitely many inferences and ends. Only that potential, and the nature of biological causality it realizes, may be conceived differently by a small-scale society and an industrialized scientific community (as well as folk communities influenced by science).

For scientific systematics the goal is to maximize inductive potential *regardless* of human interest. The motivating idea is to understand nature as it is "in itself," independently of the human observer (as far as possible). To adopt this, Itzaj would have to suspend their primary concern with ecological and morphobehavioral relationships in favor of deeper, hidden properties of greater inductive potential. But the cognitive cost would likely outweigh the benefit (Sperber and Wilson 1986), for this potential, which science strives to realize, is to a significant extent irrelevant, or only indirectly relevant, to local ecological concerns.

For scientific systematics, folkbiology may represent a ladder to be discarded after it has been climbed, or at least set aside while scientists surf the cosmos. But those who lack traditional folk knowledge, or implicit appreciation of it, may be left in the crack between science and common sense. For an increasingly urbanized and formally educated people, who are often unwittingly ruinous of the environment, no amount of cosmically valid scientific reasoning skill may be able to compensate the local loss of ecological awareness.

For the Itzaj, and arguably for other small-scale societies, folkbiological taxonomy works to maximize inductive potential *relative* to human interests. Here folkbiological taxonomy provides a well-structured but adaptable framework. It allows people to explore the causal relevance to them—including the ecological relevance—of the natural world, and in indefinitely many and hitherto unforeseen ways. Maximizing the human relevance of the local biological world—its categories and generalizable properties (including those yet undiscovered)—does not mean assigning predefined purposes or functional signatures to it. Instead, it implies providing a sound conceptual infrastructure for the widest range of human adaptation to surrounding environmental conditions, within the limits of culturally acceptable behavior and understanding.

## Appendix Listing of Itzaj Birds (from the Aggregate Sorting)

Card number = *Species name* (ORDER: Family) = English name = *Spanish name* = consensual Itzaj name

34 = *Ceryle torquata* (Coraciiformes: Alcedenidae) = Ringed kingfisher = *martín pescador* = aj-noj[+]ch'el

35 = *Chloroceryle amazona* (Coraciiformes: Alcedenidae) = Amazon kingfisher = *martín pescador* = aj-ya'ax[+]ch'el

103 = *Egretta alba* (Ciconiiformes: Ardeidae) = Great egret = *garza real* = aj/ix-säk[+]säk~b'ok

102 = *Egretta caerula* (Ciconiiformes: Ardeidae) = Little blue heron = *garza* = aj/ix-b'ox[+]säk~b'ok

54 = *Cochlearius cochlearius* (Ciconiiformes: Ardeidae) Southern boat-billed heron = *garza* = aj/ix-t'on~k'uum = aj-kuchaaraj

5= *Tigrisoma lineatum* (Ciconiiformes: Ardeidae) = Banded-tiger heron = *garza* = aj/ix-t'on~k'uum = aj-jo'jo'

104 = *Anas discors* (Anseriformes: Anatidae) = Blue-winged teal = *pato* = u-kutz-il~ja'/paatoj ("water turkey")

53 = *Jacana spinosa* (Charadriiformes: Jacanidae) = Northern Jacana = *gallito* = ix-ch'iich-il~naab' (sometimes applied to *Aramides cajanea* = Gray-necked wood-rail = gallinola = ix-gayinoolaj)

66 = *Ortalis vetula* (Galliformes: Cracidae) = Plain chachalaca *chachalaca* = ix-b'ach

16 = *Columba nigrirostris* (Columbiformes: Columbidae) = Short-billed pigeon = *paloma* = ix-ku'uk~tzu'uy~een ("squirrel tricked me," onomatopoeic)/ix-k'uk'~suku'un ("budding brother," onomatopoeic)

15 = *Columba speciosa* (Columbiformes: Columbidae) = Scaled pigeon = *paloma* = ix-chukib'/ix-chäk~koj ("red bill")

19 = *Leptotila plumbeiceps* (Columbiformes: Columbidae) = Grey-headed dove = *paloma* = ix-säk~nej ("white tail/tip")/ix-tzu~tzuy~een ("tricked me," onomatopoeic)

69 = *Claravis pretiosa* (Columbiformes: Columbidae) = Blue ground-dove = *paloma* = ix-kuut/ix-tuut

17=*Columbina talpacoti* (Columbiformes: Columbidae)=Ruddy ground-dove = *tortolita* = ix-puruwok (onomatopoeic)/ix-mukuy (onomatopoeic)

18 = *Geotrygon montana* (Columbiformes: Columbidae) = Ruddy quail-dove = *paloma de monte* = ix-k'än~ka' ("yellow grinding stone," for yellowish eyes but onomatopoeic)/ix-tuut (onomatopoeic)

61 = *Odontophorus guttatus* (Galliformes: Phasiandae) = Spotted wood quail = *codorniz* = ix-kob'an~chaakoj/ix-b'olon~chaak ("nine thunder," onomatopoeic)

3 = *Crypturellus soui* (Galliformes: Tinamidae) = Little tinamou = *perdiz* = ix-noom

60 = *Dactylortyx thoracicus* (Galliformes: Phasiandae) = Long-toed partridge = *codorniz* = **ix-chulul/ix-chilu'**

1 = *Crypturellus boucardi* (Galliformes: Tinamidae) = Slaty-breasted tinamou = *perdiz* = **ix-noom/ix-b'aalej**

2 = *Crypturellus cinnamomeus* (Galliformes: Tinamidae) = Rufescent tinamou = *perdiz* = **ix-noom**

4 = *Tinamous major* (Galliformes: Tinamidae) = Great tinamou = *perdiz grande* = **ix-män~kolol**

68 = *Penelope purpurascens* (Galliformes: Cracidae) = Crested guan = *cojolito* = **aj-kox**

67 = *Crax rubra* (Galliformes: Cracidae) = Great curassow *faisán* = **k'äm~b'ul/aj-b'ox[+]k'äm~b'ul/aj-b'ox~chiich'** ("yellow bean," bulbous yellow knob above bill for male only, as opposed to knobless rusty brown female = **aj-chäk[+]k'äm~b'ul/aj-chäk~'chiich'/aj-b'olon~chan**)

31 = *Meleagris ocellata* (Galliformes: Phasiandae) = Ocellated turkey = *pavo real* = **u-kutz-il(+)k'aax**

38 = *Centurus pucherani* (Piciformes: Picidae) = Black-cheeked woodpecker = *carpintero* = **aj-ch'uut/aj-ch'eje'/aj-chejun**

39 = *Centurus aurifrons* (Piciformes: Picidae) = Gold-fronted woodpecker = *carpintero* = **aj-ch'uut/aj-ch'eje'/aj-chejun**

36 = *Celeus castaneus* (Piciformes: Picidae) = Chestnut-colored woodpecker = *carpintero* = **aj-ch'eje'[+]b'oneetej**

37 = *Piculus rubiginosus* (Piciformes: Picidae) = Golden-olive woodpecker = *carpintero* = **aj-k'än[+]ch'eje'** = **aj-ch'ej~nek'** ("seed pecker")

41 = *Campephilus guatemalensis* (Piciformes: Picidae) = Pale-billed woodpecker = *carpintero grande* = **aj-noj(+)kolon~te'** = **aj-b'ox[+]**

40 = *Dryocopus lineatus* (Piciformes: Picidae) = Lineated woodpecker = *carpintero grande* = **aj-noj(+)kolon~te'** = **aj-b'ox[+]**

78 = *Pteroglossus torquatus* (Piciformes: Ramphastidae) = Collared aracari = *pito* = **aj-pichik'** (onomatopoeic)

75 = *Aulacorhynchus prasinus* (Piciformes: Ramphastidae) = Emerald toucanet = *pito verde* = **aj-ya'ax[+]pichik'** (onomatopoeic)

79 = *Ramphastos sulfuratus* (Piciformes: Ramphastidae) = Keel-billed toucan = *pito real* = **aj-piitoj**

62 = *Ara macao* (Psittaciformes: Psittacidae) = Scarlet macaw *guacamaya* = **aj-mo'**

21 = *Aratinga aztec* (Psittaciformes: Psittacidae) = Olive-throated parrot = *lorito* = **ix-p'ili'** (onomatopoeic)

63 = *Aratinga nana* (Psittaciformes: Psittacidae) = Green parakeet = *perica* = **ix-p'ili'** (onomatopoeic)

65 = *Amazona viridigenalis* (Psittaciformes: Psittacidae) = Red-crowned parrot = *loro* = **ix-t'ut'** (species not found in Peten)

22 = *Pionus senilis* (Psittaciformes: Psittacidae) = White-crowned parrot = *loro* = **ix-kuyutz'** (onomatopoeic)

23 = *Pionopsitta haematotis* (Psittaciformes: Psittacidae) = Brown-hooded parrot = *loro* = **ix-kuyutz'** (onomatopoeic)

20 = *Amazona albifrons* (Psittaciformes: Psittacidae) = White-fronted parrot = *loro maizero* = **ix-janä~näl** ("corn-eater")

24 = *Amazona autumnalis* (Psittaciformes: Psittacidae) = Red-lored parrot/Yellow-cheeked parrot = *loro zapatero* = **ix-janä~ya'** ("chicle-eater")/**ix-kolix** (onomatopoeic)

25 = *Amazona farinosa* (Psittaciformes: Psittacidae) = Blue-crowned parrot = *loro* = **ix-kocha'** (onomatopoeic)

33 = *Trogon massena* (Trogoniformes: Trogonidae) = Slaty-tailed trogon = *aurora* = **ix-koko~chan** (onomatopoeic)

83 = *Pharomachrus mocinno* (Trogoniformes: Togonidae) = Quetzal = *quetzal* = **ketzal/uy-utzil~maayaj** ("Maya beauty")

58 = *Sarcoramphus papa* (Falconiformes: Cathartidae) = King vulture = *zopilote rey* = **aj-'usil/aj-chäk[+]ch'om[[+]]'usil/aj-noj[[+]]chäk[+]-ch'om** ("large-red vulture")

56 = *Cathartes burrovianus* (Falconiformes: Cathartidae) = Lesser yellowhead vulture = *zopilote* = **aj-chäk[+]pol[[+]]ch'om** ("red-headed vulture")

94 = *Cathartes aura* (Falconiformes: Cathartidae) = Turkey vulture = *zopilote negro (cabeza colorada)* = **aj-b'ox[+]ch'om** (Note: the picture used in the stimulus set was a grey-headed juvenile; red-headed adults are called **aj-b'ox[+]ch'om[[+]]chäk u-pol**, "red-headed black vulture")

95 = *Coragyps atratus* (Falconiformes: Cathartidae) = Black vulture = *zopilote negro* = **aj-b'ox[+]ch'om/aj'-b'ox[+]ch'om[[+]]b'ox u-pol** ("black-headed black vulture")

97 = *Tyto alba* (Strigiformes: Tytonidae) = Barn owl = *lechuza* = **aj-xooch'** (onomatopoeic)

71 = *Strix virgata* (Strigiformes: Strigidae) = *tecolote* = **aj-b'uj** (onomatopoeic)

70 = *Strix nigrolineata* (Strigiformes: Strigidae) = Black-and-white wood owl = *tecolote* = **aj-b'uj** (onomatopoeic)

74 = *Otus guatemalae* (Strigiformes: Strigidae) = Vermiculated screech-owl = *tecolote* = **aj-b'uj[+]kaachoj/aj-kukus[+]b'uj**

98 = *Bubo virginianus* (Strigiformes: Strigidae) = Great horned owl = *tecolote* = aj-b'uj[+]kaachoj/aj-kukus[+]b'uj (Note: species not present in Peten)

72 = *Glaucidium brasilianum* (Strigiformes: Strigidae) = Ferruginous pygmy owl = *la viuda* = ix-nuk

7 = *Rostrhamus socialibis* (Falconiformes: Accipitridae) = Snail kite = *gavilán caracolero* = aj-ch'uuy[+]t'ot' ("snail raptor")

11 = *spizaëtus tyrannus* (Falconiformes: Accipitridae) = Black hawk-eagle = *gavilán* = aj-jun~k'uuk' ("one sprout"/"griffin," also occasionally applied to Ornate hawk-eagle = *S. ornatus*)

6 = *Chondrohierax uncinatus* (Falconiformes: Accipitridae) = Hook-billed kite = *gavilán* = aj-ch'uuy/aj-mujan

12 = **Micrastur semi-torquatus** (Falconiformes: Falconidae) = Collared forest falcon = *gavilán* = aj-ch'uuy/aj-mujan

9 = *Buteogallus urubitinga* (Falconiformes: Accipitridae) = Great black hawk = *gavilán* = jach ch'uuy/jach mujan ("true raptor") = aj- noj[+] ch'uuy (Note: some informants contrast this species, as aj-noj[[+]b'ox[+] ch'uuy, to the smaller Common black hawk, aj- mejen[[+]]b'ox[+] ch'uuy; but sorting with unscaled picture exemplars did not always coincide with nomenclatural contrasts)

8 = *Buteogallus anthracinus* (Falconiformes: Accipitridae) = Common black hawk = *gavilán* = aj-b'ox[+]ch'uuy

14 = *Falco rufiguralis* (Falconiformes: Accipitridae) = Bat falcon = *gavilán avado* = aj-'ab'aad'oj[+]ch'uuy ("mottled raptor")

13 = *Micrastur ruficollis* (Falconiformes: Falconidae) = Barred forest-falcon = *gavilán* = aj-'ii' (onomatopoeic)/aj-ch'uuy(+)'ii'

10 = *Buteo magnirostris* (Falconiformes: Accipitridae) = Roadside hawk = *gavilán* = aj-'ii' (onomatopoeic)/aj-ch'uuy(+)'ii' (Note: although similar to the Barred forest-falcon in size and coloring, its call and behavior differ greatly; it alone answers to Itzaj descriptions of the drawn-out scream "iiii!")

96 = *Falco sparverius* (Falconiformes: Falconidae) = American sparrow-hawk/kestrel = *gavilán clis-clis* = aj-k'il~k'il ("the wounder")

57 = *Herpetotheres cachinnans* (Falconiformes: Falconidae) = Laughing falcon = *guaco* = aj-b'ak~b'ak (onomatopoeic) = aj-päy~ja' ("the rain caller/announcer")

55 = *Leptodon cayanensis* (Falconiformes: Accipitridae) = Cayenne kite = *gavilán/guaco* = aj-b'ak~b'ak (onomatopoeic) (Note: although similar to the Laughing falcon in size, and somewhat in its laughing call, it soars and behaves very differently, and is quite rare)

59 = *Spizaëtus ornatus* (Falconiformes: Accipitridae) = Ornate hawk-eagle = *aguilucho* = **aj-b'ox(+)mujan/aj-ch'uuy(+)kaachoj**     ("horned raptor")/**aj-jun~k'uuk'** (see *S. tyrranus*)

76 = *Crotophaga sulcirostris* (Cuculiformes: Cuculidae) = Groove-billed ani = *garrapatero* = **aj-ch'ik~b'ul** ("flea-full," onomatopoeic) (Note: this picture was often misidentified as a raptor, although all informants know that the ani is not a raptor)

81 = *Nyctiphrynus yucatanicus* (Caprimulgiformes: Caprimulgidae) = Yucatan poorwill = *tapacaminos* = **aj-pujuy** (more common in Gentral Peten is the Northern Whip-poor-will, *Caprimulgus vociferus*) (onomatopoeic)

73 = *Nyctibius griseus* (Caprimulgiformes: Nyctibiidae) = Common potoo = *hormiguero* = **aj-pujuy/ix-sut** ("the visitor," because not common to Central Peten)/**ch'iich'-il~sakal** ("army-ant bird," perhaps confounded also with antshrikes)

43 = *Pachyramphus aglaiae* (Passeriformes: Cotingidae) = Becard = *mosquero/canario* = **aj-b'ox(+)ch'iich'** ("black bird," for black males only)/ **ix-ma'~tuch** ("no gizzard," for brown females, onomatopoeic)

85 = *Pitangus sulfuratus* (Passeriformes: Tyrannidae) = Derby flycatcher = *mosquero/canario* = **ix-reeynaj[+]wirisu'**

84 = *Myiozatetes similis* (Passeriformes: Tyrannidae) = Giraud's flycatcher = *mosquero/canario* = **ix-reeynaj[+]wirisu'**

44 = *Myarchus crinitus* (Passeriformes: Tyrannidae) = Great-crested flycatcher = *mosquero/canario* = **ix-wirisu'**

47 = *Myarchus yucatensis* (Passeriformes: Tyrannidae) = Yucatan flycatcher = *mosquero/canario* = **ix-wirisu'**

46 = *Myarchus tyrannulus* (Passeriformes: Tyrannidae) = Brown-crested flycatcher = *mosquero/canario* = **ix-wirisu'**

45 = *Myarchus tuberculifer* (Passeriformes: Tyrannidae) = Dusty-capped flycatcher = *mosquero/canario* = **ix-wirisu'**

48 = *Icterus mesomelas* (Passeriformes: Icteridae) = Yellow-tailed oriole = *calandre/canario* = **ix-wirisu'/ix-tzi'il**

49 = *Icterus chrysater* (Passeriformes: Icteridae) = Yellow-backed oriole = *calandre/canario* = **ix-wirisu'/ix-tzi'il**

90 = *Turdus albicolis* (Passeriformes: Turdidae) = White-throated robin = *canario* = **ix- k'ok'** (onomatopoeic)

64 = *Turdis nudigensis* (Passeriformes: Turdidae) = Clay-colored robin = *canario* = **ix-k'ok'** (onomatopoeic)

101 = *Cyancorax yncas* (Passeriformes: Corvidae) = Green jay = *canario* = **ix-k'ok'** (misidentification?)

50 = *Thraupis abbas* (Passeriformes: Thraupidae) = Yellow-winged tanager = *canario/taquilla* = **ix-wirisu'/ix-k'än~tzeem** ("yellow breast," because of lemon wing coverts)

89 = *Psilorhinus morio* (Passeriformes: Corvidae) = Brown jay = *pea* = **aj-pa'ap** (onomatopoeic)/**ix-wirisu'** (Note: probably some misclassification based on judgments of morphological similarity alone; all informants recognize the distinctive call of the Brown jay, which they compare to that of the chachalaca)

52 = *Passerina caerulea* (Passeriformes: Fringillidae) = Blue grosbeak = *canario/taquilla* = **ix-wirisu'**

51 = *Habia rubica* (Passeriformes: Thraupidae) = Red-crowned ant-tanager = *canario* = **ix-chäk~tun~p'irich** ("red-stone," onomatopoeic)

42 = *Automolus ochrolaemus* (Passeriformes: Furnariidae) = Buff-throated foliage-gleaner = *canario* = **ix-pitz'il~'oox** (onomatopoeic) (Note: **ix-pitz'il~'oox** applies to warblers in general)

87 = *Progne subis* (Passeriformes: Hirundinidae) = Purple martin = *tijera* = **ix-nukuch[+]kusam**

86 = *Progne chalybea* (Passeriformes: Hirundinidae) = Grey-breasted martin = *tijera* = **ix-nukuch[+]kusam**

88 = *Steligidepteryx ruficollis* (Passeriformes: Hirundinidae) = Rough-winged swallow = *tijera* = **ix-kusam**

99 = *Chaetura vauxi* (Apodiformes: Apodidae) = Vaux's swift = *tijera* = **ix-mejen[+]kusam**

100 = *Hirundo rustica* (Passeriformes: Hirundinidae) = Barn swallow = *tijera* = **ix-kusam**

82 = *Panyptila cayannensis* (Apodiformes: Apodidae) = Lesser swallow-tailed swift = *tijera* = **ix-kusam**

80 = *Chaetura pelagica* (Apodiformes: Apodidae) = Chimney swift = *tijera* = **ix-kusam**

92 = *Dives dives* (Passeriformes: Icteridae) a = Melodius blackbird = *tordo cantor* = **aj-pich'** (sometimes applied to the male *Ouiscalus mexicanus* = Great-tailed grackle = *sanate* = **aj-sanaatej**)

77 = *Pinya cayana* (Cuculiformes: Cuculidae) = Cayenne squirrel-cuckoo = *mosquitero* = **aj-käpäk~cho'** (onomatopoeic)

93 = *Gymnostinops montezuma* (Icteridae: Passeriformes) = Montezuma oropendola = *oropéndula* = **aj-k'ub'ul**

91 = *Zarhynchus wagleri* (Icteridae: Passeriformes) = Chestnut-headed oropendola = *oropéndula* = **aj-k'ub'ul**

32 = *Momotus momota* (Coraciiformes: Momotidae) = Blue-crowned motmot = **aj-b'uk~pik** (onomatopoeic)

26 = *Phaeochroa cuvierii* (Apodiformes: Trochilidae) = Scaley-breasted hummingbird = *chupaflor* **tz'unu'un**

27 = *Chlorostilban canivetti* (Apodiformes: Trochilidae) = Fork-tailed emerald = *chupaflor* = **tz'unu'un**

28 = *Florisuga mellivora* (Apodiformes: Trochilidae) = White-necked jacobin = *chupaflor* = **tz'unu'un**

30 = *Heliothryx barroti* (Apodiformes: Trochilidae) = Purple-crowned fairy = *chupaflor* = **tz'unu'un**

29 = *Anthracothorax prevostii* (Apodiformes: Trochilidae) = Green-breasted mango = *chupaflor* = **tz'unu'un**

105 = *Desmodus rotundus* (Chiroptera: Desmontidae) = Vampire bat = *vampiro* = **aj-tz'utz'~k'ik'[+]** ("blood sucker")

106 = *Artibeus jamaicensis* (Chiroptera: Stenodermatinae) = Large fruit-eating bat = *murciélago* = **aj-nojoch[+]sotz'**

## Notes

1. Comparisons between folkbiological systems are often based on analyses of a specious level of folk taxonomy called "terminal contrast." Terminal contrast occurs between named groupings that include no additional named groupings. For example, among folk in Michigan the class of terminal contrast includes bat, squirrel, weasel, beaver, beagle (dog), poodle (dog), calico (cat), short-haired tabby (cat), and long-haired tabby (cat). There is little systematic relation between terminal folk taxa and corresponding scientific taxa. Thus bat includes a variety of different scientific families, genera and species in the order Chiroptera, many of which are locally represented in Michigan. Squirrel includes different local genera and species of the family Sciuridae. Weasel encompasses two local species of the genus *Mustela*. Beaver corresponds to the single local species *Castor canadensis*. Beagle and poodle denote two "varieties" of the species *Canis familiaris*. Calico refers to a "variety" of *Felis cattus*, whereas short-haired tabby and long-haired tabby are (mongrelized) "races" of the species. Using terminal contrast as the focus of comparison between folkbiology and scientific systematics thus reveals little relationship. In fact several studies in psychology and anthropology that purport to compare the "taxonomic structure" of folk and scientific biology use terminal contrast as the basis of analysis (Conklin 1962; Lévi-Strauss 1966; Rosch 1975a). This is unfortunate because terminal contrast is a purely (ethno) linguistic feature that has little direct significance for the structure of living kind taxonomies. As a result the profound similarities between Linnaean and folk-biological taxonomies have often been ignored.

2. English speakers ambiguously use "animal" to refer to at least three distinct classes of living things: nonhuman animals, animals including humans, and mammals (prototypical animals). "Beast" seems to pick out nonhuman animals

in English but is seldom used today. "Plant" is ambiguously used to refer to the plant kingdom, or to members of that kingdom that are not trees.

3. Like other folk who have not been exposed to the Western tradition dating to Aristotle, Itzaj consider humans ontologically distinct from other living kinds (Atran 1985; see also Kesby 1979; Posey 1981). Itzaj believe that all living kinds (humans, animals, and plants) have a "heart/essence" (*puksik'al*) that makes any individual the kind of living thing it is. But only animals and plants are always exclusively individuated in terms of their unique generic-species essence, whereas humans are variously individuated as both individual agents and as social actors in accordance with inferred intentions rather than expected clusters of body parts. Itzaj, like folk everywhere, always identify an individual animal or plant, first and foremost, as a member of the generic species that presumably causes that individual to be. But Itzaj, like most people in the world, individuate humans, or *winik*, without exclusive recourse to a single superordinate level of superordinate existence, such as the level of species. Depending on context, a person may be Itzaj or Yukatek, Maya or Ladino, man or woman, mother or godmother, neighbor or stranger, hunter and/or farmer, or some combination which presumably determines that person's intentional self.

4. Life forms vary across culture. Ancient Hebrew or modern Rangi (Tanzania) include herpetofauna (reptiles and amphibians) with insects, worms, and other "creeping crawlers" (Kesby 1979), whereas Itzaj Maya and (until recently) most Western cultures include herpetofauna with mammals as "quadrupeds." Itzaj place phenomenally isolated mammals like the bat with birds, just as Rofaifo (New Guinea) place phenomenally isolated birds like cassowaries with mammals (Dwyer 1976). Whatever the content of life-form *taxa*, the life-form level, or *rank*, universally partitions the living world into broadly equivalent divisions.

5. According to Brown (1982: 102), Itzaj see mammals as part of an unnamed "residual category" that includes invertebrates save worms. For Mayan languages generally, he claims that mammal is a residual life form encompassing creatures left over after encoding bird, fish, and snake. The evidence for the former claim comes from Otto Schumann's (1971) brief lexicon and the unpublished notes of Pierre Ventur (Brown 1979: 382). Evidence for the latter claim comes secondhand, via dictionaries. Overall, our experiments show that patterns of induction among mammals are the same as those for bird, fish, tree, or vine (Atran et al. 1998). In sorting tasks, mammals are always isolated from the other animals as an exclusive group, with two exceptions: the bat (*aj-sotz'*) is always classified with the birds, and the otter (*u-pek'-il ja'*) is always classified with other mammals but occasionally crossed-classified with some water-dwelling reptiles (crocodiles and turtles, but not water snakes). Brown also relies on linguistic evidence to claim that *kan* (snakes) is an Itzaj life form. But sorting and inference tasks (see figure 6.7 below) clearly indicate that snakes and lizards (*uy-et'-ok juj*) are taxonomically closer to one another than either of these intermediates is to other intermediates of the herpetofauna life form (*b'a'al~che'+k-u-jil-t-ik u-b'aj*), such as turtles (*aak*) or amphibians (*b'a'al~che'+k-u-siit'*).

6. Mammals and herpetofauna also appear to be embedded under the mutually exclusive category quadruped (i.e., *b'a'al∽che'* sense 2), which can be explicitly rendered as *a'-b'a'al∽che' yan uy-ok* ("animals having feet") or *kän-taach uy-ok* ("four-footed"). More often *kän-taach uy-ok* refers exclusively to the herpeto-fauna, much as the old Yukatek terms *xaknal* or *xakatnal* might be translated as *cuadrúpedo* but refer only to herps (Beltrán [1742] 1859: 228). Snakes are thought to have "hidden" feet that "only the speechless can see" (*chen ch'uch'k-u-cha'an-t-ik uy-ok* kan).

7. In the logical structure of folk taxonomy, outliers may be considered mono-typic life forms with only one generic species (for a formalism, see the appendix in Atran 1995).

8. Botanists and ethnobotanists see privileged folkbiological groups as akin to scientific genera (Bartlett 1940; Berlin 1972; Greene 1983). Plant genera espe-cially are often readily recognized morphologically without technical aids (Lin-naeus 1751). Zoologists and ethnozoologists view them as more like scientific species, where reproductive and geographical isolation are more readily identified in terms of behavior (Simpson 1961; Diamond 1966; Bulmer 1970).

9. Contrast this with *tzimin∽che'*, the "tapir-tree" (*Vatairea lundelli*), so called because tapirs seek out the bark of its large buttresses for nourishment. Such names reflect ecological relations.

10. For "all" responses the overall Itzaj and Michigan patterns were nearly identical, indicating that generic species are inductively privileged regardless of whether people are perceptually familiar with them (Itzaj) or not (Americans).

11. Moving vertically within each graph corresponds to changing the premise category while holding the conclusion category constant. This allows us to test the similarity-coverage model of category-based reasoning (Osherson et al. 1990). In this model the closer the premise category is to the conclusion category, the stronger the induction should be. Our results show only weak evidence for this general reasoning heuristic, which fails entirely to account for the various "jumps" in inductive strength that indicate absolute or relative privilege.

12. Consider the relative cognitive advantages of perceptual ease and familiarity in handling living-kind categories versus an appropriate anticipation of where biologically relevant properties will likely cluster. For convenience, call the first perceptual privilege, the second inductive privilege. Perceptual privilege facilitates access to, and use of, knowledge of the day-to-day world we usually experience, and is associated with ease of communication, category recognition, and recall. Inductive privilege allows us to go beyond the information that experience privi-leges and into the realm of reasonable expectations about the causal under-pinnings of natural categories.

From an evolutionary standpoint, both forms of cognitive privilege make sense: perceptual privilege adaptively harnesses experience with nature, whereas induc-tive privilege adaptively harnesses expectation about nature. If such expectation is always focused on the folk-generic level, it is arguably because that level cap-tures aspects of biological reality that are both causally recurrent and especially relevant to the emergence of human life and cognition. In small-scale "traditional" societies, as perhaps in ancestral hominid environments, relatively short-term experience with the ambient world of plants and animals, which is intimate and intensive, could privilege the same level of biological awareness that relatively long-term considerations of causal importance and relevance would. For large-scale industrialized societies, a cognitive division of labor could develop to manage the psychological requirements of appreciating and dealing with what we most readily experience versus what is likely to matter most in the run of life.

If so, then at least for the domain of living kinds, we should expect perceptual privilege and inductive privilege to somewhat diverge in focus and target along the lines that our results indicate. But regardless of perceptual experience or familiarity, inductive privilege at the generic-species should generally dominate exploration of the biological world, and inferences in the face of uncertainty. This is because the generic-species level generally corresponds to that cut in nature where the biological properties and causes most relevant to long-term human survival and apprehension of nature tend to maximally cluster and most likely recur.

13. For each subject we have a square symmetric data matrix, where number of rows and columns is equal to the number of generic species sorted. Subjects' taxonomic distance matrices were correlated with each other, yielding a pairwise subject-by-subject correlation matrix representing the degree to which each subject's taxonomy agreed with each other subject's taxonomy. Principal component factor analyses were then performed on the intersubject correlation matrix for each group of informants to determine whether there was a "cultural consensus" in informant responses. A cultural consensus is plausible if the factor analysis results in a single factor solution. If a single dimension underlies patterns of agreement within a domain, then consensus can be assumed for that domain, and the dimension can be thought of as reflecting the degree to which each subject shares in the consensual knowledge (Romney, Batchelder, and Weller 1986). Consensus is indicated by a strong single factor solution in which (1) the first latent root (eigenvalue) is large compared to the rest, (2) all scores on the first factor are positive, and (3) the first factor accounts for most of the variance. To the extent some individuals agree more often with the consensus than others, they may be considered more "culturally competent" than others with respect to the domain. Estimation of individual knowledge levels, or competencies, is given by each subject's first factor scores. This represents the degree to which that subject's responses agree with the consensus. In other words, the pattern of correlations among informants should owe entirely to the extent to which each knows the common (cultrually relative) "truth." The mean taken from all first-factor scores provides an overall measure of consensus.

14. Including the generic-species level yields a higher correlation because it involves filling in the respective matrices' diagonal cells (e.g., bat-bat). For folk matrices, diagonal cells are always 0 because the folk distance between a folk-taxon and itself is 0. For the corresponding scientific matrix, diagonal cells are usually 0, but not always so. When the scientific difference between a generic

species and itself is not 0, it is because the scientific extension of that folktaxon and itself crosses one or more scientific levels. For example, in Michigan, "bat" exemplars extend over several genera of the same family (second level); so the most conservative estimate of scientific distance between any two "bat" exemplars is 2 rather than 0. Likewise, in Peten, "bat" exemplars extend over two suborders of the same order (fourth level); so the estimate of scientific distance between any two "bat" exemplars for Itzaj is 4 rather than 0. In many cases where the diagonal is greater than 0, folk—particularly Itzaj—clearly distinguish between all the scientific species and provide binomial names for them; however, these distinctions do not exist at the generic-species level but at the subordinate level of folk specific. In these instances folk consider the distinction between the scientific species to be finer than the distinction between folk-generic species.

15. Other factors in the divergence between folk and scientific taxonomies are related both to science's global perspective in classifying local biota and to its reliance on biologically "deep," theoretically weighted properties of internal anatomy and physiology. Thus the opossum is the only marsupial in North and Central America. Both Itzaj and midwesterners relate the opossum to skunks and procupines because all share readily perceptible features of morphology and behavior. From a scientific vantage, however, the opossum is taxonomically isolated from all the other locally represented mammals in a subclass of its own. One factor mitigating the ability of Itzaj or midwesterners to appreciate the opossum as scientists do is the absence of other locally present marsupials to relate the opossum to. As a result both Michigan students and Itzaj are apparently unaware of the deeper biological significance of the opossum's lack of a placenta.

16. Figure 6.8 shows only prototypical species of the most frequently cited Itzaj snake taxa. We have yet to determine the full extension of these taxa. Itzaj use other snake categories as well, but our biological inventories of them are too incomplete to allow their inclusion at this time.

17. That Itzaj and scientists discern broadly similar groups in nature does not entail that they are observing what science views as "objectively out there." It could indicate that both perspectives share the same phenomenal bias to see the world in peculiarly human ways. For example, Maya and American folk, as well as scientists, tend to underdifferentiate the large order of passerines as a group relative to the bigger, more distinctively colored or more vocally apparent birds (see Boster 1988). Phylogenetically minded systematists may seek to "correct" this cognitively motivated historical bias, which places more than half of all living birds in a single order. But given the "classic" ornithological classifications that now exist as a basis for comparisons in psychology and anthropology, any correspondence between scientific and folk classifications in the literature must be interpreted with caution as to what it tells us about reality.

Research was funded by NSF (SBR 93-19798, 94-22587) and France's Research and Education Ministry (CNRS 92-C-0758). Comparative studies were co-directed with Douglas Medin. Participants in this project on biological understanding across cultures include John Coley and Elizabeth Lynch, (psychology, Northwestern University), Alejandro López (psychology, Max Planck), Ximena Lois (linguistics, Crea-Ecole Polytechnique), Edilberto Ucan Ek' (Herbolaria Maya, Mérida), Valentina Vapnarsky (anthropology, University of Paris X), Edward Smith and Paul Estin (psychology, University of Michigan), David Taylor (biology, University of Michigan), and Brian Smith (biology, University of Texas, Arlington). For several years we have been gathering material on Itzaj Maya natural history. Our data baseline includes herbaria (on deposit with the Comité Bio-Itza and the University of Michigan), archival and fieldwork on Itzaj history and ethnography, an Itzaj grammar and an Itzaj/Spanish dictionary focusing on natural history (folkbiology, ethnomedicine, and cosmology). The research agenda includes comparative study of folkbiology and folkecology among native Lowland Maya, immigrant Highland Maya, and Spanish-speaking Ladinos.

## References

Atran, S. 1983. Covert fragmenta and the origins of the botanical family. *Man* 18: 51–71.

Atran, S. 1985. Pre-theoretical aspects of Aristotelian definition and classification of animals. *Studies in History and Philosophy of Science* 16: 113–63.

Atran, S. 1987. Origins of the species and genus concepts. *Journal of the History of Biology* 20: 195–279.

Atran, S. 1990. *Cognitive Foundations of Natural History* Cambridge: Cambridge University.

Atran, S. 1993. Itza Maya tropical agro-forestry. *Current Anthropology* 34: 633–700.

Atran, S. 1994. Core domains versus scientific theories. In L. Hirschfeld and S. Gelman, eds., *Mapping the Mind*. Cambridge: Cambridge University Press.

Atran, S. 1995. Classifying nature across cultures. In D. Osherson and E. Smith, eds., *Invitation to Cognitive Science*: *Thinking*, vol. 3. Cambridge: MIT Press.

Atran, S. 1998. Folk biology and the anthropology of science: *Behavioral and Brain Sciences* 21: 547–611.

Atran, S., and E. Ucan Ek'. 1999. Classification of useful plants by the northern Peten Maya. In C. White, ed., *Ancient Maya Diet*. Salt Lake City: University of Utah Press.

Atran, S., P. Estin, J. Coley, and Medin, D. 1997. Generic species and basic levels: Essence and appearance in folk biology. *Journal of Ethnobiology* 17: 22–45.

Atran, S., and D. Medin. 1997. Knowledge and action: Cultural models of nature and resource management in Mesoamerica. In M. Bazerman, D. Messick, A. Tinbrunsel, and K. Wayde-Benzoni, eds., *Environment, Ethics, and Behavior*. San Francisco: New Lexington Press.

Barrera Marín, A., A. Barrera Vásquez, and R. López Franco. 1976. *Nomenclatura etnobotánica Maya*. Mexico City: INAH.

Barsalou, L. 1985. Ideals, central tendency, and frequency of instantiation as determinants of graded structure in categories. *Journal of Experimental Psychology: Learning, Memory, and Cognition* 11: 629–54.

Bartlett, H. 1940. History of the generic concept in botany. *Bulletin of the Torrey Botanical Club* 47: 319–62.

Beltrán, Fray Pedro de. 1859 [1742]. *Arte del idoma Maya* 2d ed. Mérida: J.D. Espinosa.

Berlin, B. 1972. Speculations on the growth of ethnobotanical nomenclature. *Language and Society* 1: 63–98.

Berlin, B. 1992. *Ethnobiological Classification*. Princeton: Princeton University.

Berlin, B., D. Breedlove, and P. Raven. 1973. General principles of classification and nomenclature in folk biology. *American Anthropologist* 74: 214–42.

Berlin, B., D. Breedlove, and P. Raven. 1974. *Principles of Tzeltal Plant Classification*. New York: Academic Press.

Boster, J. 1988. Natural sources of internal category structure. *Memory and Cognition* 16: 258–70.

Brown, C. 1979. Growth and development of folk botanical life-forms in the Mayan language family. *American Ethnologist* 6: 366–85.

Brown, C. 1982. Growth and development of folk zoological life-forms in the Mayan language family. *American Ethnologist* 9: 97–111.

Brown, C. 1984. *Language and Living Things*. New Brunswick: Rutgers University Press.

Bruce, R. 1968. *Gramática Lacandón*. Mexico City: INAH.

Bulmer, R. 1970. Which came first, the chicken or the egg-head? In J. Pouillon and P. Maranda, eds., *Echanges et communications: mélanges offerts à Claude Lévi-Strauss*. The Hague: Mouton.

Cain, A. 1956. The genus in evolutionary taxonomy. *Systematic Zoology* 5: 97–109.

Campbell, J., and W. Lamar. 1989. *The Venomous Reptiles of Latin America*. Ithaca: Cornell University Press.

Carey, S. 1996. Cognitive domains as modes of thought. In D. Olson and N. Torrance, eds., *Modes of Thought*. Cambridge: Cambridge University Press.

Coley, J., D. Medin, and S. Atran. 1997. Does privilege have is rank? Inductive inferences within folkbiological taxonomies. *Cognition* 63: 73–112.

Conklin, H. 1962. Lexicographical treatment of folk taxonomies. In F. Householder and S. Saporta, eds., *Problems in lexicography*. Report of the Conference on Lexicography, 11–12 November 1960. Bloomington: Indiana University Press.

Darwin, C. 1859. *On the Origins of Species by Natural Selection*. London: Murray.

Diamond, J. 1966. Zoological classification of a primitive people. *Science* 151: 1102–04.

Diver, C. 1940. The problem of closely related species living in the same area. In J. Huxley, ed., *The New Systematics*. Oxford: Clarendon.

Donnellan, K. 1971. Necessity and criteria. In J. Rosenberg and C. Travis, eds., *Readings in the Philosophy of Language*. Englewood-Cliffs, NJ: Prentice Hall.

Dougherty, J. 1979. Learning names for plants and plants for names. *Anthropological Linguistics* 21: 298–315.

Dwyer, P. 1976. An analysis of Rofaifo mammal taxonomy. *American Ethnologist* 3: 425–45.

Dupré, J. 1981. Natural kinds and biological taxa. *Philosophical Review* 90: 66–90.

Ellen, R. 1993. *The Cultural Relations of Classification*. Cambridge: Cambridge University Press.

Gelman, S., and Wellman, H. 1991. Insides and essences. *Cognition* 38: 214–44.

Gilmour, J., and S. Walters. 1964. Philosophy and classification. In W. Turrill, ed., *Vistas in Botany: Recent Researches in Plant Taxonomy*, vol. 4. Oxford: Pergamon Press.

Greene, E. 1983. *Landmarks in Botany*, 2 vols. Stanford: Stanford University.

Hatano, G. and K. Inagaki. 1996. Cognitive and cultural factors in the acquisition of intuitive biology. In D. Olson and N. Torrance, eds., *The Handbook of Education and Human Development*. Oxford: Blackwell.

Henley, N. 1969. A psychological study of the semantics of animal terms. *Journal of Verbal Learning and Verbal Behavior* 8: 176–84.

Hellmuth, N. 1977. Cholti-Lacandon (Chiapas) and Petén-Ytzá agriculture, settlement pattern and population. In N. Hammond, ed., *Social Process in Maya Prehistory*. London: Academic Press.

Herrera Castro, N. 1994. Los heurtos familiares mayas en el oriente de Yucatán. *Etnoflora Yucatense*, fasículo 9. Mérida: Universidad Autónoma de Yucatán.

Hickling, A., and S. Gelman. 1995. How does your garden grow? Evidence of an early conception of plants as biological kinds. *Child Development* 66: 856–76.

Hunn, E. 1976. Toward a perceptual model of folk biological classification. *American Ethnologist*: 3: 508–24.

Hunn, E. 1977. *Tzeltal Folk Zoology*. New York: Academic Press.

Hunn, E. 1982. The utilitarian factor in folk biological clasification. *American Anthropologist* 84: 830–47.

Keil, F. 1979. *Semantic and Conceptual Development: An Ontological Perspective*. Cambridge: Harvard University Press.

Keil, F. 1994. The birth and nurturance of concepts by domains. In L. Hirschfeld and S. Gelman, eds., *Mapping the Mind*. Cambridge: Cambridge University Press.

Kesby, J. 1979. Rangi classification of animals and plants. In R. Reason and D. Ellen, eds., *Classifications in Their Social Contexts*. New York: Academic Press.

Lévi-Strauss, C. 1966. *The Savage Mind*. Chicago: University of Chicago Press.

Linnaeus, C. 1751. *Philosophia Botanica*. Stockholm: G. Kiesewetter.

Lois, X. 1988. Gender markers as "rigid determiners" of the Itzaj Maya world. *International Journal of American Linguistics* 64: 224–82.

López, A., S. Atran, J. Coley, D. Medin, and E. Smith, 1997. The Tree of Life: Universals of Folkbiological Taxonomies and Inductions. *Cognitive Psychology* 32: 251–95.

Landa, Diego de. 1985[1566]. *Relación de la cosas de Yucatán*, ed. M. Rivera Dorado. Crónicas de America, no. 7. Madrid: Historia 16.

Mandler, J., P. Bauer, and L. McDonough. 1991. Separating the sheep from the goats: Differentiating global categories. *Cognitive Psychology* 23: 263–98.

Marks, I. 1987. *Fears, Phobias, and Rituals*. Oxford: Oxford University Press.

Mayr, E. 1969. *Principles of Systematic Zoology*. New York: McGraw-Hill.

Medin, D., E. Lynch, J. Coley, and S. Atran. 1997. Categorization and reasoning among tree experts: Do all roads lead to Rome? *Cognitive Psychology* 32: 49–96.

Nations, J. 1992. Vocabulario Lacandón: Plantas y animales. Paper prepared for Conservation International, April 1992, Washington, D.C.

Nations, J., and R. Nigh. 1980. Evolutionary potential of Lacandon Maya sustained-yield tropical forest agriculture. *Journal of Anthropological Research* 36: 1–30.

Osherson, D., E. Smith, O. Wilkie, A. López, and E. Shafir, 1990. Category-based induction. *Psychological Review* 97: 85–200.

Posey, D. 1981. Wasps, warriors and fearless men: Ethnoentomology of the Kayapó Indians of Central Brazil. *Journal of Ethnobiology* 1: 165–74.

Rips, L., E. Shoben, and E. Smith. 1973. Semantic distance and the verification of semantic relations. *Journal of Verbal Learning and Verbal Behavior* 12: 1–20.

Romney, A. K., S. Weller, and W. Batchelder. 1986. Culture as consensus: A theory of culture and informant accuracy. *American Anthropologist* 88: 313–38.

Rosch, E. 1975a. Universals and cultural specifics in categorization. In R. Brislin, S. Bochner, and W. Lonner, eds., *Cross-cultural Perspectives on Learning*. New York: Halstead.

Rosch, E. 1975b. Cognitive representations of semantic categories. *Journal of Experimental Psychology* 104: 192–233.

Rosch, E., C. Mervis, W. Grey, D. Johnson, and P. Boyes-Braem. 1976. Basic objects in natural categories. *Cognitive Psychology* 8: 382–439.

Roys, R. 1931. *Ethno-botany of the Maya*. Middle America Research Institute Publication 2. New Orleans: Tulane University Press.

Russell, B. 1958. *The ABC of Relativity*. London: Allen and Unwin.

Schumann, O. 1971. *Descripción estructural del Maya Itza del Petén*. Centro de Estudios Mayas, Cuaderno 6. Mexico City: UNAM.

Seligman, M. 1971. Phobias and preparedness. *Behavioral Therapy* 2: 307–20.

Simpson, G. 1961. *Principles of animal taxonomy*. New York: Columbia University Press.

Sloman, S. 1993. Feature-based induction. *Cognitive Psychology* 25: 231–80.

Sperber, D., and D. Wilson. 1986. *Relevance* London: Blackwell.

Standley, P., and J. Steyermark. 1946–1977. *Flora of Guatemala*, vol. 24, parts 1–13. Chicago: Field Museum of Natural History.

Stevens, P. 1994. Berlin's "ethnobiological classification." *Systematic Biology* 43: 293–95.

Stross, B. 1973. Acquisition of botanical terminology by Tzeltal children. In M. Edmonson, ed., *Meaning in Mayan Languages*. The Hague: Mouton.

Villagutierre Soto-Mayor, Juan de. 1985 [1701]. *Historia de la conquista de Itzá*, ed. J. García Añoveros. Crónicas de America, no. 13. Madrid: Historia 16.

Wallace, A. 1889. *Darwinism*. London: Macmillan.

Warburton, F. 1967. The purposes of classification. *Systematic Zoology* 16: 241–45.

# 7

# Inductive Reasoning in Folkbiological Thought

John D. Coley, Douglas L. Medin, Julia Beth Proffitt, Elizabeth Lynch, and Scott Atran

How do people understand the world of plants and animals and in what specific ways do these understandings vary with culture, experience, or expertise? These are the basic questions addressed by researchers in the field of folkbiology, originally by cognitive anthropologists and more recently by cognitive and developmental psychologists. We see our work, like the other chapters in this volume, as bringing together contributions from anthropology and psychology (and perhaps linguistics and philosophy as well) to support an inter-disciplinary cognitive ethnoscience. Each of these disciplines brings strengths—and weaknesses—to the task; by incorporating their complementary perspectives, we gain a clearer vision of the phenomena under study.

Cognitive anthropology is responsible for initially mapping out folkbiology as a field of study (Conklin 1962). Anthropological studies reveal the richness of folkbiological thought. They consider context and provide thoughtful, detailed analyses of entire systems of folkbiological categories. By investigating disparate cultures in many parts of the world, this research has also revealed universal principles underlying folkbiological category organization (see Atran 1990; Berlin 1992; Malt 1995, for reviews). However, anthropological research also has limitations. For example, the methods for eliciting names and identifications of flora and fauna are sometimes quite informal, and it is often unclear whether the informant or informants comprise a representative sample of the general population or merely a select set of local experts. Indeed, variation within a culture is rarely of interest (see Boster 1995 for an exception). More generally, description tends to be at the level of culture rather than the individual, which makes it difficult for psychologists to extract individual psychological processes. Moreover the very methods that provide rich anthropological data can be a limitation from an experimental point of view; lack of methodological rigor can raise skepticism about the conclusions drawn. Overall the data are rich but perhaps not as "hard" as psychologists would like, nor analyzed with the sort of precision required to yield tightly constrained models of cognition.

Thus, from a psychologist's perspective, ethnobiological studies have certain limitations. Experimental psychology has different strengths and weaknesses. Laboratory studies of conceptual structure allow for tight experimental controls and for precise tests of well-articulated models of categorization and reasoning. However, tightly controlled paradigms and methodologies may actually prevent informants from displaying forms of knowledge that would be most incisive for the questions under consideration. In addition stimulus materials are often selected with little concern for representativeness or systematic sampling. Finally the heavy use of college sophomores as research participants reflects great faith in the generality of any findings, a faith that is rarely subjected to empirical test.

We believe that cross-fertilization of these two fields is critical to advance our understanding of human cognition. To give but one example, Brent Berlin and his colleagues found one level (or rank) in a folktaxonomic hierarchy that is especially salient and psychologically privileged (Berlin, Breedlove, and Raven 1973). This important idea was transported to psychology and elaborated in an important series of studies by Eleanor Rosch and her associates (Rosch et al. 1976) which continue to influence psychological research on concepts (e.g., Medin and Coley, 1998). More generally, cross-cultural studies of cognition by anthropologists help establish (or undermine) claims about generality or universality of psychological models.

We believe that there is much to be gained by applying field methods in the laboratory and laboratory methods in the field. In our own research, we have employed methods that combine tests bearing directly on computational models of cognition with more open-ended, less-constrained procedures that often prove to be more informative. In many respects we have come to view our research participants more as collaborators than as subjects. The difficulties in carrying out these intentions completely undermine any smugness, and our goal is to make "stumbling progress" (the stumbling part is guaranteed).

Our overall aim has been to use cross-cultural comparisons of folk-biological taxonomic systems and associated reasoning processes to better understand universal and culturally specific aspects of folkbiology. Our initial studies compared Itzaj Maya from Petén, Guatemala, who know a great deal about the natural world, with American undergraduate students, who do not. For a variety of reasons our research has quickly evolved to a "triangulation strategy" where the third group of informants consists of different types of American experts (e.g., people who know a lot about trees). As we will see, often the within-culture differences are more striking than the cross-cultural ones.

In the present chapter we focus on two findings having to do with patterns of inductive inference. A great deal of research in ethnoscience has been devoted to describing and explaining the structure of folkbiological taxonomies (e.g., Berlin, 1992; Brown 1984; Hunn 1977). However, much less research has examined how such categories are used in reasoning. Some psychologists (e.g., Anderson 1990) have even argued that the single most important purpose of categories is to support predictions and inferences. By inductive reasoning we mean the process by which people generalize from a particular instance or category to another, often more inclusive one. For example, using the knowledge that a white oak benefits from a certain fertilizer to infer that other oaks would also benefit is category-based induction. Much of what we take to be true about the world we have learned through induction; indeed it would be impossible to learn that, for example, "snakes bite" or "dogs bark"—without having encountered all snakes or all dogs—unless we could readily infer a general principle on the basis of limited experience with a few exemplars. Thus induction is too important a function of concepts to be ignored.

The organization of this chapter is as follows: First we describe research we've done on the relation between privileged levels in a conceptual hierarchy and inductive inference. This research reveals surprising cross-cultural agreement as to which level is inductively privileged, and a surprising dissociation of knowledge and expectation for Americans. Then we turn to a further inductive phenomenon associated with a formal model for category-based induction. Here we find complex patterns of group commonalities and differences that defy easy explanation but certainly raise some new puzzles. Although we do not resolve these puzzles, the results point to some further avenues of exploration. Both sets of studies demonstrate that by looking at how categories guide induction, and by combining the richness of field anthropology with the precision of experimental psychology, progress in understanding the nature of folkbiological thought can be made.

## 7.1    Privileged Levels and Induction

Both psychologists and ethnobiologists take it as given that humans spontaneously organize categories into hierarchical taxonomic systems. Moreover, as we suggested earlier, both disciplines claim that a specific level within the folkbiological taxonomy is privileged—most important, salient, and useful. Ethnobiologists studying systems of classification among traditional peoples (e.g., Berlin 1976, 1978, 1992; Berlin, Breedlove, and Raven 1973; Brown 1984; Bulmer 1967; Bulmer and Tyler 1968; Diamond 1966; Hays 1983, Hunn 1977) have argued that the core of any folkbiological taxonomy, is the *folk-generic* rank. Folk generics are named by *primary lexemes* (unanalyzable names, e.g., *tiger*, *trout*, *oak*) and tend to correspond to biological genera or species. Berlin (1992) argues that:

… in the categorization of plants and animals by peoples living in traditional societies, there exists a specifiable and partially predictable set of plant and animal taxa that represent the smallest fundamental biological discontinuities easily recognizable in any particular habitat. This large but finite set of taxa is special in each system in that its members stand out as beacons on the landscape of biological reality, figuratively crying out to be named. These groupings are the generic taxa of all such systems of ethnobiological classification, and their names are precisely the names of common speech. (p. 53)

According to Berlin, folk-generic categories are perceptually salient and identifiable without close study. Generic names are the first offered and the most frequently used in everyday discourse. Among the traditional societies studied by Berlin and colleagues, folk-generic taxa may be among the first learned by children (Stross 1973).

In a now classic paper, Rosch, Mervis, and their associates (Rosch et al. 1976) set out to test Berlin's notion that a single taxonomic level is psychologically privileged. They argued that "in the real world information-rich bundles of perceptual and functional attributes occur that form natural discontinuities and that basic cuts in categorization are made at these discontinuities" (p. 385). In a series of experiments they present evidence that the "basic level" is the most inclusive level at which (1) many common features are listed for categories, (2) consistent motor programs are employed for objects in the category, (3) category members have similar shapes, and (4) it is possible to recognize an average shape of the category. In all of these experiments, the logic of locating the basic level was the same; the basic level was the level above which much information was lost, and below which little information was gained. For instance, in a feature-listing task, subjects listed a mean of 3 common features for the superordinate category *furniture*, a mean of 9 features for basic level furniture categories (e.g., *table*), and an average of 10.3 features for subordinate furniture categories (e.g., *kitchen table*). There was a large gain in information when going from the superordinate to the basic level (6 new common features are added in this example), and only a slight gain going from the basic to the subordinate (1.3 features).

Surprisingly, for biological taxonomies, Rosch et al.'s "basic level" failed to correspond to Berlin's privileged "folk-generic" rank; instead of *maple* and *trout*, Rosch et al. found that *tree* and *fish* functioned as basic-level categories for Berkeley undergraduates. Rosch et al.'s basic level for living kinds corresponds to Berlin's life-form level, superordinate to the folk-generic level. Thus, while both endorse the existence of a privileged level, the disciplines diverge with respect to exactly which level they identify as privileged. Why do anthropological and psychological observations fail to converge on a single privileged level?

One possibility is that differences in the location of the basic level could be a function of differences in expertise (e.g., Dougherty 1978; Johnson and Mervis 1997; Mervis and Rosch 1981; Tanaka and Taylor 1991). If members of traditional societies—like those that make up the bulk of subjects of ethnobiological research—have more expertise than the Berkeley undergraduates that were Rosch's subjects, and expertise leads to more specific basic levels, then the apparent discrepancy may be an expertise effect. If this were the case, however, it would challenge the view that basic-level categories reflect natural discontinuities in the world.

We set out to explore the relation between privileged levels and inductive inference. (For a more detailed report of this research, see Coley, Medin, and Atran et al. 1997; Atran et al. 1997). By examining the perceived strength of inductive inferences to categories of different folkbiological ranks, we hoped to discover whether one hierarchical level is psychologically privileged with respect to induction. As argued above, Rosch et al. characterize "basic" categories as those that are (1) more informative than less specific categories, and (2) not much less informative than more specific ones. Extending this logic to induction, inductive inferences to a privileged category should be significantly stronger than inferences to more general categories, but not significantly weaker than inferences to more specific categories. To return to the example of furniture, if *table* (as opposed to *kitchen table* or *furniture*) is privileged for induction, then inferences about tables should be roughly as strong as inferences about kitchen tables, and much stronger than inferences about furniture. In other words, we will consider the most specific level in folkbiological taxonomy above which a significant breakpoint in inductive strength occurs to be inductively privileged.

Given this logic, a privileged level would be the highest or most abstract level at which inductive confidence is strong. At more inclusive levels confidence should take a sharp drop. Furthermore, if knowledge or societal expertise is driving the apparent difference in "basic" levels between Rosch's Berkeley undergraduates and ethnobiologists' informants, and the basic level is also privileged for induction, then we would expect a corresponding difference in patterns of reasoning. Specifically, the privileged level for members of a traditional society should be subordinate to the privileged level for industrialized urban-dwellers; one group may privilege *oak* (a folk-generic category) and the other *tree* (a more abstract life form). Thus we were also interested in comparing the inductively privileged level for Americans and Itzaj. Differences in the location of an inductively privileged level would lend support to the "cultural differences are expertise differences" perspective.

To test these predictions, we examined patterns of inference among the Itzaj Maya and Northwestern University undergraduates. The Itzaj Maya inhabit the Petén rain forest region of Guatemala. The Itzaj are Mayan Amerindians; their ancestors were the last independent native polity in

Mesoamerica to be conquered by the Spaniards. The Itzaj of today have retained mastery of most of the ethnobiological knowledge that the Spaniards reported collecting from native people at the time of the initial conquest (Atran 1993). Men divide their time between agriculture (agroforestry) and hunting, while women are responsible for the myriad tasks required to run households that lack electricity and running water. In terms of age and (lack of) knowledge of the natural world, the Northwestern University students were fairly homogeneous.[1]

We asked members of both populations to rate the relative strength of inferences from taxa of one rank to taxa of the next higher rank. For example, a participant might be told that all members of a given folk-generic taxa have a certain property, and then asked to think how likely it is that all members of the appropriate life-form taxa would also share that property (e.g., "All *trout* have enzyme X. How likely is it that all *fish* have enzyme X?"). For Northwestern undergraduates, properties involved unspecified enzymes, proteins, and disease. Students rated the likelihood of the arguments on a scale of 1 (not very likely) to 9 (extremely likely).

For the Maya participants, we used folkbiological taxa familiar to them, and we phrased the questions a bit differently. All properties involved were unfamiliar diseases; participants were given the premise, and then queried with possible conclusions (e.g., "All *green agoutis* are susceptible to a disease of the heart called eta. If all *green agoutis* are susceptible this disease, do you think *all other agoutis* are susceptible to this disease? [If the response is "no,"] Do you think *some other agoutis* are susceptible?").

By systematically presenting participants with a number of inferences at different levels of the folkbiological hierarchy, and varying the life forms presented in those inferences, we were able to get a good look at perceived strength of inductive inferences to different folkbiological ranks. The results are summarized in figure 7.1. They clearly show that folk-generic categories (e.g., *trout*, *oak*) were inductively privileged for both the Itzaj and for American undergraduates. For both groups, inferences to folk-generic categories were consistently stronger than inferences to more general (life-form or folk-kingdom) categories, and no weaker than inferences to more specific (folk-specific) categories. For both

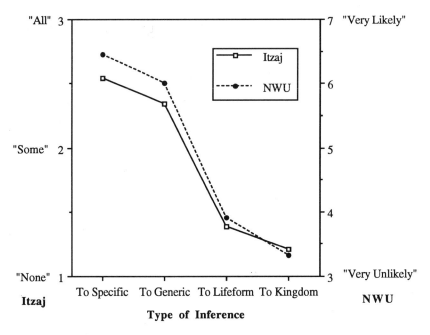

**Figure 7.1**
Induction patterns from Northwestern Students and Itzaj Maya compared

groups, the gain in inductive strength was greatest moving from life-form to folk-generic categories, suggesting that folk-generic categories are psychologically privileged with respect to induction.

We expected this pattern for the Itzaj; it is consistent with Berlin's characterization of the folk-generic rank as psychologically privileged for members of traditional societies. We did not expect it for the Americans. Indeed, this result is surprising given Rosch's findings that the basic level for American students is at the life-form level for biological categories, which would lead one to expect that American students would also show inductive privilege at the life-form level, not the folk-generic level. So, rather than resolving the discrepancy between Rosch's and Berlin's notions of privilege, we appear to have complicated it: Why do we find a discrepancy among American undergraduates between the level privileged for induction and that privileged for other cognitive measures? Why do members of two such different cultural groups—with such radically different knowledge about and experience with nature—show such similar patterns of reasoning about folkbiological categories, when their "basic" levels are presumably different?

The answer to these questions may lie in a distinction between *knowledge* and *expectation*. We suspect that Roschian tasks measuring the "basic level" and our induction task are tapping different competencies, resulting in the discrepancy between the level identified as privileged by the two sets of tasks. Most of Rosch's tasks—and Berlin's too, for that matter—required *knowledge* (either in terms of generating information corresponding to labels, or identifying pictures on the basis of labels) or the ability to make perceptual discriminations. Thus for biological categories Rosch's results show that (1) the folk-generic level is not the locus of knowledge for urban Americans and (2) the folk-generic is not the most perceptually differentiated level for Americans.

In contrast, rather than having participants list features that they knew to be true of categories, we asked them to project properties expressly designed to be unknown. Instead of testing participants' knowledge, we tested their *expectations*. Our results show that despite lack of knowledge and perceptual differentiation, Americans *expect* that the folk-generic level is most useful for inductive inference. Although both Itzaj and undergraduates are going beyond their knowledge to make inferences about novel properties, we suspect that they may be doing so for different reasons. Americans' expectation may be guided by implicit assumptions about the way that language constrains categories, whereas the same expectation on the part of the Itzaj may be bolstered by knowledge and personal experience.

Implicit assumptions that members of named categories share important properties and explicit knowledge about how language marks hierarchical taxonomic relations might drive the undergraduates' expectation that folk-generic taxa are inductively strong. As Berlin et al. document, below the level of folk generic, the nomenclatural pattern tends to mark relative subordinate relationships (e.g., *oak, red oak, northern red oak*). Thus, knowing that an oak is a tree marks *oak* as a folk generic—the lowest level at which things have unique names—because subordinate relations are often given in the nomenclature. More generally, implicitly learning the logic of nomenclatural patterns of inclusion ("a red oak is a kind of oak"), and explicitly learning inclusion relations of folk generics under life forms ("an oak is a kind of tree") may be enough to set up a semblance of a folkbiological taxonomy and to flag the folk-generic level despite little experience with members of the categories.

Sensitivity to such nomenclatural patterns begins early in development (Gelman, Wilcox, and Clark, 1989). Moreover developmental evidence shows that labels can be important indicators of taxonomic categories (Waxman 1991). Children take labels as signals to look for commonalities among otherwise disparate objects. Further children as young as two years expect that members of the same category, despite perceptual dissimilarities, will share underlying properties. Thus labels may "stake out" a category, despite lack of specific knowledge about members of that category (Gelman and Coley 1990, 1991). This may include the assumptions that the category will be coherent, category members will share many underlying properties beyond what meets the eye, and that in effect, here is "where the conceptual action is." In other words, labels may signal categories that are believed to embody an essence (e.g., Gelman and Coley 1991; Gelman, Coley, and Gottfried 1994; Medin and Ortony 1989). These mechanisms are available early and may represent underlying, basic assumptions about how language organizes experience. These assumptions may well have led to expectations of inductive privilege of folk-generic taxa despite little direct experience with those taxa. The notion of *expectation* is crucial here. Our task— inductive inference concerning virtually blank biological predicates— relies on expectations about the categories involved. We are not claiming that our American participants *knew* that maples or trout share important clusters of properties. On the contrary, we argue that in many cases, what little knowledge subjects possessed about maples and trout led them to *expect* that important property clusters would cohere at that level. Indeed Rosch sums it up very well: "For humans, the major part of the classification system is probably neither biologically fixed nor created anew by each individual, but is provided by the culture and language into which the individual is born" (Rosch 1975, p. 177).

Thus perhaps we can characterize American performance as reflecting this divergence of knowledge and expectation. On one hand, Americans may *know* more features and perceptual affinities at the more abstract level of *tree* and *fish*. Nevertheless, they may *expect* the strongest clusters of properties to cohere at the folk-generic level, even if they have little specific knowledge about most folkbiological categories at that level.

This discrepancy may not characterize the folkbiological knowledge of the Itzaj. In situations where people are likely to be well acquainted with local living kinds, as in "traditional" societies like the Itzaj, ethnobiological evidence argues that perceptual cues converge on folk generics as being psychologically basic. In other words, for the Itzaj, knowledge may converge with expectations. This rests on the presumption that the Itzaj, and indeed the other groups that provided the basis for Berlin's system, would in fact show a "basic" level on Roschian tasks subordinate to that of American college students because the Itzaj are folkbiological experts. This presumption remains to be tested. Rosch et al. (1976; Mervis and Rosch 1981) suggest that the basic level may change with expertise; Tanaka and Taylor (1991) and Johnson and Mervis (1997) offer empirical support for this hypothesis, showing that experts may have basic levels subordinate to those of nonexperts. If members of traditional societies can be considered folkbiological experts, they may have a basic-level (folk-generic) advantage for both perceptual and knowledge-based tasks.

The Itzaj pattern may well represent the default case for human understanding of living kinds under normal (evolutionarily attuned) environmental conditions in which personal knowledge of the natural world converges with expectations derived from societal systems of nomenclature and cognitive expectations about the properties of named categories. The divergence for Americans may in turn represent a "devolved" or degenerate state of folkbiological knowledge based on the poor environmental conditions of urbanized societies. ·

### Summary
We examined the relation between privileged levels and inductive inference, expecting that the basic level in folkbiological taxonomy (life forms for American undergraduates based on empirical work, folk generics for the Itzaj, based on some anthropological data and presumption) would also be inductively privileged. The results present a much more complicated picture. The folk-generic level was inductively privileged for both the Itzaj and for American undergraduates. For the Itzaj, this is in accord

with the location of the presumptive basic level for traditional societies. For the Americans, it does not correspond to the empirically established basic level, suggesting a dissociation between knowledge, organized at the life-form rank (*fish, tree*), and expectations of shared properties, category coherence, and perhaps even essence, which is maximized at the folk-generic rank (*trout, oak*).

These results suggest that characterizing cultural differences in terms of expertise-driven differences in the location of a single, monolithic "basic level" is an oversimplification. Americans and Itzaj appear to differ in the level at which knowledge is most readily organized and accessed, but not in the level at which expectations about inductive strength are strongest. Thus it may be more accurate to characterize cultural differences in terms of the degree to which knowledge and experience correspond than as differences in the location of a single privileged level. This research also demonstrates the more general point of how combining anthropological insight with psychological methodology can lead to discoveries that enhance our understanding of the complexity of folkbiological thought. We now turn to another such example.

## 7.2   Diversity-Based Reasoning

An important function of taxonomic classification is enabling generalizations between categories. Osherson et al. (1990) identify a set of phenomena that characterize category-based inferences in adults, and they formalize a model that predicts the strength of those inferences. Osherson et al. discuss inductive "arguments" in which facts used to generate the inference play the role of premises, and the inference itself plays the role of conclusion.

(i)  Hyenas have an ileal vein
     *Cows have an ileal vein*
     Wolves have an ileal vein.

This argument is strong to the extent that belief in the premises leads to belief in the conclusion. To promote reasoning based solely on the categories, the properties (e.g., have ulnar arteries) are "blank," that is, plausible but unfamiliar biological properties. There are two components to Osherson et al's (1990) similarity-coverage model (SCM). Subjects may infer that wolves have an ileal vein because they are similar to hyenas, or they may infer it because they have inferred that all mammals share the property given that hyenas and cows do. Thus the first component of the model, *similarity*, calculates the maximum similarity of the premise categories to the conclusion category; the greater this similarity, the stronger the argument. In this example hyenas are more similar to wolves than cows are, hence similarity is calculated for hyenas. The second component, *coverage*, calculates the average maximum similarity of premise categories to members of the "inclusive category"—the lowest category that includes both premise and conclusion categories. For argument (i) the inclusive category is presumably *mammal*. In our research the inclusive category is simply the conclusion category. The greater the coverage of the inclusive category by the premise categories, the stronger is the argument. Sloman (1993) presents an alternative model, but for our purposes his computation of coverage makes the same predictions as Osherson et al.

We use the SCM to compare patterns of inference based on taxonomic categories by testing for three category-based induction phenomena: similarity, typicality, and diversity. These phenomena can be accounted for in terms of the two main features of the SCM: the similarity component and the coverage component. Not surprisingly, the similarity component drives the similarity phenomenon, which predicts that the stronger inference is the one whose the premise is most similar to the conclusion.

In contrast, typicality and diversity hinge on coverage. The typicality phenomenon predicts that a more typical instance promotes stronger inferences than a less typical instance. Typicality in this case is computed in terms of central tendency; the typicality of an item is the average taxonomic distance of that item to all other items in the inclusive category. The higher the average similarity of that item to other members of the category, the more typical it is. Thus more typical items provide greater coverage than less typical ones.

Like typicality, diversity is a measure of category coverage. The diversity phenomenon predicts that an argument will be inductively strong to the degree that categories mentioned in its premises are similar to different instances of the conclusion category. For example, consider arguments in (ii):

(iia)  Jaguars have protein Y
       *Leopards have protein Y*
       All mammals have protein Y.

(iib)  Jaguars have protein Y
       *Mice have protein Y*
       All mammals have protein Y.

The SCM predicts that that the categories mentioned in the premise of (iib) provide greater *coverage* of the conclusion category *mammal*—that they are more similar to more mammals—than the categories mentioned in the premises of (iia), thus making (iib) the stronger argument. Indeed most subjects agree that the (iib) is stronger than (iia) (López 1995; Osherson et al. 1990; Smith, López, and Osherson 1992). In general, diversity predicts that an argument with more diverse premises will be evaluated as stronger than an argument with more similar premises.

For the purposes of this chapter, we focus on our findings regarding diversity. This phenomenon has been well documented among American college student subjects but has received no cross-cultural validation. As part of a larger, comprehensive comparison of categorization and reasoning about mammals (López et al. 1997), we compared diversity-based reasoning among two groups: the Itzaj Maya natives of Petén, Guatemala, and University of Michigan undergraduates. To generate sets of premises that informants would judge to differ in diversity, we first need a measure of similarity. To this end, we asked each participant to sort cards corresponding to local mammal species into categories by "putting the things together that go together by nature." We then asked participants to successively lump and split categories to produce a hierarchical taxonomy. Each group showed a high consensus on sorting, and we therefore used group patterns of sorting to establish similarity relations among the mammals of each locale. Specifically, our measure of similarity was the folktaxonomic distance derived from these sortings. One advantage of the sorting measure of similarity is that it directly links folktaxono mies with patterns of reasoning.

Using these similarity ratings—based on the participants' own folk-taxonomies—we created pairs of arguments where the categories mentioned in the premise of one argument were more similar than the categories mentioned in the correspond ing argument. Participants were then asked which pair provided a better basis for a generalization. Questions concerned hypothetical diseases among populations of famil-iar mammals "on an island in Ontario" for Michigan students or "on an island in Yucatan" for Itzaj participants. For example, one item for the Michigan participants was: "Wolves and deer have a disease. Wolves and coyotes have another disease. Do you think all other mammals on this island have the disease of wolves and deer or the disease of wolves and coyotes?" In this case, since Michigan students deem wolves and deer to be more diverse than wolves and coyotes (based on their sorting data), they cover the conclusion category *mammal* better. Therefore the diversity principle predicts that Michigan students should choose the disease of wolves and deer. Structurally identical items were derived for the Itzaj participants from their sortings of Petén mammals. It should be emphasized that there is no obviously correct answer to the diversity problems; preference for the more diverse argument is simply a phe-nomenon predicted by the SCM and validated empirically with American undergraduate populations (e.g., Osherson et al. 1990).

Each participant was given four diversity problems, along with other reasoning problems. We were interested in how often participants in each group would favor the argument with the more diverse premise. The results were striking: Michigan participants overwhelmingly favored the more diverse premise, c hoosing it on 96 percent of trials. In contrast, Itzaj participants chose the more diverse premise on only 35 percent of trials. Both groups were reliably different from chance performance. Why did this significant difference in performance emerge?

Two possibilities can be ruled out immediately. First, the difference did not stem from an unwillingness on the part of the Itzaj to reason hypo-thetically. On the other reasoning problems included with the task—those involving similarity and typicality—the Itzaj performed identically to the Michigan students. Second, the Itzaj do not lack the ability to use diversity as a reasoning strategy. On other real-world reasoning prob-lems where a diverse sample would lead to a more robust con clusion, (e.g., "Imagine you want to buy several bags of corn from a given person. Before buying them, this person will show you only two cobs of corn to check whether all the corn is good. Do you prefer him to show you two cobs from one and the same bag, or do you prefer him to show you one cob from one bag and another cob from another bag?"), the Itzaj showed a reliable preference for the more diverse sampling strategy. Of course it is not entirely clear that this sort of "spatial" diversity is the same kind of process as category-based diversity; nevertheless, performance on these problems indicates that the Itzaj do have an understanding of sampling.

Although we can safely rule out these two potential explanations, a myriad of differences remain between the Itzaj and Michigan students which might explain or contribute to an explanation of the differences in diversity-based reasoning. Chief among these is expertise. The Itzaj have a great deal of contact, and a correspond ingly vast store of knowledge about the mammals of the forest, including ecological relationships that exist among species (see Atran 1994; López et al. 1997). In contrast, Michigan students have little contact and little knowledge about native mammals. To get a better idea about why the Itzaj show negative category-based diversity, we turn a more detailed analysis of the justifications they provided for their judgments and how these might reflect differences in the kind of knowledge possessed by the Itzaj.

The Itzaj justified their responses to the reasoning items on the basis of specific ecological knowledge, often leading them to conclude that the more diverse premise was the weaker of the two choices. For example, given the argument that rats and mice have one disease and tapirs and squirrels have another, one Itzaj participant favored the rats and mice argument, which is less diverse. She explained that tapirs and squirrels are less likely to pass on the disease because they probably required an ecological agent (a bat biting them) to get the disease in the first place, whereas rats and pocket mice are close enough "companions" that they need no such intervention. In other cases the more similar pair had a more different range and habitat (according to the justifications) than the other pair such that using diversity based on ecology would yield negative diversity according to categorical similarity. This suggests that the Itzaj may be using a diversity-based reasoning process, but using different kinds of categories (i.e., ecological ones). A follow-up study testing the

Itzaj on different palms also failed to show (category-based) diversity and produced justifications that again were causal/ecological in character. Informants appealed to range, abundance, and causal potency (e.g., tall palms can affect short palms more readily than the converse) as well as other ecological factors to reason about the hypothetical disease. In short, the Itzaj justifications revealed that the novel disease may not in fact function as a blank property but rather as a trigger for ecologically-based inductions.

Results from the sorting task provide converging evidence for the role of ecology. Many of the Itzaj groupings had an explicitly ecological nature. For example, many Itzaj classified the spider monkey, howler monkey, kinkajou, coatimundi, and other climbing mammals together as *arboreal mammals*, based on habitat and behavior. Likewise the otter— the only aquatic mammal in our set—was isolated because of habitat instead of being classified with other morphologically similar mustelids. In contrast, the undergraduate sorts were based almost entirely on morphology, and more specifically, on size. In addition sorting justifications were much more likely to include detailed ecological information for the Itzaj than for the undergraduates (López et al. 1997). Whereas the Itzaj sort mammals into relational (ecological) categories and justify their diversity responses using relational (ecological) information, the undergraduates do neither.

In addition the density of the Itzaj's ecological knowledge about individual folk genera may block the salience of more abstract categories like *mammal* as the basis for induction. It's possible that given their knowledge of individual species, the Itzaj find higher-order groups of mammals—a necessary component of diversity-based reasoning—less salient than do the Michigan students, who have little knowledge of individual species but have some ideas about taxonomic relations at higher levels. Indeed, consistent with this interpretation, Michigan students were more likely to sort mammals into a few, higher-order groups than were Itzaj participants; thus higher-order classes seem more salient for the Michigan participants.

Thus is appears that differences in patterns of reasoning may be attributable to the higher levels of ecological knowledge possessed by the Itzaj. Of course there are myriad of other differences between Maya elders and University of Michigan undergraduates that could account for these differences. Here is where our triangulation research comes into play: if knowledge blocks the use of diversity-based reasoning, then American experts may also fail to show diversity.

To address this question, we are exploring the impact of different kinds of expertise on categorization and reasoning about trees (see Medin et al. and Atran 1997). We have recently collected data on diversity-based reasoning from Chicago-area tree experts. Their educational backgrounds are diverse; some never completed high school, while others have earned advanced degrees. They are ethnically diverse, predominantly male, and range in age from twenty-nine to seventy-six years old. For present purposes we focus on three types of tree experts: maintenance personnel, landscapers, and taxonomists. Parks maintenance personnel are primarily involved with removing damaged and diseased trees, planting new trees, and pruning and treating trees in public parks and along streets. Landscapers tend to be concerned with utilitarian aspects of trees and with placing suitable (low-maintenance, disease-resistant) trees in appropriate, aesthetically pleasing settings. Taxonomists tend to be involved in research, consulting, and a variety of educational activities. Members of each group have had ten or more years of experience working with trees, which qualifies each participant as a knowledgeable expert.

Each of these experts was given a number of diversity-based reasoning problems. As with the mammal problems, diversity was computed based on the aggregated sortings of the experts themselves. Problems involved two newly discovered tree diseases. The only information available to the expert was that one disease affected one pair of trees, while the other disease affected a different pair. For example, in one item, experts were told that "disease A affects eastern white pine and weeping willow; disease B affects white birch and river birch." The expert was then asked which disease would be more likely to affect more other kinds of trees. In this case the first pair is more dissimilar and therefore provides better coverage of the conclusion category *tree*, than the second, so a diversity-based response would be that disease A was more likely to affect more other kinds of trees.

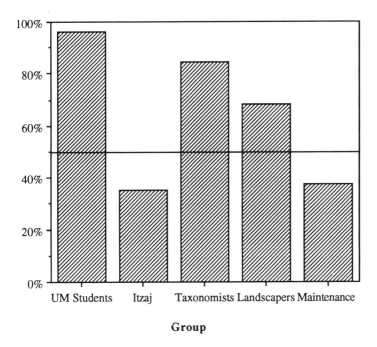

**Figure 7.2**
Percentage of diversity-based responses from different groups

The results are presented in figure 7.2, along with the responses of the UM students and Itzaj to the mammal diversity items mentioned above. (The horizontal line at 50 percent represents chance responding across all items.) As can be seen in figure 7.2, there were clear differences in diversity-based reasoning among the three expert groups. Specifically, taxonomists and landscapers chose the more diverse pair at levels that were reliably above chance (86 and 71 percent, respectively) and reliably more often than maintenance workers. Maintenance workers' responses, like the Itzaj, were significantly below chance (27 percent), indicating that they showed a reliable preference for the more similar pair. Thus, expert groups clearly differed in their use of diversity as a basis for induction.

These results from tree experts allow us to rule out several possible explanations for the discrepancy in the use of diversity between the Itzaj and the Michigan students. First, general differences between Maya and

Americans cannot explain the result; results from the tree experts show that some Americans use diversity, and some do not. Second, expertise or quantity of knowledge does not necessarily block the use of diversity. All of our tree experts have a good deal of knowledge about trees, but some used diversity and some did not.

In other words, the conditions that lead one to use diversity as an inductive reasoning heuristic are not as straightforward as we might have thought. To get some better insights into the basis of performance, we again turn to the justifications given for judgments, which reveal distinct strategies. Many of the taxonomists and some of the landscapers explicitly mentioned diversity as the basis for their choice. But some of the taxonomists and many of the landscapers employed causal/ecological justifications on at least some of the tests. For example, they might mention range, numbers or frequency of a kind, and susceptibility to disease. In short, for these experts, diversity was one strategy among several.

In contrast, maintenance personnel rarely mentioned anything that could be construed as diversity or, in terms of the SCM, coverage, and instead revealed predominately causal/ecological strategies.[2] For example, on the item contrasting two birches with a pine and a willow, almost all maintenance personnel responded that more other trees were likely to get the disease associated with the birches (the less diverse pair), often arguing that birches are very susceptible and widely planted so that there would be more opportunities for the disease to spread. Generally, the justifications were remarkably parallel to those of the Itzaj on mammals and palms, including in a few cases the idea that a disease will spread more readily from a big tree to a small than from a small tree to a big one.

Although it appears that diversity is one strategy among many and that it may be blocked by alternative patterns of reasoning, we still do not have a good understanding of the differences associated with type of expertise. In general, our landscapers and taxonomists have had more formal education than our maintenance workers. There are exceptions, however, and our sample includes both landscapers and taxonomists who have do not have college degrees, and maintenance workers who do. This allowed us to compare diversity-based reasoning among those experts who have a college degree or more with those who have less than a college degree without duplicating our previous analysis. Were education the major determinant in the use of diversity in induction, the more educated group should show more use of diversity. Results suggest that this is not the case; there were no reliable differences in the use of diversity as a function of education. This also makes it unlikely that differences between Michigan students and Itzaj are attributable to disparities in formal education.

What then drives the differences in the use of diversity-based reasoning? What do the Itzaj and tree maintenance workers have in common that differs from landscapers, taxonomists, and university undergraduates? One speculation is that it may relate to how knowledge that is specifically relevant to our questions is acquired. Taxonomists and landscapers are probably more likely to learn about trees formally than are maintenance workers, who may have well received the bulk of their training on the job. Similarly the Itzaj acquire their knowledge of mammals through first-hand experience or orally-transmitted lore, whereas what UM students know about local mammals is probably picked up in school, at the zoo, or on TV, rather than in local woods and fields. Perhaps it is the way that domain-specific knowledge is acquired, rather than the level of education in general, that predicts diversity-based reasoning. A related possibility is that the diversity-users may have had more experience—at least in educational settings—with taxonomic categories superordinate to the genus level. This may also contribute to diversity-based induction. It may be that the use of ecological knowledge versus "coverage" depends on the relative accessibility of taxonomic versus ecological information. One observation consistent with this competing strategy view (noted earlier) is that some of the maintenance personnel did use coverage as a justification on other reasoning trials that were not tests of diversity. Obviously this is a puzzle that awaits further exploration.

## Summary

In comparing category-based induction across cultures, we found that Itzaj Maya and Michigan undergraduates both showed similarity and typicality phenomenon but that the Michigan participants showed diversity-based reasoning, whereas the Itzaj did not and indeed showed reliable antidiversity. This seems attributable in part to the Itzaj's relatively large store of ecological knowledge but is viewed very differently when one notes that American tree maintenance personnel—but not landscapers or taxonomists—also show negative diversity. Thus our "triangulation" strategy allows us to rule out several potential explanations for our findings.

Together, our studies of diversity-based reasoning provide an intriguing perspective on the similarity-coverage model (and associated models). First of all, diversity is not a universal—there are alternative reasoning strategies that may be triggered by what are nominally "blank" properties. We believe that ecological reasoning is important in and of itself, and we have launched a separate line of research aimed at analyzing folkecology (e.g., Atran and Medin 1997). Second, the apparent competition of strategies raises new questions about the memory organization and the role of hierarchical taxonomies in retrieval which we are also aiming to pursue. Last, our results are leading us to take a closer look at the notion of diversity itself. Should it be equated with coverage? We suspect, for example, that undergraduates might show diversity-based reasoning even when they know too little about the referents of folkbiological terms to assess something like coverage (similarity). Answers to these sorts of questions await further investigation.

### 7.3    Summary, Conclusions, Further Questions

In this chapter we have discussed two cases in which examining the use of folkbiological categories in inductive inference has yielded insights that mere description of folktaxonomy might have missed. The first set of findings involved a surprising cross-cultural convergence. Previous research leads to the prediction that Northwestern undergraduates would privilege more general categories for induction than the Itzaj. Instead, we found that despite large disparities in experience and knowledge of the natural world, folk-generic taxa were inductively privileged for both groups. Indeed superimposed data from the two groups are nearly identical.

Second, we related findings that University of Michigan undergraduates, but not Itzaj Maya, evaluated arguments in accord with the principle of diversity. This initial divergence seemed strange; to us, the argument with the more diverse premises seems intuitively much stronger. However, after further research, it turns out that this antidiversity pattern is not peculiar to the lowland rainforests of Guatemala. Illinois tree maintenance workers showed the same patterns of reasoning, and landscapers and taxonomists displayed similar strategies at least some of the time.

Taken together, what do these results tell us about the nature of folkbiological thought? First, we find group convergences and divergences that are not simply a function of culture or experience. Itzaj folkbiological "experts" resemble American "novices" in some respects (privileged levels) but not in others (diversity-based reasoning); with respect to diversity-based reasoning, they resemble s ome American experts (maintenance workers) but not others (landscapers, taxonomists). In other words, when reasoning is examined, a broad construal of "culture" seems not to be the largest predictor of performance.

Second, experience may have a differential impact on different aspects of folkbiological reasoning. On one hand, folk-generic taxa appear to be inductively privileged for individuals whether or not those individuals have had much experience with the organisms so classified or not. For the Itzaj, experience may converge with language and expectation to privilege the folk generic. For American college students, language and expectations appear to be enough to overcome lack of experience and similarly mark the folk generic as privileged. Thus different experiences appear to lead to similar outcomes.

On the other hand, diversity-based reasoning seems quite susceptible to the effects of experience. Itzaj and American college students show radically different patterns of performance on diversity-based reasoning items. Taxonomists and landscapers show a pattern of reasoning intermediate to that of undergraduates and Maya, while the behavior of American maintenance experts is strikingly similar to that of the Itzaj. Clearly in this case experience has a large impact on reasoning patterns; it remains to be seen exactly what aspects of experience have this effect.

Finally this sampling of results yields important avenues of future research. First, although we do find many cross-cultural similarities with respect to folkbiological reasoning, we are in no position to claim that members of different cultures do not differ fundamentally with respect to other aspects of folkbiological thought. The abilities that we have measured may well be the very ones that are most likely to show universality. Moreover constraints inherent to our methods may reinforce this apparent finding. In this light it is vital to look at beliefs, naive theories, and the explanatory networks in which folkbiological categories are embedded (e.g., Carey 1985; Keil 1994; Hatano and Inagaki 1994). Further exploration of these issues may well reveal deep cultural differences. Another important future direction is to look at less "taxonomic" ways of organizing folkbiological knowledge (e.g., ecological webs). Again, it may be that by focusing on taxonomies we are overlooking important sources of cultural differences in folkbiological thought.

Further research is needed regarding the development of folkbiological thought. Our findings point to salient differences in patterns of reasoning and also to unexpected commonalities. In either case we are left wondering how different learning conditions might contribute to the differences in patterns of reasoning, or how developmental patterns result in similar outcomes despite marked differences in environment and experience. These are essentially developmental questions, and research on the changes in folkbiological reasoning and thought over time is needed to answer them.

Apart from expanding and challenging our knowledge about folkbiology, these results make a methodological point about the investigation of folkbiology in general: investigations of inductive reasoning complement, expand, and enrich studies of categorization. It is important to describe folk taxonomy, but it is equally important to document how folk taxa are used in everyday thought and interaction with the world. Moreover this research demonstrates the value of a multidisciplinary approach to the study of folkbiological thought. Without a detailed analysis of the systems in which these categories are situated, or the justifications that our informants provide along with their responses to our items, we could not have made the progress that we have to date. Moreover our cross-cultural and cross-experiential evidence provides a clear challenge for existing models of inductive reasoning. Our work on folkbiological induction is far from complete, but the fragmentary evidence we have gathered adds depth and complexity to our understanding of folkbiological thought.

# Notes

1. In a recent survey of Northwestern undergraduates, we presented the names of 80 trees and asked the students to circle the trees that they had *heard of* before, regardless of whether they knew anything about them. More than 90 percent said they had heard of Birch, Cedar, Chestnut, Fig, Hickory, Maple, Oak, Pine, and Spruce, but fewer than half indicated any familiarity with Alder, Buckeye (despite the fact that the Ohio State Buckeyes are in the Big Ten conference along with Northwestern), Catalpa, Hackberry, Hawthorn, Honeylocust, Horsechestnut, Larch, Linden, Mountain Ash, Sweetgum, or Tuliptree—all of which are common to the Evanston area, and many of which they see nearly every day on the Northwestern campus.

In another survey, we presented names of 56 plants (trees, bushes, flowers), and 56 animals (mammals, birds, fish) with distractors to Northwestern undergraduates. Their task was to indicate which of the items belonged to which categories (i.e., is a *tapir* a mammal, fish, bird, or none of the above? Is a *catalpa* a tree, bush, flower, or none of the above?). Mean performance (51 percent correct) was just different from chance, but obviously left a great deal to be desired.

2. Interestingly, the large majority of maintenance personnel did employ coverage-like justifications on some reasoning tasks. However, these tended to appear on typicality tests, not diversity tests. Thus on a trial involving Silver Maple getting one disease and Kentucky Coffee tree another, the disease of the Silver Maple might be selected by maintenance because "the maple family is bigger" (maintenance personnel tend to use "family" to refer to scientific genera). Assuming that "coverage" mediates diversity, maintenance personnel should have diversity *available* as a strategy but it appears to be blocked by other factors such as causal/ecological reasoning.

# References

Anderson, J. R. 1990. *The Adaptive Character of Thought*. Hillsdale, NJ: Lawrence Erlbaum.

Atran, S. 1990. *Cognitive foundations of natural history: Towards an anthropology of science*. Cambridge: Cambridge University Press.

Atran, S. 1993. Itzaj-Maya tropical agro-forestry. *Current Anthropology* 34: 633–700.

Atran, S. 1994. Core domains versus scientific theories: Evidence from systematics and Maya folkbiology. In L. Hirschfeld and S. Gelman, eds., *Mapping the Mind: Domain Specificity in Cognition and Culture*. New York: Cambridge University Press.

Atran, S., P. Estin, J. D. Coley, and D. L. Medin 1997. Generic species and basic levels: Essence and appearance in folk biology. *Journal of Ethnobiology* 17: 22–45.

Atran, S., and D. L. Medin, 1997. Knowledge and action: Cultural models of nature and resource management in Mesoamerica. In M. Bazerman, D. Messick, A. Tinbrusel, and K. Wayde-Benzoni, eds., *Psychological Perspectives to Environment and Ethics in Management*. San Francisco: Jossey-Bass, pp. 171–208.

Berlin, B. 1976. The concept of rank in ethnobiological classification: Some evidence from Aguaruna folk biology. *American Ethnologist* 3: 381–99.

Berlin, B. 1978. Ethnobiological classification. In E. Rosch and B. Lloyd, eds., *Cognition and Categorization*. Hillsdale: Lawrence Erlbaum, pp. 9–26.

Berlin, B. 1992. *Ethnobiological Classification: Principles of Categorization of Plants and Animals in Traditional Societies*. Princeton: Princeton University Press.

Berlin, B., D. E. Breedlove, and P. H. Raven. 1973. General principles of classification and nomenclature in folk biology. *American Anthropologist* 75: 214–42.

Boster, J. S. 1995. The information economy model applied to biological similarity judgment. In J. Levine, L. Resnick, and S. Behrend, eds., *Socially Shared Cognition*. Washington: American Psychological Association.

Brown, C. H. 1984. *Language and Living Things: Uniformities in Folk Classification and Naming*. New Brunswick, NJ: Rutgers University Press.

Bulmer, R. 1967. Why is the cassowary not a bird? A problem of zoological taxonomy among the Karam of the New Guinea Highlands. *Man* 2: 5–25.

Bulmer, R., and M. J. Tyler. 1968. Karam classification of frogs. *Journal of Polynesian Society* 77: 333–85.

Carey, S. 1985. *Conceptual Change in Childhood*. Cambridge: MIT Press.

Coley, J. D., D. L. Medin, and S. Atran. 1997. Does rank have its privilege? Inductive inferences within folkbiological taxonomies. *Cognition* 64: 73–112.

Conklin, H. C. 1962. The lexicographical treatment of folk taxonomies. *International Journal of American Linguistics* 28: 119–41.

Diamond, J. 1966. Zoological classification of a primitive people. *Science* 151: 1102–1104.

Dougherty, J. W. 1978. Salience and relativity in classification. *American Ethnologist* 5: 66–80.

Gelman, S. A., and J. D. Coley. 1990. The importance of knowing a dodo is a bird: Categories and inferences in 2-year-old children. *Developmental Psychology* 26: 796–804.

Gelman, S. A., and J. D. Coley. 1991. Language and categorization: The acquisition of natural kind terms. In J. P. Byrnes and S. A. Gelman, eds., *Perspectives on Language and Thought: Interrelations in Development*. Cambridge: Cambridge University Press, pp. 146–96.

Gelman, S. A., J. D. Coley, and G. M. Gottfried. 1994. Essentialist beliefs in children: The acquisition of concepts and theories. In L. W. Hirschfeld and S. A. Gelman, eds., *Mapping the Mind: Domain Specificity in Cognition and Culture*. Cambridge: Cambridge University Press, pp. 341–65.

Gelman, S. A., S. A. Wilcox, and E. V. Clark. 1989. Conceptual and lexical hierarchies in young children. *Cognitive Development* 4: 309–26.

Hatano, G., and K. Inagaki. 1994. Young children's naive theory of biology. *Cognition* 50: 171–88.

Hays, T. E. 1983. Ndumba folk biology and general principles of ethnobiological classification and nomenclature. *American Anthropologist* 85: 592–611.

Hunn, E. S. 1977. *Tzeltal Folk Zoology: The Classification of Discontinuities in Nature.* New York: Academic Press.

Johnson, K. E., and C. B. Mervis. 1997. Effects of varying levels of expertise on the basic level of categorization. *Journal of Experimental Psychology* 126: 1248–77.

Keil, F. 1994. The birth and nurturance of concepts by domains: The origins of concepts of living things. In L. A. Hirschfeld and S. A. Gelman eds., *Mapping the Mind: Domain Specificity in Cognition and Culture* (234–254). Cambridge: Cambridge University Press, pp. 234–54.

López, A. 1995. The diversity principle in the testing of arguments. *Memory and Cognition* 23: 372–82.

López, A., S. Atran, J. D. Coley, D. Medin, and E. E. Smith. 1997. The tree of life: Universals of folkbiological taxonomies and inductions. *Cognitive Psychology* 32: 251–95.

Malt, B. C. 1995. Category coherence in crosscultural perspective. *Cognitive Psychology* 29: 85–148.

Medin, D. L., and J. D. Coley. 1998. Concepts and categorization. In J. Hochberg and J. E. Cutting, eds., *Handbook of perception and Cognition, Perception and Cognition at Century's End: History, Philosophy, Theory.* San Diego: Academic Press.

Medin, D. L., and A. Ortony. 1989. Psychological essentialism. In S. Vosniadou and A. Ortony, eds., *Similarity and Analogical Reasoning.* Cambridge: Cambridge University Press, pp. 179–95.

Medin, D. L., E. B. Lynch, J. D. Coley, and S. Atran. 1997. Categorization and reasoning among tree experts: Do all roads lead to Rome? *Cognitive Psychology* 32: 49–96.

Mervis, C. B., and E. Rosch. 1981. Categorization of natural objects. *Annual Review of Psychology* 32: 89–115.

Osherson, D. N., E. E. Smith, O. Wilkie, A. López, and E. Shafir. 1990. Category-based induction. *Psychological Review* 97: 185–200.

Rosch, E. 1975. Universals and cultural specifics in human categorization. In R. W. Brislin, S. Bochner, and W. J. Lanner, eds., *Cross-cultural Perspectives on Learning.* New York: Wiley, pp. 177–206.

Rosch, E., C. B. Mervis, W. D. Gray, D. M. Johnson, and P. Boyes-Braem. 1976. Basic objects in natural categories. *Cognitive Psychology* 8: 382–439.

Sloman, S. A. 1993. Feature-based induction. *Cognitive Psychology* 25: 231–80.

Stross, B. 1973. Acquisition of botanical terminology by Tzeltal children. In M. Edmonson, ed., *Meaning in Mayan languages*. The Hague: Mouton, pp. 107–42.

Tanaka, J. B., and M. Taylor. 1991. Object categories and expertise: Is the basic level in the eye of the beholder? *Cognitive Psychology* 23: 457–82.

Smith, E. E., A. López, and D. Osherson. 1992. Category membership, similarity, and naive induction. In A. Healy, S. Kosslyn, and R. Shiffrin, eds., *Essays in Honor of W. K. Estes*. Hillsdale, NJ: Lawrence Erlbaum.

Waxman, S. R. 1991. Convergences between semantic and conceptual organization in the preschool years. In S. A. Gelman and J. P. Byrnes, eds., *Persepectives on Language and Thought: Interrelations in Development*. Cambridge: Cambridge University Press, pp. 107–45.

# 8

# The Dubbing Ceremony Revisited: Object Naming and Categorization in Infancy and Early Childhood

Sandra R. Waxman

This Chapter is dedicated to Roger Brown for his profound influence.

An Itzaj infant rests on his mother's back as she walks through a village in Guatemala's Petén region. A North American infant sits in his stroller as his father walks past a pet store on his way to rent a video. Each infant will grow up in a world that the other cannot imagine, amid objects and events that the other has not experienced, and with words that the other cannot understand. And yet there will be striking similarities in the most fundamental aspects of their conceptual and language development. Within the first year of life, each of these infants will form categories to capture both the similarities and differences among the various objects they encounter. Most of these early object categories will be at an intermediate level of abstraction (i.e., dog,[1] rather than the more inclusive animal or the more specific terrier), known as the basic, or folk-generic, level in psychology and anthropology, respectively. These early categories will serve as an inductive base, permitting the infants to make inferences about the behaviors and properties of new objects. In addition to these conceptual advances, each infant will acquire his native language naturally, at a remarkable pace. By 12 months of age, each will begin to produce words, and included among these will be names for important people, for salient relations (e.g., hot, uh-oh), and for the basic level categories of objects that capture their interest. Each will add new words, and by 24 months of age, each will have productive command of hundreds of words and will begin to combine these to produce short, well-formed phrases.

This vignette reveals that although infants across the world's communities are exposed to widely varying types of experiences, they follow strikingly similar paths in cognitive and language development. Early cognitive and language development unfold naturally in humans, but these advances are also shaped in important ways by the people, the objects, and the events that the infant encounters. Therefore developmental theories must take into account both the natural endowments of the human infant and the shaping role of the environment.

To meet this challenge, I have woven together several lines of interdisciplinary work to cast light on the evolution of object categorization and object naming in infants and young children. This research has led me to the conclusion that object categorization and naming are tightly linked in human development. From the onset of acquisition, there are powerful, implicit links between these two uniquely human capacities. For infants who are on threshold of object naming, novel words highlight commonalities among objects and, in this way, foster the formation of object categories. This initial expectation is powerful. It guides infants in their first efforts to map words to their meanings. It also guides the acquisition of stable conceptual systems. However, this initial expectation is modified as a result of infants' experience with the range of objects and the structure of the native language they encounter (Waxman 1998).

## 8.1   Categorization, Naming, and the Establishment of Hierarchical Systems: Some Central Issues

### Hierarchical Systems Established Universally

Extensive research in cognitive psychology, anthropology, and linguistics has revealed that people across the world establish hierarchical systems or taxonomies to capture important relations among objects (Atran, 1990; 1995; Berlin 1992; C. Brown 1977; Coley Medin Atran 1997; Frake 1962; Keil 1995; Lopez Atran Coley Medin, and Smith 1997; but see Burling 1964; Dupre 1981, and Lancy 1983 for arguments against this universalist position). Some of the most compelling evidence comes from detailed examinations of folkbiological knowledge from such disparate cultures and locales as the American Southwest (Hage and Miller 1976; Wyman and Bailey 1964), Guatemala (Atran 1990), Mexico

(Berlin, Breedlove, and Raven 1974; Berlin 1992; Hunn 1977), China (Anderson 1967), the New Guinea highlands (Bulmer and Tyler 1968), and college-educated North American adults (see Medin and Heit 1995; Smith and Medin 1981; Rosch, Mervis, Gray, Johnson, and Boyes-Braem 1976). Findings like these are intriguing, for they suggest that people immersed in vastly different cultures, living in vastly different locales, and exposed to vastly different amounts of formal schooling settle on a similar solution to the cognitive problem of organizing information efficiently. And because the categories within such systems support inductive inference, they motivate us to extend existing knowledge beyond that which we may have observed directly (S. Gelman and Medin 1993; Lopez et al. 1997.).

### Privileged Status of the Basic, or Folk-Generic, Level

There is also strong evidence that across cultures, categories at an intermediate level of abstraction—known as the basic level in psychology (Rosch et al. 1976) and the folk-generic level in anthropology (Atran 1990; Berlin, 1992)—enjoy a privileged status. Descriptively this privileged level occupies a middle position within a hierarchical system (e.g., dog, rather than the more specific terrier, or the more inclusive mammal or animal; see Rosch et al. 1976 for a detailed description of the evidence). Briefly stated, under most circumstances, adults prefer to categorize and label objects at this level, and they are quickest to identify objects at this level. In addition these mid-level categories appear to have greater inductive potential than higher- and lower-order object categories (S. Gelman 1988; Coley et al. 1997).

Beyond such descriptions, precise formal characterizations of the privileged status of these mid-level categories have been difficult to achieve. Also at issue is the precise location of this privileged level within a given object hierarchy. Atran (1990) and Medin et al. (1997) have documented that there are "shifts" as a function of expertise. For example, for tree experts, the category oak may be privileged with regard to naming and induction, while for novices, the more inclusive category tree may serve this function (Atran 1990; Medin et al. 1997; Johnson and Mervis 1994; Mervis Johnson, and Mervis 1994). These controversies notwithstanding, the construct of a basic level has proved useful as a description or heuristic in research with adults and children alike (see Berlin 1992; Armstrong, Gleitman, and Gleitman 1983; Medin and Heit 1995; Waxman 1990).

### Developmental Primacy of the Basic, or Folk-Generic, Level

Of particular interest is the developmental evidence for a basic level advantage in object categorization, object naming, and induction. Developmentally, object categorization and naming at the basic level precedes that at higher- and lower-order levels within a hierarchy. Basic level object categories are formed early in infancy (Quinn, Eimas, and Rosenkrantz 1993); basic level categories and their names are acquired long before those at nonbasic levels (Rosch et al. 1976; Waxman 1990; Markman 1989; Mervis and Crisafi 1982; Anglin 1977; Brown 1958; Dougherty 1979; Mervis 1987; Stross 1973; Waxman and Hatch 1992); basic level names provide criteria for object individuation and object identity (Hall and Waxman 1993; Hall 1993; Macnamara 1986). Moreover basic level object categories serve as children's first and strongest basis for inductive inference (S. Gelman 1988; Waxman et al. 1997).

This is not to say that early category knowledge is limited to the basic level. This is clearly not the case. Infants and children also appreciate more abstract (e.g., <u>animal</u>) and more specific (e.g., <u>collie, Thompson (green) grapes</u>) object categories (Mandler 1992; Waxman 1990; Waxman and Markow 1995). Findings like these are testimony to the richness and flexibility of infants' early perceptual and conceptual abilities, and their ability to recruit these abilities in the service of object categorization. However, there are several indications that these nonbasic level categories do not enjoy the privileged status accorded to those at the basic level. Nonbasic level object categories are named later in development than those at the basic level, and they do not serve as the primary basis for inductive inference (Waxman et al. 1997; Gelman 1988). Thus the ability to form nonbasic level categories does not, in itself, preclude the argument for the developmental primacy of the basic level. On the contrary, the weight of the evidence (from a psychological, linguistic, philosophical, and anthropological perspective) supports the developmental primacy of the basic level in object categorization, naming, and induction (Waxman 1998).

### Systematic Relation between Hierarchical Level and Linguistic Form

Further support for both universality of hierarchical systems and the privileged status of the basic level comes from cross-linguistic analyses of object naming and categorization. Berlin (1992) and his colleagues (C. Brown 1977; Hunn 1977) have discovered a systematic relation between the hierarchical level of an object category and the linguistic form of its label. This striking relation has been documented in adult speakers of diverse languages (see Berlin 1973). According to Berlin (1973; 1992), there are two important cross-linguistic observations regarding the basic or folk-generic level. First, across languages, categories at the basic level are named. Indeed Berlin (1973) has argued that classes at this level are so salient that they are "... crying out to be named." A second observation is that across languages, names for basic level categories have a consistent linguistic form. They tend to be simple (monomorphemic) count nouns. Examples from American English folk-biology are nondecomposable count nouns such as *grape, orchid*, and *whale*.

There are two key distinctions between the nomenclatural patterns associated with basic versus nonbasic level categories (Berlin 1973; 1992). First, unlike basic level categories, many nonbasic level categories remain unnamed. For example, in several folkbiological systems, the categories <u>plant</u> and <u>animal</u> are not lexicalized. (The psychological status of these covert categories will be discussed in the final section of this chapter.) Second, when nonbasic level categories <u>are</u> named, the linguistic form of their names differs systematically from those at the basic level. In contrast to the basic level, nonbasic level categories tend to be named with more complex, polymorphemic forms. For example, categories at the more abstract levels (e.g., the family, life form, and unique beginner ranks in ethnobiology, or the superordinate and global level categories in psychology) are typically named with count nouns, that are more complex morphologically than those at the basic level. This complexity appears to be a consequence of linguistic constructions such as compounding (see Lyons 1977 or Marchand 1969 for a full discussion of morphological complexity and other derivational forms). Names associated with the more specific levels (e.g., the specific and varietal ranks, or the subordinate level) exhibit a different nomenclatural pattern entirely. These tend to be marked with phrases in which a modifier is used in conjunction with a simple count noun to denote a specific type of the basic level category marked by the noun alone. Examples from American English folk biology include names such as *Concord grape, humpback whale*, or *cymbidium orchid*.

In brief, this ethnobiological program of research has revealed striking uniformity across diverse languages regarding (1) the categories that are most likely to be lexicalized, and (2) the linguistic form of the names associated with categories at each hierarchical level. Evidence from American sign language (ASL) suggests that these convergences between nomenclatural patterns and object categorization are not a consequence of the particular modalities (visuomotor or auditory-vocal) through which a language is transmitted but are instead a more general feature of language and conceptual organization (Newport and Bellugi 1976; Waxman 1990).

### Identifying Sources of Uniformities in Classification and Naming

What are the sources underlying these uniformities in folk classification and naming? Do these uniformities reflect the structural regularities among objects found within the natural world (see Berlin 1973; 1992; Rosch et al. 1976)? Do they arise as a consequence of the organizational tendencies (or constraints) imposed by the human mind? Although we do not yet have an answer to these questions, it is apparent that these sources are not mutually exclusive. Therefore several different research strategies have been mined to gain insights into the relative contributions of each.

One strategy has been to identify similarities and differences among hierarchical systems that have been established by adults *across* diverse cultures. Thanks to the painstaking and extensive research conducted by primarily by ethnobiologists, we now have elaborate descriptions of folktaxonomic knowledge across cultures. These comprehensive analyses of entire folkbiological systems have made it possible to speculate about factors within a given environment that may contribute to cross-cultural differences.

Another productive research strategy has been to compare, *within* a particular culture, the knowledge systems of groups of individuals with different kinds of expertise. Chi (1983), Medin (Medin et al. 1997; Coley et al. 1997), and Mervis (Johnson and Mervis 1994; Mervis et al. 1994) have each pioneered this approach within the psychological literature. They have shown that experts and novices differ in the amount of knowledge that they have acquired within a domain. As a consequence the taxonomies constructed by experts have greater detail than those of novices. In addition the inductive force of their knowledge within that expert domain also differs. Further the precise location of the privileged level may shift as a function of expertise (Coley et al. 1997; Medin et al. 1997). Nonetheless, the similarities between experts and novices appear to outstrip their differences. Both groups form hierarchical systems and use categories within these systems as an inductive base. For both groups, mid-level object categories within these hierarchical systems appear to be privileged with respect to object naming, categorization and induction.

### Necessity of Adopting a Developmental Approach

The research strategies described thus far amplify the uniformities and also reveal fascinating divergences across cultures or groups of individuals. However, there is an inherent limitation in these approaches that can only be overcome by adopting a developmental approach. For no matter how carefully an ethnobiological record is constructed and analyzed, or how elegantly an experiment is designed, evidence from adults cannot reveal the origins of knowledge or the mechanisms responsible for its unfolding. It is impossible to discern the initial state of a system from an examination of its mature state. To understand the origins and emergence of a system, one must begin at the beginning.

The power and necessity of adopting a developmental approach to questions of acquisition has been recognized across disciplines. See, for example, the elegant work of Marler (1991) on the acquisition of song in the white-crowned sparrow, Held and Hein (1963) on the acquisition of depth perception in kittens, Baillargeon (1993) and Spelke (1993) on infants' acquisition of physical knowledge about objects, and R. Gelman (1991) on the acquisition of number concepts in humans. Although these programs of research focus on different topics, they share with each other, and with research on folkbiology, a commitment to characterizing the rapid acquisition of complex, sophisticated systems. They also share a commitment to considering carefully the relative contributions both of the amount and type of information present in the environment and of the structure imposed by the learner. (See Gallistel et al. 1991 for an extended discussion of this topic.)

In my research program I have adopted a similar approach to examine the origin and emergence of the relation between object categorization and naming. I argue for an integrative account that embraces at once the importance of *constraints* or *expectations* inherent in the child and *learning* on the basis of the child's experience.

### Clarifying the Notion of Constraints within the Child

The interplay between constraints and learning is essential. Children raised in different communities and cultures will encounter different objects, will acquire different languages, and will be presented with different types of instruction and training (Cole et al. 1971; Laboratory of Comparative Human Cognition 1983; Lave 1991; Rogoff 1990). Acquisition must be sufficiently constrained to permit the child to form fundamental categories of objects and to acquire their native language, yet sufficiently flexible to accommodate the systematic variations that occur across cultures and languages.

Therefore an argument for constraints on acquisition is not a polarized argument that locates the engine of acquisition solely within the mind of the child. Neither does it preclude the indisputable fact that the kinds of input that children receive will shape their knowledge. Rather, the argument is that these constraints or expectations direct infants' attention toward precisely the sort of information and regularities in the environment that will make possible the rapid acquisition of complex systems of knowledge, including the acquisition of word meaning and the establishment of object categories (Gelman and Williams 1998; Waxman 1998). Notice also that this is a dynamic account: the initial constraints that we observe in infants at the outset of acquisition are not rigidly fixed. They do not exert a uniform influence throughout development. On the contrary, the infants' expectations regarding the specific relations between word meaning and conceptual organization become modified over the course of development. Thus any thorough account of acquisition will consider both factors within the child and factors within the child's environment (including the objects the child encounters, the native language under acquisition, and the people transmitting knowledge from one individual to another, from one generation to another).

## The Dubbing Ceremony

This essential interaction between constraints within the child and learning comes into sharp focus when viewed through the lens of a simple and culturally widespread naming ritual known as the Original Word Game (Brown 1958) or the Dubbing Ceremony (Putnam 1975). This is a natural interchange involving a young child and a caretaker (an adult, or an older child). Typically one individual (e.g., an adult) points to an object (e.g., a tapir) and provides its name ("Ila' a' tzimin∼che' je'lo'" [in Itzaj] or "Look, a tapir" [in English]). This simple ceremony is nothing more (or less) than an ostensive definition, embedded within a social exchange.

Considered from a social and cultural vantage point, the dubbing ceremony reveals the status accorded to naming across human society and the role that adults naturally assume in transmitting knowledge. The ceremony also captures the strong intuition that naming and categorization are not independent. By providing distinct names for two objects (e.g., "This is a *horse*; that is a *tapir*"), we highlight the conceptual distinctions between them. By providing a common name for these objects (e.g., "These are *animals*"), we highlight the conceptual commonalities among them. Thus names offer tacit information about relevant commonalities and distinctions among objects. Naming, then, is itself an act of categorization. Adults' naming practices help to shape the boundaries of children's object categories and their names. In this way the dubbing ceremony illustrates the vital contribution of parents and other caretakers in the child's acquisition of object categories and their names.

A thorough consideration of this ceremony also underscores the contribution of factors within the child. Despite wide variations in cultural practices associated with early naming, there is remarkable cross-cultural consistency in the timing and in the composition of the early lexicon. For example, in some cultures (e.g., middle- to upper-class communities in North America), caretakers begin naming objects for their infants well before the infants themselves can speak. In other communities (Kahluli; see Ochs and Schieffelin 1984), caretakers speak directly to infants only once the infants themselves have begun to speak. Another source of variation comes from the structure of the language presented to infants. Infants as young as eight months of age are especially attentive to novel words, particularly those that occur at the end of a sentence or phrase boundary, such as "See the *tapir*?" (Fernald 1992; Jusczyk and Aslin 1995; Newsome and Jusczyk 1994). In many languages (e.g., English, Spanish, French), names of objects typically occupy this privileged phrase–final position. However, in other languages such as Mandarin Chinese (Tardif 1996), Korean (Au, Dapretto, and Song 1994; Choi and Gopnik 1996), and apparently Itzaj, this is less often the case.

Despite these cross-linguistic variations in the prevalence of naming routines and the linguistic structure in which names are embedded, infants acquire words for objects and categories of objects rapidly (Gentner 1982; Gleitman 1990; Goldin-Meadow, Seligman, and Gelman 1976; Huttenlocher and Smiley 1987; Macnamara 1982; Nelson 1973; Saah, Waxman, and Johnson 1996). This consistency in the timing and the composition of the early lexicon suggests that there are also strong factors within the child that support the acquisition of object categories and their names (Newport 1991; Gentner 1982; Waxman and Markow 1995).

**Mapping Problem**    Perhaps the most compelling evidence of the child's contribution to acquisition comes from an analysis of the "mapping problem" (Gleitman and Wanner 1982). Consider, once again, the infant who hears "Ila' a' tzimin~che' je'lo'" as a tapir disappears behind a knoll. If the dubbing ceremony is to be informative at all, the infant must solve a difficult three-part task. First, the infant must parse the relevant word (*tzimin~che* or *tapir*) from the continuous speech stream; second, the infant must identify the relevant entity(ies) (the tapir) in the scenario; third, the infant must establish a <u>word-to-object</u> mapping between the two. In essence infants must discover the relevant linguistic units, the relevant conceptual units, and the precise mappings between them.

It is remarkable that by 12 months of age, infants are able to accomplish this task, keeping track of numerous new words and mapping them correctly to the objects upon which they were introduced. (See Carey 1978; Dromi 1987; Goldfield and Reznick 1990; Heibeck and Markman

1987; Waxman and Hall 1993; Woodward, Markman, and Fitzsimmons 1994 for discussions of fast mapping and the rapid acquisition of a lexicon.) But even more remarkable is the fact that infants, like adults, readily and spontaneously extend words beyond the instances upon which they were taught, and that they do so in a systematic and principled fashion.

**From Word-to-Object to Word-to-Object Category Mappings**    When a child applies the name *tapir* to a new and (as yet) unlabeled object, that child has made an inference regarding the extension of that name to other novel objects.[2] Such spontaneous and principled extensions indicate that infants go well beyond word-to-object mappings to establish word-to-object category mappings. This is an impressive feat, particularly because there is a crucial distinction between an individual object and an object category. An individual object is a perceptually salient entity that can be partitioned amid the ongoing stream of activity. This perceptual salience of objects is likely a factor in infants' rapid acquisition of names for individual objects (as compared to words for actions and other relations; Gentner 1982). But this observation about individual objects cannot account for the acquisition of names for object categories. This is because an object category, unlike an individual object, is not a perceptually salient whole. On the contrary, members of object categories are distinct, and often disparate, individuals that tend to appear at different times and places. Moreover, it would be logically impossible for caretakers to assemble together all members of an object category to model explicitly the extension of the category name. Therefore, infants' spontaneous and principled extension of a novel word to an object category must reflect, in large part, their implicit expectations regarding a relation between object naming and categorization.

**Induction Problem: Extension, Intension, and Indeterminacy of Meaning**
This discussion exposes an essential dialectic between extension (roughly, the entities included in a given category, or subsumed under a given category name) and intension (roughly, the meaning or concept underlying a category or its name). The extension of the concept or word *tapir* includes all members of the concept *tapir* and excludes all other individ-

uals; the intension of the concept or word *tapir* incorporates the criteria for inclusion in the lexical or conceptual category. But neither intension nor extension is revealed explicitly in the dubbing ceremony or in any other overt act of naming. Such acts do nothing more than indicate, via ostension, a name for an individual object. How then does the child discover the proper extension or intension for a novel word?

We know that the perceptual and conceptual repertoires of infants and young children permit them to appreciate many different kinds of properties of objects and relations among them. In principle, infants' rich and flexible repertoires should complicate the task of mapping a word to its meaning. How do infants select among the various kinds of properties and relations when seeking to determine the intension and extension of a word? How do they so rapidly learn that a given word (e.g., *tapir*) will apply to a particular whole object and can be extended to other members of its kind (e.g., other tapirs; perhaps other quadrupeds), but not to salient parts or properties of the object (e.g., it's long snout or lackluster color), to salient actions in which it may be engaged (e.g., foraging in the ferns), or to other salient thematic or associative relations involving the named object? If infants had to rule out these (and countless other) candidate meanings, word learning would be a laborious task, and would likely proceed at a sluggish pace. Yet this description does not fit. Infants and toddlers acquire words, especially words for objects and object categories, at a remarkably brisk pace.

**Solving the Induction Problem: Contribution of the Child**    To reconcile the disparity between the logical difficulty of this task and infants' seemingly effortless solution, several scholars have proposed that infants are guided by certain constraints, or expectations, that lead them to favor some types of conceptual relations over others in mapping words to their meanings (Chomsky 1986; Landau and Gleitman 1985; Pinker 1984; Markman 1989; Waxman 1990 1991). There is now substantial evidence for this position. For example, infants and toddlers reveal a strong expectation that the *first* word applied to an object will refer to that whole object and will be extended to other members of the same object category (Markman and Wachtel 1988; Taylor and Gelman 1988; Hall, Waxman, and Hurwitz 1993; Markman 1989; Waxman and Hall 1993).

For the most part their extensions are roughly equivalent to basic level categories. To be sure, adults and other caretakers shape the extension and intension of children's categories an names. But in their first efforts, children typically map names to categories at a mid-level category (Mervis and Mervis 1988; Waxman and Senghas 1992). This suggests that there is a strong priority for establishing names for basic level kinds.

The bias to extend novel words to (roughly) basic level categories appears to reflect both the infants' appreciation of the perceptual and conceptual salience of groupings at the basic or folk-generic level, and the naming strategies of the adult community. (Recall that across languages, adults prefer to label objects at the basic level.) Thus the priority for establishing basic level names likely reflects a coordination between parental input and the child's interpretive biases in the acquisition of object categories and their names.

Moreover English-speaking children as young as two and a half years of age consistently use the grammatical form of a novel word as a clue to its meaning. For example, preschool-aged English speakers expect that count nouns will refer to objects and object categories (e.g., tapir, mammal, animal), that proper nouns will refer only to the named individual and not to other members of its kind (Hall 1991; 1994; Katz, Baker and Macnamara 1974; Gelman and Taylor 1984), and that adjectives (and other modifiers) will mark object properties or distinctions within a basic level kind (Markman and Hutchinson 1984; Taylor and Gelman 1988; Waxman 1990).

One important caveat bears mention: Children will use syntactic form as a cue to meaning only if they are already familiar with a basic level name for the object(s) under consideration (Au 1990; Au and Markman 1987; Hall 1991; Hall et al. 1993; Markman and Wachtel 1988; Taylor and Gelman 1988). When children hear a new word (be it a count noun, mass noun, proper noun, or adjective) applied to a familiar object (e.g., a horse), their interpretation varies appropriately as a function of its grammatical form, as described above. But when a new word is applied to an unfamiliar object (e.g., an armadillo), preschoolers reveal a strong tendency to interpret the novel word, independent of its grammatical form, as referring to the basic level object kind. Thus children's interpretation of a novel word applied ostensively to an object is mediated by their familiarity with a basic level name for that object. This is consistent with the claim that there is a strong *conceptual priority* for establishing names for basic level kinds. It supports the argument that basic level names provide principles of object individuation and object identity (Hall 1993; Hall and Waxman 1993; Macnamara 1982) and set the stage for the acquisition of higher- and lower-order category names.

In sum, evidence from several different laboratories using several different experimental techniques converges on a common conclusion: Children have implicit expectations regarding the relation between object naming and categorization. They focus their attention differently when an object is named than when it is not named. Moreover their expectations concerning the extensions of novel words are guided, at least in part, by grammatical form (Brown 1957).

These expectations or linkages between particular types of words (count nouns, proper nouns, adjectives) and particular types of conceptual relations (object categories, individual objects, object properties) are impressive. And they have often been invoked to help explain how children so rapidly map novel words to their meanings and so successfully construct hierarchical systems of knowledge. What is the empirical evidence for this view?

## 8.2   Relation between Object Categorization and Naming in Development: Empirical Evidence

This section illustrates, primarily with examples from my research program, the nature of the empirical evidence regarding the origin and emergence of a relation between object categorization and naming in the developing mind. I discuss three series of experiments, each of which draws on different experimental methods and different subject populations. Several common threads tie these experiments together. All of the experiments are essentially object categorization tasks, tailored to the particular population under investigation. In each experiment I observe the relation between object naming and categorization by comparing subjects' object categorization in "neutral" conditions involving no object names with their performance when they are introduced to names for the object categories under consideration. Performance in the neutral conditions permits an assessment of how readily infants and children establish categories at various levels within a hierarchy; performance in the naming context permits an assessment of the role of naming in this important endeavor.

In the first series of experiments, I describe some foundational research with preschool-aged children acquiring English as their native language. These experiments reveal that novel count nouns support the establishment of object categories at the basic and superordinate levels, and that novel adjectives support the establishment of object categories at the more specific subordinate levels.

## Constructive Influence of Naming: Evidence from English-speaking Preschoolers

In an early study R. Gelman and I took as our starting point the well-documented finding that young children succeed in categorizing objects at the basic level before they do so at nonbasic levels. We were especially intrigued at their difficulty in forming superordinate level categories. According to most traditional developmental accounts (e.g., Inhelder and Piaget 1964; Bruner, Goodnow, and Austin 1956; Vygotsky 1962), this was interpreted as evidence of young children's general inability to appreciate abstract relations. However, a more thorough consideration of preschoolers' behavior casts doubt on this strong conclusion.

Consider children's behavior in naming. It is not uncommon for a toddler to overextend the word *doggie* to refer to a horse, or for a preschooler to overextend the word *squirrel* to refer to a lemur. These overextensions, which permit the child to remark on an object for which they do not have an existing name, are revealing because they often respect the boundaries of object categories at a superordinate level. More recent evidence, gleaned from directed interviews as well as from object categorization tasks, offers direct support for the intuition that preschoolers do appreciate such abstract distinctions as that between animate and inanimate objects (R. Gelman 1990; S. Gelman 1988; Keil 1989; Mandler 1993). This suggests that although preschoolers appreciate nonbasic level object categories, they have difficulty recruiting this knowledge in the standard classification tasks.

To test this hypothesis, we designed a highly structured classification task (Waxman and Gelman 1986) in which an experimenter introduced preschool children to some "very picky" puppets who "only wanted a certain kind of thing." To indicate the type of thing that each puppet wanted, the experimenter displayed three typical instances (e.g., a dog, a horse, a duck) of a superordinate level category (e.g., animal), and then asked children to sort additional items for each puppet. To examine the influence of novel words, we compared performance in a Novel Noun and No Word (control) condition. Children in the No Word condition were introduced to the instances and were told, "Look at these." Children in the Novel Noun condition were introduced to the same instances but were told, "These are *dobutsus*."

Despite the fact that this task was so highly structured, children in the No Word condition still had difficulty forming superordinate level categories. This result is consistent with the traditional accounts of preschoolers' conceptual difficulties forming object categories at the superordinate level (Inhelder and Piaget 1964; Rosch et al. 1976). In sharp contrast, children in the Novel Noun condition were extremely successful. They classified objects consistently into superordinate level categories. In fact children in the Novel Noun condition were as successful as another group of children who had been provided with the familiar English superordinate labels for the classes (e.g., "These are *animals*").

Thus providing a name (even a novel one) effectively oriented preschool children toward commonalities among the objects and licensed the induction of superordinate level categories. Markman and Hutchinson (1984) have reported a similar pattern of findings, indicating that novel count nouns also augmented basic level object categorization in preschool-aged children. These findings indicate that preschoolers do indeed appreciate superordinate level object categories, but that superordinate relations are heightened in the context of learning a novel word (Waxman 1994).

In a subsequent series of experiments, I examined the *specificity* of this linkage between object categorization and naming. First, we asked whether novel count nouns draw attention to object categories at all hierarchical levels. Second, we asked whether object categorization is

**HIERARCHICAL LEVEL**

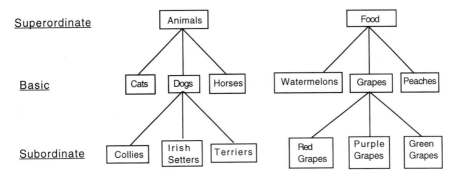

**Figure 8.1**
Representation of an object hierarchy

facilitated by novel words in general, or whether this focus is specific to learning novel nouns.

To address these questions, we systematically compared the effect of introducing novel words in a multiple-level classification task (Waxman 1990). Children were asked to sort pictures of objects at three different hierarchical levels (subordinate, basic and superordinate) within two different natural kind hierarchies (animals and food). See figure 8.1. As in the previous experiment (Waxman and Gelman 1986), the experimenter introduced three "very picky" puppets along with three typical members of each category. Children in the No Word condition sorted with no further instructions. To examine the influence of naming on object categorization, children in the Novel Noun condition heard a novel noun in conjunction with the photographs from each category (e.g., "These are the *dobus*"). To examine the specificity of these naming effects, we also examined the influence of introducing novel adjectives. Children in the Novel Adjective condition heard novel words that were presented in syntactic frames appropriate for adjectives (e.g., "These are the *dob-ish ones*").

The results of this experiment revealed (1) the facility with which children form basic level categories, (2) the important role of naming in the formation of nonbasic level object categories, and (3) the specificity of children's expectations about the relation between object categorization and naming. Children in all three conditions formed the basic level categories successfully. At nonbasic levels, performance varied as a function of condition, and the influence of novel words on object categorization became apparent. The children were highly sensitive to the linguistic form in which a novel word is introduced. Novel nouns facilitated categorization at the superordinate, but not the subordinate, level. This pattern was completely reversed for children hearing novel adjectives. Unlike nouns, novel adjectives facilitated categorization at the subordinate, but not superordinate, level.

Preschool-aged children thus have both the *linguistic* capacity to distinguish among the relevant syntactic forms (count noun vs. adjective) and the *conceptual* or *perceptual* ability to appreciate both superordinate and subordinate level relations object categories. Further they have a tacit expectation that these linguistic and conceptual abilities are interwoven. They expect that novel count nouns will refer to object categories at the superordinate level and that novel adjectival phrases will refer to object categories at subordinate levels.

This clear pattern bears a striking resemblance to the systematic relation between object classification and naming that has been documented in the ethnobiological record (Berlin, 1992). In fact the convergences between the developmental and ethnobiological work suggest at least one way in which the labelling practices of the adult community will shape the semantic and conceptual categories formed by children: particular linguistic forms (count nouns vs. adjectives) will focus children's attention on object categories at particular hierarchical levels (superordinate vs. subordinate).

However, neither the ethnobiological nor the developmental research described thus far can reveal the origins, emergence, and universality of these linkages between object naming and categorization. Because the developmental evidence is derived almost exclusively from preschool-aged children, and because these individuals have already made significant linguistic and conceptual advances, it is unclear how and when these precise linkages between object naming and categorization emerge in the developing child. (See Nelson 1988 for an extended discussion of this point.) Therefore, to ascertain which linkages (if any) guide acquisition from the outset, and how these are shaped by experience, it is important to examine infants on the threshold of language acquisition. Second, because very little work in ethnobiology has involved children (but see Dougherty 1979 and Stross 1973 for two noteworthy exceptions), and very little work in developmental psychology has involved children acquiring languages other than English, the extant evidence is based almost exclusively on children acquiring English. This is a serious limitation. It is therefore unclear which (if any) of these linkages are universal features of human development, which are specific to the English language, and how these linkages are shaped by language-specific learning. It is crucial that we examine children acquiring languages other than English. A developmental, cross-linguistic program will permit us to trace the origins of this phenomenon and to examine the constructive role of the native language under acquisition.

## Developmental, Crosslinguistic Proposal

### A précis of the Crosslinguistic and Developmental Literatures    A review of the crosslinguistic and developmental literatures offered some signposts for our investigations. Briefly stated, this review suggested that the expectation linking count nouns and object categories was stable across languages and across development. There are universal features inherent in the design of language that appear to support this expectation. The grammatical category <u>noun</u> is unique for its stability across languages and across development. All known human languages have fully developed grammatical category <u>noun</u>, and across languages, this grammatical category includes the names for object categories (Dixon 1982; Gentner 1981; 1982; Greenberg 1963; Macnamara 1982; Maratsos 1991; Wierzbicka 1986; Gleitman 1990; Jackendoff 1990). There is also developmental stability for this grammatical category. Infants appear to have a special talent for mapping words to object categories, particularly those at the basic level. As a result names for object categories tend to be the most prevalent form in the early lexicon (Au et al. 1994; Gentner 1982; Saah et al. 1996; but see Bloom, Tinker and Margulis 1993; Gopnik and Choi 1991 and Tardif 1996 for a different view). In addition the mappings between count nouns and object categories can be established independently of the other grammatical categories. Other grammatical

categories (e.g., adjectives, verbs) appear to be semantically, morphologically, and syntactically dependent on nouns (Fisher 1996; Gleitman 1990; Hall et al. 1993; Maratsos 1991; Waxman and Markow, 1996).

In contrast to this stability of the grammatical category *noun*, there is substantially more variation across languages and across development associated with the grammatical category *adjective* (Bowerman 1985; Choi and Bowerman 1991; Gentner 1981; 1982; Maratsos 1991; Maratsos and Chalkley 1980; Talmy 1985; Wierzbicka 1986). Languages vary in the extent to which a grammatical category adjective is developed. Although many languages (like English) have a richly developed open-class adjective system, other languages have only a sparse set of adjectives. For example, most Bantu languages include between 10 and 50 adjectives. This is related to the crosslinguistic variability associated with this grammatical form. The meanings conveyed with an adjective in one language may be conveyed with a different grammatical form in another. There is also developmental variation in the adjective system. Adjectives tend to be acquired later than nouns (Bloom et al. 1993; Fenson et al. 1994; Gentner 1982; Waxman and Markow 1996). Early in acquisition, children tend to interpret adjectives (erroneously) as referring to object categories. For example, anecdotal evidence suggests that infants extend novel adjectives (e.g., "hot!") as referring to an object or object category (e.g., cup or stove) rather than to a salient property of the named object (e.g., its temperature). Observations like these are consistent with experimental evidence. There is a systematic bias to interpret the first word applied to an object as referring to the object category rather than to an object property (Hall et al. 1993; Waxman and Markow, 1996).

**A Developmental, Crosslinguistic Proposal** The developmental and crosslinguistic evidence suggests that all children, independent of the language under acquisition, will find support for an expectation that a novel noun (applied to an object) will refer to that object and will be extended to other members of its kind. As a result the expectation that count nouns refer to object categories is likely to play an instrumental role across development and across languages (Gleitman 1990; Maratsos 1991; Pinker 1994; Waxman 1994; Waxman and Markow 1996). In contrast, the crosslinguistic variability associated with the adjective system suggests that the mappings between adjectives and their associated meanings will neither be uniform across development nor across languages. Instead, the specific expectations regarding the types of meaning associated with adjectives should emerge later in development, should rely on an existing base of linguistic and conceptual knowledge, and should vary according to the particulars of the language under acquisition (Dixon 1982; Waxman and Markow 1998; Wierzbicka 1986).

Based on these patterns, I have proposed that (1) infants commence the process of acquisition equipped with an initially general expectation linking words to object categories, and (2) more finely tuned expectations linking specific linguistic forms (e.g., count nouns, proper nouns, adjectives) with specific types of meaning (e.g., object categories, individual objects, object properties, respectively) will emerge later, shaped by the infant's language-specific experience (Waxman 1994; Waxman and Markow 1995; Waxman, Senghas et al. 1997). One strength of this proposal is that an initially general expectation guides infants in their first efforts to map words to their meanings, supporting the ability to establish reference and setting the stage for the more specific linkages. Another strength is that it accommodates the fact that infants will acquire the particular syntactic distinctions drawn in their native language and will learn the range of meanings associated with each grammatical form. Finally this proposal embraces at once the notion of constraints within the child and learning on the basis of experience.

## 8.3    Empirical Evidence for the Proposal

### Characterizing the Initial Expectations: Evidence from Infants Acquiring English

According to the proposal, infants on the brink of language acquisition should reveal evidence of an initial, general expectation that novel words (both count nouns and adjectives), applied to individual objects, will refer to object categories. To test this proposal, we therefore designed a procedure for infants (ranging from 12 to 14 months of age) who were just beginning to produce their first words (Waxman and Markow 1995).

To discover whether infants at this early point in acquisition would be guided by a general expectation that words refer to object categories, we adapted an object manipulation task, analogous to the more standard novelty-preference paradigms used in infancy research (see Waxman and Markow 1995 for a complete description of the method and results). The task involved two phases. See figure 8.2. In the *familiarization* phase an experimenter offered an infant four different toys from a given category (e.g., four different animals), one at a time in random order. This was immediately followed by a *test phase* in which the experimenter presented both a new member of the given category (e.g., another animal) and an object from a novel contrasting category (e.g., a fruit). Each infant completed the task with four different sets of objects: two involved categorization at the basic level (e.g., cars vs. airplanes; horses vs. cats) and two involved categorization at the superordinate level (e.g., animals vs. fruit; tools vs. vehicles). Infants manipulated the toys freely during this procedure, and their manipulation served as the dependent measure in our analyses.

If the infant detects the commonality or shared category relation among the objects presented during the familiarization phase, then the infant's attention during this phase will wane. At test, when two objects are presented simultaneously, if the infant notices that one object is a member of the now-familiar category, attention to that object should remain relatively low. In contrast, if the infant notices that one object is from a novel category, then attention to that object should be relatively high. Therefore, if an infant has formed an object category, that infant should reveal a decrease in attention during the familiarization phase, and a preference for the novel object at test.

To test the proposed influence of novel words on object categorization, we randomly assigned infants to one of three conditions, which differed only in the experimenter's comments about the objects presented during the *familiarization phase*. In the No Word condition (control), she said, "See here?" as she introduced the objects; in the Novel Noun condition, she said, "See the *daxin*?"; In the Novel Adjective condition, she said, "See the *dax-ish* one?" In the test phase, infants in all conditions heard precisely the same phrase ("See what I have?").

## Familiarization Phase

Familiarization Trial 1
(Animal vs. Fruit)

NOUN: "See the <u>fauna</u>?"
ADJECTIVE: "See the <u>faunish one</u>?"
NO WORD: "See <u>here</u>?"

Familiarization Trial 2
(Animal vs. Fruit)

NOUN: "See the <u>fauna</u>?"
ADJECTIVE: "See the <u>faunish one</u>?"
NO WORD: "See <u>here</u>?"

Familiarization Trial 3
(Animal vs. Fruit)

"See what I have"

Familiarization Trial 4
(Animal vs. Fruit)

NOUN: "See the <u>fauna</u>?"
ADJECTIVE: "See the <u>faunish one</u>?"
NO WORD: "See <u>here</u>?"

## Test Phase

Test Trial
(Animal vs. Fruit)

"See what I have?"

Figure 8.2
Design of experiment from Waxman and Markow (1995)

If infants begin the process of lexical acquisition with no expectations regarding the extension of object names to object categories, then novel words should exert no influence on categorization: performance in all three conditions should be comparable. However, if novel words direct infants' attention to object categories, then infants who hear novel words in conjunction with the objects presented during familiarization should be more likely than those in the No Word condition to form object categories. Including both a Novel Noun and Novel Adjective condition permits us to test the specificity of this initial expectation. If, as I have proposed, the expectation is general, then infants in both the Noun and Adjective conditions should be more likely to form object categories than should those in the No Word control condition.

The data were entirely consistent with this proposal. Infants hearing novel words were more likely to form object categories than were their age-mates in the No Word control condition. Consider first the results from the *familiarization phase* (figure 8.3). On basic level trials, infants in all three conditions exhibited a significant decrease in attention. On superordinate level trials, the facilitative effect of the novel words became apparent: infants in the Novel Noun and Novel Adjective conditions showed a decrease in attention. Only infants in the No Word condition failed to exhibit such a trend. In the test phase (figure 8.4), the influence of novel words on object categorization was also evident. On basic level trials, infants in both the Novel Noun and Novel Adjective conditions showed reliable preference for the novel object. Infants in the No Word condition showed only a weak novelty preference. At the superordinate level, infants in the Novel Noun condition revealed a clear novelty preference, while those in the Novel Adjective condition revealed a trend in this direction. In contrast, infants in the No Word condition revealed no preference for the novel test object. To amplify these results, which are based on summaries over groups of subjects, we also examined the patterns displayed by each individual subject included in the experiment. We found that this phenomenon held up consistently across subjects.

In a series of subsequent experiments, we have begun to examine the influence of novel words on object categorization in infants as young as 9 months of age (Balaban and Waxman 1996; Waxman and Balaban 1996). In a procedure very much like the one described above, we find

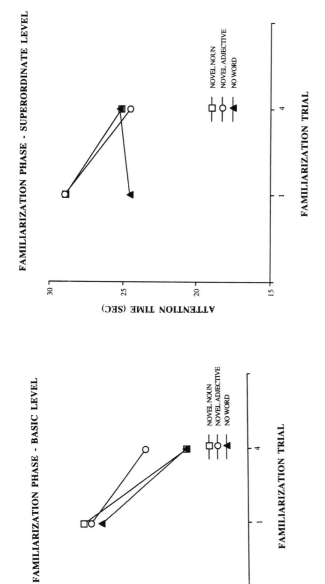

**Figure 8.3**
Familiarization phase from Waxman and Markow (1995)

**TEST TRIALS**

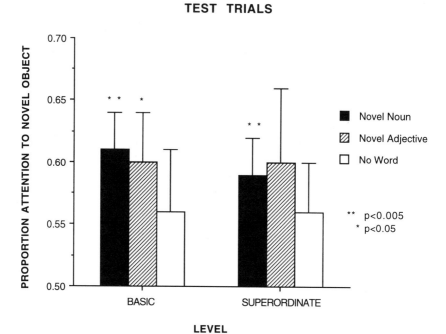

Figure 8.4
Test phase from Waxman and Markow (1995)

that novel nouns facilitate the formation of object categories at the basic and superordinate level, relative to performance in a No Word control condition. And in another series of experiments, using a forced-choice procedure, we have demonstrated that novel nouns focus attention on object categories for infants ranging from 16 to 30 months of age as well (Waxman and Hall 1993; Waxman, Stote and Philippe 1996).

In sum, the data from these experiments reveal that infants on the threshold of producing language harbor a broad, initial expectation that words (presented either as nouns or as adjectives) applied to objects will refer to those individual objects and will be extended to refer to other members of the same category. This developmental pattern illustrates three complementary points.

First, these results are relevant to the question concerning the early acquisition of basic level categories. Recall that at 12 months infants in all conditions formed basic level categories successfully. That is, novel words did not influence performance at this level. In contrast, novel words exerted a clear facilitative effect on object categorization at the more abstract superordinate levels. This result suggests that object names serve as a catalyst for object categorization, particularly when the perceptual or conceptual support for a category is not as compelling as at the basic level. This is consistent with the prevalent psychological and anthropological notion that basic level categories are especially salient groupings, for infants and adults alike.

Second, these results support the proposal that acquisition is guided by an initial, general expectation on the part of the learner. It is unlikely that this initial expectation could have been learned or induced by the infant on the basis of observations of their existing word-meaning mappings (as suggested by Nelson 1988), for very few such mappings (if any) have been established by 9 months of age. From the outset, then, novel words direct infants' attention to object categories. The power of the dubbing ceremony derives, in large part, from the infants' a priori expectation that novel words, applied to individual objects, will refer to those objects and to other members of the same category. This initial rudimentary linkage between words and object categories serves a crucial function: it guides infants in their earliest efforts to map words to categories of objects, and it sets the stage for the emergence of a more specific set of expectations regarding particular types of words (e.g., nouns, adjectives, verbs) and particular types of conceptual relations (e.g., object categories, object properties, events).

Third, these findings with infants reveal a substantial role for learning and experience. For although infants treat novel words presented as nouns or adjectives identically with respect to object categorization, by two and a half years of age, this pattern changes. Toddlers and preschoolers acquiring English distinguish novel nouns from adjectives, and assign each particular types of meanings (e.g., Taylor and Gelman 1988; Waxman 1990). Clearly, then, between infancy and the preschool years, there is a burgeoning sensitivity to using linguistic form as a cue to word meaning. The more specific expectations linking novel adjectives to their associated meanings appear to emerge later, once the process of lexical acquisition is underway.

## Modification of Initial Expectations: Evidence from Toddlers Acquiring English

To begin to understand how the infants' initial broad expectation becomes fine-tuned over the course of development, we have initiated a series of cross-sectional experiments to determine when, and under what circumstances, English-speaking subjects develop the more specific expectation that count nouns, but not adjectives, refer to object categories. I selected a group of 21- and 30-month-olds, suspecting that both their lexical and syntactic advances would permit them to tease apart the distinction between words presented as nouns and adjectives. We predicted that during this developmental period, count nouns would continue to promote object categorization, but that novel adjectives would no longer be expected to serve this function. And we expected that this distinction between novel nouns and adjectives vis-à-vis object categorization would be more apparent with familiar than with unfamiliar objects.

My colleagues and I tested this hypothesis using a forced-choice task in which an experimenter presented subjects with a target object (e.g., a horse) and two alternatives—one from the same object category as the target (e.g., another horse) and other from a contrasting object category (e.g., a bear; Waxman, Stote, and Philippe 1996). Each subject completed this task on eight different sets of objects, four involving categorization at the basic level and four involving categorization at the superordinate level. At each level two sets included familiar objects, and two included unfamiliar objects (for which the children had no existing category name).

We compared toddlers' performance in a Novel Noun, Novel Adjective, and No Word condition. In the Novel Noun condition, the experimenter introduced the target saying, "This one is a *daxin*." She introduced the choices, saying, "Can you find another *daxin*?" In the Novel Adjective condition, she said, "This one is *dakish*. Can you find another *dakish* one?" In the No Word condition, she said, "Look at this one. Can you find another one?"

Our results indicated that the specific expectation that novel nouns (but not adjectives) refer to categories of objects begins to emerge at about 21 months of age in children acquiring English and becomes more entrained with age. At both 21 and 30 months, subjects in the Novel

Noun condition were more likely than those in either the Novel Adjective or No Word conditions to consistently select the alternative from the same object category as the target. This provides the earliest documentation to date of infants' emerging ability to distinguish the grammatical category *noun* from *adjective*, and to assign each distinct types of meaning. (See Bowerman 1996a, and Waxman and Markow 1996 for evidence of other related semantic-syntactic distinctions that emerge at this developmental moment.)

In sum, this developmental program of research begins to document the manner in which an initial and general linkage between words and object categories can give way to a more specific set of expectations regarding the particular types of meaning associated with novel words from different syntactic categories in English. These experiments permit us to test the hypothesis that language-specific learning is essential in the modification of the initially broad expectation linking words and object categories. However, to fully understand whether and how these expectations are shaped by the structure of the language under acquisition, it is crucial that we examine children acquiring languages other than English. Therefore my colleagues and I have asked whether the linkages that we have observed in infants and children acquiring English are evident in children acquiring other languages as well.

### Constructive Role of Language: Cross-linguistic Evidence from Children Acquiring English, French, or Spanish

If the proposal that I have articulated is correct, then children's expectations regarding count nouns and object categories should be consistent across languages. In contrast, their expectations concerning the types of meaning associated with adjectives should vary as a function of the language under acquisition. To test this proposal, we have compared the influence of novel words presented as nouns or as adjectives on object categorization in young monolingual children acquiring either English, French (from Montreal, Canada) or Spanish (from Buenos Aires, Argentina) as their native language.

Although these three languages are closely related to one another, they provide an interesting set of cross-linguistic comparisons, primarily because of differences in the grammatical use and referential status associated with the grammatical category <u>adjective</u> (see Waxman, Senghas et al. 1997 for a more detailed account of this difference and for a more thorough discussion of the cross-linguistic studies). In Spanish, nouns are omitted when the grammatical subject of a sentence is evident from the context. To get a flavor of this phenomenon, consider a scenario in which there are several different baskets lying in a corner of a room. In English, speakers distinguish these linguistically by modifying a noun (or pronoun) with an adjective (e.g., "the *smooth* basket" or "the *smooth* one"). In Spanish, the head noun in the phrase is omitted, leaving the determiner and adjective (e.g., "el *suave*") alone to refer to the intended basket. This results in a determiner-adjective (det + A) construction. In Spanish, det + A constructions are ubiquitous. In fact, if the head noun is not dropped under such circumstances, the sentence is judged to be awkward or ungrammatical by native adult speakers. Det − A constrictions are spontaneously productive in Spanish-speaking children as young as two and a half years of age. Of course, det − A constructions are sometimes permissible in English and, to a somewhat greater degree, in French.[3] However, in both English and French, det − A constructions occur only under restricted sets of circumstances; the this form is <u>not</u> spontaneously productive.

Therefore, in Spanish (more than in English or French), adjectives often appear in a syntactic frame that is identical to that for count nouns. Moreover, in these det + A constructions, adjectives are extended to members of the object categories denoted by a named property. As a result in Spanish there is considerable overlap in the syntactic privileges of occurrence and the extensions associated with count nouns and adjectives applied ostensively to objects.

We suspected that this difference might have consequences for children's interpretations of novel words applied to objects. In particular, we hypothesized that experience with these different native languages would lead to different outcomes in the expectations concerning the range of meanings associated with the grammatical form *adjective*. If this is the case children acquiring French (like those acquiring English) should learn that adjectives do not, as a rule, refer to object kinds. However, children acquiring Spanish should learn to use adjectives in a way that English- and French-speakers do not. In Spanish, where both nouns and adjectives are permitted to convey information concerning object categories, children may learn that novel adjectives, like nouns, can be extended to refer to objects and categories of objects.

To test these predictions, we designed a five-item forced-choice procedure. We focused exclusively on the influence of introducing novel nouns and novel adjectives on children's tendency to form object categories at the superordinate level. We used essentially the same methodology for children acquiring English, French, and Spanish, but we modified the materials slightly in two ways. First, we selected objects that would be familiar to children growing up in each of the three locales. For example, we found that squirrels were familiar to children growing up in Boston, Chicago, and Montreal but not to those from Buenos Aires. Second, we selected objects that would permit us to assess the role of grammatical gender in French- and Spanish-speakers' performance. Briefly stated, there was no evidence that children's choices were influenced by grammatical gender.

In each experiment a child sat individually with an experimenter to "read" through a picture book that we had created. On each page there were five different pictures, including a target object (e.g., a cow), two objects from the same superordinate category as the target (e.g., a fox and a zebra), and two objects that were thematically related to the target (e.g., a barn and milk). Children participated in one of three conditions, which differed only in the way the experimenter introduced the target object. In the Novel Noun condition, she said, for example, "See this 'fopin'? Can you find another 'fopin'?" In the Novel Adjective condition, she said, for example, "See this 'fopish' one? Can you show me another one that is 'fopish'?" In the No Word (control) condition, the experimenter pointed to the target and said, "See this? Can you find another one?" The child and experimenter went through the book two times. On the second reading, the experimenter reminded the children of their first choices and asked them to select another from the remaining (3) alternatives.

The results of these experiments were consistent with the previously presented proposal. See figure 8.5. Performance in the Novel Noun condition was uniform across all three languages. Children hearing a target labeled with a novel noun revealed a strong inclination to select the

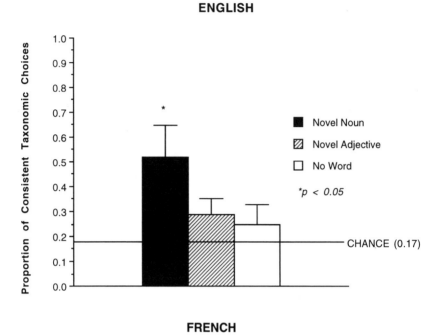

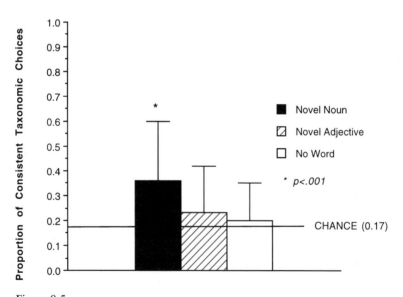

**Figure 8.5**
Proportion of consistently taxonomic selections is performance in (5a) English, (5b) French, and (5c) Spanish. From Waxman, Senghas, and Benveniste (1996)

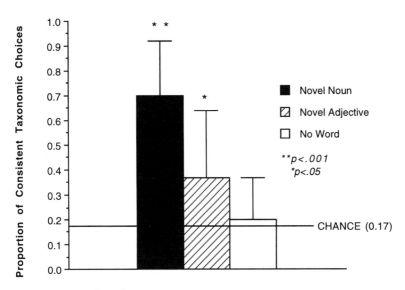

**SPANISH**

Figure 8.5 (continued)

alternatives that were from the same object category as the target. Performance in the No Word condition was also uniform across languages. Children in this control condition revealed no preference for either the taxonomic or thematic alternatives.

However, performance in the Novel Adjective condition varied systematically as a function of the language under acquisition. Children acquiring French (like those acquiring English) performed at chance in the Novel Adjective condition, revealing no preference for either the taxonomic or thematic alternatives. This indicates that they had learned that adjectives do not, as a rule, refer to object kinds. In contrast, Spanish-speaking children displayed a strong inclination to extend novel adjectives (like a novel nouns) to other members of the same superordinate level object category. This inclination to extend novel adjectives to object categories was apparent whether the novel adjectives were presented within det + A phrases or whether they were presented in conjunction with an overt noun or pronoun. This pattern of performance, which we have now replicated in four different studies, suggests that

Spanish-speaking children have learned that both count nouns and adjectives, applied ostensively to an individual object, can be extended to other members of a superordinate level object category.

**Integrating the Developmental and Cross-linguistic Evidence**    Together, the developmental and cross-linguistic findings support the proposal that (1) early conceptual and language development unfold under the guidance of an initial set of broad constraints or expectations that are inherent in the child, (2) these initial constraints are themselves modified as a result of experience with both the range of objects and the structure of the native language that the infant encounters, and (3) throughout the course of development, there are strong but implicit linkages between object categorization and naming, and these foster the establishment of increasingly sophisticated hierarchical systems of knowledge.

Let us consider each aspect of this proposal in turn. First, our results support the argument that infants begin the process of lexical acquisition with an initially general expectation linking words to objects and categories. The fact this expectation is evident at 9 and 12 months of age reveals that it is available to guide infants in their early efforts to map words to their meanings (Balaban and Waxman 1996; Waxman and Markow 1995; Waxman and Hall 1993). This challenges directly the claim that this linkage is unavailable at the onset of lexical acquisition, that it is learned or constructed as a consequence or by-product of word learning (Bloom et al. 1993; Nelson 1988; Smith 1995). In addition the fact that this expectation is initially general (evident with novel words presented either as nouns or as adjectives) is consistent with developmental work. At 12 months of age, infants have probably not yet identified the relevant surface cues to permit them to distinguish among the particular grammatical categories (e.g., nouns, adjectives) as they are presented in the stream of language. Our results are also consistent with the crosslinguistic fact that languages converge in the mappings between nouns and categories of objects.

In fact it may be to infants' advantage to begin with an initially general expectation—an expectation that will guide them in establishing early word-meaning mappings and that can then be tailored to suit the particular variations encountered in their native language. In other words, this account is flexible enough to accommodate the fact that infants naturally acquire languages that differ among themselves in the ways in which they recruit particular grammatical categories to convey particular types of meaning.

The second aspect of our proposal focused on the manner in which this broad initial expectation would be modified or refined. We argued that the more specific linkages between particular types of words (e.g., nouns, adjectives) and particular types of meaning (e.g., object categories, object properties) would emerge as a function of infants' experience with the particular grammatical distinctions drawn in their language and their familiarity with labels for object kinds. The evidence is consistent with this position. We proposed that the linkage between count nouns and object categories would be uniform across development and across languages. Consistent with this proposal, we discovered that the expectation that a novel word (presented as a count noun and applied to an individual object) will be extended to include that object and other members of its superordinate level kind was evident in French- and Spanish-speaking children, just as it has been evident in English-speaking children (Markman and Hutchinson 1984; Waxman 1990; Waxman and Kosowski 1990) and in infants in an English-speaking environment (Waxman and Balaban 1992; Waxman and Hall 1993; Waxman and Markow 1995). There is consistency across development and across languages in children's expectations concerning the type of meaning associated with novel count nouns.

We also suggested that the more specific mappings between adjectives and their associated meanings would emerge later in development and would vary according to the structure of the native language under acquisition. Consistent with this proposal, we discovered children's expectations concerning the meaning associated with novel adjectives did change over early development (Waxman and Markow 1995; Waxman et al., 1996) and did vary across languages (Waxman et al. 1997). There is variation across development and across languages in children's expectations concerning the range of meanings associated with novel adjectives. Infants' initial expectations are subsequently shaped by the structure of the native language under acquisition and become more entrained with age.

The third aspect of our proposal asserts that throughout the course of development, linkages between object categorization and object naming will foster the establishment of increasingly sophisticated hierarchical systems of knowledge. The ethnobiological evidence suggested that across the world's languages, adults tend to label basic and superordinate level object categories with count nouns, and subordinate level object categories with modifier-noun phrases. The developmental data suggested that infants universally expect that count nouns, applied to individual objects, will refer to that whole object and to other members of the same basic or superordinate level object category. In addition, the developmental data indicate that once a basic level term has been acquired, infants interpret novel adjectives as referring to salient object properties, as opposed to object categories (Waxman and Markow 1996; Waxman et al. 1996). In this way adults' naming practices and infants' implicit expectations converge to support the establishment of rudimentary hierarchical systems.

Taken together, these developmental and crosslinguistic results advance substantially our theories of the acquisition. These results also illustrate the importance of considering carefully the interplay between constraints within the child and input from the language environment.

## 8.4    Further Considerations

### Cognitive Consequences of Naming

I have argued that object naming plays an instrumental and specific role in establishing object categories within a hierarchical or taxonomic system. However, there is another aspect of the relation between object names and categories that I have not addressed directly. This is the notion that deep intuitions—sometimes known as essentialist beliefs—are conferred in the act of naming. Because this is the case, naming promotes not only the formation of an object category but also promotes the inductive potential of that category. Essentialist beliefs appear to be especially strong for natural kind terms (Keil 1989; Kripke 1972; Putnam 1975), particularly those referring to basic level categories (S. Gelman 1988; Waxman et al. 1996).

**Words as Invitations to Form Categories**    These two important consequences of naming—that naming promotes the formation of object categories and that named categories serve as a powerful inductive base—have led me to argue that words serve as invitations to form categories (Waxman and Markow 1995). Words focus infants' attention on commonalities among objects, highlighting these especially in cases where the perceptual or conceptual similarities may not be as apparent as at the basic, or folk-generic, level. At superordinate levels, for example, the presence of a common word for a set of objects invites infants and children to assemble together objects that they might otherwise consider to be rather distinct entities. Naming, then, promotes comparison of objects in the child's mind (Gentner and Waxman 1994; Waxman and Markow 1996). This can have dramatic consequences, inviting the child to notice deeper and more subtle commonalities than those that served as the initial basis of the grouping. In this way, naming may itself help to advance the child beyond perceptible commonalities among objects, pointing them toward a richer appreciation of the deeper, nonperceptible commonalities that characterize human concepts (Gelman 1988; Gelman and Coley 1990; Gelman and Markman 1987; Shipley 1989).

I suspect that even at the basic level, where infants and children readily form object categories (even in the No Word conditions), naming will serve a crucial inductive role. Naming may engender a search for the nonobvious commonalities, and this may contribute to the acquisition of the elaborate information, richly interconnected theories, and inductive depth that are the hallmarks of this preferred level (Gentner and Waxman 1994; Keil 1987; Murphy and Medin 1985).

**Words as an Obstacle in Forming Categories**    The argument that words serve as an invitation to form categories helps to account for the rapid establishment of hierarchical systems and for the inductive strength of the object categories within these systems. At the same time, however, naming may serve as a conservative force with respect to object categorization.

If naming leads to a search for commonalities and coherence among category members, then it may be difficult to change or modify those object categories that have been named. There is some evidence for this conservative force in naming. Although novel nouns facilitate classifica-tion at the superordinate level, they put children at a disadvantage in classification at the subordinate level (Waxman 1990; Waxman, Shipley and Shepperson 1991). Children hearing novel nouns in the context of a classification task were less successful in forming subordinate level categories than were their peers hearing no novel words. Because the novel nouns drew children's attention toward the commonalities among objects at the basic level, they may have made children less likely to attend to the perceptible distinctions among subordinate level categories. From this observation, several points follow.

First, it may be difficult for children to partition an inductively rich named category. In particular, it may be difficult to partition basic level categories and to establish subordinate level categories as a basis for inductive inference. There are several indications that this may be the case. Although preschool-aged children notice the perceptual distinctions among subordinate level categories (e.g., terriers vs. collies; red grapes vs. green grapes; see Waxman 1990; Waxman et al. 1991), these perceptu-ally based groupings do not support induction. Instead, the basic level categories (e.g., dog or grape) tend to serve as the basis for children's inductive inferences. Preschool-aged children require additional concep-tual information about the subordinate level distinctions before they can use subordinate level categories as an inductive base (Waxman et al. 1997).

Another example of this conservative force comes from the observa-tion that named categories may be resistant to change. The named cate-gories tree and flower may serve as a case in point. Neither of these categories is actually a bona fide scientific category. But it is hard to convince people—especially people living in urban and suburban com-munities—that this is the case. For in addition to the perceptible com-monalities among members of each of these categories, I suspect that the prevalence of a common name ensures a continued commitment to con-struing each as a unified grouping in categorization and in induction.

### Mistaking the Map for the Territory: Issues of Measurement

At its best, research on folkbiology is a joint enterprise involving anthropology, cognitive and developmental psychology, linguistics, and philosophy. Each of these disciplines shares a commitment to understanding the same phenomenon, each brings a unique perspective to the issues. In addition to our common interests, researchers in these disciplines encounter common obstacles in interpreting the evidence before us. Because our subject matter cannot be observed directly, we must depend on overt behaviors (including e.g., object naming, object categorization, typicality judgments, induction tasks) to draw inferences about the underlying organization of object categories in the human mind. Although our research tools have become increasingly sophisticated and our hypotheses have become increasingly precise, the inferential nature of this joint endeavor remains a challenge.

When, and on what basis, can we credit subjects with an appreciation of a category or concept? This question has generated extensive debate. Generally, our decisions in such matters are based on subjects' overt behavior. For example, when a subject places objects together in a categorization task, or when a subject produces a common name for a group of different objects, we infer that the overt behavior reflects an appreciation of an underlying (covert) category. Notice that this logic applies to studies of infants as well as adults. At this stage in our interdisciplinary enterprise, many different kinds of measurements have been introduced, each of which enriches our approach to the task at hand. However, these various measures are all subject to many of the same critical interpretive problems.

**What Constitutes Empirical Evidence for a Category?**    First, when a subject fails to provide a common response to a given set of objects, this does not in itself warrant the conclusion that the subject fails to represent the category in question. For example, an adult may appreciate the category <u>animal</u> but may fail to provide a common behavioral response to all members of that category. She may produce one overt behavior (e.g., running rapidly, or producing an elevated galvanic skin response) in response to some members (e.g., a leopard and a spider), but not to others (e.g., a cow and a ladybug). Similarly an infant or young child may appreciate the category <u>animal</u> but fail to group them together on some behavioral task. The point here is that failure to provide a common response does not license the conclusion that the subject (be it an adult or a child) fails to represent the category in question.

Conversely, when a subject succeeds in producing a common response (e.g., uttering a label, producing a physical grouping of objects), this does not constitute evidence that the subject represents the underlying category in question. For example, a subject may produce a common response (rapid running or elevated galvanic skin response) to a leopard and to a city bus that is about to drive away.

Likewise evidence of identical performance (e.g., in object categorization, object naming, induction) within two different individuals or within two different populations (e.g., infants vs. adults in a given culture; Itzaj Maya vs. U.S. adults; bird experts vs. novices) does not constitute evidence that the underlying structure of knowledge is the same in each. For example, although 12-month-olds may be capable of grouping instances of the category <u>animal</u> in precisely the same ways as adults, the underlying knowledge associated with that grouping is surely more elaborate in the adult. And although third graders and biologists may identify some of the same individuals as members of the category <u>bird,</u> the underlying knowledge is surely more detailed in the mind of the biologist.

**Covert Categories**    Scholars from various disciplines have devoted considerable attention to studying the relation between object naming and categorization; most have converged on the idea that these capacities are inextricably linked in humans. Although it is not within the scope of this chapter to discuss this topic fully, it is important to point out some core interdisciplinary ideas that are relevant to issues of acquisition. One key idea that has been articulated within cognitive psychology and anthropology is the notion that performance on naming and categorization tasks provide converging measures of the same underlying conceptual structure (Medin et al. 1997; Rosch et al. 1976; Medin and Waxman 1998). But there is also evidence to suggest that these are not perfectly convergent.

Covert (or unnamed) categories serve as one especially intriguing example. If naming and categorization are perfectly converging measures, then there should be no cognitive difference between those categories that are named and those that remain unnamed. However, some have argued that only named categories have the status of a true category within a given culture (C. Brown 1977; Burling 1964; Hunn 1977). Others (Berlin 1978; Kay 1971; Taylor 1984) have asserted that this criterion is too restrictive, that "... although a name may be an unambiguous indicator of a category, the absence of a name does not necessarily imply the absence of a category" (Berlin 1978, p. 12).

To support this assertion that covert categories are not unrecognized, Berlin garnered additional evidence. For example, he argued that although there are no overt labels denoting the categories plant or animal in Tzeltal, there are other indexes that these categories are part of the conceptual repertoire of people in this Mayan language community. For example, all plants take the classifier *tehk*; all animals take the classifier *koht*. This type of evidence is persuasive, but it is not unimpeachable. There is no compelling reason to assume that a group of objects whose labels take a particular classifier term constitute the same sort of category as do a group of objects that share a common label. Lakoff (1988) provides a fascinating example. In Dyirbal (an aboriginal Australian language) the classifier *balan* accompanies the names referring to women, fire, scorpions, and other dangerous things. The mechanisms linking this diverse set of objects together must be quite different than those underlying taxonomic categories (e.g., plant, animal). As a consequence the argument that objects denoted by a common classifier term have the same conceptual status as those denoted by a common label seems to be a vulnerable one. This is an argument that is certainly worth testing.

Covert categories provide a fascinating example of problems with measurement and inference. Although covert categories have been discussed primarily in the anthropological literature, they have important implications in cognitive and developmental psychology as well. Of particular interest is the fact that early in lexical development, most nonbasic level categories remain unnamed (Anglin 1977; Brown 1957; Mervis and Crisafi 1982; Waxman and Hatch 1992). We have argued that there are many other behavioral indexes (e.g., semantic overextensions, novelty-preference tasks, semantic clustering techniques) that suggest that children's failure to label an object category does not necessarily constitute a failure to appreciate that category. However, it is very much an open question whether these (as yet) unnamed categories share the same status as labeled categories.

## 8.5  Conclusions

The recent renewal of interdisciplinary interest in the relation between naming and categorization provides us with exciting opportunities and difficult challenges. The most recent evidence comes from diverse populations; it is gathered using diverse research tools. One challenge is to integrate these diverse findings and to use them as a basis upon which to generate additional theoretical and empirical work. A related challenge is to avoid the more general debates of the past, in favor of articulating more precise hypotheses regarding the relation between language and categorization. The current mandate is not to decide whether language influences categorization or whether categorization influences language. Rather, it is to specify how, when, and under what specific circumstances language and categorization exert their influences in acquisition.

In this chapter, I have focused primarily on the role of specific linguistic forms (e.g., count nouns, adjectives) in the establishment of object categories at specific levels within a taxonomy (e.g., subordinate, basic, superordinate). I have argued that from the onset of acquisition, there are precise and powerful relations linking linguistic and conceptual development and that these support the establishment of hierarchical systems of knowledge. I have asserted that although it has been difficult to formalize our notions of the basic level, categories at this level form the core of object categorization. I have demonstrated that language plays a constructive role, particularly in the acquisition of nonbasic levels, and that count nouns and adjectives support the acquisition of categories at the superordinate and subordinate level, respectively.

The objects that an infant encounters may differ across cultures. There will be tapirs and kinkajous in the rain forest, and squirrels and bluejays in North American backyards. And the names for objects will differ across languages. But the fundamental process of mapping words to their meaning is similar across cultures and languages. Infants systematically and naturally extend words, applied to individual objects, to other members of an object category, and these named categories go on to support inference and induction. From infancy, then, the dubbing ceremony serves as a powerful catalyst in object naming, object categorization and object induction.

## Notes

1. I use underlining to refer to an object category and *italics* to refer to the category name.

2. Of course the young word learners' extensions do not always converge precisely with those of the adult community. For example, both over- and under-extensions are observed in child language (Merriman 1986; Mervis and Mervis 1982, 1988; Waxman and Senghas 1992). In overextensions, the infant extends a word more widely than in the adult language (e.g., an infant may use the word *doggie* to refer to most furry four-legged creatures); in underextensions, the infant is more restricted than the adult in extension (e.g., an infant may apply the word *doggie* to some instances of the adult category dog but not others). These extensions will be shaped over time as the infants' learn the range or boundaries of a name. Notice, however, that the very fact that infants readily extend words beyond the referents upon which they were taught is important, for to accomplish this task, infants must use some sense of the word's meaning or its intension.

3. I am excluding for present discussion, phrases that are interpretable with an elliptical context as well as those that become acceptable only when they are produced with contrastive stress. See Waxman et al. (1996) for a more thorough discussion.

## References

Anderson, E. N. 1967. *The Ethnoicthyology of the Hong Kong Boat People.* Unpublished PhD dissertation. University of California, Berkeley.

Anglin, J. M. 1977. *Word, Object, and Conceptual Development.* New York: Norton.

Armstrong, S. L., Gleitman, L. R., and H. Gleitman. 1983. What some concepts might not be. *Cognition* 13: 262–308.

Atran, S. 1990. *Cognitive Foundations of Natural History: Towards an Anthropology of Science.* Cambridge: Cambridge University Press.

Au, T. K. 1990. Children's use of information in word learning. *Journal of Child Language* 17: 393–416.

Au, T. K., M. Dapretto, and Y. K. Song. 1994. Input versus constraints: Early word acquisition in Korean and English. *Journal of Memory and Language* 33: 567–82.

Au, T. K., and E. M. Markman. 1987. Acquiring word meanings via linguistic contrast. *Cognitive Development* 2: 217–36.

Baillargeon, R. 1993. The object concept revisited: New directions in the investigation of infants' physical knowledge. In C. E. Granrud, ed., *Visual Perception and Cognition in Infancy*. Hillsdale, NJ: Lawrence Erlbaum, pp. 265–315.

Balaban, M. T., and S. R. Waxman. 1996. An examination of the factors underlying the facilitative effect of word phrases on object categorization in 9-month-old infants. In A. Stringfellow, D. Cahana-Amitay, E. Hughes, and A. Zukowski, eds., *Proceedings of the 20th Boston University Conference on Language Development*, vol. 1. Somerville, MA: Cascadilla Press, pp. 483–93.

Balaban, M. T., and S. R. Waxman. 1997. Do word labels facilitate categorization in 9-month-old infants? *Journal of Experimental Child Psychology* 64: 3–26.

Berlin, B. 1973. The relation of folk systematic to biological classification and nomenclature. *Annual Review of Systematic and Ecology* 4: 259–71.

Berlin, B. 1978. Ethnobiological classification. In E. Rosch and B. B. Lloyd, eds., *Cognition and Categorization*. Hillsdale, NJ: Lawrence Erlbaum, pp. 9–26.

Berlin, B. 1992. *Ethnobiological classification: Principles of categorization of plants and animals in traditional societies*. Princeton: Princeton University Press.

Berlin, B., D. E. Breedlove, and P. Raven. 1974. *Principles of Tzeltal Plant Classification*. New York: Academic Press.

Bloom, L., E. Tinker, and C. Margulis. 1993. The words children learn: Evidence against a noun bias in early vocabularies. *Cognitive Development* 8: 431–50.

Bowerman, M. 1985. What shapes children's grammars? In D. I. Slobin, ed., *The Crosslinguistic Study of Language Acquisition: Theoretical issues*, vol. 2 Hillsdale, NJ: Lawrence Erlbaum, pp. 1257–1319.

Bowerman, M. 1996a. Learning how to structure space for language: A crosslinguistic perspective. In P. Bloom, M. A. Peterson, L. Nadel, and M. F. Garrett, eds., *Language and Space: Language, Speech, and Communication*. Cambridge: MIT Press, pp. 385–436.

Bowerman, M. 1996b. The origins of children's spatial semantic categories: Cognitive versus linguistic determinants. In J. J. Gumperz and S. C. Levinson eds., *Rethinking Linguistic Relativity: Studies in the Social and Cultural Foundations of Language*, no. 17. Cambridge: Cambridge University Press, pp. 145–76.

Brown, C. H. 1977. Folk botanical life-forms: Their universality and growth. *American Anthropologist* 79: 317–432.

Brown, R. 1957. Linguistic determinism and the part of speech. *Journal of Abnormal and Social Psychology* 55: 1–5.

Brown, R. 1958. *Words and Things: An Introduction to Language*. New York: Macmillan.

Bruner, J. S., J. J. Goodnow, and G. A. Austin. 1956. *A Study of Thinking*. New York: Wiley.

Bulmer, R., and M. Tyler. 1968. Karam classification of frogs. *Journal of Polynesian Society* 77: 333–85.

Burling, R. 1964. Cognition and componential analysis: God's truth or hocuspocus? *American Anthropologist* 66: 20–28.

Carey, S. 1978. The child as word learner. In M. Halle, J. Bresnan, and G. A. Miller, eds., *Linguistic Theory and Psychological Reality*. Cambridge: MIT Press, pp. 264–93.

Chi, M. T. H. 1983. Knowledge-derived categorization in young children. In D. R. Rogers and J. A. Sloboda, eds., *The Acquisition of Symbolic Skill*. New York: Plenum Press, pp. 327–32.

Choi, S., and M. Bowerman. 1991. Learning to express motion events in English and Korean: The influence of language-specific lexicalization patterns. *Cognition* 41: 83–121.

Choi, S., and A. Gopnik. 1995. Early acquisition of verbs in Korean: A crosslinguistic study. *Journal of Child Language* 22: 497–529.

Chomsky, N. 1986. *Knowledge of Language: Its Nature, Origin, and Use*. Westport, CT: Praeger.

Cole, M., J. Gay, J. A. Glick, and D. W. Sharp. 1971. *The Cultural Context of Learning and Thinking*. New York: Basic Books.

Coley, J. D., D. L. Medin, and S. Atran. 1997. Does rank have its privilege: Inductive inferences within folkbiological taxonomies. *Cognition* 64: 73–112.

Dixon, R. M. W. 1982. *Where Have All the Adjectives Gone?* New York: Mouton.

Dougherty, J. W. D. 1979. Learning names for plants and plants for names. *Anthropological Linguistics* 21: 298–315.

Dromi, E. 1987. *Early Lexical Development*. Cambridge: Cambridge University Press.

Dupre, J. 1981. Natural kinds and biological taxa. *Philosophical Review* 90: 66–90.

Fenson, L., P. S. Dale, J. S. Reznick, E. Bates, D. J. Thal, and S. J. Pethick. 1994. Variability in early communicative development. *Monographs of the Society for Research in Child Development* 5: 1–185.

Fernald, A. 1992. Meaningful melodies in mothers' speech to infants. In H. Papousek, U. Jurgens, and M. Papousek, eds., *Nonverbal Vocal Communication: Comparative and Developmental Approaches. Studies in Emotion and Social Interaction*. New York: Cambridge University Press, pp. 262–82.

Fisher, C. 1996. Structural limits on verb mapping: The role of analogy in children's interpretations of sentences. *Cognitive Psychology* 31: 41–81.

Frake, C. O. 1962. The ethnographic study of cognitive systems. In T. Gladwin and W. C. Sturtevant, eds., *Anthropology and Human Behavior.* Washington, DC: Anthropological Society of Washington, pp. 72–85.

Gallistel, C. R., A. L. Brown, S. Carey, R. Gelman, and F. C. Keil. 1991. Lessons from animal learning for the study of cognitive development. In S. Carey and R. Gelman, eds., *The Epigenesis of Mind: Essays on Biology and Cognition. The Jean Piaget Symposium Series.* Hillsdale, NJ: Lawrence Erlbaum, pp. 3–36.

Gelman, R. 1990. First principles organize attention to and learning about relevant data: Number and the animate/inanimate distinction as examples. *Cognitive Science* 14: 79–106.

Gelman, R. 1991. Epigenetic foundations of knowledge structures: Initial and transcendent constructions. In S. Carey and R. Gelman, eds., *The Epigenesis of Mind: Essays on Biology and Cognition.* Hillsdale, NJ: Lawrence Erlbaum.

Gelman, R., and E. M. Williams. 1999. Enabling constraints for cognitive development and learning: A domain-specific epigenetic theory. In D. Kuhn and R. Siegler, eds., *Handbook of Child Psychology: Vol. 5. Cognition, perception and language, Vol. 2.*

Gelman, S. A. 1988. The development of induction within natural kind and artifact categories. *Cognitive Psychology* 20: 65–95.

Gelman, S. A., and J. D. Coley. 1990. The importance of knowing a dodo is a bird: Categories and inferences in 2-year-old children. *Developmental Psychology* 26: 796–804.

Gelman, S. A., and E. M. Markman. 1987. Young children's inductions from natural kinds: The role of categories and appearances. *Child Development* 58: 1532–41.

Gelman, S. A., and D. L. Medin. 1993. What's so essential about essentialism? A different perspective on the interaction of perception, language, and conceptual knowledge. *Cognitive Development* 8: 157–68.

Gelman, S. A., and M. Taylor. 1984. How two-year-old children interpret proper and common nouns for unfamiliar objects. *Child Development* 55: 1535–40.

Gentner, D. 1981. Some interesting differences between verbs and nouns. *Cognition and Brain Theory* 4: 161–78.

Gentner, D. 1982. Why nouns are learned before verbs: Linguistic relativity versus natural partitioning. In S. Kuczaj, ed., *Language development: Language, thought, and culture,* vol. 2. Hillsdale, NJ: Lawrence Erlbaum, pp. 301–34.

Gentner, D., and S. R. Waxman. 1994. *Perceptual and conceptual bootstrapping in early word meaning.* Paper presented at the International Conference on Infancy Studies, June, Paris, France.

Gleitman, L. R. 1990. The structural sources of word meaning. *Language Acquisition* 1: 3–55.

Gleitman, L. R., and E. Wanner. 1982. Language acquisition: The state of the state of art. In E. Wanner and L. Gleitman, eds., *Language acquisition: The state of the art.* Cambridge: Cambridge University Press, pp. 3–48.

Goldfield, B. A., and J. S. Reznick. 1990. Early lexical acquisition: Rate, content, and the vocabulary spurt. *Journal of Child Language* 17: 171–83.

Goldin-Meadow, S., M. E. Seligman, and R. Gelman. 1976. Language in the two-year-old. *Cognition* 4: 189–202.

Gopnik, A., and S. Choi. 1990. Do linguistic differences lead to cognitive differences? A cross-linguistic study of semantics and cognitive development. *First Language* 10: 199–215.

Greenberg, J. H. 1963. Some universals of grammar with particular reference to the order of meaningful elements. In J. H. Greenberg, ed., *Universals of Language.* Cambridge: MIT Press.

Hage, P., and W. R. Miller. 1976. 'Eagle' = 'bird': A note on the structure and evolution of Shoshoni ethnoornithological nomenclature. *American Ethnologist* 3: 481–88.

Hall, D. G. 1991. Acquiring proper nouns for familiar and unfamiliar animate objects: Two-year-olds' word learning biases. *Child Development* 62: 1142–54.

Hall, D. G. 1993. Basic-level individuals. *Cognition* 48: 199–221.

Hall, D. G. 1994. How children learn common nouns and proper names. In J. Macnamara and G. Reyes, eds., *The Logical Foundations of Cognition.* Oxford, England: Oxford University Press, pp. 212–40.

Hall, D. G., and S. R. Waxman. 1993. Assumptions about word meaning: Individual and basic-level kinds. *Child Development* 64: 1550–70.

Hall, D. G., S. R. Waxman, and W. R. Hurwitz. 1993. How 2- and 4-year-old children interpret adjectives and count nouns. *Child Development* 64: 1661–64.

Heibeck, T. H., and E. M. Markman. 1987. Word learning in children: An examination of fast mapping. *Child Development* 58: 1021–34.

Held, R., and A. Hein. 1963. Movement-produced stimulation in the development of visually guided behavior. *Journal of Comparative and Physiological Psychology* 56: 872–76.

Hunn, E. S. 1977. *Tzeltal Folk Zoology: The Classification of Discontinuities in Nature.* New York: Academic Press.

Huttenlocher, J., and P. Smiley. 1987. Early word meaning: The case of object names. *Cognitive Psychology* 19: 63–89.

Imai, M., and D. Gentner. 1993. What we think, what we mean, and how we say it: papers from the parasession on the correspondence of conceptual, semantic, and grammatical representations. In *Proceedings of the Chicago Linguistic Society* 29.

Inhelder, B., and J. Piaget. 1964. *The Early Growth of Logic in the Child.* New York: Norton.

Jackendoff, R. 1990. *Semantic Structures.* Cambridge: MIT Press.

Johnson, K. E., and C. B. Mervis. 1994. Microgenetic analysis of first steps in children's acquisition of expertise on shorebirds. *Developmental Psychology* 30: 418–35.

Jusczyk, P., and R. N. Aslin. 1995. Infants' detection of the sound patterns of words in fluent speech. *Cognitive Psychology* 29: 1–23.

Katz, N., E. Baker, and J. MacNamara. 1974. What's in a name? A study of how children learn common and proper names. *Child Development* 45: 469–73.

Kay, P. 1971. On taxonomy and semantic contrast. *Language* 47: 866–87.

Keil, F. C. 1987. Conceptual development and category structure. In U. Neisser, ed., *Concepts and Conceptual Development: Ecological and Intellectual Factors in Categorization.* New York: Cambridge University Press, pp. 175–200.

Keil, F. C. 1989. *Concepts, Kinds and Cognitive Development.* Cambridge: MIT Press.

Keil, F. C. 1995. The growth of causal understandings of natural kinds. In D. Sperber, D. Premack, and A. J. Premack, eds., *Causal Cognition: A Multi-disciplinary Debate. Symposia of the Fyssen Foundation.* New York: Clarendon Press, pp. 234–67.

Kripke, S. 1972. Naming and necessity. In D. Davidson and G. Harman, eds., *Semantics of Natural Language.* New York: Humanities Press, pp. 253–355.

Laboratory of Comparative Human Cognition. 1983. Culture and cognitive development. In P. Mussen, ed., *Handbook of Child Psychology: History, Theory, and Methods,* vol. 1. New York: Wiley.

Lancy, D. F. 1983. *Cross-cultural Studies in Cognition and Mathematics.* New York: Academic Press.

Landau, B., and L. R. Gleitman. 1985. *Language and Experience: Evidence from the Blind Child.* Cambridge: Harvard University Press.

Lave, J. 1991. Situating learning in communities of practice. In L. B. Resnick, J. M. Levine, and S. D. Teasley, eds. *Perspectives on Socially Shared Cognition.* Washington, DC: American Psychological Association, pp. 63–82.

Lopez, A., S. Atran, J. D. Coley, D. L. Medin, and E. E. Smith. 1997. The tree of life: Universal and cultural features of folkbiological taxonomies and induction. *Cognitive Psychology* 32: 251–95.

Lyons, J. 1977. *Semantics.* Cambridge University Press.

Macario, J. F., and E. F. Shipley, and D. O. Billman. 1990. Induction from a single instance: Formation of a novel category. *Journal of Experimental Child Psychology* 50: 179–99.

Macnamara, J. 1982. *Names for Things.* Cambridge: MIT Press.

Macnamara, J. 1986. *A Border Dispute: The Place of Logic in Psychology.* Cambridge: MIT Press.

Mandler, J. M. 1992. The foundations of conceptual thought in infancy. *Cognitive Development* 7: 273–85.

Mandler, J. M. 1993. On concepts. *Cognitive Development* 8: 141–48.

Maratsos, M. P. 1991. How the acquisition of nouns may be different from that of verbs. In N. A. Krasnegor, D. M. Runbaugh, R. L. Schiefelbusch, and M.

Studdart-Kennedy, eds., *Biological and Behavioral Determinants of Language Development*. Hillsdale, NJ: Lawrence Erlbaum, pp. 67–88.

Maratsos, M., and M. A. Chalkley. 1980. The internal language of children's syntax: The ontogenesis and representation of syntactic categories. In K. Nelson, ed., *Children's Language*, vol. 2. New York: Gardner Press.

Marchand, H. 1969. *The Categories and Types of Present-day English Word-Formation*. Munich: Beck.

Markman, E. M. 1989. *Categorization and Naming in Children: Problems of Induction*. Cambridge: MIT Press.

Markman, E. M., and J. E. Hutchinson. 1984. Children's sensitivity to constraints on word meaning: Taxonomic vs. thematic relations. *Cognitive Psychology* 16: 1–27.

Markman, E. M., and G. F. Wachtel. 1988. Children's use of mutual exclusivity to constrain the meanings of words. *Cognitive Psychology* 20: 121–157.

Marler, P. 1991. The instinct to learn. In S. Carey and R. Gelman, eds., *The Epigenesis of mind: Essays on biology and cognition*. Hillsdale, NJ: Lawrence Erlbaum.

Medin, D. L., and E. Heit. 1995. Categorization. In D. E. Rumelhart and B. O. Martin, eds., *Handbook of Cognition and Perception: Cognitive Science*. San Diego: Academic Press.

Medin, D. L., E. B. Lynch, J. D. Coley, and S. Atran. 1997. Categorization and reasoning among tree experts: Do all roads lead to Rome? *Cognitive Psychology* 32: 49–96.

Medin, D. L., and S. R. Waxman, 1999. Cross-disciplinary perspectives on conceptual organization. To appear in W. Bechtel and G. Graham, eds., *A Companion to Cognitive Science*. Oxford: Blackwell.

Merriman, W. E. 1986. Some reasons for the occurrence and eventual correction of children's naming errors. *Child Development* 57: 942–52.

Mervis, C. B. 1987. Child-basic object categories and early lexical development. In U. Neisser, ed., *Concepts and Conceptual Development: Ecological and Intellectual Factors in Categorization*. Emory symposia in Cognition, 1, pp. 201–233. New York: Cambridge University Press.

Mervis, C. B., and M. A. Crisafi, 1982. Order of acquisition of subordinate-, basic-, and superordinate-level categories. *Child Development* 53: 258–66.

Mervis, C. B., K. E. Johnson, and C. A. Mervis. 1994. Acquisition of subordinate categories by 3-year-olds: The roles of attribute salience, linguistic input and child characteristics. *Cognitive Development* 9: 211–34.

Mervis, C. B., and C. A. Mervis. 1982. Leopards are kitty-cats: Object labeling by mothers for their thirteen-month olds. *Child Development* 53: 267–73.

Mervis, C. B., and C. A. Mervis. 1988. Role of adult input in young children's category evolution: I. An observational study. *Journal of Child Language* 15: 257–72.

Murphy, G. L., and D. L. Medin. 1985. The role of theories in conceptual coherence. *Psychological Review* 92: 289–316.

Nelson, K. 1973. Some evidence for the cognitive primacy of categorization and its functional basis. *Merrill-Palmer Quarterly of Behavior and Development* 19: 21–39.

Nelson, K. 1988. Constraints on word learning? *Cognitive Development* 3: 221–46.

Newport, E. L. 1991. Contrasting conceptions of the critical period for language. In S. Carey and R. Gelman, eds., *The Epigenesis of Mind: Essays on Biology and Cognition.* Hillsdale, NJ: Lawrence Erlbaum.

Newport, E. L., and U. Bellugi. 1978. Linguistic expression of category levels in a visual-gestural language: A flower is a flower is a flower. In E. Rosch and B. B. Lloyd, eds., *Cognition and categorization.* Hillsdale, NJ: Lawrence Erlbaum, pp. 49–71.

Newsome, M., and P. Jusczyk. 1994. *Infants' ability to learn and parse words.* Paper presented at the 127th Meeting of the Acoustical Society of America, Cambridge, MA.

Ochs, E., and B. Schieffelin. 1984. Language acquisition and socialization. Three developmental stories and their implications. In R. Shweder and R. LeVine, eds., *Culture Theory.* Cambridge: Cambridge University Press.

Pinker, S. 1984. *Language Learnability and Language Development.* Cambridge: Harvard University Press.

Pinker, S. 1994. How could a child use verb syntax to learn verb semantics? *Lingua* 92: 377–410.

Putnam, H. 1975. *Mind, Language and Reality: Philosophical Papers*, vol. 2. Cambridge: Cambridge University Press.

Quinn, P. C., P. D. Eimas, and S. L. Rosenkrantz. 1993. Evidence for representations of perceptually similar natural categories by 3-month-old and 4-month-old infants. *Perception* 22: 463–75.

Rogoff, B. 1990. *Apprenticeship in Thinking: Cognitive Development in Social Context.* Oxford: Oxford University Press.

Rosch, E., C. B. Mervis, W. D. Gray, D. M. Johnson, and P. Boyes-Braem. 1976. Basic objects in natural categories. *Cognitive Psychology* 8: 382–439.

Saah, M. I., S. R. Waxman, and J. Johnson. 1996. *The composition of children's early lexicons as a function of age and vocabulary size.* Paper presented at the 21st Boston University Conference on Language Development, Boston, MA.

Shipley, E. F. 1989. Two kinds of hierarchies: Class inclusion hierarchies and kind hierarchies. *Genetic Epistemologist* 17: 31–39.

Slobin, D. I. 1985. Cross-linguistic evidence for the language-making capacity. In D. I. Slobin, ed., *The Cross-linguistic Study of Language Acquisition: Theoretical issues*, vol. 2. Hillsdale, NJ: Lawrence Erlbaum.

Smith, E. E., and D. L. Medin. 1981. *Categories and Concepts*. Cambridge: Harvard University Press.

Smith, L. B. 1995. Self-organizing processes in learning to learn words: development is not induction. In *The Minnesota Symposium on Child Psychology: Basic and Applied Perspectives on Learning, Cognition, and Development*, vol. 28. Marwah, NJ: Lawrence Erlbaum, pp. 1–32.

Spelke, E. S. 1993. Object perception. In A. I. Goldman, ed., *Readings in Philosophy and Cognitive Science*. Cambridge: MIT Press, pp. 447–60.

Stross, B. 1973. Acquisition of botanical terminology by Tzeltal children. In M. S. Edmonson, ed., *Meanings in Mayan Languages*. The Hague: Mouton, pp. 107–42.

Talmy, L. 1985. Lexicalization patterns: Semantic structure in lexical forms. In T. Shopen, ed., *Language typology and syntactic description*, vol. 3. Cambridge: Cambridge University Press, pp. 57–149.

Tardif, T. 1996. Nouns are not always learned before verbs: Evidence from Mandarin speakers' early vocabularies. *Developmental Psychology* 32: 492–504.

Taylor, P. M. 1984. "Covert categories" reconsidered: Identifying unlabeled classes in Tobelo folk biological classification. *Journal of Ethnobiology* 4: 105–22.

Taylor, M., and S. A. Gelman. (1988). Adjectives and nouns: Children's strategies for learning new words. *Child Development* 59: 411–19.

Vygotsky, L. S. 1962. *Thought and Language*. Cambridge: MIT Press.

Waxman, S. R. 1990. Linguistic biases and the establishment of conceptual hierarchies: Evidence from preschool children. *Cognitive Development* 5: 123–50.

Waxman, S. R. 1991. Convergences between semantic and conceptual organization in the preschool years. In S. A. Gelman and J. P. Byrnes, eds., *Perspectives on Language and Cognition: Interrelations in Development*. Cambridge: Cambridge University Press, pp. 107–145.

Waxman, S. R. 1994. The development of an appreciation of specific linkages between linguistic and conceptual organization. *Lingua* 92: 229–57.

Waxman, S. R., and M. T. Balaban. 1992. The influence of words vs. tones on infants' categorization. Paper presented at the Eighth International Conference on Infant Studies, Miami, FL.

Waxman, S. R., and M. T. Balaban. 1996. Ursines and felines: Novel words support object categorization in 9 month old infants. Paper presented at the International Conference on Infancy Studies, Providence, RI.

Waxman, S. R., and R. Gelman. 1986. Preschoolers' use of superordinate relations in classification and language. *Cognitive Development* 1: 129–56.

Waxman, S. R., and D. G. Hall. 1993. The development of a linkage between count nouns and object categories: Evidence from 16- to 21-month-old infants. *Child Development* 64: 1224–41.

Waxman, S. R., and T. Hatch. 1992. Beyond the basics: Preschool children label objects flexibly at multiple hierarchical levels. *Journal of Child Language* 19: 153–66.

Waxman, S. R., and T. D. Kosowski. 1990. Nouns mark category relations: Toddlers' and preschoolers' word-learning biases. *Child Development* 61: 1461–73.

Waxman, S. R., E. B. Lynch, K. L. Casey, and L. Baer. 1997. Setter and samoyeds: The emergence of subordinate level categories as a basis for inductive inference. *Developmental Psychology* 33: 1074–90.

Waxman, S. R., and D. B. Markow. 1995. Words as invitations to form categories: Evidence from 12- to 13-month-old infants. *Cognitive Psychology* 29: 257–302.

Waxman, S. R., and D. B. Markow. 1996. Soft ice cream and soft slippers: The role of object kind in mapping adjectives to object properties. Paper presented at the meeting of the Society for Research in Child Development, Washington, DC.

Waxman, S. R., and D. B. Markow. 1999. Object properties and object kind: 21-month-old infants' extension of novel adjectives. *Child Development*, in press.

Waxman, S. R., and A. Senghas. 1992. Relations among word meanings in early lexical development. *Developmental Psychology* 28: 862–73.

Waxman, S. R., A. Senghas, and S. Benveniste. 1997. A cross-linguistic examination of the noun-category bias: Evidence from French- and Spanish-speaking preschool-aged children. *Cognitive Psychology* 43: 183–218.

Waxman, S. R., E. F. Shipley, and B. Shepperson. 1991. Establishing new subcategories: The role of category labels and existing knowledge. *Child Development* 62: 127–38.

Waxman, S. R., R. Stote, and M. Philippe. 1996. Count nouns and object categories: Modifications in word-learners' expectations from infancy through the preschool years. Poster presented at the meeting of the Society for Research in Child Development, Washington, DC.

Wierzbicka, A. 1986. What's in a noun? (or: How do nouns differ in meaning from adjectives?). *Studies in Language* 10: 353–89.

Woodward, A. L., E. M. Markman, and C. M. Fitzsimmons. 1994. Rapid word-learning in 13- and 18-month-olds. *Developmental Psychology* 30: 553–66.

Wyman, L. C., and F. L. Bailey. 1964. *Navaho Indian Ethnoentomology.* Publications in Anthropology no. 12. Albuquerque: University of New Mexico.

# 9

# Mechanism and Explanation in the Development of Biological Thought: The Case of Disease

Frank C. Keil, Daniel T. Levin, Bethany A. Richman, and Grant Gutheil

It has become increasingly tempting in recent years to consider children as intuitive theorists or little scientists. This temptation seems to be both well justified and clearly groundless. On the positive side, we know that even young infants have clear expectations that allow them to understand and differentiate their physical and social worlds. A six-month-old for example, seems to possess a naive "theory" of mechanics within which she is able to predict the behaviors of physical objects using basic principles governing interactions of bounded solids (Spelke 1991). Infants also seem to understand that social beings interact in ways that go beyond these principles, and are instead governed by a naive psychology. For example, people can act on each other at a distance while simple objects cannot (Woodward, Phillips, and Spelke 1993). Even hands are interpreted in a goal-directed way while perceptually similar rods are not (Woodward 1995).

On the other hand, there is no evidence that infants have theories that include explicit sets of rules, or that they generate precise hypotheses in anything like the manner suggested by traditional accounts of how science works. In fact even older children often seem surprisingly ignorant of many seemingly critical and specific details of how things work in a given domain. Five-year-olds, for example, seem to have little understanding of how most machines work, how chemicals react, or how the sun and planets move. This ignorance isn't especially surprising given how little opportunity children have had to observe the inner workings of machines, and chemical reactions, or to learn the details of astronomy, but it points out a problem. It seems highly implausible that children have theories or act like scientists if we mean they have the kind of detailed accounts of mechanisms so common in mature sciences, yet it seems equally unlikely that they move from complete ignorance to full scientific theories in a single discontinuous leap. How then are we to characterize the developmental progression in which all of us, young child or novice adult, come to grasp both the specific factual information relevant to a given domain, and integrate that information into the causal structure underlying that domain? Some kind of intermediate level of sophistication would seem helpful to organize children's expectations regarding natural phenomena.

The most common account of this progression assumes that causal theorylike knowledge reflects a kind of abstraction from concrete detailed instances that takes years to develop, especially for knowledge of abstract principles that is acquired without explicit instruction (e.g., Keil 1987). One area in which extensive investigation of this process has taken place is in the domain of naive biological reasoning. The emergence of knowledge and explanation are especially relevant to the case of biological thought. The living world is all around us, while the mature science of biology provides both detailed mechanisms and abstract theoretical principles for phenomena in physiology, reproduction, evolution, and disease. If there is a developmental pattern concerning knowledge of detailed mechanisms or abstract principles, biology is an excellent place to look. Research in the area, however, has evolved in such a way that studies often seem to be at odds with each other.

One proposal, largely consistent with the concrete to abstract shift hypothesis, argues that not until the elementary school years do children really start to have any sort of distinctively biological theory. Prior to that time, they are either largely atheoretical (e.g., Gentner and Toupin 1988) or attempt to understand biological phenomena in terms of better-developed systems of explanation in other areas, such as folk psychology or physical mechanics (Carey 1985, 1995). Researchers in this tradition point out all the spectacular ways in which children as old as six or seven fail to understand some very obvious things about biological kinds and/ or fail to differentiate them from nonbiological kinds. There is no question that such children do give very different patterns of answers on these tasks than older children and adults (Inagaki and Hatano 1993).

In a different tradition, many recent studies suggest that even young preschoolers view living kinds as a distinct class of things with their own special principles and interrelations. Although they clearly misunderstand, or do not know, significant information concerning specific biological mechanism, preschoolers seem to have clear expectations at a more general level in several areas of biological understanding such as the special properties of biological growth, and various aspects of reproduction and contamination, among many others. For example, children understand that the process of biological growth implies that an organism becomes larger over time while aging in artifacts does not entail this kind of change (Rosengren et al. 1991).

In contrast to the first research tradition discussed, these results seem to indicate that preschoolers' grasp of biology is both theoretically driven and distinct from their understanding of social/psychological phenomena. It is seems then that despite the long-standing intuitive appeal of the concrete to abstract shift proposal, there can be glaring exceptions to this framework. Within language acquisition, for example, children likely start with a set of abstract principles and expectations that gradually get filled in with concrete details. Within biological reasoning, preschoolers have surprising difficulty judging if specific, clearly machinelike parts (i.e., gears) belong inside animals, while at the same time clearly grasping abstract relations that distinguish the insides of machines from the insides of animals (Simons and Keil 1995).

Given these findings, we propose that rather than a concrete to abstract shift in development, abstract principles are among the first patterns to be learned and remembered by young children. These patterns are not formal rules connected in a nomological-deductive manner but rather are likely represented in a more informal manner that is abstract and distanced from specific instances. Throughout development, specific information is learned and incorporated into this existing framework. This developmental progression would foster exactly the seemingly conflicting pattern of results discussed above: significant grasp of abstract relations governing a specific domain, coupled with robust errors concerning specific concrete mechanism in that domain. To further assess the validity of this proposal, and better understand how such developmental progression could occur, we focus here on one area of biology, disease.

## 9.1   Disease and Contagion

Everyone gets sick. Some are lucky and have only experienced the occasional cold while others are plagued by serious and life-threatening illnesses. Also common is the experience of observing illness in others. It therefore likely that children in just about any culture will invariably have had such experiences several times before they even start talking. Conceptions of illness accordingly provide a way of asking how one central aspect of biological thought might emerge in childhood. In addition disease, especially issues concerning its transmission to others, provides a domain in which notions of mechanism, cause, and explanation all figure prominently. Finally as adults we make a number of principled distinctions between different kinds of abnormalities and their transmission. For example, we take considerable pains to distinguish aberrant mental states from aberrant bodily states. Even in the context of medical models of mental illness, no adult considers mental states, or the contents of our beliefs, as transmitted in anything like the same manner as variations in our bodily states. For these reasons studies of developing knowledge about transmission of unusual mental states and bodily states offer a potentially revealing insight into how explanations in different domains become distinct and at what level of analysis such distinctions occur.

In this chapter we consider how concepts of disease develop in the broader context of how intuitive theories and causal understanding might emerge in childhood and come to form distinct domains of thought. As mentioned above, the study of biological thought has in recent years become an active arena for asking these broader questions about conceptual change. We focus here on contagion both as a way of looking at biological thought in more specific terms and as a way of tying it to the broader context of conceptual change.

## 9.2   Views of Disease and Contagion Prior to Germ Theory

Disease is from of old and nothing about it has changed. It is we who change as we learn to recognize what was formerly imperceptible—Charcot

If a naive biology that includes an understanding of contagion is a central organizing principle in cognitive development, then why is explicit understanding of contagion historically so recent a development? In many ways views of disease and contagion seem to have changed dramatically in the last few hundred years. For example, the germ theory of disease is not even 150 years old, and the history of medicine and biology is full of examples of religious and mystical beliefs very different from twentieth century Western biology and medicine. These apparently irrational beliefs regarding the concrete mechanisms behind disease transmission may, however, coexist with a more biologically grounded set of broader and more abstract framing beliefs about disease and contagion. Indeed, even current medicine sometimes appeals to social influences, or in some cases religious influences on the disease process. It is therefore useful to consider a few examples of pre-germ theory beliefs about disease and contagion to better understand how concrete detailed mechanisms and more abstract understanding of biology might interact.

The germ theory of disease, given to us by Pasteur in the nineteenth century, is an encompassing theory that makes concrete the idea that tiny microbes, or germs as he called them, are involved in the etiology of many serious diseases. Until this time disease was seen as intricately linked with religion, magic, and the occult (Atkinson 1956). Sickness and disease, along with other misfortunes, were punishment by a higher being or force. Yet some basic understanding of disease transmission must have been present since the beginning of civilization. Although Pasteur introduced the terminology and concrete mechanisms associated with disease, the theory of contagion has much older roots.

Before the discovery of the microscope, it is not surprising that most people attributed sickness to otherworldly phenomena. Religion and magic were such intricate parts of everyday life that these explanatory systems, often with explicit causal mechanisms, were called upon to fill in unknown details of disease transmission. The availability of this powerful explanatory framework could go so far as to override or supplant more implicitly held theories about general biological phenomena. People then, like people today, wanted satisfying and explicit answers to help them understand the often overwhelming dramas of everyday life and their religions often offered explanations invoking all-powerful agents whose scope of efficacy left few phenomena unexplained.

Despite the presence of religious and magical explanation for disease, it is possible to trace the roots of a more biological theory to the beginnings of civilization. Even prior to the beginning of written history, a rudimentary knowledge of functional anatomy guided the treatment for a variety of ailments (Atkinson 1956; Manger 1992). For example, trephening, an operation where circular sections of the skull are cut out, was thought to cure what we today would call a migraine, or an epileptic attack. While such operations were seen as liberating the skull, and thereby the individual, from evil demons, they also show that more than 20,000 years ago people correctly associated pain and unusual behavior with a fundamentally somatic treatment. Additional prehistoric evidence indicates a basic knowledge of the bodily function. For example, remains unearthed in England show a skull with bony destruction due to a jaw abscess which also showed evidence of being operated on (Atkinson 1956). Evidence has also been found of well-healed bone fractures which had been set in splints (Venzmer 1968). In addition to surgical solutions, early humans also sought out chemical remedies, namely the herbs and roots around them, to try and cure the sickness and ills that existed. These chemical remedies were often effective, and though their putative mechanisms may have been partially mediated by demons, there appeared to be some sense that different substances had different physiological/functional effects (Atkinson 1956).

Because disease and sickness were usually attributed to the supernatural, magic was often invoked as treatment. If a disease existed that had no obvious etiology, it was attributed to some kind of sorcery. It was the medicine man, or shaman, who was responsible for supervising the healing process. This involved giving the patient a disguise or prescribing deleterious medicines so that the patient's body was no longer a desirable host for the entity causing the illness (Haggare 1933). The body as the host for the disease-causing entity is a theme that is repeated throughout ancient civilizations. In this sense the demon can be seen as a much larger more intelligent "germ" with powerful physical/spatial abilities that allowed it to inhabit or "infect" bodies.

In Babylon hundreds of years before the birth of Christ, Hammurabi's code of laws included many rules that applied to physicians, most of which were intended to regulate magical methods of overcoming disease. In addition cures were often brought about by lay people. The custom was to have the sick placed outside where passersby could stop and give advice regarding their ailments (Atkinson 1956). Thus nonphysicians had, if not a formal theory of disease, at least an idea of what it was to feel sick and certain experiences to draw upon to find remedies and were able to share them with others. Interestingly the disease we now call epilepsy was considered contagious by the Babylonians, although demons were thought to actually cause the seizures.

Although medicine in the ancient civilizations might be seen to consist only of magic, this is not true. In ancient Mesopotamia, for example, anyone wanting to devote themselves to medicine was required to have both a precise knowledge of magical ceremonies used to bring about a cure and knowledge of anatomy, surgery, and basic remedies (Venzmer 1968). The doctors of this time also knew enough about disease vectors to appreciate the connection between mosquitoes and fevers. Although flies were associated with harmful demons, the boils they were known to cause were treated using physical remedies, such as compresses. Doctors of ancient times also differentiated the clinical indicators of various infections and diseases such as tuberculosis, pneumonia, and gastrointestinal afflictions (Venzmer 1968). Thus physicians in ancient Mesopotamia developed rational, observation-based methods of treating illness while retaining magical and religious explanations to fill in specific mechanisms.

The ancient Egyptians also displayed a functional knowledge of disease and medicine that coexisted with beliefs about magic and mysticism. Ancient Egyptian papyrus scrolls included detailed beliefs about gods, demons, and magical spells side by side with a more physiologically based medical doctrine. For example, one scroll dating back to 3000–2500 BC, outlines the measures that were taken to care for illness and injury (Ackerknecht 1968). Sutures and plasters were used to treat wounds, and broken bones were placed into splints made from hallowed ox bones. Egyptian knowledge of anatomy, including that of the brain, was also quite impressive. In addition the Ebers Papyrus (Atkinson 1956) documents a list of remedies for various ailments such as indigestion, poisonous bites, burns, and delaying or hastening labor. One of the most fascinating aspects of this document is that many of the medical substances used then such as castor oil are actually still in use now (Venzmer 1968).

Ancient India developed a system of traditional medicine which is widely practiced there today. Those training to be doctors had a thorough knowledge of anatomy which was obtained by studying corpses. Thus the Indians became excellent surgeons and were able to perform complex procedures such as skin grafts. They were also familiar with diseases such as diabetes, and were adept at diagnosing it by the "honey" or sweet taste of a patient's urine (Venzmer 1968). One of the medical philosophies important to the Indians was the Ayurvedic philosophy, which said that all essential bodily functions could be explained in terms of the three "dosas." These dosas were the three primary humors (fluids) of bile, wind, and phlegm. A variety of factors including accidents or demonic possession could disturb the delicate balance of the primary humors, leading to poor health. This humoral pathology is also the basis of Greek and Roman medicine, which provided the foundations for modern Western medicine (Manger 1992).

Greek medicine was one of the first recorded medical approaches not interwoven with religion. Greek philosophers attempted to explain the workings of the world in terms of everyday experiences instead of through divine interventions, which led them to focus on maintaining the body's harmony. Pythagoras and Alcmaeon of Croton believed that pairs of opposites defined existence, and that one was in good health when these pairs were in balance. As a result disease was caused by an excess in one member of a pair. For example, a fever occurred when there was an excess of heat, while chills occurred when there was an excess of cold (Phillips 1973).

The central figure in Greek medicine, Hippocrates, believed it was essential to understand that disease was a natural process rather than a supernatural one. The guiding force behind a patient's treatment was knowledge of that individual's constitution and balance. To Hippocrates, disease was caused by an imbalance of a person's humors—blood, phlegm, black bile, and yellow bile. An ailment was not isolated to any part of a person but affected the whole person. The body's immune system attempted to eliminate disease by utilizing normal physiological processes in a dramatic fashion. In essence, sickness was a result of difficulty in maintaining balance in the victim's surroundings. Balance was restored when "morbid" elements in the humors had been eliminated from the body, through bleeding, secretions, or excretions. Humors were believed responsible for almost every serious affliction, mental or physical. Hippocrates is also believed to have focused on environmental causes of illness. For example, although he could not pinpoint the exact source, he associated malaria with marshes (Manger 1992).

The transition facilitated by Hippocrates from mechanisms that invoke demons and religious deities to ones that carefully avoided such invocations may not be so much a transition from prebiological to biological thought as it was the emergence of a new more powerful and more local causal theory referring to humors. In this sense, older magical and religious explanations were also biological in that they specified an interaction between the demon and functional biological systems in ways not possible in nonliving systems. For example, ancient Egyptian priests performed healings by simultaneously invoking God and administering medicinal substances (Haggare 1933).

If a series of biologically grounded principles existed as common knowledge or intuition prior to their formalization, then the discoveries of Hippocrates and the others who followed can be seen as resting upon a series of assumptions without which the search for a coherent explanation of disease would have been hopeless. These assumptions can support a whole range of particular theories, correct or not. For example, Claudius Galen, a figure synonymous with early Roman medicine, was able to demonstrate that arteries are filled with blood, and not air, as was believed by Aristotle. Galen taught that the arteries carried blood that was charged with a vital spirit as it passed through the lungs. Clearly, even though the particulars regarding the behavior of vital spirits were incorrect, this was an important precursor to later discoveries regarding the particular mechanisms involved in respiration. Equally important, however, is that this discovery would not have happened without a series of more basic biological assumptions. For example, would Galen have come up with an adequate functional analysis if he had believed that the properties of biological organisms exist to serve the needs of external agents such as gods? This would have been an understandable assumption if Galen had used the same kind of reasoning with disease as might be used with human made objects whose properties tend to serve their makers (Keil 1994).

It is thought that Marcus Terentius Varro (116–27 BC) anticipated the germ theory of disease by recognizing the possibility that living matter might be involved in the etiology of disease (Scarborough 1969). He thought that swampy places were inhabited by very small animals that could enter the body, either through the mouth or nose, and cause serious illness. This was of obvious interest to the ancient Romans who were starting to make hygienic advances with public baths and latrines and were concerned about the purity of water and the sanitation of such dwellings. Again, this kind of reasoning is biologically grounded and reveals the appeal of humoral models of physiology. These specify a set of fluids similar to the bodily fluids that transmit disease. Therefore humoral theory can connect with a set of reasonable and useful assumptions about contagion. For example, if one sees yellow bile or phlegm, avoiding it will prevent buildup of like substances in your one's own body. Thus the theory, incorrect at a specific factual level, still could accurately guide behavior regarding isolation of ill individuals.

During the Middle Ages, Europe suffered from many epidemic diseases, the most well-known being the bubonic plague. Although the exact nature of these diseases was not understood, people realized that individuals afflicted with the plague had to be isolated. These individuals could not enter cities or sell articles of food or drink. It is therefore evident that the people of this time understood the contagiousness and lethality of this disease. They thought that it could be passed from person to person and noticed that a lack of cleanliness helped to spread the plague, so strict regulations controlling hygiene were introduced into the cities. Unfortunately, they failed to understand the mediating role of vermin in contagion.

Probably the greatest scourge during the Renaissance was syphilis. Girolamo Fracastro closely studied the disease and is credited with the popular mercury treatment for curing syphilis. Fracastro later broadened the scope of his research to many other infectious diseases, such as anthrax, leprosy, tuberculosis, and typhus. He believed that all of these diseases were due to an infecting agent, or contagium, and thought it could be transmitted in three different ways (Buck 1979). The first was physical contact between two people, and the second was by using objects that were contaminated by the infecting agent. The last was by breathing air that could contain this contagium. It is here during the Renaissance in the 1400s, that we see clear precursors of the germ theory of disease.

At the end of the sixteenth century, the discovery of the microscope transformed the study of disease. Before this time it was understandable that people did not have a firm grasp of the agents that were making them ill because they were simply impossible to see. The microscope revealed the existence tiny microbes, able to multiply at a very rapid rate, that could plausibly serve as a concrete mechanism to explain the invisible transmission of illness.

This discovery led to a series of scientific advances in the nineteenth century that finally produced the "germ theory" of disease. The work of three men in particular was central to these discoveries: Agostino Bassi, Louis Pasteur, and Robert Koch. Bassi focused on the silkworm disease of muscardine. He was able to transfer this disease to healthy silkworms by injecting matter from dead silkworms that had been infected. He further ascertained that a small plant or fungus was responsible for causing muscardine. From his findings, he conjectured that other diseases could be caused by such parasites.

Pasteur studied fermentation, and determined that microorganisms (or ferments) were responsible for this process. He extrapolated this idea to infectious diseases, arguing that microorganisms caused those as well. Although Pasteur's ideas met with much resistance, he sought to discredit the magical beliefs of his opponents by demonstrating that microbes (bacteria) did not arise via spontaneous generation in inorganic matter (Manger 1992). In 1862 he completed a successful series of experiments showing that the theory of spontaneous generation was incorrect. In 1864, when disease spread among silkworms in France, Pasteur had yet another opportunity to prove his theories. He found that indeed, the disease was not a punishment from God but rather was due to tangible causes that could be controlled.

Finally Robert Koch was responsible for discovering the anthrax germ. He identified the germ, but more important, he determined how it was transmitted. Even before Koch, it was known that a sick animal could transmit anthrax to a healthy one, but the manner in which this took place was a mystery. Koch discovered that after infected animals died, the anthrax germs changed into inert spores capable of surviving indefinitely. A healthy animal could pick up these spores, which would then change back into germs, and infect a new victim. Koch thereby illustrated the importance of understanding modes of transmission of disease. In other words, once the microscope allowed a concrete way of talking about unseen agents theories of disease expanded greatly with detailed accounts at the microscopic level. But all these later accounts had far more continuity with earlier ones than popular notions of the novelty of germ theory would suggest.

In appears that humans, throughout time, have always had an idea of what disease was, how it could affect their lives, and most important, how to match somatic complaints with the correct disease-producing behaviors such as physical contact with sick persons. These basic intuitions combined with useful terminology and equipment, such as the microscope, converged to provide a concrete explanation. Prior to the availability of this concrete explanation for disease transmission, religious beliefs served a filling-in function, providing details where intuition failed. It is interesting to note that the filling-in function of religion can logically exist today, even in individuals such as doctors who have extensive knowledge about contagion. This is because concrete explanation is limited in a variety of ways, in particular because this kind of explanation usually specifies a set of limiting conditions that restricts the scope of any given set of knowledge. Religious or metaphysical explanations are more flexible and can extend to situations where empirically based explanations are not available or cannot in principle be used. Therefore, when one looks back to primitive civilizations, religious and magical beliefs were not so irrational. They were, instead, an example of borrowing from a powerful and flexible system of explanation to fill in what were surely terrifying gaps in explanation for often fatal illnesses. This kind of explanation is also invoked when a victim asks the obvious question "Why am I sick?" The answer to this kind of question almost always involves a normative component no matter how sophisticated and concrete an understanding of contagion is brought to bear. The history of medicine might not therefore be an example of a long struggle toward a finally correct set of concrete mechanisms. Instead, it is better represented by the interplay of different coexisting systems of explanation, each filling a role where the other fails.

If the historical development of knowledge about disease can be seen in terms of the coexistence of different systems of explanation, then anthropological data from traditional societies converge on the same notion. In fact understanding this kind of coexistence is seen as pivotal in the field of medical anthropology (Loveland 1976). Although individuals in many traditional cultures hold a variety of beliefs about supernatural causation, it is important to distinguish between a culture's tendency to use demonlike terms in discourse and a deeper simultaneous understanding of more biological/functional models of disease. In a recent linguistic analysis of disease relevant discourse among the Tzeltal Maya, Maffi (1994) shows that while one set of terms refers to supernatural agents, a different set refers to more natural mechanisms. Green, Jurg, and Dgedge (1993) provide converging evidence for the coexistence of spiritual and more biological explanations of illness in traditional societies. They found that traditional healers in Mozambique believe that one class of ailment is caused by "kohma," an invisible microscopic agent found in bodily fluids. However, another less serious class of ailment is caused by an unhappy "nyoka" which healers describe as a spirit inhabiting the body. Quintanilla (1976) describes a similar dichotomy among the Kechua and Aymara Indians in southern Peru. In this society several classes of illness are seen as naturally caused and amenable to somatic treatment. Other illnesses, however, are caused by the loss of one's spirit or soul and require elaborate rituals by the local healer to entice the victim's soul to return to his body. These Indians were willing to accept biological explanations and treatments when they observed their efficacy, but retained their belief in their local healers for other ailments which did not seem amenable to the physicians pills.

In other cases dual modes of explanation can be seen for the same illness. For example, Pakistani mothers interviewed by Mull and Mull (1994) believe that pneumonia can have a number of different causes including an imbalance in bodily temperature which they explain in terms very much like the disruption in a homeostatic process. This imbalance is most frequently caused by excess "coldness" in which the body is somehow disrupted by something that is too cold. This can include exposure to a draft, cold weather, or breast milk from a woman who has gotten too cold. This theory is accompanied by a set of remedies and preventive measures that range from avoiding chills and wet feet to acceptance of antibiotics from a physician. On the other hand, these same mothers also believe that pneumonia can be caused by the shadow of a supernatural spirit. In such situations treatment from a holy man is sought.

More generally, cross-cultural observation emphasizes that mystical beliefs about every day causation are not necessarily associated with immaturity. For example, Mead (1932) observed that young Manus children almost exclusively referred to natural causes when explaining everyday occurrences. It was the adults who referred to mischievous spirits or engaged in other animistic reasoning when some item was lost, or when an unknown sound emanated from the trees. In a simple experiment Mead told the children stories which baited them to engage in supernatural animistic reasoning. In one of them, a boy named Popoli loses his canoe because it drifts away. Mead suggested to them that the canoe might be "bad," but the children would have none of this kind of explanation. A typical retort was, "Popoli is a stupid boy; he doesn't know how to fasten a canoe; when I fasten a canoe it doesn't drift; I understand" (p. 185).

In short, three themes seem to run through both the history of thought about disease and observations of traditional cultures:

1. In many cases demons and supernatural agents seemed to play the role of germs in most older historical lay accounts. These were the invisible autonomous entities that acted on biological functional systems whether they be organs, "humors," or musculoskeletal interaction. While it is likely true that modern lay persons consider germs in a more biologically specific way than the older supernatural agents, the pattern of inference in both cases is specifically biological. In this way talk of supernatural agents has considerable continuity with modern day germ accounts.

2. The supernatural was often invoked as default option where more precise options were not available. When an illness could not be understood at all, the magical omnipotent nature of some supernatural agent was available to fill the void just as they are today for some modern medical professionals who refer to miracles from God as ways of talking about the unexplainable. This is not very different from substituting supernatural agents for germs.

3. Talk of supernatural agents and talk of natural causes are neither mutually exclusive nor necessarily contradictory. One can fill in for gaps left by the other; and equally important, they can reflect different styles of discourse used in different settings with different aspects of understanding being captured for posterity. It is also clear that cross-cultural work on conceptions of disease will help us better understand its historical development.

### 9.3   Children's Understanding of Contamination and Contagion

Research on children's understanding of contagion and contamination has evolved over the past fifty years essentially in parallel with major theories of cognitive development. Initially a Piagetian approach tied development of children's understanding of contagion to the development of domain-general competencies and focused on children's use of immanent justice explanations for illness (Piaget 1932). This approach was based on unstructured interviews where children often claimed that illness could be brought on by naughty behavior, and consequently that ill individuals were being punished. Although recent evidence runs against this conceptualization (Springer and Rukel 1992), it is does resonate strongly with the kind of victim blaming that is evident in the case of AIDS. Relatively recent incarnations of this kind of model emphasize a stagelike developmental sequence that is more closely tied to the particulars of the disease process (Bibace and Walsh 1981). In both cases, however, domain-general principles are activated to explain children's understanding of illness.

One of the major methodological weakness with initial research supporting immanent justice and the Piagetian models is that it depended on use of open-ended questioning procedures where children were asked to explain why either they or someone in a story got sick. The results of these studies can be very difficult to interpret. For example, when asked why they were ill, diabetic children responded that it was a punishment for eating too much sugar (Beverley 1936). However, what these children mean by "punishment" is unclear. This may indicate immanent justice, or simply be a convenient metaphoric label for a biological process they are quite aware of (Springer and Rukel 1992). Further, in open-ended situations children are highly susceptible to demand characteristics and will base their responses on any salient part of the story that seems to signal the experimenter's intent. Therefore, if a character in a story who gets sick is prominently associated with bad behavior, the child will mention this in his/her response. Perhaps they believe that there is a moral to be had in the story and report their understanding as such. This research might therefore have led to the false conclusion that children knew little about the true mechanisms behind the transmission of illness until they reached the appropriate stage in development.

Rather than asking open-ended questions, children could be asked to choose one of two different explanations for the transmission of illness. In this case subjects can contrast two relevant options and choose the one they think best explains the illness, rather than providing the explanation themselves. When this method is used, children consistently reject immanent justice explanations for illness, referring instead to biological causes such as germs (Springer and Rukel 1992).

In the case of contamination, research initially suggested that young children were unsophisticated in their understanding of the consequences of contact between a disgusting substance (feces) and potential food. Fallon, Rozin, and Pliner (1984) asked children aged 3 to 12 if they would drink contaminated juice under a number of circumstances. Most children passed the simplest tests and claimed they wouldn't drink juice with a small bit of feces in the bottom. They also claimed that they wouldn't drink juice from the top of the glass using a straw. The youngest children did, however, say that they would drink the juice if the contaminant were removed with a spoon. Only by age 10 did children strongly reject this method of removing the contamination. Fallon et al. suggest that these findings imply that young children understand that the contaminant might be present throughout the liquid, but that they incorrectly believe the contamination to be reversible. They go on to argue that young children do not fundamentally distinguish between the category of disgusting things and other things that have negative valences associated with them.

The pragmatics of the experimental situation may, however, have influenced children's responses in these studies. The youngest children may have believed that any adult asking them about drinking feces laden juice would only do so if it were okay. In addition the repeated questioning may have implied that the adult was offering to put in considerable effort to make the juice acceptable by providing a straw, getting a spoon, and even spilling the juice and replacing it for the picky child. At some point politeness would demand that the child drink the juice unless they realized that it was all just a test. Siegal (1988) avoided this problem by asking the children if a character in a story would get sick by drinking the juice. In this case children indicated that drinking contaminated juice, even after removal of the contaminant with a spoon, would cause illness.

This research indicates that children produce the correct rejection behavior based on knowledge regarding the process of contamination. Additional evidence provided by Au, Sidle, and Rollins (1993) shows that children have some understanding of the possibility that invisible particles of contaminant can affect a drink. Siegal and Share (1990) also find that children appreciate the potentially harmful nature of the invisible. The children in this experiment correctly predicted hypothetical health outcomes involving invisible particles and further refused to eat moldy bread even when the mold was covered up with a much liked spread. Children are also able to put principled limits on the spread of germs. Springer and Belk (1994) found that children believe that mere proximity is insufficient for a contaminant to ruin their drink, and Kalish (1996) found that children believe that invisible contaminants can cause illness.

Children also seem to understand the difference between the emotional response to contamination, and the physical one of getting ill. Kalish (1997) asked children if a character was disgusted and was made ill in response to a contaminated bit of food. Children heard stories in which the character did or did not know if the food was contaminated, and did or did not eat the food. In the most interesting contrast, children said the character was more likely to get sick than depressed if they did eat the food, but did not know it was contaminated, and also said that the character was more depressed than sick if they did know it was contaminated but did not eat the food. Children seem aware that emotional effects are more likely to arise from knowing that one has eaten contaminated substances, and the physical effects are more likely caused by actually having eaten the food. They therefore do not blindly assume that eating contaminated food causes just any problem. Rather, they have some notion that the particular set of effects induced by the episode depends on a both psychological and physical factors. Further a subset of 5-year-olds consistently responded that physical illness is more likely to occur after a delay as compared with the emotional response to the disgusting substance. The younger children (mean age 3:8) believed that both the emotional response and illness would occur immediately after eating the food.

If children understand something of the difference between mental and physical effects of eating contaminated food, then they might be able to correctly understand other mental/physical distinctions relevant to contagion. Of particular interest here is the difference between mental and physical routes of illness transmission. This contrast is particularly interesting given the claim that a naive theory of biology does not develop until middle childhood and arises primarily from an earlier theory of psychology (Carey 1985). Under this conceptualization young children should use a psychological theory to explain contagion. At first glance this conflicts with Kalish's data which indicates that children differentiate the two domains at some level. It would, however, be easy to argue that the knowledge children exhibit in the contamination and contagion studies is not a coherent theory specific to biology. It is, rather, a set of isolated facts that make no contact with each other and that are not exclusively applied to biological phenomena (Solomon and Cassamatis 1995). The degree to which this is plausible given the complete set of competencies that children reveal will be discussed later, but for now it is important to note that the data reviewed to this point are highly interesting but clearly not conclusive.

In particular, most of the findings reviewed here test children's knowledge about everyday situations they are likely to have experienced directly. Children may have experienced ruined food and been told that eating it will cause illness. In the case of the Kalish studies, for example, children's ability to differentiate the emotional and physical effects of contamination may be directly based on experiencing the depression of watching a favorite drink disappear as mom tosses it out after a meeting with a fly, or witnessing the chaos that ensues after sneezing into a big serving bowl of chili. Such experiences are likely to be accompanied by extensive explanation about the possibility of getting sick from germs on the fly, and detailed story justifying the necessity of sending out for pizza. These experiences may form a data set which the children can apply directly to experimental situations that mimic them almost exactly. In such situations the competencies could plausibly be based on simple association with past experiences and therefore miss tapping the key properties of a systematic naive biology.

One way of attempting to stretch children's knowledge is to assess the degree to which they appropriately apply abstract principles to new situations. Carey's (1985) classic studies use this strategy by teaching children a new property for a living kind and testing the degree to which they generalize it to other entities. In this situation at least part of the problem cannot be drawn directly from past experience, and it therefore requires some kind of appropriate abstraction or generalization. The same could be said for novel situations testing children's understanding of contamination. The studies that follow therefore test children's understanding of contagion by asking them to predict the likely route of transmission for novel biological diseases that they are not likely to have experienced directly. In order for children to correctly respond in these cases, they must make a series of inferences that cannot be guided by direct reference to particular experiences. Instead, they must assess the degree to which a novel malady fits their notion of a biological illness and use this match to correctly predict a route of transmission. The particular contrast assessed will be between social and physical routes of transmission for mental and physical afflictions.

In summary, most psychologists would agree that children do not use an immanent justice explanation for illness and that they seem to understand more about illness then models assuming the necessity of domain general competencies would appear to allow. There is, however, substantial disagreement regarding the proper conceptualization of these early competencies. Two basic camps appear to have evolved. First, there are researchers who believe that children have a specific explanatory system for biological phenomena. According to this conceptualization, children's correct judgments about contagion and contamination are inferences based on a comparatively abstract and uniquely biological set of beliefs. On the other hand, some researchers consider children's biological knowledge to be a set of relatively uncoordinated facts that they will not limit to biology. The studies presented here attempt to evaluate children's beliefs about contagion using a set of novel afflictions and require children to evaluate the plausibility of different means of illness transmission. A key question concerns whether it is possible to have some systematic explanatory notions concerning disease without having an understanding of detailed mechanisms. This seems possible given the history of biological thought and could serve as an organizing principle in development as well.

## 9.4    Study 1

In the first study children heard a series of stories describing people with either a biological or a mental ailment. The biological ailments were skin conditions including yellow skin, wrinkles, and blue spots. The mental conditions were false beliefs. For example, one character thinks that Big Bird follows him around and talks to him. The stories reinforced the idea that the beliefs were signs of mental illness and were explicitly described as false. Children also often commented that they were "silly" or "crazy." Two events were then described in which the afflicted individual came into contact with a potential receiver of the illness. In one of the situations, the contact was exclusively physical, and in the other it was exclusively social. For example, one of the stories described a child who woke up in the morning with yellow skin, a presumptively biological affliction. Later in the day, when riding on the train she looked through the window and saw a friend in another car. They interacted by talking through an intercom but did not come into physical contact. After this introduction, she got to summer camp and accidentally slept in someone else's sleeping bag and used their toothbrush, but did not otherwise come into contact with the other camper. Each of the stories was accompanied by a series of drawings depicting the social and physical interactions. These interactions are shown schematically in figure 9.1.

At the end of the story, the children were asked who would catch the main character's illness: the individual who engaged only in the social interaction, or the one who only had the physical interaction. They were also asked to justify their responses. Correct answers were judged to be ones where the child successfully matched the mental affliction with the social interaction, or the physical affliction with the physical interaction. It should be noted that it is not necessarily true that a mental illness can *only* be caused by a social interaction, but as will be seen, adult intuition leans strongly in this direction. Therefore, for the example story above, a correct answer would required that the child match the biological nature of the skin affliction with the indirect physical interaction implied by the event where the character mistakenly uses another's sleeping bag. Each child heard six different stories, three describing mental afflictions, and three describing physical ones. The accuracy of children's intuitions are summarized by a score from zero to three for each kind of story with each point reflecting a choice that correctly matches a means of transmission with a kind of affliction.

Four groups of children (age 3/4, 5/6, 7/8, and 9/10) along with a group of college students participated in the study. The results of the forced choice response are summarized in figure 9.2 which shows several interesting patterns. First, the youngest group of children seemed somewhat able to match each kind of illness with the most likely method of transmission. For both story types, their performance was significantly above chance with 67 percent accuracy in the biological illness stories, $t(47) = 4.308$, $p = 0.0001$; one-tailed $t$-tests in all cases, and 60 percent accuracy in the mental illness stories, $t(47) = 2.022$, $p = 0.0244$. Accuracy for the biological stories showed a relatively smooth progression of improvement throughout development, but this seems to have come at the cost of overgeneralization as is evident in below-chance performance in the mental illness stories in the three older groups of children. Surprisingly, older children seem to have thought that physical contact was necessary to catch both biological *and* mental afflictions.

The protocols collected in response to open-ended justifications support the notion that the older children were using their understanding of

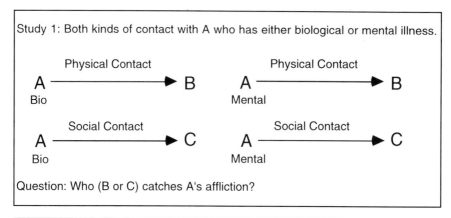

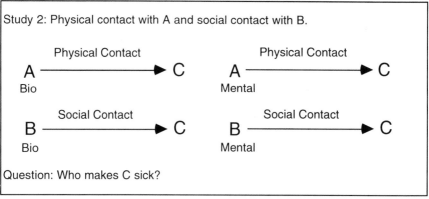

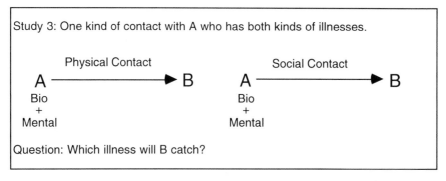

**Figure 9.1**
Methods used in studies 1, 2, and 3

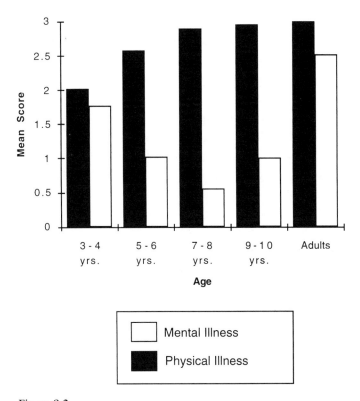

**Figure 9.2**
Mean number of correct transmission choices out of three possible in study 1

biological illnesses to explain the mental afflictions. These were coded for the presence of statements invoking germs as an explanation for transmission. The majority (67.4 percent) of older children's responses for the mental affliction included the notion of germs. (The youngest children said just about nothing in response to this question.) This is only a bit less frequent than reference to germs for the biological stories (in which 81 percent mentioned germs).

The results of Study 1 form a U-shaped developmental curve for responses on the mental anomalies, where performance shows a drop during a middle period of development. Such curves have long been of interest in the history of developmental psychology (e.g., Richards and Siegler 1982; Stavey et al. 1982) with many possible interpretations ranging from changing sets of rules in a production system to reorganizations of connectionist networks. Here the children's responses suggest that the change is caused by a move from an abstract understanding of biological and mental disorders to a more concrete model and mechanism. Unfortunately, the new mechanism, "germs," when it first is incorporated, is incorrectly construed in such a manner as to cause an overgeneralization of their mediating power to mental contents. It appears as if children who first learn about germs use a rule roughly of the sort that germs mediate physical transmission of anomalies (not social transmission) and that they can transmit all anomalies. The children are correct in limiting the method of transmission of germs to physical contact, but their conceptions of germs themselves and what they can transmit seem to be much less constrained.

As children grow older, they start to limit the germ explanation to biological illness, apparently because they have a more accurate notion of mechanism. The youngest children, also do better on the mental items because they haven't yet incorporated a germ model and rely on a more abstract and vaguer sense that mental and biological anomalies are fundamentally different and that the mental is more associated with social contexts and the biological with more physical contexts.

One problem with accepting a substantive developmental explanation for findings of Study 1 is that the pattern of overgeneralization of the germ explanation might be due to the particular structure of the stories themselves. First, the physical contact may make the character at the receiving end more salient. This is particularly problematic because the response the child must make depends on a choice between the two potential victims. Although the physical content event usually involved characters that were not present, the narrative structure of the stories could have any number of unpredictable effects on children's choices. Study 2 therefore uses a narrative that is essentially the reverse of that used in Study 1. Instead of a single source and two potential receivers, two sources and one receiver are used. Instead of choosing between two victims, the child attempts to trace the source of the illness.

## 9.5 Study 2

Six new stories were created which included only one potential victim who experienced two different contact events (again one social and one physical) with two different sources of illness (see figure 9.1). Both sources had the same biological or mental illnesses. For example, in one story two children named John and Henry are described who both falsely believe they have treasure buried in their backyards. They then have separate interactions with Ted, a friend of theirs. In one interaction, Ted uses John's football helmet and mouth guard right after John used it. In the other, Ted plays with Henry using walkie talkies to communicate while they stay in their respective bedrooms. While talking, Henry tells Ted about the treasure. The next day, Ted believes there's treasure in his yard. Children were then asked from whom Ted got his idea.

Two groups of children (age 5, $n = 20$ and 6, $n = 20$) heard three stories describing transmission of each kind of affliction. Results confirmed the findings of Study 1. For the biological afflictions the 5-year-olds chose the physical route for an average of 2.6 out of three the biological ailment stories, while they chose the social route for an average of 0.74 of the three mental illness stories. The 6-year-olds chose the biological route for 2.88 of the biological stories, and chose the social route for 0.82 of the mental illness stories. This closely replicates the findings of Study 1 where the 5- and 6-year-olds chose an average of 2.58 out of three physical routes for the biological stories, and 1.02 out of three social routes for the mental stories. Again, children frequently mentioned germs to explain transmission of mental illnesses. Ninety-five percent of the children mentioned germs in at least one physical ailment story, and 68 percent mentioned germs in at least one mental ailment story.

## 9.6   Study 3

If the overgeneralization observed in Studies 1 and 2 covers up an early understanding of specifically biological contagion, then it should be possible to design stimuli that sufficiently reduce the demand to consider biological mechanisms to allow performance that is above chance for the biological stories while performance on the mental stories does not fall below chance. One factor that might tempt children to overgeneralize biological mechanisms is the presence of a series of cues in both kinds of stories which point to biological transmission. For all stories in Studies 1 and 2, a physical contact is included that may be strongly associated with poor heath practice and therefore illness. For example, in a mental illness story the character may have shared a toothbrush with someone who is described as sick or at least abnormal. This might be enough to consistently invoke a biological model of contagion even given an illness for which the child might not otherwise infer a biological mechanism.

Study 3 therefore tested four groups of childrens' (age 3–4, $n = 13$; 5, $n = 28$; 6–7, $n = 26$; 8–9, $n = 18$) intuitions about contagion using stories designed to include fewer cues that imply biological contagion. In this case all scenarios described only one contact event which was either physical or social. The source individual had both a mental affliction and a biological one, and the child's task was to determine which illness would be transmitted given the type of contact that occurred. For these narratives, therefore, the mental stories contained no contacts characteristic of biological contagion. As in Studies 1 and 2 the narrative was accompanied by pictures. Children gave a response by witnessing two puppets expressing different opinions regarding which illness would be transmitted and pointing to the puppet they thought correct. They then justified their response.

As can be seen in figure 9.3, one of the most notable features of these data is that the stories were particularly difficult for the children to apprehend. In Studies 1 and 2, children were able to correctly identify the physical contact route of transmission on at least 2.5 out of 3 stories by age 5, whereas in the present study they did not reach a comparable level of performance until age 8–9. Therefore the difficult narrative structure of these stories may account for the poor performance on the part of the 3- to 4-year-olds (who did not differ significantly from chance in either condition).

The most important feature of these data is that in no case was less than chance performance observed in the mental stories suggesting that children overgeneralized much less than in the previous two studies. This impression is strongly confirmed by the justifications children gave. Only 15 percent of children responded that germs were involved in the social contact stories while 79 percent said that germs were responsible in the physical contact stories. Although responses were not unequivocal, all groups except the 3–4 year olds showed above chance performance in the physical contact stories ($p < 0.05$, one-tailed $t$-tests in all cases). By

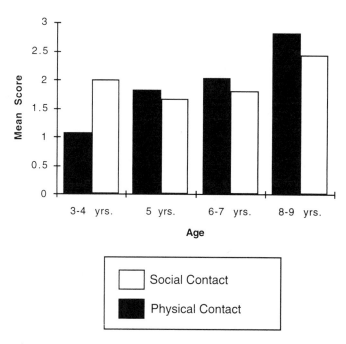

**Figure 9.3**
Mean number of correct transmission choices out of three possible in study 3

age 6–7, children achieved an average of 2 in 3 stories correct in the case of physical transmission, and 1.8 out of 3 correct for the mental transmission stories. These data also appear to replicate the U-shaped developmental curve that was observed in Study 1. By age 8–9 the children responded accurately for both types of transmission and mentioned germs in only 17 percent of mental illness stories. These results stand in contrast to the findings of Studies 1 and 2 where children as old as 9–10 appeared to overgeneralize the biological mechanism, responding at less than chance levels for social transmission stories and mentioning germs in 75 percent of mental illness stories.

At the most basic level Study 3 demonstrates that attempts to assess children's intuitions about biology, and for that matter in any domain, almost inevitably must confront the balance children strike between local heuristics and strategies and a more principled refusal to apply knowledge where they do not believe it fits. Especially in cases where unusual situations are involved, children are likely to search the stimulus materials themselves for cues that can guide application of core theories. In the case of contagion, they appear to pick up on physical contact as a characteristic indicator of biological disease transmission because their intuitions do not provide a solid set of rules for mental illnesses. In this context it is important to note that none of the subjects, even the adults in Study 1, had completely consistent intuitions regarding the most likely mechanism for contagion of false beliefs. It is certainly not inconsistent with a mature conception of biology that mental illness in general can be transmitted via germs, although germ based transmission of the particular contents of the beliefs does seem very odd. In the absence of strong intuitions it is only reasonable to search the particular situation described in the stimulus stories for cues regarding transmission.

In trying to understand children's theories about biology, then, overgeneralization should not always be seen as evidence for the absence of a coherent theory. For example, in other studies children were found unable to distinguish between illnesses caused by germs and those caused by poisons in that they believed both to be contagious (Solomon and Cassimatis 1995). Children might seem to think that germs are not part of a specifically biological system. Rather, the knowledge that germs cause illness might be an isolated fact. Presumably the isolated status of knowledge about germs renders it unable to accurately guide inference in new situations because generalization could only occur based on domain-general principles of structural similarity between a new situation and the current knowledge. This kind of similarity would not prevent incorrect generalization to poison because it is not bound by a theory that can isolate poison's nonbiologial status. However, according to the above reasoning the same could easily be true of a fact that is fundamentally attached to a more general biological knowledge. If certain features of a situation signal applicability of a theory then it should be activated and tested for the degree to which unknowns can be incorporated.

Take for example, a story from Solomon and Cassamatis (1995) in which a character comes in contact with either germs or poison, then gets sick and meets a friend:

A girl named Beth breathed in some germs [or poison] and pretty soon she got a runny nose and had to stay home from school. If a friend of hers, named Gavin, came over to visit and hung out with her for while do you think that Gavin could catch having a runny nose from Beth?

In this story several strong cues point to transmission of a common cold, a situation that is probably well known to children. A child gets characteristic symptoms and engages in characteristic contact with another child. Both of these facts can be expected to strongly activate a biological contagion theory. The presence of poison, a concept with unknown relation to contagion, gives the child three choices. The child can vacate his/her theory of contagion and make no prediction regarding transmission. He/she can require that a known contaminant be present and in its absence predict no transmission. Finally he/she can apply the theory in the presence of incomplete information and predict transmission. The first option is analytically weak. Making no commitment in the presence of a series of theory-relevant facts causes the child to miss out on an opportunity to refine his/her knowledge regarding transmission. The second option implies use of a strict criterion that several known elements must be present in order for contagion to occur. With poison, a concept not part of the known set of biological agents, in the place of expected information regarding a source for the illness a negative prediction is made. This strategy also cripples the process of expanding the child's understanding of biology because, like the first option, it requires information to be present that is often not available. As pointed out by Millikan (1993), concepts specify sets of features that are often not present in any given situation or precept. This is in fact what makes them useful. If some subset of features are present, then activation of the more abstract conceptual representation allows inference of the presence of other (nonpresent) features, and further allows inferences based on those features. The filling-in function of the conceptual apparatus implies the advantages of the child's third option—treating the theory-relevant features (runny nose and contact) as sufficient to generate the prediction of contagion.

The more general point is that several distinct strategies can be brought to bear on cases where one is confronted with incomplete information, and developmental changes in which strategies are used first should not be confused with deeper patterns of understanding. With biological thought, and in these cases with contagion, we can think of the developmental change in two ways that are interrelated. One involves change that occurs as children start to learn about a new more detailed mechanism. Prior to learning about the mechanism, they might have some strong sense about the more general causal properties of a domain. They might know, for example, that biological phenomena involve physical entities that act on each other directly and that biological organisms and systems have functional roles, even though they don't necessarily have minds. They might see such relations as importantly distinct from those in the social realm, which involve nonphysical entities, causal actions at a distance, and very different sorts of functional relations. There is in fact considerable evidence that preschoolers have just this sort of abstract knowledge (Simons and Keil 1995; Gutheil, Vera, and Keil 1998).

When a child first tries to incorporate the notion of germs, it seems that a common pattern is to posit a very simple and powerful mechanism along the lines that germs are physical entities that can transmit disease through physical contact and that they can transmit any sort of anomalous state, whether biological or mental. This sort of mechanism would account for the U-shaped curve that is sometimes observed. Does it mean that the children have no sense of biology or that they don't understand germs as biological entities? This conclusion is consistent with findings that children seem to rely on mechanical reasoning instead of uniquely biological reasoning when trying to understand biological phenomena (chapter 11, this volume). Such a conclusion is, however, not entirely necessary. Children might have abstract expectations about biology but not yet understand whether germs are within that realm. Alternatively, they might assume that germs are like people, embodying of both biological patterns of causation and psychological ones. This situation would be very similar to the coexistence of different systems of reasoning discussed here with reference to the historical development of medical knowledge and in traditional cultures. Moreover, on occasions where children do treat poison like germs, they might be simply misattributing poison to the same category as germs rather than lacking any understanding of the living nonliving distinction. As children get still older, they seem to reify their notion of how germs work such that they can only transmit factors that contribute to altered biological states, not mental ones. It seems that they gradually come to understand how to fit particular mechanisms into their broader senses of how living things work.

The second way of thinking about the developmental change focuses more on the sorts of local strategies that a child might use to fill in gaps of missing information. Thus, when children start to think about germs, they might assume that germs are involved in transmitting ailments in all situations that pass a certain threshold of overall similarity to the most familiar known case involving germs and contagion. Such a case might involve the common cold and being told that either touching a sick person or an object that they have contaminated will cause one to pick up their sickness. When confronted with a novel situation, the child looks for overall similarity to the common cold cases and, if the similarity is high enough, judges that the described ailment will be transmitted. It is important to see, however, that a simple similarity strategy cannot work in isolation. Some assumptions about germs and mechanisms seem to also be necessary. Thus, when children are comparing the new situation to old familiar ones involving contagion, they seem to be primarily weighting the kind of interaction between the two individuals. They may consider whether there is physical contact, whether it is direct or indirect, and even whether some sort of ingestion is involved. If everything is similar in those respects, they will often infer contagion regardless of how dissimilar the affliction might be to known cases. They therefore must discount similarity of affliction and emphasize similarity of transmission. To do so, they must have some hunches about what issues are relevant to how germs work.

## 9.7   Mechanism, Explanation, and Understanding

The case of emerging beliefs about disease, and of beliefs about living kinds in general, highlights a central problem in current research on cognitive development. There is now a strong consensus that even very young children's concepts, and the broader knowledge systems in which those concepts are embedded, must involve some understanding of causal relations among properties, larger property clusters, and individuals. At the same time young children, and for that matter sophisticated adults, cannot have exhaustive knowledge of all causal relations and must surely continue to learn as experience in a domain accumulates. The problem lies in trying to characterize how such knowledge might change with development. Traditionally there has been an assumption that causal understanding must arise from and/or be equivalent to clear notions of specific mechanisms, in essence highly concrete mental models of how things work in a particular area. For example, Au and Romo (chapter 11, this volume) argue that mechanical reasoning is used to the exclusion of any understanding of uniquely biological mechanisms, in both children and lay adults. This account assumes that knowledge of concrete mechanisms must precede abstract understandings, and when the former are found lacking, the latter must be even further beyond the realm of comprehension. Here we argue that one can have some understanding of likely causal patterns without having any particular mechanisms in mind and that, indeed, sometimes the first concrete mechanisms can lead one astray and cause errors in judgment.

A key challenge is to better specify what sorts of knowledge enable one to prefer some classes of explanations over others without having specific mechanisms in mind. In addition we need to better understand how these sorts of knowledge interact with and help guide the more specific mechanisms. Elsewhere, the notion of "modes of construal" has been offered as way of describing how a young child might have a sense of the kind of causal patternings and properties that are most relevant to reasonable explanations in a domain (Keil 1995). Such modes may not only be necessary for understanding how knowledge grows and changes in development but also how we learn and develop new explanations in adulthood. Our point in this chapter is to illustrate in the very specific case of beliefs about disease, how this much more general question of the relations between explanation, mechanism, and understanding is one of the most fundamental and important issues in current work on cognitive development. Moreover some of the most interesting and provocative insights are emerging in the realm of biological thought.

## Note

Research in this chapter was supported by NIH grant R01-HD23922.

## References

Ackerknecht, E. H. 1968. *A Short History of Medicine*. New York: Ronald Press.

Atkinson, D. T. 1956. *Magic, Myth and Medicine*. New York: World Publishing.

Au, T. K., A. L. Sidle, and K. Rollins. 1993. Developing an understanding of conservation and contamination: Invisible particles as a plausible mechanism, *Developmental Psychology* 2: 286–99.

Beverly, B. L. 1936. The effect of illness on emotional development. *Journal of Pediatrics* 8: 533–43.

Bibace, R., and M. E. Walsh. 1981. Children's conceptions of illness. In R. Bibace, and M. E. Walsh, eds., Children's *Conceptions of Health, Illness, and Bodily Functions*. New Directions for Child Development. San Francisco: Jossey-Bass.

Buck, A. H. 1979. *The Growth of Medicine from the Earliest Times to about 1800*. New Haven: Yale University Press.

Carey, S. 1985. *Conceptual Change in Childhood*, Cambridge: MIT Press.

Carey, S. 1995. On the origin of causal understanding. In D. Sperber, D. Premack and A. J. Premack, eds., *Causal Cognition: A Multidisciplinary Approach*. New York: Oxford University Press, pp. 268–303.

Fallon, A. E., P. Rozin, and P. Pliner. 1984. The child's conception of food: The development of food rejections with special reference to disgust and contamination sensitivity. *Child Development* 55: 366–75.

Gentner, D., and C. Toupin. 1988. Systematicity and surface similarity in the development of analogy. *Cognitive Science* 10: 277–300.

Green, E. C., A. Jurg, and A. Djedje. 1993. Sexually-transmitted diseases, AIDS and traditional healers in Mozambique. *Medical Anthropology* 15: 261–81.

Gutheil, G., A. Vera, and F. C. Keil. 1998. Do Houseflies think? Patterns of induction and biological beliefs in development. *Cognition* 66: 33–49.

Haggare, H. W. 1933. *Mystery, Magic, and Medicine*. Garden City, NY: Doubleday, Doran.

Inagaki, K., and G. Hatano. 1993. Young childrens' understanding of the mind-body distinction. *Child Development* 64: 1535–49.

Kalish, C. W. 1996. Preschoolers' understanding of germs as invisible mechanisms. *Cognitive Development* 11: 83–106.

Kalish, C. W. 1997. Preschoolers' understanding of mental and bodily reactions to contamination: What you don't know can hurt you, but cannot sadden you. *Developmental Psychology* 33: 79–91.

Keil, F. C. 1987. Conceptual development and category structure. In U. Neisser ed., *Concepts and Conceptual Development*. New York: Cambridge University Press, pp. 175–200.

Keil, F. C. 1994. Explanation, association, and the acquisition of word meaning. *Lingua* 92: 169–96.

Keil, F. C. 1995. The growth of causal understanding of natural kinds: Modes of construal and the emergence of biological thought. In A. Premack and D. Sperber, eds., *Causal Cognition*. Oxford: Oxford University Press, pp. 234–62.

Loveland, F. O. 1976. Snakebite cure among the Rama indians of Nicaragua. In F. X. Grollig and H. B. Haley, eds., *Medical Anthropology*. Paris: Mouton, pp. 81–102.

Maffi, L. 1994. A linguistic analysis of Tzeltal Maya ethnosymptomatology. *Dissertation Abstracts International* 55: 9504901.

Magner, L. N. 1992. *A History of Medicine*. New York: Marcel Dekker.

Mead, M. 1932. An investigation of the thought of primitive children with special reference to animism. *Royal Anthropological Institute Journal* 62: 173–90.

Millikan, R. 1993. Synthetic concepts: Philosophical thoughts on categorization. Unpublished manuscript.

Mull, D. S., and J. D. Mull. 1994. Insights from community-based research on child pneumonia in Pakistan. *Medical Anthropology* 15: 335–52.

Phillips, E. D. 1973. *Greek Medicine*. London: Thames and Hudson.

Piaget, J. 1932. *The Moral Judgement of the Child*. London: Kegan, Paul, Trench, Trubner.

Quintanilla, A. 1976. Effect of rural-urban migration on beliefs and attitudes toward disease and medicine in southern Peru. In F. X. Grollig and H. B. Haley, eds., *Medical Anthropology*. Paris: Mouton, pp. 393–401.

Richards, D. D., and R. S. Sielger. 1982. U-shaped behavioral curves: It's not whether you're right or wrong, it's why. In S. Strauss, and R. Stavy, eds., U-*Shaped Behavioral Growth*. New York: Academic Press, pp. 37–61.

Rosengren, K. S., S. A. Gelman, C. W. Kalish, and M. McCormick. 1991. As time goes by: Children's early understanding of growth in animals. *Child Development* 62: 1302–20.

Rozin, P., A. Fallon, and M. Augustoni-Ziskind. 1986. The child's conception of food: The development of categories of acceptable and rejected substances. *Journal of Nutrition Education* 18: 75–81.

Scarborough, J. 1969. *Roman Medicine*. Ithaca: Cornell University Press.

Siegal, M. 1988. Children's understanding of contageon and contamination as causes of illness. *Child Development* 59: 1353–59.

Siegal, M., and D. L. Share. 1990. Contamination sensitivity in young children. *Developmental Psychology* 26: 455–58.

Simons, D. J., and F. C. Keil. 1995. An abstract to concrete shift in the development of biological thought: The insides story. *Cognition* 56: 129–63.

Solomon, G. E. A., and N. L. Cassimatis. 1995. On young children's understanding of germs as biological causes of illness. Paper presented at the meetings of the Society for Research in Child Development, Indianapolis, IN.

Spelke, E. S. 1991. Physical knowledge in infancy: Reflections on Piaget's theory. In S. Carey and R. Gelman eds., *Epigenesis of Mind: Studies in Biology and Cognition* Hillsdale, NJ: Lawrence Erlbaum.

Springer, K., and J. Ruckel. 1992. Early beliefs about the causailty of illness: Immanent justice revisited and rejected. *Cognitive Development* 7: 429–43.

Springer, K., and A. Belk. 1994. The role of physical contact and association in early contamination sensitivity. *Developmental Psychology* 30: 864–68.

Stavy, R., S. Strauss, N. Orpaz, and G. Carmi. 1982. U-shaped behavioral growth. In S. Strauss, and R. Stavey, eds., U-*Shaped Behavioral Growth*. New York: Academic Press, pp. 11–36.

Venzmer, G. 1968. *Five Thousand Years of Medicine*. New York: Taplinger.

Woodward, A. L., A. Phillips, and E. S. Spelke. 1993. Infants' expectations about the motion of animate versus inanimate objects. *Proceedings of the 15th Annual Conference of the Cognitive Science Society*, Hillsdale, NJ: Lawrence Erlbaum, pp. 1087–92.

Woodward, A. L. 1995. Infants' reasoning about the goals of a human actor. Poster session presented at the Biennial meetings of the Society for Research in Child Development, Indianapolis, IN.

# 10

# A Developmental Perspective on Informal Biology

Giyoo Hatano and Kayoko Inagaki

Until very recently there have been few interactions between anthropological studies dealing with biological understanding among people living in small communities without modern science and technology (i.e., folkbiology) and developmental studies on naive biology of children growing up in technologically advanced societies. Only after Atran (1990), investigators in these two research areas, separated by the disciplinary boundary, have recognized the conceptual relevance of each other's work. Folkbiology and naive biology have in fact many similarities because both of them are the product of human minds that are endowed with innate constraints or learning biases for biological entities and phenomena, and neither of them is much influenced by the modern science of biology. However, these two forms of informal biology are not alike in every aspect. Whereas folkbiology reflects rich direct and indirect experience with biological kinds in the indigenous culture, naive biology is usually built upon a limited experiential database. Therefore, although it seems that pieces of folkbiological knowledge that are essentially universal across cultures are acquired quite early in the development of naive biology, and vice versa, this is not always the case.

Let us first discuss similarities and differences between folkbiology and naive biology, as the starting point for more systematic comparisons to be made later in this chapter. We assume that there are a few striking commonalities between them due to the shared sources for their acquisition. First, in both folkbiology and naive biology entities in the world are divided into four ontological categories, that is, humans, other animals, plants, and nonliving things (Atran 1998). This is because humans are supposed to have domain-specific schemata of mind through which they "conceptually perceive" different aspects of the world differently (Atran 1998). Humans can distinguish humans from all other things, and animals from nonliving things including artifacts, primarily in terms of the spontaneous movement (Gelman 1990). They can also separate plants from nonliving things because plants grow though they do not move (Inagaki and Hatano 1996, Experiment 1).

Second, both of these forms of informal biology rely on global and intuitive modes of understanding (e.g., various forms of vitalism) because neither indigenous people nor children in our society possess the set of conceptual tools that has been accumulated in modern biology. Although both folkbiology and naive biology are theories about biological entities and phenomena, not just collections of observed facts and effective procedures, young children or indigenous people have to make sense of their observations without being helped by the modern science of biology.

We also assume that there are marked differences between folkbiology and naive biology, due to the different sources for their acquisition. Young children have little firsthand experience with nonhuman animals and plants, whereas indigenous adults in small communities are experts on living kinds in their ecological niche. Thus it is not surprising that indigenous adults everywhere possess "similar folkbiological structures composed of essence-based species and ranking of species" (Atran 1998, p. 1) as joint products between their expertise and the domain-specific schemata of human cognition. In contrast, young children, though they may have some abstract or global understanding of what animals or plants are like (Simons and Keil 1995), lack concrete or specific pieces of knowledge about each living thing.

This difference in the experiential database produces another important difference: young children's biology must be personifying, whereas indigenous adults' biology can be category based. Young children may know that for instance, a gazelle belongs to the same group as deer and that therefore a gazelle's behavior can be better predicted by an inference based on his or her knowledge about a deer than by personification. However, unless this knowledge about a deer or the genus of deers is rich and active, he or she has to rely on personification.

In this chapter we would like to examine in detail the interface between folkbiology and naive biology that we have been studying, relying on the rough sketch of similarities and differences between them described above. In some cases where folkbiological knowledge is clear and known to us, we will examine whether or not it can be applied to naive biology. In other cases, based on the above analyses of similarities and differences and our experimental findings of naive biology, we will make predictions for folkbiology or try to give suggestions for research to folkbiologists.

## 10.1  Classifying Objects into Four Ontological Categories

According to Atran (1998), in cultures throughout the world it is common to classify all entities into four ontological categories: humans, nonhuman animals, plants, and inanimate objects including artifacts. Is this classification easy for young children as well, at least regarding typical examples of those categories?

### Children Six Years of Age and Older

The most relevant data to this issue have been obtained from our cross-national study including Israel, Japan, and the United States (see Hatano et al. 1993). Participants, who were 6, 8, and 10 years old, were asked whether each of eight objects possessed each of 16 attributes. The objects were typical entities of the four ontological categories: people (a woman, a girl), other animals (a rabbit, a pigeon), plants (a tree, a tulip), and inanimate objects (a stone, a chair). The 16 attributes could be divided into seven clusters including (1) life status (is alive), (2) unobservable animal attributes (has a heart, has bones, has a brain), (3) sensory attributes (can feel that it is cold, can feel pain if we hit it with a stick), and (4) attributes true of all living things (grows, dies/withers).

Questions about the eight objects were presented in random order. All 16 questions were asked about each object before proceeding to the next object. The 16 questions about the presence of the attributes were asked in a different random order for each object, except that the last question was always whether the object was alive. This was done to minimize the effect of children's answers to this question on their judgments of the presence of other attributes.

Let us examine the accuracy of judgments for four clusters of attributes (all-living-thing, unobservable animal part, sensory, and life status) to the four classes of objects (people, other animals, plants, and inanimate objects). Percentages of incorrect responses are tabulated for each country by age group in table 10.1. Children's judgments of attributes of all-living-things and of being alive were judged as correct if they were reported as present in people, other animals, and plants, and absent in inanimate things. Their judgments of unobservable animal properties and of sensory attributes were judged to be correct if these attributes were reported to be present in people and other animals but not in plants and inanimate objects.

Table 10.1 reveals four general trends. First, the accuracy of judgments was generally high even among the 6-year-olds, who were accurate more than 85 percent of the time when aggregating the percentage correct across the object classes and the four property clusters.

Second, the accuracies varied considerably among the object classes. Specifically, judgments regarding people were almost perfectly accurate for all attribute clusters (aggregated percentage correct, 99 percent), and these were significantly different from those for animals (91 percent) and inanimate objects (95 percent), both of which were quite high among the 6-year-olds and very high among the 8- and 10-year-olds. The proportion of correct judgments for plants was 84 percent, which was the lowest in accuracy of the above four classes.

Third, as children grew older, their judgments became more accurate. However, attributing life status or sensory properties was not very accurate even among the 10-year-olds, probably due to the ambiguity of the questions posed to them. The term "alive" is especially complex and contains multiple definitions that children may find confusing.

Fourth, when there were cross-national differences in accuracy, American children outperformed both Israeli and Japanese children. Israeli children were the least accurate in attributing all-living-thing properties and life status to plants; only 51 percent of Israeli 10-year-olds correctly attributed life status to plants. This point will be discussed later.

To summarize, the above data support the assumption that it is fairly easy for children to distinguish typical instances of the four ontological categories in attributing properties, though this study did not examine whether the children could classify those instances.

**Table 10.1**
Mean percentages of incorrect judgments of clusters of properties for each class of entity by age and country

| Age property | People | | | Other animals | | | Plants | | | Inanimates | | |
|---|---|---|---|---|---|---|---|---|---|---|---|---|
| | I | J | US | I | J | US | I | J | US | I | J | US |
| **6** Alive | 8 | 0 | 0 | 8 | 2 | 1 | 42 | 34 | 32 | 18 | 20 | 4 |
| Animal properties | 3 | 1 | 0 | 28 | 32 | 18 | 5 | 9 | 4 | 3 | 12 | 3 |
| Sensory properties | 3 | 1 | 3 | 26 | 24 | 8 | 24 | 31 | 30 | 8 | 22 | 11 |
| All-living-things properties | 8 | 3 | 4 | 22 | 24 | 12 | 28 | 22 | 8 | 2 | 8 | 1 |
| **8** Alive | 0 | 0 | 0 | 0 | 3 | 1 | 41 | 28 | 12 | 2 | 6 | 1 |
| Animal properties | 0 | 0 | 1 | 13 | 3 | 4 | 4 | 10 | 3 | 0 | 2 | 0 |
| Sensory properties | 0 | 0 | 0 | 16 | 6 | 6 | 23 | 21 | 19 | 7 | 3 | 0 |
| All-living-things properties | 0 | 1 | 1 | 1 | 2 | 1 | 17 | 3 | 2 | 2 | 4 | 1 |
| **10** Alive | 0 | 0 | 1 | 0 | 0 | 0 | 41 | 9 | 2 | 0 | 8 | 0 |
| Animal properties | 0 | 0 | 1 | 16 | 7 | 4 | 1 | 0 | 1 | 0 | 0 | 1 |
| Sensory properties | 0 | 0 | 0 | 12 | 10 | 4 | 12 | 20 | 17 | 1 | 9 | 1 |
| All-living-things properties | 1 | 0 | 1 | 9 | 3 | 2 | 21 | 5 | 0 | 0 | 8 | 1 |

Note: I = Israel; J = Japan; US = United States.

## Younger Children

Inagaki and Hatano (1993a) administered the same set of questions to younger Japanese children, specifically, to 36 four-year-olds (mean age was 4 years 1 month; range, 3 years 7 months to 4 years 6 months). These children were tested again at 5 years 1 month (range, 4 years 8 months to 5 years 6 months) and at 6 years 1 month (5 years 7 months to 6 years 6 months). Table 10.2 shows the percentages of incorrect responses at each testing. (The data on the attribute of having a brain were not analyzed here because many 4-year-olds failed to understand the term "brain.") We can see two trends in table 10.2. First, these younger children were moderately accurate in their judgments except when they were 4 years of age (aggregated percentages correct were 66, 79, and 90 percent, respectively, at ages 4, 5, and 6). Second, the accuracies in judgments varied markedly between humans and the other three classes of entities. Specifically, even at 4 years of age judgments on humans were accurate for all attribute clusters (84 percent), whereas those on the other three classes were not accurate: 64 percent for the inanimate objects, 60 percent for plants, and 57 percent for other animals.

Although the above results from aggregated percentages correct seem to indicate that younger children before 6 years of age did not differentiate among nonhuman animals, plants and inanimates, results from a rule assessment showed that this was not the case. Rule analyses (Richards and Siegler 1984) were performed on the pattern of each child's responses for each of the three property clusters: unobservable animal, sensory, and all-living-thing properties.

It was judged whether each child's pattern of attributions for the four ontological classes roughly conformed to one of four anticipated rules. They were as follows: (1) The humans rule (humans alone possess the property, H-rule), (2) The humans and animals rule (humans and other animals alone possess the property, A-rule), (3) The all-living-things rule (humans, other animals and plants possess the property, L-rule), and (4) the everything rule (everything including nonliving things possess the property, E-rule). Patterns of attributions that did not meet any of these rules were put into the residual category ("others").

**Table 10.2**
Mean percentages of incorrect judgments of clusters of properties for each class of entity at each testing

| | People | | | Other animals | | | Plants | | | Inanimates | | |
|---|---|---|---|---|---|---|---|---|---|---|---|---|
| Age at testing | 4 yrs | 5 yrs | 6 yrs | 4 yrs | 5 yrs | 6 yrs | 4 yrs | 5 yrs | 6 yrs | 4 yrs | 5 yrs | 6 yrs |
| **Properties** | | | | | | | | | | | | |
| All living things | 20 | 5 | 0 | 51 | 32 | 14 | 39 | 22 | 9 | 23 | 13 | 4 |
| Unobserved animal | 19 | 3 | 1 | 57 | 40 | 22 | 23 | 15 | 6 | 39 | 13 | 0 |
| Sensory | 13 | 6 | 0 | 36 | 22 | 15 | 50 | 45 | 25 | 38 | 36 | 14 |
| Life status | 10 | 4 | 0 | 15 | 8 | 1 | 54 | 38 | 38 | 54 | 38 | 24 |
| Means | 16 | 5 | 0 | 43 | 28 | 15 | 40 | 29 | 17 | 36 | 23 | 9 |

For the unobservable animal properties, the A-rule (correct attribution response) and the H-rule (underattribution response) were used more often than the others at age 4, though responses that could not be identified as one of the rules were also found often. Although users of the H-rule were still found at age 5, more than 50 percent at this age correctly used the A-rule, and at age 6 a great majority of them (86 percent) adopted it.

For the sensory properties, children used the E-rule (overattribution response) at a substantial rate at both ages 4 and 5, but few children did so at age 6; more than 80 percent of the children at age 6 used either the A-rule or the L-rule, though many fewer (20 percent) used the latter. This finding suggests that the children differentiated animals and plants from nonliving things in terms of their ability to feel sensation, though attributing sensations to plants is not scientifically correct.

For the all-living-things property, about 30 percent (10/36) used the L-rule (correct attribution) at age 4; major incorrect rules at this age 4 were the E-rule (overattribution) and the A-rule (underattribution), and quite a number of the children could not be classified as users of any specific rule at age 4. However, the users of the L-rule markedly increased at ages 5 and 6, specifically, 72 percent at age 5 and 94 percent at age 6. This result suggests, contrary to previous studies (e.g., Carey 1985), that children can distinguish living things (animals and plants) from nonliving things, at least in terms of growth and death, by age 5. This point will be discussed further in a later section.

### Combining Two or Three Ontological Categories

Correct biological understanding requires us to integrate the categories of humans and other animals into the category of animals, and those of animals and plants into the category of living things. If the taxonomy of entities in the four ontological categories is based on human domain-specific schemata, such integrations should be rather difficult.

Atran (1998) claims that in virtually no culture do people consider that humans and nonhuman living kinds belong to the same ontological category. This may also be true for young children growing up in technologically advanced societies. In fact Johnson, Mervis, and Boster (1992) found that, whereas 10-year-olds and adults possess a category of primates and include humans in it, 7-year-olds regard humans as very different from even a monkey. Carey (1985) also reported that when 4-year-olds were taught some novel properties about people, they attributed them to other animals to a much greater extent than when taught about dogs. In contrast, 10-year-olds and adults who were taught about dogs were hardly distinguishable in attributional patterns from those taught about people. These results indicate that humans have some special status among animals if they are included in that category.

However, it doesn't seem difficult for young children to recognize some commonalities between humans and other animals. Young children often rely on the person analogy for predicting behaviors of an animal in unfamiliar situations, as will be shown below. They also tend to project human attributes to animals, especially mammals (Carey 1985; Inagaki and Sugiyama 1988). Moreover Vera and Keil (1988) have shown that giving a context referring to a person's living better or becoming more active produced more extended and accurate inductive projections to a variety of animals. It is likely that young children regard a human as something special, but at the same time that they treat a human as prototype of animals.

Is it possible for young children to recognize commonalities between animals and plants? Some investigators are skeptical. For example, Carey (1985) claims that young children do not possess an integrated category of living things, since they are totally ignorant of their histologically or physiologically shared bases.

However, we believe that young children have grasped commonalities between animals and plants at a functional level that may be taken as biological long before they recognize histological or physiological commonalities. Let us present some of our recent findings (Inagaki and Hatano 1996). One experiment examined whether children before age 6 distinguished plants and animals from nonliving things in terms of growth (i.e., changes in size over time). Children of ages 4 and 5 were presented with a picture of a flower's sprout (or a new artifact or a young animal) as the standard stimulus picture and then asked to choose which of two other pictures would represent the same plant (or artifact or animal) a few hours later and several months/years later (see figure 10.1).

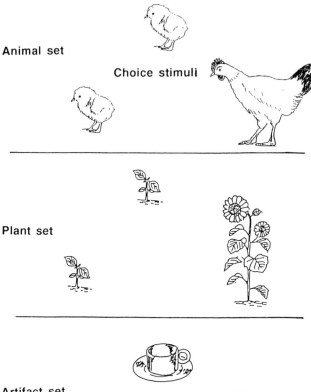

**Standard stimulus**

**Animal set**

**Choice stimuli**

**Plant set**

**Artifact set**

**Figure 10.1**
Example set of standard stimulus and choice stimulus cards for plants, artifacts, and animals

Results indicated that the children show "invariance" patterns (i.e., no change in size both a few hours later and several months/years later for all the items) for artifacts but "growth" patterns (i.e., increase in size either/both a few hours later or/and several months/years later) for plants and animals.

Another experiment indicated that 5-year-olds constrained inductive projections of not only growth but also other properties such as taking food and water, using the category of living things, when given brief vitalistic descriptions about them. Here half of the children were given contexts by short vitalistic descriptions about target properties, such as for growth, "A person becomes bigger and bigger, *by taking in energy from food and water*," whereas the other half were not given such descriptions (the italic part in the above example was not given). Then both groups of the children were required to attribute these properties to three animals, three plants, and three inanimate objects presented in a mixed order, in a question such as "Does X grow?" The results indicated that biological contexts helped the children extend given properties, especially growth and the taking of food and water, to both animals and plants but not to nonliving things. This finding suggests that the biological context activated the category of living things that the children already possessed, since each description for creating the biological context took only seconds.

Still another experiment strongly suggested the possibility that young children have consciously grasped commonalities between animals and plants. Another group of 5-year-olds was directly asked whether plants or inanimate objects would show similar phenomena to those observed for animals. They responded affirmatively only for plants and could offer some specific phenomena for growth, feeding, and aging/dying in support of their answers; for example, many children indicated that watering for plants was analogous to feeding for animals.

It will be intriguing to investigate whether indigenous adults also possess categories of animals (including both humans and other animals) and of living things. If they do, perception of living kinds is surely guided conceptually, since these categories cannot be formed based on similarities in appearance, motion, or style of life only.

## 10.2    Taxonomy of Animals

Atran (1998) claims that teleological schemata, the domain-specific processing apparatus unique to the conceptual module of folkbiology, generate almost universally across cultures, categories of living things that roughly correspond to biological species and higher-order groupings. In fact he and his associates have found that the Itzaj Maya Indians classify mammals in good accordance with scientific (evolutionary) classifications; their classification is a little more accurate than American college students' classification.

This system for biological classification will not hold for young children, however. Young children have very limited direct contact with most animals except for pets. Thus we assume that though they may have similar teleological schemata to those of indigenous adults, young children's classification of mammals in particular or animals in general are not scientifically accurate. Young children may be easily distracted by some surface similarities. Let us examine this assumption by analyzing data obtained in one of our studies on naive biology.

### Finding Pairs of Animals

Inagaki and Hatano (1988) examined whether elementary school children would attribute human properties more often to the more humanlike member of a pair of animals than the less humanlike one, even when they knew these members belonged to the same category. Thirty-three second-graders (mean age 8 years 2 months, range 7 years 8 months to 8 years 7 months), 34 fourth-graders (mean age 10 years 2 months, range 9 years 8 months to 10 years 7 months), 26 students from a national university, and 47 from a private university served as subjects. Most students from the national university took qualifying examinations on a variety of subjects including biology to enter the university, whereas those from the private university did not, and thus the latter students were considered biologically less knowledgeable than the former. None of the college students majored in biology.

Inagaki and Hatano used five pairs of animals belonging to the same higher-order categories that are different in similarity to people. These were an elephant and a mouse (mammals), a penguin and a swallow

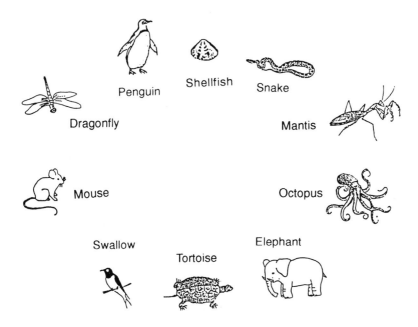

**Figure 10.2**
Drawings of ten animals used in the grouping task

(birds), a tortoise and a snake (reptiles), a mantis and a dragonfly (insects), and an octopus and shellfish (mollusks). After being asked six property questions, "Does *X* have a property *Y*?" or "Does *X* do *Y*?" in printed form, the students were given a grouping task to examine whether they could classify the ten animals into the five higher-order categories. They were first given two practice tasks, using four kinds of animals that were not used in the main task, to confirm that they understood how to group the same kinds. Then they moved on to the main task in which they were shown drawings of the above ten animals arranged in a circle and required to group animals of the same kind by drawing lines (see Figure 10.2). They were not told how many groups they should make, nor how many animals would be in each group. They were instructed to leave out animals that did not go together with any of the others.

Classifications were judged as correct when pairings based on higher-order categories were made, and as incorrect when an animal was grouped with two other animals belonging to different categories, even if one of the pairings was correct (e.g., a dragonfly was paired correctly with a mantis, but also with a swallow, and the mantis and swallow were not paired). Proportions of correct classifications were 40.2 percent for the second-graders, 47.8 percent for the fourth-graders, 69.1 percent for the students from the private university, and 90.4 percent for the national university students. This result indicates that the classification based on higher-order categories was difficult for the second- and fourth-graders, and even for some college students.

What kinds of errors did these students make? We found three major types of errors, and all types were observed among not only the elementary school children but also the private university students, though the occurrence rates were lower among the latter. The first type was an error produced by grouping based on where animals can be seen. Specifically, these students tended to group animals that were observed at a zoo into the same category; for example, about one-third of the second- and the fourth-graders paired a snake with an elephant or a mouse, and 24 percent of the second-graders, 29 percent of the fourth-graders, and 28 percent of the private university students grouped a penguin with an elephant or a mouse. These are all animals that students living in big, clean cities can observe only at a zoo.

The second type of error was due to grouping based on capabilities, that is, linking animals that can fly, animals that can swim, and so on. One-third of the second-graders and one-fifth of the fourth-graders paired a dragonfly with a swallow, and two students from the private university did so. One-fourth of the second-graders and the fourth-graders grouped a penguin with a tortoise or an octopus, and 4 out of the 47 private university students did so.

The third type was an error generated by grouping based on the appearance of animals. For example, some students paired a snake and an octopus probably because these animals twist and turn, and a tortoise was sometimes put together with a shellfish.

It is not very surprising that the children had difficulty classifying animals, considering that they had very limited direct experience with them. They were in fact easily distracted by some surface similarities and/or shared associations. However, the private university students, who had

had biology classes in junior high and high school, although they probably had not studied hard, unexpectedly showed only slightly more accuracy in their classifications than the elementary school children. Patterns of erroneous pairings by these children and adults are especially intriguing. Both groups often considered where animals are raised and how they move as important characteristics.

How can we reconcile children's rather inaccurate classifications with the respectable accuracy of the classification of mammals by the Itzaj Maya Indians? One plausible answer is in terms of the different amount of experience. Another is that whereas humans can classify animals belonging to a single class (e.g., mammalia) fairly accurately by observing and weighing various dimensions of similarity, they are prone to make erroneous groupings across classes depending on such salient similarities as living in the same place and moving in the same way. In other words, life forms that are cross-culturally variable (Atran 1998) do not necessarily correspond with any scientific categories. Atran (1998) reports that a bat is classified as a bird among the Itzaj. Similarly a life form of creeping things may include an earthworm, a leech, or even a snake, in addition to a variety of bugs (as in ancient China).

## 10.3  Taxonomy-Based versus Similarity-Based Inference

As mentioned at the beginning of this chapter, young children's prediction and explanation of an unfamiliar living thing's properties and behaviors are based on its similarity to people, not based on its higher-order category membership and category-property associations. This seems inevitable, since they do not have a well-developed taxonomy of animals and plants nor rich knowledge about higher-order categories. However, young children are so familiar with humans that they can use their knowledge about humans as a source for analogically attributing properties to less familiar animate objects or for predicting the reactions of such objects to novel situations. It should be noted that they do not use their knowledge about humans indiscriminately. In other words, they can use personification or the person analogy in an adaptive way in that they generate reasonable answers without committing many overpersonifying errors. How is it possible for young children who have not acquired an articulated taxonomy of properties (all-living-thing properties, animal properties, etc.) to do so? They seem to be helped by two constraints when they transfer knowledge about humans to other animate objects.

One is a differential application or similarity constraint, which requires the target object to be more or less similar to a human in order for the person analogy to be applied to it. As Vosniadou (1989) asserts, children tend to apply an analogy on the basis of salient similarity between the target and the source, though the "depth" of this perceived similarity varies with the richness and structuredness of the knowledge base children have. Generally, the closer the target object is biologically to a human being, the more often children recognize its similarity and thus apply the person analogy.

The other constraint in young children's person analogy is a factual check or feasibility constraint, proposed by Inagaki and Hatano (1987, 1991). This requires that the predicted behavior of the target object through the person analogy be feasible, and that, if not, the prediction be rejected. It is claimed that this constraint works after the person analogy is attempted, that is, one examines whether the analogical inference is tenable on the basis of factual knowledge about the target object. Even young children often know specific facts about "observable attributes" of an animate object, for example, whether or not it has a mouth, walks, or speaks to humans (e.g., Gelman, Spelke, and Meck 1983; Inagaki and Hatano 1987). Thus they may use this knowledge to check the plausibility of predictions reached by the person analogy, even though the knowledge is not powerful enough to generate predictions in itself.

**Personification of Animals and Plants**

In Inagaki and Hatano (1991) children of age 6 were asked to predict a grasshopper's or a tulip's reactions to three types of novel situations: (1) similar situations in which a human being and the target object behave similarly, and thus the person analogy generates predictions plausible to them in light of their specific knowledge, (2) contradictory situations where the target object and a human react differently, and predictions based on the person analogy contradict children's specific knowledge about the target, and (3) compatible situations where the object and a human being in fact react differently, but predictions obtained through the person analogy do not seem implausible to them. Example questions for these situations are as follows: "We usually feed a grasshopper once or twice a day when we raise it at home. What will happen with it if we feed it ten times a day?" [In the case of a tulip, the word *water* was used instead of *feed.*] (a similar situation). "Suppose that a woman buys a grasshopper. On her way home she drops in at a store with this caged grasshopper. After shopping she is about to leave the store without the grasshopper. What will the grasshopper do?" (contradictory). "Does a grasshopper feel something if the person who has been taking care of it daily dies?" [If the subject's answer is yes] "How does it feel?" (compatible).

Results indicated that for the similar situations many of the children generated reasonable predictions with some explanations by using person analogies, whereas they did not give personified predictions for the contradictory situations. As expected, they produced unreasonable predictions for the compatible situations, where they were unable to check the plausibility of products of person analogies because they lacked adequate knowledge, for example, about the relationship between the brain and feeling (Johnson and Wellman 1982).

The following examples clearly indicate how young children could generate more or less "reasonable" responses to a set of questions about a grasshopper or about a tulip.

*M.K. (6 years, 3 months):* For the "too-much-eating" question of the similar situation, "The grasshopper will be dizzy and die, 'cause the grasshopper, though it is an insect, is like a person (in this point)"; for the "left-behind" question of the contradictory situation, "The grasshopper will be picked up by someone, 'cause it cannot open the cage." ["*If someone does not pick up the cage, what will the grasshopper do?*"] "The grasshopper will just stay there." ["*Why doesn't the grasshopper do anything? Why does it just stay there?*"] "It cannot (go out of the cage and) walk, unlike a person"; for the caretaker's death question of the compatible situation, "The grasshopper will feel unhappy."

*Y.S. (6 years, 0 months):* For the too-much eating question, "The tulip will go bad. ["*Why?*"] If we water the tulip too much, it cannot drink the water so much, so it will wither"; for the left-behind question, "The tulip doesn't speak.... Someone will bring the (potted) tulip to the police office, as a lost thing. ["*If there is no one who does such a thing, what will the tulip do? Is there anything the tulip can do?"*] The tulip cannot move, because it has no feet"; for the caretaker's death question, "The tulip will surely be sad. It cannot say 'sad,' but it will feel so inside."

Generally speaking, children generate reasonable predictions, using person analogies in a constrained way, and the person analogy may be misleading only where they lack (biological) knowledge to check analogy-based predictions.

**Projection Based on Similarity to a Person**
Young children's frequent use of personification is also suggested from studies using the inductive projection paradigm, that is, when a child is asked to judge whether a set of animate and inanimate objects has target properties that he or she knows a human possesses. Both Carey (1985) and Inagaki and Sugiyama (1988) showed that when asked to attribute biological properties that humans possess to varied animate objects, preschoolers reveal a gradually decreasing pattern of attribution from humans to those objects that are arranged on a continuum according to the phylogenetic affinity to a person, whereas adults tend to show a flat attributional pattern with an abrupt change (Carey 1985; Inagaki and Sugiyama 1988). Here it is assumed that the gradually decreasing patterns are generated by subjects who attribute properties that they know humans possess to other animate objects to the extent that they perceive similarity between humans and the target objects, whereas the flat patterns involving an abrupt decrease are products of a deductive attribution arrived at by relying on the higher-order category membership and category-attribute associations. In other words, the gradually decreasing pattern is assumed to represent similarity-based inferences (Inagaki and Sugiyama 1988) or the comparison-to-people model (Carey 1985), and the flat pattern involving an abrupt decrease reflects category-based inferences.

Carey (1985) found, through analyses of group data, that 4-year-olds made similarity-based inferences, while 10-year-olds relied little on this process. Inagaki and Sugiyama (1988) revealed, through analyses of individual data as well as group data, that ways of inference changed from preschoolers' reliance on similarity-based to adults' category-based; in addition elementary school children (second- and fourth-graders) used an intermediate form of inference, which might be called "constrained similarity-based inference," namely inference primarily based on similarity but constrained by higher-order categorical knowledge (e.g., the animal-plant distinction). This shift was observed for not only anatomical/physiological properties but also mental ones, though the shift for the latter occurred later in life.

The person analogy is not limited to biological inference, it is observed in other behavioral domains. However, it is a very useful tool in biological inference because humans are a species of advanced animals, and they have a body and exhibit biological phenomena like other animals. It is an interesting question whether indigenous adults may rely on the person analogy when they do not know much about the target property. It is true that they possess a well-developed taxonomy of animals and plants and usually make category-based inferences using the taxonomy. However, they may not know some category-property associations. It is likely that they rely on personification in that case as a default strategy. In fact Inagaki and Sugiyama (1988) found that even some college students make similarity-based inferences for mental properties, for which they have not been taught category boundaries.

Another interesting question is whether indigenous children respond in a similar fashion to children in technologically advanced societies. If so, it would support our assumption that the shift from similarity-based to category-based inference is universal and does not require school instruction (Hatano and Inagaki 1996).

## 10.4   Mind-Body or Psychology-Biology Differentiation

Folkbiological studies have concentrated almost exclusively on indigenous adults' grasp of nonhuman animals and plants, especially their taxonomy and taxonomy-based inferences (e.g., inductive projection of a property from one category to another). Whether indigenous people distinguish between mind and body or separate biology from psychology has not been an issue in these studies. This is because those people appear to surely possess a form of biology, that is, a rich body of knowledge about the properties and behaviors of animals and plants. In addition folkbiologists have paid little attention to these people's comprehension of human bodily processes. In contrast, in conceptual developmental research, the question of whether young children distinguish between mind and body is critical in relation to the hot issue of whether they possess an autonomous biology (Carey 1985; Coley 1995; Inagaki and Hatano 1993b; Springer and Keil 1989).

A promising approach to the problem of the mind-body distinction is to examine whether different types of causal explanations are given for bodily versus mental processes or biological versus psychological attributes. More specifically, it has been debated whether young children apply nonintentional causality for biological phenomena and intentional causality for psychological ones. Two notions have been proposed as candidates for such nonintentional (yet nonmechanistic) causality (Carey 1995): teleological mode of construal (Keil 1992) and vitalistic causality (Inagaki and Hatano 1993b). We will focus on the latter notion, which we proposed, and then refer to its possible relationships with the former.

Carey (1985) claimed that children before age 10 base their explanations of biological phenomena on an intentional causality because they are ignorant of the physiological mechanisms involved. However, Inagaki and Hatano (1993b) claimed that young children before schooling can apply vitalistic (i.e., nonintentional) causality in explaining biological phenomena, and thus they have a form of biology that is differentiated from psychology.

Young children cannot give articulated mechanical explanations when asked to explain biological phenomena (e.g., bodily processes mediating input-output relations) in an open-ended interview (e.g., Gellert 1962); sometimes they try to explain them using the language of person-intentional causality (Carey 1985). These findings apparently support the claim that young children do not yet have biology as an autonomous domain. It seems inevitable to accept this claim as long as we assume only two types of causalities, namely intentional causality versus mechanical causality, as represented by Carey (1985). However, Inagaki and Hatano (1993b) propose that children who are reluctant to rely on intentional causality for biological phenomena but who are not as yet able to use mechanical causality often use an intermediate form of causality that might be called "vitalistic causality."

Intentional causality means that a person's intention causes the target phenomenon, whereas mechanical causality means that physiological mechanisms cause the target phenomenon. For instance, a specific bodily system enables a person, irrespective of his or her intention, to exchange substances with the environment or to carry them to and from bodily parts. In contrast, vitalistic causality indicates that the target phenomenon is caused by the activity of an internal organ, which has, like a living thing, "agency" (i.e., a tendency to initiate and sustain behaviors). The activity is often described as a transmission or exchange of the "vital force," which can be conceptualized as unspecified substance, energy, or information. Vitalistic causality is clearly different from person-intentional causality in the sense that the organ's activities inducing the phenomenon are independent of the intention of the person who possesses the organ.

**Naive Biology Is Vitalistic**
In one of our studies (Inagaki and Hatano 1990) some of the children 5 to 8 years of age gave explanations referring to something like vital force as a mediator when given novel questions about bodily processes, such as, what effect the cessation of blood circulation would have; for example, one child said, "If blood does not come to the hands, they will die, because the blood does not carry energies to them, " and another child, "We wouldn't be able to move our hands, because energies fade away if blood does not come there." However, since the number of the children who spontanously gave vitalistic explanations was small, another experiment was done to ask children to choose a plausible explanation out of the presented ones.

We predicted that even if young children could not generate vitalistic causal explanations for themselves, they would prefer vitalistic explanations to intentional ones for bodily processes when asked to choose one from among several possibilities (Inagaki and Hatano 1993b, Experiment 2). Twenty each of 6-year-olds, 8-year-olds, and college students were asked to choose one from three possible explanations each for six bodily phenomena, such as blood circulation, and respiration. The three explanations represented intentional, vitalistic and mechanical causality, respectively. An example question on respiration with three alternative

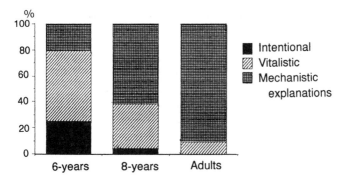

**Figure 10.3**
Percentages of choices for different types of causal explanations

explanations was as follows: Why do we take in air? (1) Because we want to feel good [intentional]. (2) Because our chest takes in vital power from the air [vitalistic]. (3) Because the lungs take in oxygen and change it into useless carbon dioxide [mechanical].

Results indicated that the 6-year-olds chose vitalistic explanations as most plausible most often (54 percent of the time). With increasing age the subjects came to choose mechanical explanations most often. It should be noted that the 6-year-olds chose nonintentional (vitalistic plus mechanical) causal explanations 75 percent of the time, though they were more apt to adopt intentional causality than the 8-year-olds or adults (see figure 10.3).

Young children seem to rely on vitalistic causality only for biological phenomena. They seldom attribute social-psychological behavior, which is optional and not needed for survival, to the agency of a bodily organ or part, as revealed by Inagaki and Hatano (1993b, Experiments 3 and 3a). The following is an example question for such behavior used in the study: When a pretty girl entered the room, Taro came near her. Why did he do so? Eighty percent of the 6-year-olds chose "Because Taro wanted to become a friend of hers" [intentional explanation], whereas only 20 percent opted for "Because Taro's heart urged him to go near her" [vitalistic]. For biological phenomenon questions, which were almost the same as those used in Experiment 2 of Inagaki and Hatano (1993b) except for excluding the mechanical causal explanation, they tended to choose vitalistic explanations rather than intentional ones.

Although young children's use of vitalistic causality falsifies the claim that they interpret biological phenomena entirely within the framework of psychology, it is possible that they find organ-intentional vitalistic explanations appealing for biological phenomena. If this is the case, we must conclude that young children's biology is still "psychological" in the sense that it involves intentional states, though the domain of bodily processes is differentiated from that of voluntary actions.

Thus, in one of our recent studies (Hatano and Inagaki 1994), we asked children aged 5 to 6 years to choose between two types of vitalistic explanations, the organ-intentional and the organ-agential. An example question was as follows: "Why does a baby become bigger and bigger?" (1) Because the baby's body wants to become bigger [organ-intentional]. (2) Because the baby's body takes in energy for becoming bigger from milk [organ-agential]. For this question 80 percent of not only the 6-year-olds but also the 5-year-olds preferred the organ-agential explanation as plausible. For the other five questions, 6-year-olds chose the organ-agential explanations consistently and 5-year-olds tended to do so. Thus the possibility that children's biology is "psychological" is low for 5-year-olds and older. How about the biology of 4-year-olds and younger?

### Younger Children Possess "Psychological" Biology

Inagaki (1997) examined whether younger children would recognize that the workings of internal organs cannot generally be controlled by the intention of the person who has them. Children aged 3 to 5 years were asked questions, such as, "Taro wants to stop breathing from morning till night. Can he do that?" or "Taro falls down and hurts his knee. If he speaks to the hurt, 'Pain, Pain, go away quickly,' will he become free from the pain?" Results indicated that whereas a majority of the 4- and 5-year-olds recognized that the heartbeat or breathing cannot be controlled by a person's intention, the 3-year-olds did not understand it. In addition, 70 percent of the 3-year-olds answered that they could get rid of the pain or the itch by ordering it to disappear, and 80 percent of them answered that they could order their stomach to work harder when they wanted to eat more. In contrast, only 40 percent of the 4-year-olds gave such answers for the above phenomena. A majority of the 5-year-olds recognized that they could not get rid of the pain by strong desire nor order their stomach to work harder.

Awareness of their own bodily processes was markedly lower among the 3-year-olds than the 4- and the 5-year-olds. It was assessed by questions, such as, "Can you show me how you breathe?" A significant positive correlation was found between the degree of the awareness of bodily processes and the number of correct responses to questions about the mind's lack of the ability to control bodily processes. These results suggest that very young children's characterization of bodily processes is not clearly separated from that of mental states.

Vitalistic causality is certainly based on the presumption that different cause-effect relationships have to be applied to biological kinds from nonliving entities (Atran 1998). It is probably derived from a general mechanism of personification that young children are prone to rely on. One who has no means for observing the opaque inside or details of the target object often tries to understand it in a global fashion, by assuming it or its parts to be humanlike (Ohmori 1985). Hence young children try to understand the workings of internal bodily organs by regarding them as humanlike (but noncommunicative) agents and by assigning to their activities global life-sustaining characteristics, which results in vitalistic causality for bodily processes. We can see a similar mode of explanation in Japanese endogenous science before the Meiji restoration (and the beginning of rapid modernization), which had evolved with medicine and agriculture as its core (Hatano and Inagaki 1987). It is likely that in other cultures people may have differently instantiated forms of vitalism, in other words, explanatory frameworks for not only treating biological kinds differently from nonliving things but also assigning some agency to living things and their constituent parts.

What is the relationship between the vitalistic explanation for biological phenomena and the teleological-functional explanation for biological properties (Keil 1992) or the teleological presumption for morphological characteristics (Atran 1998)? Both certainly fall between the intentional and the mechanical, and both seem to afford valid perspectives of the biological world. One interpretation is that they are essentially the same idea with different emphases; the teleological is more concerned with the "why" or the cause, whereas the vitalistic is concerned more with the "how" or the process. Another interpretation is that because the vitalistic explanation refers to the activity of the responsible organ or bodily part (implicitly for sustaining life), it is closer to mechanical causality than is the teleological one, which refers only to the necessity. Carey (1995) indicates that what is teleological is not necessarily biological. Teleological explanations can aptly be applied to artifacts as well as biological kinds. We guess that the teleological presumption is tightly associated with the biological world only in small communities where people are not surrounded by a variety of complex artifacts. Anyway, it will be intriguing to examine these characterizations of "biological" explanations in concrete experimental studies for both children and adults in different cultures.

## 10.5   Where Culture Makes a Difference

So far we have compared folkbiology in general and naive biology in general, assuming that their major characteristics are more or less universal. However, it is true that there are some significant and interpretable variations in both of them. Although Atran (1998) believes that the taxonomies of living kinds are more or less universal and that these taxonomies are "products of an autonomous, natural classification scheme of the human mind" (p. 23), he now admits that prototypes may differ from culture to culture; frequency of contact, number of properties shared with other members, and ecological significance all contribute to which taxa are considered to be the most typical or truly representative. Similarly Dougherty (1978) claimed that which level of conceptual organization becomes salient depends on the richness of relevant knowledge in the domain. Likewise the naive biology of young children may take slightly or considerably different forms because skeletal innate constraints can be instantiated differently depending on sociocultural constraints (Hatano 1995). In this section we will discuss the issue of cultural variation in young children's biological understanding.

### Raised Animals as the Source
We can reasonably assume that engaging in activities involving raising animals and plants may make the target living thing become prototypical for young children. Inagaki (1990) compared the biological knowledge of kindergartners who had actively engaged in raising goldfish for an

extended period at home with that of the children of the same age who had never raised any animal. Although these two groups of children did not differ in factual knowledge about typical mammals, the goldfish-raisers had much richer procedural, factual, and conceptual knowledge about goldfish. More interestingly, the goldfish-raisers used their knowledge about goldfish as a source for analogies in predicting the reactions of an unfamiliar "aquatic" animal (i.e., a frog), one that they had never raised, and produced reasonable predictions with some explanations for it. For example, one of the raisers, when asked whether we could keep a baby frog in the same size forever, answered, "No, we can't, because a frog will grow bigger as goldfish grew bigger. My goldfish were small before, but now they are big." It might be added that the goldfish-raisers tended to use person analogies as well as goldfish analogies for a frog. In other words, the goldfish-raisers could use two sources for making analogical predictions.

This effect of familiarity on the selection of the source was confirmed in another study (Inagaki 1996; see also Hatano and Inagaki 1992). More specifically, this study revealed that having two highly familiar domains of animals, namely of a human and a raised animal, helped young children to enlarge their narrow conception of animals. Previous studies have reported that young children tend to underattribute unobservable animal properties (shared by all animals, e.g., breathing), especially to animals that are phylogenetically far from and dissimilar to people (Carey 1985; Inagaki and Sugiyama 1988). Contrary to these findings, young children who had raised goldfish attributed to goldfish at a high rate properties of having a heart, blood, breathing, and excreting, which are all possessed by humans. In addition, when asked to attribute those properties to a variety of animals including a tortoise, a frog, and a carp, goldfish-raisers were superior in attributing them to animals that fall phylogenetically between humans and goldfish. This effect was marked for aquatic animals. Thus the raised animal served as another prototype for animals.

The above findings in naive biology are probably consistent with folkbiological observations. Although indigenous adults seldom make the raised animal analogy across genera, it is highly likely that the raised animal becomes a prototype within the genus.

## Psychological Distance between Categories

Another aspect that may be influenced markedly by culture is the distance between ontological categories. As mentioned in the first section, these categories are likely to be products of a natural classification scheme of the human mind and thus are universal across cultures. However, how these four categories are arranged may vary from culture to culture. For example, in some cultures plants may be regarded similar to humans and animals, whereas in others they may be considered very close to nonliving kinds, or some nonliving entities may be treated somewhat similar to living things.

In the study cited in the first section, Hatano et al. (1993) tried to differentiate between the universal aspects and the culturally specific aspects of children's conceptions of life and their understanding of the attributes of living things by comparing 6-, 8-, and 10-year-olds from Israel, Japan, and the United States. The children were asked whether two typical entities each of the four ontological categories (people, nonhuman animals, plants, and inanimates) possessed each of 16 attributes, including life status (being alive), unobservable animal attributes (e.g., has a heart), sensory attributes (e.g., feels pain), and attributes true of all living things (e.g., grows).

The results illustrate both similarities and differences across cultures in children's biological understanding. Here we focus on cultural differences. As predicted from cultural analyses, Israeli children were considerably more likely not to attribute to plants life status and other properties that are shared by all living things, whereas Japanese children, whose overall accuracy was comparable to that of the Israeli children, were considerably more likely to attribute to inanimate objects properties that are unique to living things.

These differences are especially interesting because they suggest that children's naive biology is influenced by beliefs within the culture in which they grow up. Features of culture and language may account for Israeli children being less apt than American or Japanese children to attribute to plants life status and properties of living things. Stavy and Wax (1989) suggested that within the Israeli culture, plants are regarded as very different from humans and other animals in their life status. This cultural attitude parallels that of a Biblical passage (Genesis, 1, 30), well known to Israeli students, indicating that plants were created as food for living things including animals, birds, and insects. Adding to, or perhaps reflecting, their cultural beliefs, the Hebrew word for "animal" is very close to that for "living" and "alive." In contrast the word for "plant" has no obvious relation to such terms (Stavy and Wax 1989).

From a similar perspective, we can interpret why Japanese children might be more likely than children in the United States or Israel to view plants or inanimate objects as alive and having attributes of living things. Japanese culture includes a belief that plants are much like human beings. This attitude is represented by the Buddhist idea that even a tree or blade of grass has a mind. In Japanese folk psychology, even inanimate objects are sometimes considered to have minds. For example, it is at least not a silly idea for Japanese to assign life or divinity not only to plants but also to inanimate objects, especially big or old ones. In addition linguistic factors seem to influence Japanese children's attributional judgments.

It is very interesting to find general principles of classification as has been attempted by folkbiologists (Berlin, Breedlove and Raven 1973). It is also interesting, however, to examine how flexibly these general principles are applied to the biological world depending on cultural beliefs and linguistic devices.

## 10.6    Conclusion: The Nature of Informal Biology

In this final section we will examine two topics based on the review and discussion in the preceding sections: First, the nature of informal biology will be discussed in the light of findings in both naive biology and folkbiology, and second, the possibility of cross-fertilization between studies of these two forms of informal biology will be examined.

### Nature of Informal Biology

One of the most important questions regarding the characterizations of informal biology is whether biology is a privileged domain, that is, whether humans are endowed with constraints for acquiring a form of biology. A sociobiological perspective suggests an affirmative answer to this question. For humans as a species it has been essential to have some knowledge about animals and plants as potential foods (Wellman and Gelman 1992) and also knowledge about our bodily functions to maintain health (Hatano 1989; Inagaki and Hatano 1993b). If this is true, then we can expect that biology is acquired early in life as well as universally across cultures.

How early does naive biology emerge? Most investigators in conceptual development (including Carey 1995) have agreed that lower elementary school children possess a form of biology. Moreover it is agreed almost unanimously that even younger children have a body of knowledge about biological phenomena that constitutes a theory or is theorylike and that is differentiated from psychology or an explanatory framework in terms of desire and belief. What is still debatable is whether this body of knowledge is truly biological (Carey 1995; Keil 1992; Solomon et al. 1996).

Recent empirical studies in folkbiology and naive biology offer a more differentiated notion of "truly biological" and thus provide better answers to the "whether privileged" and "how early" questions. They strongly suggest, as we have reviewed, that humans are born to classify entities into the four ontological categories and to acquire, through experiences, a more or less universal taxonomy within the categories of animals and plants. However, humans are not born to develop an elaborated causal explanatory framework for biological properties and processes.

There is some evidence that even infants can distinguish objects having a capacity for self-initiated movement from those not having it (e.g., Golinkoff et al. 1984). This could be taken as the first step toward the acquisition of naive biology. The differentiation of plants from nonliving things could also be achieved early, since it is a product of the natural classification scheme of the human mind.

However, classifying animals or plants into genera and building a hierarchical structure of them would take a longer time, since it involves the learning of what kinds of similarity metrics should be used at each level of the hierarchy. Understanding bodily processes would be delayed too, since it presupposes the awareness of the processes, many of which are not accompanied by pain or other distinctive indicators. Infants seldom need biological knowledge of this sort, since they do not need to take care of their health nor try to find food themselves. Moreover a more or less complete form of autonomous biology has to deal with entities that have agency (i.e., initiate and maintain activity without external forces) but that cannot communicate with humans, and thus has to apply a form of causality that is neither intentional nor mechanical in nature. It also presupposes the construction of an integrated category of living things including animals and plants, which appear very different.

Whether informal biology gradually emerges out of psychology (Carey 1985) or is a distinct theory or mode of construal from the start (Keil 1992) constitutes another important question for its characterization. The answer to this question also depends on our criteria for defining the domain of biology. We assume that there are innate constraints unique to the domain of biology, which lead to the construction of a distinct theory from very early years. The natural classification scheme is the best example of such constraints. Skeletal principles differentiating between animate and inanimate entities (Gelman 1990) and abstract knowledge assuming different internal structures for natural kinds versus artifacts (Simons and Keil 1995) also seem to constitute innate constraints, since they are taken for granted before a large amount of factual knowledge has been accumulated.

However, a theory or causal explanatory framework for biological properties and processes has to be constructed more gradually, and its construction can be affected by acquired knowledge, among others, knowledge concerning how the mind works or psychology, which has been established earlier. It is at least possible that both indigenous adults and young children, whose knowledge about biological causality is scarce, are tempted to interpret biological phenomena by borrowing psychological knowledge.

It may even be possible to claim that biology and psychology, or the mind and the body, are never completely differentiated in human cognition except in the Western modern sciences. It is perfectly natural for lay people to assume, as psychosomatic medicine has proved, that the mind and the body are correlated; that is, the mind influences the body as well as is influenced by it. The following examples could be regarded as good psychological explanations for the biological phenomena of reproduction and disease: Mr. and Mrs. Smith had six children because they loved each other so much; Mr. Smith had a stomachache because he had been terribly anxious about the business. We believe that young children possess a form of autonomous biology, but like ordinary adults' biology, it may be affected by psychology to some extent.

### Cross-fertilization of Naive Biological and Folkbiological Research

The preceding discussion reveals that enhanced interactions between folkbiologists and researchers of naive biology are beneficial to both for at least two reasons. First, these two forms of informal biology are so similar that findings in one could meaningfully be tested in the other. In many cases we will find commonalities that can serve as a cross-check. More important, however, when we find differences between them, we can better conceptualize what variables play an important role in the acquisition of informal biology. For example, young children are universal novices, whereas indigenous adults are experts in their ecological niche. Thus the acquisition of folkbiology is a process of gaining expertise in the domain, though it is based on domain-specific schemata of the human mind. Studying these two forms of informal biology in close connection, we can better understand the contributions of innate constraints and experiences. Another example is the study of the possible effects of scientific biological concepts and expressions that may be transmitted to young children through mass media. Although it is generally assumed that young children are totally inaccessible to scientific biology, they may have learned some of its vocabulary and concepts. Indigenous adults are much less likely to be exposed to such pieces of information.

Second, both researchers of naive biology and folkbiologists may recognize, through interactions between them, some important topics that have been neglected for historical reasons. We have tried in the preceding sections to derive such suggestions from folkbiology to research on naive biology. We would like to end this chapter by offering a suggestion for future research in folkbiology.

Topics of research on folkbiology seem to be somewhat limited. For example, folk medicine or indigenous people's understanding of bodily functions and diseases is not included in the research. This is probably because these topics belong in another branch of anthropology. In contrast, recent studies on naive biology have examined such specific issues as bodily processes, diseases, reproduction, and parent-offspring similarities, as well as the classification of animals and plants, within a framework theory of biology. We believe it would be intriguing to investigate how indigenous people conceptualize their own bodily processes and how they apply this conceptualization to their teleological construal of the properties and behaviors of animals and plants.

## References

Atran, S. 1990. *Cognitive Foundations of Natural History: Towards an Anthropology of Science*. Cambridge: Cambridge University Press.

Atran, S. 1998. Folk biology and the anthropology of science. *Behavioral and Brain Sciences* 21: 597–611.

Berlin, B., D. Breedlove, and P. Raven. 1973. General principles of classification and nomenclature in folk biology. *American Anthropologist* 74: 214–42.

Carey, S. 1985. *Conceptual Change in Childhood*. Cambridge: MIT Press.

Carey, S. 1995. On the origin of causal understanding. In D. Sperber, D. Premack and A. J. Premack, eds., *Causal Cognition*. Oxford: Clarendon Press, pp. 268–302.

Coley, J. D. 1995. Emerging differentiation of folkbiology and folkpsychology: Attributions of biological and psychological properties to living things. *Child Development* 66: 1856–74.

Dougherty, J. W. D. 1978. Salience and relativity in classification. *American Ethnologist* 5: 66–80.

Gellert, E. 1962. Children's conceptions of the content and functions of the human body. *Genetic Psychology Monographs* 65: 291–411.

Gelman, R. 1990. First principles organize attention to and learning about relevant data: Number and the animate-inanimate distinction as examples. *Cognitive Science* 14: 79–106.

Gelman, R., E. Spelke, and E. Meck. 1983. What preschoolers know about animate and inanimate objects. In D. Rogers and J. A. Sloboda, eds., *The Acquisition of Symbolic Skills*. New York: Plenum, pp. 297–326.

Golinkoff, R. M., C. G. Harding, V. Carlson, and M. E. Sexton. 1984. The infant's perception of causal events: the distinction between animate and inanimate objects. In L. P. Lipsitt and C. Rovee-Collier, eds., *Advances in Infancy Research* vol. 3. Norwood, NJ: Ablex, pp. 145–65.

Hatano, G. 1989. Language is not the only universal knowledge system: A view from "everyday cognition." *Dokkyo Studies in Data Processing and Computer Science* 7: 69–76.

Hatano, G. 1995. Cultural psychology of conceptual development: The need for numbers and narratives. Paper presented at the biennial meeting of the Society for Research in Child Development, Indianapolis, IN.

Hatano, G., and K. Inagaki. 1987. Everyday biology and school biology: How do they interact? *Quarterly Newsletter of the Laboratory of Comparative Human Cognition* 9: 120–28.

Hatano, G., and K. Inagaki. 1992. Desituating cognition through the construction of conceptual knowledge. In P. Light and G. Butterworthi eds., *Context and Cognition: Ways of Learning and Knowing*. London: Harvester/Wheatsheaf, pp. 115–33.

Hatano, G., and K. Inagaki. 1994. Bodily organ's "intention" in vitalistic causal explanations. [in Japanese]. Paper presented at the 36th annual meeting of Japanese Educational Psychology Association.

Hatano, G., and K. Inagaki. 1996. Cognitive and cultural factors in the acquisition of intuitive biology. In D. R. Olson, and N. Torrance, eds., *Handbook of Education and Human Development: New Models of Learning, Teaching and Schooling*. Cambridge, MA: Blackwell, pp. 683–708.

Hatano, G., R. S. Siegler, D. D. Richards, K. Inagaki, R. Stavy, and N. Wax. 1993. The development of biological knowledge: A multi-national study. *Cognitive Development* 8: 47–62.

Inagaki, K. 1990. The effects of raising animals on children's biological knowledge. *British Journal of Developmental Psychology* 8: 119–29.

Inagaki, K. 1996. Effects of raising goldfish on young children's grasp of common characteristics of animals. Paper presented at the 26th International Congress of Psychology, Montreal.

Inagaki, K. 1997. Emerging distinctions between naive biology and naive psychology. In H. M. Wellman and K. Inagaki, eds., *The Emergence of Core Domains of Thought: Children's Reasoning about Physical, Psychological, and Biological Phenomena*. New Directions for Child Development, no. 75. San Francisco: Jossey-Bass Publishers, pp. 27–44.

Inagaki, K., and G. Hatano. 1987. Young children's spontaneous personification as analogy. Child Development 58: 1013–20.

Inagaki, K., and G. Hatano. 1988. Developmental changes in biological attribution [in Japanese]. Paper presented at the 30th annual convention of the Japanese Association of Educational Psychology, Naruto.

Inagaki, K., and G. Hatano. 1990. Development of explanations for bodily functions [in Japanese]. Paper presented at the 32nd annual convention of the Japanese Association of Educational Psychology, Osaka.

Inagaki, K., and G. Hatano. 1991. Constrained person analogy in young children's biological inference. *Cognitive Development* 6: 219–31.

Inagaki, K., and G. Hatano. 1993a. Developmental changes in biological attributions by young children: A longitudinal study. Paper presented at the Meeting of the Society for Research in Child Development, New Orleans.

Inagaki, K., and G. Hatano. 1993b. Young children's understanding of the mind-body distinction. *Child Development* 64: 1534–49.

Inagaki, K., and G. Hatano. 1996. Young children's recognition of commonalities between animals and plants. *Child Development* 67: 2823–40.

Inagaki, K., and K. Sugiyama. 1988. Attributing human characteristics: Developmental changes in over- and underattribution. *Cognitive Development* 3: 55–70.

Johnson, C. N., and H. M. Wellman. 1982. Children's developing conceptions of the mind and brain. *Child Development* 53: 222–34.

Johnson, K. E., C. B. Mervis, and J. S. Boster. 1992. Developmental changes within the structure of the mammal domain. *Developmental Psychology* 28: 74–83.

Keil, F. C. 1992. The origins of an autonomous biology. In M. R. Gunnar and M. Maratsos, eds., *Modularity and Constraints in Language and Cognition; The Minnesota Symposia on Child Psychology*, vol. 25. Hillsdale, NJ: Lawrence Erlbaum, pp. 103–37.

Ohmori, S. 1985. *The Structure of Knowledge and Science* [in Japanese]. Tokyo: Nihon Hoso Shuppan Kyokai.

Richards, D. D., and R. S. Siegler. 1984. The effects of task requirements on children's life judgments. *Child Development* 55: 1687–96.

Simons, D. J., and F. C. Keil. 1995. An abstract to concrete shift in the development of biological thought: The insides story. *Cognition* 56: 129–63.

Solomon, G., S. Johnson, D. Zaitchik, and S. Carey. 1996. Like father, like son: Young children's understanding of how and why offspring resemble their parents. *Child Development* 67: 151–71.

Springer, K. and F. C. Keil. 1989. On the development of biologically specific beliefs: The case of inheritance. *Child Development* 60: 637–48.

Stavy, R., and N. Wax. 1989. Children's conceptions of plants as living things. *Human Development* 32: 88–94.

Vera, A. H., and F. C. Keil. 1988. The development of inductions about biological kinds: The nature of the conceptual base. Paper presented at the 29th meeting of the Psychonomic Society, Chicago.

Vosniadou, S. 1989. Analogical reasoning as a mechanism in knowledge acquisition: A developmental perspective. In S. Vosniadou and A. Ortony, eds., *Similarity and Analogical Reasoning*. Cambridge: Cambridge University Press, pp. 413–37.

Wellman, H. M., and S. A. Gelman. 1992. Cognitive development: Foundational theories of core domains. *Annual Review of Psychology* 43: 337–75.

# 11

## Mechanical Causality in Children's "Folkbiology"

Terry Kit-fong Au and Laura F. Romo

### 11.1 Do Children Have Folkbiology?

How do children explain and reason about biological phenomena? One idea that has set much of the research agenda for this topic since mid 1980s—put forth by Carey (1985, 1991)—is that young children use their knowledge about people to do the job. So children may confuse biology with psychology, and they may think that all animate phenomena (e.g., growth, biological inheritance, life, death, illness) are governed by sociopsychological factors (e.g., motivations, feelings, beliefs, morality and social convention). For instance, preschool children talk about the origin of babies mostly in terms of the parents' intentional behavior such as going out to a store to buy a baby or making a baby and placing it in the mother's tummy (Bernstein and Cowan 1975; Goldman and Goldman 1982). Carey (1985, 1991) concluded from an extensive review of previous research that children do not seem to understand any uniquely biological causal mechanisms prior to age ten. Moreover young children seem to use people as a prototype for reasoning about novel and non-obvious attributes of biological kinds (Carey 1985). For example, preschool children often generalize a novel property such as "has a spleen" from people to other animals (e.g., dogs, birds, bees) primarily on the basis of how similar the other animals are to people. Such inductive inferences are quite sensible, even though not always correct. But interestingly, if the property is taught on dogs or bees, preschool children do not generalize it to people and other kinds of animals. Based on these and other kinds of evidence, Carey (1985, 1991) argued that a folkbiology might emerge from a folk psychology (or a folk theory of people), and children might not construct their first autonomous biology until age ten or so.

In response to this important and controversial proposal, considerable research efforts have been devoted to studying children's early knowledge about biological kinds. To date, there is rather compelling evidence that children begin to distinguish plants and animals from human artifacts by age three or four (e.g., Backscheider, Shatz, and Gelman 1993; Hickling and Gelman 1995; Keil 1994); some children can apply their inchoate understanding of the biological-nonbiological distinction to novel entities (e.g., germs) as well as familiar ones by age five (Au and Romo 1996; see also Keil 1992). In other words, even before school age, children begin to sort out the ontologicial categories "biological kinds" and "nonbiological kinds" (see also Gelman 1996; Wellman and Gelman 1997).

In addition to outlining the ontology in a domain, a framework theory should specify basic causal devices in that domain in order to offer coherent bases for reasoning about relevant phenomena (e.g., Brewer and Samarapungavan 1991; Wellman 1990; Wellman and Gelman 1992). To be credited with a folkbiology, children have to go beyond making an ontological distinction between biological and nonbiological kinds. They must also have some ideas about causal devices or mechanisms that apply only to biological phenomena. Given the importance of uniquely biological causal mechanisms in deciding whether a set of beliefs qualifies as a folkbiology, it is no coincidence that such mechanisms constitute a major battleground for the debate on when children construct their first autonomous biology.

## 11.2    Do Children Know Any Uniquely Biological Causal Mechanisms?

Researchers including Hatano and Inagaki (1994), Keil (1992, 1994), and Springer (1995; Springer and Keil 1991; Springer, Nguyen, Samaniego 1996; Springer and Ruckel 1992) have argued that prior to age six or seven, children understand some causal principles in the domain of biological kinds. On the other hand, Carey (1985, 1991, 1995; Carey and Spelke 1994), Atran (1994), and Solomon (Solomon and Cassimatis 1995; Solomon, Johnson, Zaitchik, and Carey 1996) have argued that children's early knowledge of biological kinds does not include explicit biological causal principles. But underneath all the arguments between these two camps lies a consensus (see also Au and Romo 1996). Namely most, if not all, participants of this debate seem to agree that by age six or seven, children can understand some causal principles for explaining biological phenomena—now that Carey and her colleagues (1995; Carey and Spelke 1994; Solomon et al. 1996) put the probable age onset at six or seven to accommodate recent evidence of early inchoate biological knowledge (e.g., Gelman 1996; Inagaki and Hatano 1993; Keil 1992; Springer and Keil 1991; Wellman and Gelman 1997; see also chapter 10, this volume).

We actually want to go against the tide by arguing that an understanding of any true biological causal mechanism is not something children pick up intuitively in everyday life. Even what Carey and her colleagues are willing to accept as evidence for such understanding— which we will review presently—is not about causal mechanisms per se. Rather, it is about causal input-output relations. Now is probably as good a time as any to explain why we put quotation marks around "folkbiology" in the title of this chapter. We did so because we are not convinced that children, or adults for that matter, spontaneously construct uniquely biological causal mechanisms from their everyday experience. No study that we know of has demonstrated that children or adults—without the benefit of science education—make use of such causal mechanisms to explain or reason about biological phenomena. So, if domain-specific causal devices constitute an integral part of any folk theory, then none of the folk conceptions about biological kinds documented to date seem to qualify as a folk theory (see Atran 1994, 1995; see also chapter 6, this volume). Where does this line of argument lead us? Not a very enviable spot, we must say. In some sense we are questioning whether *folkbiology*—the very title of this edited volume—might be a contradiction in term. If neither children nor adults spontaneously construct uniquely biological causal mechanisms from everyday experience, can we really consider their folk conceptions about biological kinds to be folkbiologies? Because we are taking a rather precarious (if not indeed radical) position, we had better build our case carefully to make sure that our chapter will not be pulled from this collection of essays on folkbiology.

Much of the research on children's understanding of biological phenomena has focused on biological processes, input-output relations, causal agents (e.g., vital force, essence, innards), and so forth, rather than causal devices or mechanisms per se. Since comprehensive reviews of this research literature already exist (Gelman 1996; Wellman and Gelman, 1997; see also chapter 10, this volume), we will try to be selective here.

**Biological versus Psychological Processes**
Children begin to distinguish *biological processes* from psychological ones by age four or five. They appreciate that some processes (e.g., growth, breathing) cannot be stopped by intention alone. For instance, people cannot prevent an animal from growing bigger and old, just because they want it to remain small and cute (Inagaki and Hatano 1987). They also recognize that bodily processes such as running speed and psychological processes such as forgetfulness tend to be modified by different means—in these examples, by exercise and mental monitoring, respectively (Inagaki and Hatano 1993). Moreover 6-year-olds tend to attribute biological properties such as "has blood" and "sleeps" to predatory and domestic animals at the same rate, but they attribute psychological properties such as "can feel happy" and "can feel scared" more to domestic animals. By age eight, children use taxonomic groups (e.g., mammals, birds, reptile, fish) as a basis for attributing biological but not psychological properties. They use the predatory versus domestic distinction to attribute psychological (e.g., "can feel pain," "is smart," "can feel scared") but not biological properties (Coley 1995).

In several ecologically significant areas—growth, illness, kinship—children show rather impressive understanding from their preschool years on. For instance, preschool children know that "growth" and "self-healing" are unique to plants and animals (Carey 1985; Rosengren, Gelman, Kalish, and McCormick 1991; Backscheider, Shatz, and Gelman 1993). From age six on, some children spontaneously attribute "can grow bigger" to novel entities such as germs (Au and Romo 1996). Preschoolers also know about constraints on growth and development: Animals get bigger not smaller and become structurally more complex not simpler (e.g., from caterpillar to butterfly, and not vice versa; Rosengren et al. 1991).

In the domain of illness, preschool children appreciate that illness and contamination can be caused by germs. Because germs are so tiny that they are not readily perceptible, children probably learn about germs primarily through language. Nonetheless, by age six, children manage to construct rather sophisticated beliefs about germs: germs exist despite absence of perceptible evidence; germs can live, die, and grow bigger; germs can make people sick (e.g., Au and Romo 1996; Au, Sidle, and Rollins 1993; Kalish 1996; Siegal 1988; Rosen and Rozin 1993).

Children's early knowledge of parent-child resemblance is equally impressive. For instance, preschool children expect that animals of the same family, more so than unrelated but similar looking animals, to share certain properties such as tiny bones, or an ability to see in the dark (Springer 1992). They also expect that underlying essential nature is inherited and unaffected by upbringing. That is, a calf raised among pigs will grow up to moo and have a straight tail (Gelman and Wellman 1991); a human baby shares racial characteristics with the biological parents rather than adoptive parents (Hirschfeld 1994; see also chapter 12, this volume). Whether children project novel, inherent characteristics from birth parents but not adoptive parents to birth/adoptive children remains an open question (e.g., Solomon et al. 1996; Springer 1995). Nonetheless, children's inchoate understanding of parent-child resemblance seems to include some kind of causal input-output relations (i.e., input = some characteristics of the parents; output = similar characteristics in their baby). How the input is turned into the output—the causal mechanism—however, remains unspecified (Au and Romo 1996; Carey 1995).

To characterize children's early knowledge about biological kinds, there are several proposals about underlying causal principles: vitalistic causality (Hatano and Inagaki 1994; Inagaki and Hatano 1993), functional-teleological explanations (Keil 1992 1994), essence (S. Gelman, Coley, and Gottfried 1994), innards (e.g., R. Gelman 1990). While each proposal has considerable empirical support, it remains unclear to what extent these proposed *causal agents* are uniquely biological. How different is vital force from fuel in getting some machinery (human and otherwise) to work? How different is the role of function in driving the evolution of biological kinds and the evolution of technology and artifacts? How different is the essence for biological kinds from that for chemicals? How do innards differ for biological versus nonbiological kinds? Are these proposed causal agents different primarily in their domain of application (e.g., vital force for biological kinds and fuel for artifacts) but analogous in other ways (e.g., causal mechanisms for how they affect entities in their domain of application)? Perhaps, more important, none of the proposed causal principles offers any explicit causal mechanisms. What might the causal chain of events look like? How do the proposed causal agents such as "vital force," "function," "essence," or "innards" work? (see also Au 1994; Au and Romo 1996; Wellman and Gelman 1997).

## 11.3  Do Adults Readily Construct Uniquely Biological Causal Mechanisms?

One way to study folkbiology is to explore children's beliefs about biological kinds and processes; another way is to study adults who have not received much or any science education. We have just begun to read about studies using the latter approach, so our knowledge in this area is bound to be patchy and limited. Our initial impression is that published reports of such studies tended to focus on causal agents and/or input-output causal relations rather than causal mechanisms. In the domain of illness, for instance, Nichter and Nichter (1994) reported that mothers in a rural area in the Philippines linked most respiratory conditions to sudden changes body temperature due to sun, rain, wind, bathing, and so on. A study of Latino adults beliefs about *empacho* (roughly means "blocked digestion") revealed that it generally believed to be caused by "a bolus of food that sticks to the wall of the intestine, usually as a result of dietary indiscretion or swallowing a lot of saliva" (Weller et al., 1993). Some African communities were reported to believe that diarrhea can be caused by teething, intestinal worms, eating bad food, drinking too much water, ingesting dirt, being touched by a father who has just committed adultery, worrying too much, being hit on the buttocks, and so forth (Green, Jurg, and Djedje 1994; Yoder 1995). See D' Andrade (1976) and Murdock (1980) for additional examples of studies focusing on causal agents and input-output causal relations rather than causal mechanisms.

It is perhaps no accident that people across cultures have rich beliefs about what might cause a person to have certain illness symptoms, what effect a treatment might have, and so forth. Such beliefs about input-output relations in the domain of illness—if roughly on the right track—can be very useful in illness prevention and treatment (e.g., see Berlin and Berlin, 1996). Beliefs about causal mechanisms of illness (or other biological phenomena for that matter), by contrast, seem more like a luxury than a necessity in everyday life. For example, the belief "smoking can cause lung cancer" could save lives if people act on this belief sensibly, with or without understanding any causal mechanism for how smoking might cause lung cancer. Lack of ecological significance, then, might be why causal mechanisms for biological phenomena are much less thought about in everyday life and much less documented in anthropological studies. Nonetheless, we did come across some published narratives revealing the informants' beliefs about causal mechanisms for specific illness.

### Gastrointestinal Problems

Consider this narrative collected in El Salvador:

In the stomach, food is cooked (*se cuecen los alimentos*) and therefore the stomach has to stay warm. When the climate turns cool, the stomach gets cold, letting food leave the stomach undigested. If you eat food with cold properties during the cold season you can also get stomach problems. Food which is considered cold, even though heated in the fire, always maintains this property. Tamales, beef or pork consommé and chicken soup are all considered cold food. In addition to these foods cucumbers and tomatoes are cool. The outside surface of the bean sticks in the stomach and for this reason it is not recommended to give children beans at nighttime, because the night is cold and the food is cold, thereby making the child sick. (Bonilla, Alferez de Castilo, and Piñeda 1987; translated by and quoted in Kendall 1990, pp. 183–184).

Temperature (i.e., hot, cold) and adhesiveness (e.g., the cold surface of bean sticking in the stomach) figure prominently in this account of causal chain of events that can lead to stomach problems. Note that temperature and adhesiveness are mechanical/physical rather than biochemical properties of substances. Similarly naive mechanics also seems to be recruited by Latino adults to explain the symptoms of *empacho*. This illness is characterized by a cluster of symptoms including stomach aches and bloating, vomiting, cramps, diarrhea, constipation, and lack of appetite (Weller et al. 1993). As noted earlier, it is generally believed to be caused by a blockage of food in the stomach or intestines. For many Mexican-Americans, the recommended treatments include stomach massages, rolling an egg on the stomach, and popping the skin on the small of the back to dislodge the food blockage, or drinking olive oil or herbal teas to loosen the food (Trotter 1991). In this case mechanical causal devices rather than uniquely biological causal devices are invoked when the informants tried to specify the causal chain of events that can lead to these symptoms and how the recommended treatments work to relieve the symptoms.

A third example of invoking mechanical causality in reasoning about treatment for gastrointestinal illness can be found among indigenous healers in Mozambique. When traditional African medicine fails to cure a child's diarrhea, indigenous healers consider "the child being without water" to be the cause of symptoms such as white eyes, edema in limbs, loss of appetite, loss of skin elasticity, general weakness, and thirst. The mechanical path of how water gets into the child is believed to matter a great deal. For instance, some healers noted that they can give a child water, but this will not do because the water will just swell up his stomach. Instead, "the child must be taken to a hospital quickly, where doctors 'will put water' (or 'blood') into the child by a needle in the arm" (p. 16, Green et al., 1994).

## Breast Cancer

In a study of twenty-six African-American women in rural North Carolina with advanced breast cancer, 62 percent of these women seemed to believe that their cancerous lumps were triggered by a bump or blow to the body which causes some impurities in the blood to clump together in one place (Mathews, Lannin, and Mitchell, 1994). Here are some examples of how these women talked about the cause of their breast cancer (p. 793):

May: I "noticed a knot in my breast in 1989, but it didn't hurt. It just came from bumping into the bed so I put it out of my mind."
Jean: "I had a sore spot on my breast that came from bumping into the car door with my groceries. A lump came up there but it never bothered me."

Clara: "I had a pain in my arm for five years.... I also had a knot in my breast all that time, but it would come and go.... But then I noticed a few months ago that there was a big knot on my right breast where Mr. Jones (an Alzheimer's patient she sits for) had been hitting me on the side. You know, if you get a hard enough blow, it makes some kind of blood clot, and if it stays there long enough it's going to form something else."

Lucille: "That knot I had came and went. If you have dirty blood, the impurities have to go somewhere. And once I passed the change (i.e., menopause), that blood just stayed in me all the time. It was mounting up. When I fell down that day in the garden, they all came up to that bruise and they made a lump. That's what made it so big."

More generally, our glimpse of the medical anthropology literature suggests that while people can often come up with reasonable lists of causes, symptoms, and recommended treatments for various salient illnesses in their communities, their repertoire does not seem to include biological causal mechanisms for *how* specific causes can lead to specific symptoms or *how* specific treatments work. When they do manage to talk about causal mechanisms linking the causes and treatments to symptoms, they often fall back on their naive mechanics (e.g., temperature and stickiness of food, mechanical blows on the body). Even when they attribute an illness to moral transgression (e.g., a child's diarrhea caused by the child's father's adultery) or negligence (e.g., a child's diarrhea caused by the child's mother stepping into milk expressed from a woman who has had a miscarriage), mechanic transfer of contaminants or impurities is often implicated (e.g., the adulterous father touching the child; the careless mother nursing the child). When mechanical causality is not recruited to fill in specific causal chains of events for natural or supernatural causation of illness, typically little else is offered in terms of explicit causal mechanisms (e.g., see Murdock 1980).

## 11.4 Mechanical Causality in Children's "Folkbiology"

To date, only a few studies have explicitly examined children's beliefs about causal mechanisms for biological phenomena. In one study, Inagaki and Hatano (1993) compared children's preference for intentional, vitalistic, and mechanical causal explanations for biological phenomena. They asked children, for instance, why we eat food everyday. Children were asked to choose among three explanations: "Because we want to eat tasty food" (intentional); "Because our stomach takes in vital power from the food" (vitalistic); "Because we take the food into our body after its form is changed in the stomach and bowels" (mechanical). Likewise, when asked why we take in air, children were asked to choose from: "Because we want to feel good" (intentional); "Because our chest takes in vital power from the air" (vitalistic); "Because the lungs take in oxygen and change it into useless carbon dioxide" (mechanical). In this study 6-year-olds chose vitalistic explanations as most plausible most often (54 percent of the time). Eight-year-olds chose vitalistic explanations only 34 percent of the time; they generally preferred mechanical explanations (62 percent). Adults overwhelmingly preferred mechanical explanations (96 percent).

Springer and Keil (1991) also found that 6- and 7-year-olds favored mechanical causality over other kinds of causal mechanisms (e.g., genetic, intentional) in explaining, for instance, how a baby flower may get its blue color or how a puppy may get its brown fur color. Children in this study were offered three kinds of possible explanations: Intentional, mechanical, and genetic. One example: "The mother flower wanted her baby to be blue just like her. Because she wanted the baby to be blue, she gave it some very tiny things that went into the seed and turned the baby flower blue" (intentional); "Some very tiny blue pieces went from the mother to the baby flower. These tiny blue pieces went into the seed and got all over the baby flower. Because they got into the baby flower's petals, the baby flower turned blue" (mechanical); "Some very tiny colorless things went from the mother to the baby flower. These tiny things put the blue color together in the baby flower. Even though these tiny things aren't any color, they could make the baby flower blue" (genetic). The mechanical account (or what Springer and Keil called the "gemmulic account") was judged best by the 6-year-olds nearly 80% of the time. An important difference between the winner and the losers is that the mechanical account specifies a simple mechanical transfer of color pigment, whereas the genetic and the intentional accounts did not.

Together, these studies suggest that mechanical causality is the mechanism of choice during middle childhood for explaining biological phenomena. Our quick survey of medical anthropological studies also hints at adults' reliance on mechanical causality when pressed to speculate on specific chains of causal events inside the human body—if scientific accounts are not in the adults' repertoire. One caveat: In Inagaki and Hatano's (1993) and Springer and Keil's (1991) studies, children were asked to choose among several possible mechanisms, rather than to generate one on their own. As Carey (1995) pointed out, it is very difficult to make different explanation types comparable with respect to the informativeness of the explanation and familiarity with the information it contains. So, when children chose one type of explanation over another, it is not always clear why they did so.

Nonetheless, we suspect that mechanical causality is the mechanism of choice for children and adults—especially those without the benefit of science education—in their attempts to make sense of biological phenomena. For one thing, from infancy on, children know and rapidly learn quite a lot about how objects and substances behave in terms of mechanics. Their naive mechanics allows them to appreciate that physical entities will move according to principles such as cohesion, solidity, contact, and continuity (e.g., Carey and Spelke 1994; Spelke and Hermer 1996; Wellman and Gelman 1992, 1997). Although children and even adults make erroneous predictions about the dynamics of more complex systems (e.g., wheels and pulleys), they are generally quite good at reasoning about whether an object or a portion of substance will stay put or be set in motion, how it will move (as long as the entity can be thought of as a single particle of mass), and so forth (e.g., McCloskey 1983; Proffitt, Kaiser, and Whelan 1990). So, before children and adults understand any uniquely biological mechanisms, it makes sense for them to apply their naive mechanics—a rather well-worked-out foundational theory— to reason about living things as well as nonliving things. Indeed, as discussed earlier, adults from different cultures seem to recruit their naive mechanics to explain causal links between causes, symptoms, and treatments of illness.

**Psychological Causality: Another Contender**
Another obvious source for causal mechanisms at children's disposal, as Carey (1985, 1991, 1995) pointed out, is naive psychology. But by age six or so, as discussed earlier, children can grasp the conceptual distinction between biological and nonbiological kinds and that between bio-

logical and psychological processes. They recognize that bodily processes and psychological processes tend to be modified by different means. From that point on, it is unlikely that children confuse folkbiology with folk psychology. So, when they offer a sociopsychological explanation for a biological phenomenon (e.g., John has a cold today because yesterday he played with Mary, who kept coughing and sneezing while playing with him), it does not necessarily mean that psychological causality is the only game in town. At a different level of analysis, children could be thinking about Mary passing some of her cold germs to John when she accidentally sneezed or coughed at him. In other words, children's use of sociopsychological explanations for biological phenomena cannot by itself be taken as *prima facie* evidence for children confusing folk psychology with folkbiology.

What about children under age six? If children have to stretch either their naive psychology or naive mechanics to reason about biological processes, it seems plausible that they would opt for naive mechanics. For one thing, even preschoolers can distinguish mental and physical entities (e.g., a cookie in a dream vs. a cookie in real life) and processes (e.g., thinking about eating a cookie vs. actually eating a cookie; Wellman 1990; Wellman and Estes 1986). Note that, like mechanical processes, most biological processes (e.g., growth, healing, reproduction) act on physical rather than metaphysical matter. By contrast, psychological processes typically affect thoughts, feelings, and at times behaviors. So, before children understand any causal mechanisms that are uniquely biological, it seems more natural for them to stretch their naive mechanics rather than naive psychology to explain biological phenomena.

### In Children's Own Words

Earlier we offered some suggestive evidence that without the benefit of science education, adults in different cultures invoke mechanical causality to explain the causes, symptoms, and treatments of illness. Inagaki and Hatano's (1993) and Springer and Keil's (1991) studies also suggest that mechanical causality is the mechanism of choice during middle childhood for explaining biological phenomena. But children in these two studies did not have to generate their own explanations; they were asked to choose among several possible mechanisms. Given the methodological concern raised by Carey (1995), namely the comparability of different explanations types for extraneous factors, it would be helpful to hear what kinds of explanations children can come up with on their own.

## A Case Study

**Reproduction** We have been following one child's quest for biological knowledge for some time. The first report was filed in 1996 (by Au and Romo, p. 210):

A child we know asked, at age 2 years 9 months, where she was when her mother planted the orange tree in their backyard and was told that she was in her mother's tummy. She then wanted to know where she was when her mother planted the lemon tree in their front yard. The mother said, "You weren't even in my tummy yet." The child was visibly upset about her nonexistence once upon a time. The mother relented and explained, "Half of you was in my tummy; the other half, in Daddy's tummy." The child went away happy but came back in a few minutes to ask, "Were my feet in Daddy's tummy?" The mother was determined to help the child supplant this mechanical explanation with a proper one, namely, a biological one. She explained that the two halves did not have arms and legs; instead each half was like a little egg (without the shell, she emphasized); the two little eggs mixed together and then grew into a baby. The toddler nodded and talked about this matter-of-factly a few times in the ensuing weeks. Her mother was pleased with the progress until the child asked one day, "How did I get into your tummy? Did Dr. Wilkinson cut open your tummy to put me inside?"

The notion of procreation is difficult to grasp. How can the concept of object permanence—at the core of naive mechanics—be reconciled with the transition from nonexistence to existence in reproduction of biological kinds? This child in this case went with her intuitions about mechanical causality. Understanding such a transition can be difficult even for adults. Just think about how intellectually unsatisfying the notion of "spontaneous generation" is for explaining generation of bacteria and fungi from apparently nothing. One could almost imagine the scientific community's collective sigh of relief in 1862 when Pasteur finally managed to show experimentally that microorganisms came only from other microorganisms; that a completely sterile solution will remain so unless contaminated by some microorganisms (e.g., Pruves, Orians, and Heller, 1992). Consider also the biblical account for the origin of the human species. To create Adam, God took some dust from the ground and shaped it into a human figure. To effect the nonbiological to biological transformation, God then breathed into it life and created a man. To create Eve, a rib was taken from Adam and transformed into a woman. In this account, biological beings were created by transforming physical matter (i.e., dust, air in a breath, rib bone) rather than by spontaneous generation of some sort. These two events—one in the history of science and the other in religion—are so different and yet so alike. They both illustrate people's tenacious hold onto their naive mechanics and their reluctance to cross the ontological boundary of physical and metaphysical matter in tracing the history of an individual entity.

**Illness**   We revisited the child a few days after she had celebrated her fourth birthday. By then, according to diary records kept by the mother of the child's speech, this 4-year-old seemed to know quite a lot about germs, infections, and relevant treatments. For instance, she often talked about good germs that can be used for making yogurt and bread, and bad germs that can get into people's bodies to make them sick. She knew that germs need nutrients in order to multiply (by splitting themselves into baby germs). She knew that soap can help wash germs off people's hands and bodies, that brushing one's teeth with toothpaste can help wash germs off the teeth. She knew that there are different kinds of bad germs. For instance, at age 3 years 9 months, her mother explained to her that the Los Angeles Zoo decided to give up its penguin exhibit and moved it to another zoo because the penguins kept getting sick, perhaps because Los Angeles is too warm for penguins. The child asked, "Is it because the germs that make penguins sick are different from the germs that make people sick?" The mother asked, "Why do you think so?" The child explained, "Because people get sick when it's too cold; penguins get sick it's too warm!"

This child also knew that some medicine can kill certain kinds of germs but not others. For instance, when she was told that her eyes seemed pink one morning, she asked, "Are my eyes crusty too? Do you have to give me the eyedrops?" (age 3 years 10 months). As it turned out, her mother had explained to her during her previous episode of conjunctivitis that the medicine in the eyedrops could kill only the kind of germ that causes pink and crusty eyes, that it could not kill the kind of germ that causes only pink but not crusty eyes. This distinction between bacterial and viral infection was of great interest to her because she hated eyedrops.

Her knowledge of germs, infections, and germ-killing medicine seems to have behavioral consequences. At age 3 years 10 months, when her pink eyes turned out to be also crusty, her mother had a hard time (as usual) convincing her to cooperate with the administration of the eyedrops. Until the mother offered the following explanation, that is. She explained, "This morning, you let me put some eyedrops in your eyes. The medicine killed some of the germs, and your eyes are now less pink and crusty. But there are still germs in your eyes. If you don't kill the rest with more eyedrops, the germs will split into more baby germs, and they will make your eyes pinker and more crusty again." This explanation seemed to be effective enough to get the child to lie still for the mother to administer the eyedrops, although not enough to stop the child from cringing in anticipation of the pain inflicted by the eyedrops. This child's knowledge of germs and illness also seems to be useful in other ways. For instance, she is very good about brushing her teeth twice a day and washing her hands before meals. When she discovered that someone she knew brushed his teeth only at bedtime, she told him, "You should brush your teeth in the morning too. When you brush you teeth at night, you can't brush all the bad germs and food off. The bad germs can split into baby germs when you sleep. So there will be lots of germs in you teeth in the morning!" (age 3 year 11 months).

Her knowledge of germs inside the human body also seemed quite sophisticated. For instance, when she scraped her knees or had some other minor wounds, she often talked about the pink and slightly swollen area around the wound. She would explain to whoever might be interested that there were still bad germs in the wound, that white blood cells were needed to kill the germs, that the wounded area was pink and swollen because the body had to let more blood—which carried white blood cells—to go there. In short, this child seemed to understand some biological mechanisms in this domain. Briefly, she seemed to know that germs are biological kinds that can live and die, that different germs can thrive in different conditions (e.g., penguin germs in warm weather; human germs in cold weather), that germs can reproduce by dividing into baby germs, that germs need nutrients for survival and reproduction, that germs can be killed by medicine and white blood cells, that dead germs are harmless.... This set of beliefs allowed her to reason about the causes, treatments, and symptoms of infections quite coherently and sensibly.

We want to make two points with this case study. First, understanding and making use of biological causal mechanisms for reasoning about biological phenomena are possible even during the preschool years if appropriate input from adults is available. So, for most children, the relatively late emergence of an autonomous biology—compared to naive mechanics—may have to do with the timing of input from science education rather than some domain-general cognitive limitations that prevent children from understanding simple biological causal mechanisms.

This brings us to the second point. Namely the input for developing an understanding of uniquely biological causal mechanisms is probably not available to most children in their everyday life. In fact we would venture as far as suggesting that an understanding of biological causal mechanisms is a luxury rather than a necessity during early and middle childhood. Children can do quite well in predicting biological phenomena by learning about causal agents and input-output relations. When pressed to be explicit about the causal chain of events between the input and output, they can always fall back on mechanical causality. A case in point: The 4-year-old in this case study once explained to her mother why she could not sit up straight in a restaurant. (The child and her father had just picked up the mother from the airport.) She explained, "When you were in Washington, DC, at your meeting, I started coughing and having a runny nose. Now there are so many germs moving this way and that way! They keep pushing me this way and that way, so I can't sit still." She then plopped down on her mother's lap.

## How School-Age Children Explain the "Incubation of Germs" Phenomenon

We (Au and Romo 1996) asked thirty-five 8- and 9-year-olds, "There are a few germs on a piece of fish inside a plastic bag. What will happen in a couple of days? Will there be more germs, fewer germs, or the same number of germs? Why?" About 26 percent of the children explained their predictions about the number of germs by invoking mechanical causality. Some examples are: "Same number of germs—because no germs can get through the plastic;" "More germs—because the fish will get more germs from the plain plastic bag. There might be dirt in that bag." About 17 percent correctly explained that there would be more germs because the germs would divide or multiply.

We also asked these children to consider, "Some bad germs got inside a kid's body. She felt okay for a day. But then the next day she started to feel sick all over her whole body. Why did it take a whole day for her to feel sick after the germs got inside her body?" Most of the children failed to give any meaningful explanation. But 34 percent of them did explain either that it took time for enough germs to get inside the girl's body or that it took time for the germs to get to different parts of the girl's body. Only 6 percent of them explained that it took time for the germs to multiply/reproduce inside the girl's body. There seemed, then, to be considerable interest in the paths traversed by the cold germs (i.e., getting into the body, going to different parts of the girl's body) and the time required by such traveling. Our findings about food spoilage and contagion are consistent with Springer and Belk's (1994) finding that some preschoolers and most 7- and 8-year-olds recognized the need for physical contact between a contaminant-carrying bug and food for the food to become contaminated. That is, most school-age children seem to believe that the mechanical paths traced by germs and/or contaminants are crucial for predicting whether contagion/contamination will occur.

### How School-Age Children Explain HIV Transmission

In assessing an experimental AIDS curriculum for fourth- to eighth-grade children, we asked children to explain their judgments of AIDS risk in the novel situations (Au and Romo 1996). The experimental curriculum focused on a biological causal mechanism of HIV transmission, and so we expected that it would get children to mention the biology of HIV more than an existing curriculum would. We divided children's explanations into these four categories:

1. Mentioning the biology of HIV (die, survive, or reproduce). *For example*, "I said no because the saliva on the toothbrush bristles connected with air, so the AIDS in the saliva are dead;" "No, because it dies in the water. We always rinse with water and it [HIV on a toothbrush] dies;" "No, because AIDS can die in water."

2. Mentioning the mechanical path traversed by the HIV. *For example*, "Because if you wipe a person who has a bloody nose and you have a cut on your hand, the infected blood can get into you;" "The AIDS virus can get from the needle to the other person."

3. Mentioning the media (substances surrounding the HIV). *For example*, "No, because there is no blood involved;" "Yes, because you can only get AIDS through blood."

4. No or irrelevant/uninformative explanation. *For example*, "I said no because you can't get AIDS by tattooing anywhere, maybe something else."

About 46 percent of the explanations invoked mechanical causality to talk about the path traversed by the AIDS virus. Only 17 percent mentioned the biology of the AIDS virus; only 11 percent mentioned just the media of the virus. The remaining 26 percent were "I don't know" or irrelevant explanations. Interestingly children's tendency to offer a mechanical causal explanation did not vary much across grades or conditions (experimental vs. existing curriculum), even though the experimental curriculum succeeded in getting children to give biological explanations more often. These findings suggest that the tendency to invoke mechanical causality to explain AIDS—and perhaps more generally infection—transmission is rather robust during middle childhood and early adolescence.

### Interim Conclusions

In this section we showed how children explained in their own words various biological phenomena. Mechanical causality was often invoked in their explanations. This finding is in line with the suggestive evidence that school-age children tend to choose, in forced-choice tasks, mechanical causal explanations over other kinds of explanations (e.g., genetic, intentional, or vitalistic) for biological phenomena (Inagaki and Hatano 1993; Springer and Keil 1991). Despite young children's rather impressive knowledge about biological kinds, we need to be cautious in attributing the status of an autonomous theory to such knowledge structure (see also Atran 1994, 1995; Carey 1995; Solomon et al. 1996). We need to know what its domain-specific causal devices and mechanisms might look like. That was what we tried to find out in the two studies to be reported here.

## 11.5 Study 1: Children's Explanations for Illness, Food Spoilage, Death, Inheritance

How robust is children's tendency to invoke mechanic causality in explaining biological phenomena? While our case study and the two larger studies just summarized suggest that children from a wide age range (ages 3 to 14) stretch their naive mechanics into the domain of biology, it is obvious that we need more comprehensive evidence. In this study we set out to listen to more children talking about more biological phenomena.

### Method

**Participants**   One hundred and five children (48 boys, 57 girls) in kindergarten through sixth grade were interviewed at their school, which was a parochial school serving primarily a low-income, Latino community in East Los Angeles. We chose this school because we were interested children's intuitive explanations for illness causation, food spoilage, death, and genetic inheritance. Two teachers at the school told us that the children had received very little, if any, health instruction either at home or school and that the school was in the process of developing a health education program. The sample size and mean age (and age ranges) in each grade were: 22 kindergartners, 5:8 (i.e., 5 years 8 months, ranging from 5:1 to 6:5), 14 first graders, 6:6 (6:2 to 7:2), 18 second graders, 7:6 (7:0 to 8:8), 15 third graders, 8:7 (8:2 to 9:2), 16 fourth graders, 9:7 (9:2 to 10:6), 10 fifth graders, 10:8 (10:5 to 11:7), 10 sixth graders, 11:7 (11:2 to 12:2).

**Procedure**   Children were interviewed individually in a quiet corner of their school. Each interview lasted about 10 to 15 minutes and was audiotaped and later transcribed. During the interview, an experimenter showed a child colored drawings depicting four stories (illness, food spoilage, death, inheritance). For each story, the experimenter narrated the picture(s) according to a well-rehearsed script and then asked a set of yes/no and open-ended questions about the story. The order of the stories was randomized and counterbalanced across children.

To create a comfortable atmosphere for the younger children, we sat next to the children to share a "picture book" (i.e., our stimulus book). To keep children interested in this book-reading task, some of the pictures included pop-up details (e.g., lifting a paper hat off a baby's head to examine her hair color, opening a freezer door to look inside). All children were interviewed according to the same protocol and using the same stimulus book.

We always followed up our yes/no questions with open-ended ones (e.g., "Why do you think that happened?"). To encourage children to tell us more, we probed for additional information after each explanation offered by a child (e.g., "That's interesting. Can you explain a little more about how that works?"). We probed only as long as each child had new information to offer. So, when children repeated a previous response, said that they had finished answering or didn't know the answer to the question, or changed the topic of the question, we moved on to the next question in the story or to the next story.

All interviews were transcribed and then coded according to the coding systems to be described presently. Because the questions and coding systems vary considerably from story to story, we will present the stimulus stories, questions, coding systems, and results one story at a time.

## Illness

### Story and Questions

*Scene 1* (a smiling boy talking to a girl holding a handkerchief to her face): "This is a picture of John and this is Mary. John is visiting Mary today. But poor Mary had a cold. She was sneezing and sneezing, and some bad germs got into John's body. But John felt fine, and they played for a little while, and then he went home."

*Scene 2* (John holding his hand to his throat looking unhappy): "The next day when John woke up, he had a sore throat! Now remember when John was playing with Mary? Some bad germs got into his body, yet he felt fine. But the next day, he woke up with a sore throat. Why do you think that happened? *Why did it take a whole day for John to get a sore throa?*"

*Scene 3* (John lying in bed looking miserable): "That night, John felt worse. Not only did his throat hurt, but now his ears hurt, his head hurt, and his whole body felt tired all over. Why do you think that happened? *Why did John feel sick all over?"*

## Coding System

1. "Biology" of germs or white blood cells (including biological processes or animate functions such as growing, dying, reproducing, fighting, eating). *For example,* "The germs are growing and growing and making him more sick;" "It takes time for the cells to die off when bacteria strikes;" "Maybe the virus gets into one of his cells, and the cells keep reproducing, and then he will get more germs;" "The germs needed time to travel when they fight with your white blood cells, and then take effect."

2. Explicit mechanical transfer of germs. *For example,* "Germs spread all over his body;" "The germs went into his throat;" "Germs settle in;" "Germs barely got in;" "It takes a while for the germs to get there."

3. Explicit movement of unspecified entities (e.g., sickness, cough, sneeze, it, they). *For example,* "He got sick because it went into his neck;" "The sneeze little by little came in through his body;" "The cough went all through his body and made him sick."

4. Only people's behaviors or characteristics. *For example,* "Mary sneezed on him;" "When he was talking to Mary, it got all over him;" "Mary was sneezing/had a cold/wasn't feeling well;" "John was talking to/visiting Mary;" "John was playing and talking too much/didn't rest/ didn't take medicine/didn't wear a jacket/went outside too long;" "The body gets weaker and weaker;" "He might have been healthy enough that it, well, because it takes time for colds and other sorts of sicknesses to take over your immune system;" "He did not feel he had the germs . . . and then in the morning, he realized that he was cold and he got sick."

5. Other/irrelevant/uninformative/other/no explanations.

Category 1 (biology) supersedes category 2 (explicit mechanical transfer), which supersedes category 3 (movement of unspecified entities), which in turn supersedes category 4 (people). This coding system was applied to both questions: "Why did it take a whole day (or, in study 2, "so much time") for John to get a sore throat?" and "Why did John feel sick all over (or, in study 2, "in so many parts of his body")?" Responses from all of the children in this and the next study were coded by the same coder. A second coder went over 33 percent (85 out of the 260 children in these two studies combined) of the responses independently for the first question and 38 percent of the responses for the second question. The two coders agreed on 92 and 91 percent of the cases, respectively (Cohen's Kappas = 0.89 and 0.86).

**Results**    Only 6 percent of the 105 children in this study talked about the "biology" of germs or white blood cells (dying, growing bigger/ stronger, breeding, fighting, eating) when they tried to explain "Why did it take a whole day for John to get a sore throat?" Only 4 percent of the children did so when they tried to explain "Why did John feel sick all over?" This tiny minority of children came from second through sixth-grade classes (i.e., age seven and older).

By contrast, 35 percent of the children invoked mechanical transfer of germs to explain why it took a whole day for John to get a sore throat (e.g., "The germs went into his throat;" "It takes a while for the germs to get there"), and 42 percent did so to explain why John felt sick all over (e.g., "Germs spread all over his body"). This kind of explanation accounts for a majority of the older children's responses: 63 percent (fourth grade), 70 percent (fifth grade), 80 percent (sixth grade).

Many children—especially the younger ones—did not go much beyond talking about people's behaviors (e.g., "Mary was sneezing on him;" "John was talking to Mary") or characteristics (e.g., "the body gets weaker and weaker"). Overall, 39 percent of the children gave this kind of "people" explanations for the "took a whole day" question, and 30 percent did so for the "sick all over" question. Such explanation talked about pertinent input-output relations at best; they did not offer any causal mechanism for the incubation period of infectious diseases. Table 11.1 summarizes the results on illness.

## Food Spoilage

### Story and Questions

*Scene 1* (a family gathering around the kitchen table, with parents wrapping up food in foil): "This is a picture of Karla and this is her family. They had fish for dinner tonight. Karla's mother and father are wrapping up the leftover fish. They wrapped the fish up tightly in foil and put it in the freezer."

**Table 11.1**
Percentage of children in study 1 giving various explanations for illness

| Explanation type | Grade =<br>N = | K<br>22 | 1st<br>14 | 2nd<br>18 | 3rd<br>15 | 4th<br>16 | 5th<br>10 | 6th<br>10 | All<br>105 |
|---|---|---|---|---|---|---|---|---|---|
| **Incubation period of colds** | | | | | | | | | |
| Biology | | 0 | 0 | 17% | 0 | 6% | 10% | 10% | 6% |
| Movement of germs | | 14% | 14% | 17% | 27% | 63% | 70% | 80% | 35% |
| Movement of sickness, etc. | | 5% | 0 | 22% | 7% | 6% | 10% | 0 | 8% |
| People's behaviors, etc. | | 55% | 57% | 33% | 60% | 25% | 10% | 10% | 39% |
| **Spreading of symptoms to different parts of the body** | | | | | | | | | |
| Biology | | 0 | 0 | 17% | 0 | 0 | 10% | 0 | 4% |
| Movement of germs | | 27% | 7% | 28% | 47% | 63% | 70% | 80% | 42% |
| Movement of sickness, etc. | | 0 | 7% | 17% | 13% | 6% | 10% | 0 | 8% |
| People's behaviors, etc. | | 36% | 50% | 33% | 27% | 19% | 10% | 20% | 30% |

*Scene 2* (kitchen scene, a covered plate is on the table and a covered plate is in the freezer): "The next day, when Karla went to the freezer, she saw the wrapped fish. But look—some wrapped fish was left on the table! It was left there all night long. *Do you think this fish has more germs than it did last night?* (if "yes") *How did more germs get on the fish?* (if "no") *Why not?"* (experimenter opening the freezer) "What about the fish in the freezer? *Do you think this fish has more germs than it did last night?* (if "yes") *How did more germs get on the fish?* (if "no") *Why not?"*

**Coding System**

1. Biology of germs. *For example*, "The germs can die because it's very cold in the freezer;" "The germs will breed."

2. Explicit mechanical transfer of additional germs. *For example*, "Bugs got in and spread germs onto the fish;" "Germs are everywhere and get on the fish;" "The freezer is closed/sealed so germs cannot get on the fish;" "This has been sitting out, and it's been exposed to bacteria;" "Bacteria can flow through many places. Like if there's a broken plate, it can still flow in through the broken part."

3. Implicit mechanical transfer of germs: Discussing a source of additional germs without spelling out the mechanical path. *For example*, "The house is covered with germs and bacteria;" "They left it out on the table and outside there are germs;" "There is no germs in the cold and so it's protected from germs;" "The freezer doesn't have germs (and tables do)."

4. Observable events.

4a. Relevant to mechanical transfer of additional germs: Mentioning possible sources or carriers of germs without using the term *germ*. *For example*, "The table is dirty;" "It was in the freezer, and the freezer is closed;" "The freezer door doesn't have holes;" "Nobody touched it, sneezed on it, or coughed on it;" "Bugs could land on it."

4b. People's behaviors: Discussing food storage and food contamination via saliva. *For example*, "It was left it out on the table;" "They didn't put it in the freezer;" "Karla's family ate it and germs went onto the fish;"

4a. Macroscopic description of the fish. *For example*, "The fish stayed fresh;" "It's in the freezer. It's keeping it not to be rotten."

5. Other/irrelevant/uninformative/no explanations.

In this coding system category 1 (biology) supersedes category 2 (explicit mechanical transfer), which supersedes category 3 (implicit mechanical transfer), which in turn supersedes category 4 (observable events). Within category 4, 4a supersedes 4b, which supersedes 4c. This system was applied to responses given to "Do you think this fish has more germs than it did last night? (if "yes") How did more germs get on the fish? (if "no") Why not?" for both the fish in the freezer and the fish left out on the table. Responses from all of the children in both studies 1 and 2 were coded by the same coder. For the "fish on the table" question, a second coder went over 41 percent (105 out of the 260 children in these two studies) of the data independently, and the two coders agreed on 94 percent of the cases (Cohen's Kappa = 0.92). For the "fish in the freezer" question, a second coder went over 38 percent of the data independently, and the two coders agreed on 85 percent of the cases (Cohen's Kappa = 0.81).

**Results** None of the children in this study, not even the sixth graders, invoked a biological causal mechanism to explain why there were more (or no more) germs in the fish after being left out on the table overnight. When asked to explain why there were more (or no more) germs in the fish after being stored in the freezer overnight, only 5 of the 105 children in this study—one each in second, third, four, fifth, and sixth grade— talked about the biology of germs (e.g., the germs died in the freezer).

Most of the children talked about observable events: potential source of germs (e.g., "the table is dirty"), people's behaviors (e.g., "they didn't put it in the freezer"), or the fish (e.g., "The fish stayed fresh/became soggy"). These explanations reflect what children could readily observe in daily life: the input-output relation of food storage practices and the subsequent condition of food. By themselves, such explanations do not offer any causal mechanism for food spoilage or its prevention.

Of the 105 children, 26 percent did manage to offer explicit causal mechanisms for why the fish had more (or, for a small number of children, no more) germs after being left out on the table overnight. All of them invoked mechanical causality: "Bugs got in and spread germs onto the fish;" "Germs are everywhere and get on the fish;" "Germs couldn't get in because the fish was wrapped;" and so forth. To explain why the fish in the freezer had no more (or, for a small number of children, more) germs after being stored there overnight, 32 percent of the 105 children offered an explicit causal mechanism. As noted earlier, only 5 percent of the children invoked biology (e.g., death of germs). The remaining 27 percent of the children invoked mechanics (e.g., "The freezer is closed/sealed so germs cannot get on the fish"). Table 11.2 summarizes the results on food spoilage.

### Death

**Story and Questions**   Picture of an insect: "What is this? That's right. And when [child's label for the insect in plural form, e.g., grasshoppers] are alive, we know that they can move, they can eat, and they can breathe. *Do you think a [child's label, e.g., grasshopper] can live forever? Why?*"

### Coding System

1. Biological processes without causal mechanism (e.g., life span). *For example*, "Part of cycle of life;" "Because you have to die sometimes;" "No one could live forever;" "Because everything has a time to die;" "It could get old."
2. Mechanical causes: Discussing outside mechanical forces that could crush the insect. *For example*, "If you step on it;" "Some animals could eat them;" "It got smashed."
3. Other observable events without explicitly mentioning any mechanical cause of death. *For example*, "It gets hurt;" "It can be killed;" "Eating poison food and eating poison things;" "Go in water;" "It has no food;" "It's too hot or too cold;" "In winter when it's snowing."
4. Other/irrelevant/uninformative/no explanations.

Category 1 (biological processes) supersedes category 2 (mechanical), which supersedes category 3 (other observable events). This coding system was applied to responses given to "Do you think a [child's label, e.g., grasshopper] can live forever? Why?" Only explanations from children who had correctly said "no" to the yes/no question were coded. Two coders independently went over all such explanations (altogether 224 explanations in studies 1 and 2 combined). They agreed on 93 percent of the cases (Cohen's Kappa = 0.90).

Table 11.2
Percentage of children in study 1 giving various explanations for food spoilage

| Explanation type | Grade =<br>N = | K<br>22 | 1st<br>14 | 2nd<br>18 | 3rd<br>15 | 4th<br>16 | 5th<br>10 | 6th<br>10 | All<br>105 |
|---|---|---|---|---|---|---|---|---|---|
| **Fish on the table** | | | | | | | | | |
| Biology | | 0 | 0 | 0 | 0 | 0 | 0 | 0 | 0 |
| Explicit movement of germs | | 18% | 7% | 50% | 27% | 25% | 20% | 30% | 26% |
| Implicit movement of germs | | 0 | 0 | 6% | 0 | 0 | 0 | 0 | 1% |
| Observable events | | | | | | | | | |
| Relevant to mechanical transfer | | 36% | 36% | 11% | 40% | 31% | 60% | 50% | 35% |
| People's behaviors | | 27% | 43% | 28% | 13% | 44% | 20% | 20% | 29% |
| Condition of fish | | 0 | 7% | 0 | 13% | 0 | 0 | 0 | 3% |
| **Fish in the freezer** | | | | | | | | | |
| Biology | | 0 | 0 | 6% | 7% | 6% | 10% | 10% | 5% |
| Explicit movement of germs | | 9% | 21% | 33% | 20% | 38% | 30% | 50% | 27% |
| Implicit movement of germs | | 0 | 7% | 6% | 13% | 0 | 0 | 10% | 5% |
| Observable events | | | | | | | | | |
| Relevant to mechanical transfer | | 45% | 29% | 22% | 33% | 50% | 40% | 30% | 36% |
| People's behaviors | | 23% | 29% | 28% | 13% | 6% | 10% | 0 | 17% |
| Condition of fish | | 0 | 0 | 0 | 7% | 0 | 0 | 0 | 1% |

**Results**   In this study, 25 (or 24 percent) of the 105 children incorrectly answered "yes" to the question, "Can grasshoppers/crickets/bugs live forever?" Twelve of them were in kindergarten, 7 in first grade, 4 in second grade, and 2 in fourth grade. This finding is reminiscent of our earlier finding that most children in a low-income Latino sample could not appropriately apply the attribute "will die someday" to plants and animals and not minerals and artifacts until age seven or so, lagging by about two years behind a university lab school sample (Au and Romo 1996).

For the 80 children who answered "no", the two most popular kinds of explanations for why an insect cannot live forever were: life span (38 percent; e.g., "everything has a time to die") and mechanical causes (30 percent; e.g., "if you step on it"). As, shown in table 11.3, explanations invoking life span became prevalent by second grade (about age seven). The percentage of children in each grade giving this kind of explanation varied from 36 percent to 60 percent in second through sixth grades. From kindergarten on, explanations invoking mechanical causality had a substantial presence, ranging from 20 percent to 57 percent in each grade. Most of the remaining children mentioned observable events that were not explicitly mechanical (e.g., "it has no food"). Note that neither the explanations invoking life span nor those mentioning nonmechanical events offered any explicit causal mechanism. Again, the only explanations that did so invoked mechanical causality.

## Inheritance

### Story and Questions

*Scene 1*   (a black-haired woman holding a baby with a hat on): "This is a picture of a baby, and this is his mom. What color hair do you think this baby has? Why don't you check under the hat and see? Yes, you were right—this baby has black hair just like his mother."

*Scene 2*   (a brown-haired woman holding a baby with a hat on): "Here's another baby, and this is her mom. What color hair do you think this baby has? Let's check under the hat and see. Yes, you were right— this baby has brown hair just like her mother. Why do you think that happened? *Why does this baby and her mom have the same hair color?*"

Table 11.3
Percentage of children in study 1 giving various explanations for an insect's death

| Explanation type | Grade =<br>N = | K<br>10 | 1st<br>7 | 2nd<br>14 | 3rd<br>15 | 4th<br>14 | 5th<br>10 | 6th<br>10 | All<br>80 |
|---|---|---|---|---|---|---|---|---|---|
| Life span/getting old | | 0 | 14% | 36% | 40% | 50% | 60% | 50% | 38% |
| Mechanical causes | | 40% | 57% | 21% | 20% | 29% | 30% | 30% | 30% |
| Observable nonmechanical causes | | 40% | 0 | 21% | 20% | 14% | 10% | 10% | 18% |

**Coding System**

1. Biology: Transfer of information through genes. *For example*, "The genes from the mother and the chromosomes mix with the father and give the genetic code of the what the baby's going to look like."

2. Explicit mechanical transfer of substance to the baby. *For example*, "The mother's cells/genes/DNA/blood/food went into the baby;" "A piece of the mother's hair fell onto the baby;" "Blood mixed together and went into the baby;" "The baby has the mother's blood/genes;" "The mother painted or dyed the baby's hair."

3. Only implicit mechanical transfer of substance to the baby: Noting the mother-child proximity or connection during gestation/birth without explicitly mentioning transfer of substance. *For example*, "The baby was in the mommy's stomach;" "The baby was connected to the mother;" "The baby is a part of the mom;" "The baby was born from the mother;" "The baby came from the mother;" "They were a part of each other;" "The baby is part of the mother."

4. Only parent-child relations. *For example*, "Because it's the mom's baby;" "Because they are related/the same family;" "Because they live together;" "Mothers/Parents and babies are supposed to have the same hair color" "Black hair is passed down from generation to generation;" "The mom and dad made the baby;" "The dad got the mom pregnant;" "Because the mother and the baby are both girls;" "Because they are Filipino."

5. Other/irrelevant/uninformative/no explanations.

Category 1 (biology) supersedes category 2 (explicit mechanical transfer), which supersedes category 3 (implicit mechanical transfer), which in turn supersedes category 4 (parent-child relations). This coding system was applied to children's explanations for "Why does this baby and her mom have the same hair color?" Responses from all of the children in both studies 1 and 2 were coded by the same coder. A second coder went over 44 percent (114 out of the 260 children in these two studies) of the data independently, and the two coders agreed on 90 percent of the cases (Cohen's Kappa = 0.87).

**Results**    None of the children in this study, not even the sixth graders, invoked a biological causal mechanism to explain parent-child resemblance of hair color. (The example used for illustrating this category in the coding system was actually taken from study 2.) While some children used scientific jargon such as *genes*, they only talked about parent-child relations and/or the mechanical transfer of genes without explaining how genes can determine hair color (i.e., by transfering information/ instruction for making color pigment rather than by transfering color pigment itself). For example, one explanation coded as "parent-child relations" was, "My brother got the same genes as my dad, and I got the same genes as my mom." An example for the "mechanical transfer of genes" was "It could be through their genes.... The genes go into the baby's body because they are from the same family."

Virtually all of the children talked about family relations in explaining parent-child resemblance in hair color. Some children did go beyond that to talked about an explicit causal mechanism, which was invariably mechanical in nature. They talked about explicit mechanical transfer of substances such as blood, food, part of the mother's body, mother's hair, genes, and stuff carried by sperms/eggs. Such explanations were prevalent among the third, fifth, and sixth (although not fourth) graders—ranging from 33 percent to 40 percent in each of these three grades (see table 11.4).

Another popular explanation type had to do with the baby's extreme proximity to the mother during gestation or birth (e.g., the baby was inside the mother/came out of the mother). Even though such explanations did not talk about transfer of substance explicitly, they may have reflected beliefs about such transfer (e.g., food, blood, body stuff) from the mother to the baby. The percentage of children giving this kind of explanation for each grade (K–6) ranged from 18 percent to 50 percent, accounting for 30 percent of children's responses in this study.

### Conclusions from Study 1

Several conclusions can be drawn from these findings pertaining to four different biological phenomena: illness, food spoilage, death, inheritance. First, children very rarely, if at all, invoked uniquely biological causal mechanisms in their attempt to explain these phenomena. Those who did tended to come from the upper grades and to use scientific jargon— probably reflecting input from science classes rather than folk beliefs developed from everyday experience. In other words, there is little evidence that kindergarteners or grade school children have any *bona fide*

**Table 11.4**
Percentage of children in study 1 giving various explanations for mother-child resemblance of hair color

| Explanation type | Grade =<br>N = | K<br>22 | 1st<br>14 | 2nd<br>18 | 3rd<br>15 | 4th<br>16 | 5th<br>10 | 6th<br>10 | All<br>105 |
|---|---|---|---|---|---|---|---|---|---|
| Biology | | 0 | 0 | 0 | 0 | 0 | 0 | 0 | 0 |
| Explicit transfer of substance | | 14% | 7% | 11% | 33% | 19% | 40% | 40% | 21% |
| Implicit transfer of substance | | 18% | 21% | 33% | 33% | 25% | 50% | 40% | 30% |
| Parent-child relations | | 18% | 36% | 39% | 27% | 56% | 10% | 20% | 30% |

folkbiology—if inclusion of domain-specific causal mechanisms is to be considered crucial for any folk theory. Second, as Carey (1985, 1991, 1995) would have predicted, many children talked about people's behaviors, relations, and characteristics. Such explanations at best, however, were about input-output causal relations. Such talk about people (and other observable events) generally offered no explicit causal mechanism for explaining the biological phenomena examined in this study. Third, when children managed to offer explicit causal mechanisms, they almost always invoked mechanical causality (e.g., movement of germs that can cause illness and food spoilage, mechanical forces that can cause death, transfer of substances that affect a baby's hair color).

## 11.6 Study 2: A Replication

The children in study 1 primarily came from low-income Latino families. Study 2 examined children's beliefs in other socioeconomic and ethnic groups.

### Method

**Participants** In one school serving primarily middle class families, 66 children (18 boys, 48 girls) were interviewed. There were roughly 38 percent Anglo, 24 percent Filipino, and 20 percent Latino children; the remaining children came from other ethnic backgrounds. The sample size and mean age (and age ranges) in each of these grades were 21 first graders, 7:1 (6:6 to 8:3), 20 third graders, 9:1 (8:7 to 9:10), and 25 fifth graders, 11:0 (10:7 to 12:5). In another school, which serves primarily lower-middle class families, 89 children (41 boys, 48 girls) were interviewed. The ethnic makeup of the students was roughly 17 percent Anglo, 52 percent Filipino, and 31 percent Latino. The sample size and mean age (and age ranges) in each of these grades were 19 kindergartners, 5:8 (5:4 to 6:7), 22 first graders, 6:9 (6:6 to 7:4), 19 third graders, 8:8 (8:3 to 9:3), 16 fifth graders, 10:8, (10:4 to 11:4), and 13 seventh graders, 13:1 (12:6 to 13:4).

**Procedure** The procedure was the same as that of study 1, except for some wording changes in the research protocol for the illness, food spoilage, and death stories. (The protocol for the inheritance story remained unchanged.)

*Illness*  In study 1, some children did not talk about the incubation period even though we had asked them, "Why did it take *a whole day* for John to get a sore throat?" Many of them seemed to treat our question as, "Why did John get a sore throat?" In study 2, we asked instead, "Why did it take *so much time* for John to get a sore throat?" Also, in study 1, we had asked, "Why did John feel sick all over?" Again, some children seemed to ignore the "all over" part of the question. In study 2, we asked instead, "Remember here in the morning, he felt a little sick just in his throat. But that night, John felt sick in many parts of his body. So how do you think that happened? Why did John feel sick *in so many parts of his body?*"

*Food Spoilage*  In study 1, we had asked, "Do you think this fish has more germs than it did last night? (if "yes,") How did more germs get on the fish? (if "no,") Why not?" Our probe for a "yes" answer may have biased children to talk about mechanical transfer of additional germs because of the wording in the probe (i.e., "get on"). In study 2, we asked instead, "Do you think this fish has more germs than it did last night? (yes/no) Why do you think so?"

*Death*  In study 1, the questions "Do you think a grasshopper/cricket/ bug (child's label) can live forever? Why?" did not elicit very much talk about possible causes of death. In study 2, we added, "What are some ways a grasshopper/cricket/bug could die?"

## Results

Illness  The main findings of study 1 on illness were replicated with these two samples from more diverse ethnic and higher socioeconomic backgrounds. That is, only a small number of children—mostly in the upper grade—talked about the biology of germs to explain the incubation period of an infectious disease and the spreading of symptoms to different parts of the body. By contrast, a substantial number of children invoked mechanical causality to talk about the movement of germs when they tried to explain these phenomena. The remaining children tended to talk only about what they can readily observe in daily life. Table 11.5 summarizes the results on illness in this study.

**Food Spoilage** The main findings of study 1 on food spoilage were replicated in this study with one exception. Namely most of the 25 fifth graders in the school serving primarily middle-class families talked about the biology of germs (e.g., death, breeding) when they tried to explain why there would be more (or no more) germs on the fish. About the fish that was left out on the table overnight, 72 percent of these fifth graders talked about a biological causal mechanism; about the fish that was stored in the freezer, 76 percent did so. So these children outperformed their peers and older children in the low-income sample of study 1 (fifth and sixth graders) and those in the lower-middle class sample of this study (fifth and seventh graders). As it turned out, the fifth-graders in the middle-class sample had recently seen a film on germ multiplication and the environments (at various temperatures: body temperature, room temperature, hot and cold places) where germs can live and die. Such school input was rare or entirely absent in the low-income sample, the lower-middle class sample, and in the first and third grade of this middle-class sample. These findings are consistent with our speculation (noted earlier) that the relatively late emergence of an autonomous biology—compared to that of naive mechanics —may have much to do with the timing of science education input. The results on food spoilage for this study are summarized in table 11.6.

**Death** In this study ten of the 89 children (or 11 percent) from the lower-middle class sample and one of the 66 children (or 2 percent) in the middle class sample incorrectly answered "yes" to the question, "Do you think a grasshopper/cricket/bug can live forever?" All but one of these children was in kindergarten or first grade.

As in study 1, for the children who answered "no," the two most popular kinds of explanations for why an insect cannot live forever were life span (26 percent for the lower-middle class sample and 42 percent for the middle-class sample) and mechanical causes (30 percent and 52 percent, respectively for the two samples). Most of the remaining children mentioned observable events that were not explicitly mechanical (e.g.,

**Table 11.5**
Percentage of children in study 2 giving various explanations for illness

| Explanation type | Grade = <br> N = | Middle-class sample | | | Lower-middle-class sample | | | | | All |
| | | 1st <br> 21 | 3rd <br> 20 | 5th <br> 25 | K <br> 19 | 1st <br> 22 | 3rd <br> 19 | 5th <br> 16 | 7th <br> 13 | 155 |
|---|---|---|---|---|---|---|---|---|---|---|
| **Incubation period of colds** | | | | | | | | | | |
| Biology | | 0 | 5% | 32% | 0 | 0 | 5% | 13% | 31% | 10% |
| Movement of germs | | 33% | 60% | 48% | 21% | 23% | 42% | 38% | 38% | 38% |
| Movement of sickness, etc. | | 10% | 5% | 0 | 5% | 5% | 0 | 6% | 8% | 5% |
| People's behaviors, etc. | | 33% | 20% | 20% | 63% | 59% | 21% | 38% | 23% | 35% |
| **Spreading of symptoms to different parts of the body** | | | | | | | | | | |
| Biology | | 0 | 0 | 24% | 0 | 0 | 5% | 6% | 8% | 6% |
| Movement of germs | | 38% | 70% | 56% | 21% | 23% | 58% | 56% | 69% | 48% |
| Movement of sickness, etc. | | 14% | 5% | 8% | 5% | 14% | 11% | 19% | 8% | 10% |
| People's behaviors, etc. | | 19% | 25% | 12% | 68% | 59% | 21% | 19% | 15% | 30% |

Table 11.6
Percentage of children in study 2 giving various explanations for food spoilage

| Explanation type | Middle-class sample | | | Lower-middle-class sample | | | | | |
|---|---|---|---|---|---|---|---|---|---|
| Grade = | 1st | 3rd | 5th | K | 1st | 3rd | 5th | 7th | All |
| N = | 21 | 20 | 25 | 19 | 22 | 19 | 16 | 13 | 155 |
| **Fish on the table** | | | | | | | | | |
| Biology | 0 | 0 | 72% | 0 | 0 | 0 | 6% | 0 | 12% |
| Explicit movement of germs | 14% | 30% | 16% | 26% | 14% | 63% | 50% | 54% | 31% |
| Implicit movement of germs | 5% | 0 | 4% | 0 | 14% | 0 | 6% | 8% | 5% |
| Observable events | | | | | | | | | |
| Relevant to mechanical transfer | 33% | 40% | 0 | 16% | 32% | 21% | 38% | 23% | 25% |
| People's behaviors | 29% | 25% | 8% | 53% | 18% | 16% | 0 | 8% | 20% |
| Condition of fish | 5% | 5% | 0 | 0 | 0 | 0 | 0 | 8% | 2% |
| **Fish in the freezer** | | | | | | | | | |
| Biology | 0 | 10% | 76% | 0 | 0 | 11% | 6% | 15% | 17% |
| Explicit movement of germs | 14% | 20% | 12% | 11% | 18% | 42% | 50% | 23% | 23% |
| Implicit movement of germs | 0 | 5% | 4% | 16% | 9% | 5% | 6% | 8% | 6% |
| Observable events | | | | | | | | | |
| Relevant to mechanical transfer | 29% | 35% | 0 | 32% | 32% | 21% | 38% | 23% | 25% |
| People's behaviors | 43% | 25% | 4% | 37% | 36% | 11% | 0 | 23% | 23% |
| Condition of fish | 0 | 0 | 0 | 0 | 5% | 0 | 0 | 8% | 1% |

"it has no food"). Again, neither the explanations invoking life span nor those mentioning nonmechanical events offered any explicit causal mechanism. The only explanations that did so invoked mechanical causality. Table 11.7 summarizes the results on death for this study.

**Inheritance**   Only one child (a seventh grader in the middle-class school) among the 155 children in this study talked about the transfer of information about hair color from the mother to the baby: "The genes from the mother and the chromosomes mix with the father and give the genetic code of the what the baby's going to look like." The use of jardon speaks clearly for the influence of science education; it certainly does not look like something spontaneously constructed by a child from everyday experience.

Most of the children's explanations fell roughly equally often into one of these three categories: explicit mechanical transfer of substances (28 percent for the lower-middle class sample, $N = 89$; 18 percent for the middle class sample, $N = 66$), mother-child proximity during pregnancy or birth (26 percent and 30 percent, respectively), and only parent-child relations (24 and 35 percent, respectively). Again, when children explicitly talked about a causal mechanism for mother-child resemblance of hair color, they virtually always talked about mechanical transfer of substance such as blood, body parts, hair, and food. Table 11.8 summarizes the results on inheritance for this study.

### Individual Children's Response Patterns

Do most children invoke mechanical causality to explain biological phenomena some of the time? Or, do most of the "mechanical" explanations found in these two studies concentrated on the same group of children? What about explanations invoking biological causal mechanisms? What about explanations that focus on only people's behaviors, characteristics, relations, or other observable events? To address these questions, we computed the number of explanations in these three categories given by each child across biological phenomena.

Included as "biological causal mechanisms" are biology of germs for the illness and food spoilage stories, and transfer of information/instruction about hair color for the inheritance story. (The death story is not included

**Table 11.7**
Percentage of children in study 2 giving various explanations for an insect's death

| | | Middle-class sample | | | Lower-middle-class sample | | | | | |
|---|---|---|---|---|---|---|---|---|---|---|
| Explanation type | Grade = N = | 1st 20 | 3rd 20 | 5th 25 | K 14 | 1st 18 | 3rd 18 | 5th 16 | 7th 13 | All 144 |
| Life span/getting old | | 24% | 30% | 64% | 5% | 9% | 32% | 56% | 62% | 38% |
| Mechanical causes | | 62% | 55% | 36% | 11% | 27% | 37% | 38% | 23% | 39% |
| Observable nonmechanical causes | | 5% | 15% | 0 | 11% | 14% | 11% | 0 | 15% | 9% |

**Table 11.8**
Percentage of children in study 2 giving various explanations for mother-child resemblance of hair color

| | | Middle-class sample | | | Lower-middle-class sample | | | | | |
|---|---|---|---|---|---|---|---|---|---|---|
| Explanation type | Grade = N = | 1st 21 | 3rd 20 | 5th 25 | K 19 | 1st 22 | 3rd 19 | 5th 16 | 7th 13 | All 155 |
| Biology | | 0 | 0 | 0 | 0 | 0 | 0 | 0 | 8% | 1% |
| Explicit transfer of substance | | 0 | 15% | 36% | 11% | 9% | 21% | 50% | 69% | 24% |
| Implicit transfer of substance | | 38% | 30% | 24% | 5% | 45% | 47% | 19% | 0 | 28% |
| Parent-child relations | | 38% | 35% | 32% | 37% | 27% | 5% | 25% | 23% | 28% |

because no child offered any truly biological causal mechanism for that phenomenon.) Table 11.9 presents the percentage of children in each grade, with studies 1 and 2 combined, giving various numbers of explanations invoking a biological causal mechanism. Overall, 80 percent of children gave no such explanation ($N = 260$). Only from second grade on did some children manage to offer at least one such explanation (possible maximum = 5).

Included as "mechanical causal mechanisms" are explicit mechanical transfer of germs for the illness and food spoilage stories, mechanical forces that can cause death, and mechanical transfer of substances from mother to baby. In sharp contrast to the pattern of results for "biology" explanations, 77 percent of the children invoked mechanical causality at least once. They gave anywhere from one to five such explanations (maximum = 6; see table 11.9).

Included as "only people's behaviors, characteristics, relations, and other observable events" are only people's behaviors and characteristics for the illness story, only observable events for the food spoilage story, only observable events without explicit mention of mechanical forces for the death story, and only parent-child relations for the inheritance story. Like mechanical causality, people's behaviors and other observable events were invoked as the sole explanation for at least one biological phenomenon by 77 percent of the children. These children gave anywhere from one to six such explanations (maximum = 6; see table 11.9).

Taken together, these patterns of results suggest that most of children invoke mechanical causality to explain a biological phenomenon some of the time. Most of the children also sometimes talk *only* about people's behaviors and other observable events. Finally most children invoked no biological causal mechanism in these two studies.

## 11.7  Concluding Remarks

Now we feel that we have probably earned the privilege to put quotation marks around "folkbiology" in the title of this chapter. Our case study of a preschool child's quest for biological knowledge, our survey of folk explanations for illness in medical anthropology research, our review of previous experimental studies of conceptual development in the domain

**Table 11.9**
Percentage of children in both studies giving various "biological," "mechanical," and "people/observable event" explanations

| Number of explanations | Grade =<br>N = | K<br>41 | 1st<br>57 | 2nd<br>18 | 3rd<br>54 | 4th<br>16 | 5th<br>51 | 6th<br>10 | 7th<br>13 | All<br>260 |
|---|---|---|---|---|---|---|---|---|---|---|
| **Biological** | | | | | | | | | | |
| 0 | | 100% | 100% | 78% | 85% | 88% | 45% | 80% | 46% | 80% |
| 1 | | 0 | 0 | 11% | 15% | 13% | 18% | 20% | 38% | 11% |
| 2 | | 0 | 0 | 6% | 0 | 0 | 18% | 0 | 15% | 5% |
| 3 | | 0 | 0 | 6% | 0 | 0 | 14% | 0 | 0 | 3% |
| 4 | | 0 | 0 | 0 | 0 | 0 | 4% | 0 | 0 | 1% |
| 5 | | 0 | 0 | 0 | 0 | 0 | 2% | 0 | 0 | 0 |
| **Mechanical** | | | | | | | | | | |
| 0 | | 49% | 37% | 28% | 19% | 13% | 6% | 0 | 0 | 23% |
| 1 | | 22% | 25% | 28% | 11% | 13% | 16% | 20% | 8% | 18% |
| 2 | | 15% | 25% | 6% | 24% | 13% | 31% | 20% | 38% | 23% |
| 3 | | 10% | 7% | 39% | 22% | 56% | 25% | 20% | 31% | 21% |
| 4 | | 5% | 5% | 0 | 15% | 6% | 18% | 10% | 15% | 10% |
| 5 | | 0 | 2% | 0 | 9% | 0 | 4% | 30% | 8% | 5% |
| 6 | | 0 | 0 | 0 | 0 | 0 | 0 | 0 | 0 | 0 |
| **People/observable event** | | | | | | | | | | |
| 0 | | 12% | 7% | 11% | 28% | 19% | 43% | 60% | 23% | 23% |
| 1 | | 20% | 32% | 33% | 31% | 6% | 22% | 10% | 31% | 25% |
| 2 | | 22% | 26% | 17% | 13% | 38% | 25% | 20% | 31% | 23% |
| 3 | | 20% | 19% | 28% | 17% | 31% | 2% | 10% | 15% | 16% |
| 4 | | 15% | 7% | 6% | 9% | 6% | 4% | 0 | 0 | 7% |
| 5 | | 7% | 7% | 6% | 2% | 0 | 2% | 0 | 0 | 4% |
| 6 | | 5% | 2% | 0 | 0 | 0 | 2% | 0 | 0 | 2% |

of biology, and the two new studies reported here all converge to the same conclusions. First, children and adults do not seem to construct uniquely biological causal mechanisms from their everyday experience. If inclusion of domain-specific causal devices or mechanisms is crucial for determining whether a set of folk beliefs qualifies as a folk theory, then most children and probably even adults do not develop a "folkbiology" unless given science input.

We must confess that we oscillate almost daily between thinking that (1) children clearly have no folk theory in the domain of biological kinds and (2) we are being too harsh. One difficulty with taking a hard line on folkbiology is that we may be forced to say that children (and most adults for that matter) do not have a naive psychology either. Research on naive "psychology" to date has focused on causal relations among beliefs, feelings, and behaviors (e.g., Wellman, 1990; Wellman and Gelman 1998). It has offered no clue for what folk psychological causal mechanisms might look like. So, in our more lenient moments, we ponder whether a foundational theory must include domain-specific causal mechanisms. Might inclusion of input-output causal relations and causal agents suffice? Should some day enough researchers be willing to abandon inclusion of domain-specific causal mechanisms as a necessary criterion for folk theories, or more specifically, for folkbiology (e.g., Atran 1998), we will probably be willing to credit children as well as adults with folkbiology. But until then....

Second, Carey (1981, 1991, 1995) cannot be more correct in saying that children draw on their knowledge of people (and other everyday observable behaviors) to reason about biological phenomena. However, such explanations are at best about input-output causal relations. They do not provide causal mechanisms per se.

Third, when children do talk about causal mechanisms in their attempts to make sense of biological phenomena, they almost always fall back on a folk theory that they know well—namely naive mechanics. Such reliance on mechanical causality is pervasive; it is evident among children across a rather wide age range (from preschool years through adolescence), different ethnic backgrounds, and different socioeconomic backgrounds. To be honest, we were quite surprised that our study 2 replicated all of the main findings of study 1. Our team of interviewers and transcribers was convinced that we would find major differences between our low-income sample (study 1) and the two samples from higher socioeconomic backgrounds (study 2). They noted that the children from the low-income sample were hard to interview because the children, especially the younger ones, would just sit there and say very little (see also Brice 1983). Nonetheless, when those children talked—however inarticulate they may have seemed—they revealed much the same kinds of beliefs as the children from the higher-income samples.

We rest our case.

## Note

We thank the children, staff, and parents of All Souls Elementary School, Our Lady of Lourdes Elementary School, St. Finbar's Elementary School, and St. Genevieve's Elementary School for their support and cooperation. We are grateful to Gery Ryan for helpful discussion and to Nina Bermudez, Jennifer DeWitt, Sun Mee Lee, Iling Lin, Marlene Martinez, Natalie May, Denise Piñon, Cristy Scoville, Jeanine Wan, and Caryn Wernle for their helpful input for designing the studies and their invaluable assistance in data collection, transcription, and coding.

## References

Atran, S. 1994. Core domains versus scientific theories: evidence from systematics and Itza-Maya folkbiology. In L. A. Hirschfeld and S. A. Gelman, eds., *Domain Specificity in Cognition and Culture*. New York: Cambridge University Press, pp. 316–40.

Atran, S. 1995. Causal constraints on categories and categorical constraints on biological reasoning across cultures. In S. Sperber, D. Premack, and A. J. Premack, eds, *Causal Cognition*. Oxford: Clarendon Press, pp. 205–33.

Atran, S. 1998. Folk biology and the anthropology of science: Cognitive universals and cultural particulars. *Behavioral and Brain Sciences* 21: 547–611.

Au, T. K. 1994. Developing an intuitive understanding of substance kinds. *Cognitive Psychology* 27: 71–111.

Au, T. K., and L. F. Romo. 1996. Building a coherent conception of HIV transmission: A new approach to AIDS education. In D. Medin, ed., *The Psychology of Learning and Motivation,* vol. 35. San Diego: Academic Press, pp. 193–241.

Au, T. K., A. L. Sidle, and K. B. Rollins. 1993. Developing an intuitive understanding of conservation and contamination: Invisible particles as a plausible mechanism. *Developmental Psychology* 29: 286–99.

Backscheider, A. G., M. Shatz, and S. A. Gelman. 1993. Preschoolers' ability to distinguish living kinds as a function of regrowth. *Child Development* 64: 1242–57.

Berlin, E. A., and B. Berlin. 1996. *Medical Ethnobiology of the Highland Maya of Chiapas, Mexico: The Gastrointestinal Diseases*. Princeton: Princeton University Press.

Bernstein, A. C., and P. A. Cowan. 1975. Children's concepts of how people get babies. *Child Development* 46: 77–91.

Bonilla, D. E., M. Alferez de Castillo, and F. Piñeda. 1987a. *Informe Final de la Investigación Antropológica Realizada en el Cantón Chanmico, San Juan Opica, La Libertad*. Ministerio de Salud Pública y Asistencia Social de El Salvador, Instituto de Nutrición de Centro América y Panamá (INCAP).

Brewer, W., and A. Samarapungavan. 1991. Children's theories vs. scientific theories: Differences in reasoning or differences in knowledge? In R. Hoffman and D. Palermo, eds., *Cognition and the Symbolic Processes*. Hillsdale, NJ: Lawrence Erlbaum, pp. 209–32.

Brice, S. H. 1983. *Ways with Words: Language, Life, and Work in Communities and Classrooms*. Cambridge: Cambridge University Press.

Carey, S. 1985. *Conceptual Change in Childhood*. Cambridge: MIT Press.

Carey, S. 1991. Knowledge acquisition: Enrichment or conceptual change? In S. Carey and R. Gelman, eds., *The Epigenesis of Mind: Essays on Biology and Cognition*. Hillsdale, NJ: Lawrence Erlbaum, pp. 257–91.

Carey, S. 1995. On the origin of causal understanding. In S. Sperber, D. Premack, and A. J. Premack, eds, *Causal Cognition*. Oxford: Clarendon Press, pp. 268–302.

Carey, S., and E. Spelke. 1994. Domain specific knowledge and conceptual change. In L. A. Hirschfeld and S. A. Gelman, eds., *Domain specificity in cognition and culture*. New York: Cambridge University Press, pp. 169–200.

Coley, J. D. 1995. Emerging differentiation of folkbiology and folkpsychology: Attributions of biological and psychological properties to living things. *Child Development* 66: 1856–74.

D'Andrade, R. G. 1976. A propositional analysis of U.S. American beliefs about illness. In K. Basso and H. A. Selby, eds., *Meaning in Anthropology*. Albuquerque: University of New Mexico Press, pp. 155–247.

Gelman, R. 1990. First principles organize attention to and learning about relevant data: Number and the animate-inanimate distinction as examples. *Cognitive Science* 14: 79–106.

Gelman, S. A. 1996. Concepts and theories. In R. Gelman and T. K. Au, eds., *Handbook of Perception and Cognition: Perceptual and Cognitive Development*, 2nd ed. San Diego: Academic Press, pp. 117–150.

Gelman, S. A., J. D. Coley, and G. M. Gottfried. 1994. Essentialist beliefs in children: The acquisition of concepts and theories. In L. A. Hirschfeld and S. A.

Gelman, eds., *Domain Specificity in Cognition and Culture*. New York: Cambridge University Press, pp. 169–200.

Gelman, S. A., and H. M. Wellman. 1991. Insides and essences: Early understandings of the non-obvious. *Cognition* 38: 213–44.

Goldman, R. J., and J. D. G. Goldman. 1982. How children perceive the origin of babies and the roles of mothers and fathers in procreation: A cross-national study. *Child Development* 53: 491–504.

Green, E. C., A. Jurg, and A. Djedje. 1994. The snake in stomach: Child diarrhea in central Mozambigque. *Medical Anthropology Quarterly* 8: 4–24.

Hatano, G., and K. Inagaki. 1994. Young children's naive theory of biology. *Cognition* 50: 171–88.

Hickling, A. K., and S. A. Gelman. 1995. How does your garden grow? Evidence of an early conception of plants as biological kinds. *Child Development* 66: 856–76.

Hirschfeld, L. A. 1994. The child's representation of human groups. In D. Medin, ed., *The Psychology of Learning and Motivation: Advances in Research and Theory*, vol. 31. San Diego: Academic Press, pp. 133–85.

Hirschfeld, L. A. 1996. *Race in the Making*. Cambridge: MIT Press.

Inagaki, K., and G. Hatano. 1987. Young children's spontaneous personification as analogy. *Child Development* 58: 1013–20.

Inagaki, K., and G. Hatano. 1993. Young children's understanding of the mind-body distinction. *Child Development* 64: 1534–49.

Kalish, C. 1996. Preschoolers' understanding of germs as invisible mechanisms. *Cognitive Development* 11: 83–106.

Kendall, C. 1990. Public health and the domestic domain: Lessons from anthropological research on diarrheal diseases. In J. Coreil and D. Mull, eds., *Anthropology and Primary Health Care*. Boulder, CO: Westview Press, pp. 173–95.

Keil, F. C. 1992. The origins of an autonomous biology. In M. R. Gunnar and M. Maratsos. eds., *Modularity and Constraints in Language and Cognition. Minnesota Symposia on Child Psychology*, vol. 25. Hillsdale, NJ: Lawrence Erlbaum, pp. 103–37.

Keil, F. C. 1994. The birth and nurturance of concepts by domains: The origins of concepts of living things. In L. A. Hirschfeld and S. A. Gelman, eds., *Domain Specificity in Cognition and Culture*. New York: Cambridge University Press, pp. 234–54.

Mathews, H. F., D. R. Lannin, and J. P. Mitchell. 1994. Coming to terms with advanced breast cancer: Black women's narratives from eastern North Carolina. *Social Science and Medicine* 38: 789–800.

McCloskey, M. 1983. Naive theories of motion. In D. Gentner and A. Stevens, eds., *Mental Models*. Hillsdale, NJ: Lawence Erlbaum, pp. 299–324.

Murdock, G. P. 1980. *Theories of Illness: A World Survey*. Pittsburgh: Pittsburgh University Press.

Nichter, M., and M. Nichter. 1994. Acute respiratory illness: Popular health culture and mother's knowledge in the Philippines. *Medical Anthropology* 15: 353–75.

Proffitt, D. R., M. K. Kaiser, and S. M. Whelan. 1990. Understanding wheel dynamics. *Cognitive Psychology* 22: 342–73.

Purves, W. K., G. H. Orians, and H. C. Heller. 1992. *Life: The Science of Biology.* San Francisco: W.H. Freeman.

Rosengren, K. S., S. A. Gelman, C. W. Kalish, and M. McCormick. 1991. As time goes by: Children's early understanding of growth in animals. *Child Development.* 62: 1302–20.

Solomon, G. E. A., and N. L. Cassimatis. 1995. On young children's understanding of germs as biological causes of illness. Poster presented at Society for Research in Child Development, Indianapolis.

Solomon, G. E. A., S. C. Johnson, D. Zaitchik, and S. Carey. 1996. Like father, like son: Young children's understanding of how and who offspring resemble their parents. *Child Development* 67: 151–71.

Spelke, E. S., and L. Hermer. 1996. Early cognitive development: Objects and space. In R. Gelman and T. K. Au, eds., *Handbook of Perception and Cognition: Perceptual and Cognitive Development,* 2nd ed. San Diego: Academic Press, pp. 71–114.

Springer, K. 1992. Children's awareness of the biological implications of kinship. *Child Development* 63: 950–59.

Springer, K. 1995. The role of factual knowledge in a naive theory of biology. Paper presented at the symposium on Characterizing Young Children's Knowledge of Biology. Society for Research in Child Development, Indianapolis.

Springer, K., and F. C. Keil. 1991. Early differentiation of causal mechanisms appropriate to biological and non-biological kinds. *Child Developmental* 62: 767–81.

Springer, K., T. Nguyen, and R. Samaniego. 1996. Early awareness of decomposition as a distinctive property of biological kinds: Evidence for a naive theory. *Cognitive Development* 11: 65–82.

Springer, K., and J. Ruckel. 1992. Early beliefs about the cause of illness: Evidence against immanent justice. *Cognitive Development* 7: 429–43.

Trotter, R. T. 1991. A survey of four illnesses and their relationship to intra-cultural variation in a Mexican-American community. *American Anthropologist* 93: 115–125.

Vosniadou, S., and W. F. Brewer. 1992. Mental models of the earth: A study of conceptual change in childhood. *Cognitive Psychology* 24: 535–85.

Weller, S. C., L. M. Pachter, R. T. Trotter II, and R. D. Baer. 1993. Empacho in four Latino groups: A study of intra- and inter-cultural variation in beliefs. *Medical Anthropology* 15: 109–36.

Wellman, H. M. 1990. *The Child's Theory of Mind.* Cambridge: MIT Press.

Wellman, H. M., and D. Estes, 1986. Early understanding of mental entities: A reexamination of childhood realism. *Child Development* 57: 910–23.

Wellman, H. M., and S. A. Gelman. 1992. Cognitive development: Foundational theories of core domains. *Annual Review of Psychology* 43: 337–75.

Wellman, H. M., and S. A. Gelman. 1997. Knowledge acquisition. In D. Kuhn and R. Siegler eds., *Handbook of Child Psychology: Cognitive Development*, 5th ed. New York: Wiley, pp. 523–73.

Yoder, P. S. 1995. Examining ethnomedical diagnoses and treatment choices for diarrheal disorders in Lubumbashi Swahili. *Medical Anthropology* 16: 211–47.

# 12

# How Biological Is Essentialism?

Susan A. Gelman and Lawrence A. Hirschfeld

One of the most striking qualities of living things is their constancy over variation, both variation over time and variation over individuals. Thus a newborn infant becomes an adult, a sprout becomes an apple tree, a caterpillar turns into a butterfly—and these are not just accidental, idiosyncratic changes but ones that characterizes the life history of each and every adult human, apple tree, or butterfly. Similarly a hummingbird, ostrich, falcon, and sparrow differ to an extraordinary degree from one to another, yet they all share certain core properties that allow us to say that they are all birds (and that bats are not). An intuitive notion of "essence" has been posited to account for how humans understand this constancy. According to this view, humans are predisposed to notice that members of a biological kind have a hidden essence that remains unchanged across outward changes such as growth and reproduction (Atran 1990; Pinker 1994). It is thus perhaps not surprising that essentialism has been argued to be a central component of folkbiology, along with structured taxonomies (Atran 1990; Berlin 1978) and causal explanatory frameworks (chapter 11, this volume).

We resist tying essentialism too closely to folkbiology, however, for several reasons. First, the notion has a long history of links to other domains, and indeed much of the evidence for essentialism comes from outside the domain of folkbiology. People appear to attribute hidden essences to social categories such as race, gender, and personality (see Allport 1954, Banton 1987; Stoler 1995 for race; Fuss 1989 and Taylor 1994 for gender; and Gelman 1992 for personality). Racial, gender, or personality "essences" may be analogical extensions from a folkbiological notion (Atran 1990; Guillaumin 1980), but race, gender, and personality are not themselves biological categories. Similarly, claims of essentialism in language extend to words such as proper names (Kripke 1972) and artifacts (Putnam 1975). Given these controversies, the present chapter examines the evidence for essentialism and addresses whether essentialism is plausibly a core component of folkbiology: whether it is an untutored belief, universal, and/or biologically specific.

First, what is an essence? As noted above, in the realm of folkbiology, it is taken to be that hidden, identity-determining aspect of an organism that remains unchanged over growth, morphological transformations, and reproduction. Pinker (1994) refers to the essence as what determines that "a caterpillar, chrysalis, and butterfly are in a crucial sense the same animal" (p. 422). However, outside the realm of folk biology, the range of uses of "essence" and claims about its origins are staggeringly broad. When we co-taught a graduate seminar in 1996 on essentialism, and read sources from ancient Greek philosophers to postmodern feminist theorists, we were overwhelmed by the scope, richness, and variety in arguments about essentialism. We read authors who treated essences as a property of the real world, others who treated essences as an inevitable product of the human mind, and still others who treated essences as a historical construction imposed on people for political ends. Some scholars asserted that essentialism is a core component of a naive-biology module; others, that it is domain-general property of language.

Reeling from the variability and seeming contradictions in these claims, the students in the seminar repeatedly and persistently asked us to define "essence," and to answer once and for all the question of whether the authors on the syllabus were all talking about the same thing. While struggling to address these questions, we also found ourselves being reminded of other curious phenomena *not* discussed in readings on essentialism yet sharing many of its features—including contagion, contamination, art forgeries, and the vast sums people pay to purchase Jackie Onassis's faux-pearl necklace. Are these phenomena interpreted within the same mode of reasoning, and if so, are they biological?

This chapter is, in a sense, a response to the seminar. We will argue for a notion of "essence" that is both broader and more contained than we have found in the literature. It is more contained in that some of the senses in the literature, though relevant to metaphysical discussions, have little relevance for psychological or anthropological portrayals. At the same time the interpretation we propose in this chapter is broader because biological essentialism appears to be one of a class of phenomena in which small causes are thought to have powerful, far-ranging effects. Examining essentialism within this broader set also has implications for the issue of domain specificity.

## 12.1 Containing the Notion of Essence

One of the reasons the notion of essence is interesting is that it is remarkably pervasive despite its conflicts with reality. It has been pervasive across time (discussed at least over the past 2,400 years), across radically different philosophical traditions (e.g., embraced by both Plato and Locke), and across cultures. However, biologists insist that biological species do not truly have essences (Sober 1994; Mayr 1982), and certainly other essentialized categories such as race lack biological coherence (Hirschfeld 1996). Still, despite the fact that essentialism may yield little insight about the nature of the world, it promises to yield insights on how the human mind constructs reality, a point to which we return later in the chapter.

Just how pervasive the notion (of essence) is depends largely on whether different people are referring to the same thing. There are at least three distinct types of "essence" in the literature: sortal, causal, and ideal (see also Hirschfeld 1996).

1. *Sortal essence.* The sortal essence is the set of defining characteristics that all and only members of a category share. Aristotle in *Metaphysics* makes a distinction between essential and accidental properties (see Keil 1989 on defining vs. characteristic properties) such that the essential properties constitute the essence. For example, the essence of a grandmother would be the property of being the mother of a person's parent (rather than the accidental or characteristic properties of wearing glasses and having gray hair; see Landau 1982). Sortal essence is a restatement of this classical view of concepts. Meaning (or identity) is supplied by a set of necessary and sufficient features that determine whether an entity does or does not belong in a category (Smith and Medin 1981). Specific essentialist accounts provide arguments concerning which sorts of features are essential.

2. *Causal essence.*   The causal essence is the substance, power, quality, process, relationship, or entity that *causes* other category-typical properties to emerge and be sustained and confers identity. Locke in his *Essay Concerning Human Understanding* (bk. 3, p. 26) describes it as "the very being of anything, whereby it is what it is. And thus the real internal, but generally ... unknown constitution of things, whereon their discoverable qualities depend, may be called their essence." The causal essence is used to explain why things are the way they are. Whereas the sortal essence could apply to any entity (pencils, wastebaskets, tigers are all categories for which certain properties may be "essential," i.e., crucial for determining category membership), the causal essence applies only to entities for which inherent, hidden properties determine observable qualities. For example, the causal essence of water may be something like $H_2O$, which is responsible for various observable properties that water has. Note that the cluster of properties "odorless, tasteless, and colorless" is not an essence of water, despite being true of all members of the category WATER, since the properties "odorless, tasteless, and colorless" lack causal force.

3. *Ideal essence.*   The ideal essence is ideal in the sense of not having a real instantiation in the world. For example, the essence of "goodness" is some pure, abstract quality that is imperfectly realized in real-world instances of people doing good deeds. None of these good deeds perfectly embodies "the good," but each reflects some aspect of it. Plato's cave allegory (in which what we see of the world are mere shadows of what is real and true) exemplifies this view. The ideal essence thus contrasts with both the sortal and the causal essences, which concern qualities of real-world entities.

Accounts differ concerning the question of where the essence (of whatever type) is located. Is it located in the world (metaphysical essentialism) or is it a representation of some sort, either conceptual (psychological essentialism), embedded in language (nominal essentialism), or located in cultural practices (cultural essentialism)? Thus there are at least twelve different senses of "essence":

|                  | Sortal | Causal | Ideal |
|------------------|--------|--------|-------|
| Metaphysical     | x      | x      | x     |
| Representational |        |        |       |
| Psychological    | x      | x      | x     |
| Nominal          | x      | x      | x     |
| Cultural         | x      | x      | x     |

We focus on those senses of "essence" marked by the large bold x's. Metaphysical essentialism is beyond the scope of this chapter, both because there are compelling reasons to doubt the reality of essences from a biological perspective, as mentioned above, and because current psychological methods are not designed to shed light on these issues. The empirical studies reviewed here focus on beliefs about pigs, for example, not on pigs themselves. We also decline to consider sortal essences, primarily because they seem implausible from both a psychological and a linguistic perspective. Given the past thirty years of research on categorization, it is extremely unlikely that people represent features that can identify all and only members of a category (see Rosch and Mervis 1975 for review), regardless of how confident they are that such features exist (McNamara and Sternberg 1983; Malt 1994).

Ideal essences have been virtually ignored in studies of concept representation (but see Sperber 1975). If anything, people's representations of most object concepts seem to be based on the structure and variability of what they encounter rather than nonrealized ideals. That is, when people are asked to rate the typicality of various instances of a category, their ratings usually reflect central tendencies rather than ideals (Rosch and Mervis 1975). Interestingly, however, other kinds of categories do elicit ideals rather than central tendencies—such as the prototype of a rich person is fabulously rich and not "average" rich (Barsalou 1985), suggesting that it may be feasible to examine notions of ideal essence in some content domains.

## 12.2   How Essential Is Essentialism?

Distinguishing among sortal, causal, and ideal versions of essentialism allows us to better assess recent arguments *against* the claim that an essentialist presumption is part of our conceptual repertoire. Specifically, although various lines of evidence argue against essences as determining word use, the findings speak only against the attribution of sortal not causal essences.

For example, Malt (1994) demonstrates that speakers of English use the word "water" to refer to liquids that are not pure $H_2O$. Because the most plausible account available for a metaphysical essence for water has been $H_2O$, Malt interprets the evidence as damaging to an essentialist theory.[1] Specifically, she has shown that people do not endorse $H_2O$ as either necessary or sufficient for "water" when the word is used at a superordinate level (including pond water, polluted water, etc.; although her own data suggest that there is a subordinate-level usage, "pure water," which is more or less equivalent to $H_2O$). Critically $H_2O$ represents a sortal not causal essence, and accordingly her study provides evidence only against the classical view of category meaning.

Braisby, Franks, and Hampton (1996) similarly question whether the empirical evidence supports essentialist predictions. The essentialist predictions they consider all target sortal essences, as can be seen in how they characterize the essentialist view: "Essentialism's proposal [is] that actual essences alone determine a word's reference" (p. 249), and "classification of entities as members or non-members of the kind category will be determined according to their possession of the essence" (p. 251). They examine subjects' intuitions about the application of various category names (cat, water, tiger, gold, bronze, lemon, and oak) following a set of counterfactual demonstrations. For example, in one scenario subjects hear, "You have a female pet cat named Tibby who has been rather unwell of late. Although cats are known to be mammals, the vet, on examining Tibby carefully, finds that she is, in fact, a robot controlled from Mars." Subjects are asked to judge the truth or falsehood of statements such as "Tibby is a cat, though we were wrong about her being a mammal." If being a mammal is an essential feature of cats, then subjects should judge this statement as false. Overall, the results did conform to the essentialist predictions—despite the ambiguity in the questions (e.g., some subjects may have assumed that Tibby is a cat, despite not being a mammal, because this was stated in the first line of the scenario) and despite the heavy information-processing demands (e.g., essentialist responses required subjects to apply double negatives—judging a negative statement ["Tibby is not a cat ..."] as false). However, the less-than-perfect responses led Braisby et al. (1996) to conclude that "words and concepts are not used in accordance with essentialism" (p. 247). On a *causal* essentialist view, the essence need not provide necessary and sufficient clues for determining reference (see also Medin, 1989), and accordingly the experiments are relevant to a sortal (not causal) essentialist view.

Another objection that has been raised to essentialism concerns the prediction that speakers should treat essentialized categories as having sharp boundaries—something either is or is not a member of the essentialized kind depending on whether or not it has the essential feature. Kalish (1995) conducted a series of experiments examining this question and found that, in general, subjects were willing to rate category membership as "graded" (nonabsolute). For example, subjects judged that a mule is neither entirely a horse nor entirely not-a-horse. Again, we have some disagreements with the specifics of how the study was conducted,[2] but the more general point is that the studies do not test causal essentialism. Specifically, subjects may believe that a certain inner quality or process of inheritance is needed in order for an animal to be a horse, but that in the real world different instances possess that quality or participate in that process to various degrees (e.g., a mule is half-horse because it is literally a hybrid, the offspring of a horse and a donkey). This possibility can be seen most clearly when one considers concepts that are essentialized yet graded, such as kinship. Siblings are more closely related than second-cousins, yet in both cases there is commonly believed to be a shared (family) essence.

## 12.3   Evidence for Essentialist Representations

In order to make a convincing case for essentialism as a fundamental folk notion, it is obviously crucial to provide evidence regarding the beliefs of ordinary folk. (Here we distinguish between "ordinary folk" and such luminaries as Aristotle, Plato, or Locke.) Although philosophical insights help sharpen questions of what essentialism is, they do not tell us whether people typically construe the world in these terms. Indeed, the notions sketched above may seem at first arcane and *counter to* common sense. What is commonsensical about invisible qualities that one can never know completely? Here it is important not to confuse the direct observability of the central construct with its status as common sense. Religious concepts provide an apt analogue: God is a mysterious concept, yet one that is readily embraced in folk theories (Boyer 1994).

Indeed essentialism is surrounded by a web of common sense, intuitive beliefs that are fully consistent with it. For example, the appearance-reality distinction posits that reality may be other than what the eyes perceive, and by 4 years of age children firmly grasp the distinction (Flavell, Flavell, and Green 1983). The notion of identity as persistent and resistant to change is also achieved early in childhood (by age 6 or 7 [Kohlberg 1966] if not earlier [Bem 1989]). Children by $2\frac{1}{2}$ or 3 years of age seem to share the belief that the world has natural discontinuities and that "natural kinds" are highly predictive of other properties (Markman 1989; Wierzbicka 1994; Gelman 1999). Furthermore there is evidence that throughout life, people expect and search for causes of events and regularities in the world (Bullock, Gelman, and Baillargeon 1982; Brown 1990). Even the seemingly sophisticated notion that unobservable entities can have massive effects is robust and early emerging, as can be seen with early beliefs about mental states (Gopnik and Wellman 1994). All of these ideas, though not necessarily constituting or causing essentialism, provide a framework within which essentialism can sit comfortably. Thus they provide a plausibility argument for suggesting that essentialism may draw on common sense. We now turn to the evidence, from research on social practices and individual performances, particularly of young children.

**Observations of Social Practice**
As already noted, the possibility that each biological species has a unique essence was entertained in literate Western cultures at least as far back as ancient Greece. There is further considerable literature suggesting that peoples the world over produce public representations that either explicitly or tacitly support the claim that essentialism is a widely recurrent strategy for thinking about many aspects of the world (Allport 1954; Guillaumin 1980; Stoler 1995; Fuss 1989; Rorty 1979). How to interpret this recurrence, however, is a matter of some controversy.

One school of thought is that essentialism is universally embraced, in cultures varying widely on dimensions of geography, technology, scientific sophistication, and economy. One form of support for this is indirect, from how people organize their knowledge of plants and animals into classification systems. Atran (1990) notes two distinct aspects of systems of folk biological classification: a taxonomic principle and a causal principle. On the one hand, people classify animals and plants into shallow and ranked taxonomies that exhaustively partition any local environment (Berlin 1978). These classifications are based in significant part on morphological and other structural similarities—as opposed to utilitarian or symbolic associations—between category members. Such taxonomies pull together diverse instances under a single label, thereby treating them as if the same—and this is not the only logical system possible (i.e., the universality is not required by logical constraints). On the other hand, an essentialist causal schema is universally applied to thinking about the creatures sorted into these taxonomies. According to this schema, members of each taxon share an essence or "nature" or underlying propensity to develop the appearance, behaviors, and ecological proclivities typical of that category.

Atran (1995) suggests that the taxonomic and essentialist principles are related in two ways (indeed Atran et al. [in press] has recently argued that the essentialist principle may be derived from the taxonomic one). First, the essentialist presumption (that holds that any living kind, all things being equal, will develop in a species-typical way) explains how creatures fit into the supposedly well-bounded categories of folk biological taxonomies despite obvious physical aberrations (e.g., three-legged, albino tigers). Second, the categories of folk taxonomies (i.e., the taxa of any given taxonomic array) are generally good predictors of underlying shared properties. It is important to note, however, that though the evidence for universal taxonomic sortings is vast, the evidence for a universal essentialist presumption in folk biology is sparse, consisting of conjecture in Western philosophy and natural science, on the one hand, and vague and passing speculations in the ethnographic record, on the other.

Other sources suggest that whereas the predilection for essentialism may be universal, instantiations of essentialism are culture specific. Thus, although ethnographies report that widely different societies discuss entities that to our minds seem essencelike (e.g., Daniel's [1985] discussion of *kunam* among Tamil-speakers in southern India as compared to Yengoyan's (forthcoming) discussion of blood among the Aborigines of Australia), each system of essentialist belief seems significantly distinct. Still it is the task of ethnographers generally to highlight the distinctiveness of each cultural formation, and from ethnographic data alone it is not possible to determine how widespread these concepts are. More important, it is not yet known if each instance represents the same notion of essences (e.g., the Tamil *kunam* are obtained from contact with the land rather than from inheritance; the *bope* component, which Crocker 1979 describes for the Bororo, are generally found in all animals rather than differing by species). Nonetheless, such appeals to nonvisible, causally efficacious inner qualities are intriguing.

In contrast to universalist claims, relativist accounts posit that essentialism is culturally specific. One set of arguments attempts to demonstrate that essentialism emerged only at particular historical moments (e.g., Rorty 1979), often emphasizing the role that systems of essentialist belief play in supporting and furthering the political and economic aims of specific groups. (Guillaumin's 1980 discussion of racial essentialism and Fuss's 1989 of gender essentialism are good examples.) While acknowledging the specificity of each system of belief, Hirschfeld (1996) interprets the same historic specificity somewhat differently. He notes that while these ideological couplings may be historically unique, they nonetheless all represent cultural or political recruitments of a universal predilection for essentializing human difference.

Another important concern when examining different systems of social practice for universal properties is the possibility that common threads across systems of belief and practice are more apparent than real. Studies of kinship are a case in point. For many decades anthropologists analyzed kinship (i.e., systems of social practice and belief that organize individuals into groups based on principles of descent and alliance) as if each kinship system were of a universal kind. The major empirical goal was to discover universal principles of kinship. Serious doubts, however, came to be been raised about whether or not these various systems of belief and practice were in fact of a single kind (Schneider 1968; Needham 1974). Although this debate is not resolved, at the very least, it highlights the growing consensus among cultural theorists that phenomena may appear quite similar yet represent fundamentally distinct conceptualizations. In any event, we can conclude that while cross-cultural investigations of essentialism have the potential to shed considerable light on questions of universality, at the moment the question remains understudied and unresolved.

## Individual Performances

Taken together, the concerns raised in the previous section make clear that more precise data are needed in order to compare across essentialistlike phenomena. Happily such evidence exists. Psychological studies of individual performance provide compelling, although indirect, evidence consistent with an essentialist bias. On these tasks, subjects reveal that they look beyond surface similarity when reasoning about categories. Much of this work is with children, who provide an interesting and strong test, given the demonstrated attention young children pay to outward appearances on a broad spectrum of cognitive tasks (Inhelder and Piaget 1964). Despite their focus on superficial cues in a range of contexts (see Jones and Smith 1993), $2\frac{1}{2}$-year-old children appreciate that animal categories support inductive inferences regarding familiar properties (Gelman and Coley 1990), and 3- and 4-year-olds use categories (animals, plants, substances, and artifacts) to guide inferences about novel properties (Gelman 1988; Gelman and Markman 1986, 1987; Carey 1985)—even when surface appearances compete. Four-year-old children also appreciate the importance of internal, intrinsic causal mechanisms for living things and artifacts. For example, children report that a bird flies because of its heart and muscles, that a car moves uphill because of its motor, and that a flower blooms on its own (Gelman and Kremer 1991; see also R. Gelman 1990). Children also realize that human intervention has limited effects in the natural world (Gelman and Kremer 1991; Inagaki and Hatano 1993). The common thread running through all these findings is that children attribute unseen constructs to account for observable phenomena. See Gelman and Coley (1991) for a more detailed review of these lines of evidence.

Three more direct lines of evidence for essentialism demonstrate that (1) maintenance of identity over superficial transformations, (2) appeal to invisible causal mechanisms, and (3) assumption of innate dispositions or potential among living things.

## Maintenance of Identity

The attribution of an underlying essence allows people to imagine that individuals undergo marked change yet retain their identity. We know that adults in our culture believe that radical changes, such as metamorphosis, are possible (Rips 1989; Rips and Collins 1993). Along the same lines, Keil (1989) found that second-graders (though not preschoolers) realize that animals but not artifacts can maintain identity over such transformations. Children were shown pictures of animals, then told about transformations performed by doctors that changed the characteristic features of the animal into those of another animal. For example, a tiger had its fur bleached and a mane sewed on, so that it now resembled a lion. Children were then asked whether the post-transformation animal was a lion or a tiger. Second- and fourth-graders maintained that the animal's identity would not change. Importantly, when asked about artifacts, subjects did not show this pattern (e.g., coffee pot could readily be transformed into a bird feeder). This finding indicates an early-developing belief that animals (but not human-made objects) possess essences that are responsible for maintenance of identity.

Subsequent work with younger children demonstrates a similar kind of understanding. When the transformations involve costume changes, even 3- and 4-year-olds recognize that identity is maintained (Keil 1989). In the same vein Gelman and Wellman (1991) used a paradigm very similar to that of Keil but with simpler transformations: Each item had either its "insides" or its "outsides" removed. Test items were selected to be clear-cut examples (for adults) of objects for which insides, but not outsides, are essential. For example, blood is more important than fur to a dog; the engine of a car is more important than the paint. Four- and 5-year-old children treated removal of insides (e.g., blood and bones of a dog) as disastrous to the identity and functioning of an item (e.g., it is no longer a dog, and can no longer bark or eat dog food), whereas removal of outsides (e.g., fur) was not. Children also rely heavily on insides when learning new words; specifically, they are better able to overcome the mutual exclusivity error when learning that animals from contrasting subtypes share internal similarities with one another (e.g., that a flying squirrel has the same internal structure as a typical squirrel; Diesendruck, Gelman, and Lebowitz 1996).

An additional series of studies by Rosengren et al. (1991) examines children's understanding of maintenance of identity over, using the natural biological transformation of growth rather than more contrived situations. Rosengren et al. reasoned that an important piece that may be missing from past research is what *mechanism* is underlying the change. In other words, children may be sensitive to whether the mechanism is a natural biological transformation or one that defies biological laws. The implication is that even though children report that some transformations lead to identity change, they may realize that natural transformations (e.g., growth) do not. To examine this question Rosengren et al. showed 3-year-olds, 5-year-olds, and adults a picture of an animal and told, "Here is a picture of Sally when Sally was a baby. Now Sally is an adult." They were then shown two pictures: one identical to the original and one the same but larger, and were asked which was a picture of Sally "as an adult." At all age groups, subjects tended to choose the larger picture, showing that they expected the object to undergo change in size with growth. Results of another condition showed that by 5 years of age, children realize that growth is inevitable. In this condition children saw a picture of a juvenile of a species that undergoes radical metamorphosis (e.g., a caterpillar). They then saw a picture of the same creature, only smaller (e.g., a smaller caterpillar), and a picture of a larger animal differing in shape (e.g., a moth). Again, subjects were asked to choose which picture represented the animal after it became an adult. Three-year-olds were at chance, but 5-year-olds chose the metamorphosized animal significantly above chance levels. By the age of 5 years, then, children believe that an individual can naturally undergo even substantial shape changes over time.

Do children have similar expectations about the immutability of social identity? The question is of interest because adults attribute racial and gender properties to hidden essences that are fixed at birth, presumably because adult common sense about race and gender is grounded in biology. It has been suggested, however, that children do not have similar expectations about the immutability of racial and gender identities because they tend to interpret these identities as social rather than biological phenomena (see Katz 1982; Aboud 1988 for reviews).

In a series of studies Hirschfeld (1995a, 1996) explored whether preschoolers in fact believe that all social identities are equally changeable. Using children's expectation about natural changes in outward appearance over time, he asked 3-, 4-, and 7-year-olds whether a person's race or physique was likely to change as he or she grew older. Even 3-year-olds believed that race was less likely to change than physique (despite the fact that physique is both inherited and relatively constant over the life span). In another condition Hirschfeld asked children whether parents and offspring were more likely to resemble each other racially or in terms of body build. As they did in the growth condition, even 3-year-olds judged a person's race as more constant than his or her physique. In fact children's inferences about the inheritance of racial and body build were indistinguishable from their inferences about the growth of racial and body build properties, providing evidence that both causal processes (i.e., growth and inheritance) are governed by the same essentialist presumption.

These data are demonstrational in that they constitute an existence proof. The studies conducted by Gelman and Wellman (1991) and by Keil (1989) show that children realize that sometimes, the features most critical to an object's identity may be internal and nonobvious. The experiments of Rosengren et al. (1991) demonstrate maintenance of identity over changes wrought by growth. Hirschfeld's (1995a, 1996) findings reveal that racial identity is treated much like biological category identity, being both fixed at birth and impervious to change over time. In all three cases, children endorse the possibility that objects have important underlying properties. A further question is whether they believe these underlying properties have special causal force.

### Causal Explanations

A critical aspect of essences is their causal force. Locke talks about the essence as the causal mechanism that gives rise to those properties that we can see. If children are essentialists, they should search for underlying causes that result in observable features (e.g., assuming some underlying nature that causes category members to be alike). "Features" include not only perceptual appearances but also behaviors and/or events that are shared by category members. For example, the essence of a tiger causes it to have stripes, large size, capacity to roar, and so on. There is some hint in the literature that children assume that events have intervening causal mechanisms (Bullock, Gelman, and Baillargeon 1982). There is also evidence that when explaining events with no observable cause, children appeal to underlying causes (Shultz 1982; Chandler and LaLonde 1994).

For example, on viewing a radiometer (a device that spins when light is beamed on it), children as young as 4 years of age typically said "yes" when asked if there was "some invisible thing that goes from the light to the propeller." Children impute underlying causes (particularly immanence) for self-initiated movement and do so in a domain-specific way (differently for animals vs. artifacts; Gelman and Gottfried 1996). Children regularly appeal to intrinsic factors even without knowing the internal mechanism (e.g., responding "it just did it itself"). Thus children seem to be displaying a belief in some underlying causal mechanism, without necessarily knowing how that mechanism works.

## Innate Potential

Essentialism encompasses a commitment to a particular kind of underlying causal relation, that is, innate potential, the belief that a set of characteristics will unfold with maturation, even though they show no sign at birth. For example, a lion cub has the potential to grow into something large and fierce, even though it is small and helpless at birth. The fact that such characteristic attributes emerge so predictably suggests that the individual possesses nonobvious, intrinsic qualities. To explain developmental changes like this, we as adults might say that lions have an essential nature that is responsible for how they grow.

To test whether preschool children have an idea of innate potential, Gelman and Wellman (1991) conducted a study that can be thought of as pitting nature against nurture. On each of a series of items, 4-year-old children learned about a baby animal that was raised among members of a different species in an environment more suited to the adoptive species. For example, children first saw a picture of a baby kangaroo, learned that the baby kangaroo was taken to a goat farm when she was a baby, and raised by goats. Children were asked about how the animal would be after it grew up. In this case they heard, (1) Was she good at hopping or good at climbing? (2) Did she have a pouch or was she without a pouch?

Children nearly always answered on the basis of category membership or innate potential. For example, they said that a baby kangaroo raised among goats will grow up to hop and have a pouch. An analogous study with seeds showed similar results, indicating that the results with animals are not simply due to providing the category label—because specifying the origin of a seed does not entail stating its category identity (e.g., "comes from an apple" differs from its original identity of "apple seed" and its future identity of "apple tree"). In addition a seed looks nothing like its eventual end state (plant or tree). Finally the use of seeds allows examination of a very different kind of parent-offspring relationship, in which characteristics cannot be transmitted by means of modeling, reinforcement, or training. Results of this study showed that older 4-year-olds answered primarily on the basis of innate potential. The mixed performance of young 4-year-olds appeared to be due to a less developed understanding of the relation between seeds and plants at that age (Hickling and Gelman 1995). Nonetheless, it is striking that most of the children consistently reported that a seed has the innate potential to develop in accordance with the parent species. Four-year-old children act like essentialists, assuming that members of a category share an innate potential and that innate potential can overcome a powerful environment.

Carey and her collaborators (Carey and Spelke 1994; Carey 1995; Solomon et al. 1996) cautioned that a biological notion of innate poten-tial is not required to account for these findings and that at least some of them might be attributed to children's expectations that identity is maintained over time (in as much as the animal was labeled as being a member of a particular species, e.g., a kangaroo, children may have assumed that it would continue to have kangaroo properties without reasoning about the mechanism involved). In subsequent studies, how-ever, Hirschfeld (1995a, 1995b, 1996) and Springer (1995) used a pro-cedure in which subjects were *not* told the category identity of the infant. In one series of studies, Hirschfeld (1995a, 1995b) showed preschoolers pictures of two families, one black and the other white, whose newborns were inadvertently switched in the hospital. Each family took home and raised the other's infant. Children were then shown pictures of two school-aged children, one black and the other white, and asked which was the child when he/she grew up and began school. Three-year-olds chose at chance, but 4-year-olds relied overwhelmingly on a nativist (essentialist) reasoning strategy, choosing the child who racially matched the birth parents, not the adopted parents. In a subsequent experiment Springer (1995) replicated this finding and extended it, demonstrating that 5-year-olds believe that not only race but also a range of biological (though not psychological) properties are fixed at birth and immutable over the life span. Here again the data support the essentialist interpretation. Children reasoned that category identity is determined at birth and its development is impervious to environmental influences. Moreover both sets of studies show that an essentialist notion of innate potential governs children's expectations about racial identity.

In another study we asked preschoolers what social categories, including race, might be associated with differences in language spoken (Hirschfeld and Gelman 1997). Again the question is of interest because adults often link language differences with cultural and racial differences. Moreover anecdotal data suggest the possibility that adults believe that some aspects of language may also be "natural" in the sense of fixed at birth. In the study we found that children readily expect people of different *races* to speak different languages. However, they do not expect people of different *ages* to speak different languages; thus the inference is not simply that any social category differences will predict differences in language spoken.

We speculated that this specific pairing of language and race might occur because children treat both language and race as "natural" categories and thus might be similarly distributed across populations. To test this possibility, we conducted a switched-at-birth experiment using language as the contrast. Preschoolers were told about two couples, one who spoke English and one who spoke Portuguese. As in Hirschfeld and Springer's studies, children were told that the newborn of each couple was switched with the infant of the other couple. Children were then played two audiotape speech samples, one in English and the other in Portuguese, and were asked to choose which was the language that the switched-at-birth child spoke when it grew up. While 3-year-olds performed at chance, 5-year-olds consistently selected the language of the birth parents.

One intriguing aspect of the developmental work is how powerful children's essentialist interpretations are, at such a young age. Indeed for some domains they may be even more essentialist than those of older children and adults. Taylor (1996) examined essentialist beliefs about gender in subjects ranging from preschool to college age. The task was again a nature-nurture task similar to those described above. Subjects were told about an infant boy who was raised from birth by his aunt on an island populated entirely by girls and women. (Another item concerned an infant girl who was raised from birth by her uncle on an island containing only boys and men.) Subjects were then asked to infer various properties of the boy (or girl) when he/she was 10 years old (e.g., would he play with trucks or dolls?). There were two notable findings from this study: First, the youngest subjects inferred that gender-linked properties were inherent in the child and not determined by the environment (e.g., they typically inferred that the boy raised with females would play with trucks and be good at football). Second, the strongest evidence of essentializing was with the youngest subjects; by roughly 9 to 10 years of age, subjects began to incorporate socialization and interactionist explanations.

Thus by late preschool, children reliably use a nature over nurture strategy for reasoning about race, language, and gender, suggesting that an essentialist bias for innate potential may shape children's expectations about a broad range of phenomena, not simply living things under the guise of a folkbiology. On this account, biological kinds may be distinguished by the strict taxonomic hierarchies in which they are sorted (Atran 1990; but see Carey 1995, regarding lack of developmental evidence) but not by essentialist reasoning. We are not claiming that folkbiology does not encompass a coherent domain (nor are we denying that it might). Rather, we suggest that if it does encompass a coherent domain in early childhood it is not in virtue of a specific mode of essentialist reasoning.

The apparent early convergence between essentialist reasoning about nonliving kinds and about human kinds gains further support in an argument proposed by Hirschfeld (1989) concerning children's understanding of kinship. Notably kinship has some of the features of both category identity (i.e., type identity in the sense that one of us is a white, male, *Homo sapiens*) and individual identity (i.e., token identity in the sense that other of us is named Susan and was born in Bristol, Pennsylvania). Like category identities, kinship roles pick out groups of people (those who are my kinfolk versus those who are not). But unlike species identity (in which something is typically either an $X$ or a $Y$ but not some mix of both), kinship identity is graded. For instance, an individual and his or her sibling are typically thought to share more family "essence" than an individual and his or her cousin. Indeed a tension between category and individual aspects of kinship identity is fundamental to the domain of kinship. Kin *groups* are defined with respect to an *individual* ego such that the collectivity can never be logically separated from the individual (and its boundaries can never be fixed independent of some given individual). Biological identity, in contrast, is organized around category identities that are independent of individuals, to the extent that a plausible argument has been made for treating each species as a whole as an individual (chapter 13, this volume; Sober 1994).

Thus we find little support for the argument, cited above, that essentialism spreads by analogical transfer. There is scant development evidence to support the claim that essentialism is transferred from its "proper" domain (i.e., folkbiology) to other domains (e.g., race, language, gender, or kinship). Instead, the early and nearly parallel emergence of essentialist reasoning in these different domains is consistent with the maturation of a single conceptual bias for essentialist reasoning. An alternative interpretation of the convergence of essentialist reasoning about nonhuman living kinds, human races, language, gender, and kinship is that these all of these kinds could fall within a single domain of folkbiology (at the very least, the human races and gender are psychologically fundamental kinds of living things). Although the "proper" boundaries of folkbiology remain unsettled, human races and gender have not been considered part of folkbiology for three reasons. First, children seem to treat humans as ontologically distinct from nonhuman natural kinds (Johnson, Mervis, and Boster 1992; Jackendoff 1992; Carey 1985; Keil 1979). Second, by middle childhood, children's reasoning about biological properties such as heritability and growth differ for human races and animals (Hirschfeld 1996). Third, there appears to be no corresponding notion of taxonomic "rank" for humans, as there so clearly are for nonhuman living kinds.

## 12.4   Sources of Essentialist Representations

The question of whether essentialism is biological is embedded in larger questions regarding source. Put crudely, four major claims are that essentialism is in the world, in the mind, in language, or in culture. Of course, essentialism could result from an interaction of two or more factors (as with the evolutionary story that the mind is adapted so as to identify regularities in the natural world), and we suspect that any reasonable person is to some degree an interactionist. Nonetheless, there is considerable room for disagreement. Any answer to this question will have to satisfy two observations: there are remarkable similarities across domains—in how people essentialize animal species and human personality types, for example; yet there are compelling differences across domains—in how people construe animal species and artifacts, for example.

Assuming that one grants that children are essentialist (see Jones and Smith 1993, for a dissenting view), the major arguments against considering essentialism to be a childhood construction is that essentialism is imparted to children from elsewhere, either from the structure of the world or from the information that parents provide. Both of these simple scenarios seem insufficient, as briefly reviewed below.

### Is Essentialism Provided by the Structure of the World?

It may seem as if essentialism is compatible with scientific descriptions of the world, and even paves the way for scientific advances: Ordinary people thought all along that water, tigers, gold, for example, had nonobvious causal properties, and lo! science tells us that it's so (molecular structure of water as $H_2O$; biological structure is governed by DNA; Putnam 1975). On this view, people's essentialist views may derive from real-world properties. However tempting it may be to suppose that the world provides us with real essences, studies of essentialist construals and of biological species strongly suggest that essentialism does not reside in the objects of the world.

First, the strongest version of essentialism (in which species are immutable categories of existence) is incompatible with evolutionary theory, which posits continual change over time (Mayr 1991). Clearly one can be essentialist without believing that essentialized categories are unchanging (Sober 1994). However, Sober rejects a metaphysical reality to essentialism for another reason: essentialism assumes that the essence resides in each individual organism—that it is a property of each organism. In contrast, according to evolutionary theory, species cannot be characterized in terms of properties of individual members but rather in terms of properties of the population. To use familiar Kuhnian terminology, there was a paradigm shift in how biologists think about species, and essentialism revealed itself to be dependent on the old paradigm. Taking a somewhat different (and perhaps more controversial) approach, Dupré (1993) suggests that species are real, just not in the sense we usually assume. He argues that each organism belongs to numerous natural kinds, each with its own essence (a view he calls "promiscuous realism"), thus undermining the notion of a single real category (or single real essence) for each organism. Arguably the most striking evidence against the reality of essences is the evidence discussed earlier, that people essentialize nonbiological categories. In particular, a considerable literature documents the willingness, at least of modern folk, to apply an essentialist presumption to race (Allport 1954; Guillaumin 1980; Banton 1987; Goldberg 1993; Stoler 1995), despite the fact that racial categories do not capture reliable biological variation.

Indeed, even if the world were composed of real essences, this is a far cry from demonstrating that such essences are available to young children. What the world does seem to provide are natural perceptual discontinuities (Berlin 1978) which humans are predisposed to note. However, this falls far short of an *essence*—an invisible causal mechanism that accounts for such discontinuities. The child looking at and listening to the natural world will never see or hear an essence directly.

**Is Essentialism Provided by the Structure of the Input?**
If essentialism is not simply a reading off of regularities in the world, is it instead directly provided to children, at least in this highly technological culture? Essentialist accounts seem to be ubiquitous in middle-class adult causal explanatory accounts (ranging from scientific attempts to map out the genetic contribution to IQ, alcoholism, and shyness, to the play *The Bad Seed*). Furthermore, as noted earlier, commonsense interpretations of scientific biology often tend (erroneously) toward an essentialist reading. It seems plausible, then, that children learn their essentialist beliefs from the messages directed toward them by mass media (including educational books and TV programs as well as popular fiction) and by

parents. However, to date little information is available concerning the sorts of messages provided to children related to this topic. Casual observation suggests that, at the very least, some powerful counter-essentialist imagery is provided in children's fiction. Dr. Seuss's *Horton Hears a Who* and the hit movie *Babe* are both highly popular examples of antiessentialist accounts provided to young children.

In order to gain a more systematic portrait of parental input in a highly essentialized culture, Gelman et al. (1996) studied how highly educated parents in a middle-class U.S. university town talk about essentialized and nonessentialized categories (animals and artifacts). The parents were talking to their 20- and 35-month-old children, as essentialist beliefs have been documented by roughly 30 months of age. The study was designed to examine whether parents directly teach children the content of essentialist beliefs. Do they teach them, for example, that insides are more important than outsides, that characteristics are inherited, or that for some categories all instances are alike in fundamental nonobvious ways?

Mother-child pairs were videotaped while looking through two picture books together. The books were created specifically for the study and were designed to elicit essentializing talk and explanations by providing appearance-reality contrasts in which superficial properties alone could not explain the basis of how items are classified (e.g., one page included a bird and two bats). Indeed, the books elicited frequent naming errors from the children, thus providing ample opportunities for parents to explain why and how, for example, a bat is not a bird. One book focused on animals, the other on artifacts, with the assumption that animals are more highly essentialized and that therefore domain differences in parental speech would be revealing of ways that parents convey essentialist notions.

Parents did talk differently about animals and artifacts, but not by alluding to essences. Parents gestured more toward same-category members for animal categories than for artifact categories, they produced more utterances that linked together multiple members of the same category for animal categories than for artifact categories, and they produced more generic statements (e.g., "Bats live in caves"; Carlson and Pelletier 1995) for animal categories than for artifact categories. These are all devices for drawing children's attention to animal categories, and arguably they imply a certain coherence to the animal categories. Still, they do not constitute essentialist explanations, nor do they provide causal mechanisms for why animal categories cohere.

In contrast, on the rare occasions when parents did talk about the topics one might consider essentializing (e.g., kinship, internal parts, origins, teleology, and inductive potential), they did so in sketchy, elusive ways. Here is a representative sample of what parents actually said concerning these topics: "Batteries go in the car and the other car and the clock" [insides]; "There's the mother cat and there's the baby" [kinship]; "These look like snakes, but they're called eels" [appearance-reality contrast]. As should be clear from the examples, parents' talk about these topics were rather vague. Appearance-reality statements were somewhat more common, and were significantly more frequent for animals than artifacts. But parents never resolved appearance-reality contrasts in terms of internal parts, inheritance, or the like. Altogether, mention of all these topics combined accounted for less than 2 percent of parents' speech; even this small proportion could not be said to be informative.

This study provides an initial glimpse into the kind of input children are receiving. If it turns out to be representative, it suggests that the input children receive about essentialist beliefs is indirect at best, thus affirming the importance of children's own constructions.

The role of children's own constructions is brought into even broader relief when we examine how children acquire knowledge of naturalized social categories such as race and possibly language. Although race is thought to be tethered directly and unproblematically to perceptual experience, there is considerable evidence that this is not the case. First, as just observed, the social category "race" is neither biologically coherent nor does it capture interesting or even consistent variation in biological properties. Second, the distribution of traits and features relevant to racial categorization (e.g., skin color or hair texture and color) are not associated with the distribution of "deeper" or hidden properties. Thus there is little opportunity for the external world to shape racial categorization in the unmediated sense that underlies virtually all work on the psychology of race (see Hirschfeld 1996, for an extended discussion). Finally, despite the tendency to view race as a visual ideology (i.e., an ideology rich in visual correlates and expectations), the attributions of the nonobvious and the unseen are much more central to racial reasoning than attributions of the perceptible (Stoler 1995; Hirschfeld 1996).

This is evident when we examine the development of children's beliefs about race. Many people (and most researchers) assume that (1) because adult racial discourse is so closely tied to the visual level and (2) because racial variation seems directly perceptible, children initially learn about race by focusing on differences in people's appearance. Yet in a direct test of this assumption, Hirschfeld (1993) found that preschoolers' first racial categories are actually not rich in perceptual information. In fact he found that young children's attention is centered less on visual cues than on verbal cues. This finding is consistent with the idea that adults, through their speech and customary practices, play a central role in the development of children's racial beliefs. Other studies, however, indicate that this sort of direct parental modeling is not the case. Parents very rarely speak to their children about race (Kofkin et al. 1995), and when they do—as when they directly intervene in attempts to shape their children's racial beliefs and attitudes—they have little effect (Spencer 1983; Branch and Newcombe 1980, 1986). Rather children seem to construct racial categories and elaborate racial beliefs in significant measure on their own.

## 12.5    Broadening the Notion of Essence

The paradigm example of essentialism, particularly in the psychological literature, is that of a biological species: Tigers have in common an essence that causes a rich set of properties (both observable and unknown) to be shared among members of the kind. However, at least for adults, essentialism also appears outside the realm of biological species, to play a role in our understanding of what it means to be kinfolk and what it means to be an individual. Kinship essences and individual essences call into question the notion that essentialism is a biologically specific notion. On the other hand, some scholars propose that kinship and individual essences are *derived from* an understanding of biological species essence (Atran 1990; Rothbart and Taylor 1990)—or at least that one should assume that biological essentializing and nonbiological essentializing are distinct unless provided with compelling evidence to the contrary.

Perhaps even more challenging to the notion of essence as a biologically specific notion is the observation that essentialism appears to fall squarely within a larger class of related phenomena. Consider first the properties that essences share:

1. There is a nonvisible part/substance/quality in each individual (as an individual or as a member of a category).
2. This part/substance/quality is inherent and very difficult to remove.
3. The part/substance/quality has the property of transferability—it is passed along from parent/host to offspring/client typically at a specific moment or brief period.
4. This transfer from parent/host to offspring/client does not diminish the amount of essence or its consequences for identity in the parent/host.
5. This nonvisible part/substance/quality has vast, diffuse, unknown causal implications.
6. The implications include authenticity and identity.

It is striking that, as a package, this causal[3] account differs markedly from those in most physical domains such as naive mechanics (e.g., energy can be transferred from one object to another, but the amount of energy in that case is diminished). These are not properties of the world at large.

At the same time the properties listed above are shared by a set of other phenomena quite distinct from the realm of biology, including contamination, fetishes, and blessings (see table 12.1). To illustrate, we compare contagion by germs to contamination. Germs, like essences, are nonvisible (see Au, Sidle, and Rollins 1993; Kalish 1996), are very difficult to remove (Rozin and Nemeroff 1990), are transferrable to others, and have broad, diffuse, unknown effects (including effects on identity; e.g., consider how one changes category by contracting cancer or AIDS). Although one could consider germs themselves to be biological entities, one finds precisely the same set of properties when considering the phenomenon of nonbiological contamination. Rozin and Nemeroff (1990) provide the example of people feeling uncomfortable with the notion of wearing Hitler's sweater. There is some quality in the sweater (let's call it "negative value"—intriguingly Rozin and Nemeroff call it "essence") that is nonvisible, very difficult to remove (e.g., the sweater is still noxious even after being sterilized in boiling water or gashed with scissors),

**Table 12.1**

| Phenomenon | Nonvisible agent | Embodied in: | Transfer process | Causal implications |
|---|---|---|---|---|
| Essentialism | Essence | Tigers | Inheritance | Morphology, behavior, etc. |
| Contagion | Germs | Sick person | Coughing | Illness |
| Contamination | Value | Hitler's sweater | Wearing | |
| Fetish | Value | Jackie O's pearls | Owning | |
| Blessing | Value | Pope | Touching | |

transferrable to others (e.g., by wearing the sweater; although note that the transfer process does not remove the negative value from the sweater nor even from the previous wearer), and having broad, diffuse, unknown causal implications (e.g., vaguely, that something bad may happen). Finally the invisible quality is central to the identity of the item.

We are not suggesting that essentialism is the *only* way to account for such evaluation. Indeed there are simpler possibilities. Consider the case of Jackie Onassis's faux-pearls that recently fetched a small fortune at auction. You might like Jackie Onassis and therefore assume that you'll like her faux-pearls, you might think that she had extraordinary taste, or you might note that lots of people hold Jackie Onassis in high regard and imagine that a well-motivated market strategy is to buy her things in anticipation of being able to sell them for a profit later. We acknowledge that essentializing her pearls is only one explanation for wanting to own them. Importantly, however, these alternative accounts are insufficient, particularly to explain the peculiar significance of direct physical contact with the objects in question.

Consider once again the Pope's robe or Hitler's sweater. The value of these objects is contingent on *touching* them, not simply owning them. Moreover touching them is more valuable (or more negatively valuable in the case of Hitler's sweater) than just seeing them or standing next to them. The importance of physical contact makes sense only on an essentialist account; it is wholly unpredicted by accounts that involve common liking, confidence in another's judgment, or principles of market speculation. And we suspect that this will be true of Jackie O's pearls.

## How Are These Phenomena Related?

There are at least three possibilities for explaining how these diverse phenomena converge: (1) They may be wholly distinct entities that are only coincidentally similar. (2) One of these phenomena may be conceptually prior, with the others being similar because they borrow or analogize from the central example. (3) They may all be instantiations of a single framework for causal interpretation.

In favor of the first possibility, there are certainly differences among the phenomena. They differ in whether they involve a category (species essence), an individual (contagion), or something intermediate (kinship essence). They also differ in their gradedness (e.g., species essence is presumably nongraded, but see Kalish 1995), whereas kinship essence and fetishizing admit of degrees (e.g., seeing vs. touching vs. owning the Pope's robe). And they differ in terms of which domains are implicated (e.g., species essences seem relevant for living or natural things, not artifacts, whereas contamination, fetishizing, blessing, and contagion may all involve artifacts somewhere along the causal chain). These phenomena are thus not identical. Nonetheless, the strongest argument against treating these as distinct is that none of these examples is independently motivated from evidence in the world. Given the lack of an *external* source, it is plausible to hypothesize some sort of common cognitive motivation.

As noted earlier, this common motivation might involve analogies from a base to more peripheral domains. Indeed a frequently encountered explanation for the recurrence of essentialist reasoning across content areas in *adult* cognition is analogical transfer. On this interpretation, essentialism is a domain-specific assumption which then is "borrowed" by other domains via analogical transfer (see Allport 1954, Atran 1990, Boyer 1990, and Rothbart and Taylor 1990, for cognitive versions of this view; see Guillaumin 1980, and Banton 1987, for historical versions).

Atran (1990) proposes that this is the best *developmental* account as well: Essentialism begins (ontogenetically) as a domain-specific biological assumption and then is adopted by other domains. Thus, "apparent morphological distinctions between human groups are readily (but not necessarily) conceived as apparent morphological distinctions between animal species" (Atran 1990: 78), causing essentialist principles initially limited to folk biology to transfer to social cognition. This explanation is supported only if essentialism in fact develops first in folkbiology and subsequently emerges in other domains.

While no one yet has done the sorts of careful studies needed to examine children's reasoning *across* domains, the available evidence strongly argues *against* the transfer-by-analogy account. Children appear to construe several phenomena in essentialistlike ways quite early. Au et al. (1993) showed that by 3 years of age, children appeal to invisible particles in explaining how a substance can continue to exist despite visual disappearance (e.g., when explaining why water in which sugar has been dissolved still tastes sweet). Fetishizing also emerges early with many children's attachment to transitional objects (e.g., a particular soft blanket; Litt 1986; Passman 1987). Although the meaning children associate with such attachments is unclear, it is worth noting that the traditional interpretation is that children conceive of the object as taking the place of the mother, in a sense invested with the mother's essence (Winnicott 1969). While such a claim clearly speculates about the child's conceptualization far beyond the evidence, intriguingly a major cultural determinant of children's attachments to transitional objects is whether the young child and the mother sleep together or in separate beds (Wolf and Lozoff 1989).

Similarly evidence supports the idea that essentialist beliefs about contamination and contagion emerge early in the preschool years, at much the same age as essentialism in biology, race, and gender. For example, Siegal and Share (1990) found that 3-year-olds discriminate contaminated from safe substances, even when the outward appearances of the two substances are identical (e.g., moldy bread with jam concealing the mold vs. unmoldy bread with jam spread on it). In a study examining children's explanations for disease, Springer and Ruckel (1992) found that most children, even those who appear to be relying on a notion of immanent justice, attribute illness to germs and other unseen agents (see also Kalish 1996). The similarities between disease and inheritance explanations did not escape Springer and Ruckel's notice: Although the "transmission" of disease from one person to another is very different from the genetic "transmission" of properties from parents to offspring, children's reasoning about inheritance and disease may nonetheless reflect the same underlying belief system, and these beliefs may (or may not) be specific to the domain of biology (1992: 440–41).

Together, these data suggest a close developmental convergence in the emergence of essentialist reasoning in several independent content areas. By 3 to 4 years of age, children appeal to essentialism or essentialist-like notions in reasoning about biological species, race, gender, and kinship, on the one hand, and contamination, contagion, and (perhaps) fetishes, on the other. This pattern is more likely to reflect the multiple instantiation of an essentialist bias across several domains rather than the penetration of biological reasoning into other conceptual systems.

### Architecture of Multiple Instantiations

Gelman et al. (1994) suggest at least two readings of early cross-domain instantiations of essentialism. First, essentialism might emerge in several domains more or less independently. They caution that for reasons of parsimony, the appeal of this interpretation is limited if too many distinct kinds of domains were implicated. If our proposal here is correct—that essentialist reasoning about biological species, gender, race, kinship, contagion, contamination, fetishization, and the like, cannot in structure or development be clearly distinguished—this concern is well-grounded. The second reading they propose is that essentialism is a domain-general assumption that is invoked differentially in different domains depending on the causal structure of each domain. They argue that, while speculative, this is the more compelling account in part because it predicts a broad yet not promiscuous application of essentialism.

Sperber (1994), Leslie (1994), and Keil (1994) provide a view of cognitive architecture that is consistent with this suggestion. On their view, many domain differences lie neither at the level of perceptual structure nor conceptual organization of the domain itself, but at the level of more abstract mechanisms or modes of understanding that come to be incorporated in different domains. To date a relatively small number of modes of understanding (or modes of construal) have been proposed: an intentional mode, a mechanical mode, a teleological mode, an essentialist mode, perhaps a vitalistic mode (Inagaki and Hatano 1993), and a deontological mode (Atran 1996). Importantly these modes are distinct from specific causal principles.

There are explanatory networks for steam-heating systems known only to plumbers, with many unique terms that are functionally defined in terms of other terms unique to boilers, such as the Hartford loop which is a special convolution of pipe designed for certain pressure gradients. Cardiologists have similar clusters of terms and laws for hearts, as do myriad other professionals and experts. In most of these cases some terms can only be understood by knowing how they are embedded in the larger system of causal relations of that domain. Are wide-ranging areas of expertise to be considered on the same terms as a naive psychology, physics, or biology? An alternative model would maintain that the handful of fundamental modes of construal has a distinct status that makes these importantly different from local areas of expertise. The plumber's expertise sits inside a more basic framework of causal understandings involving fluids and containers, which must be presupposed for the more specific beliefs to be meaningful (Keil 1995: 259).

The same issue arises when considering the specific causal relations associated with a particular conceptual domain as well as those associated with local expertise. For instance, American folk biology captures a number of related but independent causal relations concerning growth, inheritance, contagion, and the like. There is no a priori reason to assume that patterns of causal reasoning about growth will be much like those about inheritance, yet as already observed, even 3-year-olds treat the two causal relations as having similar outcomes (Hirschfeld 1995a). In part, this finding is surprising because the mechanisms underlying growth and inheritance are poorly understood on a commonsense level (and were poorly understood on a scientific level until relatively recently). One plausible explanation for this convergence in reasoning about growth and inheritance is that children apply an essentialist assumption to both causal relations. There is patterned resemblance over time in growth because of continuity in an individual's essence. By the same token there is patterned resemblance between parent and offspring because of shared species (or racial or family) essence.

It is also not the case that a specific inventory of causal principles (or the phenomena that they are meant to interpret)[4] necessarily requires a particular framework for causal interpretation (or mode of construal). Indeed the controversy about when folkbiology becomes a distinct domain relative to folk psychology illustrates the fact that many causal principles, including those that explain continuity in inheritance and growth, can have both intentional (i.e., psychological) and essentialist (i.e., biological) interpretations (compare Gelman and Wellman 1991; Hirschfeld 1995a; Springer 1995 to Carey 1985, 1995; Carey and Spelke 1994; and Solomon et al. 1996; see also Schult and Wellman 1997; Hickling 1996).

### How Does a Mode of Construal Become Associated with a Particular Domain?

In several publications Keil suggests that the linkage between mode of construal and domain occurs as children and adults search for resonances between modes of construal and the "real world structure" (1994: 252). Elsewhere he elaborates, proposing that "much of our adult intellectual adventures involve trying to see which mode of construal best fits a phenomenon, sometimes trying several different ones, such as thinking of a computer in anthropomorphic 'folk-psychology' terms, in fluid dynamic terms, or in physical-mechanical terms" (1995: 260). Gelman et al. (1994) make a similar point about essences and living kinds:

> In the case of an animal, the child would notice the animal moving on its own, would see no apparent external cause (either human or mechanical), and so would conclude that some inner, inherent nature is responsible for its movement.... In contrast, in the case of a wastebasket, any behaviors or functions of the object could be readily traced to the people who made and use the wastebasket; hence there would be no need to appeal to properties inherent in the object or a wastebasket essence" (1994: 358–59).

It seems plausible that resonance with "real world structure" provides the motivation to link a domain with an essentialist mode of construal for some domains (as has already been noted, the natural discontinuities in morphology, behavior, and ecological proclivities in nonhuman living things are good predictors of many other underlying shared properties). However, it is not obvious that "real world structure" directly motivates an essentialist interpretation of contaminants, disease, or fetishes.

What accounts for the attribution of an essentialist mode in these cases? The answer is not obvious. We agree with Gelman et al.'s speculation that domains are essentialized to the extent that other causal accounts are poorly supported. But we believe that more is involved; otherwise, essentialist accounts would emerge wherever knowledge is sparse (e.g., to explain garage-door openers, TV remote control devices, and light switches).

We acknowledge that a fully specified set of conditions on an essentialist mapping remains to be determined, but we offer some speculation. An essentialist mode of construal is likely to be recruited under at least two conditions: first, when the entities of a domain undergo regular and radical transformation, inexplicable with reference to any other causal mode, and second, when the event being explained is unpredicted or causally anomalous with respect to other events in the same domain.

**First Condition: Regular and Radical Transformation**    Consider living kinds as an example of the first condition. The most compelling reason to essentialize living kinds lies in the regular changes in outward appearance and behavior that an individual creature undergoes during growth. All living kinds of interest to humans grow and transform themselves substantially over their lifetimes. Virtually all have immature and mature forms. Moreover many plants have variants that flower, bear fruit, or otherwise change in appearance depending on the time of year or conditions of growth (e.g., levels of sun and water).

A further motivation for essentializing living things is the variation encountered within any given living kind category. On the one hand, dodos and robins are both birds, yet the two sorts of creatures are very different on most attention-demanding dimensions. On the other hand, there is also marked variation among individuals within a living kind category: Three-legged tigers are still tigers, bonsai maples are still maples, bleached skunks are still skunks.[5]

*Race*    Perhaps a better illustration of this condition is race. The major task that essentialism performs in racial thinking is to resolve the paradox between two fundamental aspects of racial concepts. On the one hand, race is a visual phenomenon, rooted in the way people look. On the other hand, we cannot assign people to racial categories simply on visual inspection alone: the way people look is often racially misleading, so that in at least some systems of racial thinking "passing" is a possibility. The insufficiency of the visual is an important theme in much racial discourse, and it concerns how to integrate the visual with the system of classification that dominates much colonial writing (Stoler 1995). Racial discourse is so concerned with the marginal cases and anomalous appearances because neither are predictable from the center. Races don't merge into one another in people's minds (though they do in fact). Rather, they contain seeming anomalies that are difficult to predict and explain without reference to something like hidden racial essences.

It is important to keep in mind that it is not the essentialization of race that causes visually atypical members to be put in the same categories with visually more typical members. Rather, it is the existence of such hybrid categories that causes an essentialist presumption to be recruited, as a means of *explaining* these sorting choices. The reason one encounters anomalies to begin with, discussed in detail in Hirschfeld (1996), is that racial categories are about two things: beliefs about human physical variation (and its supposed causes) and the distribution of power and authority. Race indexes the way power and authority are distributed, but only imperfectly. Thus the distribution of people (agents of power and authority) is often peculiar from the perspective of the system of racial belief itself (e.g., the one-drop of blood rule for deciding the racial status of mixed-race individuals). What essentialism does is give a coherent explanation for the imperfect mapping of race to power. That is, essentialism does not cause race to be visually incoherent; visual incoherence causes essentialism to be triggered.

The point here is that learning about living things and learning about races is much easier given an essentialist assumption. With it, learning systems of exception becomes learning a causally coherent, if perceptually surprising, story. Whales are mammals not because of some shared mammalian essence; whales are mammals because they possess certain relevant properties with other mammals. We *explain* this with reference to a whale essence that causes it to develop these properties and sustain them over time. We readily think this because we are willing, indeed even eager, to believe that essentialist causality is a good explanation for why the marginal cases are included at all. We don't learn these things because they are essentialized (recall that there is little evidence that essentialization is socialized explicitly or directly); rather, we essentialize these things because we have learned something about them that becomes particularly explicable under an essentialist interpretation.

**Second Condition: Causal Anomaly**   The second condition that may trigger an essentialist presumption—when an event is unpredicted or causally anomalous with respect to other events in the same domain—is more difficult to convey, in part because the notions of "unpredicted" and "causally anomalous" suggest intuitions that are broader than we have in mind.

It might be easier to characterize this condition by pointing out at least one kind of anomaly that we do *not* have in mind here. Beanbag chairs are admittedly anomalous in many respects: they lack legs, rigid seats and backs, and so on. However, they are not anomalous from the perspective of the teleological causal logic that defines artifact categories: a beanbag chair *looks* anomalous but is a perfectly functional seating device. Contrast this with Jackie Onassis's pearls. We speculate that these pearls are essentialized because they gain their special value through contact with Jackie Onassis, a contact that is thought to endure somehow in the object. That is to say, this particular string of pearls is hypervalued with respect to others. But this hypervaluation is not a function of those things that typically determine variation in value among members of an artifact category: nothing about the materials from which they are manufactured gives them special value, their intrinsic aesthetic value is not particularly great, and presumably they are no more a "success" as accessories than other faux-pearls. Instead, they are causally anomalous. Explaining their value is facilitated by imagining that they are imbued with something of Jackie O's essence (just as Hitler's sweater has high negative value because some part of Hitler's being, his nature, indeed his essence, infects it).

*Hypervaluation*   The argument sketched out above is missing a crucial piece, namely, why it is that Jackie O's pearls are hypervalued to begin with if not as a result of essentialism. Plausibly the initial impetus is associationist: The pearls are attractive because they have come into close contact with her (an attractive, famous person). Similar sorts of associative preferences and avoidances are found in a variety of species as in classical conditioning, and they are often difficult to modify. However, vague associations do not provide satisfying causal accounts, so the story does not end there: The associative preference then calls out for a causal explanation (in this case, an essentialist one), which then leads to even greater valuation, in an increasing spiral. This search for a causal account may be further heightened by Onassis's prominence in the public sphere. In a moment we will discuss a number of ways in which a celebrity's possession might become especially highly valued. For now, we want to suggest only that as this value became more recognized, it *demanded* a causal explanation. The "best" one available, we further suggest, is essentialist.

An alternative account is that person-to-artifact essentialism is a version of biological essentialism, one in which either species or individual essences are thought to be so highly contagious and permeable that they could be transmitted by incidental contact (as well as by inheritance). Some evidence does indicate that inheritance is not, according to folk belief, the sole means by which species (and possibly individual) essences pass from individual to individual. Jacques Guillemeau, a seventeenth-century French physician, provided an anecdote of an often encountered notion: "It is an accepted thing that milk ... has the power to make children resemble their nurses in mind and body, just as the seed makes them resemble their mother and father" (quoted in Fairchild 1984: 195). Similarly there is evidence that the Dutch colonial administration in the nineteenth-century was convinced (or worried) that too long an exposure to Javanese culture and climate would cause Dutch settlers to become Javanese in some sense (Stoler 1995). While these essential transmissions are clearly outside the framework of biological reproduction, Hirschfeld (1996) has argued that they are not outside the framework of *natural* reproduction. Nonetheless, we are unaware of any data, anecdotal or otherwise, suggesting that a natural or biological essence regularly transmigrates from persons to objects. Cases in which it occurs are, as we contend, limited to fetishization, contamination/pollution, or blessings.

An important correlate to the importance of the hypothesized triggering conditions is that essentialism may not map cleanly onto domains. Events and specific entities (with specific biographies) may be essentialized without essentializing the larger domain of which it is part. Thus the fact that something is essentialized cannot (or cannot solely) be a function of the domain to which it belongs, nor to the closeness between that domain and another, more basically essentialized domain, as Atran (1990) has proposed for the essentialization of race.

## 12.6    Conclusions

The question we posed with this chapter—how biological is essentialism?—was meant to provoke discussion of several issues. First, how well-motivated is the attention that folkbiology has received in research on essentialist reasoning? And conversely, how well-motivated is the attention that essentialism has received in research on folkbiology? We would probably have to conclude that the motivation is better with respect to the latter than the former. Essentialism is an essential part of folkbiology. A crucial aspect of the way living kinds are organized and reasoned over in our mind's eye is explicable only when an essentialist presumption is acknowledged. Adults construct highly articulated essentialist discourses about biological things. Children seldom if ever articulate their essentialist assumptions about living things (or other domains, for that matter), yet the discovery that their reasoning is imbued with essentialism has been a striking finding.

However, this does not mean that folkbiology is critical to understanding essentialism. Indeed, assuming that essentialism is fundamentally biological may have limited our understanding of what psychological essentialism is. By speculating that essentialism is not uniquely tethered to the folkbiological, we are not suggesting that it is a domain-general effect. Again, not every domain is essentialized or even potentially essentializable. Essentialism is a mode of understanding invoked when ontological commitments (e.g., that caterpillars and butterflies are the same creature) or biographical saliencies (e.g., Jackie Onassis's prior possession of certain objets d'art) are otherwise causally unexplained. Essentialism is an instrumental doctrine. It provides coherence to folk theories, explains consistency in otherwise diverse folk collections, and invests importance in events where the world fails to deliver.

## Notes

Support for writing this chapter was provided by NSF grant BNS-9100348, NICHD grant R01-HD36043, and a J. S. Guggenheim fellowship to Gelman and by NSF grant SBR-9319796 to Hirschfeld and NSF grant SBR-9319798 to Atran, Hirschfeld, Medin, and Smith. We thank the members of our graduate seminar (Winter 1996), "Essentialism in cognition and culture"—Todd DeKay, Gil Diesendruck, Martie Haselton, Gail Heyman, Melissa Koenig, Barlow LeVold, Brian Malley, Ivelisse Martinez, Janet McIntosh, John Opfer, Tom Rodriguez, and Julie King Watson—for their insightful discussions. We are particularly grateful to Janet McIntosh for her important contributions, several of which we have tried to develop here. We also thank Scott Atran, Doug Medin, and Dan Sperber for their helpful comments on an earlier draft.

1. The claim that $H_2O$ is the essence of water has been most clearly elaborated in an influential paper by Putnam (1975). However, it is important to keep in mind that in Putnam's view, $H_2O$ is the *metaphysical*, not psychological, essence of water. Furthermore Putnam notes that this metaphysical essence is known (or at least understood) only by experts, not most layfolk. This scientific claim is itself corrigible and so may turn out in the final analysis not to be the "true" essence of water. Thus Malt's experiments do not constitute a test of Putnam's arguments— and to our view do not provide a compelling test of psychological essentialism more generally.

2. For example, Kalish included neither positive examples (e.g., three-legged horse, two-foot-high horse) nor familiar subtypes (e.g., penguins or ostriches as kinds of birds), although our intuitions suggest that subjects would have supplied more absolute responses in such cases.

3. One question that arises is whether all of these examples should be considered causal. Certainly in all of the examples listed above, the causal mechanism is un-known: we don't know exactly how essences result in morphology and behaviors, why eating dirt leads to illness, or precisely what happens after we kiss the hem of the pope's robe. Thus these phenomena are similar to what Au and Romo (chapter 11, this volume) call "input-output relations" rather than articulated causal mechanisms. Why, then, call these causal, as opposed to stimulus-response pairings of the sort that lead to "superstitious" behavior in pigeons (as Skinner has shown)? Whereas the pigeons' "superstitions" were based on observable stimulus-response pairings, the causal links discussed here are theorized even in the absence of evidence. Moreover people start building stories to fill in the gaps: they attribute theorized causal agents (essences, germs, personality, gods) to do the work. These theorized components are neither observed nor known (e.g., we don't know what the essence is, and we don't know what happens if we own Jackie O's necklace). That people appeal to these causal chains nonetheless sug-gests that people may have a propensity to invoke unobservable causal constructs (Tomasello, personal communication).

4. Depending on the level of specificity, the causal principle may commit one to a particular mode of construal. Here, however, we have in mind phenomena such as inheritance rather than specific causal principles such as gene transmission or socialization.

5. Bear in mind that recognizing token identity constancy for species that undergo radical transformations or individuals across the lifespan does not require essen-tialization. Many primate species seem to recognize both, presumably without adopting an essentialist presumption.

6. Faculties, competencies, and task-specific algorithms do not map cleanly or directly on to other dimensions relevant to domain specificity. For instance, faculties include structures that have been described as both modules (e.g., language) and theories (i.e., theory of mind or folk psychology); competencies include both areas of expertise as well as some specific aspects of modules (e.g., certain color memory proclivities), while task-specific algorithms are generally not discussed as domains in and other themselves but rather are seen as constituent devices within a domain. Jackendoff (1992) distinguishes two sorts of modules: the first, input-output modules (which would fall under our "task-specific algorithms"), target and process specific kinds of information; the second, central modules (which would fall under our "faculties"), "integrate information provided by disparate input modules into a unified modality-independent conception of the world" (p. 70). The importance of our third type of domain-specific device, competencies, is evident when we consider the various proclivities and capacities that are included in the domain of color. First, the domain of color perception might reasonably be thought to fall under a faculty of vision. Second, some aspects of color perception presumably involve task-specific algorithms (e.g., the mnemonic salience of focal colors). Third, and most important, other aspects of color processing (e.g., constraints on the order in which basic color terms enter a language) don't seem to fall under either task-specific algorithms or faculties but represent distinct competencies.

## References

Aboud, F. E. 1988. *Children and Pejudice*. Cambridge, MA: Basil Blackwell.

Allport, G. 1954. *The Nature of Prejudice*. Reading, MA: Addison-Wesley.

Aristotle. 1924. *Metaphysics*. Oxford: Clarendon Press.

Atran, S. 1990. *Cognitive Foundations of Natural History*. Cambridge: Cambridge University Press.

Atran, S. 1996. Modes of thinking about living kinds: science, symbolism, and common sense. In. D. Olson and N. Torrance, eds., *Modes of Thought: Explorations in Culture and Cognition*. Cambridge: Cambridge University Press.

Atran, S. 1995. Classifying nature across cultures. In D. Osherson and E. Smith, eds., *Invitation to Cognitive Science: Thinking* vol. 3, 2nd ed. Cambridge: MIT Press.

Atran, S., P. Estin, J. Coley, and D. Medin. 1999. Generic species and basic levels: essence and appearance in folk biology. *Journal of Ethnobiology*, in press.

Au, T., A. Sidle, and K. Rollins, 1993. Developing an intuitive understanding of conservation and contamination: Invisible particles as a plausible mechanism. *Developmental Psychology* 29: 286–98.

Banton, M. 1987. *Racial Theories*. Cambridge: Cambridge University Press.

Barsalou, L. W. 1985. Ideals, central tendency, and frequency of instantiation as determinants of graded structure in categories. *Journal of Experimental Psychology: Learning, Memory, and Cognition* 11: 629–54.

Bem, S. 1989. Genital knowledge and gender constancy in preschool children. *Child Development* 60: 649–20.

Berlin, B. 1978. Ethnobiological classification. In E. Rosch and B. Lloyd, eds., *Cognition and categorization.* Hillsdale, NJ: Lawrence Erlbaum.

Berlin, B. 1992. *Ethnobiological Classification.* Princeton: Princeton University Press.

Boyer, P. 1990. *Tradition as Truth and Communication.* New York: Cambridge University Press.

Braisby, N., B. Franks, and J. Hampton. 1996. Essentialism, word use, and concepts. *Cognition* 59: 247–74.

Branch, C., and N. Newcombe. 1980. Racial attitudes of black preschoolers as related to parental civil rights activism. *Merrill-Palmer Quarterly* 26: 425–28.

Branch, C., and N. Newcombe. 1986. Racial attitude development among young black children as a function of parental attitudes. *Child Development* 57: 712-21.

Brown, A. L. 1990. Domain-specific principles affect learning and transfer in children. *Cognitive Science* 14: 107–33.

Bullock, M., R. Gelman, and R. Baillargeon. 1982. The development of causal reasoning. In W. J. Friedman, ed., *The Developmental Psychology of Time.* New York: Academic Press, pp. 209–54.

Carey, S. 1985. *Conceptual Development in Childhood.* Cambridge: MIT Press.

Carey, S. 1995. On the origins of causal understanding. In D. Sperber, D. Premack, and A. J. Premack, eds., *Causal Cognition: A Multi-disciplinary Approach.* Oxford: Clarendon Press, pp. 268–308.

Carey, S., and E. Spelke. 1994. Domain specific knowledge and conceptual change. In L. A. Hirschfeld and S. A. Gelman, eds., *Mapping the Mind: Domain Specificity in Cognition and Culture.* New York: Cambridge University Press.

Carlson, G. N., and F. J. Pelletier, eds., 1995. *The Generic Book.* Chicago: University of Chicago Press.

Chandler, M. J., and C. E. Lalonde. 1994. Surprising, magical and miraculous turns of events: Children's reactions to violations of their early theories of mind and matter. *British Journal of Developmental Psychology* 12: 83–95.

Crocker, J. C. 1979. Selves and alters among the Eastern Bororo. In D. Maybury-Lewis, ed., *Dialectical Societies: The Ge and Bororo of Central Brazil.* Cambridge: Harvard University Press, pp. 249–300.

Daniel, E. 1984. *Fluid Signs: Being a Person the Tamil Way.* Berkeley: University of California Press.

Diesendruck, G., S. A. Gelman, and K. Lebowitz. 1996. *Conceptual and Linguistic Biases in Children's Word Learning.* Unpublished manuscript. University of Michigan.

Dupré, J. 1993. *The Disorder of Things: Metaphysical Foundations of the Disunity of Science.* Cambridge: Harvard University Press.

Fairchild, C. 1984. *Domestic Enemies: Servants and Their Masters in Old Regime France*. Baltimore: Johns Hopkins Press.

Flavell, J. H., E. R. Flavell, and F. L. Green. 1983. Development of the appearance-reality distinction. *Cognitive Psychology* 15: 95–120.

Fuss, D. 1989. *Essentially Speaking: Feminism, Nature, and Difference*. New York: Routledge.

Gelman, R. 1990. First principles organize attention to and learning about relevant data: Number and the animate-inanimate distinction as examples. *Cognitive Science* 14: 79–106.

Gelman, S. A. 1988. The development of induction within natural kind and artifact categories. *Cognitive Psychology* 20: 65–96.

Gelman, S. A. 1992. Children's conception of personality traits—Commentary. *Human Development* 35: 280–85.

Gelman, S. A. 1999. Developing a doctrine of natural kinds. *Psychology of Communication and Language*, in press.

Gelman, S. A., and J. D. Coley. 1990. The importance of knowing a dodo is a bird: Categories and inferences in 2-year-old children. *Developmental Psychology* 26: 796–804.

Gelman, S. A., and J. D. Coley. 1991. Language and categorization: The acquisition of natural kind terms. In S. A. Gelman and J. P. Byrnes, eds., *Perspectives on language and thought: Interrelations in development*. Cambridge: Cambridge University Press, pp. 146–96.

Gelman, S. A., J. D. Coley, and G. M. Gottfried. 1994. Essentialist beliefs in children: The acquisition of concepts and theories. In L. A. Hirschfeld and S. A. Gelman, eds., *Mapping the Mind: Domain Specificity in Cognition and Culture*. New York: Cambridge University Press, pp. 341–66.

Gelman, S. A., and K. E. Kremer. 1991. Understanding natural cause: Children's explanations of how objects and their properties originate. *Child Development* 62: 396–414.

Gelman, S. A., and E. M. Markman. 1986. Categories and induction in young children. *Cognition* 23: 183–209.

Gelman, S. A., and E. M. Markman. 1987. Young children's inductions from natural kinds: The role of categories and appearances. *Child Development* 58: 1532–41.

Gelman, S. A., and H. M. Wellman. 1991. Insides and essences: Early understandings of the nonobvious. *Cognition* 38: 213–44.

Gelman, S. A., J. D. Coley, K. S. Rosengren, E. Hartman, and A. Pappas. 1996. *Beyond Labeling: The Role of Parental Input in the Acquisition of Richly-Structured Categories*. Unpublished manuscript. University of Michigan.

Gelman, S. A., and G. M. Gottfried. 1996. Children's causal explanations of animate and inanimate motion. *Child Development* 35: 28–34.

Goldberg, T. 1993. *Racist Culture: Philosophy and the Politics of Meaning.* New York: Basil Blackwell.

Gopnik, A., and H. Wellman. 1994. The theory theory. In L. A. Hirschfeld and S. A. Gelman, eds., *Mapping the Mind: Domain Specificity in Cognition and Culture.* New York: Cambridge University Press.

Guillaumin, C. 1980. The idea of race and its elevation to autonomous scientific and legal status. *Sociological Theories: Race and Colonialism.* Paris: UNESCO, pp. 37–68.

Hickling, A. K. 1996. The emergence of causal explanation in everyday thought: Evidence from ordinary conversation. Unpublished PhD dissertation. University of Michigan.

Hickling, A. K., and S. A. Gelman. 1995. How does your garden grow? Evidence of an early conception of plants as biological kinds. *Child Development* 66: 856–76.

Hirschfeld, L. 1989. Discovering linguistic differences: Domain specificity and the young child's awareness of multiple languages. *Human Development* 32: 223–36.

Hirschfeld, L. 1993. Discovering social difference: The role of appearance in the development of racial awareness. *Cognitive Psychology* 25: 317–50.

Hirschfeld, L. 1995a. Do children have a theory of race? *Cognition* 54: 209–52.

Hirschfeld, L. 1995b. Anthropology, psychology, and the meanings of social causality. In D. Sperber, D. Premack, and A. Premack, eds., *Causal cognition: A multidisciplinary debate.* New York: Oxford University Press, pp. 313–50.

Hirschfeld, L. 1996. *Race in the Making: Cognition, Culture, and the Child's Construction of Human Kinds.* Cambridge: MIT Press.

Hirschfeld, L. A., and S. A. Gelman. 1994. Toward a typography of the mind: An introduction to domain-specificity. In L. A. Hirschfeld and S. A. Gelman, eds., *Mapping the Mind: Domain Specificity in Cognition and Culture.* New York: Cambridge University Press.

Hirschfeld, L. A., and S. A. Gelman. 1997. What young children think about the relation between language variation and social difference. *Cognitive Development* 12: 213–38.

Inagaki, K., and G. Hatano. 1993. Young children's understanding of the mind-body distinction. *Child Development* 64: 1534–49.

Inhelder, B., and J. Piaget. 1964. *The Early Growth of Logic in the Child.* New York: Norton.

Jackendoff, R. 1992. *Languages of the Mind: Essays on Mental Representation.* Cambridge: MIT Press.

Johnson, K., C. Mervis, and J. Boster. 1992. Developmental changes within the structure of the mammal domain. *Developmental Psychology* 28: 74–83.

Jones, S., and L. Smith. 1993. The place of perception in children's concepts. *Cognitive Development* 8: 113–39.

Kalish, C. 1995. Essentialism and graded membership in animal and artifact categories. *Memory and Cognition* 23: 335–53.

Kalish, C. 1996. Causes and symptoms in preschoolers' conceptions of illness. *Child Development* 67: 1647–70.

Katz, P. 1982. Development of children's racial awareness and intergroup attitudes. In L. Katz, ed., *Current topics in early childhood education*, vol. 4. Norwood, NJ: Ablex, pp. 16–54.

Keil, F. 1979. *Semantic and Conceptual Development: An Ontological Perspective*. Cambridge: Harvard University Press.

Keil, F. 1989. *Concepts, Kinds, and Cognitive Development*. Cambridge: MIT Press.

Keil, F. 1994. The birth and nurturance of concepts by domains: The origins of concepts of living things. In L. A. Hirschfeld and S. A. Gelman, eds., *Mapping the Mind: Domain Specificity in Cognition and Culture*. New York: Cambridge University Press.

Keil, F. 1995. The growth of causal understandings of natural kinds. In D. Sperber, D. Premack, and A. Premack, eds., *Causal cognition: A multidisciplinary debate*. Oxford: Oxford University Press.

Kohlberg, L. 1966. A cognitive-developmental analysis of children's sex-role concepts and attitudes. In E. Maccoby, ed., *The Development of Sex Differences*. Palo Alto: Stanford University Press.

Kofkin, J., P. Katz, and E. Downey. 1995. Family discourse about race and the development of children's racial attitudes. Paper presented at the Bienniel Meetings of the Society for Research in Child Development. Indianapolis.

Kripke, S. 1972. Naming and necessity. In D. Davidson and G. Harman, eds., *Semantics of Natural Language*. Dordrecht: Reidel.

Landau, B. 1982. Will the real grandmother please stand up? The psychological reality of dual meaning representations. *Journal of Psycholinguistic Research* 11: 47–62.

Leslie, A. 1994. ToMM, ToBy, and agency: Core architecture and domain specificity. In L. A. Hirschfeld and S. A. Gelman, eds., *Mapping the Mind: Domain Specificity in Cognition and Culture*. New York: Cambridge University Press.

Liberman, A., and I. Mattingly. 1989. A specialization for speech perception. *Science* 243: 489–94.

Litt, C. J. 1986. Theories of transitional object attachment: An overview. *International Journal of Behavioral Development* 9: 383–99.

Locke, J. [1671] 1959. *An Essay Concerning Human Understanding*, vol. 2. New York: Dover.

McNamara, T. P., and R. J. Sternberg. 1983. Mental models of word meaning. *Journal of Verbal Learning and Verbal Behavior* 22: 449–74.

Malt, B. 1994. Water is not $H_2O$. *Cognitive Psychology* 27: 41–70.

Markman, E. M. 1989. *Categorization and Naming in Children: Problems in Induction.* Cambridge: MIT Press.

Mayr, E. 1982. *The Growth of Biological Thought.* Cambridge: Harvard University Press.

Mayr, R. 1991. *One Long Argument: Charles Darwin and the Genesis of Modern Evolutionary Thought.* Cambridge: Harvard University Press.

Medin, D. 1989. Concepts and conceptual structure. *American Psychologist* 44: 1469–81.

Needham, R. 1974. *Remarks and Inventions: Skeptical Essays about Kinship.* London: Tavistock.

Passman, R. H. 1987. Attachments to inanimate objects: Are children who have security blankets insecure? *Journal of Consulting and Clinical Psychology* 55: 825–30.

Pinker, S. 1994. *The Language Instinct.* New York: Morrow.

Putnam, H. 1975. The meaning of "meaning." In H. Putnam, ed., *Mind, Language and Reality: Philosophical Papers*, vol. 2. New York: Cambridge University Press.

Rips, L. J. 1989. Similarity, typicality, and categorization. In S. Vosniadou and A. Ortony, eds., *Similarity and Analogical Reasoning.* New York: Cambridge University Press, pp. 21–59.

Rips, L. J., and A. Collins. 1993. Categories and resemblance. *Journal of Experimental Psychology: General* 122: 468–86.

Rorty, R. 1979. *Philosophy and the Mirror of Nature.* Princeton: Princeton University Press.

Rosch, E., and C. Mervis. 1975. Family resemblances: Studies in the internal structure of natural categories. *Cognitive Psychology* 8: 382–439.

Rosengren, K., S. Gelman, C. Kalish, and M. McCormick. 1991. As time goes by: Children's early understanding of growth in animals. *Child Development* 62: 1302–20.

Rothbart, M., and M. Taylor. 1990. Category labels and social reality: Do we view social categories as natural kinds? In G. Semin and K. Fiedler, eds., *Language and Social Cognition.* London: Sage.

Rozin, P., and C. Nemeroff. 1990. The laws of sympathetic magic: A psychological analysis of similarity and contagion. In. J. Stigler, R. Shweder, and G. Herdt, eds., *Cultural Psychology: Essays on Comparative Human Development.* New York: Cambridge University Press.

Schneider, D. 1968. *American Kinship: A Cultural Account.* Englewood Cliffs, NJ: Prentice-Hall.

Schult, C. A., and H. M. Wellman. 1997. Explaining human movements and actions. *Cognition* 62: 291–324.

Siegal, M., and D. Share. 1990. Contamination sensitivity in young children. *Developmental Psychology* 26: 455–58.

Smith, E. E., and D. L. Medin. 1981. *Categories and Concepts.* Cambridge: Harvard University Press.

Sober, E. 1994. *From a Biological Point of View.* New York: Cambridge University Press.

Solomon, G. E. A., S. C. Johnson, D. Zaitchik, and S. Carey. 1996. Like father, like son: Young children's understanding of how and why offspring resemble their parents. *Child Development* 67: 151–71.

Spencer, M. 1983. Children's cultural values and parental child rearing strategies. *Developmental Review* 3: 351–70.

Sperber, D. 1975b. Pourquoi les animaux parfaits, les hybrides et les monstres sont-ils bon à penser symboliquement? *L'Homme* 15: 5–24.

Sperber, D. 1994. The modularity of thought and the epidemiology of representations. In L. A. Hirschfeld and S. A. Gelman, eds., *Mapping the Mind: Domain Specificity in Cognition and Culture.* New York: Cambridge University Press, pp. 39–67.

Springer, K. 1995. The role of factual knowledge in a naive theory of biology. Paper presented at meeting of the Society for Research in Child Development, Indianapolis.

Springer, K., and J. Ruckel. 1992. Early beliefs about the cause of illness: Evidence against immanent justice. *Cognitive Development* 7: 429–43.

Stoler, A. 1995. *Race and the Education of Desire: A Colonial of Foucault's History of Sexuality.* Durham: Duke University Press.

Taylor, M. 1996. The development of children's beliefs about social and biological aspects of gender differences. *Child Development* 67: 1555–71.

Wierzbicka, A. 1994. The universality of taxonomic categorization and the indispensability of the concept "kind." *Rivista di Linguistica* 6: 347–64.

Winnicott, D. W. 1969. *The Child, the Family, and the Outside World.* Baltimore: Penguin Books.

Wolf, A. W., and B. Lozoff. 1989. Object attachment, thumbsucking, and the passage to sleep. *Journal of the American Academy of Child and Adolescent Psychiatry* 28: 287–92.

Yengoyan, A. 1999. Essentialisms of aboriginality: Blood/race, history, and the state in Australia. In. R. Grew and A. Burguière, eds., *The Invention of Minorities.* Ann Arbor: University of Michigan Press.

# 13

# Natural Kinds and Supraorganismal Individuals

Michael T. Ghiselin

There is folk taxonomy, on the one hand, and taxonomy as it is practiced by professional systematic biologists, on the other. Not surprisingly there has been a great deal of speculation about the similarities and differences between the two, sometimes backed up by extensive historical investigation (Atran 1990). At a bare minimum there seems to be a certain amount of continuity, insofar as scientists have taken the existing folk classifications as a starting point for developing something rather different.

In the past anthropologists tended to stress the differences, especially the utilitarian and social aspects of folk taxonomy or the realism of scientific taxonomy. This tradition has by no means died out, but the relativist version formulated by the sociologist Émile Durkheim (Durkheim and Mauss 1903, translation 1963) has generally been rejected as too extreme, even by those who find it useful (Douglas 1986).

Empirical investigation during more recent years has indicated that irrespective of culture, *Homo taxonomicus* classifies plants and animals in much the same way, and does so using a hierarchical structure that crudely approximates the Linnaean hierarchy (Brown 1984; Berlin 1992; D'Andrade 1995). The observations of field biologists that primitive hunters and gatherers are very good at distinguishing what experts consider biological species (Mayr 1942; Diamond 1965) have been supported by specialists on ethnobotany and ethnozoology (e.g., Hunn 1975), though not without some opposition (Armstrong, Gleitman, and Gleitman 1983).

The shift to realism occurred despite serious misconceptions about the metaphysics of taxonomy. In particular, there was the philosophy inherent in the early writings of Berlin and his collaborators (Berlin,

Breedlove, and Raven 1968) which was repudiated as a result of empirical investigations. The basic thesis of the "pheneticist school" that classification has to be based upon something called "overall similarity" never had a very large following among systematic biologists and was soon discredited. However, pheneticism influenced a wide variety of other disciplines, and some of its assumptions were taken over quite uncritically.

Students of folk taxonomy and of what cognitive psychologists call "categorization" have paid little attention to another serious misconception about classification, namely the notion that biological species and other taxa are so-called natural kinds. The term "natural kind" was introduced into the philosophy of science by the English philosopher John Stuart Mill as a general term that designates classes of objects with certain scientifically important properties in common. Such kinds of entities have many similar properties and they have them of physical necessity. Bromine, for example, has a particular atomic number, atomic weight, valence, and so forth. The laws of nature are such that bromine must have certain properties, irrespective of time and place.

Biological species are "natural" in contradistinction to "artificial": they are something that we discover rather than create. They are not, however, kinds, or classes, of organisms, or of anything else. They are wholes composed of organisms, or to put it in slightly different terms, they are individuals at a supraorganismal level. Here "individual" is used not in the more familiar (biological) sense of an organism but in the traditional (ontological) sense of a concrete particular. Although conceiving of species as ontological individuals has a long history (see Mayr 1987; Ghiselin 1987a,b), it was not a serious topic of discussion among theoreticians of taxonomy until I at last managed to get the point across using a rather forced analogy with such firms as General Motors (Ghiselin 1974).

What later came to be called the "individuality thesis" attracted the attention of the philosopher David Hull when he referred to the first publication in which I discussed the topic (Ghiselin 1966). At first he rejected the individuality thesis, but he soon changed his mind and was instrumental in getting it understood and generally accepted by philosophers of biology (Hull 1975, 1976, 1978). He also applied it to intellectual history (Hull 1988). My own publications on the individuality thesis have considered the implications for cognitive psychology at some length (Ghiselin 1981, 1987c, 1997).

Two things initially convinced me that species are individuals. First, it follows deductively from the technical definitions of "individual" and "species" that are used by metaphysicians and systematists respectively. Second, their names are defined ostensively, like proper names (i.e., those of individuals) in general: we sort of "point" at the thing that the name refers to.

What convinced Hull was the fact that there are no laws of nature for particular species. This made perfectly good sense because there are no laws of nature for any individuals whatsoever. Laws of nature, which are necessarily true of everything to which they apply, irrespective of time and place, are about classes, such as "planet" or "species" in general, and make no reference to individuals such as "Jupiter" or "*Homo sapiens.*"

On the other hand, although an individual has a history, a class does not. We can track organisms and species through time because, unlike classes, they have definite locations and periods where and when they exist. Now, since natural kinds are supposedly consequences of the laws of nature, whereas the order with which systematic biology deals is a matter of history rather than law, there is no way in which such groups as Mammalia can be interpreted as natural kinds. There is a fundamentally different causal nexus underlying their various properties.

Classes are abstractions, and as such they cannot "do" anything. At the organismal level this seems obvious: organism in the abstract cannot reproduce—only an individual organism can do that. If species were classes, then they could not do anything either: such as evolve, speciate, or become extinct. The fact that they do things like that suffices to show that they are not natural kinds.

Interestingly John Stuart Mill (1872: 17, and other editions) explained the difference between a natural kind and a supraorganismal individual quite well, despite believing that species are classes. This he did with the example of a military unit, which is a social individual. According to Mill, the 76th regiment of foot in the British Army is not a general but a particular term, with a proper name. One can easily come up with further examples of "groups" that are really composite wholes made up of parts rather than classes with members. Canada, for instance, is not a class of provinces. You are not a class of cells.

One can easily show that everyone, at least tacitly, routinely makes such an ontological distinction. Parts of a whole function quite differently in our thinking from members of a class. This point becomes quite obvious when we realize that unlike classes individuals have no instances. For example, we do not say that my left hand is a Michael Ghiselin. Pressing the example, were my right hand also a Michael Ghiselin, there would be at least two Michael Ghiselins. By the same token we may argue that Ontario is not a Canada. And for exactly the same reasons I am not a *Homo sapiens* or a Mammalia. (At least if I use language like the competent scientist I am supposed to be.)

One might object that such terms as "human being" and "mammal" seem, at least, to function like ordinary class names. "Human being," however, is not a synonym for "*Homo sapiens*" but a collective term for certain of its parts. There are many wholes for which we have what I call "componential sortals": terms for the individuals that are parts of some larger individual. In other words, a human being is an organism-level component of *Homo sapiens*, and a mammal is an organism-level component of Mammalia. If we needed such terms for our own organs or cells we could invent them. When parts of a whole have something in common, we can process them logically as if they were members of a class. For many purposes one can treat classes as if they were individuals or individuals as if they were classes, and it does not make much difference.

Indeed for some purposes it actually helps to treat classes as if they were individuals. That is why Venn diagrams are so useful in visualizing logical relationships: they depict class inclusion as if it were a whole-part relation. Branching diagrams likewise can depict purely logical relationships such as class inclusion as well as concrete connections such as genealogies. Nor has this point altogether escaped the attention of cognitive psychologists. Markman (1973, 1979) found that children were better able to think in terms of families and other wholes than of classes. Unfortunately, her contribution has not received anywhere near the attention that it deserves, and even she has persisted in treating the generality of groups as if they were natural kinds (Markman 1989). I do not believe that her neologism "collection" strictly corresponds to "individual" in the ontological sense that I have used, but it comes close.

Theoreticians of systematics have long made a reasonably clear distinction between *classification*, on the one hand, and *identification*, on the other. Classification is a creative process whereby the materials are arranged in some kind of order, or system, perhaps providing names for groups of them. Identification is the assignment of an individual such as a botanical specimen to a place in a preexisting system, and perhaps to decide that a name applies to it. In general, cognitive psychologists conflate these two very different operations under a single term: categorization. But the term is often restricted to identification (Smith and Medin 1981: 7). Because of the resulting confusion, and also because of other equivocations, it might be a good idea to drop this use of "category" altogether.

If, as is so often the approach, one attempts to understand cognition from the point of view of language acquisition, the confusion between classification and identification becomes compounded. There is no particular connection between how somebody classifies and whether he can identify an "instance" of a named group in somebody else's classification. And given the multiplicity of ways in which even a single organism classifies a given body of material, the pitfalls should be all too obvious.

The state of confusion between language as it is used by semieducated laypersons, on the one hand, and language as it is used by professional systematists, on the other, creates additional problems. Consider the following sentence by one of my favorite culinary authors, the late James Beard (1974: 170): "Did you know that the strawberry, which grows all over the world, is not really a true fruit in the strict botanical sense, but a member of the rose family, the genus *Fragaria*?" Somehow he has taken the fact that a strawberry, which is an organ and not a taxonomic group in the first place, is not a berry but a receptacle, to mean that a strawberry is not a fruit, assuming that there is in fact a taxon that corresponds to fruit! As somebody who really understands zoological discourse, I am amazed that cognitive psychologists make as much sense of their data as they do. At least they are better off than the professors of philosophy who make fantastic claims about tigers from other planets.

Systematic biologists are beginning to make a clear distinction between *defining* properties and *diagnostic* ones (Ghiselin 1984). A defining property is one that an entity must possess if a name is to apply to it. This is a logical "must"—it is logically impossible for a bachelor to be married. A diagnostic property is one that is highly reliable in identification but is not logically necessary. Things could be otherwise, and perhaps occasionally they are. Like the symptoms that are "diagnostic" of a disease, they are very useful, but they may or may not be present. More important, however, although species and other taxonomic groups do have diagnostic properties, they have no defining ones. And this is because, like France and George Washington, they are individuals, with names that are not defined in terms of properties. Cognitive psychologists do make the distinction between properties that are and are not defining. But they rarely if ever consider the possibility that a group has no defining properties whatsoever. On the other hand, they seem to be giving up on defining properties where, it seems to me, they perhaps exist in subtler form (Medin 1989). Cognitive psychology has been heavily burdened with phenomenalism as a metaphysical presupposition. Only gradually has it managed to get away from the sort of naive empiricism that systematic biology got rid of two decades ago in favor of etiological classification. To be sure, it has been well substantiated that people if asked will at least try to put objects together on the basis of what is called "similarity"—yet they prefer to group things according to common causes. Nonetheless, the groups in question are still called "natural kinds" despite the profound distinction between the results of history and the results of laws of nature.

Insofar as the individuality thesis has received grudging recognition outside of biology, we are told that yes, this is something that scientists do, but hardly what one would expect of our unlettered brethren and sisters (Atran 1990: 265). It seems to me much more reasonable, however, to assume that *Homo taxonomicus* has been classifying in more or less the same way all along, and that when attempting to classify upon an etiological basis, both natural kinds and ontological individuals have been viable alternatives.

If we want to understand classification properly, we need to look upon individuals as the fundamental ontological inhabitants of an organism's world, and by the same token to consider identifying them as a crucial step in cognition. Our ability to make such judgments must have originated well over a billion years ago. The natural order has created selection pressures, such that there is a great advantage to being able to identify instances of natural kinds, on the one hand, and individuals, on the other. Selection therefore may well have created a system of classification such that the organisms identify instances of such classes as food and prey. But it also would seem to have created the capacity to identify individuals. The immune system, which distinguishes self from nonself is very old. Older still is the capacity of DNA to recognize parts of lineages of which it is a component. Such recognition is particularly important in meiosis and in other processes having to do with sex. Unicellular organisms and the gametes of multicellular ones are very adept at identifying other components of their own species. The capacity to distinguish degrees of proximity in the genealogical nexus is also well documented among a wide range of animals and plants. Crucial to many organisms is the ability to identify one's parent and one's offspring: other components, in other words, of an individual called a "lineage." Likewise animals routinely identify individuals of which organisms are parts, such as flocks, herds, and other social units. Individuals of which an animal is not a part may be added to the list: its nest, its territory, the pond in which it dwells. Whether or not cognitive maps really exist, each such map is an individual map that maps an individual territory.

To some people it has seemed rather a puzzle as to how we know that we are able to identify an individual. Sometimes we are indeed fooled, as in the case of identical twins. On the other hand, individuality is not a kind of similarity. Individuals are single things and spatiotemporally restricted. In the case of one's self, they do not go away and return. One might be fooled by a pair of identical twins if one encountered them at different times, but never if one saw the two of them at once. Not only are we familiar with such individuals as our selves, we are likewise familiar with individuals that are parts of our selves, such as our own left hand and right. That these are indeed parts with wholes is recognized by students of cognition and folk anatomy. Indeed Ellen (1977) seems to make very much the kind of distinction between wholes and classes that I do. No doubt a considerable amount of background knowledge about functional anatomy is brought to bear upon our decisions about classification. People have a lot of tacit knowledge about organisms and what they do.

The extent to which *Homo academicus* is able to ignore the phenomena of reproduction and sex can be truly amazing. However, one does not have to be a professional genital anatomist like me to be at least vaguely aware of them. Many people not only know about procreation but actually participate in it. Likewise the fact that people and other animals change as they get older is by no means a secret, nor is the fact that there are important differences between males and females. Therefore it would be most remarkable if folk taxonomy never recognized that organisms of different sexes may be conspecific despite sexual dimorphism and other forms of intraspecific variation. The marine biologist R. E, Johannes (1981) spent a lot of time studying the native fishermen of Palau in the West Caroline Islands. He was most impressed with their knowledge of feeding and reproduction, including the fact that color variants are males and females. As to birds, they often form biparental families that provide care for the young, much as we do. The developmental stages of birds are also widely known. One does not have to know about the so-called law of von Baer (1828) to realize that however "atypical" or sexually dimorphic adult birds may seem, the eggs and chicks are significantly less divergent.

Those who created the scientific classification of animals and plants were obviously not oblivious to the phenomena of procreation. To be sure, there was a long tradition of belief in spontaneous generation on the part of the simpler forms of life. Be this as it may, pre-evolutionary species concepts did include the notion that conspecifics breed successfully only with conspecifics. And the sterility of mules tended to reinforce such notions. There is no reason why breeding communities of wildlife could not be conceptualized as individuals, by analogy with domesticated breeds that are kept separate by human artifice rather than isolating mechanisms. Nor is there any reason why such units would have to be evolutionary ones. They could be the products of Special Creation, perhaps originating as single pairs, and change within species might occur only within certain limits.

That pre-Darwinian systematists did in fact interpret taxa as individuals is manifest from the Strickland Code of zoological nomenclature (Strickland et al. 1843) which was developed by a committee of the British Association for the Advancement of Science. It refers to the names of species as "proper" names. By definition, a proper name is the name of an individual. (By "pre-Darwinian" I of course mean prior to 1859, and I should point out that Darwin was on the committee.)

The use of certain metaphors suggests that the taxa of early systematists could at least be analogized with individuals. The empire, the kingdom, and the family, in their nontaxonomic sense, are all classes of supraorganismal individuals. So why should there be any difficulty in thinking about Plantae or *Homo sapiens* as the sort of concrete particular thing that England is? Or the House of Saxe-Coburg and Gotha? Or the British Army with its regiments and soldiers? The language of discourse among taxonomists was transformed in part by taking metaphorical expressions in a literal sense. Genealogy is part of every normal human being's daily routine, and we all have the capacity to think about it. The informants of ethnobotanists and ethnozoologists often assert the existence of a close relationship between two groups of organisms by such expressions as saying that they are "brothers" (Berlin 1992: 145).

The "natural kind" view of taxonomy is obviously misleading at best, and a lot that has been taken for granted is clearly wrong. But cognitive psychologists have been remarkable resistant to criticism of their more fundamental assumptions. If one examines the books and journals in these genres, one readily sees that virtually everything that gets cited on the science of taxonomy is long out of date and largely discredited. The relevant literature on the philosophy of systematics, literature that has appeared in the most reputable scholarly journals, is passed over unmentioned (anthology: Ereshefsky 1992). Readers are not told about the cladistic revolution, nor are they given the slightest hint that a new generation of textbooks has been written to accommodate it, both by its proponents (Hennig 1966; Wiley 1981; Ax 1987) and its critics (Mayr and Ashlock 1991).

As to possible causes of what looks on the face of it like a conspiracy of silence, it would seem that the cognitive approach has been burdened by some unfortunate metaphysical commitments. The academic tradition in the philosophy of science that began to fall apart over thirty years ago presupposed phenomenalistic and set-theoretical metaphysics. The set-theoretical approach of Gregg (1954), for example, was enthusiastically endorsed by Kay (1971). Such preferences are reinforced by efforts to use computers and artificial intelligence as a model for cognitive processes. Small wonder therefore that a lot of people who might have been more critical were taken in by the pheneticists, who tried to base classification on overall similarity and have computers do the work. Small wonder too that they embraced a lot of misguided notions about disjunctive definitions, fuzzy sets, and family resemblances.

Likewise, although ostensive definitions work quite well for such individuals as organisms, species, and continents, efforts by philosophers to define the names of elements and other classes that way were a complete disaster. But it was a move that provided a superficially attractive way to be a realist out of one side of one's mouth and a nominalist out of the other. Psychologists and anthropologists, after all, are natural scientists and they don't want classification to be altogether arbitrary. Hence the attractiveness of the natural kind notion as presented by such philosophers as Kripke and Goodman (anthology: Schwartz 1977). As Hull (1992) has lately stressed, the individuality thesis has rendered that literature obsolete.

The hypothesis that human beings think typologically is perfectly reasonable, and there is plenty of empirical evidence indicating that all too often they do think typologically. Thinking in terms of stereotypes and screening out diversity is part of everybody's cognitive routine. But I can see no justification, other than bad metaphysics, for presupposing that human cognition lacks flexibility and that its possessors have no access to alternative ways of thinking. A certain inflexibility does characterize many of my own reflexes, and for all I know the entire conduct of many an insect's life. And I freely admit that much of my own behavior has a genetic basis. For example, when I go to New Guinea with my colleague Terrence Gosliner in order to study the pretty little marine gastropods called "nudibranchs" that interest us, we behave somewhat differently. We both take notes, but he photographs the animals and I draw them. He has a gene for photographing nudibranchs, whereas I have a gene for drawing nudibranchs. The alleles in question are located on our X chromosomes, to judge from the fact that my colleague's brother is color-blind too.

Granted what everybody knows about the physiology of color vision, it stands to reason that people will behave with a certain amount of uniformity with respect to the taxonomy of color. I would be surprised, for example, to find terms for "ultraviolet" in the folk taxonomies of unlettered New Guinea tribesmen, though I am sure that the notion can be expressed in Tok Pisin (Neo-Papuan). Therefore a lot of the cross-cultural uniformity that has been found in the nomenclature of color makes perfectly good sense (Berlin and Kay 1969). It is easy to see, however, that one might extrapolate to the point of finding genes "for" all sorts of things. The mere fact that people classify in the same way does not really tell us what role inheritance plays in their doing so, and more important, whether they might do otherwise under certain circumstances.

Even if we do have some sort of hereditary predisposition to classify certain kinds of objects in a particular way, we may also have other hereditary capacities to classify those very same objects in a somewhat different way. As a highly visual, diurnal animal with good color vision, I rely heavily upon that kind of sensory information when dealing with nudibranchs. However, the animals are often loaded with chemicals that protect them from predators. Consequently they can often be identified by their smell. We can obviously use all sorts of sensory channels when classifying and identifying the objects in our environment. It seems perfectly reasonable that we should employ a wide range of cognitive mechanisms as well.

What sort of mechanisms are involved? It looks to me as if Atran has been trying to endow the genome with something like a textbook of Aristotelian philosophy, complete with intuition as the fundamental source of knowledge. For all I know there may be a great deal of truth in all that. But even so, we may wonder what gets intuited, beyond a range of possibilities. Our capacity to deal with basic ontological concepts, such as the categories of substance, process, and attribute, has been admirably documented by Keil (1979, 1989), however much one may disagree about the details (Ghiselin 1987). One does not have to be a professional metaphysician to see the absurdity of saying that a walk can be purple or that today is heavier than yesterday.

Intuition tells professional metaphysicians, cognitive psychologists, anthropologists, and all sorts of other intellectuals that biological species are natural kinds. To treat species as individuals is, for most persons at least, counterintuitive. But our intuitions all too often lead us astray, and most of us learn from experience not to trust them. If we want to discover the foundations of knowledge, we had better not seek them in the attic.

## References

Armstrong, S. L., L. R. Gleitman, and H. Gleitman. 1983. What some concepts might not be. *Cognition* 13: 263–308.

Atran, S. 1990. *Cognitive Foundations of Natural History. Towards an Anthropology of Science.* Cambridge: Cambridge University Press.

Ax, P. 1987. *The Phylogenetic System: The Systematization of Organisms on the Basis of Their Phylogenesis*, 2nd ed., trans. by R. P. S. Jeffries. New York: Wiley.

Beard, J. 1974. *Beard on Food.* New York: Knopf.

Berlin, B. 1992. *Ethnobiological Classification: Principles of Categorization of Plants and Animals in Traditional Societies.* Princeton: Princeton University Press.

Berlin, B., D. E. Breedlove, and P. H. Raven. 1968. Covert categories and folk taxonomies. *American Anthropologist* 70: 290–99.

Berlin, B., and P. Kay. 1969. *Basic Color Terms: Their Universality and Evolution.* Berkeley: University of California Press.

Brown, C. H. 1984. *Language and Living Things: Uniformities in Folk Classification and Naming.* New Brunswick, NJ: Rutgers University Press.

D'Andrade, R. 1995. *The Development of Cognitive Anthropology.* Cambridge: Cambridge University Press.

Diamond, J. M. 1965. Zoological classification system of a primitive people. *Science* 151: 1102–04.

Douglas, M. 1986. *How Institutions Think.* Syracuse: Syracuse University Press.

Durkheim, É., and M. Mauss. 1963 *Primitive Classification*, 2nd ed, trans. and Intro. by R. Needham. Chicago: University of Chicago Press.

Ellen, R. F. 1977. Anatomical classification and the semiotics of the body. In J. Blacking, ed., *The Anthropology of the Body.* New York: Academic Press, pp. 343–73.

Ereshefsky, M., ed. 1992. *The Units of Evolution: Essays on the Nature of Species.* Cambridge: MIT Press.

Ghiselin, M. T. 1966. On psychologism in the logic of taxonomic controversies. *Systematic Zoology* 15: 207–15.

Ghiselin, M. T. 1974. A radical solution to the species problem. *Systematic Zoology* 23: 536–44.

Ghiselin, M. T. 1981 Categories, life, and thinking (with commentary). *The Behavioral and Brain Sciences* 4: 269–313.

Ghiselin, M. T. 1984. "Definition," "character," and other equivocal terms. *Systematic Zoology* 33: 104–10.

Ghiselin, M. T. 1987a. Species concepts, individuality, and objectivity. *Biology and Philosophy* 2: 127–43.

Ghiselin, M. T. 1987b. Response to commentary on the individuality of species. *Biology and Philosophy* 2: 207–12.

Ghiselin, M. T. 1987c. Classification as an evolutionary problem. In A. Costall, and A. Still, eds., *Cognitive Psychology in Question*. Brighton: Harvester Press, pp. 70–86.

Ghiselin, M. T. 1997. *Metaphysics and the Origin of Species*. Albany: State University of New York Press.

Gregg, J. R. 1954. *The Language of Taxonomy: an Application of Symbolic Logic to the Study of Classificatory Systems*. New York: Columbia University Press.

Hennig, W. 1966. *Phylogenetic Systematics*, 2nd ed, trans. by D. Dwight Davis and Rainer Zangerl. Urbana: University of Illinois Press.

Hull, D. L. 1975. Central subjects and historical naratives. *History and Theory* 14: 253–74.

Hull, D. L. 1976. Are species really individuals? *Systematic Zoology* 25: 174–91.

Hull, D. L. 1978. A matter of individuality. *Philosophy of Science* 45: 335–60.

Hull, D. L. 1988. *Science as a Process: An Evolutionary Account of the Social and Conceptual Development of Science*. Chicago: University of Chicago Press.

Hull, D. L. 1992. Biological species: An inductivist's nightmare. In M. Douglas and D. Hull, eds., *How Classification Works: Nelson Goodman among the Social Sciences*. Edinburgh: Edinburgh University Press, pp. 42–68.

Hunn, E. S. 1975. A measure of the degree of correspondence of folk to scientific biological classification. *American Ethnologist* 2: 309–27.

Johannes, R. E. 1981. *Words of the Lagoon: Fishing and Marine Lore in the Palau District of Micronesia*. Berkeley: University of California Press.

Kay, P. 1971. Taxonomy and semantic contrast. *Language* 47: 866–87.

Keil, F. C. 1979. *Semantic and Conceptual Development: An Ontological Perspective*. Cambridge: Harvard University Press.

Keil, F. C. 1989. *Concepts, Kinds, and Cognitive Development*. Cambridge: MIT Press.

Markman, E. 1973. Facilitation of part-whole comparisons by use of the collective noun "family". *Child Development* 44: 837–40.

Markman, E. 1979. Classes and collections: Conceptual organization and numerical abilities. *Cognitive Psychology* 11: 395–411.

Markman, E. M. 1989. *Categorization and Naming in Children: Problems of Induction.* Cambridge: MIT Press.

Mayr, E. 1942. *Systematics and the Origin of Species.* New York: Columbia University Press.

Mayr, E. 1987. The ontological status of species: Scientific progress and philosophical terminology. *Biology and Philosophy* 2: 145–66.

Mayr, E., and P. D. Ashlock. 1991. *Principles of Systematic Zoology,* 2nd ed. New York: McGraw-Hill.

Medin, D. L. 1989. Concepts and conceptual structure. *American Psychologist* 44: 1469–81.

Mill, J. S. 1872. *A System of Logic Ratiocinative and Inductive Being a Connected View of the Principles of Evidence and the Methods of Scientific Investigation,* 8th ed. London: Longmans, Green.

Schwartz, S. P., ed. 1977. *Naming, Necessity, and Natural Kinds.* Ithaca: Cornell University Press.

Smith, E. E., and D. L. Medin. 1981. *Categories and Concepts.* Cambridge: Harvard University Press.

Strickland, H. E., J. Phillips, J. Richardson, R. Owen, L. Jenyns, W. J. Broderip, J. S. Henslow, W. E. Shuckard, G. R. Waterhouse.

Von Baer, K. E. 1828. *Über Entwickelungsgeschichte der Thiere. Beobachtung und Reflexion,* vol. 1. Königsberg: Gebrüder Bornträger.

W. Yarrell, C. Darwin, J. O. Westwood. 1843. Report of a committee appointed " to consider of the rules by which the nomenclature of zoology may be established on a uniform and permanent basis. *Report of the British Association for the Advancement of Science* 12: 104–21.

Wiley, E. O. 1981. *Phylogenetics: The Theory and Practice of Phylogenetic Systematics.* New York: Wiley.

# 14

# Are Whales Fish?

John Dupré

The whale, the limpet, the tortoise, and the oyster ... as men have been willing to give them the name of fishes, it is wisest for us to conform.
Oliver Goldsmith (1728–1774; quoted in the *Oxford English Dictionary*)

This chapter discusses the relationship between ordinary language classification of biological organisms and scientific classification. In a recent book (Dupré 1993) I argued at length for a pluralistic view of biological classification. This thesis has two parts, a pluralism about biological taxonomy and the insistence that folk taxonomies are as legitimate, and can be interpreted as realistically, as scientific taxonomies. A consequence of this, which I shall emphasize in this chapter, is that there is no reason to expect folkbiological categories to converge toward scientifically recognized kinds. Although there are certainly cases in which this happens, the removal of whales from the category of fish being a standard example which I shall consider in some detail, I argue that such changes are, at least, philosophically unmotivated.

The first thesis, that there is no unique and privileged biological classification, is somewhat less controversial. A similar position has been endorsed by some philosophers (Kitcher 1984; Ereshefsky 1992; but see Sober 1984), and a related, if qualified, version has been accepted by some systematists (Mishler and Donoghue 1982). Although in many cases, when we look at organisms in a restricted spatial and temporal location, biological distinctions are unambiguous, even overdetermined, there is no reason to expect this to be the case as we extend our perspective spatially and temporally. This follows directly from our current understanding of the evolutionary process. Given this indeterminacy of kinds in nature, we should anticipate that different biological interests, for example, evolutionary versus ecological or morphological, will often dictate different taxonomies. Moreover there is no reason to be concerned by the fact that biologists concerned with very different classes of organisms often appeal to different classificatory principles. Whereas a classification aimed at reflecting phylogenetic history may have much to commend it for the study of birds or mammals, it may be neither feasible nor even useful for microorganisms or, perhaps, flowering plants.[1]

The topic of this chapter, however, is the more controversial claim that folk classifications should be treated on a par with scientific classifications.[2] Scientific classifications, I argue, are driven by specific, if often purely epistemic, purposes, and there is nothing fundamentally distinguishing such purposes from the more mundane rationales underlying folk classifications. The opposite view has been promoted among philosophers in highly influential writings by Kripke (1972) and, especially, Putnam (1975). Putnam treated folk classifications as first approximations to scientific taxonomies and argued that it was inherent in our use of everyday natural kind terms that they be subject to refinement as scientific taxonomies were developed and improved. However, in presenting this argument, Putnam assumed erroneously that biological natural kind terms in ordinary language typically approximated scientific biological taxa. In fact this is not at all generally the case (Dupré 1981).

Systematic divergence between scientific and folkbiological classification is readily documented for both Western and other indigenous peoples. It is sometimes suggested that similarities between scientific and indigenous taxonomies are so striking as to suggest some unique and objective set of facts by which both are determined. But closer examination shows this appearance to be illusory. First, most folk taxonomies are applied only to quite restricted areas of space and time, and as I have noted, from such a limited perspective morphological gaps between some kinds of organisms will be striking and unequivocal. Second, and more important, the large majority of folk taxonomy occurs at levels above that of the species, and higher-level classifications are not generally held to have much objective significance from a scientific point of view.[3] Only in restricted biological domains—birds, mammals, some reptiles, and some flowering plants—do folk classifications sometimes extend down to the level of the species. Even in these domains, with the possible exception of mammals, species-specific terms are the exception rather than the rule. In our own culture many people can identify, more or less, a mouse, a sparrow, a frog, or a marigold. A Dusky Seaside Sparrow (*Ammospiza nigrescens*) or a Prickly Fetid Marigold (*Dyssodia acerosa*) is another matter. Indeed it is misleading to think of these latter as terms of general folkbiology. They are rather parts of the highly specialized vocabularies of birdwatchers and wildflower enthusiasts, folk who, despite the low esteem with which their activities are sometimes regarded by professional biologists, have a special concern to remain scientifically *au courant*. At any rate more familiar folkbiological terms correspond, at best, to higher-level categories such as the genus or family and frequently, as I shall illustrate, to no recognizable scientific category at all.

Let me add two parenthetical comments. First, the case of bird-watchers and other biological amateurs should remind us of the very important point that science does not have a monopoly on specialized vocabularies. It would be very interesting to compare the vocabularies of furriers, timber-merchants, or herbalists with those of both biologists and ordinary folk. It seems likely, for example, that the rather disparate set of species that are referred to by the word "cedar" owe their association to an interest in a particular kind of timber. Second, no doubt hunter-gatherer societies have more sophisticated resources for describing their biological environment than do typical Western suburbanites. I take it, though, that this amounts to no more than a matter of degree, and has no bearing on the contrast I want to draw between scientific and folk taxonomies. Hunter-gatherers, presumably, make fine distinctions among the plants and animals in their immediate environment because of a pressing interest in eating them or putting them to other practical uses. I take it that they would be less inclined than Westerners to defer to scientific revisions of their taxonomy unless persuaded of some practical benefit to be obtained from such a revision. In this regard, as I shall argue, I would take them to be revealing superior philosophical sophistication.

Returning to the main thread of the argument, I noted that most terms of folkbiology are not terms for species. Where folk taxa do refer to species, it is generally plausible to take the folk and biological terms as coextensive (though one might note that the two would respond differently to such scientific changes as the identification of sibling species). However, for very many cases in which the folk term refers to a higher level in the taxonomic hierarchy, there is not even a candidate referent from scientific biology. Two examples will be discussed in much more detail below. One very typical pattern is that a higher-level biological taxon will be divided into several folk taxa for reasons that have little or no biological salience. A few examples are frogs and toads, titmice and chickadees, hares and rabbits, or onions, garlics, leeks, and other more decorative lily relatives. The last example illustrates that often there are good nonbiological reasons for such distinctions, in this case culinary. Other cases are more complicated. Petrels, for example, all of which are Tubenoses (order Procellariiformes), include the Storm Petrels (family Hydrobatidae) and the Large Petrels, the latter comprising a few species in the family Procellariidae, the family that also includes all Fulmars and Shearwaters. And so on. At the opposite end of the spectrum we might finally note the various forms of *Brassica oleracea*—cabbage, kale, Brussels sprouts, cauliflower, broccoli, and the like, the last two even being assigned to the same subspecies, *botrytis*, which we certainly have ample reason to distinguish for more mundane, again culinary, purposes.

The general point then is that science and ordinary life provide disjoint taxonomies of the biological world. If, as Putnam suggests, we have linguistic intentions, implicit in our use of biological kind words, to refer to the kinds that science will eventually privilege as real, then these intentions will be radically subversive of ordinary language. Since there are often good and obvious reasons for our ordinary language distinctions, such subversion will be generally regrettable. Better then to resist these subversive intentions, and better yet to deny that anything so undesirable should be acknowledged as among our pretheoretical linguistic intentions. Nevertheless, although our biological and folk taxonomies are disjoint, they often overlap locally and interact with one another in various interesting ways. I shall explore these interactions with reference to my main present example.

## 14.1  Why Whales Should Be Fish

In a paper some years ago (1981) I claimed that, contrary to a widely held misapprehension, whales were perfectly respectable fish. I must confess, however, that I have since come to doubt this claim about whales. The reason for this, though, is not that I have come to see that the march of science was indeed irresistible. It is rather that I have come to doubt whether there is any sense in which such a well-entrenched tenet of folk-biology as that which excludes whales from the ranks of fish could be shown to be wrong. Thus I still think that folk once believed that whales were fish, and that they were duped into changing that belief for bad reasons. Before this unfortunate occurrence, whales indeed were fish. But I take it that now almost all educated people are quite confident that whales *aren't* fish. And this, I now think, is enough to show that they are right that whales are now no longer fish.

Let me begin by considering briefly what is a whale and what is a fish. We may, I think, be quite confident that these are terms of ordinary language. My four-year-old son is a quite competent user of both, and I take it that he is not especially precocious in this regard. To begin with whales, I suppose that many, in the scientistic spirit theorized by Putnam, would now try to identify whales with the order Cetacea. In support of my strong intuition that dolphins and porpoises are not whales, however, I am pleased to note that Webster's defines whale as "any of the larger marine mammals of the order Cetacea, esp. as distinguished from the smaller dolphins...." Dolphins and porpoises do not form any significant subgroup of the order Cetacea. This order is, indeed, commonly divided into two suborders, namely the Toothed whales and the Baleen whales. Although dolphins and porpoises may constitute a specific lineage of the Toothed whales, proposing a dichotomy between this lineage, on the one hand, and all other lineages of toothed whales plus all the Baleen whales, on the other, makes no biological sense. Note also that dolphins are more closely related phylogenetically to Toothed whales than these latter are to Baleen whales. In sum, then, the category of whales is a biologically arbitrary one. In agreement with Webster's we may plausibly conclude that the reason dolphins and porpoises are not whales is much more prosaic: they aren't big enough. Very large size is central to the ordinary language concept of a whale. In fact the word "whale" is often used as a metaphor for largeness or excess as, for instance, in "a whale of a time."

Similar remarks apply to the concept of fish. As the quotation at the beginning of this chapter suggests, the term is sometimes used very widely for any aquatic animal. This usage is suggested by the various aquatic animals, such as starfish, cuttlefish, crayfish, and generically, shellfish, whose names contain the suffix fish but which most people would decisively exclude from the extension of that term. The OED in fact does offer the definition as "any animal living exclusively in the water" for popular language but adds a "scientific" usage which restricts the term to cold-blooded vertebrates with gills. Webster's begins with a version of this scientific definition and adds "(loosely) any of a variety of aquatic animals." This scientific definition applies to members of the classes Chondrichthyes[4] (cartilaginous fishes), Osteichthyes (bony fishes), and Agnatha (jawless fishes). But there is little or no biological rationale for a category containing just these groups. The primitive and rather unpleasant species in the class Agnatha (lampreys, hagfishes, and slime eels) have little in common with a state-of-the-art carp or tuna. Sometimes, it is true, the agnaths are distinguished from the other two classes, only the later being denominated "true fish". But in fact a shark and a salmon are barely more closely related to one another than either is to a lamprey.

Thus the notion that there is a "scientific" usage of the word "fish" is a decidedly suspect one.[5] The appeal in the definition to such technical matters as the possession of gills or cold-bloodedness seems rather a quasi-scientific rationalization of an extra-scientific linguistic intuition than the report of a genuinely scientific usage. Indeed, as is so commonly the case with attempts to define biological kinds, it is not even strictly true of all its intended referents. Some species of tuna maintain body temperatures as much as 20 degrees higher then their surroundings, and so should qualify as warm-blooded. And the lungfish *Protopterus* has been shown to get only 10 percent of its oxygen from water through its reduced gills. If its gills were to disappear completely at a subsequent evolutionary stage, I doubt whether it would thereby cease to be a fish. Given, then, that neither "whale" nor "fish" is really a scientific term, the rationale for the dictum taught religiously to all our children that whales are not fish (and it is interesting that it is something that reliably requires to be taught) is more than a little unclear.

I have not attempted to do a historical study of this usage, but it is clear that whales have not always been nonfish. The whale and the sturgeon were once known as the royal fish. The great fish that swallowed Jonah is also referred to as a whale. And so on. Moreover there are obvious reasons for including whales in the (nonscientific) category of fish. A dolphin is in many ways a similar beast to a tuna. Both are superbly adapted to swimming at high speeds, and consequently they show considerable analogous evolution in superficial morphology. Certainly they are a lot more superficially similar than either is to an eel, a sea horse, or a ratfish, or, for that matter, to a bat, a rabbit, or a sloth. Given, then, that whales were once seen as fish, and that neither "whale" nor "fish" is in any serious sense a scientific taxonomic term, it is interesting to speculate, at least, as to how they became nonfish.

## 14.2   Why Whales Are Not Fish

Despite the foregoing considerations, I have already conceded the obvious fact that whales are not fish. Why not? We might ask both why this fact is obvious, and why it came to be a fact at all. The first question is easy enough. Educated speakers will, I suspect, almost unanimously refuse to apply the word "fish" to, Blue whales, Killer whales, and similar creatures and, for that matter, to dolphins. Ultimately I suppose that this is the only relevant evidence, and that it is decisive. On the other hand, I also suspect that if pushed to rationalize this linguistic intuition, most people will be found to believe that scientists have found out what fish are, and what whales are, and that the latter are distinct from the former. Here, as I have argued, they would be mistaken. What a fish is is not the sort of thing a scientist (except, perhaps, a linguist) could find out.

  Much more interesting, then, is the second question. Is there a good reason for teaching our children that whales are not fish? Even if these are not scientific categories, one might argue that some useful scientific knowledge is transmitted by using them this way. Whales are, after all, mammals, and no other mammals are much like fish. Being mammals ourselves, we tend to know quite a bit about this class of organisms, and we certainly learn a good deal about whales by knowing that they are mammals. But this argument is not compelling. The obvious rejoinder is that some mammals are fish. In fact, if we taught our children that whales were mammalian fish, they would both learn to apply general knowledge about mammals to whales (they bear live young and suckle them, are warm-blooded, etc.) and might also learn that "fish," unlike "mammal," was not a term for any coherent scientific grouping of organisms but a loose everyday term for (perhaps) any aquatic vertebrate. Indeed, the argument that because whales are mammals they cannot be fish seems to me to be a paradigm for the confusion between scientific and ordinary language biological kinds. (I shall return to this point in the next section.)

In some ways a more satisfactory answer to the present question might be a moral one. Certainly our sense of appropriate treatment of cetaceans is greatly influenced by the conviction that whales are not fish. Nowadays, if one offers someone the choice between a tuna sandwich or a whale steak, one will notice a strong tendency to choose the former and even some degree of outrage at being offered the latter. Even some people with moral objections to eating any mammals will sometimes consider it acceptable to eat fish. This perhaps points toward the greatest respect in which whales really do diverge from typical stereotypes of fish. We think of fish as being fairly stupid creatures and of whales, even by mammalian standards, as being decidedly bright. Although no doubt the emphasis on intelligence in deciding how bad it is to kill and eat something has an anthropocentric aspect—intelligence being of course what we take to be so special about ourselves—there is surely something plausible to the idea. Killing a highly intelligent animal will perhaps cause great grief to its relatives and school-friends, and perhaps even will put an end to a more intrinsically valuable life. But certainly this point has at most rhetorical force. There is no reason why some kinds of fish should not be much more intelligent than others. Certainly there are such differences among mammals (between a human or whale, say, and a shrew) and perhaps there are comparable distinctions in intelligence between different kinds of non-cetacean fish. Moreover I take it that whales ceased to be fish long before anyone was much troubled by eating them—indeed in many countries it appears that they are still not much troubled by doing so. So certainly this is not the historical explanation for the change.

For want of a better explanation, I conclude that the exclusion of whales from the category of fish developed as a response to greater scientific knowledge of the nature of whales, which was, as I have argued, a somewhat misguided response. No doubt such infiltrations of ordinary language by science are common enough. So I now turn to a more general consideration of the relation between scientific and ordinary language terms for biological kinds.

## 14.3 Science and Ordinary Language

The general point of the discussion so far is to insist that ordinary language and science provide largely independent and often disjoint ways of classifying the biological world. Where ordinary language biological kinds are distinct in extension from any coherent scientific kind, the attempt to revise them in accord with supposedly scientific discoveries can promote only confusion. Moreover, as I have argued elsewhere (1981, 1993), I take it that ordinary language classifications are typically quite as well-motivated, and the kinds to which they refer may be just as objectively real, as biological classifications. It is just that they are differently motivated. Thus onions may constitute a perfectly real class of organisms, but not one that biologists have found any good reason to classify together. There are presumably objective facts about organisms of certain species that make them suitable for flavoring stews though I must admit that I cannot confidently vouch for the fact that all the species referred to as onions meet this condition. Similarly with fish, though the rationale for this much broader category is perhaps a lot vaguer. On the other hand, it is clear that to call these systems of classification *wholly* independent would be an exaggeration. For better or worse, as the principle example in this chapter illustrates, the development of scientific thinking sometimes has an impact on ordinary language usage.

One important aspect of this interaction is the importation of relatively pure scientific categories from scientific taxonomy into ordinary language. I have already suggested that this is the way that many species terms should be understood. Here the amateur naturalists who are the primary users of such terms have an explicit interest in distinguishing those species recognized by professional biologists, and ordinary language terms are treated as synonyms for Latin binomials. Perhaps of greater interest are the constructions of ordinary language terms to acknowledge higher-level taxonomic distinctions developed by biologists. Several examples have occurred in the foregoing discussion. One of the most familiar examples is "mammal." This, surely, is a term imported into common usage from scientific taxonomy. Less familiar, but similar, examples are the jawless fish, cartilaginous fish, and bony fish also mentioned above. The point of these terms is to be able to make biologically significant distinctions in somewhat more user-friendly ways than by learning terms such as Osteichthyes or Chondricthyes. Whereas the latter serve purposes such as international standardization important for biologists, the former are both easier to remember and more informative for less technical scientific or quasi-scientific discourse. I take it, however, that "is a member of the class Agnatha" and "is a jawless fish" are perfect synonyms, with scientific practice determining the reference. (Being a jawless fish does not mean being a fish and being jawless, or it would apply to all those bony fishes on the fishmonger's slab that have had their heads cut off.)

I want to claim, however, that these imported terms from scientific discourse should be understood quite differently from more familiar and well-entrenched ordinary language terms, and that the failure to make this distinction indicates a significant confusion common to many philosophers and lexicographers. Whereas the definition of mammal as, say, "warm-blooded, hairy vertebrate with a four-chambered heart and which nourishes its young with milk from maternal mammary glands" is entirely appropriate, the definition of fish as "cold-blooded, aquatic vertebrate with gills, and (usually) scales, fins, etc." is much more questionable. These definitions look very much alike. But, I have suggested, the terms to which they apply are of quite different kinds. Thus, while it is quite appropriate to say that it is a scientifically attested fact that all mammals have four-chambered hearts, it seems to me something like a category mistake to say that it is a scientific fact that all fish have gills—not because they might not but because science has nothing to say about all fish.

This last remark perhaps gets to the heart of the present problem. It is, I think, not widely accepted that there are any matters of much importance about which science has nothing to say. And certainly the question, What kind does this organism belong to? will strike most people as paradigmatically the kind of question about which science must be the only authoritative arbiter (e.g., see again Putnam 1975). Ironically, perhaps, the idea of an authoritative and unique answer to such a question really assumes some version of essentialism, the idea that some fundamental, essential property of a thing makes it the kind of thing it is, and essentialism was central to the Aristotelian and Scholastic views of knowledge against which modern science developed in large part as a critical reaction. Essentialism in biology, more specifically, was delivered its death blow by the triumph of Darwinism, and the consequent recognition that an organism might belong to a quite different kind from its ancestors, and that variation rather than uniformity was the norm for a biological kind. In a biology premised on variation and change, there is no reason to expect any unique answer to questions about how organisms should be grouped together, and a fortiori, there is no reason to expect science to provide such answers.

I do not want to deny the possibility that there might be scientifically motivated revisions of ordinary language biological kinds for which the revision might be sufficiently justified by some biological knowledge that it would somehow convey, though I am not convinced that there are such. Certainly there are many cases in which we change our views as to what higher level, scientifically defined, kinds familiar ordinary language kinds belong. But as in the case of whales and fish, whereas it is certainly of interest to recognize that whales are mammals, this fact has no bearing that I can see on whether they are fish. The majority of cases that come to mind are of just this kind. So, for instance, it is sometimes said that marsupial mice are not really mice. The point, of course, is that Australian mice are very distantly related to mice in most of the rest of the world. For the slightly more technical this reflects the divide between marsupial and placental mammals, and I take it that these kinds, unlike mice, certainly, are pure scientific imports. (Indeed I take it that while the notion of a marsupial is a fairly familiar one, many fewer people can correctly contrast it with a placental. Poststructuralists might note this as a case of an unmarked category—like male or white—which is invisible because assumed by default.) Since "mouse," on the contrary, is an ancient and well-entrenched term of ordinary language, the denial that marsupial mice are real mice is again based on an illegitimate interplay between categories of quite different kinds.

It may be that excessive scientism, whether among lexicographers, high school science teachers, or just regular folk, will continue to favor a continuing convergence between scientific and ordinary language taxonomies. If this is the case, it does not reflect a gradual Piercean convergence on some objective reality but, rather, the hegemonic power of one, sometimes imperialistic, method of knowledge production. Perhaps for most folk in the West such imperialism is relatively harmless; for most of us urban and suburban folk what we call organisms doesn't matter very much. And even for folk more intimately connected with nature, I do not suppose that adopting Western scientific modes of classification would be very damaging to their dealings with natural objects. Probably in those cases in which they would be damaging, folk will refuse to adopt them.

Nevertheless, there are reasons for resisting, or at least pointing out, this imperialism. With regard to its effects on Western culture, the main such reason is simply to resist the excesses of scientism. The achievements and successes of science are amply evident, but it is also important that human culture has aims and projects that are distinct from and incommensurable with those of science, and science does not hold the answer to every question of human interest. Quasi-scientific doctrines such as that whales have been discovered not to be fish help to obscure this point. With regard to our view of non-Western biological classification, this moral may be more important. Especially in relation to cultures with more regular and direct interaction with nature, we would do well to explore thoroughly the basis and function of such classifications before criticizing them for their nonconvergence on our own scientific categories. Once again, the perception of the value of Western science will hardly be enhanced by insisting on unsubstantiated claims to insight where this is not to be had.

## 14.4  Promiscuous Realism

I conclude this chapter with some brief remarks of a more purely philosophical character. Views about classification tend to assume a strictly dichotomous form. On the one hand, there is a strongly realist view.

Things belong to natural kinds, and it is part of the agenda of science to discover what these kinds are. Such a view is naturally, though not invariably, associated with essentialism: discovery of a natural kind involves discovering the essential property that qualifies a thing as a member of the kind. On the other hand, there are strong forms of constructivism. Kinds, on such views, are not natural but reflect grids imposed upon nature by humans. Nature is seen as amorphous until structure is imposed on it by us. It is generally assumed that such a view makes classification in some sense arbitrary. Perhaps there are human ends that favor one scheme of classification over another, but at any rate nature is equally amenable to any such scheme. I have advocated an intermediate view, however, which I have called promiscuous realism (Dupré 1981, 1993).

According to promiscuous realism, there are many, perhaps very many, possible ways of classifying naturally occurring objects that reflect real divisions among the objects. But not just any arbitrary classification will reflect real such divisions. Thus my position is realist, in that I insist that there is something in nature that legitimates a good set of classifications; in fact I see no harm in claiming that good classifications reflect natural kinds so long as the conception of natural kind in question is sharply separated from any connection with essentialism, and so long as it is recognized that a thing may belong to many different natural kinds. But the position also recognizes an ineliminable role for human classifiers in selecting a particular classification scheme from among the many licensed by natural similarities and differences. This selection will of course depend crucially on the purposes for which the classification is intended. Indeed it might be that relative to a particular purpose there is a uniquely best scheme of classification. What is excluded is that there should be a uniquely best system of classification for all purposes or, which comes to the same thing, independent of any particular purpose. The underlying philosophical view I have criticized as scientistic in preceding parts of this chapter is the view that science can be expected to provide just such a goal-independent set of classifications. The reason I reject this idea is not, as is generally supposed by constructivists, that nature provides no objective divisions between kinds but rather that it provides far too many. This is the promiscuity in the thesis of promiscuous realism.

Biology provides the central illustration of this view. Both scientific and extrascientific discourses provide a variety of different ways of classifying organisms. I argue that the classifications favored by science are distinguished from the rest not by their superior objectivity but simply by the specific, though various, goals that characterize scientific investigation of nature. If biological science could lay claim to a uniquely correct scheme of classification, it might be hard to resist the claim that this was in some sense *the* uniquely correct scheme for all purposes.[6] It is therefore important to the defense of promiscuous realism that there are good grounds for denying the existence of any such unique classificatory scheme even for biological science (see above, and for more detail, Dupré 1993, ch. 2, 1999). If different theoretical or practical scientific goals dictate different principles of classification, it is difficult to see why the various schemes of biological classification in ordinary language or in technical but nonscientific domains should not be accorded equal objective legitimacy.

Thus, finally, as well as misrepresenting in detail the scope of biological discovery, the denial that whales are fish propagates, in my view, bad philosophy. It reflects the assumption that inclusion of one kind within another can only reflect a positioning of the subordinate kind within a unique hierarchy of kinds, the hierarchy gradually being disclosed by biological science. But in fact there are many such partially overlapping and intersecting hierarchies. This situation would be usefully highlighted by the much more perspicuous claim that whales (and dolphins and porpoises) were mammalian fish.

Regrettably, I have had to admit that whales are not fish, for the sufficient reason that almost everyone in our culture, ignoring the partially excellent advice of Goldsmith, agrees not to call them so. Most folk assume, I take it, that biological kinds either fully include one another or are wholly disjoint. And thus since certainly not all mammals are fish (and vice versa), none can be. It would be futile and ridiculous for me to attempt a campaign for the reinstatement of whales into the realm of fish. Nevertheless, the recognition that there is no good reason for their having been excluded from this category would be salutary.

## Notes

1. A detailed defence of taxonomic pluralism is provided in Dupré (1999).

2. The equal legitimacy of scientific and folk biological classifications is also argued by Atran (1999), who also argues that scientific classifications are, in an important sense, grounded on an antecedent folkbiology. Atran bases the autonomy of folkbiology, in part, on an innate cognitive structure, a thesis about which I am rather more skeptical, however.

3. One classic study of folk classification argues that genera are the predominant level at which such classifications are made (Berlin, Breedlove, and Raven 1974). My impression is that the situation is much more varied for Western folk classifications, though this may very well reflect the more haphazard relations between contemporary urbanized people and the natural world.

4. This class is sometimes subdivided into two full classes, Selachii (sharks and rays) and Holocephali (rabbit-fishes, such as the grotesque *Chimaera.*)

5. I should note that this conclusion, as also the earlier one about whales, is quite independent of any special view about the nature of species.

6. I say it *might* be hard. Actually I am not at all sure it might not nevertheless be possible and desirable to resist this claim. It is widely assumed that chemistry has provided just such a uniquely best scheme for classifying kinds of stuff by reference to chemical structure. But there are purposes for which it would be quite wrong—legally and economically, for example—to classify diamonds and graphite together, despite both being forms of elemental carbon. In the other direction, an example that has been discussed in the philosophical literature is that of jade, which comes in two quite distinct chemical forms, jadeite and nephrite, which are not relevantly different in terms of their properties as semiprecious stones.

## References

Atran, S. 1998. Folk biology and the anthropology of science. *Behavioral and Brain Sciences* 21: 547–611.

Berlin, B., D. E. Breedlove, and P. H. Raven. 1974. *Principles of Tzeltal Plant Classification*. New York: Academic Press.

Dupré, J. 1981. Natural kinds and biological taxa. *Philosophical Review* 90: 66–90.

Dupré, J. 1993. *The Disorder of Things: Metaphysical Foundations of the Disunity of Science*. Cambridge: Harvard University Press.

Dupré, J. 1999. On the impossibility of a monistic account of species. In R. A. Wilson, ed., *Species: New Interdisciplinary Essays*, Cambridge: Cambridge University Press.

Ereshefsky, M. 1992. Eliminative pluralism. *Philosophy of Science* 59: 671–90.

Kitcher, P. 1984. Species. *Philosophy of Science* 51: 308–33.

Kripke, S. 1972. Naming and necessity. In D. Davidson and G. Harman, eds., *Semantics of Natural Language*. Dordrecht: Reidel.

Mishler, B. D., and M. J. Donoghue. 1982. Species concepts: A case for pluralism. *Systematic Zoology* 31: 491–503.

Putnam, H. 1975. The meaning of "Meaning." In *Mind, Language, and Reality. Philosophical Papers*, vol. 2. Cambridge: Cambridge University Press.

Sober, E. 1984. Sets, species, and evolution: Comments on Philip Kitcher's "Species." *Philosophy of Science* 51: 334–41.

# 15

## Interdisciplinary Dissonance

David L. Hull

We all know that those scholars whose work is genuinely interdisciplinary are the last hired and first fired in academia (Derricourt 1996: 9). Even so we keep repeating the mantra about the need for more interdisciplinary work to bridge the gaps between our overspecialized fields. Perhaps not all areas of intellectual activity can be unified into a single discipline, but unification when it is possible is a virtue.

One problem with interdisciplinary work is the standards by which it should be evaluated. Hard-liners insist that interdisciplinary work must meet the highest standards of all the disciplines to which it contributes. A philosopher writing on the cost of meiosis must meet the same high standards as a population geneticist who works exclusively on this topic, and the philosophy of any scientist who enters into a philosophical discussion had better be as sophisticated as that produced by a philosopher who has spent his entire career working in philosophy. Those of us who are more lenient are willing to give a little. For a philosopher, the evolutionary biology is not so bad, or for an anthropologist, the philosophy is sophisticated enough. The principle of linguistic charity should be applied to interdisciplinary work as well as to issues of meaning in general.

A second problem with interdisciplinary work is that people from different disciplines frequently have very different interests and values. Evolutionary biologists are not likely to modify their views of biological species because of the beliefs of ordinary folk. The converse inference is not so straightforward. We live in the scientific age. In a host of ways, science takes precedence to other activities. We spend considerable time educating our children to think "scientifically," even if it means abandoning cherished ideas. Many children are taught in Sunday school that

God created all species of plants and animals 10,000 years ago in the Garden of Eden, but when these students take courses in biology, they are taught that species have evolved over long stretches of time. Similarly various sorts of ordinary folk perceive plants and animals as belonging to species that do not always coincide with those of professional systematists. One of the central problems in this volume is what to do when different disciplines conflict or when professional opinions differ from those of ordinary people.

One way out of this apparent conflict is to reject interdisciplinary work. Pluralism is preferable to unification. Interdisciplinary work is downright evil. Biologists, various peoples around the world, and protestant creationists have their own species concepts, and no inferences can be drawn from one area to another. Biological species evolve, folk species are Aristotelian, and creationist species are eternal and immutable. There are no contradictions here because no one is talking about the same things. For those who take this alternative, this chapter will contain nothing of interest because in it I assume that interdisciplinary work is not only possible but also valuable. People working in different disciplines can learn from each other in the absence of reduction.

Several of the authors in this volume have produced bodies of work that are genuinely interdisciplinary, combining anthropology, evolutionary biology, cognitive psychology, history of science, and even philosophy. In this chapter I compare the views about species of plants and animals expressed by three of the contributors to this volume: an evolutionary biologist (Michael Ghiselin), an anthropologist (Scott Atran), and a philosopher (John Dupré). The purpose of this exercise is to see what sorts of enlightenment interdisciplinary work can provide and how differences of opinion among scholars of such diverse backgrounds, interests, and standards can be reconciled.

Unfortunately, these comparisons turn out not to be strictly parallel. Biology and anthropology are both sciences and as such share certain basic beliefs. Ghiselin is interested in species as the things that evolve, Atran is interested in the groupings of plants and animals produced by various folk around the world, but both men support their interpretations by reference to evidence. If biologists discover that selection does not play a major role in evolution, then Ghiselin is in trouble. Similarly Atran's investigations of native peoples led him to successively modify his stand on folk taxonomy. Because evolutionary biology and ethnobiology are scientific disciplines, the issue of interdisciplinary work is limited at least to science.

But Ghiselin and Atran also deal with problems that have traditionally been considered the province of philosophers. Ghiselin's contrast between spatiotemporally localized entities (individuals) and the sorts of classes that function in natural regularities has been a staple of philosophy for the past two thousand years, and Atran sets out a philosophical view that clearly has its origins in Aristotle. Ghiselin and Atran are engaged not only in science but also in philosophy. Dupré in turn is a philosopher, not a scientist. He is not interested in species for their own sake but rather in the implications that they have for Hilary Putnam's principle of the division of linguistic labor. According to Putnam (1975), ordinary language evolves by means of various sorts of experts emerging and taking control of certain areas of intellectual endeavor, including cooking, forestry, ballroom dancing, and the like. According to Putnam, nonexperts should defer to the linguistic usage of these experts when conflicts arise. Dupré is primarily concerned to reject this philosophical principle.

Neither evolutionary biologists nor cultural anthropologists are in total agreement over the basics of their respective fields. Even so, stereotypes of evolutionary biologists and cultural anthropologists can be discussed with some profit, but we philosophers are such a heterogeneous lot that terming anyone a "philosopher" imparts almost no information. The most that I can say is that we deal with such "fundamental" issues as the mind-body problem, free will, determinism, and so on. Nothing can be said about the *methods* that we use. Some of us, especially philosophers of science, take the findings of science very seriously; most philosophers do not. For example, philosophers who know no physics whatsoever happily teach courses on space and time. A phenomenologist's view of space and time is quite different from that of a physicist.

Some philosophers take linguistic usage very seriously. They are interested in following out all the implications of a particular language, whether that language is the esoteric language used by cognitive psychologists or one of the more common dialects spoken by ordinary people. One group of philosophers in the recent past have labeled their program "ordinary language philosophy"—a period that Marjorie Grene (1995: 55) wickedly terms the "Bertie Wooster season in philosophy." In the early years of this movement, ordinary language philosophers sought to solve or, at least, dissolve traditional philosophical problems by reference to ordinary language. Many, possibly all, philosophical problems arise when philosophers misuse ordinary language. For example, in most cases, when people say that they "know" something, they do not think that they are infallible. "Yes, I know which train to take to the Arsenal stop on the Victoria Line, but I could be mistaken." However, so ordinary language philosophers claim, traditional philosophers have introduced endless confusion by running together the various ways in which ordinary people use the term "know" with one particular and peculiar philosophical usage.

The main sticking point for ordinary language philosophy has been problems about what precisely counts as "ordinary" language. One might think that whatever dialects or idiolects ordinary people happen to speak count as ordinary language. If so, then the literature in ethnobiology should be of central interest to ordinary language philosophers, but such is not the case. Rarely, if ever, do ordinary language philosophers do the sort of empirical research necessary to find out about the wide variety of uses common in various sectors of any language community. Nor do they seem to be especially interested in the work of others who do. Instead, ordinary language has evolved into a highly esoteric and intricate language invented by ordinary language philosophers, a language that is anything but ordinary.

Other philosophers take "intuition" very seriously. At bottom, the only way that a philosopher can choose between different positions is according to his or her own intuitions, and some philosophers have much better intuitions than others. "How can you tell?" I just can. If depending ultimately on intuitions were not depressing enough, most philosophers rarely mention the criteria that they use in philosophical inquiries. If scientists depend on one cluster of methods and philosophers depend on a different cluster of methods, comparing the results of these two endeavors might well be difficult, but not impossible. Ghiselin and Atran are sufficiently clear about how we are to judge their *scientific* work, but none of the three authors in this volume whose work I am comparing say very much about how we are to evaluate their more *philosophical* claims. In this chapter, I try to extract the methods that these three authors use in justifying their philosophical preferences. The issue of interdisciplinary work within the confines of science is difficult enough. When one of the disciplines is philosophy, difficulties are only magnified.

At bottom, the chief point of disagreement between Ghiselin, Atran, and Dupré is the relative priority of certain ways of conceptualizing the living world. Ghiselin leans toward a scientific perspective, while Atran and Dupré lean more toward the conceptions of ordinary people. According to anthropologists such as Atran, evolutionary biologists are just one more exotic tribe on a par with all other peoples. Dupré in turn stands up for all those people who speak ordinary English against the onslaught of the scientific juggernaut. In this connection Atran is in somewhat of a bind. He himself is a professional scientist, albeit a scientist who investigates nonprofessional scientists. As scientists, anthropologists have developed their own jargon that differs significantly from the dialects of their subjects. Anthropologists are no more inclined to give up their own conceptual systems in the face of differences with their subjects than evolutionary biologists are likely to change their technical vocabulary to make it accord with the languages spoken by ordinary people.

## 15.1 Evolutionary Biology

Michael Ghiselin has contributed to a wide spectrum of disciplines, from the biology of nudibranchs to evolutionary theory, economics, cognitive psychology, history of science, and philosophy. What does he think species are? For well over two thousand years, species have been construed in the West to be kinds. Kinds have been treated in a wide variety of ways and distinguished from particulars in almost as many different ways, yet few topics in the past two millennia have been treated in as univocal a way as the metaphysical status of biological species. They are kinds. To use contemporary logical terms, an organism is a member of its species. Periodically a biologist has questioned this consensus, but not until Ghiselin began beating his contemporaries over the head with a two-by-four did the message get through. After a couple of decades of debate, a new consensus seems to have emerged (Wilson 1996). Species as the things that evolve are not kinds but individuals. An organism is *part* of its species, not a *member*.

From the preceding discussion of Ghiselin's work, the interdisciplinary character of his radical solution to the species problem is clear. The metaphysical distinction between kinds and individuals plays as big a role in his discussion as do the details of the evolutionary process. On one reading all Ghiselin is arguing is that given the traditional distinction between kinds and individuals, we have had one of our examples wrong. Species do not belong in the metaphysical category "kind" but in the complementary metaphysical category "individual." On this weak interpretation Ghiselin did not rework philosophical categories but took them for granted. Species as the things that evolve have more of the characteristics of individuals than of kinds.

As "weak" as this interpretation may be, it is still quite an accomplishment to change people's minds on such a basic and pervasive issue. Many scholars, especially philosophers, find such a conceptual shift with respect to species too difficult. They were raised at their mother's knee to think in a particular way, and that is that. To them conceptualizing species as individuals is too counterintuitive. They also see all sorts of implications of this position that strike them as unacceptable. For example, if species are individuals, then no laws of nature can make uneliminable reference to species as taxa. It may well be true that armadillos always give birth to quadruplets, but this regularity cannot count as a law of nature akin to the laws of Newton, Boyle, Darwin, Mendel, and Einstein.

To me, at least, this implication seems perfectly acceptable. Whatever laws of nature may be, they do not include the millions of correlations that biologists have found with respect to taxa. However, even if we accept Ghiselin's position, biology is not totally bereft of laws. Statements about species taxa are not candidates for laws, but if we go up a level to the species category itself, laws are still possible. For example, the role of peripheral isolation in the formation of new species may be lawful. The process of character displacement may also lend itself to a characterization in terms of laws. With respect to these putative laws, particular species are instances.

Some evolutionary biologists agree with Ghiselin that species should be treated as the things that evolve but disagree with him about what this position entails. For example, the spatiotemporal character of species follows from the role of selection in evolution. If species evolve via natural selection, then they must be individuals. If, however, selection does not play the major role in the evolutionary process that Ghiselin thinks that it does, then species as the things that evolve need not be treated as individuals, though they still may. The role of natural selection in evolution is sufficient for treating species as individuals but not necessary. Other possible mechanisms might have this same implication for the ontological status of species.

But Ghiselin's species concept is not the only species concept loose in the the biological community. Some of these species concepts are compatible with species being individuals, some not. Here the differences arise from the heterogeneous character of biology. Perhaps a complete unification of biology into a single conceptual system is a long-term goal, but until that golden day arrives, biologists are forced to live with disparate species concepts. Different areas of biology require dividing up nature in different ways. Evolutionary theory requires genealogical kinds, while the science of form needs kinds that have no genealogical dimension. All of this variation in goals and needs has led some philosophers to suggest that biology is not a single discipline but many (Wilson 1996: 315; see also chapter 14, this volume).

On a stronger interpretation, Ghiselin is attempting something more ambitious—he intends to contribute not just to evolutionary biology but more generally to philosophy. For example, in his early paper on species, Ghiselin (1974) notes one philosophical implication of taking species to be individuals. The reality of species has always been argued in the context of kinds. Realists argue that kinds really do exist out there in nature. They lay in wait for us to discover them. Nominalists, to the contrary, think that nature has no joints to be discovered. We can impose any sort of classification that we please on a nature that is as seamless as gruel. Ghiselin (1974: 542) argues that on his proposal the preceding debate is otiose. If species are not kinds, then all the controversy about the reality of kinds is irrelevant to the reality of species. The issue for Ghiselin is the reality of individuals. Do individuals really exist? Are there "natural" individuals?

Since the publication of his seminal paper, Ghiselin has continued to discuss the ontological status of species and has addressed issues that are properly termed "philosophical." For example, a common complaint raised by philosophers with respect to the entire discussion about species as individuals is that the distinction between kinds and individuals is too simple. A much more sophisticated system of metaphysical categories is needed.[1] At the very least, so certain philosophers have complained, Ghiselin needs to pay attention to such traditional philosophical distinctions as count nouns versus mass nouns, classes versus properties, extensionally defined sets versus intensionally defined classes, and so on. In his chapter in this volume, Ghiselin only touches on such broad philosophical issues (e.g., his discussion of "componential sortals"). He addresses these issues much more extensively in *Metaphysics and the Origin of Species* (1997). His philosophical views must be evaluated in the same ways that all philosophical theses are evaluated—whatever these ways may be.

With respect to the subject of this volume, Ghiselin notes that early systematists no doubt took "existing folk classifications as a starting point for developing something rather different." The hierarchical classifications that anthropologists have discerned in a variety of cultures crudely approximate the Linnean hierarchy of professional systematists. However, according to Ghiselin, the claim that folk classifications and the classifications produced by professional systematists approximate each other is based on two serious mistakes. First, anthropologists acknowledge a certain amount of variation in folk classifications but neglect to mention that comparable differences of opinion exist among professional systematists. Instead, anthropologists treat the scientific species concept as if it were univocal, when it is anything but. The real comparison should be among the various classifications and species concepts of ordinary folk, on the one hand, and the equally extensive variety of classifications and species concepts urged on us by professional systematists, on the other hand.

When the issue is the concordance between folk species and the species of professional systematists, anthropologists tend to have phenetic species in mind, as if virtually all systematists adhered to the principles of numerical phenetics. Although no one has any hard figures on the topic, my best guess is that, of the various general views of systematics currently extant, phenetics comes in a poor third after cladistics and evolutionary systematics. If ethnobiologists are really interested in similarities and differences between folk classifications and those of professional systematists, they need to expand their studies to include the most prevalent views among biologists about species. Atran does just this for evolutionary taxonomy (see Atran 1998).

However, Ghiselin maintains that neither professional systematists nor ordinary people have been all that consistent through the years in how they have viewed species. Sometimes they have treated species as individuals and sometimes as kinds. For example, ordinary people agree with professional systematists that males and females belong in the same species with each other and their progeny no matter how much they might differ in their appearance. They are part of a genealogical nexus. Yet both professional systematists and ordinary people have also viewed species as composed of organisms exhibiting a certain degree of morphological similarity with each other and morphological gaps between them and other closely related species. The major sticking point is what to do when genealogy does not accord nicely with similarity. Evolutionary biologists have excellent reasons to give priority to genealogy. How about ordinary people?

Anthropologists raised the issue of possible correspondences among various folk classifications. Biologists are the ones who raised the issue of any additional correspondence (or lack thereof) between folk classification and those produced by professional systematists. This second issue first arose in connection with the work of Ernst Mayr, the father of the biological species concept. In the 1930s, while studying the birds of New Guinea, Mayr discovered that the woodsmen and hunters of a particular tribe in the Arfak Mountains recognized 136 of the 137 species that he, a trained ornithologist, recognized (Mayr, Linsley, and Usinger 1953: 5; Mayr 1963: 17).

Thirty years later, Jared Diamond repeated this exercise for one North Fore village in the New Guinea Highlands with much the same result. Of the 120 species that he recognized, local people recognized 110. In 93 cases there was a one-to-one correspondence between the two. Diamond (1966: 1104) reasoned from this strong correlation to the reality of species. The argument seemed to be that if two such disparate groups of people as European systematists and the local people of New Guinea recognize the same groups of birds, then this distinction is unlikely to be a function of some similarity in their social backgrounds but really must be out there in nature. Species really exist.

However, both the preceding studies and the conclusion about the reality of species need to be examined a bit more carefully. The correlations claimed by Mayr and Diamond concern what Mayr terms "non-dimensional" species, that is, species extended only minimally in space and time, such as the crows in my valley in my lifetime. If species are viewed as being extended extensively in space so that the same species of crow might live in Indiana and Indonesia, correlations between folk species and those of professional systematists are greatly reduced. If species are also viewed as being extended in time so that the elephants that Hannibal dragged over the Alps can belong to the same species as those in my local zoo, these correlations are even less neat and clean.

But regardless of how much concordance exists between species recognized by ordinary folk and by professional systematists, the issue of the reality of species remains. One general principle in logic is that if heads I win, then tails I have to lose. That is, if a particular state of affairs confirms my hypothesis, then the opposite state of affairs must count against it. Diamond was willing to reason from the agreement between his recognition of species and those of the local people to the reality of species. Now, what if he had discovered a strong *dis*cordance between the species he recognized and those of the local people? Would he had concluded that species are not real? I strongly doubt it. Hence the form of this argument seems to be, heads I win, tails I don't lose—a nice game if you can sucker others into playing it with you.

In sum, Ghiselin urges his ontological views on other *biologists* because of the increased coherence that this perspective brings to the biological literature, especially in evolutionary biology. Anything like direct evidence is very difficult to bring to bear on such deep philosophical issues. No crucial experiments are possible. Ghiselin (1998) does claim that everyone routinely distinguishes between individuals and kinds. He

(1998) also notes that children are better able to think in terms of families than in terms of abstract classes. "Genealogy is part of every normal human being's daily routine." People may well not conceive of species as individuals, but when they attempt to classify etiologically, it is more reasonable to assume that both perspectives have always been "viable alternatives."

None of the preceding observations provide very strong evidence for Ghiselin's position. All of these claims could be mistaken and not put his individuality thesis into much jeopardy. His thesis stands or falls on its integration into contemporary evolutionary biology, not on the way that ordinary people may or may not conceive of species. Nor does Ghiselin insist that all people, no matter where or when, *must* view species as individuals. He argues that evolutionary biologists must, but that is all. In fact, for most people, treating species as individuals is strongly counterintuitive. But our intuitions "all too often lead us astray" (p. 16). Our intuitions lead us astray if by "species" we mean the things that evolve. They may be very dependable with respect to things like all the crows in my valley.

## 15.2   Anthropology

Are species cross-cultural universals? As the literature in ethnobiology has proceeded on this topic, the positions urged have grown progressively weaker. The initial hypothesis was that species as taxa are cross-cultural universals. Ordinary people in different cultures make roughly the same cuts when it comes to species of plants and animals. Correlations with respect to higher taxa are not nearly so tight. After additional investigations, ethnobiologists have modified their position so that it applies only to species of relatively large, phenomenally salient organisms, especially if they are of importance to the local people. But even among this tiny percentage of organisms, agreement among people living in different societies is not as tight as one might like.

When we turn from ordinary people to systematists, the story changes appreciably. Atran (1990) restructured the debate over species by limiting himself to Mayr's nondimensional species (Atran 1990: 12). If one follows a species throughout its geographic range or through time, the borders between closely related species blur appreciably. However, at any one location, usually only a single species of a genus is present. Hence at any one locale these generic species are easy to distinguish. Thus, according to Atran, the appropriate contrast is between the non-dimensional species recognized by trained systematists and the generic species recognized by ordinary people.

Although this move does significantly improve the correlation under discussion, it has one unfortunate consequence: species taxa cannot possibly be cross-cultural universals. If the notion of nondimensional species is taken seriously, no professional systematist can claim that organisms living in different locations belong to the same nondimensional species. Perhaps ordinary folk as they visit relatives in nearby valleys are willing to recognize birds in the two valleys as belonging to the same species (as they conceive of species), but professional systematists cannot.

In sum, as far as species as taxa are concerned, ethnobiologists continue to disagree about how extensive the overlap is both among folk species and between folk species and the species recognized by professional systematists. If ethnobiologists limit themselves to nondimensional species, then the concordance between species recognized by local folk and the nondimensional species of any systematist that might happen to wander into their locale is greatly increased. However, this increase in concordance is purchased at a serious price: nondimensional species can occur only in a single location. The crows living in my valley cannot possibly belong to the same nondimensional species as the crows living in your valley, no matter how similar they might be, no matter if these crows on occasion happen to fly from valley to valley to mate.

Difficulties in finding correlations among folk species forced Atran to move up a metaphysical level to the level of "categories," namely to the level of species as the class of all species. Perhaps species *taxa* are not cultural universals, but the species *category* itself is. According to Atran, all people share a strong tendency to classify living creatures hierarchically, to believe that something internal to organisms makes them into the kinds of organisms they are (in Aristotelian terms, their "essence"), and to treat the species level as being more "real" than other levels in the hierarchy:

... cultures across the world organize readily perceptible organisms into a system of hierarchical levels that are designed to represent the embedded structure of life around us, with generic-species level being the most informative (Atran et al. 1998: 6).

The purpose of Atran's paper with Paul Estin, John Coley, and Douglas Medin is to test this group of interrelated hypotheses. Do college students raised in rural Michigan treat generic species in the same way as do the Itzaj Maya of the Peten rain forest? Atran et al. use the alacrity with which their subjects are willing to make inductive inferences to discover which levels of the taxonomic hierarchy are psychologically privileged. Although Atran et al. found that life-form categories are inductively stronger for industrialized Americans (college students raised in rural Michigan) than for the Itzaj Maya adults living in a small-scale subsistence society, both groups treat generic species as being most privileged as far as making inductive inferences are concerned.

As in the case of Ghiselin, Atran is not just a narrow specialist. To be sure, he counts as a professional ethnobiologist, but he has also published extensively in history and philosophy of science. In his *Cognitive Foundation of Natural History: Towards an Anthropology of Science* (1990), he argues for a fundamental epistemological thesis about knowledge acquisition that applies to scientists and to nonscientists alike. According to Atran, theory-neutral generic species are both epistemologically and temporally prior to any "theories" that people (including scientists) might develop to explain the apparent similarities and differences between these generic species. As he characterizes this thesis, the "very possibility of such theorizing would not exist if generic species were not present to provide the trans-theoretical basis for scientific speculation about the biological world" (Atran et al., p. 5).

More generally, the cognitive structures of ordinary conceptual domains not only constrain the initial elaboration of the corresponding fields but in addition, by doing so, render them possible (Atran, p. 2; see also Atran, pp. 11, 24). Atran postulates the existence of something he terms "common sense" that is indubitable because it is "restricted to the manifestly visible dimensions of the everyday world, that is, to *phenomenal* reality" (Atran 1990: 3). The phenomenal world of ordinary human experience, in turn, refers only to the "cognitive 'givens' of our species"

(p. xi), "the 'bare' facts of common sense" (p. 6). In this respect, "certain basic notions in science are more hostage to the dictates of common sense than the other way around" (Atran, p. 47). However, common sense is not all-powerful. Sometimes, with almost superhuman effort, we can "transcend" it (Atran, p. 12).

As the discussion in the preceding two paragraphs clearly indicates, Atran has switched from science to philosophy. He brings lots of evidence to bear on his *scientific* views, but how are we to evaluate his *philosophical* views? Scientists are very strongly predisposed to a combination of two philosophical views commonly referred to as "empiricism" and "inductivism." Real scientists must begin with indubitable facts and nothing but indubitable facts, and only after the massive accumulation of such facts are scientists warranted in "speculating" about more general features of the world. This highly inductive interpretation of science remains extremely popular among scientists to the present. Most recently numerical pheneticists (Sneath and Sokal 1973), pattern cladists (Nelson and Platnick 1981), and ideal morphologists (Webster and Goodwin 1996) have championed such a view.

I know how to evaluate the scientific work of scientists when they are engaged in science, but the evaluation of their philosophical tenets is a good deal more problematic. Certain groups of scientists are strongly predisposed to a combination of inductivism and empiricism, while professional philosophers almost to the person not only reject this philosophical view but do so with derision. Although the existence of indubitable phenomenal givens looked promising to some philosophers a couple of generations ago, this promise was never realized. No one has been able to come up with a single example of such indubitable phenomenal givens that satisfies even the most enthusiastic supporters of this philosophical research program, let alone its critics (Earman 1993: 13). But just because the brightest philosophers who have ever lived failed in their attempts to elucidate a particular philosophical view does not mean that Atran must also fail.

A common argument form turns on self-reference. If all universal claims are false, then so is this one. In response to the claim by social relativists that we are all forced to hold the beliefs that we do by our social upbringing, the obvious reply is, so is this belief. If social constructivists can rise above their social upbringing, then so can others. A similar argument applies to Atran. In his own investigations did Atran actually begin with phenomenal givens and hold off "speculating" about them until he has accumulated massive numbers of such givens? I have read quite a few of Atran's papers and have been able to find only a very few examples of anything that might be considered indubitable phenomenal givens (e.g., grass is green). Perhaps the masses of Atran's phenomenal givens remain buried in his field notes, or possibly he himself has not bothered to discern and record the foundations on which all knowledge is based, including his own.[2]

In sum, the strongest part of Atran's work is the data that he brings to bear on his scientific claims. Not only does he use the data gathered by others, but also he himself is willing to get his own hands dirty. In the absence of research in ethnobiology, we would all remain ignorant of folk classifications, and the absence of such knowledge would be a great loss. The problem is to find some reason to accept Atran's more philosophical views, such as his belief in the indubitable phenomenal givens that underlie all the "theorizing" that comprises science.

Some scientists claim that scientific concepts are more fundamental than those drawn from any other area of human endeavor. Their slogan seems to be "science *über alles.*" Atran agrees that one set of concepts underlies all others, but for him these concepts are philosophical, not scientific. His slogan seems to be "phenomenal givens *über alles.*" Both Ghiselin (1998) and Dupré (1998) agree that scientific classifications are in some sense "grounded" in antecedent folk classifications, but Ghiselin (1998) objects to Atran endowing the "genome with something like a textbook of Aristotelian philosophy, complete with intuition as the fundamental source of knowledge." And Dupré (1998) is skeptical of Atran's claim that all human beings share an "innate cognitive structure."

## 15.3 Philosophy

Anyone taken aback by the numerous "schools" that exist in science, whether in systematics or ethnobiology, is likely to be dismayed at the even more numerous schools of philosophy. To make matters worse, philosophers and scientists have pooled their efforts in setting out methods for evaluating scientific claims, while no one has been all that vocal about ways in which philosophical claims are to be evaluated. This unfortunate situation can be seen in Dupré's contribution to this volume. Dupré's main contention in chapter 14 is that scientific usage, contrary to Putnam (1975), need not and should not supersede all other usages, including various sorts of ordinary usage. His primary example is whales.

Because of Dupré's repeated reference to "ordinary language" and his recourse to dictionaries, one might suspect that he is an advocate of some sort of ordinary language philosophy—not "ordinary language philosophy" as it has become in the etiolated hands of English dons, but "ordinary language" in a robust, literal sense. For example, in connection with the issue of whether whales are fish or mammals, Dupré apologizes for not doing a "historical study" of the ways in which "whale" and "fish" have been used in the past. Instead, he makes recourse to dictionaries of the English language (the whale/fish issue has a long history; e.g., Whewell 1840: 1: 456).

In an early paper on natural kinds and biological taxa, Dupré (1981: 65–76) argued that whales are fish and not, as scientific imperialists would have us believe, mammals. Apparently, this observation met with a storm of protest. As a result Dupré has been reluctantly forced to "admit that whales are not fish, for the sufficient reason that almost everyone in our culture ... agrees to call them so" (p. 18). At times Dupré (1998) does not sound quite so egalitarian as he observes that "now almost all educated people are quite confident that whales aren't fish. And this, I now think, is enough to show that they are right that whales aren't fish."

With respect to the whale example, Dupré has given in. Since scientists have forced almost everyone in our culture, in particular, educated people, into thinking that whales are not fish, then Dupré is willing to concede that whales are not fish. Even so, Dupré still retains his antipathy to scientific imperialism with respect to ordinary language. "Whale" and "fish" used to have a perfectly good usage in ordinary language, and ordinary English has been impoverished by the change foisted upon us by scientists.

With respect to this issue, I am of two minds. Many, probably most, of the distinctions made by scientists are of little or no concern to ordinary people. I see no reason to laden ordinary discourse with all these distinctions. For example, the term "work" occurs both in physics and in ordinary English. According to the scientific usage, someone who carries a heavy box up a flight of stairs is engaged in work, but if he carries it across the floor, he is not! Clearly we need a notion of work that departs from the technical usage in physics. Similarly botanists have a technical conception of fruit that departs significantly from ordinary usage. According to botanists all sorts of things are "fruit," including tomatoes. Should we abandon our ordinary use of "fruit" for the scientific usage? I see no reason why. The two terms have very different but equally legitimate uses. We need some word to refer to the things that we are inclined to put in a fruit cocktail even if all of them are not technically "fruit." With respect to this thesis, I find myself in total agreement with Dupré.

However, I think that all languages, including ordinary languages, are in need of constant reformulation, and science is only one source of these changes. The sort of academic dialect that I use in conversing with my colleagues has been "enriched" in the past decade or so with all sorts of terms from computer science. Some jar with my own idiolect; most do not. Macintosh windows are not "windows" as far as I am concerned, but no one else seems to care about my preferences in these matters. When I was in school, I was taught never to split an infinitive. As far as I can tell, the current rule is to always split infinitives—as I just did.

But not all changes are so benign. "Unique" used to be unique. As it has come to mean "rare," no substitute for the original usage has arisen. The loss is significant, The distinction between "that" and "which" is disappearing. Even the contrast between "who" and "whom" is going by the boards. I don't like it, but future generations will not care in the least. The only trace of previous uses will be in old unread books (the old canon) and references in dictionaries to "archaic" usage.

The point of all the preceding is that all sorts of forces produce changes in ordinary English. It is a hodgepodge of old and new uses. Try as we might, we cannot stem such changes. With great effort, we can consciously direct the course of language here and there, such as substituting "Down syndrome" for "mongoloid." The most significant effort in recent history to improve English has been motivated by social sensitivity as we replace such offensive terms as "mailman" and "Oriental." But in general, as the French have discovered, languages have lives of their own.

As people discover what condition "Down syndrome" refers to, this term accumulates the same negative connotations that the old, offensive term possessed, and the name must be changed again, this time to "twenty-one trisomy." A similar changing of names can be found with respect to undertakers, janitors, and garbage collectors. Changing language may change society to some extent, but not much.

Dupré mentions all sorts of concerns that influence language. For example, bird watchers, wild flower enthusiasts, furriers, timber-merchants, and herbalists all develop the vocabularies that they need. Of all the various forces that produce linguistic change, Dupré selects science for special condemnation, but I fail to see what is wrong with languages evolving and why the influence of science on languages is so special. Dupré and I were taught significantly different languages as children. As he was brought up in England, "clever" had no negative connotations, but for many Americans it does. So? In addition the English think that their version of English is more basic or more correct than other versions. For their part, Americans tend to smile at this conviction with some degree of superiority, knowing that our usage will eventually win out by sheer force of numbers and dollars.

To return to the whale example, scientists are very far from having won this particular battle. Several senses of "animal," "fish," and "mammal" remain in ordinary English. For several years, a TV series about a boy and his dolphin was introduced by this budding pedant informing a friend that Flipper is not a fish but an animal. That this claim gives most of us no pause indicates that the relevant scientific distinctions have yet to be assimilated in their entirety by the general public. Time and again people contrast people with animals, as if we were not animals. If Dupré objects to whales being termed mammals, then he must be even more irate at people being called animals.

Of course anthropologists such as Atran are interested in how people actually use the terms they employ. I have no problems here. I can also identify with the anxiety that anthropologists feel about the massive "pollution" that is going on with respect to various native peoples. Their customs and languages are as endangered as the snail darter and spotted owl. That anthropologists themselves are one factor in this pollution makes the problem especially poignant. From a philosophical perspective, I fail to see why Dupré treats the hodgepodge commonly known as ordinary English with such deference.

Dupré makes an occasional reference to dictionaries. For example, he has the "strong intuition that dolphins and porpoises are not whales," and he supports this intuition by reference to Webster's dictionary. I can see why I should pay attention to dictionaries when I am interested in linguistic usage. I am also committed to taking seriously the results of extensive empirical investigations into usage of the sort carried out by Atran. One goal of dictionaries is to chronicle the vicissitudes of linguistic usage, but like it or not, dictionaries must be updated periodically. We can no more stop social, cultural, and linguistic change in their tracks than we can stop biological evolution. Even influencing the direction of this change is extremely difficult, probably in most cases impossible. Like it or not, languages continue to evolve, and science is a factor, but only one factor, in this change.

However, the ultimate evaluative term in Dupré's dialect is "intuition." If Dupré were an ordinary language philosopher in the technical sense, then the intuitions of those people who have internalized this highly technical and esoteric language are worth something. Just as all triangles have three sides in the context of euclidean geometry, "know" is a success term in certain philosophical systems. Linguistic intuitions count for something within a particular linguistic context, but Dupré mentions no particular context in which his intuitions function. As best as I can tell, the context for his linguistic intuitions is ordinary English, but ordinary English is too complicated, not to mention downright messy, to support very many intuitions. Given the idiosyncrasies of our linguistic upbringing, Dupré has his intuitions, I have mine, and that is pretty much that.

When Ghiselin began to wonder whether species are best viewed as individuals or classes, I doubt that he was in the least inclined to look up these terms in a dictionary. Even if he had, he would not have felt bound by the various definitions that he found there. Dictionaries register various past and current uses. Ghiselin was not interested in registering accepted usage but attempting to *change* it. One reason why Ghiselin is not in the least enamored of anything that might be termed ordinary language or linguistic intuitions is that he has spent the last thirty years urging a decidedly counterintuitive position on species, first, on evolutionary biologists and then on a much larger audience. Time and again, he was met with the objection "But that just don't sound right."

One of the most important functions of intellectual activity, in particular, science, is to *change* what sounds right. Some people believe that all truth has been known for a long time, usually set out in some great book whether it was authored by Aristotle or God, but for those of us who think that we can increase our understanding of the world in which we live, we must be prepared to change our minds even about deeply held beliefs. Common sense, intuitions, and ordinary usage do not have to be mistaken all the time, but at least sometimes they are. The claim that species are individuals certainly runs counter to ordinary usage. It also seriously challenges common sense. I take neither of these observations to count in the least against Ghiselin's claim.

### 15.4   Summary Evaluation

Ghiselin, Atran, and Dupré all discuss species of plants and animals. Is there anything to be learned by similarities and differences in the methodologies that they use and the conclusions that they reach? Some claims are unproblematically empirical and can be tested by the sorts of procedures perfected by scientists. For example, Ghiselin claims that in the context of evolutionary theory, species must be treated as spatiotemporally localized individuals. Fairly direct evidence can be brought to bear on the role of selection in evolution. However, the most powerful support that Ghiselin's conceptual reformation can receive is any increased internal coherence it can bring to evolutionary biology. If those evolutionary biologists who use his metaphysical reformulation produce simpler, more powerful versions of evolutionary theory, then this success is as definitive a consideration as can be brought to bear on the subject.

Atran's claim that all people recognize generic species is straightforwardly empirical, and Atran has set himself the task of testing it. But mixed in with these empirical claims are assertions that are not in any straightforward sense empirical. For example, Atran reiterates his belief that generic species provide the transtheoretical basis for scientific speculation about the biological world and that, in the absence of generic species, theorizing about the biological world would be impossible (see chapter 6, this volume). The work that would be required to test this claim would be massive. In addition the opportunities for introducing ad hoc hypotheses would be extensive. Once again, the strongest support that Atran's theory can receive flows from the increased coherence and power that it brings to anthropology.

Some of the claims that Dupré makes about ordinary usage are empirical. He thought that support for the claim that whales are fish was widespread. He discovered that apparently it was not. But Dupré does not think of himself as being totally hostage to usage. Instead, intuitions are the ultimate arbiters. The question then becomes the source and justification of these intuitions. If these intuitions are purely idiosyncratic, then I see no reason why I or anyone else should pay them much attention. If they stem from a general, well-formulated philosophical worldview, then they have more force depending on how well this worldview has stood up to criticism. Unfortunately, right now in the history of philosophy, worldviews are very definitely out of fashion. Instead, we work here and there on bits and pieces. Hence this source of justification is denied us.

Dupré does not offer his readers much in the way of hints as to how he can justify his claims. Reference to "intuition" serves only to name the problem, not solve it. In this respect he is far from alone. Previously I referred to self-reference. If all universal claims are false, then so is this one. I am a philosopher. If one of the glaring omissions in philosophy is the failure to show how philosophical claims might be justified, then this is as much of a problem for me as it is for any other philosopher, and I am just as obligated to say something on this score, no matter how unsatisfactory.

One thing that a philosopher can do is to set out the basic assumptions of a particular technical endeavor. If species evolve in the way that most evolutionary biologists say that they do, then they cannot fulfill the requirements of the philosophical notion "kind." Another is to compare different disciplines to uncover certain regularities in how the practitioners think. For example, operationism has arisen sequentially in time in physics, psychology, and systematics. One thing that a philosopher can do is to set out as clearly as possible the fate of this view in previous incarnations so that later enthusiasts can come to see what likely outcomes lay in store for them. Atran's indubitable facts of common sense is another example of the sort of philosophical view that can be evaluated by reference to its past track record.

Another possibility is for philosophers to interpret their philosophical claims to be as empirical as possible and test them accordingly. Maybe evidence cannot be brought to bear all that directly on philosophical claims, but with effort some indirect tests are possible. For example, if Kuhn is right and paradigms are incommensurable, then scientists who adhere to different paradigms should have a harder time communicating with each other than with scientists who adhere to the same paradigm. Do they? If not, then perhaps incommensurability thesis may well be wrong. In order to test this view, some way has to be found to decide which scientists adhere to which paradigm and how successful they are in communicating with each other, but these are the sorts of problems that accompany any attempt at empirical testing.

Another way to test philosophical claims is to get a group of workers (e.g., scientists) to understand and adopt your view and see what happens. If these workers are more successful in fulfilling the goals of their discipline, then possibly your philosophical view has something going for them. If, to the contrary, their work grinds to a halt, maybe this philosophical thesis is mistaken. Both Atran and Ghiselin have adopted this strategy (whether consciously or not). Each has convinced other scientists to incorporate his views into their own work. The rest of us can then see what the effects of these incorporations turn out to be. I am not familiar enough with the fields that Atran's views have influenced to guess at either the extent or the effects of such adoptions. However, as far as I can tell (and I am not a disinterested third party on the topic), Ghiselin has been extremely successful in getting other biologists to adopt his views, and the results have been salutary.

I cannot pretend that the preceding suggestions are very convincing, but they are better than nothing. Interdisciplinary work is very difficult. In the cases that I have investigated, the main problem is that one of these disciplines is philosophy, and no one ever says all that much about how to test philosophical claims. If philosophy is as "basic" and "fundamental" as we philosophers claim that it is, then the difficulty that we have in justifying these foundations is understandable. Either justifications continue indefinitely or else we must stop somewhere. Atran adopts the second alternative but assumes that all justifications must stop at one place and one place only—phenomenal givens. Another alternative is that all justifications must stop somewhere—or other. Different lines of justification come to rest at different sources of justification. One of the problems of the suggestions that I have made for justifying philosophical views is that they apply most clearly and directly to philosophy of science. How someone working in ethics or aesthetics is to justify his or her views, I shudder to think.

## Notes

Thanks are owed to Scott Atran, John Dupré, Michael Ghiselin, and Peter Godfrey-Smith for reading and commenting on early drafts of this chapter.

1. As supposedly simplistic as the distinction between individuals and classes may be, numerous present-day philosophers, including Dupré (1981) and Wilson (1996), find it sufficiently sophisticated to use in their own work.

2. The use of self-reference to decrease hypocrisy applies to me as well as to the authors whose work I am discussing. I am not a disinterested observer on just about every one of the topics I discuss, in particular, the ontological status of species (Hull 1976). In addition I chastise the authors of the papers under discussion for not being more explicit about the methods that they use in deciding between philosophical positions when I have not done much better myself. My most extensive discussion of this topic can be found in Hull (1989, 1993, 1997).

## References

Atran, S. 1990. *Cognitive Foundations of Natural History: Towards an Anthropology of Science*. Cambridge: University of Cambridge Press.

Atran, S. 1998. Folk biology and the anthropology of science. *Behavioral and Brain Sciences* 21: 547–611.

Atran, S., P. Estin, J. Coley, and D. Medin. 1998. Generic species and basic levels: Essence and appearance in folk biology. *Journal of Ethnobiology* 17: 22–45.

Derricourt, R. 1996. *Author's Guide to Scholarly Publishing*. Princeton: Princeton University Press.

Diamond, J. 1966. Zoological classification system of a primitive people. *Science* 151: 1102–04.

Dupré, J. 1981. Natural kinds and biological taxa. *Philosophical Review* 90: 66–90.

Earman, J. 1993. Carnap, Kuhn, and the philosophy of scientific method, In P. Horwich, ed., *World Changes: Thomas Kuhn and the Nature of Science.* Cambridge: MIT Press, pp. 9–36.

Ghiselin, M. T. 1974. A radical solution to the species problem. *Systematic Zoology* 23: 536–544.

Ghiselin, M. 1997. *Metaphysics and the Origin of Species.* Albany: State University of New York Press.

Grene, M. 1995. *A Philosophical Testament.* Chicago: Open Court.

Hull, D. L. 1976. Are species really individuals? *Systematic Zoology* 25: 174–91.

Hull, D. L. 1989. A function for actual examples in philosophy of science. In M. Ruse, ed., *What Philosophy of Biology Is.* Dordrecht: Kluwer Academic, pp. 313–24.

Hull, D. L. 1993. Testing philosophical claims about science. In D. Hull, M. Forbes, and K. Okruhlik, eds., *PSA 1992*, vol. 2. East Lansing, MI: Philosophy of Science Association, pp. 468–75.

Hull, D. L. 1997. That just don't sound right: A plea for real examples. In J. Earman and J. D. Norton, eds., *Serious Philosophy and History of Science.* Pittsburgh: University of Pittsburgh Press.

Mayr, E. 1963. *Animal Species and Evolution.* Cambridge: Harvard University Press.

Mayr, E., E. G. Linsley, and R. Usinger. 1953. *Methods and Principles of Systematic Zoology.* New York: McGraw-Hill.

Nelson, G., and N. Platnick. 1981. *Systematics and Biogeography: Cladistics and Vicariance.* New York: Columbia University Press.

Putnam, H. 1975. The meaning of "meaning," In *Mind, Language, and Reality: Philosophical Papers*, vol. 2. Cambridge: Cambridge University Press.

Sneath, P. H. A., and R. R. Sokal. 1973. *Numerical Taxonomy.* San Francisco: W. H. Freeman.

Webster, G., and B. Goodwin. 1996. *Form and Transformation: Generative and Relational Principles in Biology.* Cambridge: Cambridge University Press.

Whewell, W. 1840. *The Philosophy of the Inductive Sciences Founded on Their History*, 2 vols. London: John W. Parker.

Wilson, B. E. 1996. Changing conceptions of species. *Biology and Philosophy* 11: 405–20.

# Index